Organized Activities
as Contexts of Development
Extracurricular Activities, After-School
and Community Programs

Organized Activities as Contexts of Development

Extracurricular Activities, After-School and Community Programs

Edited by

Joseph L. Mahoney
Yale University

Reed W. Larson
University of Illinois at Urbana-Champaign

Jacquelynne S. Eccles
University of Michigan

2005

LAWRENCE ERLBAUM ASSOCIATES, PUBLISHERS
Mahwah, New Jersey   London

Lawrence Erlbaum Associates, Inc., Publishers
10 Industrial Avenue
Mahwah, New Jersey 07430

Cover design by Kathryn Houghtaling Lacey

Library of Congress Cataloging-in-Publication Data

Organized activities as contexts of development : extracurricular ac-
    tivities, after-school and community programs / edited by Joseph
    L. Mahoney, Reed W. Larson & Jacquelynne S. Eccles.
        p. cm.
    Includes bibliographical references and index.
    ISBN 0-8058-4430-9 (cloth : alk. paper)
    ISBN 0-8058-4431-7 (pbk. : alk. paper)
        1. Student activities—United States. 2. Students—Services
    for—United States. 3. Community and school—United States.
    4. Child development—United States. 5. Youth. 6. Adolescence.
    I. Larson, Reed, 1950–   II. Eccles, Jacquelynne, S.

LB3605.O74 2004
371.8'9—dc22   2003062650
                                                                CIP

Books published by Lawrence Erlbaum Associates are printed on acid-
free paper, and their bindings are chosen for strength and durability.

Printed in the United States of America
10 9 8 7 6 5 4 3 2 1

Contents

Foreword   ix
   Promoting Positive Youth Development
   Through Community and After-School Programs
     Richard M. Lerner

I   SOCIAL AND CULTURAL PERSPECTIVES

1   Organized Activities as Development Contexts   3
    for Children and Adolescents
    Joseph L. Mahoney, Reed W. Larson, Jacquelynne S. Eccles,
    and Heather Lord

2   Historical Change in Leisure Activities During   23
    After-School Hours
    Douglas A. Kleiber and Gwynn M. Powell

3   Unstructured Leisure in the After-School Hours   45
    D. Wayne Osgood, Amy L. Anderson, and Jennifer N. Shaffer

4   Activity Participation and the Well-Being of Children   65
    and Adolescents in the Context of Welfare Reform
    David M. Casey, Marika N. Ripke, and Aletha C. Huston

5   Contexts and Correlates of Out-of-School Activity   85
    Participation Among Low-Income Urban Adolescents
    Sara Pedersen and Edward Seidman

6   Dorothy, There Is No Yellow Brick Road: The Paradox   111
of Community Youth Development Approaches for Latino
and African American Urban Youth
*Francisco A. Villarruel, Martha Montero-Sieburth, Christopher Dunbar,
and Corliss Wilson Outley*

7   Youth–Adult Research Collaborations: Bringing   131
Youth Voice to the Research Process
Ben Kirshner, Jennifer O'Donoghue, and Milbrey McLaughlin

II   DEVELOPMENTAL PROCESSES AND OUTCOMES

8   Everybody's Gotta Give: Development of Initiative   159
and Teamwork Within a Youth Program
Reed Larson, David Hansen, and Kathrin Walker

9   Benefits of Activity Participation: The Roles of Identity   185
Affirmation and Peer Group Norm Sharing
*Bonnie L. Barber, Margaret R. Stone, James E. Hunt,
and Jacquelynne S. Eccles*

10   Explaining Why a Leisure Context Is Bad for Some Girls   211
and Not for Others
*Håkan Stattin, Margaret Kerr, Joseph Mahoney, Andreas Persson,
and David Magnusson*

11   Activity Choices in Middle Childhood: The Roles of Gender,   235
Self-Beliefs, and Parents' Influence
Janis E. Jacobs, Margaret K. Vernon, and Jacquelynne S. Eccles

12   Youth Music Engagement in Diverse Contexts   255
Susan A. O'Neill

13   Participation in Sport: A Developmental Glimpse at Emotion   275
Tara K. Scanlan, Megan L. Babkes, and Lawrence A. Scanlan

14 After-School Sport for Children: Implications   311
    of a Task-Involving Motivational Climate
    Joan L. Duda and Nikos Ntoumanis

15 Community Service and Identity Formation in Adolescents   331
    Hugh McIntosh, Edward Metz, and James Youniss

16 The Present and Future of Research on Activity Settings   353
    as Developmental Contexts
    Jacquelynne S. Eccles

III   INTEGRATING RESEARCH, PRACTICE, AND POLICY

17 Developing a Comprehensive Agenda for the Out-of-School   375
    Hours: Lessons and Challenges Across Cities
    Karen Pittman, Joel Tolman, and Nicole Yohalem

18 Designing Youth Development Programs: Toward a Theory   399
    of Developmental Intentionality
    Joyce Walker, Mary Marczak, Dale Blyth, and Lynne Borden

19 Someone to Watch Over Me: Mentoring Programs   419
    in the After-School Lives of Children and Adolescents
    Jean Rhodes and Renee Spencer

20 After-School Programs for Low-Income Children: 437
    Differences in Program Quality
    Deborah Lowe Vandell, Lee Shumow, and Jill Posner

21 After-School Programs, Antisocial Behavior,   457
    and Positive Youth Development: An Exploration
    of the Relationship Between Program Implementation
    and Changes in Youth Behavior
    *Stephanie A. Gerstenblith, David A. Soulé, Denise C. Gottfredson,
    Shaoli Lu, Melissa A. Kellstrom, Shannon C. Womer, and Sean L. Bryner*

22 Building Effective Practices and Policies   479
    for Out-of-School Time
    Jane Quinn

About the Editors   497

About the Authors   499

Author Index   517

Subject Index   533

Foreword

Promoting Positive Youth Development Through Community and After-School Programs

Richard M. Lerner
Tufts University

In these early years of the 21st century a new vision for discussing young people has emerged, one that emphasizes that young people may appropriately be regarded as resources to be developed and not as problems to be managed (Roth, Brooks-Gunn, Murray, & Foster, 1998). This vision is predicated on a developmental systems theoretical view of human development that emphasizes the relative plasticity of behavior across the life span, and thus the potential for finding relations within the ecology of human development that may promote positive changes (Lerner, 2002). In addition, this view is furthered by the increasingly more collaborative contributions of scholars, practitioners, and policymakers; whether involving research or program design, implementation, or evaluation, their work is predicated on the idea that all young people have the potential for successful, positive development (e.g., see Eccles & Gootman, 2002), a potential that may be actualized if the strengths of youth are integrated with the interpersonal and institutional supports for healthy development that exist in the ecology of human development.

The present volume both reflects and significantly extends the theoretical and empirical knowledge base, and the lessons from youth program practice, that legitimate this vision. As such, this book adds substantially to the basic and the applied literatures that serve to effectively counter the deficit view of youth that, beginning with G. Stanley Hall (1904), was predominant in the study of adolescence for much of the 20th century (Lerner, 2002).

The concepts associated with a belief in the possibility of promoting positive development in all young people find their roots in the now compelling scientific literature that indicates that development across the life span is propelled by dynamic relations between an active individual and his or her complex and changing context (Lerner, 2002; Shonkoff & Phillips, 2000). This literature reflects the cutting-edge interest among developmental scientists in dynamic systems views of human behavior and development (Lerner, 2002), and underscores the fact that healthy development is made more likely when there exist developmentally supportive fits or matches between the individual biological, psychological, and behavioral characteristics of diverse youth and the assets supporting positive development that exist in the young people's families, schools, communities, social institutions, and cultures (Eccles & Gootman, 2002; Eccles, Wigfield, & Byrnes, 2003; Lerner & Benson, 2003).

For much of the past 30 to 40 years, developmental scientists have focused a great deal of their empirical energies on studying these alignments, or fits, in relation to the child's or adolescent's family relationships or, to a somewhat lesser extent, to his or her school-based relationships (Eccles et al., 2003; Lerner, Anderson, Balsano, Dowling, & Bobek, 2003). For about the past 10 years, however, there has been a burgeoning of scientific interest in the broader "ecological nutrients" for promoting positive development, that is, the assets that are found in communities in general (Benson, 2003; A. Gore & T. Gore, 2002) or in community-based programs in particular (Eccles & Gootman, 2002).

Informal educational and developmentally supportive experiences, as for instance offered to young people in the context of after-school programs or in other instances of community-based programs, have been found to be a potent source of resources increasing the probability of positive development among youth. For instance, Scales, Benson, Leffert, and Blyth (2000), in a study of the individual and ecological assets associated with thriving among 6,000 racially, ethnically, socioeconomically, and geographically diverse youth from across the United States reported that:

> Time spent in youth programs appeared to have the most pervasive positive influence in [being a] ... predictor of ... thriving outcomes ... [G]ood youth programs provide young people with access to caring adults and responsible peers, as well as skill-building activities than can reinforce the values and skills that are associated with doing well in school and maintaining good physical skills. (p. 43)

Community-based youth programs provide, then, a rich source of support for the healthy development of young people. The relationships that young people have in these facets of the ecology of development constitute potentially potent means to enhance healthy and thriving psychological and social development, including positive changes pertinent to emotional development, identity, moral development, and civic engagement. The breath of the potential impact on young people that may be associated with community programs, such as after-school or extracurricular activities, has given major impetus for scholars, practitioners, parents, and youth themselves to launch diverse scholarly and programmatic collaborations (e.g., see Damon & Gregory, 2003); these partnerships are pursued to extend the developmental knowledge base and the understanding of "best practice" in youth programming in order to better enable young people to flourish.

The present volume is an exemplar of such diverse and significant collaborations. More so than any other volume presently available, this book offers a compelling demonstration of the excellent science and service ongoing both in the United States and internationally in order to understand the processes through which youth-serving, community-based programs can promote positive development of a substantial array of individual and social characteristics among diverse youth. Moreover, this volume demonstrates how such knowledge both contributes to and derives from the ongoing efforts of practitioners to deliver youth-serving, after-school programs that are effective in enhancing health and development among diverse young people.

As also convincingly demonstrated in this book, the converging import of science and application regarding the potentially potent positive influences of after-school programs on the development of youth have important implications for social policy. Investments in community-building efforts aimed at identifying, integrating, bringing to scale, and sustaining the assets for healthy youth development present in diverse communities will result in both thriving youth and flourishing communities. As amply evidenced in this timely and significant volume, nations making such investment will not only be more likely to prevent the myriad problems often identified with young people. More than this, they will be promoting characteristics such as competence, confidence, character, positive social connections, and caring and compassion among their young people. The science and applications presented in this book indicate that these young people will, as a consequence of being involved in effective community-based youth serving programs, be more likely to become active and engaged citizens of their society, people committed to contribute in creative and enduring ways to their own healthy development and to the well being of their families, communities, and society.

The caring communities that provide developmentally supportive community-based programs for their youth will fulfill the new vision for America's and the world's young people. They will help promote the healthy development of civically engaged, thriving youth, taking leadership in furthering civil society and social justice throughout the world.

REFERENCES

Benson, P. L. (2003). Developmental assets and asset-building communities: Conceptual and empirical foundations. In R. M. Lerner & P. L. Benson (Eds.), *Developmental assets and asset-building communities: Implications for research, policy, and practice* (pp. 19–43). Norwell, MA: Kluwer.

Damon, W., & Gregory, A. (2003). Bringing in a new era in the field of youth development. In R. M. Lerner & P. L. Benson (Eds.), *Developmental assets and asset-building communities: Implications for research, policy, and practice* (pp. 47–64). Norwell, MA: Kluwer.

Eccles, J., & & Gootman, J. A. (Eds.). (2002). *Community programs to promote youth development.* Washington, DC: National Academy Press.

Eccles, J., Wigfield, A., & Byrnes, J. (2003). Cognitive development in adolescence. In R. M. Lerner, M. A. Easterbrooks , & J. Mistry (Eds.), *Handbook of psychology: Vol. 6. Developmental psychology.* (pp. 325–350). New York: Wiley.

Gore, A., & Gore, T. (2002). *Joined at the heart: The transformation of the American family.* New York: Henry Holt & Company.

Hall, G. (1904). *Adolescence.* New York: Appleton.

Lerner, R. M. (2002). *Concepts and theories of human development* (3rd ed.). Mahwah, NJ: Lawrence Erlbaum Associates.

Lerner, R. M., Anderson, P. M., Balsano, A. B., Dowling, E., & Bobek, D. (2003). Models of person–context relations: Applying developmental science to promote positive human development. In R. M. Lerner, M. A. Easterbrooks , & J. Mistry. (Eds.), *Handbook of psychology: Vol. 6. Developmental psychology* (pp. 535–558). New York: Wiley.

Lerner, R. M., & Benson, P. L. (Eds.). (2003) *Developmental assets and asset-building communities: Implications for research, policy, and practice.* Norwell, MA: Kluwer.

Roth, J., Brooks-Gunn, J., Murray, L., & Foster, W. (1998). Promoting healthy adolescents: Synthesis of youth development program evaluations. *Journal of Research on Adolescence, 8,* 423–459.

Scales, P., Benson, P., Leffert, N., & Blyth, D. A. (2000). The contribution of developmental assets to the prediction of thriving among adolescents. *Applied Developmental Science, 4,* 27–46.

Shonkoff, J. P., & Phillips, D. A. (Eds.). (2000). *From neurons to neighborhoods: The science of early childhood development.* Washington, DC: National Academy Press.

I

Social and Cultural Perspectives

1

Organized Activities as Developmental Contexts for Children and Adolescents

Joseph L. Mahoney
Yale University

Reed W. Larson
University of Illinois at Urbana-Champaign

Jacquelynne S. Eccles
University of Michigan

Heather Lord
Yale University

School-age children in the United States and other Western nations spend almost half of their waking hours in leisure activities (Larson & Verma, 1999). How young persons can best use this discretionary time has been a source of controversy. For some, out-of-school time is perceived as inconsequential or even counterproductive to the health and well-being of young persons. Consistent with this view, the past 100 years of scientific research has tended either to ignore this time or to focus selectively on the risks present during the out-of-school hours (Kleiber & Powell, chap. 2, this volume). More recently, however, there is increased interest in viewing out-of-school time as an opportunity for young persons to learn and develop competencies that are largely neglected by schools. Researchers are beginning to recognize that along with family, peers, and school, the organized activities in which some youth participate during these hours are important contexts of emotional, social, and civic development. At the same time, communities and the federal government in the United States are now channeling considerable resources into creating organized activities for young people's out-of-school time (Pittman et al., chap. 17, this volume). The primary aim of this volume is to bring scientific research to bear on how this time can be used constructively.

In this chapter, we overview central issues in the field of research on organized activities to provide a background and framework for the chapters that follow. Four main areas are addressed. First, we discuss definitional issues in the field and clarify what is meant by organized activities within this volume. Second, we outline the available research indicating that participation in these activities affects short- and long-term development. Third, we consider the features of organized activities thought to account for their developmental impact and, lastly, we review evidence on factors that influence participation in these activities and whether youth benefit from their developmental potential.

WHAT ARE ORGANIZED ACTIVITIES?

This volume focuses principally on formal activities for children 6 to 18 years of age that are not part of the school curriculum. By "organized," we refer to activities that are characterized by structure, adult-supervision, and an emphasis on skill-building (e.g., Eccles & Gootman, 2002; Larson, 2000; Roth & Brooks-Gunn, 2003). These activities are generally voluntary, have regular and scheduled meetings, maintain developmentally based expectations and rules for participants in the activity setting (and sometimes beyond it), involve several participants, offer supervision and guidance from adults, and are organized around developing particular skills and achieving goals. These activities are often characterized by challenge and complexity that increase as participants' abilities develop (e.g., Csikszentmihalyi, 1990; Larson, 1994). In general, organized activities share the broad goal of promoting positive development for the participants.

A variety of labels have been used to describe organized activities for young persons. They usually denote the *who* (school-age, child, adolescent, youth), *where* (school-based, community-based), *what* (activities, programs, organizations), and *when* (after-school, extracurricular, summer, nonschool, out-of-school) elements of participation. These descriptors are meaningful and do clarify the phenomenon of interest. Accordingly, we use the term *organized activities* to refer to these variations collectively. The word *organized* is also used to make clear that so-called *unstructured activities* (e.g., watching television, listening to music, "hanging out" with peers, and "cruising" in cars) and other forms of passive leisure (e.g., eating, resting, and personal care) are not the focus of this volume, except as a backdrop of what else youth might be doing during their after-school hours (Kleiber & Powell, chap. 2, this volume; Osgood et al., chap. 3, this volume).

Breadth and Diversity of Activities

The range of organized activities available to children and adolescents in the United States and other Western nations is substantial (Carnegie Council, 1992; Eccles & Gootman, 2002; Quinn, 1999). They include nationally sponsored youth organizations and federally funded after-school programs (e.g., Boys and Girls Clubs, YMCA, YWCA, 21st Century Community Learning Centers, 4-H, Boy/Girl Scouts, Camp Fire). They involve community, school, and locally organized programs: autonomous grassroots youth developmental organizations, faith-based youth organizations, and activities provided by parks and recreation services, museums, libraries, youth centers, youth sports organizations and amateur leagues (e.g., little league), school-sponsored extracurricular and after-school activities, and community service programs. They also include specific types of activities (e.g., sports, music, hobby clubs, social clubs, religious, service activities) that can be differentiated on the basis of activity-related goals, atmosphere, and content (Roth & Brooks-Gunn, 2003).

This volume considers organized activities across this diverse range. Methodological and logistical challenges make it difficult to study national organizations and little research is available at this level of assessment. By contrast, considerable research has been conducted on community-sponsored programs and activities (e.g., Eccles & Gootman, 2002; Kirshner et al., chap. 7, this volume; McIntosh et al., chap. 15, this volume; Stattin et al., chap. 10, this volume), and school-based extracurricular activities (e.g., Barber et al., chap. 9, this volume; Eccles & Templeton, 2002; Pedersen & Seidman, chap. 5, this volume). Recently, school-sponsored after-school programs for elementary and middle-school youth have been increasing dramatically and research is beginning to be conducted on these activities (Casey et al., chap. 4, this volume; Vandell et al., chap. 20, this volume; Weisman et al., chap. 21, this volume). Finally, developmental research that compares different types of activities is relatively new and featured in several chapters (e.g., Barber et al., chap. 9, this volume; Eccles & Barber, 1999; Hansen, Larson, & Dworkin, 2003; Jacobs et al., chap. 11, this volume; Pedersen & Seidman, chap. 5, this volume). Studies of specific activities have been common in the fields of leisure studies and sports psychology and are also considered here (e.g., Duda & Ntoumanis, chap. 4, this volume; O'Neill, chap. 12, this volume; Scanlan et al., chap. 13, this volume).

ORGANIZED ACTIVITIES AND SALIENT
DEVELOPMENTAL TASKS FOR YOUNG PERSONS

In order to evaluate how these organized activities contribute to development, scholars are examining whether they help children and adolescents address the developmental tasks associated with their age periods—how they help youth achieve age-appropriate competencies. During childhood, key developmental tasks in our society include (a) acquiring habits of physical and psychological health, (b) forming a positive orientation toward school and achievement, (c) getting along with others including peers and adults, and (d) acquiring appropriate value systems about rules and conduct across different contexts. These issues remain important during adolescence, but are renegotiated in the light of interdependent changes in the bio–psycho–social system (Eccles, Barber, Stone, & Templeton, 2003; Mahoney & Bergman, 2002). In addition, new tasks such as identity formation, personal mastery/efficacy, intimacy with peers, and preparation for the transition to adulthood and postsecondary education or work become increasingly important across adolescence (Brown, Clausen, & Eicher, 1986; Collins, 2002; Levesque, 1993). In the global world of the 21st century, the development of competencies to move between diverse contexts defined by ethnicity, religion, sexual orientation, and other forms of difference is increasingly important (Larson, Wilson, Brown, Furstenberg, & Verma, 2002).

Achieving competency at these tasks allows an individual to take advantage of personal and environmental resources that promote positive functioning in the present, reduce the risk for developing problem behaviors, and increase the likelihood for healthy adjustment in the future (Eccles et al., 2003; Mahoney & Bergman, 2002; Masten & Coatsworth, 1998). Research shows that participation in organized activities can have a range of positive influence on children and adolescence. We now highlight some of this evidence for school-sponsored extracurricular activities, and community-based and after-school programs.

Extracurricular Activities and Community Programs

Involvement in organized activities such as sports teams, lessons, and clubs is relatively common during adolescence. For example, among youth ages 12 to 17 from the National Survey of Families (NASF; 1997), 57% participated on a sports team, 29% participated in lessons, and 60% participated in clubs or organizations after school or on weekends during the last year. Recent reviews support the conclusion that participation in organized activities helps young persons negotiate the salient developmental tasks of childhood and adolescence (e.g., Eccles & Gootman, 2002; Eccles & Templeton, 2002).

Increased Educational Attainment and Achievement. A long-standing finding from quasi-experimental and experimental studies is that participation in extracurricular activities and community programs promotes education attainment. This includes low rates of school failure and dropout (e.g., Hahn, Leavitt, & Aaron, 1994; Mahoney & Cairns, 1997; McNeal, 1995), high rates of postsecondary school education, and good school achievement (e.g., Eccles & Barber, 1999; Mahoney, Cairns, & Farmer, 2003; Marsh, 1992; Otto, 1975, 1976). Explanations for these education gains include the association of participation in organized activities with heightened school engagement and attendance, better academic performance and interpersonal competence, and higher aspirations for the future (e.g., Barber, Eccles & Stone, 2001; Grossman & Tierney, 1998; Lamborn, Brown, Mounts, & Steinberg, 1992; Mahoney et al., 2003; Newman, Wehlage, & Lamborn, 1992).

Reduced Problem Behaviors. A number of studies indicate that participation in organized activities is associated with reduced problem behaviors across adolescence and into young adulthood. For instance, earlier work in sociology shows that activity participation is related to low rates of delinquency (e.g., Elliott & Voss, 1974; Hanks & Eckland, 1976). More recent developmental research shows that involvement in organized activities reduces the likelihood of developing problems with alcohol and drugs (Grossman & Tierney, 1998; Youniss, Yates, & Su, 1997, 1999), aggression, antisocial behavior, and crime (e.g., Jones & Offord, 1989; Mahoney, 2000; Rhodes & Spencer, chap. 19, this volume), or becoming a teenage parent (Allen, Philliber, Herrling, & Gabriel, 1997). Activity-related affiliations with nondeviant peers, mentoring from adult activity leaders, and the fact that organized activities represent a conventional endeavor that is highly valued, challenging, and exciting represent the main explanations why organized activities protect against problem behaviors (e.g., Barber et al., chap. 9, this volume; Fletcher, Elder, & Mekos, 2000; Larson, 2000; Rhodes & Spencer, chap. 19, this volume).

Heightened Psychosocial Competencies. Organized activity participation is positively associated with psychosocial adjustment in a number of areas (Eccles & Gootman, 2002). For instance, participation is related to low levels of negative emotions such as depressed mood and anxiety during adolescence (Barber et al., 2001; Brustad, Babkes, & Smith, 2001; Larson,

1994; Mahoney, Schweder, & Stattin, 2002). Motivation for learning and high self-efficacy is linked with participation (Catalano, Berglund, Ryan, Lonczak, & Hawkins, 1999; Duda & Ntoumanis, chap. 14, this volume). These contexts also appear ideal for promotion of a more general psychological capacity—initiative—which involves the application of extended effort to reach long-term goals (e.g., Larson, 2000; Larson et al., chap. 8, this volume). Finally, maintaining or increasing self-esteem (e.g., McLaughlin, 2000; Rhodes & Spencer, chap. 19, this volume) and developing a clear and civic-minded identity (McIntosh et al., chap. 15, this volume; Youniss, McLellan, Su, & Yates, 1999) appear to be positively influenced by activity participation. The unique combination of psychological features and opportunities for social relationships and belonging are main factors thought to impact these psychosocial processes.

Extracurricular Activities During Childhood.   Although most investigations of organized activities have been conducted with adolescents, available research suggests that children benefit from participation as well. For example, consistent participation in extracurricular activities during kindergarten and first grade is related to high reading and math achievement (National Institute of Child Health and Human Development [NICHD] Early Child Care Research Network, 2004). A moderate level of participation during the first grade has also been associated with high levels of social competence several years later (Pettit, Laird, Bates, & Dodge, 1997). Similarly, participation in extracurricular activities during middle childhood is indicative of positive achievement and emotional adjustment (McHale, Crouter, & Tucker, 2001; Posner & Vandell, 1999), and predicts perceived competence and values during adolescence (Jacobs, Lanza, Osgood, Eccles, & Wigfield, 2002; chap. 11, this volume).

After-School Programs

Owing in large part to increases in maternal employment, after-school programs now provide a common form of child care and adult supervision for over 7 million American children with working parents (Capizzano, Tout, & Adams, 2000). In addition, many after-school programs are implemented with the goal of providing safe environments and alternatives to self-care, as well to take advantage of opportunities for social and academic enrichment during the nonschool hours (Vandell et al., chap. 20, this volume). These programs are oriented to children in the elementary and middle-school years.

    Relative to children in other after-school arrangements, quasi-experimental longitudinal studies show that consistent participation in after-school programs promotes positive academic performance and reduces behavior problems such as aggression (Pettit, Laird, Bates, & Dodge, 1997; Vandell et al., chap. 20, this volume; Weisman et al., chap. 21, this volume). Similarly, formal evaluations of after-school programs comparing participants and nonparticipants over time have found fewer school absences, higher school achievement, and improved work and study habits for participants.[1] Parents of participants also report that after-school programs support their work schedules and that they worry less about their children's safety. These benefits are frequently stronger for disadvantaged children, those with social, academic, or language deficits, and families residing high-risk neighborhoods.

Overall, after-school program participation appears to promote competence in several key developmental tasks during middle childhood including academic performance, school engagement, and social behaviors and relationships. The likelihood for beneficial outcomes appears greatest for: (a) after-school programs of higher quality and those in later stages of development, (b) students who show greater consistency in their program participation, and (c) programs serving low-income and low-achieving students at high risk for developing social–academic problems. However, many after-school programs focus on academic achievement rather than aiming to promote competence in personal and interpersonal domains (Vandell et al., chap. 20, this volume). Future research will need to examine what types of programs best serve the needs of young persons in the short and long term (Quinn, chap. 22, this volume).

The 21st-Century Community Learning Centers. Funding that supports the 21st-Century Community Learning Centers (21st CCLCs) provides a major source of after-school programs in the United States. A national evaluation of the 21st CCLCs was recently undertaken by Mathematica Policy Research, Inc. A report describing the first-year findings of the evaluation purports that the 21st CCLCs had little impact on the academic or social behavior of the participating elementary and middle-school students (U.S. Department of Education, Office of Under Secretary, 2003). This provided the basis for a proposed 40% budget reduction for the 21st CCLCs in 2004 (Education Budget Summary and Background, 2003). However, there are several limitations with the evaluation. For instance, the elementary school sample was not representative of the larger population of elementary schools receiving 21st CCLC funds. Comparison groups in the middle-school sample were not equivalent; the after-school

---

[1]See, for example, after-school evaluations of the YS-CARE After School Program http://www.gse.uci.edu/asp/aspeval/resources/YSCARE13.pdf, LA's Best http://www.lasbest.org/learn/eval.html, The After-School Corporation http://www.tascorp.org/pages/promising_es1.pdf

participants were at much higher risk at the beginning of the study. The absence of certain baseline data, treatment and comparison group contamination, and issues surrounding the evaluation's timing and measurement were also methodological concerns in the National Evaluation (Bissell et al., 2003; Mahoney, 2003). Finally, the quality of the programs included in the evaluation was not systematically considered. As already noted, the quality of after-school programs is very important for their effectiveness. Due to these several limitations, making generalizations about the effectiveness of the 21st CCLCs based on the reported first-year findings do not seem warranted. Extrapolation to after-school programs in general is not possible on the basis of the 21st CCLC evaluation, particularly in light of the several carefully controlled intervention studies that provide solid evidence of the effectiveness of high quality after-school programs.

Summary

Organized activities are important contexts that help young persons build competencies and successfully negotiate the salient developmental tasks of childhood and adolescence. Participation is associated with academic success, mental health, positive social relationships and behaviors, identity development, and civic engagement. These benefits, in turn, pave the way for long-term educational success and help prepare young persons for the transition to adulthood. However, although the research findings are generally positive, variations across the types of programs and the participants suggest the need for researchers to differentiate the features of programs that facilitate development and the conditions under which the benefits is most likely to occur.

FEATURES OF ORGANIZED ACTIVITIES
THAT PROMOTE DEVELOPMENT

The preceding section makes it clear that organized activities are contexts in which children and adolescents develop a range of important competencies. But why is this so? Why should activities such as playing hockey for the school team, singing in a youth community chorus, participating in school government, or spending afternoons in after-school program activities matter?

To address this question, a committee of scholars appointed by the National Research Council and Institute of Medicine recently evaluated what features of contexts promote positive development (Eccles & Gootman, 2002). By looking at research on development in contexts such as families and schools, they derived the list of eight key features in Table 1.1 that are proven to facilitate positive growth (see also Blum, 2003;

TABLE 1.1
Features of Contexts That Promote Positive Development

1. *Physical and psychological safety.* The context provides secure and health-promoting facilities and practices, allows for safe and appropriate peer interactions, and discourages unsafe health practices and negative or confrontational social interchanges.

2. *Appropriate structure.* The context provides clear, appropriate, and consistent rules and expectations, adult supervision, guidance, and age-appropriate monitoring in a predictable social atmosphere where clear boundaries are known and respected.

3. *Supportive relationships.* The context offers stable opportunities to form relationships with peers and adults wherein social interchanges are characterized by warmth, closeness, caring, and mutual respect, and where guidance and support from adults is available, appropriate, and predictable.

4. *Opportunities for belonging.* The context emphasizes the inclusion of all members and maintains a social environment that recognizes, appreciates, and encourages individual differences in cultural values, gender, race/ethnicity, and sexual orientation.

5. *Positive social norms.* The context maintains expectations and requirements for socially appropriate behavior and encourages desirable and accepted values and morals.

6. *Support for efficacy and mattering.* The context allows for and supports autonomy, values individual expression and opinions, concentrates on growth and improvement rather than absolute performance, encourages and enables individuals to take on challenging responsibilities and to carry out actions aimed at making a difference.

7. *Opportunity for skill building.* The context offers opportunities to learn and build physical, intellectual, psychological, emotional, and social skills that facilitate well-being in the present and prepare individuals for health and competent functioning in the future.

8. *Integration of family, school, and community efforts.* The context provides opportunities for synergistic experiences that integrate transactions across family, school, and community.

Note. Taken from the findings of the Committee on Community-Level Programs for Youth (Eccles & Gootman, 2002).

Lerner, Fisher, & Weinberg, 2000; Roth & Brooks-Gunn, 2003). The panel cautioned that no single feature from this list is sufficient to ensure positive development, but also that few contexts are likely to provide optimal experiences in all of these areas. They also cautioned that future research can be expected to add to or refine this list. Nonetheless these eight features represent the state of the art for thinking about what might make organized activities such as hockey, student government, or an after-school program an effective context of development.

These features can be considered as explanatory mechanisms or mediators by which participation in organized activities affect the development process. The available research evaluating these features for organized activities is limited but generally indicates, first, that many organized activities are high on several of these features and, second, that these features are linked to the positive outcomes described. On the first point, organized activities typically offer a context of safety during the after-school hours (e.g., McLaughlin, 2000), often provide opportunities for skill building and efficacy (Larson, 2000), and are frequently important contexts of supportive relationships with adults and peers (e.g., Barber et al., chap. 9, this volume; Hansen et al., 2003; Mahoney et al., 2002; Rhodes & Spencer, chap. 19, this volume).

Although research specifically linking these features to outcomes is rare, the National Research Council committee concluded that successful youth programs are characterized by many of these features. The most successful programs provide integration between a youth's family, school, and community experiences, engage youth in relationships with caring adults, and provide many of the other positive features (Eccles & Gootman, 2002; Pittman et al., chap. 17, this volume; Walker et al., chap. 18, this volume). Targeted research that begins to critically test the specific linkage between some of these features and positive development is only beginning. As one exemplar, Mahoney et al. (2003) used longitudinal data to show that the fostering of interpersonal skills in youth programs is a mediator of high aspirations for the future in adolescence and high educational attainment—including college attendance—at young adulthood.

Furthermore, we are only beginning to understand how the different combinations of features in organized activities interact to promote positive development. For instance, although participation in organized activities appears to affect complex processes such as identity formation and the development of initiative, this seems to depend on an appropriate balance of many of the features already summarized (e.g., Barber et al., chap. 9, this volume; Larson et al., chap. 8, this volume; McIntosh et al., chap. 15, this volume). Although expert youth workers have developed a fund of practitioner wisdom for understanding these balancing processes (Pittman et al., chap. 17, this volume; Walker et al., chap. 18, this volume), researchers are far behind in subjecting this wisdom to critical test. Precisely which features are involved and how they co-act to produce specific developmental changes have not yet been evaluated. Thus, one task for researchers is to understand better the interplay between these features, which patterns are most critical for promoting different competencies, and how these relations may change over development. A second and related task will be to assess how and why some organized activity contexts are more effective at providing these positive features than others (e.g., Stattin et al., chap. 20, this volume; Vandell et al., chap. 20, this volume). Both tasks will require researchers to conduct process-oriented studies focused on individual change that are explicitly designed to assess a broad array of structural and process quality parameters in the activity context.[2]

FACTORS THAT INFLUENCE ACTIVITY PARTICIPATION AND EFFECT DEVELOPMENTAL OUTCOMES

The preceding sections have described different benefits and positive features associated with organized activity participation. However, the extent to which organized activities influence development can vary across individual youth, programs, and community contexts. To derive the greatest benefit from organized activities, a youth must participate.[3] The selection processes affecting whether an individual participates and continues to participate is complex. To begin with, the degree to which a youth can actually "select" to participate in organized activities depends on the individual considered, his or her family, and the community in which he or she resides (Caldwell & Baldwin, in press; Elder & Conger, 2000; Furstenberg, Cook, Eccles, Elder, & Sameroff, 1999). Activity selection involves a reciprocal process between contextual constraints and opportunities for participation, and the individual's motivation and ability to perceive and act on them.

---

[2]In contrast to the variety of measures for assessing program quality during early childhood, there are few established instruments to evaluate out-of-school programs for school-age children or adolescents (e.g., Harms, Jacobs, & White, 1996). The diversity of program content and goals that characterize activities and programs for older children and youth may account for this discrepancy. One possibility is to define the process quality of out-of-school activities in terms of the eight features of positive youth contexts summarized in this chapter.

[3]Intervention research shows that a treatment can be beneficial for persons who do not directly receive the treatment. This phenomenon—known as *spread of effect*—may also be true for organized activities. For example, whether or not youth participate in organized activities, problem behaviors are lower if their peer group (Mahoney, 2000) or their parents (Mahoney & Magnusson, 2001) are participants. Similarly, making organized activities available to adolescents has been linked to decreased levels of juvenile antisocial behavior in the community (Jones & Offord, 1989).

Demographic and Familial Influences

Availability and affordability of activities are the most basic factors affecting participation. The presence of resources such as parks, community
centers, playing fields, and the availability of willing and competent adults
to provide the activities are requisites. The provision of programs for
youth is generally less in poor urban neighborhoods and isolated rural areas (Carnegie Council, 1992; Pedersen & Seidman, chap. 5, this volume).
Beyond availability, factors such as transportation and a family's economic means to pay the costs of activities, as well as cultural and ethnic
factors, have considerable influence on participation rates (Elder & Conger, 2000; Furstenberg et al., 1999; Villarruel et al., chap. 7 this volume).
These factors—availability, economy, and culture—are often interrelated
and likely account for the relatively low-participation rates among economically disadvantaged children and adolescents and those from traditionally defined minority groups (e.g., Hultsman, 1992; Jackson & Rucks,
1993; Pedersen & Seidman, chap. 5, this volume). It may also explain why
income support programs and the provision of culturally appropriate activities appear to increase participation rates (Casey et al., chap. 4, this
volume; Villarruel et al., chap. 6, this volume).

Parents' desire to enroll their children in organized activities and their
ability to manage their children's participation in such activities differ. If
parents work full time and children need transportation to get to organized
activities, then it may be quite difficult for a child to get and remain involved
in such activities. Similarly, if parents fear the types of children and adolescents likely to participate in the organized activities, they may prefer to keep
their children at home (Furstenberg et al., 1999; Jarrett, 1997; Stattin et al.,
chap. 10, this volume). Finally, if parents rely on their children for help at
home, they may not encourage their children to participate in organized activities (Elder & Conger, 2000; Fletcher et al., 2000).

Individual Characteristics

An individual's competence, age, and developmental status can constrain participation in organized activities. For instance, because skill
level can determine access to some organized activities, particularly in
adolescence, early activity involvement may be required for some forms
of later activity participation (McNeal, 1998). Therefore, children who
do not (or cannot) become competent in the skills developed through
organized activities early on are likely to find that opportunities for involvement in such activities diminish across childhood and adolescence. It is no small irony that organized activities are particularly

effective at building the very competencies that would facilitate participation (Larson et al., chap. 8, this volume).

The maturity of the youth may also lead some adolescents to drop out of organized activities. In general, participation in many out-of-school organized activities declines as children move into and through adolescence (Eccles & Gootman, 2002).[4] This reflects (a) a decline in some organized programs for older children, (b) an increase in competition for membership in available activities that excludes some youth from participating, (c) the fact that programs do not always provide the kinds of activities likely to be of interest to adolescents, (d) diminished school budgets that fund extracurricular activities, and (e) the increase in adolescent employment during the nonschool hours. Programs that are successful at retaining their adolescent members offer increasing opportunities for leadership, decision making, and meaningful service (Kirshner et al., chap. 7, this volume; McLaughlin, 2000; Pittman et al., chap. 17, this volume; Walker et al., chap. 18, this volume); in other words, they offer opportunities that fit the maturing adolescents' sense of self and expertise.

In addition, individual and social-contextual factors ordinarily interact to affect opportunities for participation. Individuals participate in organized activities for different reasons. Sometimes they participate of their own volition because they want to participate (they select to be involved). In other cases, they are recruited by peers, parents, and/or activity leaders to participate based on personal characteristics, ability, or social connection (they are socialized to participate). Often, both of these processes—selection and socialization—are at work in the decision to participate. Furthermore, because participation itself is a socializing experience, experiences while involved can both increase and decrease the likelihood of continued participation. Thus, continued participation reflects both of these processes.

Finally, greater benefits tend to be evident for students who show consistent participation in organized activities. For instance, children's rate of attendance in after-school programs is positively associated with gains in school achievement and work habits (Cosden, Morrison, Albanese, & Macias, 2001; Marshall et al., 1997; NICHD Early Child Care Research Network, in press). Similarly, Barber et al. (chap. 9, this volume) and Mahoney et al. (2003) find that whether participation in school-based extracurricular activities is transient or stable affects the developmental process and related outcomes. These findings are consistent with the broader literature on effective school and community interventions (e.g., Catalano

---

[4]Participation in school-based extracurricular activities has been found to increase, rather than decline, across adolescence in some studies (e.g., Kinney, 1993; Mahoney & Cairns, 1997). The increase in participation may reflect the relatively small number of extracurricular activities available to students prior to middle school and the rapid expansion of extracurricular activities in high school.

et al., 1999; Durlak & Wells, 1997; Eccles & Gootman, 2002). Building relationships, forming new behavior patterns, and acquiring competencies take time. However, the fact that selection and socialization processes interact to initiate and maintain participation makes it difficult to evaluate the effectiveness of long-term participation in organized activities.

Program Resources and Content

As with all programs for children and adolescents, the extent to which organized activities are beneficial depends on their quality and content. Quality is partly defined by whether a program offers the eight features shown in Table 1.1. But, it is also affected by the material and human resources within a program. Indeed, these are likely to be vital to the program's ability to provide the eight features. After-school programs for children provide a good example. Considerable variation exists in program resources, as evident in child-to-staff ratios, staff education, and staff turnover. Research shows, in turn, that these are related to developmental outcomes for children in the expected direction (e.g., Vandell et al., chap. 20, this volume). Children attending programs that are low on these factors may either fail to benefit or may develop increased rates of problem behaviors relative to children in alternative and high-quality after-school arrangements. In this volume, chapter 17 by Pittman et al. provides a valuable discussion of what communities need to do to build a robust system of high-quality programs to meet the needs of youth.

The content of activities within programs is also likely to affect a youth's developmental experiences. Although there is great variability in how adult leaders organize a given activity, preliminary research suggests that differing activities may provide distinct developmental opportunities and liabilities. Associated changes in substance use, antisocial behavior, school achievement, and self-esteem vary across different activities (Barber et al. 2001, chap. 9, this volume; Pedersen & Seidman, chap. 5, this volume; Stattin et al., chap. 10, this volume). For instance, in a survey in one community, Hansen et al. (2002) found that high-school youth reported more experiences related to identity exploration and emotional learning in sports compared to other organized activities, but also more negative peer and adult interactions. Consistent with this, a controlled longitudinal study found that sports participation was associated with increases in both academic achievement and alcohol consumption (Eccles & Barber, 1999).

It is important to caution that these differences are not likely to inhere in the activity itself. They could, for example, reflect how the current generation of coaches or music directors construct the culture, values, and goals youth experience in that specific activity. They could also reflect the current peer culture associated with the activity. Finally, they may also reflect the selection of youth to activities that provide a culture and experiences in line with their current values and desires. Much future research is needed to begin to separate out how developmental opportunities are shaped by the type of activity and numerous interrelated factors.

Problematic Activities. To be sure, not all youth activities and programs are beneficial and some are quite limited in the number of positive features they possess. Some structured activities are organized in ways that do not facilitate positive development and may be harmful. One example is provided by mentoring programs. Volunteer mentors are often a valuable resource in remedying the decreased availability of adult guidance for youth and facilitate perceived self-esteem and school achievement. However, the program may pose a risk if the mentoring relationship is short-lived or fails (Rhodes & Spencer, chap. 19, this volume). A second example involves participation in youth recreation centers that provide relatively low structure and lack skill-building aims. Regular involvement in these settings appears to facilitate deviant peer relationships during adolescence and persistent criminal behavior into adulthood (e.g., Mahoney, Stattin, & Magnussen, 2001; Stattin et al., chap. 10, this volume). This is likely to be particularly true if such centers attract youth who are already involved in problematic behaviors and activities (Dishion & McMahon, 1998; Dishion, McCord, & Poulin, 1999; Dishion, Poulin, & Burraston, 2001; Marshall et al., 1997; Pettit, Bates, Dodge, & Meece, 1999; Pettit et al., 1997; Reid & Patterson, 1989). These examples serve as a powerful reminder that organizing out-of-school activities appropriately is critical and essential.

Other Factors Influencing Program Impact

There are numerous other factors that may affect the impact of organized activities. Studies have suggested that high-risk youth may benefit more from organized activities than other youth (Eccles & Templeton, 2002; Mahoney, 2000). The likely explanation is that these youth have less access in other parts of their lives to the types of resources and developmental experiences that these activities provide, thus the impact is likely to be greater (Elder & Conger, 2000). Little research has been done to evaluate how gender and ethnicity may influence a child's likelihood of gaining from a program (Pedersen & Seidman, chap. 5, this volume). It should not be assumed that a single program will be equally beneficial to youth with differing backgrounds. An important horizon of future research is to understand how the fit between a youth program and the characteristics of individuals shapes development (Eccles & Templeton, 2002).

OVERVIEW OF THE CONTENTS

This book presents conceptual, empirical, and policy-relevant advances in research on children's and adolescent's participation in the developmental contexts represented by extracurricular activities and after-school and community programs. Many of the issues brought to light in this chapter are taken up in greater detail in the chapters to follow.

The volume is organized into three main sections. Part I discusses social and cultural perspectives on organized activity participation. It begins with the historical evolution of leisure activities in the United States and the associated risks inherent in a leisure experience that is unstructured and lacks involvement in organized activities. Next, new perspectives on the role of organized activity involvement in the development of youth from low-income families and those from traditionally defined minority groups are provided. Finally, the involvement of youth as participants in the research process itself is considered. Part II provides a collection of new empirical studies on how participation in organized activities affects developmental processes and outcomes. Across the chapters, particular attention is given to the developmental experiences provided through participation in difference types of organized activities, and how the experiences translate into psychosocial adjustment and competence. It concludes with a commentary by Jacquelynne Eccles that discusses chapters in Parts I and II of this volume. Part III links the conceptual and research knowledge base on organized activities to practice and policy issues surrounding out-of-school time for young persons. This includes empirically based and practical guidance for developing effective organized activities in general, and specific insights into optimal practices for community and after-school programs. This section concludes with a commentary on out-of-school practices and policy considerations by Jane Quinn.

REFERENCES

Allen, J. P., Philliber, S., Herrling, S., & Gabriel, K. P. (1997). Preventing teen pregnancy and academic failure: Experimental evaluation of a developmentally based approach. *Child Development, 64,* 729–742.

Barber, B. L., Eccles, J. S., & Stone, M. R. (2001). Whatever happened to the jock, the brain, and the princess? Young adult pathways linked to adolescent activity involvement and social identity. *Journal of Adolescent Research: Special Issue, 16,* 429–455.

Bissell, J. S., Cross, C. T., Mapp, K., Reisner, E., Vandell, D. L., Warren, C., & Weissbourd, R. (2003, May 10). Statement released by the Members of the Scientific Advisory Board for the 21st Century Community Learning Center Evaluation.

Blum, R. W. (2003). Positive youth development: A strategy for improving adolescent health. In R. M. Lerner, F. Jacobs, & D. Wertlieb (Eds.), *Promoting positive child, ado-*

lescent, and family development: A handbook of program and policy innovations (Vol. 2, pp. 237–252). Thousand Oaks, CA: Sage.

Brown, B. B., Clasen, D., & Eicher, S. (1986). Perceptions of peer pressure, peer conformity dispositions, and self-reported behavior among adolescents. *Developmental Psychology, 22,* 521–530.

Brustad, R. J., Babkes, M. L., & Smith, A. L. (2001). Youth in sport: Psychological considerations. In R. N. Singer, H. A. Hausenblas, & C. M. Janelle (Eds.), *Handbook of sport psychology* (2nd ed., pp. 604–635). New York: Wiley.

Caldwell, L. L., & Baldwin, C. K. (in press). A developmental approach to understanding constraints to adolescent leisure. In E. Jackson (Ed.), *Constraints to leisure.* State College, PA: Venture.

Capizzano, J., Tout, K., & Adams, G., (2000). *Child care patterns of school-age children with employed mothers.* Washington, DC: The Urban Institute.

Carnegie Council. (1992). *A matter of time: Risk and opportunity in the out-of-school hours.* New York: Carnegie Corporation.

Catalano, R. F., Berglund, M.L., Ryan, J.A., Lonczak, H.S., & Hawkins, J.D. (1999). *Positive youth development in the United States: Research findings on evaluations of positive youth development programs.* Report to the US Department of Health and Human Services, Office of the Assistant Secretary for Planning and Evaluation and National Institute for Child Health and Human Development. Carnegie Council on Adolescent Development. New York: Carnegie Corporation of New York.

Collins, W. A. (April, 2002). *More than myth and metaphor: The developmental significance of adolescent romantic experiences.* Presidential address presented at the Biennial Meeting of the Society for Research on Adolescence, New Orleans, LA.

Cosden, M., Morrison, G., Albanese, A. L., & Macias, S. (2001). When homework is not home work: After-school programs for homework assistance. *Educational Psychologist, 36,* 211–221.

Csikszentmihalyi, M. (1990). *Flow: The psychology of optimal experience.* New York: Harper & Row.

Dishion, T. J., McCord, J., & Poulin, R. (1999). When interventions harm: Peer groups and problem behavior. *American Psychologist, 54,* 755–764.

Dishion, T. J., & McMahon, R. J. (1998). Parental monitoring and the prevention of child and adolescent problem behavior: A conceptual and empirical formulation. *Clinical Child and Family Psychology Review, 1,* 61–75.

Dishion, T. J., Poulin, F., & Burraston, B. (2001). Peer group dynamics associated with iatrogenic effects in group interventions with high-risk young adolescents. In D. W. Nangle & C. A. Erdley (Eds.), *The role of friendship in psychological adjustment* (pp. 79–92). San Francisco, CA: Jossey-Bass/Pfeiffer.

Durlak, J. A., & Wells, A. M. (1997). Primary prevention mental health programs for children and adolescents: A meta-analytic review. *American Journal of Community Psychology: Special Issue: Meta-Analysis of Primary Prevention Program, 25,* 115–152.

Eccles, J. S. & Barber, B. L. (1999). Student council, volunteering, basketball, or marching band: What kind of extracurricular involvement matters? *Journal of Adolescent Research, 14,* 10–43.

Eccles, J. S., Barber, B., Stone, M., & Templeton, J. (2003). Adolescence and emerging adulthood: The critical passage ways to adulthood. In M. H. Bornstein, L. Davidson, C. L. M. Keyes, K. A. Moore, & The Center for Child Well-being (Eds.), *Well-being: Positive development across the life span* (pp. 383–406). Mahwah, NJ: Lawrence Erlbaum Associates.

Eccles, J. S., & Gootman, J. A. (Eds.). (2002). *Community programs to promote youth development.* Committee on Community-Level Programs for Youth. Board on Children, Youth, and Families, Commission on Behavioral and Social Sciences and Education, National Research Council and Institute of Medicine. Washington, DC: National Academy Press.

Eccles, J. S., & Templeton, J. (2002). Extracurricular and other after-school activities for youth. *Review of Research in Education, 26,* 113–180.

Education Budget Summary and Background (2003). Retrieved May 10, 2003, from http://www.ed.gov/offices/OUS/Budget03/summary/index.html.

Elder, G. H. & Conger, R. D. (2000). *Children of the land: Adversity and success in rural America.* Chicago: University of Chicago Press.

Elliot, D., & Voss, H. (1974). *Delinquency and dropout.* Lexington, MA: Lexington Books.

Fletcher, A. C., Elder, G. H., Jr., & Mekos, D. (2000). Parental influence on adolescent involvement in community activities. *Journal of Research on Adolescence, 10,* 29–48.

Furstenberg, F., Cook, T., Eccles, J., Elder, G., & Sameroff, A. (1999). *Managing to make it: Urban families in adolescent success.* Chicago: University of Chicago Press.

Grossman, J. B., & Tierney, J. P. (1998). Does mentoring work?: An impact study of the Big Brothers Big Sisters Program. *Evaluation Review, 22,* 403–426.

Hahn, A., Leavitt, T., & Aaron, P. (1994). *Evaluation of the Quantum Opportunity Program (QOP): Did the program work?* Waltham, MA: Brandeis University, Heller Graduate School.

Hanks, M. P., & Eckland, B. K. (1976). Athletics and social participation in the educational attainment process. *Sociology of Education, 49,* 271–294.

Hansen, D., Larson, R., & Dworkin, J. (2003). What adolescents learn in organized youth activities: A survey of self-reported developmental experiences. *Journal of Research on Adolescence, 13,* 25–56.

Harms, T., Jacobs, E. V., & White, D. R. (1996). *School-Age Environment Rating Scale (SACERS).* New York: Teachers College Press, Columbia University.

Hultsman, W. Z. (1992). Constraints to activity participation in early adolescence. *Journal of Early Adolescence, 12,* 280–299.

Jackson, E. L., Rucks, V. C. (1993). Reasons for ceasing participation and barriers to participation: Further examination of constrained leisure as an internally homogeneous concept. *Leisure Sciences, 15,* 217–230.

Jacobs, J. E., Lanza, S., Osgood, D. W., Eccles, J. S., & Wigfield, A. (2002). Changes in children's self-competence and values: Gender and domain differences across grades one through twelve. *Child Development, 73,* 509–527.

Jarrett, R. L. (1997). African American family and parenting strategies in impoverished neighborhoods. *Qualitative Sociology, 20,* 275–288.

Jones, M. B., & Offord, D. R. (1989). Reduction of antisocial behavior in poor children by nonschool skill-development. *Journal of Child Psychology and Psychiatry, 30,* 737–750.

Kinney, D. A. (1993). From nerds to normals: The recovery of identity among adolescents from middle school to high schools. *Sociology of Education, 66,* 21–40.

Lamborn, S. D., Brown, B. B., Mounts, N. S., & Steinberg, L. (1992). Putting school in perspective: The influence of family, peers, extracurricular participation, and part-time work on academic engagement. In F. M. Newmann (Ed.), *Student engagement and achievement in American secondary schools* (pp. 153–181). New York: Teacher College Press.

Larson, R. W. (1994). Youth organizations, hobbies, and sports as developmental contexts. In E. R. K.. Silberiesen & E. Todt (Eds.), *Adolescence in context: The interplay of family, school, peers, and work in adjustment* (pp. 46–65). New York: Springer-Verlag.

Larson, R. W. (2000). Toward a psychology of positive youth development. *American Psychologist, 55*, 170–183.

Larson, R. W., & Verma, S. (1999). How children and adolescents spend time across the world: Work, play, and developmental opportunities. *Psychological Bulletin, 125*, 701–736.

Larson, R., Wilson, R., Brown, B. B., Furstenberg, F. F., & Verma, S. (2002). Changes in Adolescents' interpersonal experiences: Are they being prepared for adult relationships in the 21st century? *Journal of Research on Adolescence, 12*, 31–68.

Lerner, R. M., Fisher, C. B., & Weinberg, R. A. (2000). Toward a science for and of the people: Promoting civil society through the application of developmental science. *Child Development, 71*, 11–20.

Levesque, R. J. (1993). The romantic experience of adolescents in satisfying love relationships. *Journal of Youth & Adolescence, 22*, 219–251.

Mahoney, J. L. (2000). Participation in school extracurricular activities as a moderator in the development of antisocial patterns. *Child Development, 71*, 502–516.

Mahoney, J. L. (2003, Spring). A critical commentary on the National Evaluation of the 21st Century Community Learning Centers. *21 community news: A newsletter for the schools of the 21st century* (pp. 1, 6). New Haven: Schools of the 21st Century, Yale University.

Mahoney, J. L., & Bergman, L. R. (2002). Conceptual and methodological considerations in a developmental approach to the study of positive adaptation. *Journal of Applied Developmental Psychology, 23*, 195–217.

Mahoney, J. L., & Cairns, R. (1997). Do extracurricular activities protect against early school dropout? *Developmental Psychology, 33*, 241–253.

Mahoney, J. L., Cairns, B. D., & Farmer, T. (2003). Promoting interpersonal competence and educational success through extracurricular activity participation. *Journal of Educational Psychology, 95*, 409–418.

Mahoney, J. L., & Magnusson, D. (2001). Parent participation in community activities and the persistence of criminality. *Development & Psychopathology, 31*, 125–141.

Mahoney, J. L., Schweder, A. E., & Stattin, H. (2002). Structured after-school activities as a moderator of depressed mood for adolescents with detached relations to their parents. *Journal of Community Psychology, 30*, 69–86.

Mahoney, J. L., Stattin, H., & Magnusson, D. (2001). Youth recreation center participation and criminal offending: A 20-year longitudinal study of Swedish boys. *International Journal of Behavioral Development, 25*, 509–520.

Marsh, H. W. (1992). Extracurricular activities: Beneficial extension of the traditional curriculum or subversion of academic goals? *Journal of Educational Psychology, 84*, 553–562.

Marshall, N., Garcia-Coll, C., Marx, F., McCartney, K., Keefer, N. & Ruh, J. (1997). After-school time and children's behavioral adjustment. *Merrill-Palmer Quarterly, 43*, 498–514.

Masten, A. S., & Coatsworth, J. D. (1998). The development of competence in favorable and unfavorable environments. *American Psychologist, 53*, 205–220.

McHale, S. M., Crouter, A. C., & Tucker, C. J. (2001). Free-time activities in middle childhood: Links with adjustment in early adolescence. *Child Development, 72*, 1764–1778.

McLaughlin, M. W. (2000). *Community counts: How youth organizations matter for youth development*. Washington, DC: Public Education Network.

McNeal, R. B. (1995). Extracurricular activities and high school dropouts. *Sociology of Education, 68*, 62–81.

McNeal, R. B. (1998). High school extracurricular activities: Closed structures and stratifying patterns of participation. *The Journal of Educational Research, 91*, 183–191.

National Institute of Child Health and Human Development [NICHD] Early Child Care Research Network. (2004). Are child development outcomes related to before/after-school care arrangements? Results from the NICHD Study of Early Child Care. *Child Development, 75*, 280–295.

Newman, F. M., Wehlage, G. G. & Lamborn, S. D. (1992). The significance and sources of student engagement. In F. M. Newmann (Ed.), *Student engagement and achievement in American secondary schools* (pp. 11–39). New York: Teachers College Press.

Otto, L. B. (1975). Extracurricular activities in the educational attainment process. *Rural Sociology, 40*, 162–176.

Otto, L. B. (1976). Extracurricular activities and aspirations in the status attainment process. *Rural Sociology, 41*, 217–233.

Pettit, G. S., Bates, J. F., Dodge, K. A., & Meece, D. W. (1999). The impact of after-school peer contact on early adolescent externalizing problems is moderated by parental monitoring, perceived neighborhood safety, and prior adjustment. *Child Development, 70*, 768–778.

Pettit, G. S., Laird, R. D., Bates, J. E., & Dodge, K. A. (1997). Patterns of after-school care in middle childhood: Risk factors and developmental outcomes. *Merrill-Palmer Quarterly, 43*, 515–538.

Posner, J. K., & Vandell, D. L. (1999). After-school activities and the development of low-income urban children: A longitudinal study. *Developmental Psychology, 35*, 868–879.

Quinn, J. (1999). Where need meets opportunity: Youth development programs for early teens. In R. Behrman (Ed.), *The future of children: When school is out* (pp. 96–116). Washington, DC: The David and Lucile Packard Foundation.

Reid, J. B., & Patterson, G. R. (1989). The development of antisocial behavior patterns in childhood and adolescence: Personality and aggression [Special issue]. *European Journal of Personality, 3*, 107–119.

Roth, J. L., & Brooks-Gunn, J. (2003). What is a youth development program? Identification of defining principles. In R. M. Lerner, F. Jacobs, & D. Wertlieb (Eds.), *Promoting positive child, adolescent, and family development: A handbook of program and policy innovations* (Vol. 2, pp. 197–224). Thousand Oaks, CA: Sage.

U.S. Department of Education, Office of the Under Secretary. (2003). *When schools stay open late: The national evaluation of the 21st century learning centers program, first year findings*. Washington, DC: Author.

Youniss, J., McLellan, J. A., Su, Y., & Yates, M. (1999). The role of community service in identity development: Normative, unconventional, and deviant orientations. *Journal of Adolescent Research, 14*, 248–261.

Youniss, J., Yates, M., & Su, Y. (1997). Social integration: Community service and marijuana use in high school seniors. *Journal of Adolescent Research, 12*, 245–262.

2

Historical Change in Leisure Activities During After-School Hours

Douglas A. Kleiber
Gwynn M. Powell
University of Georgia

The idea of leisure was given new meaning for adults as a consequence of the industrial revolution (see, e.g., Cross, 1990; deGrazia, 1962). The advent of compulsory education brought leisure into focus for children as well. There is considerable evidence that spontaneous play and games have been common to childhood for centuries and in most cultures (e.g., Aries, 1962; I. Opie & P. Opie, 1969), but the emergence of distinguishable and identifiable free time periods has resulted from the dedication of other periods of time to obligatory purposes, in particular to work and school. Changing social institutions and the resulting changes in expectations for time use are thus central elements in the evolution of after-school leisure activities for youth.

Childhood itself was redefined to some extent in the wake of the industrial revolution when the protection of children was enacted through child labor laws that specified the age at which children could be employed and limited the number of daily hours they could work. Compulsory education was a partial answer to the freeing of children from the harsh conditions of employment, but other solutions were sought, particularly in large cities, to address the remaining hours of idleness. Thus, by the end of the 19th century, parks had been designed and playgrounds were being constructed in all major U.S. cities, and the Rational Recreation Movement was born (see, e.g., Kraus, 1997). The movement had many facets, including the so-

23

cial integration of adult immigrants through "settlement" houses and urban planning around park lands, but the occupation of unemployed and unsupervised children was a primary concern of turn-of-the-century politicians and reformers.

In addition to the shortening of the workday and the expansion of available park and playground space, the delineation of ways in which play influences development (e.g., Lee, 1915) also contributed to the redefinition of childhood in American society. Play was seen as "a critical element in children's lives" (Halpern, 2002, p. 181) especially for its value in combating the alienating conditions of urban life. But at this point, only the organized versions of play were gaining public approval and were being endorsed mostly by the more educated segments of society for the less educated; Goodman (1979) concluded that early attempts to educate the working class about how best to play and use leisure appropriately were largely ignored.

The influx of large numbers of immigrants into urban areas of the United States during this time period created still another meaning and purpose for leisure (Riess, 1989). Structured activities were used by settlement houses to teach immigrants to be "solid citizens." Organized sports in particular grew out of this climate as a vehicle of socialization for both immigrants and their children. As Riess (1989) pointed out, sport was regarded as valuable for acculturating immigrants and their progeny—or at least the male members of each group—into such "basic American values as hard work, cooperation and respect for authority" (p. 151). Physical fitness was of secondary importance; indeed, as Hardy (1982) noted, "this worship of muscular ability could lead to thousands spending a sunny afternoon *sitting* in the stands" (p. 195). But large numbers of children and youth began participating, and the sense of community sports created for adults offered "order, identity, stability, and association" in a time of uncertainty and social unrest (p. 197). The play organizers of the time recognized an opportunity "to forge a new equilibrium among cultural bipolarities … [such as] individualism versus social cooperation" (Cavallo, 1981, p. 147). And although the earliest community efforts of the time focused on activities for boys and men, by 1912, organizations such as the Girl Scouts began to develop programs for girls that would explore similar themes (Swanson & Spears, 1995). Still, opportunities for girls to be involved in sports and other forms of physical recreation were restricted, and, in spite of legislation to the contrary, continue to be to this day (cf. Anshel, 1997).

Public school reform was another process that identified leisure as an important subject. "Educating for the worthy use of leisure" was one of the seven cardinal principles published in a report of the National Education Association's Commission on the Reorganization of Secondary Education (1918). It is unclear as to whether the effective and appropriate utilization of the after-school period was envisioned for that purpose; but as is true today, it was the *misuse* of available free time—toward delinquent, criminal, anti-social, and self-destructive activities—that was of more concern to early educators and urban reformers than using the time to any particular developmental advantage. Nevertheless, the potential for play, recreation and sport to be developmentally useful was probably of as much interest to reformers in the early part of the 20th century as it is today.

Changes in labor laws, the institution of compulsory education, the demands of accommodating a large influx of immigrants, and an appreciation for the value and importance of play were thus among the critical factors creating a context for the emergence of after-school programs in the late 19th and early 20th centuries. This diversity of influences may also offer a partial explanation for the range of *purposes* that has characterized the evolution of such programs. In reviewing this history as it applied to low income children, Halpern (2002) noted that care and protection of children, the opportunity for creativity and self-expression, the deterrence of crime and delinquency, the cultivation of vocational talents (albeit differently for girls and boys) and the "Americanization" of immigrants were all reflected (though not all at once) in the implicit or explicit missions and common practices of these programs. Commenting on these purposes in later decades, Medrich, Roizen, Rubin, and Buckley (1982) differentiated them into two groups—social control and opportunity enhancement—noting that the latter better described upper income area programs whereas the former was the more overarching purpose in low-income area programs. But they also noted that all of the programs they reviewed demonstrated a mixture of both purposes.

Program foci have also been subject to more general changes in prevailing social, political, and economic conditions over the course of the last century. Halpern (2002) noted that economic depressions have, on one hand, made such programs more important as school budgets have been constrained—threatening the likes of art, music, and physical education, for example—and both parents have been forced to work. On the other hand, these same conditions have also left such programs desperately short of the resources and personnel needed to compensate and serve any of the purposes noted. At times the federal government has seen fit to provide the necessary resources; Halpern points to Roosevelt's introduction of the Works Progress Administration programs in the wake of the depression of the 1930s as a prominent example.

World War II also weighed in as influential in the evolution of after-school programs in the United States according to Halpern (2002). For one thing, it pulled a good number of women into the workforce as male workers joined the armed forces, making child care an issue as a result. Secondly, after-school programs struggled with whether to address children's war-related anxieties—with counseling, distracting activities, or dramatic war play—or to actually enlist children in the war effort by having them "make bandages and service flags, knit clothing for soldiers, and cultivate 'victory gardens'" (p. 198).

The greatly expanded female workforce created by World War II was undone to some extent when the military men returned home, but the sense of entitlement for women to work outside the home was only slightly dampened as a result (Halpern, 2002). Life had changed and other factors, such as the increase in divorce, led to a more general expectation that women would be more involved in the workforce and thus less available for childcare. Indeed, one might argue that such expectations have been largely responsible for the recent, rapid expansion of funding for after-school programs and activities in a substantial way and that such activities and services are now required rather than merely desirable for avoiding self-care arrangements for children, particularly in working-class families.

In reviewing this history and the more recent changes in after-school leisure activities, it is clear that responses have been both *formal*, with communities and schools themselves providing alternatives for children in after-school hours that would be enjoyably preoccupying, instructive, or both, and *informal*, with alternatives being defined inventively by children and youth themselves and, increasingly, by the marketplace. We review the trends in these two different categories, as well as their interrelationship and the factors influencing them, in the text that follows. We end with some policy considerations and alternative directions for after-school programs in light of more recent changes. However, we leave to the chapters that follow a more specific explication of the developmental considerations that would guide policy and practice.

THE EVOLUTION OF INFORMAL
AFTER-SCHOOL ACTIVITIES

In the course of the last 150 years, long afternoons of obligatory field or factory work for children and youth have given way to a wide variety of discretionary activities. These activities include self-directed play and games, casual socializing, gang participation, television watching, caring for siblings, participating in organized activities (to be reviewed in the next section), and the more instrumental activities of completing homework and generating spending money through paid employment. Opportunities have certainly varied by race, gender, and social class, among other factors, but it still seems reasonable to assume that gains in available time have accrued for nearly every group in society, especially among children in the United States. Assessments of time use in childhood and adolescence in the United States suggest a dramatic shift from nearly 10 hours per day spent in household and income-generating labor during early American society (Johnson,

2002) to less than 1 hour in 1998 (Larson & Verma, 1999). Other studies have revealed that contemporary youth in the United States have more discretionary time (6.5 to 8 hours per day) than youth in countries in East Asia and Europe (4 to 7.5 hours per day; Larson, 2001). And this available free time has apparently increased since 1980, when an average of 5 to 6 hours of free time per day in the United States was documented (Mauldin & Meeks, 1990). According to one recent study, only 31% of American youth spend 2 or more hours on homework per day as compared to 50 to 80% of the same-age youth in France, Russia, Spain, Israel, Hungary, and Italy (U.S. Department of Education, 1996).

Child-rearing patterns have also changed over time, of course, and have predictably influenced the free-time activity of children and youth, particularly around the subject of freedom and autonomy. A comparison of primary family values of "Middletown" parents of the early 1980s with those of the 1930s indicated a sharp decline in the importance of obedience and a comparable increase in the importance of independence (Caplow, Bahr, Chadwick, Hill, & Williamson, 1982), a trend that has likely continued with this more recent turn of the century. This change has arguably promoted a greater level of comfort with leaving children and adolescents unattended to some extent as parents work outside the home. But Elkind's (1981) assessment of this trend was that there is pressure associated with that independence expectation (which may be more a reflection of neglect in some cases) and that contemporary children are "hurried" in their emotional growth process as a result. Too much is expected of them too soon. According to Elkind, such children experience responsibility overload, change overload, and emotional overload. He argues further that the hurrying of children results in large part because parents hurry themselves (cf. Linder, 1970). This orientation also makes participation in organized activities a desirable alternative for parents, a subject we consider further in the second section of this chapter. Although some independence is sacrificed in such activities, the knowledge that children and adolescents are developing abilities of various kinds and that they are cared for in a relatively safe environment is usually sufficient justification.

Nevertheless, children and adolescents often eschew any formally arranged activities after school, given the structure and formality of the preceding hours of classroom instruction. The Mood of American Youth study (Horatio Alger Association, 1996) reported that through the 1980s and 1990s, the top three activities for adolescents were listening to music, spending time with friends, and watching television or videos. According to this investigation, while students reported spending less than 1 hour per day on homework, they spent more than 4 hours per day watching television and just slightly less listening to music. Reading for enjoyment dropped significantly from 1983 to 1996, with only 3.5 hours per week spent on that activity in 1996. "Hanging out" has been a common activity for adolescents for many years. The time spent with friends has ranged from meeting on the corner or at the fence post to "cruising the strip" in groups. Individual communication has changed as well, from pen pals to telephone calls and more recently to electronic mail and instant messaging.

Although age, gender, and parental expectations dictate the extent to which children and adolescents are free to take advantage of the freedom that after-school hours might provide, several factors have circumscribed the choices that are available to American children and adolescents. The three most significant influences in the last 50 years have been: the decrease in safe places to play; the expansion of technology; and, for adolescents, the evolution of a consumer economy that makes paid work an attractive alternative to leisure activity.

Loss of Safety, Rise of Risk

Anecdotal evidence has long suggested a decline in participation in traditional child-organized games (Devereux, 1976); yet perennial games such as "hide and seek," that have been documented as early as 1605 (Aries, 1962), continue to exist to some extent. The major changes are not necessarily in the type of play, but rather in play opportunities. Informal social play depends on a sense of safety in the immediate environment. The conversion of nearby vacant lots for other purposes and a greater prospect of crime in nearly all public settings has undermined that general sense of safety. Even where children are unafraid, parents are often unwilling to let children out of their sight. A concern for safety and supervision is among the more prominent factors leading to the steady increase in parental preference for organized activities, a subject we take up shortly; but suffice to say here about younger children that whatever gains in independence might have been sought and achieved over the years have been attenuated by a growing concern for safety, particularly in urban and suburban areas.

Unstructured outdoor play has been particularly threatened as not only vacant lots but also nearby woodlands have virtually disappeared in most locales, leading to what Rivkin (1995) referred to as a "shrinking habitat" for children. With continuing land development, there is less open space for play, and existing space is more likely to be segmented and divided by roads. This physical change coupled with the concern of caregivers for the safety of the children has severely limited the "roaming ground" of modern children. Other studies (Devereux, 1976; Mergen, 1991; Sutton-Smith, 1981) reported a decline of make-believe games and backyard games of physical skill. This is an unfortunate trend according to the proponents of outdoor play, such as Rivkin (1995), who assert that unstructured play in outdoor spaces encourages imagination and way-finding skills, and increases "tangible ways of knowing" unfiltered by adult intervention. According to Rivkin, exploring the neighborhood provides children with an opportunity "to navigate immediate environs ... [and] construct for themselves the geography of their daily life ... thereby laying the foundation for the courage ... to lead their own lives" (p. 80). Unfortunately, as available land has been converted, the critical mass of participants for such adventurous play has declined in most American neighborhoods as well, thus diminishing the "web of sociability" necessary to sustain such play (Halpern, 2002, p. 202).

Expectations for emotional independence are considerably higher for adolescents than younger children, of course, but opportunities for being adventurous have been restricted for this age group as well, though for different reasons. The safety concerns of parents that counteract independence expectations for younger children give way in adolescence to the concern about possible participation in illegal or health-compromising activities (see, e.g., Cahill, 1990). This is especially true once adolescents reach the age where they can acquire a driver's license, because parents, like the police, generally know about the relationship between driving at night and criminal activity (Osgood, Wilson, O'Malley, Bachman, & Johnston, 1996).

Full consideration of demographic changes is beyond the scope of this chapter, and so we are endeavoring to represent a generally modal position on their historical influence; but one factor that has raised considerable concern about safety in American families over the last 50 years is the increasing prevalence of divorce. Evidence about the impact of divorce on parental involvement with children in recreation and enrichment activities is equivocal (see, e.g., Key & Sanik, 1990; National Survey of America's Families, 1997), but there is at least some evidence that lower levels of parental monitoring are associated with higher levels of risky leisure activity (e.g., Meschke & Silbereisen, 1998).

To the extent that leisure is characterized by intrinsically motivated activity (e.g., Kelly, 1993; Kleiber, 1999), delinquent activities may themselves be considered within the category of leisure. And when one considers that delinquent activities may also be both ability testing and socially integrative in establishing an adolescent's status with peers (e.g., Silbereisen, Eyferth, & Rudinger, 1986; Silbereisen & Noack, 1988), their attraction is understandable. Peers often provide the appreciative audience that adolescents seek in engaging in deviant activities. The lack of an adult "guardian" is reinforcing to a sense of freedom and independence. In a longitudinal study of 1,700 18- to 26-year-olds, routine casual socializing behavior with peers was predictive of increased criminal behavior, alcohol, and drug use, and dangerous driving (Osgood et al., 1996). The investigators surmised that there is not much difference in offenders otherwise; many adolescents have an "openness to delinquency" that may simply lie dormant for lack of conducive circumstances. An encouraging and idle peer group often provides such conditions, creating what Csikszentmihalyi and Larson (1984) referred to as a "deviation amplifying" effect.

Thus, for both children and adolescents, the risks associated with free time act as deterrents to parental liberalism and independence expectations, and argue instead for supervision in the hours after school and in the evening as well. But low- and middle-income parents who are employed are often not in a position to arrange alternative supervision. "Latchkey children," usually just old enough to run the risk of being allowed home on their own, consequently become a primary target population for after-school programs among both policymakers and the children's parents. But, for better or worse, with the emergence of electronic technology, the opportunities for diversion at home have also expanded dramatically and, for some parents and children, offer a suitable alternative to paid supervision or program enrollment.

The Impact of Electronic Media on After-School Leisure Activity

From its beginnings in radio, through the advent of television, to the ever-expanding variety of computer games and communication devices, electronic media have established a ubiquitous presence in contemporary American home life, often dominating after-school hours. Television watching, especially, continues to be embraced by parents to effectively "babysit" children in their absence, a presumably safe alternative to activities that would take place outside the home. It is also far less expensive than paying for supervision or some type of instruction. Even when parents are present, the preoccupation of children with electronic media of various kinds allows parents to attend to other activities. The leisure available in the evenings and on weekends is often taken up with media of various forms, and the same can be said of after-school hours that are not committed to homework, chores, informal social interaction, or structured activities.

In the 1930s, after-school time was specifically targeted by "children's hour" radio programs, and children ages 9 to 12 were listening to 2 to 3 hours of radio per day (Paik, 2001). Television quickly replaced radio as the focus of home attention after its introduction in the early 1950s. With steady increases over subsequent decades, the amount of childhood television time in the late 1980s was estimated to be as much as 30 hours per week (Tangney & Feshbach, 1988), although this may have included passive exposure as well as intentional viewing. A more recent study established an age difference in actual television watching, with 5- to 11-year-olds watching 14 hours per week and adolescents watching between 18 and 20 hours per week (Robinson & Bianchi, 1997).

One concern about televison viewing is that it preempts more active involvement in play and other leisure activities. Recent research has added evidence in support of the suspected impact of television watching on obesity (Andersen, Crespo, Bartlett, Cheskin, & Pratt, 1998). In a study of over 4,000 children ages 8 through 16, Anderson et al. found that the 26% who watched more than 4 hours of television per day had both more body fat and a significantly higher body mass index than others watching less. On the question of preempted social interaction, an earlier study established that the play behavior of a group of preschool children was significantly less social when compared with play norms collected more than 40 years earlier, and greater exposure to television was considered as the most likely explanation (Barnes, 1970). The tremendously expanded availability of computers now gives children a more interactive relationship with the video monitor, whether it be in playing computer games or "surfing" the Internet; but the "virtual" sociability of computer interaction lacks the interactive dimensionality of face-to-face encounters.

Televisions, computers, and cellular phones have transformed the leisure patterns of virtually everyone, especially in making recreation more physically passive. Paik (2001) discussed societal changes associated with the growth of electronic media such as the decline in visiting face-to-face with friends, the postponement of bedtime (by "13 minutes"), the reduction in pleasure driving, and decreased participation in sport activities. These patterns have been further exacerbated by the emergence of the Internet, according to Paik, although it adds some unique effects as well. In the past, the introduction of new media resulted in the reduction of attention to other forms of media whereas the Internet has the capacity to subsume and extend the current media content; television, movies, and radio can be delivered through the Internet. Also, what was a clear gender gap in computer use—with boys showing considerably more use than girls (Subrahmanyam, Kraut, Greenfield, & Gross, 2001)—has now diminished to a relatively slight difference (National Science Foundation, 1997), due in part perhaps to Internet activity.

The new popularity of computer-based media has, of course, made it even more likely that a child will find himself or herself in front of a screen, inevitably preempting at least to some extent, physical activity, face-to-face communication, and academic preparation. For example, Williams, E. H. Haertel, G. D. Haertel, and Walberg (1982) found a progressively more negative effect on school performance for children who are in front of a screen for under 10 hours a week, 10 to 35 hours, and more than 35 hours per week. Although we must invoke the usual cautions about inferring causality from such correlational findings, it is reasonable to expect that there will be physical, cognitive, and social costs that come as recreation shifts from active to passive and from human contact to machine (video, computer, TV) contact (Zwingmann & Gunn, 1984). However, as Tarpley (2001) pointed out, it is also possible to use the new media in more dynamic, interactive, and even overtly physical ways: "new technologies, like old ones, are simply tools; the extent to which they improve or hinder the cognitive, behavioral, social and physical aspects of the children's lives is ultimately a function of the way in which they are used" (p. 555). After-school programs that address technological competence and media literacy may provide an important antidote to the negative effects of television watching and other forms of media preoccupation.

The Choice to Work

The rapidly approaching world of work typically changes the meaning and focus of leisure for adolescents. As with their working parents, adolescents usually contrast leisure with work—as time for relaxation and escape from expectations and structure (Kleiber, Caldwell, & Shaw, 1993). However, for many adolescents, the free time not spent in school is considered valuable for making money and/or participating at least nominally in the world of adults by doing things that have instrumental value (e.g., learning to repair cars). One study (Poole & Cooney, 1986) reported that leisure and work were viewed by adolescents as entirely segmented contexts, with little influence in either direction, while another (Chamberlain, 1983) established that, at least for working-class youth, leisure was seen as a time for enhancing job prospects. A change to valuing leisure for its relationship to work and consumption appears to be especially true in the United States. In a cross-national, time-period comparison, Stiles, Gibbons, and Peters (1993) replicated a study conducted during the 1970s of teen perceptions of work and leisure and found that 1990s teens from the United States valued and glamorized work more than the 1970s teens.

A growing number of adolescents in the United States have chosen to work in their after-school hours in spite of the fact that doing so may be of questionable developmental value (cf. Greenberger & Steinberg, 1986). The desire to have discretionary income for the purchase of entertainment, clothing, and the accouterments of contemporary youth culture is a driving force behind working. In one recent study, 65% of students surveyed who were holding jobs during the school year reported that they did not have to work but wanted the extra money (Horatio Alger Association, 2001). However, where work is tied to schooling in some meaningful way, it becomes more consistent with meeting developmental tasks and has less of a negative effect on academic performance and vocational aspirations (Stone & Mortimer, 1998). To the extent that after-school programs incorporate some attention to building work-related skills and providing work opportunities, whether paid or voluntary, they expand their potential impact dramatically.

FORMAL AFTER-SCHOOL ACTIVITIES

Skill development and social competence are cultivated in nonvocational ways as well, of course; these powerful motives regularly find expression in formal activities that are organized by adults in the after-school hours. As was noted earlier, program priorities vary considerably by region, city, and neighborhood (see Halpern, 2002; Medrich et al., 1982); but the most commonly cited reason for after-school programs is a need for supervision (Rossi, Daughtery, & Vergun, 1996), a need that is expressed more in urban than rural areas and in private rather than public schools (Medrich et al., 1982). Regardless of the demographic context, however, parents typically also look for opportunities for their children to develop skills and have experiences that will be both enjoyable and developmentally valuable.

Public schools, unfortunately, have typically assumed such responsibilities only reluctantly. Although neglect of children was a concern of early social reformers, educators were not then, nor are they today, generally eager to take up the responsibility for children and youth after that final bell rings at the completion of the formal school day. Tax-based resources for schools have never been so abundant that such responsibility could be assumed without some cost to government-mandated instructional curricula. Hence, when schools would close in the afternoon, teachers sometimes prepared for the next day, and maintenance personnel finished their assigned duties; but the school was closed at the earliest opportunity. This response was further justified in the past with the shortening of work hours and general prosperity that increased the likelihood of at least one parent being at home. Live-in grandparents and other members of extended families also afforded such supervision. This picture changed in the last 50 years due especially to the return of mothers to the workplace, the dearth of affordable supervision alternatives, and the rising interest in the skills to be shaped through co-curricular and extracurricular activities. In addition, communities continue to invest greater amounts of tax revenue into school facilities and, therefore, have increased expectations for their appropriate and productive use, not only for their custodial value, but to "encourage children to use their leisure time in a creative and self-fulfilling way" (Nieting, 1983, p. 9).

Schools have both direct effects on after-school activities, in the control of length of the school day and the provision of programming and facilities, and indirect effects, in setting expectations for time required to complete school assignments—homework—outside of regular school hours. Decisions related to U.S. schools are often handled at a local district level, but national trends are observable as well. The average length of the school term grew dramatically from 1869 (132.2 days) to 1929 (172.7 days), but has remained relatively stable since that time (179.8 in 1990) with the exception of some year-round or extended term variations (U.S. Department of Education, 1996, 1998). The amount of time in school overall has continued to increase, however, with kindergarten moving from half-day to full-day, and prekindergarten programs being added based on the successful gains associated with private preschools and public Head Start programs. Homework too has increased by some estimates; one group of investigators found that the average amount of time spent studying went from 1 hour, 25 minutes per week in 1981 to 2 hours, 14 minutes in 1997 (Cooper, Lindsay, Nye, & Greathouse, 1998). But in spite of such increases in school time and related activities, the time between the hours of 3 and 6 in the afternoon is still generally available for activities, whether organized by the schools or by others.

Extracurricular Activities in the Schools

Extracurricular activities (ECAs) usually imply activities that are done in conjunction with school, but as being supplemental and unnecessary to primary curricular activities. In fact, when extracurricular activities do have a clearer relationship with the curriculum, as with a computer club, they are often called "co-curricular" activities (Haensky, Lupkowski, & Edlind, 1986). But where a school's mission includes the development of the whole child, such a distinction loses its importance In any case, most ECAs and co-curricular activities occur in the after-school hours, although some extend to weekend activities as well, particularly in middle school and high school.

Schools in the United States have defined themselves differently over time depending on the prevailing *zeitgeist*. In the 1960s and 1970s, the mission of the school was broadened to include the development of the "whole person," whereas in the 1980s and 1990s financial constraint and general school failure combined to force a retreat "back to basics" (Holland & Andre, 1987) that continues to prevail today. Furthermore, the current emphasis on outcome assessment and accountability leads to a narrowing of purposes to those that are readily measurable and even a gaze toward after-school activities for help with that agenda (cf. Halpern, 2002). A broader mission, on the other hand, supports the usefulness of ECAs for the development of such things as initiative, leadership ability, organizational skills, and social problem-solving ability, qualities that are not generally cultivated in most classroom settings. If the mission of schools is to help student become "productive members of society and to enjoy life more fully" as was suggested by a national association for supervision and curriculum development (cited in Haensky et al., 1986), athletics, service organizations, student government, and music groups become attractive complements to regular classroom activities. However, where academic performance is the clear priority, the measure of the value of ECAs comes in how they relate to those outcomes, and there is a significant amount of research that offers insight into that relationship. The relationship takes at least five possible forms:

1.   The ECA is directly supportive of academic work. It nurtures skills that are transferable to the classroom setting, or provides a context for the practical application of skills learned in the classroom setting.
2.   The ECA is compensatory and indirectly supportive of academic work. This is the case if it serves to relax the student and offers the kind of release that restores him or her for academic work.
3.   The ECA is complementary with respect to adolescent development. In other words, it serves other aspects of adolescent development that normal classroom activity either cannot or does not because of other more narrowly defined academic priorities. These would include such things as social problem solving, strategic planning and organizing, and leadership training.
4.   The ECA is disruptive. It interferes with success in academic work and/or other adolescent tasks.
5.   The ECA is neutral with respect to other aspects of adolescent life, having little or no influence, positive or negative.

Each of these alternatives may have some degree of validity, and some of the evidence bearing on each is examined elsewhere (Holland & Andre, 1987). But the recent shift in priorities, determined as they are by economic exigencies in most cases, clearly does not do justice to the better of those alternatives. It is also worth noting that most of the attention to extracurricular activities has been addressed to the high-school level. The current growth in after-school programs for elementary and middle-school students has been driven more by a concern for the care, protection, and support of children and families than by an interest in particular activities. Nevertheless, the issues of transfer of training and impact beyond the activities on both school performance and other aspects of life apply to younger children as well. Certainly more research on after-school activities in elementary and middle schools is warranted.

Provision of After-School Activities by Nonschool Agencies

Seven to 8 hours in school is generally regarded by parents, school personnel, and certainly children and adolescents themselves, as enough time to be spent in school supervision, especially given its compulsory character. School-sponsored extracurricular activity was a partial response to the need for alternative activities in after-school hours, but as was noted, such activities are available primarily at the high school level; school-based extracurricular activities for younger children have lagged far behind those available to older brothers and sisters. Fortunately a wide variety of agencies have offered alternative venues for younger children and for older children who seek structured activities outside of the school context. These include Boys and Girls Clubs, YMCAs and YWCOs, municipal recreation and leisure service agencies, Boy Scouts and Girl Scouts, youth sport associations such as Little League, and a range of private instruction in various arts and crafts.

The greatest growth in the last 40 to 50 years has been in organized sport participation; current estimates are that over 20 million children between 6 and 12 years of age are involved (Landers-Potts & Grant, 1999). And the growth has been greatest with younger children. According to data recently collected by the Institute for Social Research at the University of Michigan, weekly participation in organized sports by children between the ages of 6 and 8 grew from around 3 hours in 1981 to over 4½ hours in 1997, although it is twice as high on weekends as in the after-school hours. After-school care in YMCAs has also increased dramatically, doubling from 25% to 50% from 1983 to 1993, according to Landers-Potts and Grant (1999; see also Jacobs, Vernon, & Eccles, chap. 11, this volume.) These increases also represent a shift from boys only to coeducational programming in sports and other outdoor adventure activities. The programs further reflect a shift from decentralized play to adult-controlled athletic programs, an unfortunate development in the eyes of many (see Devereux, 1976; Halpern, 2002; Rivkin, 1995).

One of the results of this historical shift from child-directed to adult-organized and supervised activities is the emergence of what Adler and Adler (1994) called extracurricular "careers." This childhood career begins as recreation, but progresses to less spontaneous, more rationalized, and focused competition. Adler and Adler (1994) discussed youth sports in particular as reproducing the social structure and values of corporate America with its emphasis on product (skill) development and bottom line competition. The extracurricular career is described as typically moving through four phases of play: (a) spontaneous play (with self-directed organization, negotiation, and problem-solving); (b) recreational games (centered around fitness, skill development related to coordination, companionship, and play); (c) recreational team sports (advancing skill development with scoring de-emphasized); and (d) elite competition (with effort and fairness subordinated to skillful performance and accomplishment).

Nevertheless, perhaps because of this pattern of professionalization, and in spite of increases in numbers of participants at younger ages, most children drop out of organized activities by the time they are in middle and high school (Curtis & White, 1984; Ewing & Seefeldt, 1996; Kirshnit, Ham, & Richards, 1989; Malina, 1981). In a 10-year retrospective study of sport drop-outs (Butcher, Linder, & Johns, 2002), 94% of Grade 10 students had dropped out of at least one sport. More importantly, by Grade 7, 20% had dropped out of all sports, and by Grade 10, 42% had dropped out of all sports.

The reasons for the decline in participation have been the subject of a significant amount of research (e.g., Curtis & White, 1984; Ewing & Seefeldt, 1996; Kirshnit et al., 1984). An overemphasis on winning, a lack of fun, an unwillingness to endure school-like discipline, the perceived lack of ability to be competitive at a high level, the lack of social interaction with a broader range of friends outside of the sport, and growing preferences for other activities are common reasons associated with giving up sport involvement, but the desire to move on and away from adult direction is part of it as well. With respect to girls, there is also the view that involvement in sports is inconsistent with cultivating a feminine image.

If participation in active physical activities is desirable for health benefits and other purposes, the loss of interest in sports should be of some concern. And it appears that declining interest in physical activity is not just restricted to interest in sports; it applies to nearly all physical activities and many other social and artistic activities as well (Harrell, Gansky, Bradley, & McMurray, 1997). This is another issue that makes after-school programming an important subject for research as well as for public policy.

POLICY-RELATED CONSIDERATIONS

Policy recommendations for addressing changes in the after-school lives of children and adolescents have come from a variety of sources: local school boards, national education task forces, public health agencies, and federal, state, and local recreation commissions, among others. They have been based on developmental, social, academic, fiscal, and political considerations. The scope of relevant actions extends from isolated decisions of local school boards and leisure services departments, to jointly funded and operated school–community partnerships, to federal mandates to raise test scores through after-hours extended instruction time.

As noted earlier, local school board jurisdiction covers a gamut of responsibilities including length of school day, configuration and length of school calendar, use of school grounds and facilities after hours, allocation of resources for extracurricular events, and promotion or exclusion of leisure activities of any particular type. There is also an implicit assumption that extended instruction will lead to higher academic achievement, and indications are that after-school hours are being coveted for that purpose (Halpern, 2002).

At a national level, physical activity programming is implicated in calls for a reoriented healthcare system in the United States (e.g., Andreoli & Guillory, 1983) based on the recognition that threats to human health have moved from infectious disease (bacteria and virus) to chronic disease (lifestyle factors), and more recently because of the tremendous increase in childhood obesity (Andersen et al., 1998). Regular cuts to funding for health-related public services such as school health and physical education curricula and municipal park and recreation programs, on the other hand, seriously threaten such priorities (e.g., Van Horn, 1983). In the last 10 years, policymakers have been urged to direct scarce resources to programs for youth at risk with the argument that allocation of funding to this target population would generate a wide variety of benefits while reducing both delinquent behavior and social disparities (e.g., Smith, 1991); but government responses have been sporadic and of questionable efficacy. (See Eccles & Gootman, 2002, for a more contemporary review of research and policy in this area.)

Among the more common positions of child advocacy groups with respect to leisure in childhood is the commitment to protect the "space" that children have for themselves. For example, organized sports in childhood are regularly criticized (see Kohn, 1992; Sports Illustrated, 2000) for the excess intrusion of adults in directing the play of children and imposing adult competitive objectives. Encroachment of various media, particularly televised violence, into childhood is another prominent example. In reviewing this history, Trotta (2001) identified how advocacy groups have resisted this encroachment and facilitated change through public policy initiatives, internal industry review, independent research, technical consultation, consumer movements, and news media campaigns among other measures. To the extent that the after-school period becomes more clearly targeted, it is reasonable to expect both the same kinds of encroachment threats and the same responses from advocacy groups. Organizations such as the After-School Alliance and National School-Age Care Alliance may be expected to play both a watchdog role and a development role in increasing funding, training, and awareness.

Additionally, the National Research Council (Eccles & Gootman, 2002) has begun the process of constructing a framework of features of community programs that facilitate youth development. Although the 2002 report covered a wide variety of settings, the features outlined and the recommendations offered are particularly applicable to after-school programs. The report challenges programmers and policymakers to promote development at the program level, increase research indicator and outcome documentation, and serve a diverse population. The recommended features of positive developmental settings include: physical and psychological safety, appropriate structure, supportive relationships, opportunities to belong, positive social norms, support for efficacy and mentoring, opportunities for skill building, and the integration of family, school, and community efforts. These benchmarks provide focal points for fostering positive growth and for pinpointing areas for development.

Integration of efforts, however, has not happened easily in many cases. Where communities have come together to address the needs of families, in the form of child care and developmentally appropriate program options, policies, prerogatives, and practices have often come into conflict. Although schools, churches, recreation agencies, and other public social services have been distinguishable in their general purposes and practices with respect to children, all have been able to claim responsibility for children's well-being. As Halpern (2002) pointed out, this has left after-school programs as "vulnerable and malleable institutions," (p. 204) with a legacy of ambiguity with respect to responsibility, mission, and purpose. The more positive view of this in Halpern's view, however, is that the inability of any one institutional sector to claim or be ceded the responsibility for after-school programs allows them to be "adult-directed institutions where the agenda is relatively modest" (p. 170) lest there be charges of encroachment of one set of values and purposes over another. Nevertheless, the ambiguity of purposes and responsibilities should not be justification for institutional restraint. It may be that the best work is to be done at the dialectical intersection of various agency interests and the voices of the participants themselves.

TOWARD A NEW SYNTHESIS OF LEISURE AND EDUCATION IN THE AFTER-SCHOOL PERIOD

After-school programs have great potential for reducing the risks that children and adolescents face and for contributing to their development and well being. Although the body of evidence for the value and impact of after-school programs is limited, there is enough to offer direction. The outcomes can be classified into three main categories: (a) reduction of antisocial behavior and/or enhancement of prosocial behavior (prevention of negative behaviors, increase in positive behaviors, and crime reduction); (b) enhancement of opportunities for self-expression and skill development; and (c) enhancement of school-related achievement (academic preparation, intellectual development, and academic aspiration) (see also Reno & Riley, 1998, 2000; Witt, 2001). The trends in program development center around the awareness of programmers regarding the relationship between program design and outcomes. The implementation stage of any programmatic intervention should address the deeper needs of the full range of potential participants and, as the evidence suggests, by giving special attention to utilizing competent and caring adults in the provision of opportunities and leadership of activities (Witt, 2001). But in the end, because the programs are not compulsory, children and adolescents will respond to unappealing programs by "voting with their feet" (Medrich et al., 1982).

Turn-of-the-century reformers responded to a variety of social changes by trying to increase the social capital among young people at the time; the emerging significance of the after-school period provides a similar opportunity at this point in time. Although the chapters that follow in this volume address the questions about the best way to utilize this time period, the explosion of after-school programs and participants provides a ready source of data to be analyzed and challenges to be addressed. Among the variables most likely to be critical is the balance between adult-structured activities and child-organized activities. Even in the early years of the play movement, adults came to recognize that "close supervision took some of the creativity out of play" (Riess, 1989, p. 167), thus diluting the very benefits they were trying to promote (Devereux, 1976; Halpern, 2002; Sutton-Smith, 1981). Given the changes in society, reduction in safe places to play and changes in parental expectations, perhaps the new synthesis of leisure and education during after-school time is the creation of psychological and physical space where learning is self-directed and adults are "on the sidelines," as consultants, in whatever enterprise is envisioned by those who have the advantage of a protected space. Time will tell.

REFERENCES

Adler, P. A., & Adler, P. (1994). Social reproduction and the corporate other: The institutionalization of after-school activities. *The Sociological Quarterly, 35,* 309–328.

Andersen, R. E., Crespo, C. J., Bartlett, S. J., Cheskin, L. J., & Pratt, M. (1998). Relationship of physical activity and television watching with body weight and level of fatness among children. *Journal of the American Medical Association, 279*(12), 938–942.

Andreoli, K. G., & Guillory, M. M. (1983). Arenas for practicing health promotion. *Family and Community Health, 2,* 28–40.

Anshel, M. H. (1997). *Sport psychology from theory to practice* (3rd ed.). Scottsdale, AZ: Gorsuch/Scarisbrick.

Aries, P. (1962). *Centuries of childhood: A social history of family life* (R. Baldick, Ed.). New York: Vintage Books.

Barnes, K. (1970). Preschool play norms: A replication. *Developmental Psychology, 1,* 99–103.

Butcher, J., Lindner, K. J., & Johns, D. P. (2002). Withdrawal from competitive youth sports: A retrospective ten-year study. *Journal of Sport Behavior, 25,* 145–163.

Cahill, S. (1990). Childhood and public life: Reaffirming biographical divisions. *Social Problems, 37,* 390–402.

Caplow, T., Bahr, H. M., Chadwick, B. A., Hill, R., & Williamson, M. H. (1982). *Middletown families.* Minneapolis: University of Minnesota Press.

Carnegie Council on Adolescent Development. (1992). *A matter of time: Risk and opportunity in the after-school hours.* New York: Carnegie Corporation of New York.

Cavallo, D. (1981). *Muscles and morals: Organized playgrounds and urban reform, 1880–1920.* Philadelphia: University of Pennsylvania Press.

Chamberlain, J. (1983). Adolescent perceptions of work and leisure. *Leisure Studies, 2,* 127–138.

Cooper, H., Lindsay, J. L., Nye, B., & Greathouse, S. (1998). Relationship among attitudes about homework, amount of homework assigned and completed, and student achievement. *Journal of Educational Psychology, 90,* 70–83.

Cross, G. (1990). *A social history of leisure since 1600.* State College, PA: Venture Publishing.

Csikszentmihalyi, M., & Larson, R. (1984). *Being adolescent.* New York: Basic Books.

Curtis, J. E., & White, P. T. (1984). Age and sport participation: Decline in participation or increased specialization with age? In N. Theberge & P. Donnelly (Eds.), *Sport and the sociological imagination* (pp. 273–293). New York: Texas Christian University Press.

DeGrazia, S. (1962). *Of time, work and leisure.* New York: Anchor.

Devereux, E. (1976). Backyard versus Little League: The impoverishment of children's games. In D. Landers (Ed.), *Social problems in sport* (pp. 37–56). Urbana: University of Illinois Press.

Eccles, J., & Gootman, J. A. (Eds.). (2002). *Community programs to promote youth development.* National Council on Research and Institute of Medicine. Washington, DC: National Academy Press.

Elkind, D. (1981). *The hurried child.* Boston: Addison-Wesley.

Ewing, M. E., & Seefeldt, V. (1996). Patterns of participation and attrition in American agency-sponsored youth sports. In. F. Smoll & R. Smith (Eds.), *Children and youth in sport* (pp. 115–132). Madison, WI: Brown & Benchmark.

Goodman, C. (1979). *Choosing sides.* New York: Schocken Books.

Greenberger, E., & Steinberg, L. D. (1986). *When teenagers work.* New York: Basic Books.

Haensky, P., Lupkowski, A., & Edlind, E. (1986). The role of extracurricular activities in education. *High School Journal, 69,* 110–119.

Halpern, R. (2002). A different kind of child development institution: The history of after-school programs for low-income children. *Teachers College Record, 104,* 178–211.

Hardy, S. H. (1982). *How Boston played: Sport, recreation and community 1865–1915.* Boston: Northeastern University Press.

Harrell, J. S., Gansky, S. A., Bradley, C. B., & McMurray, R. G. (1997). Leisure time activities of elementary school children. *Nursing Research, 46,* 246–253.

Holland, A., & Andre, T. (1987). Participation in extracurricular activities in the secondary school: What is known, what needs to be known? *Review of Educational Research, 57,* 437–466.

Horatio Alger Association. (1996). *The mood of American youth 1996.* Alexandria, VA: Horatio Alger Association of Distinguished Americans, Inc.

Horatio Alger Association. (2001). *The state of our nation's youth.* Alexandria, VA: Horatio Alger Association of Distinguished Americans, Inc.

Johnson, C. D. (2002). *Daily life in colonial New England*. Westport, CT: Greenwood Press.

Kelly, J. R. (1983). *Leisure identities and interaction*. London: Allen & Unwin.

Key, R. J., & Sanik, M. M. (1990). The effect of homemaker's employment status on children's time allocation in single- and two-parent families. *Lifestyles: Family and Economic Issues, 11,* 71–88.

Kirshnit, C. E., Ham, M., & Richards, M. H. (1989). The sporting life: Athletic activities during adolescence. *Journal of Youth and Adolescence, 18,* 601–616.

Kleiber, D. (1999). *Leisure experience and human development: A dialectical interpretation*. New York: Basic Books.

Kleiber, D., Caldwell, L, & Shaw, S. (1993). Leisure meanings in adolescence. *Society and Leisure, 16,* 99–104.

Kohn, A. (1992). *No contest: The case against competition*. New York: Houghton Mifflin.

Kraus, R. (1997). *Recreation and leisure in modern society*. New York: Benjamin Cummings.

Landers-Potts, M., & Grant, L. (1999). Competitive climates, athletic skill, and children's status in after-school recreational sports programs. *Social Psychology of Education, 2,* 297–313.

Larson, R. W. (2001). How U.S. children and adolescents spend time: What it does (and doesn't) tell us about their development. *Current Directions in Psychological Science 10,* 160–164.

Larson, R. W., & Verma, S. (1999). How children and adolescents spend time across the world: Work, play and developmental opportunities. *Psychological Bulletin, 125,* 701–736.

Lee, J. (1915). *Play in education*. New York: Macmillan.

Linder, S. (1970). *The harried leisure class*. New York: Columbia University Press.

Malina, R. M. (1981, April). *Cultural pluralism, physical activity and youth sports*. Paper presented at the Annual Youth Sports Forum, East Lansing, MI.

Mauldin, T., & Meeks, C. B. (1990). Sex differences in children's time use. *Sex Roles, 22,* 537–554.

Medrich, E. A., Roizen, J. A., Rubin, V., & Buckley, S. (1982). *The serious business of growing up: A study of children's lives outside of school*. Berkeley: University of California Press.

Mergen, B. (1991). Ninety-five years of historical change in the game preferences of American children. *Play and Culture, 4,* 272–283.

Meschke, L. L., & Silbereisen, R. K. (1998). The association of childhood play and adolescent-parent interactions with German adolescent leisure participation. *Journal of Adolescent Research, 13,* 458–486.

National Education Association Commission on the Reorganization of Secondary Education. (1918). *Cardinal principles of secondary education, bulletin 35*. Washington, DC: U.S. Bureau of Education.

National Survey of America's Families. (1997). 1997 NSAF benchmarking measures of child and family well-being. *NSAF Methodological Reports. Rep. No. 6: Assessing the new federalism: An urban institute program to assess changing social policies*. Washington DC: Urban Institute.

Nieting, P. L. (1983, September/October). School-age children care. *Childhood Education,* 6–11.

National Science Foundation. (1997). U.S. teens and technology. *National Science and Technology Week*. Retrieved November 12, 2002, from http:www.nsf.gov/od/lpa/nstw/teenov.htm

Opie, I., & Opie, P. (1969). *Children's games in street and playground.* Oxford, England: Clarendon Press.

Osgood, D. W., Wilson, J. K., O'Malley, P. M., Bachman, J. G., & Johnston, L. D. (1996). Routine activities and individual deviant behavior. *American Sociological Review, 61,* 635–655.

Paik, H. (2001). The history of children's use of electronic media. In D. G. Singer and J. L. Singer (Eds.), *Handbook of children and media* (pp. 7–27). Thousand Oaks, CA: Sage.

Poole, M. E., & Cooney, G. H. (1986). Work and leisure relationships: An exploration of life possibilities during adolescence. *Journal of Youth and Adolescence, 15,* 475–487.

Reno, J., & Riley, R.W. (1998). *Safe and smart: Making the after-school hours work for kids.* Washington, DC: U.S. Department of Education. Retrieved from http:www.ed.gov/pubs/SafeandSmart

Reno, J., & Riley, R.W. (2000). *Working for children and families: Safe and smart after-school programs.* Washington, DC: U.S. Department of Education. Retrieved from http:www.ed.gov/pubs/parents/SafeSmart

Riess, S. A. (1989). *City games: The evolution of American urban society and the rise of sports.* Chicago: University of Illinois Press.

Rivkin, M. S. (1995). *The great outdoors: Restoring children's right to play outside.* Washington, DC: National Association for the Education of Young Children.

Robinson, J. P., & Bianchi, S. (1997). The children's hours. *American Demographics, 19,* 20–24.

Rossi, R., Daughtery, S., & Vergun, P. (1996). *Extended-day programs in elementary and combined schools.* Washington, DC: U.S. Department of Education, Office of Educational Research and Improvement.

Silbereisen, R., Eyferth, K., & Rudinger, G. (1986). *Development as action in context: Problem behavior and normal youth development.* New York: Springer-Verlag.

Silbereisen, R., & Noack, P. (1988). On the constructive role of problem behaviors in adolescence. In N. Bolger, A. Caspi, G. Downey, & M. Moorehouse (Eds.), *Persons in context: Developmental processes* (pp. 152–180). New York: Cambridge University Press.

Smith, C. (1991). *Overview of youth recreation programs in the United States.* Washington, DC: Carnegie Council on Adolescent Development.

Sports Illustrated. (2000, July). Out of control. *Sports Illustrated,* 87–95.

Stiles, D. A., Gibbons, J. L., & Peters, E. (1993). Adolescents' views of work and leisure in the Netherlands and the United States. *Adolescence 28,* 473–489.

Stone, J. R., & Mortimer, J. T. (1998). The effect of adolescent employment on vocational development: Public and educational policy implications. *Journal of Vocational Behavior, 53,* 184–214.

Subrahmanyam, K., Kraut, R., Greenfield, P., & Gross, E. (2001). New forms of electronic media. In D. G. Singer & J. L. Singer (Eds.), *Handbook of children and media* (pp. 73–99). Thousand Oaks, CA: Sage.

Sutton-Smith, B. (1981). *A history of children's play.* Philadelphia: University of Pennsylvania Press.

Swanson, R.A., & Spears, B. (1995). *History of sport and physical education in the United States* (4th ed.). Madison, WI: Brown & Benchmark.

Tangney, J. P., & Feshbach, S. (1988). Children's television viewing frequency. *Personality and Social Psychology Bulletin, 14,* 145–158.

Tarpley, T. (2001). Children, the Internet, and other technologies. In D. G. Singer and J. L. Singer (Eds.), *Handbook of children and media* (pp. 547–556). Thousand Oaks, CA: Sage.

Trotta, L. (2001). Children's advocacy groups. In D. G. Singer & J. L. Singer (Eds.), *Handbook of children and media* (pp. 699–719). Thousand Oaks, CA: Sage.

U.S. Department of Education. (1996). *International assessment of educational progress: Learning science.* Washington, DC: National Center for Education Statistics. Retrieved May 2, 2002, from http://nces.ed.gov/pubs/yi/y9638a.html

U.S. Department of Education (1998). *Elementary and secondary education: Enrollment.* Washington, DC: National Center for Education Statistics. Retrieved May 2, 2002, from http://nces.ed.gov/pubs2001/digest/tables/PDF/table038.pdf

Van Horn, C. E. (1983). *Children's programs in an era of scarce resources.* New Brunswick, NJ: Eagleton Institute of Politics.

Williams, P. A., Haertel, E. H., Haertel, G. D., & Walberg, H. J. (1982). The impact of leisure-time television on school learning: A reading synthesis. *American Educational Research Journal 19,* 19–50.

Witt, P. (2001). Insuring after-school programs meet their intended goals. *Parks & Recreation, 36,* 32–50.

Zwingmann, C., & Gunn, A. D. G. (1884). The dangers of ill-health through recreation. *Journal of Adolescence 7,* 73–81.

3

Unstructured Leisure in the After-School Hours

D. Wayne Osgood
Pennsylvania State University

Amy L. Anderson
University of Nebraska at Omaha

Jennifer N. Shaffer
Arizona State University West

In the modern industrial world, families and schools share the responsibility for supervising children and youth. Yet there is a gap of 20 to 25 hours per week between adolescents' school schedules and parents' work schedules (U.S. Department of Education and Justice, 2000), leaving 25% to 31% of waking hours during the school week that may not be covered by either institution. The other chapters of this volume concern various structured activities for children and youth that may fill this time. The present chapter provides a context of comparison to those chapters by focusing on unstructured leisure during the after-school hours.

If it is not immediately obvious that unstructured time in the after-school hours can have profound implications for children's development and future lives, consider the following: Snyder and Sickmund (1999) were interested in the potential for late-night curfews to prevent delinquency, so they compiled data about the distribution of juvenile arrests across the hours of the week. Their results, which appear in Fig. 3.1, showed surprisingly few arrests in the late-night and early morning hours. Instead, juvenile arrests were heavily concentrated in the time between the end of the school day

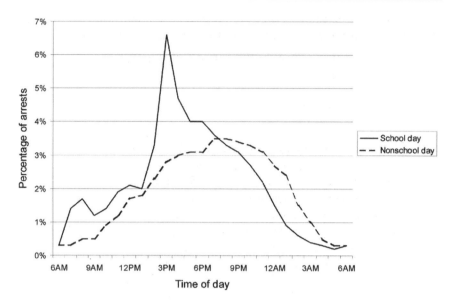

FIG. 3.1.   Juvenile arrests for aggravated assault by time of day. From "Juvenile Offenders and Victims: 1999 National Report" by H. Snyder and M. Sickmund, p. 65.
Adapted with permission.

and the dinner hour. Similarly, there is evidence suggesting that the hours
between 3 p.m. and 6 p.m. are when teenagers are most likely to engage in
sexual intercourse and the hours when many teen pregnancies may begin
(Carnegie Council on Youth Development, Task Force on Youth Development and Community Programs, 1992; Cohen, Farley, Taylor, Martin, &
Schuster, 2002). Thus, what happens during unstructured time after school
has dramatic consequences for at least some children and youth.

The present chapter addresses the nature of unstructured leisure after
school and its relationship to development, especially the development of
problem behaviors such as delinquency, substance use, and precocious sexual behavior. Our interest in this topic stems from previous work applying
criminology's routine activity perspective to individual deviance or problem
behavior (Osgood, Wilson, O'Malley, Bachman, & Johnston, 1996). We begin by considering how developmental outcomes differ between children
who are involved in structured versus unstructured activities. Doing so reveals that this relationship is best understood in the light of not only after-school care arrangements, but also more specific features of time use:
amount of structure, adult supervision, and activity choice. We then turn to
the routine activity perspective for an explanation of why that would be so,
reviewing a variety of evidence that supports the validity and utility of this

explanation. In the final section, we consider the implications of findings about unstructured leisure for policies to promote positive development.

CONTRASTS BETWEEN STRUCTURED AND UNSTRUCTURED ACTIVITIES

Care Arrangements

How is participation in unstructured activities after school related to developmental outcomes? The simplest way of answering this question is in terms of after-school care arrangements, in which case structured activities stand in contrast to adult-care and self-care activities. *Structured activities* would then be those that are organized and supervised by adults, either in a relatively public setting, such as a school, community center, or YMCA, or in a more private setting, such as music lessons or tutoring. In adult care, children or adolescents spend the after-school hours in a home where a parent or another designated adult is responsible for overseeing their activities. It is useful to distinguish two types of self-care. One type is the "latch-key" arrangement, in which children or youth return from school to a home where no adult is present. In the other type of self-care, the unstructured activities take place away from the home, and there is likely to be little constraint on how youths spend this time.

The public generally holds positive views about structured after-school activities, and there is research indicating that this care arrangement is associated with better social integration (Larson 1994), higher school performance (Fuligni & Stevenson, 1995), and fewer behavioral problems (Marshall et al., 1997). People are generally less supportive of self-care because they believe that youth are at high risk for negative outcomes when left to their own devices for long periods of time.

Consistent with this public concern, there is a substantial body of research comparing the developmental outcomes of children who take care of themselves after school with children in after-school programs. In reviewing this research, both Marshall et al. (1997) and Pettit, Laird, Bates, and Dodge (1997) concluded that the relationship between type of after-school care and children's adjustment is inconsistent across studies. To explain these varying results, researchers pointed to factors such as differing operational definitions of "self-care," varying ages of the children involved, and the inclusion of family or neighborhood characteristics as reasons for the mixed results (Belle, 1997; Cole & Rodman, 1987; Lovko & Ullman, 1989; Vandell & Shumow, 1999). For our purposes, the important point is that self-care per se does not necessarily place children and youth at risk. Thus, to understand the developmental consequences of activities in the after-school hours, we must look beyond the simple distinction of care arrangements and consider what is actually going on in those settings. As we show, a child who is home alone watching television is not at increased risk for negative developmental outcomes in the same manner as a child who is allowed to hang out with friends without an adult present.

Adult Supervision

One feature of unstructured activities that is of special interest to us is the degree to which adults are supervising or monitoring children and youth's activities. Formal, structured, after-school activities such as extracurricular sports and music lessons necessarily entail adult supervision. In adult care or self-care, however, the extent of adult oversight for children's activities can vary a great deal. For instance, many parents indirectly monitor the activities of children in self-care by telephone or by arrangements with neighbors, but others do not (e.g., Richardson, Radziszewska, Dent, & Flay, 1993; Vandell & Shumow, 1999). Furthermore, adult care does not necessarily imply that the adult who is present is paying much attention to what the child is doing. Although some parents keep a constant vigil over their children, others take little notice of what they do, allowing them to roam far and wide with no supervision and few restrictions. Furthermore, children and youth who are away from home may or may not be in a setting where there is some level of supervision by adults. For example, consider a pickup game of basketball at a Boys Club versus one at a playground. Although youth may come and go as they please in both settings, there will be adults at the Boys Club who are obligated to see that youth maintain some standard of behavior, whereas this is not as likely at the playground.

Research indicates that developmental outcomes are more closely linked to adult supervision than to care arrangements. Children in self-care who are neither directly nor indirectly monitored by adults on a consistent basis are at higher risk for negative outcomes (e.g., Richardson et al., 1993; Vandell & Shumow, 1999). For example, Steinberg (1986) reported that "self care adolescents whose parents know their whereabouts are less susceptible to peer influence than are adolescents whose parents do not know where (or presumably, how) their children spend their afternoons" (p. 438). Similarly, Mott, Crowe, Richardson, and Flay (1999) found that adolescent cigarette smoking increased substantially when self-care took place in settings that were more removed from direct or indirect adult contact. Finally, Richardson et al. (1993) reported that unsupervised youth who were monitored inconsistently or not at all had significantly higher levels of problem behavior. It is clear that adolescents who are monitored, even indirectly, are at less risk for negative developmental outcomes than those who are not.

Structure

To this point we have referred to all adult-run after-school programs as structured, but it is fruitful to give the term a more precise meaning in distinguishing among after-school activities. Specifically, an activity can be described as *structured* to the degree that it places restrictions on how time is to be spent. In this sense, after-school sports and lessons would be highly structured because adult leaders dictate that participants will engage in a highly specified series of activities. An after-school drop-in program at a community center would be comparatively unstructured if attendees could move among a variety of activities, none of which were highly scripted. Adult-care and self-care settings may typically carry less structure, although parents may still impose a degree of structure, such as maintaining high expectations for chores or homework.

Relatively little research has specifically addressed the impact that this type of structure has on developmental outcomes associated with after-school activities. A pair of studies by Mahoney and colleagues suggests that a lack of structure brings risk for antisocial behavior. Mahoney and Stattin (2000) found that youth who participated in highly structured leisure activities engaged in less antisocial behavior, whereas youth who participated in activities with little structure engaged in more antisocial behavior. Another study by Mahoney, Stattin, and Magnusson (2001) focused on youth recreation centers in Sweden that offered unstructured activities. Controlling for initial risk profiles, they found that youth who became involved in the centers subsequently committed more offenses both as juveniles and as adults. Thus, degree of structure may be critical for whether after-school activities promote or prevent problem behavior.

Socializing With Peers

Next, we consider the content of after-school activities, rather than the context of the activities (as in adult supervision) or an abstract characterization of the activities (as in degree of structure). Our interest is in leisure activities and, of course, some after-school time is devoted to nonleisure pursuits. For example, adolescents generally devote some after-school time to homework (Leone & Richards, 1989) and to household chores (Posner & Vandell, 1999; Timmer, Eccles, & O'Brien, 1985). Youth may also be involved in activities with the potential for skill building (e.g., Larson, 1994), such as art, music lessons, hobbies, or youth organizations (which children and youth may or may not regard as leisure). Most children and youth also occupy some of their time after school using media such as reading, listening to music (e.g., radio and CDs), or watching television. Watching television is by far the most frequent of these, accounting for almost 13% of their waking hours in junior high school and decreasing to just over 7% in high school (Larson & Kleiber, 1993).

Another major category of leisure activity is socializing or playing with others, which includes direct interaction or remote communication. Larson and Kleiber (1993) found that high school students spend about 16% of their waking time socializing, and this was their most frequent free-time activity. It is this last category of activities, *socializing*, that is of greatest interest to us. Research has consistently shown that children and youth who spend more time socializing with peers engage in more problem behavior. For example, high-school students who spend more time socializing with peers have poorer grades (Fuligni & Stevenson, 1995; Larson & Richards, 1991), engage in more delinquent behavior (Agnew & Petersen, 1989; Osgood et al., 1996), and more often use drugs (Wallace & Bachman, 1991). Problem behavior is especially likely when socializing with peers is combined with an absence of adult supervision (Flannery, Williams, & Vazsonyi, 1999).

A ROUTINE ACTIVITY EXPLANATION OF THE RELATIONSHIP OF TIME USE TO PROBLEM BEHAVIOR

The findings just reviewed indicate that children and adolescents have higher rates of a variety of problem behaviors when their after-school activities are less often supervised by adults, are less structured, and include more socializing with peers. The remainder of this chapter focuses on our explanation for this consistent pattern of findings, which is a variation of criminology's routine activity theory (Cohen & Felson, 1979) that Osgood and colleagues (1996) developed for explaining individual offending. The core theme of *routine activity theory* is that ordinary activities influence behavior by shaping opportunities. The individual-level version of the theory is useful here because our concern is with the connection of youths' time use to their own problem behavior.

A central concept for the individual-level version of the theory is Briar and Piliavin's (1965) idea of *situational motivation*, which is that the motivation for delinquency is inherent in the situation rather than in the person. Briar and Piliavin (1965) assumed that problem behaviors "are prompted by short-term situationally induced desires experienced by all ..." (p. 36). This view of problem behavior is also found in Gold's (1970) portrayal of delinquency as a "pickup game," analogous to a pickup game of basketball or baseball. To participate, one needs "to be there when the opportunity arises and when others are willing" (Gold, 1970. p. 94), which emphasizes that the behavior typically is casual and spontaneous.

If the motivation for deviance is inherent in situations, the question then becomes: What types of activities are most likely to bring people into contact with situational inducements to deviance? Osgood et al. (1996) provided a rationale as to why such opportunities for deviance or problem behavior would be especially prevalent during activities that combine the three characteristics already highlighted: socializing with peers, a lack of structure, and the absence of supervising adults.

The theory argues that the company of peers greatly increases situational inducements to problem behavior. Gold's (1970) pickup game analogy is useful again because it emphasizes the group nature of most deviance, which matches the abundant evidence that most problem behavior is group behavior (Erickson & Jensen, 1977). The presence of peers can make problem behavior easier and more rewarding. For example, friends may provide resources such as tobacco or alcohol, and their presence can reduce the danger inherent in fighting or stealing. More importantly, the companionship of friends is central to symbolic rewards for problem behavior because peers provide an appreciative audience so that deviant exploits can bolster a social identity as brave, adventuresome, or tough (e.g., Dishion, Spracklen, Andrews, & Patterson, 1996).

In individual-level routine activity theory, unstructured activities are those that carry no agenda for how time is to be spent (Osgood et al., 1996). The less structured an activity, the more likely a person is to encounter opportunities for problem behavior in the simple sense that he or she is not occupied doing something else. For instance, opportunities for problem behavior should be very unlikely at a basketball game that is part of an organized league, where the sequence of activities is highly scripted. The possibility of problem behavior would be somewhat greater at a pickup game, where the sport occupies most time, but the actors could shift to other pursuits at any time. The risk of problem behavior would be greatest for youth who are "hanging out," in a setting such as a park or a street corner, doing nothing in particular.

From the perspective of individual-level routine activity theory, activities are more conducive to deviance if they occur in a setting where there is no adult supervision. Supervising adults are obligated to intervene if problem behavior occurs, and there are adults in this role much of the time at school, at home, and (for employed teens) at work. Therefore, situations conducive to deviance will be most prevalent during those leisure activities away from home that are not organized by adults. Although warm relationships with parents and other adults are an important source of protection against problem behavior (Loeber & Stouthamer-Loeber, 1986), the opportunity function of supervision does not depend on a positive relationship of this sort. As Osgood and colleagues (1996) also stated: "Whether you like or dislike your father, it will be more convenient to smoke marijuana when he isn't around" (p. 640).

Individual-level routine activity theory holds that opportunities for deviance are especially concentrated in activities that combine the three elements of socializing with peers, freedom from adult supervision, and a lack of structure, whereas in isolation, each element is of limited consequence.

There is little situational inducement to problem behavior in watching television by yourself, even if that activity is unstructured and unsupervised. Nor are unsupervised adolescents especially likely to engage in problem behavior while involved in an engrossing and relatively organized activity, such as watching a movie (Osgood et al., 1996).

We believe that this explanation provides a plausible account of the concentration of problem behavior in the after-school hours, as indicated by Snyder and Sickmund (1999). For children and youth who are not participating in organized activities, the time between the end of school and parents' return from work is likely to have little structure and to be free from adult supervision. Furthermore, informal socializing with peers should be especially likely during this period. After all, schools bring children together with their age mates, and at the end of the school day they leave together en masse.

An appealing feature of individual-level routine activity theory is that the key causal variable, unstructured socializing with peers, is not in itself antisocial or deviant. Virtually everyone spends some time this way, and children and adolescents can as easily use this time for positive ends as negative ones. Indeed, many developmentalists conclude that spending at least a moderate amount of independent time with peers this way is useful for the development of social skills and peer relations (e.g., Muuss, 1980; Savin-Williams & Berndt, 1990). Furthermore, this classification of activities is sufficiently general to be applicable across time and across social groups, so it can be used in a wide variety of research, including historical and cross-cultural comparisons.

Finally, the routine activity perspective treats youths as active participants in their own development. This approach portrays environmental influences not as deterministic forces that inevitably produce certain outcomes, but rather as sources of opportunities and inducements that actors take into account in choosing among alternative actions. The amount of time that youths spend in unstructured socializing is itself in part a reflection of their personality and preferences. Macrolevel routine activity theory points to larger social forces as placing constraints on those choices (e.g., the influence of child labor laws on time available for unstructured socializing), while individual-level routine activity theory emphasizes the further consequences of activity choices for inducements to deviance.

Evidence Supporting Individual-Level Routine Activity Theory

The primary prediction of individual-level routine activity theory is that children, adolescents, and young adults who spend more time in unstructured and unsupervised socializing with peers will more often engage in problem behavior. We already noted that several studies provide evidence of that relationship. Indeed, research to date demonstrates that the relationship is robust across the range of ages 9 (Posner & Vandell, 1994) through 26 (Osgood et al., 1996), and a variety of problem behaviors (Agnew & Petersen, 1989; Hundleby, 1987; Junger & Wiegersma, 1995). Botcher's (1995) study of siblings of incarcerated offenders provides qualitative support for the relationship. In-depth interviews revealed that, among this especially high-risk group, those who were heavily involved in delinquency spent an enormous amount of time roaming with their friends, often very far from home and very late at night.

The relationship of unstructured socializing with problem behavior is also replicated by research in several different countries (Junger & Wiegersma, 1995; Riley, 1987) and by a comparison across a sample of 50 preliterate cultures (Schlegel & Barry, 1991). Schlegel and Barry concluded that problems of adolescent antisocial behavior are concentrated in those cultures where adolescents spend less time in the company of adults and more time in the company of peers. This is particularly notable because in most of those societies, independent socializing with peers occurred through participation in culturally valued religious or military activities.

Because there have been no experimental studies manipulating time use, there is no definitive evidence that the association of unstructured socializing with problem behavior is a causal relationship. Even so, the fixed effects analysis of Osgood and colleagues (1996) put the relationship to an unusually rigorous test in that this statistical approach controls for all stable individual differences that might predict who would be more likely to spend their time in an unstructured way. They found that unstructured socializing remained strongly associated with problem behavior, even when the relationship was limited to within-person change over time in this fashion.

The body of evidence on time use and problem behavior also provides discriminant validity for individual-level routine activity theory. No other type of activity is consistently associated with higher rates of problem behavior. Often problem behavior is less frequent for respondents who spend more time in activities that would reflect conventional attachments or commitments such as homework, charitable work, and family activities. Yet even these relationships were eliminated in Osgood et al.'s (1996) analysis of within-individual change. Thus, it is likely that the lower problem behavior is attributable to the social control function of those attachments and commitments (Hirschi, 1969), rather than to the activities themselves.

Haynie and Osgood's (2004) research on the combined impact of time spent with peers and the delinquency of those peers provides further support for individual-level routine activity theory. Their research probed the possibility that the association of problem behavior with unstructured socializing is a spurious result of youths who spend more time in this way having friends who are more delinquent. In that case, the association might be due to the delinquency of the peers influencing an adolescent's attitudes and behavior rather than to the opportunity processes specified by individual-level routine activity theory. Haynie and Osgood (2004) addressed this problem using a strong measure of peer delinquency, taken from the social network data of the National Longitudinal Study of Adolescent Health, and their results clearly demonstrated that this was not the case. They found that both peer delinquency and unstructured socializing with peers had substantial influence on delinquency, and those influences were independent from one another. Controlling for peer delinquency did not diminish the relationship between unstructured socializing and delinquency, and the influence of unstructured socializing did not depend on having delinquent peers. Similarly, having delinquent friends contributes to delinquency, even for adolescents who do not spend a lot of time in unstructured socializing

The Development of Unstructured Socializing

Next, we turn to the developmental pattern of unstructured socializing with friends, away from adult supervision. The standard wisdom of developmental research is that during adolescence, peers come to play a more prominent role in one's life, whereas the importance of the family diminishes (Zani, 1993). We investigated the relationship between age and time spent with peers using data from Elliott's National Youth Survey (Elliott, Huizinga, & Ageton, 1985), a representative national sample of youth ages 11 through 17. Figure 3.2 shows a substantial increase through this age span in time spent with peers on weekday evenings and weekends. Eleven year-olds reported spending 1.5 weekday evenings per week with friends, while 17-year-olds reported spending 2.4 evenings per week with friends. For weekends, the mean response of 3.3 at age 11 increased to 3.8 at age 17, for a response scale where 3 referred to *some* time on weekends and 4 referred to *quite a bit*. The growing importance of peers during adolescence is clearly reflected in time use during these two segments of the week. Interestingly, the results in Fig. 3.2 do not indicate any increase in time spent with peers during weekday afternoons, the period that is the primary focus of the present volume. Throughout this age span, respondents reported that they spent 2.6 to 3 afternoons per week with friends. By age 11, preadolescents are already with friends for a large share of their free time after school, and this does not systematically change with age.

The results of Fig. 3.2 reflect developmental trends in the amount of time spent with friends but not the conditions under which they spend time together. Individual-level routine activity theory is particularly concerned with unsupervised socializing among peers, and it would seem likely that parents would allow increasing independence from such su-

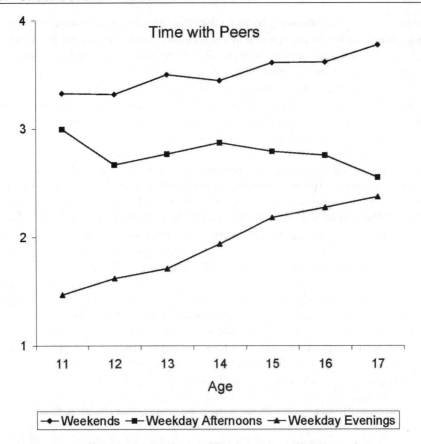

FIG. 3.2. Time with peers.

pervision as children grow older. After all, parents recognize that their children are gaining physical abilities, cognitive skills, and better judgment with age. In an unpublished paper, Jacobs and Osgood (1994) tested this proposition by examining parents' reports about how much they will permit their children to spend time with friends away from adults. They studied a random sample of adults in Nebraska, and we repeat some of their analyses here, extending them to include 477 parents reporting about their children in the range of age 5 to age 18, as opposed to the original range of age 8 to age 18.

Although it may not be surprising that the child's age is related to this type of autonomy, the strength of the relationship is remarkable. Age alone accounted for 56% of the variance in the length of time respondents allowed their children to be with friends away from adults and for 64% of the variance in parental limits on distance away from home with friends but not adults. Figure 3.3 shows developmental trends for these items, and the means vary almost the entire range of the scale. For distance from home, the response scale ranges from 1 *(not at all)* to 6 *(three miles or more)*. Age differences in means extend from 1.5 for 5-year-olds to 6 for 18-year-olds (with every parent giving the maximum response). For how long children are allowed to be with friends away from parents and other adults, the response scale ranges from 1 *(half and hour or less)* to 8 *(more than 12 hours)*, and the age specific means vary from 1.3 to 7.1.

These findings come from a representative sample of parents in Nebraska, a state with a relatively large proportion of rural rather than urban residents and a small minority population. Yet it seems likely that this pattern of results would hold more broadly. Jacobs and Osgood (1994) found that responses to these questions varied little in relation to factors such as race, income, urban versus rural residence, and the gender of either parent or child. Child's age was definitely the one dominant factor determining the amount of unsupervised socializing that parents allowed their children and adolescents.

An interesting aspect of the routine activity perspective is that patterns of time use provide a potential explanatory bridge between the social structure and individual deviant behavior, and this was a major theme of the original work in this area (Cohen & Felson, 1979). From this point of view, one reason groups differ in rates of deviant behavior is that positions in society determine conditions of life that affect how individuals spend their time, which in turn provides varying opportunities for deviance.

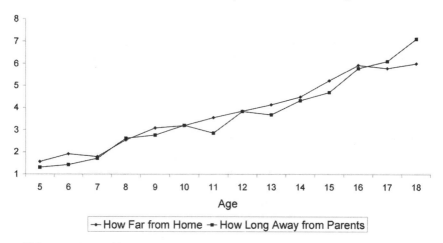

FIG. 3.3.   Parental limits on unsupervised socializing.

In this light, we ask whether individual-level routine activity theory can account for developmental trends in problem behavior. We have seen that children are allowed to spend increasing amounts of time socializing with peers away from adult supervision as they move from middle childhood through adolescence. Coinciding with this change are increasing rates of delinquency (Gottfredson & Hirschi, 1983), substance use (Johnston, O'Malley, & Bachman, 2002), and sexual behavior (Zelnik & Kantner, 1979). Therefore, the opportunity processes of routine activity theory provide a plausible account of this increase in problem behavior. This possibility is supported by Osgood et al.'s (1996) finding that unstructured socializing accounts for a sizable proportion (27% to 48%) of age trends in problem behaviors for ages 18 to 26. Nevertheless, the potential of routine activity theory to explain age trends in problem behavior has not yet been tested for the period of increasing problem behavior from middle childhood through middle to late adolescence.

Unstructured Socializing and Group Differences in Problem Behavior

Rates of unstructured socializing are also related to other group differences relevant to problem behavior. For example, boys are more likely than girls to spend time in unstructured socializing (Flannery et al., 1999; Galambos & Maggs, 1991; Steinberg, 1986). Osgood et al. (1996) found that males spend considerably more time in unstructured socializing than females, and they concluded that this difference in time use accounted for a substantial share of gender differences in problem behavior. Their estimates of the extent of mediation ranged from 16% for delinquency and dangerous driving to over 90% for illicit drug use. Although there are significant differences in the amount of time that boys and girls spend in unstructured socializing, there is clear evidence that both boys and girls who spend time this way are at risk. For example, Galambos and Maggs (1991) reported that 6th grade girls who spent after-school hours away from home without adult supervision engaged in more problem behaviors than did at-home or adult-supervised girls, and Osgood et al. (1996) reported that the relationship of unstructured socializing to problem behavior was substantial for both sexes.

The connection of unstructured socializing to race and class differences may be surprising to some. Although it is not be widely recognized, illicit drug use is considerably lower among African American youth than White youth (Johnston et al., 2002). Consistent with this, Wallace and Bachman (1991) found that African American youth spent less time in unstructured socializing than White youth, and they determined that this was an important mediator of the group difference in drug use. Similarly, Osgood et al.

(1996) found that, after controlling for school grades, students whose parents had more education (which they interpreted as a measure of social class), engaged in more of both unstructured socializing and problem behavior, with unstructured socializing serving as an important mediator of the difference in problem behavior. Osgood and colleagues (1996) interpreted this relationship as reflecting that more privileged youth are granted greater independence and have more extensive financial resources, both of which provide "resources for deviance" (Agnew, 1990) that enable more extensive unsupervised and unstructured socializing. Furthermore, Osgood and colleagues determined that a higher rate of unstructured socializing among weaker students accounts for roughly half of the relationship between poor school grades and higher levels of problem behavior.

These findings showing that youth from higher social-class backgrounds spend more time in unstructured socializing certainly do not mean that unstructured socializing is only an issue for this group. To the contrary, unstructured socializing is associated with higher rates of deviance across different race and/or ethnicity and social-class groups (e.g., Wallace & Bachman, 1991). Furthermore, Petit, Bates, Dodge, and Meece (1999) found that unstructured socializing was especially problematic for youth who live in unsafe neighborhoods, as is especially common for poor and minority youth.

There is also evidence of historical change in amounts of unstructured socializing, although there are no data to test whether this could account for trends in problem behavior. Felson and Gottfredson (1984) documented marked changes over several decades in the amount of time that teenagers in the United States have spent in unsupervised activities with peers. In a survey conducted in 1979, they asked respondents to report about their activities at age 17, and they used this retrospective data to compare activity patterns from the 1930s through the 1970s. They determined that over this period teenagers came to spend much more time away from parents and with peers, driving with friends, and out with friends after dark.

Across all of these studies relevant to individual-level routine activity theory, there is considerable evidence supporting both the validity and utility of the theory. The relationship of unstructured socializing holds for a variety of problem behaviors and many different populations, and the theory has survived several tests of whether the relationship is attributable to the causal processes specified by the theory. Furthermore, this research suggests that unstructured socializing contributes to developmental trends and several prominent group differences in problem behavior.

POLICY IMPLICATIONS

In this section, we turn our attention to the implications of findings about unstructured leisure for policies to promote positive adolescent development. The substantial time gap between parents' work schedules and children's school schedules ensures that the after-school hours provide plentiful opportunities for unstructured socializing, which helps to explain why juvenile crime is concentrated during these hours. After-school programs and other structured arrangements have the potential benefit of reducing unstructured socializing, which should in turn reduce the likelihood of problem behavior. Nevertheless, a number of potential pitfalls must be avoided in developing successful after-school programs.

First, as Mahoney and colleagues have shown (Mahoney & Stattin, 2000; Mahoney et al., 2001), programs must offer structured activities, for programs that provide unstructured activities can increase rather than decrease problem behavior. Furthermore, to reduce problem behavior, the structured, supervised activities must occupy time that otherwise would have been spent in unstructured and unsupervised socializing with peers. It is important to keep in mind that most problem behaviors are not particularly time consuming. Occupying large amounts of adolescents' time with nondeviant pursuits, by itself, will not substantially interfere with the time available to them for problem behavior (Hirschi, 1969). The idea of midnight basketball programs is useful for illustrating this dynamic (see Felson, 1994; Osgood, 1999). The premise of these programs is that 2 hours spent playing basketball means 2 fewer hours available for deviant pursuits. It is quite probable, however, that most of the program participants would otherwise have spent those 2 hours sleeping or watching television, which implies that there was little risk of problem behavior during that time in the first place. Correspondingly, school programs directed at latch-key children will not reduce problem behavior unless they recruit participants who previously were hanging out with their friends, rather than doing homework or watching television alone.

A second pitfall to avoid in designing after-school programs is the potential for inadvertently increasing unstructured socializing during nonprogram hours. Like schools, youth programs necessarily bring together groups of similarly situated adolescents, and this gathering brings the potential for unstructured socializing in adjacent hours. Returning to the midnight basketball example, the risk would be that, at the end of the supervised program activities, participants would hang out together during the early morning hours before they make their way home. If so, the program will be indirectly responsible for youths encountering new opportunities for problem behavior (Osgood et al., 1996). Thus, program designers must be cognizant of how their programs structure participants' time before and after planned activities.

After-school programs also may indirectly affect the time adolescents spend in unstructured socializing by serving as a forum in which adolescents can form and maintain peer groups. By participating in such programs, youth may enlarge their friendship networks, which could provide another source of companions when they are away from any adult supervision. Osgood (1999) argued that this type of dynamic was at work in after-school employment. Osgood demonstrated that the more hours teens devoted to employment, the more, not less, time they spent in unstructured socializing with friends. This pattern of findings may be particularly problematic for after-school programs that specifically target "at-risk" youth. Programs that bring together groups of high-risk youth may inadvertently increase opportunities for problem behavior by introducing adolescents to peers who are new resources for tobacco or alcohol and who are likely to encourage tough or adventuresome social identities.

After-school programs providing structured activities could be especially effective at preventing problem behavior if they were to target "high-risk areas," and not just at-risk youth. Osgood and Anderson (in press) found that attending a school with a high aggregate rate of unstructured socializing increased all students' risk of delinquency, even those students who spent little or no time this way themselves. Thus, the potential benefits of reducing this high-risk form of time use may extend well beyond the specific individuals who participate in a program. Also relevant to the concerns of this volume, the authors found that there was less unstructured socializing with peers when students attended schools where most parents monitored their children's behavior, whether or not their own parents kept a close watch over them (Osgood & Anderson, in press). This finding gives insight into the processes by which a high aggregate rate of unstructured socializing arises, and it could prove useful for determining what areas are most in need of programs that provide structured activities.

Osgood and Anderson (in press) also found that adolescents whose own parents monitored their behavior were at a significantly lower risk for delinquency than were adolescents whose parents did not keep a close watch over them. This finding reinforces the idea that parents and other adults have an important role to play in helping to structure adolescents' after-school time. By monitoring adolescents' activities and by encouraging them to become involved in appropriately structured after-school programs, caretakers help to reduce the amount of time adolescents spend in unstructured and/or unsupervised after-school contexts, thus reducing the potential for the development of problem behaviors. On this point, however, a cautionary note is warranted, for adolescents' activity preferences must be taken into account as well. A number of studies have found that it is not just the content or context of leisure activities that determines their relationship to delinquency, but also whether or not adolescents enjoy the activity (Agnew & Petersen, 1989; Kvaraceus, 1954). For example, Agnew and Peterson (1989) found that time spent in leisure activities that adolescents rated as their least favorite had no influence on either serious or minor delinquency and that, in some instances, leisure time spent in activities that adolescents disliked actually increased the likelihood of minor delinquent behavior.

It is important to remember that after-school programs are not the only means by which parents may limit the time their children spend in unstructured socializing. As we noted, research on children in self-care shows that indirect supervision by parents or other adults reduces negative developmental outcomes, and in Osgood and Anderson's (in press) research, it is parents' awareness of children's whereabouts, activities, and associates that is critical. Parents and other caregivers might provide indirect supervision by having youth check in with them frequently. Indeed, technological advances such as pagers and cell phones make indirect supervision an increasingly viable option for many families. Indirect supervision is probably an especially useful tool for supervising older adolescents, whose parents allow them to spend longer durations of time with friends away from adults (Jacobs & Osgood, 1994).

Finally, we want to be quite explicit that we believe that it would be inappropriate to seek to eliminate all unstructured socializing with peers. Socializing with peers away from adults is a normal part of adolescent development and helps adolescents navigate the transition from childhood to adulthood by providing opportunities to establish social identities separate from their families and to practice newly evolving adult social skills (Muuss, 1980; Savin-Williams & Berndt, 1990). Thus, moderate amounts of unstructured socializing are probably valuable for adolescents' social development, mental health, and general well-being. Moreover, many adolescents engage in a small amount of problem behavior without negative consequences (Gold, 1970). For example, some studies have found that middle class adolescents who are involved in a limited amount of minor delinquency or who experiment with low levels of drug and alcohol use are as likely to be successful in early adulthood as middle-class adolescents who are not involved in these activities (Hagan, 1991; Newcomb & Bentler, 1988). Thus, families need to find an effective balance that allows adolescents needed independence while not engendering levels of unstructured socializing that bring undue risk of problem behavior.

REFERENCES

Agnew, R. (1990). Adolescent resources and delinquency. *Criminology, 28,* 535–566.
Agnew, R., & Petersen, D. M. (1989). Leisure and delinquency. *Social Problems, 36*(4), 332–350.

Belle, D. (1997). Varieties of self-care: A qualitative look at children's experiences in the after-school hours. *Merrill Palmer Quarterly, 43*(3), 478–496.

Botcher, J. (1995). Gender as social control: A Qualitative study of incarcerated youths and their siblings in greater Sacramento. *Justice Quarterly, 12*, 33–57.

Briar, S., & Piliavin, I. (1965). Delinquency, situational inducements, and commitment to conformity. *Social Problems, 13*, 35–45.

Carnegie Council on Youth Development, Task Force on Youth Development and Community Programs (1992). *A matter of time: Risk and opportunity in the non-school hours.* New York: Carnegie Corporation of New York.

Cohen, D. A., Farley, T. A., Taylor, S. N., Martin, D. H., & Schuster, M. A. (2002). When and where do youths have sex? The potential role of adult supervision. *Pediatrics, 110*(6), Art. No. E66.

Cohen, L. E., & Felson, M. (1979). Social change and crime rate trends: A routine activity approach. *American Sociological Review, 44*, 588–609.

Cole, C., & Rodman, H. (1987). When school-age children care for themselves: Issues for family life educators and parents. *Family Relations: Journal of Applied Family and Child Studies, 36*(1), 92–96.

Dishion, T. J., Spracklen, K. M., Andrews, D. W., & Patterson, G. R. (1996). Deviancy training in male adolescent friendships. *Behavior Therapy, 27*, 373–390.

Elliott, D., Huizinga, D., & Ageton, S. S. (1985). *Explaining delinquency and drug use.* Beverly Hills, CA.: Sage.

Erickson, M. L., & Jensen, G. F. (1977). Delinquency is still group behavior!: Toward revitalizing the group premise in the sociology of deviance. *Journal of Criminal Law and Criminology, 68*, 262–273.

Felson, M. (1994). *Crime and everyday life: Insights and implications for society.* Thousand Oaks, CA: Pine Forge Press.

Felson, M., & Gottfredson, M. (1984). Social indicators of adolescent activities near peers and parents. *Journal of Marriage and the Family, 46*(3), 709–714.

Flannery, D. J., Williams, L. L., & Vazsonyi, A. T. (1999). Who are they with and what are they doing? Delinquent behavior, substance use, and early adolescents' after-school time. *American Journal of Orthopsychiatry, 69*(2), 247–253.

Fuligni, A. J., & Stevenson, H. W. (1995). Time use and mathematics achievement among American, Chinese, and Japanese high school students. *Child Development, 66*(3), 830–842.

Galambos, N. L., & Maggs, J. L. (1991). Out-of-school care of young adolescents and self-reported behavior. *Developmental Psychology, 27*(4), 644–655.

Gold, M. (1970). *Delinquent behavior in an American city.* Belmont, CA: Brooks/Cole.

Gottfredson, M. R., & Hirschi, T. (1983). Age and the explanation of crime. *American Journal of Sociology, 89*, 552–584.

Hagan, J. (1991). Destiny and drift: Subcultural preferences, status attainments, and the risks and rewards of youth. *American Sociological Review, 56*, 567–582.

Haynie, D. L., & Osgood, D. W. (2004). *Peers and delinquency reconsidered: How do peers matter for delinquency?* Unpublished manuscript.

Hirschi, T. (1969). *Causes of delinquency.* Berkeley: University of California Press.

Hundleby, J. D. (1987). Adolescent drug use in a behavioral matrix: A confirmation and comparison of the sexes. *Addictive Behaviors, 12*, 103–112.

Jacobs, J. E., & Osgood, D. W. (1994, February). *Parental limits on adolescent autonomy.* Paper presented at the meeting of the Society for Research on Adolescence, San Diego, CA.

Johnston, L. D., O'Malley, P. M., & Bachman, J. G. (2002). *The monitoring the future national survey results on adolescent drug use: Overview of key findings, 2001* (NIH Pub. No. 02–5105). Bethesda, MD: National Institute on Drug Abuse.

Junger, M., & Wiegersma, A. (1995). The relations between accidents, deviance, and leisure. *Criminal Behavior and Mental Health, 5,* 144–173.

Kvaraceus, W. C. (1954). *The community and the delinquent.* Yonkers-On-Hudson, NY: World Book Company.

Larson, R. (1994). Youth organizations, hobbies, and sports as developmental contexts. In R. K. Silbereisen & E. Todt (Eds.), *Adolescence in context : The interplay of family, school, peers, and work in adjustment* (pp. 46–65). New York: Springer-Verlag.

Larson, R., & Kleiber, D. (1993). Daily experience of adolescents. In P. H. Tolan & B. J. Cohler (Eds.), *Handbook of clinical research and practice with adolescents* (pp. 125–145). New York: Wiley.

Larson, R., & Richards, M. H. (1991). Daily companionship in late childhood and early adolescence: Changing developmental contexts. *Child Development, 62*(2), 284–300.

Leone, C. M., & Richards, M. H. (1989). Classwork and homework in early adolescence: The ecology of achievement. *Journal of Youth and Adolescence, 18*(6), 531–548.

Loeber, R., & Stouthamer-Loeber, M. (1986). Family factors as correlates and predictors of juvenile conduct problems and delinquency. In M. Tonry & N. Morris (Eds.), *Crime and justice: An annual review of the research* (Vol. 7, pp. 29–150). Chicago: University of Chicago Press.

Lovko, A. M., & Ullman, D. G. (1989). Research on the adjustment of latchkey children: Role of background/demographic and latchkey situation variables. *Journal of Clinical Child Psychology, 18*(1), 16–24.

Mahoney, J. L., & Stattin, H. (2000). Leisure activities and adolescent antisocial behavior: The role of structure and social context. *Journal of Adolescence, 23,* 113–127.

Mahoney, J. L., Stattin, H., & Magnusson, D. (2001). Youth recreation centre participation and criminal offending: A 20-year longitudinal study of Swedish boys. *International Journal of Behavioral Development, 25,* 509–520.

Marshall, N. L., Coll, C. G., Marx, F., McCartney, K., Keefe, N., & Ruh, J. (1997). After-school time and children's behavioral adjustment. *Merrill Palmer Quarterly, 43*(3), 497–514.

Mott, J. A., Crowe, P. A., Richardson, J., & Flay, B. (1999). After-school supervision and adolescent cigarette smoking: Contributions of the setting and intensity of after-school self-care. *Journal of Behavioral Medicine, 22*(1), 35–58.

Muuss, R. E. (1980). *Adolescent behavior and society.* New York: Random House.

Newcomb, M. D., & Bentler, P. M. (1988). *Consequences of adolescent drug Use: Impact on the lives of young adults.* Newbury Park, CA: Sage.

Osgood, D. W. (1999). Having the time of their lives: All work and no play? In A., Booth, A. C. Crouter, & M. J. Shanahan (Eds.), *Transitions to adulthood in a changing economy: No work, no family, no future?* (pp. 176–186). Westport, CT: Praeger.

Osgood, D. W., & Anderson, A. L. (in press). Routine activities and differences among schools in rates of delinquency. *Criminology.*

Osgood, D. W., Wilson, J. K., O'Malley, P. M., Bachman, J. G., & Johnston, L. D. (1996). Routine activities and individual deviant behavior. *American Sociological Review, 61,* 635–655.

Pettit, G. S., Bates, J. E., Dodge, K. A., & Meece, D. W. (1999). The impact of after-school peer contact on early adolescent externalizing problems is moderated by parental monitoring, perceived neighborhood safety, and prior adjustment. *Child Development, 70*(3), 768–778.

Pettit, G. S., Laird, R. D., Bates, J. E., & Dodge, K. A. (1997). Patterns of after-school care in middle childhood: Risk factors and developmental outcomes. *Merrill Palmer Quarterly, 43*(3), 515–538.

Posner, J. K., & Vandell, D. L. (1994). Low-income children's after-school care: Are there beneficial effects of after-school programs? *Child Development, 65*(2), 440–456.

Posner, J. K., & Vandell, D. L. (1999). After-school activities and the development of low-income urban children: A longitudinal study. *Developmental Psychology, 35*(3), 868–879.

Richardson, J., Radziszewska, B., Dent, C., & Flay, B. (1993). Relationship between after-school care of adolescents and substance use, risk taking, depressed mood, and academic achievement. *Pediatrics, 92*, 32–38.

Riley, D. (1987). Time and crime: The link between teenager lifestyle and delinquency. *Journal of Quantitative Criminology, 3*, 339–354.

Savin-Williams, R. C., & Berndt, T. J. (1990). Friendship and peer relations. In S. S. Feldman & G. R. Elliott (Eds.), *At the threshold: The developing adolescent*. Cambridge, MA: Harvard University Press.

Schlegel, A., & Barry, H., III (1991). *Adolescence: An anthropological inquiry*. New York: Free Press.

Snyder, H. N., & Sickmund, M. (1999). *Juvenile offenders and victims: 1999 national report*. Washington, DC: Office of Juvenile Justice and Delinquency Prevention.

Steinberg, L. (1986). Latchkey children and susceptibility to peer pressure: An ecological analysis. *Developmental Psychology, 22*(4), 433–439.

Timmer, S. G., Eccles, J., & O'Brien, K. (1985). How children use time. In F. T. Juster & F. P. Stafford (Eds.), *Time, goods, and well-being* (pp. 353–382). Ann Arbor: Institute for Social Research, The University of Michigan.

U.S. Department of Education and Justice. (2000). *Working for children and families: Safe and smart after-school programs*. Washington DC: U.S. Departments of Education and Justice.

Vandell, D. L., & Shumow, L. (1999). After-school child care programs. *Future of Children, 9*(2), 64–80.

Wallace, J. M., Jr., & Bachman, J. G. (1991). Explaining racial/ethnic differences in adolescent drug use: The impact of background and lifestyle. *Social Problems, 38*, 333–357.

Zani, B. (1993). Dating and interpersonal relationships in adolescence. In S. Jackson & H. Rodrigues-Tome (Eds.), *Adolescence and its social worlds* (pp. 95–119). Hillsdale, NJ: Lawrence Erlbaum Associates.

Zelnik, M., & Kantner, J. F. (1979). Probabilities of intercourse and conception among U.S. teenage women, 1971 and 1976. *Family Planning Perspectives, 11*, 177–183.

4

Activity Participation and the Well-Being of Children and Adolescents in the Context of Welfare Reform

David M. Casey
University of Calgary, Canada

Marika N. Ripke
Aletha C. Huston
University of Texas at Austin

Welfare reform and other policies affecting low-income families have increased employment, particularly by single parents. As parents spend more time away from home, out-of-school activities for children in middle childhood and adolescence assume a larger and more important role in children's development. Many out-of-school activities and arrangements present children with the opportunity to develop new skills, to increase their competencies in specific domains, and to form relationships with caring and supportive adults. On the other hand, there may be negative consequences of children spending too much time without adult supervision (e.g., hanging out with friends), particularly for low-income children (Posner & Vandell, 1994, 1999).

In this chapter, we examine out-of-school activities within a framework of risks and protective factors in child and adolescent development. We consider the risks posed by poverty and the potential positive and negative impacts of welfare reform and employment policies on the well-being of school-age children and adolescents in low-income families. Out-of-school, structured activities with adult supervision are conceptualized as one category of protective factors for children whose families are experiencing changing welfare and employment policies.

WELFARE REFORM

During the 1990s, federal and state policies for low-income families underwent major changes, all of which provided strong incentives for parents to leave cash assistance and to increase their involvement in paid employment. The Personal Responsibility and Work Opportunity Reconciliation Act of 1996 (PRWORA), often referred to as *welfare reform*, ended cash assistance to families with children as an entitlement program and contained numerous provisions designed to move adults from welfare to employment. At the same time, federal and state work supports for low-income parents were expanded. The maximum benefit available to low-income workers with children through the federal Earned Income Tax Credit (EITC) and through similar credits in some states more than doubled from 1993 to 2000. Federal subsidies for child care increased from $1 billion in 1991 to $1.8 billion in 2000 (Fuller, Kagan, Caspary, & Gauthier, 2002), and federal funds for 21st Century Community Learning Centers, which provide after-school programs, grew from zero to $500 million.

After 1996, the number of people receiving cash assistance declined dramatically, and rates of employment among poor single mothers increased at least through the year 2000 when the economy was strong (Crosby, Gennetian, & Huston, 2001; Greenberg et al., 2002). Poverty among children declined; the poverty rate among African American children was at the lowest level on record (Haskins & Primus, 2002). Nonetheless, there is widespread evidence that many families have remained poor, with no overall improvement in income. Of particular interest here, subsidies for child care, which can be used for any child under age 13, do not reach most eligible children. About 20% of the federally eligible children receive subsidies. Although some families, especially those with school-age children, may not need subsidies, there is evidence of a considerable unmet need in some localities (Layzer & Collins, 2001).

Impacts of Employment on Families

The changes in parents' employment brought about by welfare reform have obvious implications for family organization and for the experiences of their children. Parents not only work more hours than they did before, but approximately 40% of the low-wage jobs held by these parents have irregular or nonstandard work hours (i.e., evening and night shifts, weekend work; Presser, 2002). There is now a body of evidence showing that school-age children whose parents work in the evening perform less well in school than school-age children whose parents work conventional daytime hours (Heymann & Boynton-Jarrett, 2003; Presser, 2002). It appears that parents' absence during the evening hours makes it difficult to assure that children do their homework, get to bed on time, and the like.

Even when parents work during standard weekday hours, employment increases the need for alternatives to parental supervision during children's out-of-school time (including before and after school, summers, and school vacations). For younger children, this need is usually met by some form of child care. As children reach the late elementary school years and adolescence, structured activities and programs can play an important role in providing supervision and opportunities for youth development. The effects of parents' employment and the other changes brought about by welfare reform are likely to depend in part on the nature and quality of experiences provided for children during the times that parents are employed. The nature of these experiences changes with age.

Developmental Changes in Options for Children

Most parents arrange some form of child care for children under about age 10 or age 11. Much of this care is informal, provided in the child's home or in someone else's home; some children also attend child-care centers or out-of-school programs. There is some evidence that organized out-of-school programs can contribute to academic and social development, particularly for children from low-income families (Eccles & Gootman, 2002; Posner & Vandell, 1994, 1999). As children reach late childhood and early adolescence (roughly age 9 to age 12), they are increasingly likely to be in self-care (or care by older siblings) when their parents are working. Low-income families, especially African Americans, use less self-care than middle-income families do (Cappizano, Tout, & Adams, 2000), possibly because they consider their neighborhoods less safe. Nevertheless, many youth whose mothers are moving from welfare to work spend a significant amount of their out-of-school time in self-care (Shields & Behrman, 2002).

The shift away from child care to self-care during late childhood reflects normal developmental changes in autonomy and self-regulation. Gradually assuming responsibility for one's time and behavior is a normal and important part of becoming a mature adult. Parents can provide scaffolding for this process by allowing gradual increases in autonomy—for example, leaving children alone for short periods with a phone number or a neighbor to call in case of need, permitting children to go to locations in the neighborhood on their own, and the like. As children make this move into independence and self-direction, the qualities of the neighborhood, school, and community are likely to be increasingly important as supports or hazards influencing developmental consequences. For example, available data indicate that self-care for older school-age children and adolescents from low-income families in unsafe neighborhoods is associated with behavioral and academic problems; in contrast, time spent in self-care is not associated with negative developmental outcomes for youth from middle-income families (Kerrebrock & Lewit, 1999; Pettit, Laird, Bates, & Dodge, 1997).

When parents are employed, their ability to monitor directly this process of unfolding independence can be compromised, particularly when work conflicts with children's schedules or work conditions make it difficult to monitor from afar (e.g., by telephone). Perhaps for this reason, some research shows links between maternal employment and adolescent delinquency, due in part to lower levels of maternal supervision (Sampson & Laub, 1994), as well as decreased academic attainment (Duncan & Yeung, 1995). In general, higher levels of parental monitoring are associated with lower levels of delinquent behavior and higher levels of academic achievement among adolescents (Linver & Silverber, 1997; Patterson, 1999).

Many working parents experience gaps between their school-age children's school schedule and their work schedule, especially in cases where parents work full-time or nontraditional hours. We often focus on the after-school hours, but the hours before school may also pose a problem when parents must be at work before school is open or before the school bus comes. Summers and other school vacations also pose supervision difficulties for many parents.

By the time children reach adolescence, both parents and society assume that young people have acquired the necessary skills to function without immediate supervision. In fact, children age 13 and older are not eligible for child-care subsidies. Consequently, autonomy and self-direction are important developmental skills to be cultivated throughout early and late adolescence. In order for this process to be successful, however, the social contexts in which adolescents spend time need to support positive forms of behavior. These contexts include family, school, neighborhood, and community. In the years of middle childhood, structured child care and before-and-after-school programs provide important supports to positive development, especially when parents are working, but adolescence appears to be a period when young people in low-income families have fewer community supports for positive development (Posner & Vandell, 1994, 1999; Quinn, 1999). In a series of experiments testing welfare-to-work programs for single mothers, the effects on children's achievement and social behavior were neutral or slightly positive for children in middle childhood (roughly 6 to 10 years old; Morris, Huston, Duncan, Crosby, & Bos, 2001). For adolescents in the same families, however, there were slightly negative impacts on achievement and on some minor deviant behaviors (Gennetian et al., 2002). There are several possible reasons for these developmental differences, but they suggest a need for out-of-school contexts that promote positive youth development when parents enter welfare-to-work programs.

INCOME AND ACTIVITY PARTICIPATION

Although low-income children appear especially likely to benefit from high quality out-of-school programs, their access to these programs is limited by family resources and by the distribution of programs in the community. Poor families who use paid child care spend 18% to 30% of their incomes on child care for preschool and school-age children; in contrast, the figure for more affluent families is 5% to 7% of family income (Crosby et al., 2001; Smith, 2000). Many out-of-school programs are costly; there are enrollment costs as well as fees for uniforms, instruments, equipment, and transportation. Enrolling children in structured programs poses more of a financial barrier for poor families than it does for more affluent families. As a result, children from low-income families are less likely to be in organized out-of-school programs or enrolled in center-based care than children from middle- or higher income families (Capizzano et al., 2000). For instance, youth from low-income families participate in fewer structured activities (e.g., music lessons, art, sports) than youth from middle- and high-income families, and lower income parents rely more on community centers and national youth-serving organizations such as the Boys and Girls Clubs and YMCA (Capizzano et al., 2000; Pettit et al., 1997).

Even publicly supported activities are less available in many low-income neighborhoods than they are in higher income neighborhoods. When compared to more affluent communities, economically disadvantaged communities have fewer resources (i.e., less public support and funding), and as a result, have fewer youth organizations, sports leagues, summer camps, and out-of-school programs (Quinn, 1999). When programs are not available in the immediate neighborhood, transportation poses a greater barrier to low-income families than to affluent families, many of whom drive children to large numbers of activities after school and on weekends. This paucity of programs means that there is a smaller array of appropriate developmental opportunities for youth from low-income neighborhoods than for youth from middle-income neighborhoods.

Single mothers who increase their employment as a result of welfare reform may make use of available out-of-school activities for their children if their employment increases overall income and family resources. On average, however, moving from welfare to work does not improve overall family income. Many experiments testing welfare-to-work programs indicate that net family income does not increase when parents trade welfare for work. Income does increase when earnings are supplemented by public funds in the form of income disregards (allowing welfare recipients to keep part of their welfare grant while they earn) or the EITC (Bloom & Michalopoulos, 2001).

Family resources can also be increased by subsidies. Child-care subsidies, available for children under age 13, lead to increased use of center-based child care, after-school programs, and other formal child-care settings. Both subsidies and income resulting from earnings supplements facilitate elementary school-age children's participation in organized extracurricular activities (e.g., team sports, music lessons, clubs) that present children with developmentally enriching experiences in supervised settings (Bos et al., 1999). These findings suggest that the impacts of welfare reform on young people's activity involvement will depend partly on whether increases in parental employment are accompanied by increases in income and/or publicly supported programs that are convenient and available close to children's homes or schools.

Effects of Structured Activity Participation

Participation in organized out-of-school activities can provide children with constructive, adult-supervised ways of spending time that offer opportunities for developing prosocial skills and reducing the likelihood of involvement in deviant behavior (Carnegie Corporation, 1992; Eccles & Barber, 1999). Organized activities may contribute to positive youth development through several pathways. They provide adult supervision and guidance that may reduce the likelihood that young people will be exposed to deviant adults and deviant peer activities in their neighborhoods or communities. They offer the opportunity for youth to become involved with and to feel part of community institutions, including schools, religious organizations, and service organizations. They offer opportunities for young people to define their own identities by developing interests, finding adults and peers with whom they feel an affinity, and taking on leadership roles. Activities provide a venue in which skills and competencies other than academic success can be cultivated and valued. For a young person who is not an outstanding student, the opportunity to become really good at sports, music, or leadership may be an especially important source of self-esteem. Finally, there is extensive evidence that trajectories of social development during later childhood and adolescence depend in part on the peer group. Organized activity settings may cultivate and support peer groups with prosocial norms that support prosocial values and behavior among all of the young people participating. This last pathway is notable because it suggests that the impact of activities may be at the level of the group rather than at the level of individual children or adolescents.

Experiences in structured out-of-school environments may play an important protective role in social development and academic achievement for children from low-income families and neighborhoods because these children are at risk of low school achievement and deviant social behavior (Shields & Behrman, 2002). Participation in adult-approved, structured out-of-school programs can provide cognitive stimulation and positive adult interactions that are associated with higher grades, better peer relations, and less deviant behavior among children from low-income families (Pettit et al., 1997; Posner & Vandell, 1999). Conversely, hanging out with peers in unsupervised settings is associated with delinquency and behavior problems for adolescents from low-income families who live in dangerous neighborhoods (Eccles & Barber, 1999).

Effects of Paid Work

As children move into adolescence, many of them have jobs for pay. These range from informal employment (e.g., snow shoveling, babysitting) to formal employment in service industries (e.g., fast food restaurants, sales). On average, adolescents from affluent families engage in more paid employment than do young people from low-income families (Lerman, 2000). The costs and benefits of paid work at this age have been hotly debated. Proponents point out that employed adolescents develop a general sense of competency, efficacy, independence, and responsibility, and skills in time management, money management, and interpersonal relations. Critics caution that adolescent employment deflects youth from school, extracurricular activities, and the opportunity to develop close relationships, and encourages precocious maturity (e.g., alcohol and drug use, early sexual behavior, parenting; Bachman & Schulenberg, 1993). Indeed, adolescents who spend more time working for pay participate in fewer extracurricular activities (Anderson, Huston, Schmitt, Linebarger, & Wright, 2001).

Available evidence shows complex relations of employment to educational attainment and earnings. In a longitudinal study of a community sample, the short- and long-term correlates of adolescent employment were dependent on the intensity and duration of youth employment (Mortimer & Johnson, 1998). Boys who worked most intensively (over 20 hours per week) and continuously during high school had the highest earnings 4 years after high school, but work of high intensity curtailed young men's postsecondary schooling. Among low-income adolescents, employment is associated with higher educational attainment, but is unrelated to earnings during adulthood (Foster, 1995; Newman, 1996).

In summary, low-income school-age children and adolescents can benefit academically and socially from participation in organized out-of-school activities. The costs and benefits of employment appear to be mixed. School-age children from high-income families, however, are more likely to participate in multiple enrichment activities (e.g., sports, lessons) during their out-of-school time and to work for pay than are children from low-income families (Brimhall, Reaney, & West, 1999). We turn now to evidence from studies of welfare reform to examine two questions: What are the effects of welfare reform on children's use of out-of-school time, particularly activity participation? Does participation contribute to positive developmental outcomes for children and adolescents in low-income families affected by welfare reform?

ACTIVITY PARTICIPATION IN LOW-INCOME FAMILIES: THE NATIONAL SURVEY OF AMERICA'S FAMILIES (NSAF)

NSAF is a nationally representative study of more than 42,000 households in the United States, with an oversampling of households with incomes under 200% of the poverty level (Tout, Scarpa, & Zaslow, 2002). As part of the NSAF, information about youth's (age 6 to age 17) participation in out-of-school activities (e.g., lessons and sports) was gathered from parents. Participation rates of four groups of children were compared: (a) "welfare" families, who were receiving welfare in 1999; (b) "leavers," who left welfare between 1997 and 1999; (c) "poor nonwelfare" families, who had never received welfare benefits; and (d) "nonpoor" families with incomes at or above 200% of poverty level (Tout et al., 2002).

Participation in Structured Activities

Children from nonpoor families were more likely than any of the other groups to participate in out-of-school activities. In the nonpoor families, 90% of the children participated in at least one activity, compared to 59% of the children in welfare families, 69% in the welfare leaver families, and 65% in the poor nonwelfare families (Tout et al., 2002). In a related examination of the 1999 NSAF sample, activity participation was considered separately for children in middle childhood (age 6 to age 11) and adolescents (age 12 to age 17; Anderson Moore, Hatcher, Vandivere, & Brown, 2000). In low-income families, 67% of the middle-childhood group participated, compared to 73% for adolescents; in higher income families, 91% of children in the middle-childhood group and 89% of adolescents participated in a least one activity.

These differences in participation may be the result of numerous barriers (e.g., financial, transportation, cultural attitudes) or to the working schedules of the parent. For instance, in the NSAF sample, more than one fourth of former welfare recipients, near-poor, and low-income mothers worked shift schedules (mostly nights), which can create difficulties in coordinating work schedules and appropriate out-of-school activities and arrangements for their children (Loprest, 1999). In families with employed parents, especially single parents, older children and adolescents may take on added household responsibilities and care for younger children during the out-of-school hours, making it more difficult for them to participate in activities away from home. The combination of financial and other barriers, along with inconsistent work schedules, makes it difficult for poor parents to find appropriate structured out-of-school activities that may help to improve their school-age children's psychosocial and academic skills.

Participation in Paid Work

An analysis of a sample of the 1997 NSAF with students age 16 to age 17 from low-income and welfare families found that 31% of adolescents from families currently on welfare worked, whereas 46% of adolescents from high-income families worked (Lerman, 2000). In comparison, during this same period nationally 40% of 16- and 17-year-olds were working, with 25% of those adolescents working 20 hours or more per week. In general, there were no significant associations between school-related outcomes (e.g., completing homework, expulsions) and work, even for adolescents who worked 20 or more hours a week (Lerman, 2000). Thus, in this sample, adolescents from low-income families were less likely to be working during their out-of-school time than were adolescents from middle- or high-income families, and the amount of time adolescents spent working was not associated with academic developmental outcomes.

EXPERIMENTAL STUDIES OF WELFARE
AND EMPLOYMENT PROGRAMS

Unlike many other areas of social policy, welfare policy has been informed by random assignment experiments testing the effects of policy variations on adult labor force participation, income, and welfare receipt (Friedlander & Burtless, 1995). There have been a number of recent evaluations examining the impacts of welfare reform on both parents and children from low-income families (e.g., Bos et al., 1999; Morris et al., 2001). Some of these studies provide evidence concerning our two questions—whether welfare and employment policies affect activity participation, and if such participation contributes to children's developmental outcomes.

Because these studies are random assignment experiments, we can determine the causal effects of particular welfare and employment policies on children's participation in activities. If participation is higher in the experimental (program) group than in the control group, we can infer confidently that the policy affected participation, although we cannot determine what features of the policy were most important in creating this effect. To answer the second question—whether participation contributed to children's development—we examine two types of evidence. First, if children in the program group have higher achievement or more positive social behavior than children in the control group, we can examine what features of the children's experiences, including activity participation, were also affected by the treatment. Second, we can conduct nonexperimental analyses to determine whether children who participated more had better achievement or social behavior than did children who participated less.

What follows is a discussion of the results from two evaluations of welfare and employment programs that included measures of, among other things, children's and adolescents' participation in structured activities and developmental outcomes. These are the Self-Sufficiency Project (SSP), conducted in two Canadian provinces, and the New Hope Project, an evaluation of an employment-based, antipoverty program in Milwaukee, Wisconsin. Both of these programs strongly encouraged parental employment by making benefits contingent on full-time employment. Families who met the work requirement received wage supplements and, in the case of New Hope, other work supports that included child-care subsidies.

The Self-Sufficiency Project

The SSP was a research and evaluation project examining the impact of a temporary earnings supplement on the lives of single, low-income parents and their families who lived in New Brunswick and British Columbia, Canada. The program offered a large wage supplement to parents who left public assistance and were employed full time (30 or more hours per week). It produced a significant increase in family income. At a follow-up interview 3 years after parents were randomly assigned to be in the program group or a control group, parents and children reported on the child's activity participation in four out-of-school activities in the past year: sports with a coach, sports without a coach, lessons in music or art, and clubs or community programs. In addition, older adolescents (age 15 to age 18) were asked if they had a job; and if so, how many hours they worked per week. Developmental outcomes in three specific areas (academic and cognitive development, behavior and emotional well-being, and health and safety) were measured for children and adolescents (Morris & Michalopoulos, 2000).

The impacts on children's development varied according to age; therefore findings from the SSP were examined separately for middle-age children (age 6 to age 11), and adolescents (age 12 to age 18). Children's school achievement was measured with a math achievement test and parents' reports of their child's achievement. Parents reported on their child's behavior and emotional well-being in four specific areas: hyperactivity, conduct problems, internalizing problems, and positive social behavior. Both older children and adolescents (age 10 to age 18) were asked about their participation in minor delinquent behavior (e.g., drinking, smoking, skipping school). Adolescents age 15 to age 18 were also asked about their participation in more serious delinquent behavior such as stealing, starting fires, and using weapons (see Morris & Michalopoulos, 2000).

Developmental Outcomes and Activity Participation Among Middle-Age Children.   The SSP increased full-time maternal employment, hours of parental work, and family income. Its effects on both activity participation and developmental outcomes were different for middle-age children and adolescents. Both age groups had high base rates of participation in activities. In both program and control groups, over 85% reported some participation, and the average number of days per month of participation ranged from 13 to 17. Nevertheless, there were experimental impacts for middle-age children (age 6 to age 11).

Elementary-school-age children in the program group were more likely to participate in out-of-school activities and to perform better in school, according to parent reports and a standardized achievement test, than were children in the control group (Morris & Michalopoulos, 2000). There were no effects on their behavioral outcomes. Structured out-of-school activities may have provided children with a safe learning environment, which, in turn, had a positive impact on their development. The impacts on both activity participation and child outcomes indicate that increased participation in structured out-of-school activities by children from families in the program group may account for a portion of the increased academic and cognitive performance evidenced by children in the program group (Morris & Michalopoulos, 2000).

Developmental Outcomes and Activity Participation Among Adolescents.   By contrast, SSP had no significant impact on adolescents' (age 12 to age 18) participation in out-of-school activities, and there were negative impacts on school achievement and minor problem and delinquent behaviors. Adolescents in the program group had lower school achievement according to both parent and adolescent reports, they had more behavior problems at school, and they reported more smoking, drinking, and drug use. The 15- to 18-year-olds also reported participating in more serious delinquent behaviors such as stealing and using weapons (Morris & Michalopoulos, 2000).

The reasons for the age difference are discussed elsewhere (see Gennetian et al., 2002), but two findings concerning adolescents' use of out-of-school time are relevant to this chapter. First, program group adolescents reported more household responsibilities than did controls. If they had responsibility for housework or care of younger siblings, they may have had less opportunity to engage in outside activities even if increased family income made it possible. Second, program group adolescents were more likely than controls to be working 20 or more hours per week, leaving less time for other activities (Morris & Michalopoulos, 2000). Although paid work may have contributed to family resources or to adolescents' ability to purchase goods for themselves, it may also have exposed young people to older co-workers who smoke and drink. Some other research indicates a link between adolescent employment and such problem behavior (Lerman, 2000).

Increased parental employment and increases in income appear to have had a positive influence on elementary-school-age children but somewhat of a negative influence on adolescents (Morris, 2002). For adolescents, participation in out-of-school activities were apparently not sufficiently engaging to counteract the other impacts of the family changes induced by the SSP program. Perhaps if these adolescents had become more involved in out-of-school programs rather than such high involvement in work, the negative effect of increased parental employment would have been reduced.

The New Hope Evaluation

The New Hope Project was an experimental antipoverty demonstration program in Milwaukee, Wisconsin. It offered wage supplements, job search assistance, subsidized child care for children under age 13, and subsidized health insurance for low-income adults who worked at least 30 hours a week. The goal of the program was to raise annual household incomes above the poverty level for families with at least one adult employed 30 hours a week (Bos et al., 1999). Applicants for the program were randomly assigned to a program group that was eligible for New Hope benefits or to a control group. At a follow-up interview 2 years after parents were randomly assigned, parents and children, age 6 to age 13, reported on the child's activity participation in five structured out-of-school activities in the past year: lessons, sports with a coach, religious classes, clubs or youth groups, and recreation or community centers. *Structured activities* were defined as activities in which adults supervised and/or provided plans and guidance for the activity.

Measures of developmental outcomes fell into four broad domains: school achievement, academic and occupational motivation, psychological well-being, and social behavior. School achievement was measured by parent and teacher reports. Children's educational expectations were assessed by asking how sure they were that they would complete high school and college. Children were asked about their occupational aspirations (i.e., jobs they would like to have) and their occupational expectations (i.e., jobs they thought they would have). These were coded for occupational prestige. Measures of psychological well-being included anxiety (e.g., "have trouble going to sleep"), satisfaction with friendships (e.g., "it's easy for me to make new friends"), and scholastic and athletic competence. Parents and teachers completed scales measuring positive social behavior (e.g., "child thinks before he or she acts, usually does what I tell him or her") and externalizing behavior problems (e.g., "is aggressive toward people or objects"). Specific details of the various measures are presented in Bos et al. (1999).

Experimental Impacts.   New Hope led to increases in parent employment and to modest increases in family income. It also expanded family resources by providing a child-care subsidy that increased use of center-based care and after-school programs. Children in New Hope families participated more often in structured activities than did children in control group families; these differences were greater for boys than for girls (Bos et al., 1999). Boys in New Hope families also performed better in school and had higher educational and occupational aspirations than did boys in control families. Teachers reported that boys in New Hope families displayed more positive behavior and fewer externalizing problem behaviors at school than did control boys. Although there were some positive program effects for girls, they were weaker and less consistent than for boys. There were no program effects, however, on children's reports of psychological well-being (Huston et al., 2001).

It appears that greater economic resources, coupled with the availability of child care subsidies to New Hope participants, allowed parents to place their children in more adult-supervised, out-of-school activities. They exercised this option more for boys than for girls, and positive program effects were greater for boys than for girls.

Nonexperimental Mediation Analyses.   The experimental impacts on both activity participation and developmental outcomes provide one type of evidence for the positive influence of activity participation. A second way of examining the possible contribution of participation is nonexperimental analysis in which individual differences in participation are examined as predictors of developmental outcomes within the program and control groups. These analyses were conducted for the children age 9 to age 13, excluding the 6- to 8-year-olds, because there was little activity participation and the self-report measures of psychological well-being were not reliable for the younger group. Of the 9- to 13-year-olds, 60% participated in lessons, 58% participated in sports with a coach, 74% participated in religion classes, 59% attended a recreation or community center, and 45% participated in clubs or youth groups. Details of the data analysis are presented in Ripke, Casey, and Huston (2002).

We first tested the relations between total participation (sum of five activities) and developmental outcomes. There were no relations of activity participation to school achievement, educational and occupational motivation, or social behavior for boys or girls. Activity participation was associated with psychological well-being for boys. Boys who participated more frequently in structured activities had lower levels of perceived anxiety and higher levels of satisfaction with friendships and perceived athletic competence than did those who participated less frequently.

Separate analyses were conducted with each of the five individual activities as predictors (e.g., participation in sports). In this case, for each analysis, the independent variable was dichotomous (no participation, participation). None of the activities predicted school achievement or teacher-reported social behavior, but there were some relations of participation to children's motivation and psychological well-being. Only the results for lessons, sports, and religious classes are discussed here; there were no significant relations to developmental outcomes for youth group and community center participation.

Overall, boys who spent more time in lessons had higher occupational expectations and lower anxiety than did those who spent less time in lessons, but girls had the opposite pattern. Those who spent more time in lessons had lower occupational expectations and were more anxious. For both sexes, those who participated often in organized sports reported higher levels of occupational aspirations and expectations, lower anxiety, and less loneliness than those who participated infrequently. Children who participated often in religious classes had higher levels of perceived athletic competence than did the infrequent participators.

These nonexperimental analyses support a modest association between participation in organized, structured activities and children's psychological well-being. All of the developmental outcomes associated with participation are based on children's self-reports of motivation and psychological well-being, indicating that children who participate frequently in structured activities feel more optimistic about their futures and more satisfied with their relationships with peers. Because these analyses are nonexperimental, the causal direction for these associations cannot be determined; it is likely that children who are more optimistic and self-assured may seek out activities. In fact, the most likely scenario is probably reciprocal causation. Activities afford the opportunity to exercise and develop social and other competencies; children's own predispositions affect the extent to which they use and benefit from these opportunities.

SUMMARY OF RESULTS FROM EXPERIMENTAL STUDIES

Many discussions of out-of-school activities focus on adolescents, but the results from SSP and New Hope suggest that structured activities can play an important and positive role for children in middle childhood. In both of these programs, parents increased their hours of employment, and family income was increased. Perhaps as a result of these changes in family schedules and resources, their elementary school-age children participated more often in structured activities (i.e., lessons, organized sports) than did children in control group families (Huston et al., 2001; Morris & Michalopoulos, 2000). In fact, the rates of participation were relatively high in both program and control groups, suggesting that such activities are used by many low-income families. These findings contrast with another welfare reform experiment conducted in northern Florida, the Family Investment Program. In that experiment, welfare recipients were required to participate in employment-related activities. Although there were modest increases in both employment and income, there were no program effects on participation in structured activities by either middle-age children (age 5 to age 12) or adolescents (age 13 to age 17). Only 35% of the younger age group and 41% of the adolescents participated in any activity (Bloom et al., 2001). It is possible that activities were generally less available in the areas of Florida sampled than they were in Milwaukee or the Canadian communities in SSP.

Two types of evidence concerning the relations of activity participation and developmental outcomes were examined. First, given that both SSP and New Hope increased activity participation, these experiences may have contributed to experimental effects on children's outcomes. Both SSP and New Hope led to increased school achievement, and New Hope led to increased educational and occupational motivation and more positive social behavior in school for boys. The nonexperimental analyses in New Hope demonstrated that, within program or experimental groups, those children who participated in activities more frequently had higher levels of motivation and better psychological well-being than those who were infrequent participators. Overall, these results suggest that structured activities may make a positive contribution to children's acquisition of competence and confidence.

The results from the New Hope study suggest that structured activities play a different role in social development for girls and boys. Of the five activities examined, boys participated more than girls in clubs, sports, and community centers, whereas girls participated in lessons more than boys. Boys may seek out activities in which there are groups of peers and that involve physical activity. In any case, the structured activities investigated apparently offered opportunities for developing social competence for boys more effectively than for girls.

Evidence for adolescents is less positive than for younger children. No data on adolescents are available in New Hope, but neither SSP nor Florida's Family Transition Program increased adolescents' participation in out-of-school activities. Overall, in SSP, older adolescents (age 15 to age 18) were somewhat less likely than younger adolescents (age 12 to age 14) to engage in any of the extracurricular activities measured, and they were more likely to be working long hours for pay. Despite the likely reductions in parents' supervision produced by increased employment and increases in family income, formal out-of-school activities were either not attractive enough or not adequately accessible and available to either parents or adolescents to lead to increased participation. Given that neither SSP nor the Florida experiment increased adolescent participation in activities, it is not likely that any program effects on developmental outcomes can be attributed to formal out-of-school activities. They may, however, be linked to the adolescents' increased participation in paid work for more than 20 hours per week.

CONCLUSIONS AND POLICY IMPLICATIONS

Welfare reform and other policies designed to encourage employment for low-income single parents have increased employment. Some of these policies also increase family income by providing public supplements for earnings (e.g., the EITC). The resulting changes in family organization and parents' time at home create not only need for supervision of children when parents are working, but the opportunity for children to participate in enriching out-of-school experiences. Overall, children from low-income families spend less time in lessons, sports teams, and other extracurricular activities than do those from more affluent families. The data examined in this chapter suggest that increasing resources for families as part of welfare and employment programs increases the rates of participation for children in the middle childhood years, but not for adolescents.

The same programs that increased activity participation also increased children's achievement and positive social behavior, suggesting that activities may have played a positive role. But, social programs can only offer opportunities; children and families make the decisions about how to use those opportunities. There is undoubtedly a reciprocal relation between children's participation in activities and their social, psychological, and academic characteristics. The most reasonable conclusion appears to be that programs can offer the opportunities, and that some children will use those opportunities as a pathway to positive developmental outcomes.

One implication of these findings is that work supports for low-income parents could profitably include funding for out-of-school activities as well as more conventional child care. States now have considerable flexibility in designing child-care assistance programs that are appropriate for the families and children in their jurisdiction. As children age out of "child care," during the middle childhood years, other types of structured activities can play an important role in providing supervision as well as opportunities for recreation and learning. When welfare and employment programs contain an income-support strategy and benefits for out-of-school arrangements, they enable parents to use their increased resources to allow their children to participate in a range of programs. These resources can ensure that financial barriers do not inhibit children's opportunities to participate in beneficial activities.

Funding for programs as well as subsidies to be used by parents could increase the number and variety of activities that are available to children from low-income families. Programs that serve youth from low-income families receive at least part, if not all, of their funding from some level of government. Consequently, the availability of effective out-of-school programs for youth from low-income families is often contingent on the funding from different levels of government. Youth from more affluent families often attend out-of-school programs that are financed in large part by parent fees.

Public programs providing out-of-school activities can be especially useful for adolescents living in high-risk circumstances, but there is considerable debate about the types of programs that best serve the needs of such youth. The data reviewed here suggest that increased employment in low-income families, even with increased family resources, does not lead adolescents to participate in more out-of-school activities. Yet, there is evidence that adolescents who spend their out-of-school time hanging out with friends without adult supervision are at risk of delinquency. Ironically, increased parent employment and family resources do appear to increase the likelihood that adolescents will themselves work for pay, and there may be some negative impact of employment for these teens. More experimentally guided research examining how parents' employment and resources affect the out-of-school time of their children and adolescents would inform policymakers, funders, and program administrators about the most effective ways to ensure the availability of developmentally appropriate out-of-school activities that would attract children and adolescents as well as contributing to their overall well-being.

REFERENCES

Anderson, D. R., Huston, A. C., Schmitt, K. L., Linebarger, D. L., & Wright, J. C. (2001). Early childhood television viewing and adolescent behavior: The Recontact Study. *Monographs of the Society for Research in Child Development, 68*(1, Serial No. 264).

Anderson Moore, K., Hatcher, J. L., Vandivere, S., & Brown, B. V. (2000, October). *Children's behavior and well-being: Findings from the National Survey of America's Families* (Series Snapshots of America's Families II). Washington, DC: The Urban Institute.

Bachman, J. G., & Schulenberg, J. (1993). How part-time work intensity relates to drug use, problem behavior, time use, and satisfaction among high school seniors: Are these consequences or merely correlates? *Developmental Psychology, 29,* 220–235.

Bloom, D., Kemple, J. J., Morris, P., Scrivener, S., Verma, N., & Hendra, R. (2001). *The Family Transition Program: Final report on Florida's initial time-limited welfare program.* New York: Manpower Demonstration Research Corporation.

Bloom, D., & Michalopoulos, C. (2001). *How welfare and work policies affect employment and income: A synthesis of research.* New York: Manpower Demonstration Research Corporation.

Bos, J. M., Huston, A. C., Granger, R. C., Duncan, G. J., Brock, T. W., & McLoyd, V. C. (1999). *New hope for people with low incomes: Two-year results of a program to reduce poverty and reform welfare.* New York: Manpower Demonstration Research Corporation.

Brimhall, D., Reaney, L., & West, J. (1999). *Participation of kindergarteners through third-graders in before- and after-school care* (Rep. No. 1999-2013). Washington, DC: National Center for Education Statistics.

Capizzano, J., Tout, K., & Adams, G. (2000). *Child care patterns of school-age children with employed mothers* (Paper No. 41). Washington, DC: Urban Institute.

Carnegie Corporation. (1992). *A matter of time: Risk and opportunity in the out-of-school hours.* New York: Carnegie Corporation.

Crosby, D. A., Gennetian, L., & Huston, A. C. (2001, September). *Does child care assistance matter? The effects of welfare and employment programs on child care for preschool and young school-aged children* (Working Paper Series No. 2). New York: Manpower Demonstration Research Corporation.

Duncan, G. J., & Yeung, W. J. (1995). Extent and consequences of welfare dependence among America's children. *Children and Youth Services Review, 17,* 157–182.

Eccles, J. S., & Barber, B. L. (1999). Student council, volunteering, basketball, or marching band: What kind of extracurricular involvement matters? *Journal of Adolescent Research, 14,* 10–43.

Eccles, J. S., & Gootman, J. (Eds.). (2002). *Community programs to promote youth development: Report of the National Research Council/Institute of Medicine.* Washington, DC: National Academy Press.

Foster, E. M. (1995). Why teens do not benefit from work experience programs. Evidence from brother comparisons. *Journal of Policy Analysis and Management, 14,* 393–414.

Friedlander, D., & Burtless, G. (1995). *Five years after: The long-term effects of welfare-to-work programs.* New York: Russell Sage.

Fuller, B., Kagan, S. L., Caspary, G. L., & Gauthier, C. A. (2002). Welfare reform and child care options for low-income families. *The Future of Children, 12*(1), 97–119.

Gennetian, L. A., Duncan, G. J., Knox, V. W., Vargas, W. G., Clark-Kauffman, E., & London, A. S. (2002). *How welfare and work policies for parents affect adolescents: A synthesis of research.* New York: Manpower Demonstration Research Corporation.

Greenberg, M. H., Levin-Epstein, J., Hutson, R. Q., Ooms, T. J., Schumacher, R., Turetsky, V., & Engstrom, D. M. (2002). The 1996 welfare law: Key elements and reauthorization issues affecting children. *The Future of Children, 12*(1), 27–57.

Haskins, R., & Primus, W. (2002). Welfare reform and poverty. In I. V. Sawhill, R. K. Weaver, R. Haskins, & A. Kane (Eds.), *Welfare reform and beyond: The future of the safety net* (pp. 59–70). Washington, DC: Brookings.

Heymann, S. J., & Boynton-Jarrett, R. (2003). Managing work and caregiving after welfare reform: The importance of the quality of working conditions and social supports. In F. Wulczyn & L. Aber (Eds.), *Low income families: Coping as parents and workers.* Manuscript in preparation.

Huston, A. C., Duncan, G. J., Granger, R., Bos, J., McLoyd, V., Mistry, R., Crosby, D., Gibson, C., Magnuson, K., Romich, J., & Ventura, A. (2001). Work-based antipoverty programs for parents can enhance the school performance and social behavior of children. *Child Development, 72,* 318–336.

Kerrebrock, N., & Lewit, E. M. (1999). Child indicators: Children in self-care. *The Future of Children, 9*(2), 151–160.

Layzer, J. I., & Collins, A. (2001). *Access to child care for low-income working families report.* Washington, DC: U.S. Department of Health and Human Services.

Lerman, R. I. (2000, November). *Are teens in low-income and welfare families working too much?* (Working Paper Series B, No. B-25). Washington, DC: The Urban Institute.

Linver, M. R., & Silverberg, S. B. (1997). Maternal predictors of early adolescent achievement-related outcomes: Adolescent gender as a moderator. *Journal of Early Adolescence, 17,* 294–318.

Loprest, P. (1999, August). *How families that left welfare are doing: A national picture* (Working Paper Series B, No. B-1). Washington, DC: Urban Institute.

Morris, P. A. (2002). The effects of welfare reform policies on children. *Social Policy Report: Society for Research in Child Development, 16*(1), 4–18.

Morris, P. A., Huston, A. C., Duncan, G. J., Crosby, D., & Bos, J. M. (2001). *How welfare and work policies affect children: A synthesis of research.* New York: Manpower Demonstration Research Corporation.

Morris, P., & Michalopoulos, C. (2000). *The Self-Sufficiency Project at 36 months: Effects on children of a program that increased parental employment and income.* Ottawa: Social Research and Demonstration Corporation.

Mortimer, J., & Johnson, M. (1998). New perspectives on adolescent work and the transition to adulthood. In R. Jessor (Ed.), *New perspectives on adolescent risk behavior* (pp. 425–496). New York: Cambridge University Press.

Newman, K. S. (1996). Working poor: Low-wage employment in the lives of Harlem youth. In J. Graber, J. Brooks-Gunn, & A. Petersen (Eds.), *Transitions through adolescence: Interpersonal domains and context* (pp. 323–343). Mahwah, NJ: Lawrence Erlbaum Associates.

Patterson, G. R. (1999). A proposal relating a theory of delinquency to societal rates of juvenile crime: Putting Humpty Dumpty together again. In M. Cox & J. Brooks-Gunn (Eds.), *Conflict and cohesion in families: Causes and consequences* (pp. 11–35). Mahwah, NJ: Lawrence Erlbaum Associates.

Pettit, G. S., Laird, R. D., Bates, J. E., & Dodge, K. A. (1997). Patterns of after-school care in middle childhood: Risk factors and developmental outcomes. *Merrill-Palmer Quarterly, 43,* 515–538.

Posner, J. K., & Vandell, D. L. (1994). Low-income children's after-school care: Are there beneficial effects of after-school programs? *Child Development, 65,* 440–456.

Posner, J. K., & Vandell, D. L. (1999). After-school activities and the development of low-income urban children: A longitudinal study. *Developmental Psychology, 35,* 868–879.

Presser, H. (2002, October). *What features of work timing matter for families?* Paper presented at the conference on Work–Family Challenges for Low-Income Parents and Their Children, Pennsylvania State University, University Park, PA.

Quinn, J. (1999). Where need meets opportunity: Youth development programs for early teens. *The Future of Children, 9*(2), 96–116.

Ripke, M. N., Casey, D. M., & Huston, A. C. (2002). *Activity participation and the social development and academic achievement of low-income boys and girls.* Unpublished manuscript.

Sampson, R. J., & Laub, J. H. (1994). Urban poverty and the family context of delinquency: A new look at structure and process in a classic study. *Child Development, 65,* 523–540.

Shields, M. K., & Behrman, R. E. (2002). Children and welfare reform: Analysis and recommendations. *The Future of Children, 12*(1), 5–25.

Smith, K. (2000, Fall). *Who's minding the kids? Child care arrangements* (Current Population Rep. P70-70). Washington, DC: U.S. Department of Commerce, Economics and Statistics Administration, U.S. Census Bureau.

Tout, K., Scarpa, J., & Zaslow, M. J. (2002, March). *Children of current and former welfare recipients: Similarly at risk* (Research Brief). Washington, DC: Child Trends.

5

Contexts and Correlates of Out-of-School Activity Participation Among Low-Income Urban Adolescents

Sara Pedersen
Edward Seidman
New York University

Urban adolescents living in poverty, in contrast to their wealthier suburban peers, are exposed to a variety of risk factors that may compromise their psychosocial development. These risks include community violence, under-resourced schools, and low parental education. Historically, researchers and policymakers concerned with youth development have focused on understanding the negative individual-level outcomes associated with poverty, such as delinquency, school dropout, and teen pregnancy. More recent work, however, has examined the characteristics of contexts in which "at-risk" urban youth are embedded that actually facilitate resilience or competence (e.g., Luthar, Cicchetti, & Becker, 2000; Seidman & Pedersen, 2003). A growing body of research suggests that out-of-school activities—structured youth programs held outside of school hours—hold promise as contexts in which urban adolescent development may be supported (Barber, Eccles, & Stone, 2001; Mahoney, 2000; Mahoney & Cairns, 1997).

Increasingly, and in part in response to these studies and their findings, policymakers are expressing interest in providing young people with opportunities for growth and learning beyond school hours by establishing out-of-school activity programs. In 2001, the Younger Americans Act (H.R. 17 and S. 1005) was introduced in the U.S. House of Representatives and

85

the Senate to ensure, as a matter of national policy, that all young people would have access to five "core resources" (Sec. 102). These include "safe places with structured activities" (Sec. 102). In addition, the bill stipulates that the lion's share of program funding should go to programs serving at-risk youth, including those living in poverty.

Although many researchers and policymakers agree that out-of-school activity involvement constitutes a positive experience for young people, the associations observed between out-of-school activity participation and youth development are primarily based on research with suburban and middle class youth. The quality of out-of-school activities available to poor, urban youth, who are at heightened risk for the negative developmental outcomes out-of-school activities may guard against, has been investigated less frequently. Thus, the rates at which poor, urban youth participate in out-of-school activities embedded in different contexts (e.g., school, neighborhood, religious institution) and the benefits of participation in such activities still need to be established.

In this chapter, we first describe the rates of out-of-school activity engagement reported by inner-city youth in large-scale national surveys. Second, we review prior research on youth outcomes associated with out-of-school activity participation in four different contexts—school, the neighborhood, religious institutions, and team athletics. We highlight studies that have sampled ethnic minority, low-income, or urban youth. Third, we present the results of original analyses that assess the rates of participation in activities in each of the four contexts and the developmental correlates of participation in each context among a sample of poor, urban adolescents. In the final section, we elaborate on the implications of past research and our current findings for future studies of out-of-school activity involvement and urban youth development.

RATES OF OUT-OF-SCHOOL ACTIVITY PARTICIPATION IN ADOLESCENCE

Few prior studies have quantified the amount of time poor urban youth spend in organized out-of-school activities. Larson, Richards, Sims, and Dworkin (2001) examined the time use patterns of urban poor African American early adolescents. The urban youth spent less time in structured after-school activities (including clubs, art programs, and volunteer work) than a comparison sample of European American suburban adolescents. On average, the urban sample spent only .5% of their time engaged in such activities, compared to 1.6% among suburban youth. Interpretation of this finding is difficult due to the confounding of culture, income, and location in this sample. The authors attribute the differences between the urban and suburban teens' levels of after-school activity engagement to the urban parents' desire to maintain the safety of their children by limiting their activities outside the home. Indeed, many of the neighborhoods in which the urban sample lived had high rates of violent crime. This interpretation is also consistent with studies of parenting in violent neighborhoods. Restrictive parenting has been associated with positive youth outcomes among families in high crime inner-city neighborhoods (Gonzales, Cauce, Friedman, & Mason, 1996). Alternately, parents in high-risk neighborhoods may want their children to participate in structured activities because these activities represent safe contexts but participation rates remain low because structural barriers, such as geography and activity availability, impede youth involvement.

The findings of large-scale longitudinal surveys support the results reported by Larson and colleagues (2001). Analyses of national data collected in 1972, 1980, and 1992 on high-school seniors found that youth in the lowest socioeconomic status (SES) quartile participated in most types of school-based activities at lower rates than those in higher quartiles (National Center for Youth Statistics, 1996). For example, in 1992, roughly 20% of youth in the lowest SES quartile participated in academic clubs compared to over 30% of those in the highest quartile. Similar patterns emerged for honorary societies, student government, and newspaper/yearbook activities. In addition, although rates of participation in most school-based activities grew between 1972 and 1992 among youth in the highest quartile, low SES adolescents' participation rates declined over this period. The data reported does not establish whether the differences in school-based activity participation rates reported by low and high income youth reflect differences in the interests of these young people or the extracurricular opportunities available in their schools.

The data also indicate that Latino and African American youth engage in school-based activities at relatively low rates. For example, in 1992, 12% of Latino high-school seniors and 14% of African American seniors participated in Honorary Societies compared to 20% of European American seniors and 27% of Asian American seniors (National Center for Youth Statistics, 1996). Although participation rates have tended to decline across all groups of seniors, African American youth have experienced the most dramatic drops in participation rates. The proportion of African American high-school seniors involved in academic clubs dropped by about 36% between 1972 and 1992 (National Center for Youth Statistics, 1996).

The lower rates of school-based activity participation reported by low-income youth in the 1992 National Education Longitudinal Study (NELS) were consistent with findings from the same sample of youth surveyed 4 years earlier regarding their levels of participation in activities based outside the schools. Quinn (1997) reported that 83% of high SES 8th-grade students surveyed in the NELS of 1988 were involved in an activity outside of school compared to only 60% of low SES 8th graders. Low SES 8th graders were half as likely as high SES youth to be involved in religious youth groups and one fourth to one third less likely to be involved in scouting and team sports outside of school. In fact, although the largest proportion of low SES youth who participated in activities based outside the school were involved in team sports (almost one third of the youth report being on a sports team), over 45% of 8th graders in the top SES quartile participated in nonschool team sports. Low SES youth were, however, more likely than wealthier youth to participate in Boys and Girls Club activities, YMCA/YWCA activities, and other neighborhood-based youth groups. The results presented by Quinn (1997) were not broken down by geographic location within SES quartile. The patterns of participation among urban and suburban youth, however, mirror those for low and high SES youth.

The results of these national surveys suggest that urban poor youth evidence different patterns of participation than their wealthier and suburban peers. They are more likely to engage in neighborhood-based youth groups and less likely to participate in school-based programs. In fact, despite the seeming wholehearted support for enhanced out-of-school programming for low-income adolescents expressed by stakeholders concerned with the positive development of these youth, the discrepancy between the rates of participation in school-based activities among the poorest adolescents and the wealthiest adolescents has grown in recent years.

The participation discrepancy between low-income urban youth and wealthier suburban youth could be a reflection of the different opportunity structures in the neighborhoods and school systems in which these young people live and learn. Urban youth often attend schools with limited economic resources. These schools are less equipped to support the variety and quality of extracurricular programming available to students attending school in wealthier neighborhoods. Perhaps to compensate for this disparity, neighborhood youth organizations primarily locate themselves in low-income urban neighborhoods. Inner-city adolescents may also find that the neighborhood youth group programming is more satisfying, engaging, or enriching than the available school-based clubs. Examining the associations between out-of-school activity participation and inner-city adolescent well-being may elucidate the causal mechanisms underlying the different patterns of activity participation observed in the national data.

THE CONTEXTS AND CORRELATES
OF URBAN ADOLESCENT OUT-OF-SCHOOL
ACTIVITY PARTICIPATION

In this section, we review the correlates of activity participation within the school, religion, neighborhood, and athletic contexts. We underscore the role of race/ethnicity and gender where it has been addressed. These findings should be interpreted with caution, however, as many of the studies described (particularly those using samples of low-income youth) are cross-sectional, do not control for selection bias, and rely exclusively on self-report data.

School-Based Activity Participation

A number of large-scale longitudinal studies have found that school-based activity participation is associated with greater academic achievement and persistence and reduced antisocial behavior among working and middle-class youth (Barber et al., 2001; Eccles & Barber, 1999; Mahoney, 2000; Mahoney & Cairns, 1997). There is some suggestion in the literature that these associations may be consistent across populations of adolescents from a variety of socioeconomic backgrounds. For example, Eccles and Barber (1999) reported that the associations among involvement in student government, school spirit, or academic clubs and higher grades and greater academic persistence were independent of maternal education. In addition, two studies using related samples of rural and suburban youth, 25% of whom were African American, found that the beneficial effects of extracurricular involvement were particularly robust among youth deemed at risk for early school dropout or criminal behavior in part because of their low SES (Mahoney, 2000; Mahoney & Cairns, 1997).

Although the findings of studies with rural and suburban samples support the hypothesis that extracurricular activity involvement is as beneficial—or even more beneficial—to youth from lower SES backgrounds, the implications of these findings for low SES urban adolescents remain unclear. Urban and rural or suburban youth with similar levels of family income experience very different risks in their proximal social contexts. Disadvantaged rural and suburban adolescents are less likely to experience community violence. Even suburban schools that draw from working class or poor neighborhoods may have more resources to expend on their extracurricular programs—resulting in more numerous and higher quality activities—than inner-city schools.

In one of the few studies that explicitly examined ethnic minority urban adolescents' out-of-school activity involvement, Kahne et al. (2001) suggested that extracurricular activity involvement enhances poor urban students' perceptions of the school environment. Inner-city African American middle grades and high-school students were surveyed regarding their perceptions of the in-school and out-of-school contexts in which they were engaged. Although all youth tended to rate out-of-school activities more positively than in-school activities, participants in extracurricular activities rated in-school activities more positively and perceived the school environment as more supportive than youth who were not engaged in extracurricular activities.

Younger children from inner-city neighborhoods may also benefit from extracurricular activity engagement. In one study, low-income youth in middle childhood who engaged in formal after-school programs (primarily based in the schools) received higher grades, evidenced fewer conduct problems, were more engaged in enriching academic activities, and watched fewer hours of television than children who went home or entered into informal daycare settings (Posner & Vandell, 1994).

Neighborhood-Based Activity Participation

The relatively high participation rates reported by disadvantaged youth in neighborhood-based, out-of-school activities suggest that these programs may be particularly important contexts of urban adolescent development (Carnegie Corporation of New York, 1992; Hirsch et al., 2000; Quinn, 1997). A study by Roffman, Pagano, and Hirsch (2001) shed light on the ways in which neighborhood youth group involvement may relate to urban adolescent well-being. Differential patterns of cross-sectional associations were observed between satisfaction with the club and psychological well-being among almost 300 youth attending an urban Boys and Girls Club. Among youth who felt that club activities were unimportant to their attendance, boys reported substantially lower self-esteem than girls. Girls were more likely than boys (60% vs. 48%) and African American youth were more likely than Latino youth (60% vs. 46%) to report that the club staff members were important to their attendance of club activities. Latino youth who reported that the staff was an important reason to attend the club, however, reported fewer problems "getting into trouble" (by about one half a standard deviation) than Latino youth who felt the staff was unimportant.

Although the causal direction of the associations between club experiences and youth well-being cannot be determined from the data presented, the findings described by Roffman and colleagues (2001) suggest that neighborhood youth programs for inner-city teens may not be equally successful with all youth. Youth of different genders and racial/ethnic backgrounds may vary in the extent to which particular aspects of the program, such as the nature of the adult leadership or the type of activities offered, are beneficial to their development.

Many community-based organizations (CBOs) that serve teens also make an effort to target the families of the teens and other community members through their programming. As a result, CBO-run after-school programs not only have the potential to promote positive youth development, but also to affect change at the family, neighborhood, and community levels. One study used survey and observational methods to examine the effects of establishing Boys and Girls Clubs (BGCs) in public assistance housing developments (Schinke, Orlandi, & Cole, 1992). The authors reported that the visibility of substance use and drug-related arrests were reduced in communities in which new BGCs were established. In addition, by the final wave of data collection, reports of juvenile crime (gathered from police data) had been reduced by 13% in the neighborhoods with new clubs. No changes were observed in comparison communities in which no new clubs were established.

It should be noted that the newly established BGCs specifically targeted drug use with the SMART Moves prevention program. Not all existing BGCs, however, provided comprehensive substance abuse prevention programming. Because drug activity in housing developments with new BGCs tended, by follow-up, to be similar to those in housing with existing BGCs, the changes observed in communities with new clubs may have stemmed from club characteristics unrelated to the substance use prevention program, such as those that promoted parental involvement in club activities and an enhanced sense of community in the neighborhood.

Youth activities sponsored by CBOs, however, may not always promote positive youth development. Many CBOs sponsor unstructured, recreational "drop-in" centers that are open late and offer limited adult supervision (Stattin, Kerr, Mahoney, Persson, & Magnusson, chap. 10, this volume). Adolescents attending such centers evidence higher rates of antisocial behavior and are involved with more antisocial peers than those who do not attend (Mahoney & Stattin, 2000). Thus, the quality of the neighborhood-based activities available to adolescents may determine the extent to which involvement in such activities is associated with positive youth development.

Religious Institution-Based Participation

Greater religiosity is associated with reduced delinquency among adolescents, including lower rates of antisocial behavior and substance use (Benson, 1992; Jessor, Van Den Bos, Vanderryn, & Costa, 1995; Wallace & Bachman, 1991). These findings may be particularly relevant for adolescents living in ethnic minority communities, for whom religious involvement is often a cultural experience (Burton, Obeidallah, & Allison, 1995). However, the degree to which the reduced delinquency rates observed among religious youth may be associated with their involvement in religious youth groups is unknown.

The results of studies examining suburban working class and rural youth also suggest that diverse groups of young people, perhaps including inner-city teens, may benefit from involvement in religious youth groups. In two related studies, participation in religious or community service activities during high school was associated with lower rates of problem behavior in late adolescence and, among the same sample surveyed in young adulthood, greater academic persistence and self-esteem (Barber et al., 2001; Eccles & Barber, 1999). Further, the results of one study indicate that religious youth group involvement may contribute to the ethnic identity development of African American youth. Markstrom (1999) reported that African American high-school students who participated in religious youth groups reported higher scores on a measure of ethnic identity than African American nonparticipants. For European American students, participation and ethnic identity were unrelated. Although the population sampled in this study did not come from an urban area, Markstrom's (1999) study is one of the first empirical studies to suggest that members of different ethnic, racial, or cultural groups might experience unique benefits from participation in a particular out-of-school activity context.

Team Sports Participation

Participation in team sports has been associated with both positive and negative youth outcomes. Positive outcomes associated with sports involvement include social skills development, higher self-esteem, greater self-efficacy, and greater academic achievement, among others (Dubois, Tevendale, Burk-Braxton, Swenson, & Hardesty, 2000; Eccles & Barber, 1999; Larson, 2000; Patrick et al., 1999). For example, Eccles and Barber (1999) found that working and middle-class adolescents engaged in athletic activities evidenced greater postsecondary academic persistence than adolescents who reported similar levels of academic achievement in high school but were not engaged in athletic activities. These researchers, however, also found that youth involved in sports were more likely to use alcohol.

The rates of involvement in athletics and meaning of athletic involvement may not be the same at all stages of development for all youth. Throughout adolescence, girls participate in team sports activities at lower rates than boys—both in school and outside of school (National Center for Youth Statistics, 1996; Quinn, 1997). In one large-scale longitudinal study, girls' rates of physical activity declined dramatically between age nine and age 17 (Kimm et al., 2002). African American girls were at particular risk for low levels of physical activity: 56% of African American girls, compared to 31% of European American girls, reported no leisure-time physical activity by age 17. Girls also tend to be less confident in their athletic abilities and place a lower value on athletic achievement (Dubois et al., 2000; Fredricks & Eccles, 2002; Jacobs, Lanza, Osgood, Eccles, & Wigfield, 2002). These gender differences in sports competence beliefs are stable throughout adolescence (Fredricks & Eccles, 2002).

Although the rates of sports participation and the meaning of such participation may vary by gender, gender differences in the associations between athletic involvement and youth well-being have not been identified consistently in the literature. In one study of suburban adolescents, sports participation was associated with reduced sexual activity among girls but not boys (Miller, Sabo, Farrell, Barnes, & Melnick, 1998). Other studies, however, have observed no gender differences in the correlates of sports participation (Eccles & Barber, 1999). No studies were identified in which sports participation was more beneficial to boys than girls, suggesting that girls' lower rates of participation may constitute a risk to their positive development—at least to the degree that sports participation uniquely enhances youth well-being. For example, few activities beyond sports promote youth physical health and fitness.

Poor youth also participate in team sports at lower rates (National Center for Youth Statistics, 1996; Quinn, 1997). Very little research, however, has examined the impact of team sports participation on the development of poor youth. Hirsch et al. (2000) suggested that team sports, such as basketball, can promote energy and enthusiasm among members of the organization in which the sports team is embedded. Also, team sports were found to be the most popular activities among males attending a CBO serving low-income youth.

Inner-city girls may be at particular risk for low levels of involvement in sports, particularly in CBOs with limited funding and well-established boys' sports programs (Hirsch et al., 2000). This gender gap may limit urban girls' opportunities to develop the skills and competencies promoted by sports involvement and may affect the nature of their self-evaluations. In one study of urban girls, team sports participation in early adolescence was found to predict greater self-esteem in middle adolescence (Pedersen & Seidman, in press). Greater knowledge of the team sports opportunities available to urban adolescents of both genders and the mechanisms by which sports involvement affects their development could help schools and communities tailor their sports programs to meet the needs of youth.

NEW FINDINGS: OUT-OF-SCHOOL ACTIVITY INVOLVEMENT AND THE PSYCHOSOCIAL DEVELOPMENT OF INNER-CITY TEENS

In this section, we address some of the limitations in the existing literature by presenting the results of analyses assessing low-income urban youth's out-of-school activity participation rates and the psychosocial correlates of such participation using data from the Adolescent Pathways Project (APP). The APP examined the pathways toward positive and negative developmental outcomes of two cohorts of ethnically diverse, low-income adolescents from the public schools of New York, Washington, DC, and Baltimore (Seidman, 1991). Because poverty was the central risk condition of the APP, urban public schools in which the highest percentages of children received reduced priced/free lunch (R/FL) were chosen for study. Many of the schools were overcrowded and lacked financial and material resources. These schools were most likely to have students who grew up under conditions of extreme poverty. Indeed, 60% of the full APP sample and 79% of the African American and Latino participants lived in neighborhoods in which 20% or more of the nonelderly residents lived below the poverty line.

Previous research has not distinguished the out-of-school activity participation patterns of low-income youth at different developmental stages within adolescence. Therefore, in the following sections, we first describe the rates of participation in school-based, neighborhood, religious, and team sports activities reported by youth in each cohort across the two waves of data collection. We also examine how these longitudinal patterns of participation are associated with race/ethnicity and gender. Past literature suggests that, for example, girls participate less than boys in some types of activities, including team sports activities and neighborhood youth groups (Hirsch et al., 2000; Quinn, 1997). The findings of Hirsch and colleagues (2000) suggest that some neighborhood-based youth programs do not provide young women participants with the types of activities they rate as most desirable. Opportunities for girls to participate in sports may be further limited if neighborhood organizations earmark the majority of their athletic equipment and practice space for boys' use. In addition, Latino youth are expected to have low participation rates across most types of activities (National Center for Youth Statistics, 1996).

Second, we report the results of cross-sectional analyses that examined participation in each type of activity as a predictor of three concurrent measures of youth well-being—self-esteem, academic achievement, and antisocial behavior—in the year following a school transition.[1] Gender, race/ethnicity, and school context were also explored as moderators of the associations between participation in each type of activity and youth well-being.

---

[1]Although we describe the rates of out-of-school activity participation reported by youth in the APP sample over two waves of data collection, the analyses conducted to test the associations between out-of-school participation and the developmental correlates were cross-sectional. For these analyses, only data collected when the adolescents were in the first year of the middle grades or of high school were used. This wave of data was selected because the transitions between schools constitute risky experiences for youth—particularly those in poverty (Seidman, Aber, & French, 2004). Revealing positive associations between out-of-school activity participation and well-being during these years could help direct the actions of interventionists concerned with buffering the negative effects of school transitions.

Participation in school-based activities, religious activities, or team sports activities was expected to be positively associated with academic achievement and self-esteem. Religious participation was expected to be related to lower antisocial behavior. In contrast, research with working-class and middle-class youth suggested that sports involvement is related to problem behaviors (e.g., alcohol use) but not with a pattern of delinquent or antisocial behaviors (Barber et al., 2001; Eccles & Barber, 1999). Prior work with the current sample, however, suggests that sports participation and antisocial behavior are related for some poor urban youth (Pedersen et al., in press). Specific hypotheses regarding the direction of the associations between participation in a neighborhood youth group and the measures of well-being were not developed because past studies in this area have found both benefits (e.g., Schinke et al., 1992) and risks (e.g., Mahoney & Stattin, 2000) associated with such participation. More complex patterns of association between the different forms of participation and youth outcomes, including moderation by school context (i.e., middle grades or high school) were also explored.

Before presenting our findings, we provide descriptions of the sample and measures as well as the analyses we employ. The early adolescent or "middle grades" cohort youth ($N = 633$) were surveyed in the first 2 years of a middle-grades school, while the middle adolescent or "high school" cohort youth ($N = 315$) were surveyed in the first 2 years of senior high school. Early adolescents averaged 12.3 years ($SD = .91$) at the first wave and 13.2 years ($SD = .84$) at the second wave, whereas the middle adolescents averaged 14.9 years ($SD = .94$) at the first wave and 15.8 years ($SD = .92$) at the second wave of data collection. The sample of 948 was approximately 55% female, 29% African American, 28% European American, and 43% Latino.

At each wave of data collection, youth indicated how often they participated in school-based activities (including academic clubs, school-based volunteer activities, spirit activities, performing arts activities, school publications, and student government activities), neighborhood youth group activities, religious youth group activities, and team sports activities (see Table 5.1). The response options for the items tapping participation in school-based, neighborhood, and religious activities ranged along a 6-point scale from *Never or almost never* to *Almost every day*. Response options for the item tapping team sports participation ranged along a 5-point scale from *Once a month or less* to *Almost every day*.

We were most interested in identifying rates and correlates of regular participation in each type of activity. For school-based, neighborhood, and religious activities, youth were considered regular participants if they reported engaging in that activity at least once per month over the previous year. Because organized sports teams tend to require more frequent practices and team meetings than other clubs, however, only youth who reported playing

TABLE 5.1
Out-of-School Activity Participation Survey Items

Context	Survey Items
School-based Activities	Now we'd like to know how often you do the following activities at your school. 1. Academic activities (such as math, science club). 2. Volunteer helpers (such as peer counselsors, etc.). 3. Cheerleaders, pep club, twirlers/majorettes. 4. Musical activities (like band or chorus). 5. Debate team, drama, or theater 6. School newspaper, magazine, yearbook. 7. Student government.
Nonschool Activities	
Neighborhood	How often do these things in your neighborhood, not including your school? 1. Youth organizations in the community (like Scouts, CVC, or the Y).
Religious	These last questions are about activities at your chuch or synagogue. 1. Youth group.
Team Sports	How often do you play team sports?

team sports at least once per week were considered regular team sports participants. The proportions of regular participants in each activity context for the full sample and demographic subsamples are reported in Table 5.2.

Surveyed youth also completed items assessing their global self-esteem, antisocial behavior, and academic achievement. *Global self-esteem* was measured using the five-item global self-worth subscale of the Self-Perception Profile for Adolescents (Harter, 1988). *Academic achievement* was assessed by asking youth to respond to the question "What would you say your average grade is, if you put all your grades together?" with one of the following: *A or excellent, B or good, C or satisfactory, D or needs improvement, F or unsatisfactory.* The *antisocial behavior* measure was created by averaging three variables: (a) delinquency, based on self-reported offenses using a 10-item inventory of antisocial behaviors (e.g., *I have hit another student, I have used a weapon to steal from a person*) that were weighted according to Tracy, Wolfgang, and Figlio's (1990) seriousness of offense criteria, summed, and converted to a 0 to 5 scale to achieve a common scale of measurement; (b) alcohol use, based on 5 *yes/no* items of in-

TABLE 5.2

Inner-City Adolescents' Rates (Marginal Means) of Regular Participation in School-Based, Nonschool, and Team Sports Activities in Year 1 and Year 2

Activity Context:	School-Based[a]																Nonschool						Team Sports	
Activity Type:	Any		Academic		Volunteer/ Helpers		Spirit		Music		Debate/ Drama		News-paper		Student Gov't		Any		Neigh-borhood-based		Religious		Any	
Year:	1	2	1	2	1	2	1	2	1	2	1	2	1	2	1	2	1	2	1	2	1	2	1	2
Full sample	.47	.48	.16	.19	.20	.24	.07	.06	.21	.19	.10	.09	.05	.09	.06	.06	.21	.27	.11	.14	.16	.21	.70	.66
Female	.48	.53	.16	.20	.21	.32	.11	.10	.23	.22	.09	.10	.04	.10	.06	.06	.18	.25	.06	.11	.16	.22	.59	.54
Male	.45	.43	.17	.19	.20	.17	.02	.02	.19	.17	.11	.08	.06	.07	.06	.06	.24	.28	.16	.17	.16	.20	.81	.77
African American	.46	.48	.20	.22	.15	.19	.08	.11	.22	.22	.12	.08	.06	.11	.07	.07	.19	.32	.08	.15	.16	.26	.70	.67
Latino	.45	.47	.15	.15	.18	.24	.03	.04	.23	.22	.09	.08	.07	.08	.05	.05	.23	.18	.11	.09	.18	.15	.70	.62
European American	.49	.50	.15	.20	.28	.30	.06	.06	.18	.14	.08	.10	.04	.07	.05	.06	.21	.30	.14	.18	.14	.23	.70	.67
Middle grades	.54	.54	.20	.18	.23	.29	.08	.09	.29	.27	.11	.09	.07	.12	.08	.08	.20	.28	.11	.13	.15	.22	.77	.77
High school	.38	.42	.13	.20	.17	.19	.05	.04	.13	.12	.09	.08	.06	.04	.04	.05	.23	.26	.12	.15	.17	.20	.55	.49

Proportion Participating in Each Activity

Note. [a]The rate of participation in any school-based activity is not the sum of the rates of participation in each type of school-based activity because some young people reported engaging in more than one school-based activity. Similarly, some young people participated in both neighborhood and religious youth groups. Thus, the overall rate of engagement in nonschool activities is less than the sum of the neighborhood and religious activity participation rates.

creasing severity from 1 (*I had a sip of beer, wine, or liquor*) to 5 (*I drink alcohol at least two or three times a week*) where a score of "0" reflected no use; and (c) negative involvement with peers, the mean of three items that asked participants to indicate, on a 6-point scale (0 to 5), how often they used cigarettes or alcohol, broke the law, and destroyed others' property with their peers. Higher scores on these measures reflect higher self-esteem, greater academic achievement, and more serious antisocial behavior.

In what follows, we describe variations in the youth's rates of participation in each type of activity (e.g., school, neighborhood, religious, and team sports) across the two waves of data collection. For each activity context, a separate Repeated Measures Analysis of Variance was performed. The between-subjects factors included gender, race/ethnicity, and school context (the middle grades vs. high school). The within-subjects effect of time was also examined to reveal changes in participation rates between Time 1 and Time 2, as were the three 2-way interaction terms for time crossed with each demographic variable (e.g., gender, race, and school context) and the three 3-way interaction terms for time crossed with gender and race, gender and school context, and race and school context.

We also describe the associations between participation in each type of activity and youth well-being in the first year of the middle grades or high school. For the self-esteem, academic achievement, and delinquency outcomes, a separate cross-sectional Analysis of Variance was performed using data from Time 1. The independent variables included four dummy-coded variables representing participation versus no participation in school, neighborhood, religious, and team sports activities, as well as gender, race/ethnicity, school context and the 12 two-way interaction terms for each type of activity crossed with each demographic variable.

Means and standard errors of each developmental correlate by participation in school, neighborhood, religious, and team sports activities and youth demographic characteristics are reported in Table 5.3. Adjusting for participation in each type of activity, gender was significantly related to self-esteem and antisocial behavior, but not GPA. As expected, girls reported lower self-esteem and lower rates of antisocial behavior. Neither race/ethnicity nor school context was associated with any of the three developmental correlates. Now, the rates of out-of-school activity participation, the demographic associations with participation, and the associations between participation and the developmental correlates are described separately for each type of activity. All reported differences are significant at the $p = .05$ level unless noted otherwise.

School-Based Activity Participation

Aggregating across waves, gender and race/ethnicity interacted to predict participation in school-based activities (see Fig. 5.1a). Among African

TABLE 5.3

Adjusted Means (Standard Error) of Self-Esteem, GPA, and Antisocial Behavior by Participation in School-Based, Neighborhood, Religious, and Team Sports Activities in Year 1 and Demographic Variables (N = 903)[a]

| | Regular Engagement in Each Activity Context | | | | | | | | Demographic Variables | | | | | | |
| | School | | Neighbor-hood | | Religious Institution | | Team Sports | | Gender | | Race/Ethnicity | | | School Context | |
Outcome	P[b]	NP	P	NP	P	NP	P	NP	Female	Male	African American	Latino	European American	Middle Grades	High School
Self-Esteem	2.82 (.07)	2.76 (.07)	2.69 (.10)	2.88 (.05)	2.85 (.09)	2.72 (.06)	2.87 (.06)	2.70 (.08)	2.68 (.08)	2.90 (.09)	2.83 (.11)	2.66 (.08)	2.88 (.10)	2.85 (.07)	2.73 (.09)
GPA	3.88 (.07)	3.68 (.07)	3.64 (.11)	3.92 (.06)	3.92 (.09)	3.64 (.07)	3.87 (.07)	3.69 (.09)	3.70 (.08)	3.86 (.10)	3.69 (.12)	3.76 (.09)	3.88 (.11)	3.82 (.08)	3.74 (.10)
Antisocial Behavior	.71 (.06)	.75 (.06)	.76 (.09)	.70 (.05)	.71 (.07)	.75 (.05)	.68 (.05)	.77 (.07)	.62 (.06)	.84 (.07)	.62 (.10)	.71 (.07)	.86 (.09)	.66 (.06)	.80 (.08)

Note. [a]The sample size was reduced due to missing data on one or more variables. [b]P = participants; NP = nonparticipants.

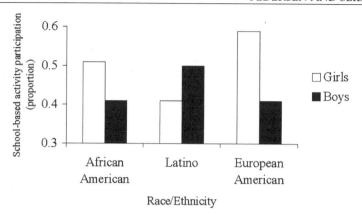

FIG. 5.1a. Gender differences in school-based activity participation rates by race/ethnicity.

American and European American youth, girls participated at higher rates than boys. Over 50% of African American girls and almost 60% of European American girls participated, compared to just over 40% of African American and European American boys. In contrast, although 50% of Latino boys participated in at least one school-based activity, only 41% of Latino girls participated in a school-based activity.

School context was also associated with average school-based activity participation. Aggregating across waves, 54% of youth in the first 2 years of the middle grades ("middle grades") and 40% of youth in the first 2 years of high school ("high school") participated in at least one school-based activity. The tendency for high-school youth to participate in school-based activities at lower rates was particularly striking among activities that usually become more competitive in high school, such as music. For example, approximately 30% of middle-grade youth were regularly engaged in school-based musical activities, such as band or chorus, compared to only 12% to 13% of the high-school sample. (As will be described later, this pattern also emerged from the team sports participation data.) Although rates of participation in debate and drama activities, spirit activities, school newspaper, magazine or yearbook, and student government were low for all youth, high-school youth also participated less in these activities.

In addition, the pattern of change over time in the school-based extracurricular participation rates of youth in the middle grades differed dramatically by gender; the same gendered pattern was not evident for the high-school cohort (see Fig. 5.1b). Over the two middle grades years, girls' participation increased whereas boys' declined. Girls in the high school sample also reported greater participation than the boys. Both high-school boys' and high-school girls' rates of engagement, however,

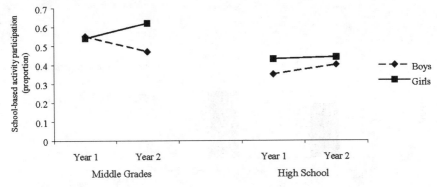

FIG. 5.1b.   Boys and girls school-based activity participation rates over time and across school context.

remained stable across time. Although the equivalence of the two samples in this study cannot be assumed, the patterns suggest that boys' disengagement from school-based activities begins in the middle grades. In contrast, girls are more likely to disengage from school-based activities on entering high school.

School-based activity participation was associated with higher grades. In contrast, no significant associations between school-based activity participation and self-esteem or antisocial behavior were observed. A trend ($p <$ .10), however, suggests that school context interacts with school-based activity participation to predict antisocial behavior (see Fig. 5.1c). Although unrelated during the first year of the middle grades, participation in school-based activities was negatively associated with antisocial behavior in the first year of high school.

Neighborhood Youth Group Participation

Aggregating across time and adjusting for school context and racial/ethnic group, boys were almost twice as likely as girls to participate regularly in neighborhood youth groups (17% of boys vs. 9% of girls). In addition, European American youth participated regularly in neighborhood youth groups at the highest rates (16%) and Latino youth participated at the lowest rates (10%). An interaction between school context and race/ethnicity suggested that these findings were mostly accounted for by the high-school sample. Among the high-school youth, 20% of the European American youth participated regularly in neighborhood youth groups, compared to less than 10% of the Latino and African American youth.

Youth reported participating in neighborhood youth groups at slightly higher rates during the second year of the study than the first. This pattern

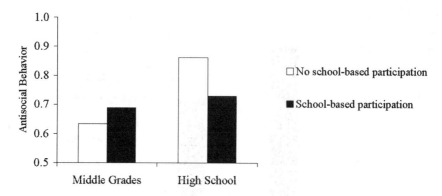

FIG. 5.1c. The association between school context and antisocial behavior by school-based activity participation.

was consistent across gender and school context, but differed by racial/ethnic group. Although African American and European American youth reported increased participation, Latino youth's rates of participation declined over time.

In contrast to the promising findings of prior work with inner-city teens in youth organizations (e.g. Hirsch et al., 2000; Schinke et al., 1992), engagement in neighborhood youth groups was negatively associated with both academic achievement and, at $p < .10$, with self-esteem. Given the cross-sectional nature of these analyses, however, we should not conclude that involvement in neighborhood youth group activities constitutes a risk for academic failure. Rather, youth who have already disengaged from school may seek out meaningful connections to peers and adults in another context, such as a neighborhood youth group. Further, youth engaged in these activities were not at greater risk for antisocial behavior.

Religious Youth Group Participation

There were no group differences in the rates of participation in a religious youth group reported by this sample when aggregating across waves of data collection. Overall, the rate of participation in a religious youth group increased over time for boys and girls and youth in each school context. In contrast, racial/ethnic differences in the pattern of change in religious youth group participation over time were observed. The participation rates of African American and European American youth increased over time; Latino youth's participation decreased.

Participation in a religious youth group was positively associated with academic achievement. Further, a significant interaction between this

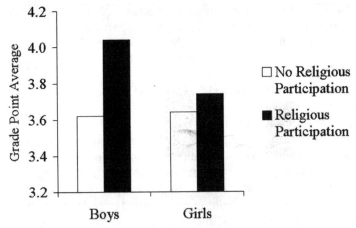

FIG. 5.2. The association between gender and GPA by religious activity participation.

religious youth group participation and the respondent's gender indicated that the positive association between such participation and academic achievement was stronger for boys than for girls, suggesting that religious youth group participation may benefit inner-city male adolescents, in particular (see Fig. 5.2).

Team Sports Participation

As expected, by far the most common activities in which the youth engaged were team sports, even though the criterion for participation was much higher. A number of interesting differences in team sports participation rates emerged. Across waves, and adjusting for school context and racial/ethnic group, more boys than girls were regular participants in team sports activities (79% vs. 56%). In addition, although almost 80% of the middle-grades sample engaged regularly in team sports, roughly one half of the high-school sample participated in such activities.

Further, the data suggest that participation in team sports may decline as youth transition from the middle grades to high school. Rates of engagement in team sports activities over time were found to differ by school context. Middle-grades youth not only participated at higher rates overall, these rates were also stable across the two waves. In contrast, high-school youth reported lower rates of engagement than middle grades youth at the first wave of data collection and the high-school students' participation rates continued to decline over time.

Engagement in team sports was associated with higher self-esteem and greater academic achievement and unrelated to antisocial behavior. No moderation by gender, race/ethnicity, or school context was observed. In light of the observed differences in team sports participation rates, these associations suggest fewer girls than boys and fewer high school youth than middle grades youth are able to benefit from team sports involvement.

SUMMARY OF FINDINGS

We found variations in the rates of participation in different activities that were consistent with our expectations based on the national data. Girls were less likely than boys to participate in team sports and Latino youth were at risk for low participation in most out-of-school activities. We also observed that rates of participation in some types of activities, including school-based activities and team sports, differed by school context.[2] In contrast, although the rates of neighborhood and religious youth group participation were low, they were stable across time and school context. Neighborhood youth group participation was particularly low.

The dramatic differences in rates of school-based and team sports activity participation among youth in the middle grades and high school are particularly striking given that the high-school sample was less representative than the middle-grades sample (Seidman, 1991). The high-school participants received better grades than their classroom peers who did not participate in the survey. Because these youth should be among the most engaged in their schools, the rates of school-based activity participation observed for this sample likely *overestimate* the true proportion of low income urban high-school students engaged in school-based activities.

The lower rates of school-based and team sports participation observed among older youth suggest that the extracurricular and athletic options available to younger adolescents are more inclusive. Middle-grades sports teams and neighborhood sports teams for early adolescents are usually open to both skilled and unskilled players. High-school sports teams and neighborhood sports teams for older teens often weed out less skilled or less committed players by requiring tryouts and attendance at frequent, demanding practices. The results of one study using data from the NELS of 1988 support the suggestion that opportunities to engage in school-based activities, including sports, cheerleading, and fine arts, close as youth enter high school

---

[2]Given the confound between school context and developmental stage, one could also argue that the differences in participation rates observed in the APP cohorts actually reflect a developmental trend toward lower participation and are not a function of school context. Although all youth were surveyed in the year after a school transition, the first time point for the middle-grades youth was either 6th or 7th grade and for the high-school youth was 9th or 10th grade. If a developmental trend toward lower participation actually existed, a linear decreasing trend in participation rates would be expected to emerge if the sample were analyzed by grade in school rather than school type. This analysis was conducted, but no linear decrease in participation emerged. The most dramatic differences were still observed between 8th-grade younger cohort students and 9th-grade older cohort students.

(McNeal, 1998). Young people who participated in one of these activities in 9th grade were highly likely to have participated in that activity in 8th grade.

It should be noted, however, that the rates of urban adolescent activity participation that we present in the current study are only for the first 2 years of the middle grades and the first 2 years of high school. During the final 2 years of high school, rates of activity participation may stabilize or grow as youth adjust to their new school and peer group environments. Awareness of out-of-school activity availability may also increase during this time.

Our findings also support the results of prior studies with middle-class samples that found out-of-school activity participation was associated with positive development. In our sample, school-based activity participants reported higher grades and, during the first year of high school, less antisocial behavior than nonparticipants. Team sports and religious youth group participation were also associated with greater academic achievement and higher self-esteem.

BUILDING BETTER OUT-OF-SCHOOL ACTIVITIES FOR INNER-CITY TEENS

The existing research and our current findings suggest a number of ways in which we may begin to provide all young people with safe places to grow and learn, achieving one of the goals of the Younger Americans Act. First, we know that young people are most likely to benefit from participation in out-of-school activities that are structured and supervised. In addition, low-income, urban youth participate in such activities at relatively low rates. Therefore, we need to ensure that all inner-city teens are offered opportunities to engage in safe, structured, and adult-supervised activities that address their diverse interests and needs by creating or modifying out-of-school settings so that they optimally foster positive development among urban youth.

Given the practical limitations of school funding for extracurricular activities in low-income, urban districts, neighborhood-based youth programs are a promising alternative to traditional school-based activities for youth living in inner cities. Our review of the existing literature revealed that poor, urban youth already participate in neighborhood-based youth programs at relatively high rates and that these programs may offer unique benefits to inner-city teens (Hirsch et al., 2000; Quinn, 1997). The results of our exploration of the developmental correlates of neighborhood activity participation, however, indicate that greater involvement is associated with lower self-esteem and academic achievement. These discrepant findings suggest that CBOs serving inner-city teens should rigorously evaluate their programming in an effort to ensure that it is structured, safe, and challenging.

Schools and other organizations offering out-of-school activities should also make an increased effort to involve all teens by developing programs that address the needs and interests of teens at risk for low levels of engagement. For example, team sports activities that appeal to girls are needed. In addition, Latinos were at particularly high risk for low engagement in school-based activities, which were also associated with the most positive developmental outcomes. Policymakers concerned with the well-being of inner-city youth should ensure that schools and youth organizations have the resources to offer activities that interest underserved populations.

Further, our past work on contextual competence suggests that positive engagement with multiple settings is likely to lead to more positive psychological outcomes than engagement in a single setting alone (Pedersen et al., in press). Creating or enhancing opportunities for youth to engage in organized, out-of-school activities in multiple settings could be one way for interventionists to maximize the benefits of engagement, especially if each setting provides a structured environment that promotes positive social transactions and fosters the development of competencies among participants (Mahoney, 2000; Mahoney & Stattin, 2000).

Although the existing literature offers some suggestions for improving the quality and diversity of youth's out-of-school activity experiences, further investigations that identify the effects of such experiences on youth development, particularly investigations that examine the critical moderators of race/ethnicity and gender, are needed. In the past, poor urban adolescents have been neglected in this small, but growing, literature. These young people, however, experience greater obstacles to success than their wealthier suburban peers—for example, poverty, violence, poor quality schooling—and, therefore, may experience even greater benefits from the additional opportunities for learning, friendship development, identity formation, and autonomy enhancement offered by many out-of-school activities.

ACKNOWLEDGMENTS

Work on this article was supported in part by grants from the National Institutes of Mental Health (MH43084) and the Carnegie Corporation (B4850) awarded to Edward Seidman, J. Lawrence Aber, LaRue Allen, and Christina Mitchell. We express our appreciation to the adolescents and schools whose cooperation made this study possible and to Jacquelynne S. Eccles and Joseph L. Mahoney for their penetrating and constructive comments on earlier drafts of the manuscript.

REFERENCES

Barber, B. L., Eccles, J. S., & Stone, M. R. (2001). Whatever happened to the jock, the brain, and the princess? Young adult pathways linked to adolescent activity involvement and social identity. *Journal of Adolescent Research, 16*(5), 429–455.

Benson, P. L. (1992). Religion and substance use. In J. F. Shumaker (Ed.), *Religion and mental health* (pp. 211–220). New York: Columbia University Press.

Burton, L. M., Obeidallah, D., & Allison, K. W. (1995). Ethnographic insights on social context and adolescent development among inner-city African-American teens. In R. Jessor, A. Colby, & R. A. Shweder (Eds.), *Ethnography and human development: Context and meaning in social inquiry* (pp. 395–418). Chicago: University of Chicago Press.

Carnegie Corporation of New York. (1992). *A matter of time: Risk and opportunity in the non-school hours.* New York: Author.

Dubois, D. L., Tevendale, H. D., Burk-Braxton, C., Swenson, L. P., & Hardesty, J. L. (2000). Self-esteem influences during early adolescence: Investigation of an integrative model. *Journal of Early Adolescence, 20,* 12–43.

Eccles, J. S., & Barber, B. L. (1999). Student council, volunteering, basketball, or marching band: What kind of extracurricular involvement matters? *Journal of Adolescent Research, 14,* 10–43.

Fredricks, J. A., & Eccles, J. S. (2002). Children's competence and value beliefs from childhood through adolescence: Growth trajectories in two male-sex-typed domains. *Developmental Psychology, 38*(4), 519–533.

Gonzales, N. A., Cauce, A. M., Friedman, R. J., & Mason, C. A. (1996). Family, peer, and neighborhood influences on academic achievement among African American adolescents: One year prospective effects. *American Journal of Community Psychology, 24,* 365–387.

Harter, S. (1988). *The self-perception profile for adolescents.* Unpublished manuscript, University of Denver, Denver, CO.

Hirsch, B. J., Roffman, J. G., Deutsch, N. L., Flynn, C. A., Loder, T. L., & Pagano, M. E. (2000). Inner-city youth development organizations: Strengthening programs for adolescent girls. *Journal of Early Adolescence, 20*(2), 210–230.

Jacobs, J. E., Lanza, S., Osgood, D. W., Eccles, J. S., & Wigfield, A. (2002). Changes in children's self-competence and values: Gender and domain differences across grades one through twelve. *Child Development, 73*(2), 509–527.

Jessor, R., Van Den Bos, J., Vanderryn, J., & Costa, F. M. (1995). Protective factors in adolescent problem behavior: Moderator effects and developmental change. *Developmental Psychology, 31*(6), 923–933.

Kahne, J., Nagaoka, J., Brown, A., O'Brien, J., Quinn, T., & Thiede, K. (2001). Assessing after-school programs as contexts for youth development. *Youth and Society, 32*(4), 421–446.

Kimm, S. Y. S., Glynn, N. W., Kriska, A. M., Barton, B. A., Kronsberg, S. S., Daniels, S. R., Crawford, P. B., Sabry, Z. I., & Liu, K. (2002). Decline in physical activity in Black girls and White girls during adolescence. *The New England Journal of Medicine, 347*(10), 709–715.

Larson, R. W. (2000). Toward a psychology of positive youth development. *American Psychologist, 55*(1), 170–183.

Larson, R. W., Richards, M. H., Sims, B., & Dworkin, J. (2001). How urban African American young adolescents spend their time: Time budgets for locations, activities, and companionship. *American Journal of Community Psychology, 29*(4), 565–597.

Luthar, S. S., Cicchetti, D., & Becker, B. (2000). The construct of resilience: A critical evaluation and guidelines for future work. *Child Development, 71,* 543–562.

Mahoney, J. L. (2000). School extracurricular activity participation as a moderator in the development of anti-social patterns. *Child Development, 71*(2), 502–516.

Mahoney, J. L., & Cairns, R. B. (1997). Do extracurricular activities protect against early school dropout? *Developmental Psychology, 33*(2), 241–253.

Mahoney, J. L., & Stattin, H. (2000). Leisure activities and adolescent antisocial behavior: The role of structure and social context. *Journal of Adolescence, 23*(2), 113–127.

Markstrom, C. (1999). Religious involvement and adolescent psychosocial development. *Journal of Adolescence, 22*(2), 205–221.

McNeal, R. B. (1998). High school extracurricular activities: Closed structures and stratifying patterns of participation. *The Journal of Educational Research, 91*(3), 183–191.

Miller, K. E., Sabo, D. F., Farrell, M. P., Barnes, G. M., & Melnick, M. J. (1998). Athletic participation and sexual behavior in adolescents: The different worlds of boys and girls. *Journal of Health and Social Behavior, 39,* 108–123.

National Center for Youth Statistics. (1996). *Youth Indicators, 1996* (OERI Pub. No. NCES 96–027). Washington, DC: Author.

Patrick, H., Ryan, A. M., Alfeld-Liro, C., Fredricks, J. A., Hruda, L., & Eccles, J. S. (1999). Adolescents' commitment to developing talent: The role of peers in continuing motivation for sports and the arts. *Journal of Youth and Adolescence, 28*(6), 741–763.

Pedersen, S. & Seidman, E. (in press). Team sports achievement and self-esteem development among urban adolescent girls. *Psychology of Women Quarterly.*

Pedersen, S., Seidman, E., Yoshikawa, H., Rivera, A. C., Allen, L., & Aber, J. L. (in press). Contextual competence: Multiple manifestations among urban adolescents. *American Journal of Community Psychology.*

Posner, J. K., & Vandell, D. L. (1994). Low-income children's after-school care: Are there beneficial effects of after-school programs? *Child Development, 65,* 440–456.

Quinn, J. (1997). Positive effects of participation in youth organizations. In M. Rutter (Ed.), *Psychosocial disturbances in young people: Challenges for prevention* (pp. 274–304). Cambridge, England: Cambridge University Press.

Roffman, J. G., Pagano, M. E., & Hirsch, B. J. (2001). Youth functioning and experiences in inner-city after-school programs among age, gender, and race groups. *Journal of Child and Family Studies, 10*(1), 85–100.

Schinke, S. P., Orlandi, M. A., & Cole, K. C. (1992). Boys and girls clubs in public housing developments: Prevention services for youth at risk. *Journal of Community Psychology, OSAP Special Issue,* 118–128.

Seidman, E. (1991). Growing up the hard way: Pathways of urban adolescents. *American Journal of Community Psychology, 19,* 169–205.

Seidman, E., Aber, J. L., & French, S. E. (2004). The organization of schooling and adolescent development. In K. Maton, C. Schellenbach, B. Leadbeater, & A. Solarz (Eds.), *Investing in children, families, and communities: Strengths-based research and policy* (pp. 233–250). Washington, DC: American Psychological Association.

Seidman, E., & Pedersen, S. (2003). Holistic contextual perspectives on risk, protection, and competency among urban adolescents. In S. S. Luthar (Ed.), *Resilience and vulnerability: Adaption in the context of childhood adversities* (pp. 318–342). Cambridge, England: Cambridge University Press.

Tracy, P. E., Wolfgang, M. E., & Figlio, R. M. (1990). *Delinquency careers in two birth co-horts*. New York: Plenum.

Wallace, J. M., & Bachman, J. G. (1991). Explaining racial/ethnic differences in adolescent drug use: The impact of background and lifestyle. *Social Problems, 38*(3), 333–357.

Younger Americans Act, S. 1005, 107th Cong. 1st Sess. (2001). Retrieved October 29, 2003, from http://www.nydic.org/nydic/s1005.htm

6

Dorothy, There Is No Yellow Brick Road: The Paradox of Community Youth Development Approaches for Latino and African American Urban Youth

Francisco A. Villarruel
Michigan State University

Martha Montero-Sieburth
University of Massachusetts–Boston

Christopher Dunbar
Michigan State University

Corliss Wilson Outley
University of Minnesota

Structured out-of-school activities have been identified as safeguards against risk-taking behavior and negative peer influence related to substance use (Hawkins, Catalano, & Olsen, 1998; Perkins & Borden, in press; Schorr, 1988; Werner & Smith, 1992; Zill, Nord, & Loomis, 1995) and have been shown to contribute to improved occupational attainment; increased scholastic performance; enhanced educational aspirations and self-concept (Marsh, 1992; McLaughlin, 2000); decreased alcohol, tobacco, and drug use (Quinn, 1999); reduced school dropout rates and ab-senteeism (Catalano, Bergund, Ryan, Lonczak, & Hawkins, 1999); lowered incidences of bullying, violence, and suicide risk (Greenberg, Domitrovich, & Bumbarger 1999); and better social skills and peer rela-tions (Posner & Vandell, 1994).

Although nearly 7 million children participate in some type of af-ter-school program (Capizzano, Tout, & Adams, 2000), only 14% of primary grade children attend such programs (Brimhall, Reaney, & West, 1999). Whereas youth from underrepresented groups can be found in almost all of these programs, youth workers and researchers have noted that ethnic minority[1] youth do not participate to the same degree as majority youth in community-based programs (U.S. Department of Agriculture Cooperative State Research, Education, and Extension Service, 2000; Villarruel, Perkins, Borden, & Keith, 2003). Lower levels of participation have led some to suggest that culturally responsive approaches, that is, approaches based on using the cultural and linguistic backgrounds of students, need to be developed in order to increase the level of participation and, subse-quently, enhance or focus on the positive developmental outcomes of underserved youth (U.S. Department of Agriculture Cooperative State Re-search, Education, and Extension Service, 2000).[2] In this chapter, we will consider these suggestions: First, we will discuss the role of urban ethnic communities in the development of African American and Latino youth growing up in the United States. We will then discuss the possible role of or-ganized positive youth development programs in the lives of these same young people, paying particular attention to the need for such programs to be culturally sensitive to people living in the communities they are meant to serve. Finally, we will offer strategies and recommendations for practitio-ners, researchers, and policymakers to begin constructing a yellow brick road (or sidewalk) for the ethnic minority youth living in urban areas.

THE ROLE OF THE COMMUNITY
IN SOCIALIZING YOUTH OF COLOR

In thinking about the role of urban communities in the lives of young peo-ple of color, one needs to consider three important aspects of communi-

---

[1]The terms *ethnic minority youth* and *youth of color* will be used interchangeably to refer, in general, to youth of African American or Latino/Hispanic background, despite their broader use with Asian Ameri-can and Native American youth.

[2]Additionally, both African American and Latino youth are overrepresented in alternative educa-tional programs (Dunbar, 2002). They are also overrepresented in the lower tracks of mathematics and science in public schools across the country (Oakes, 1997) and in the juvenile justice system (Villarruel & Walker, 2002). This inequitable treatment illustrates how practitioners and policymakers continue to overlook the need for programs, practices, and policies that can support and promote the developmental pathways of youth for underrepresented groups.

ties. First, as documented by Dunbar (2002), safe, nurturing, and caring environments allow for personal identity exploration and acceptance and, concurrently, serve as contexts in which the confusing and imposing external views of self can be understood. Moreover, Dunbar and others (e.g., Roffman, Suáurez-Orozco, & Rhodes, 2003) have argued that these contexts facilitate the development of mentor relationships, which, in turn, contribute to the development of behavioral assets (e.g., self-esteem, cultural understandings) and the promotion of healthy adjustment in their community contexts (DuBois, Neville, Parra, & Pugh-Lilly, 2002; Rhodes, 2002; Rhodes, Grossman, & Resch, 2000). Second, due to concentration of families of similar or dissimilar ethnic heritages, neighborhoods provide the backdrop for cultural identity formation. Third, due to social isolation, concentrated poverty, and public neglect, some urban neighborhoods contain many risks that can challenge positive development. All three of these neighborhood characteristics are important to consider when thinking about designing appropriate positive youth development programs for youth of color living in urban neighborhoods. We will discuss each of these characteristics briefly.

Drawing from ecological development theory (e.g., Garbarino, 1999; Hersch, 1998) and the concept of socially isolated neighborhoods, we focus on the embeddedness of youth in the context of local neighborhoods. The theory of neighborhood effects and child development elaborates on the existence of powerful relations among children, families, and contexts, and identifies the neighborhood as a critical element in development. Understanding children's perceptions of their neighborhood, their *barrio*, or their *colonias* provides the foundation for developing conceptual statements about the relationships among the environment, community development, and development of personal relationships.

Wilson (1996) theorized that the social transformation of inner cities has led to the social isolation of inner-city neighborhoods and has consequently resulted in a "concentration of poverty effects" (p. 58)—the impact of living in an impoverished neighborhood where residents' commitments to mainstream values are undermined, along with skills that permit social mobility. This has led minority children living in inner-city areas to be exposed to values, to adhere to priorities, and to adopt strategies of survival that are different from mainstream ideals. The neighborhood effect framework provides an opportunity for a new understanding about the nuances of living in inner-city environments, more specifically for understanding how structural forces impact residents, how minority children perceive their worlds and subsequently act, and how these perceptions affect their development.

According to Proshansky (1978), the physical environment associated with "big city life" (p. 152) is as important to socialization as are the norms, values, beliefs, and cultural processes associated with growing up in social groups. Similarly, David and Weinstein (1987) concluded that the built environment may engender fear of the dark, uneasiness during way finding, and a sense of social isolation. Therefore, giving attention to the impact of neighborhoods on developmental trajectories is justifiable.

Communities are also cultural contexts that can help youth define themselves in terms of their social and cultural heritage. We believe that this process of cultural and historical identity formation is a key to healthy development for adolescents of color. The extent to which the community can play this role depends on both the nature of the community in which the youth live and its association with other communities. Consider, for instance, the role of the *barrio* in socializing U.S.-born Latino youth. Some *barrios*, which have been the home and central *comunidad* for many U.S. Puerto Ricans, are now becoming populated by diverse groups from Central and South America. For example, Mexicans from the state of Puebla are slowly changing the presence of the corner *bodegas* (Puerto Rican name for grocery store) into *abbarroteras* (grocery and general store for Mexicans). These kinds of changes should produce a very different cultural socialization experience for the U.S.-born Puerto Ricans living in these *barrios*. It is likely to lead some U.S.-born Puerto Ricans to think of themselves primarily in terms of their U.S. experience (e.g., coming from the Bronx, or Long Island, rather than Puerto Rico). In contrast, the experiences of other immigrant Latinos in more homogeneous ethnic neighborhoods should lead them to identify strongly with the town, region, and/or locality from whence they came. The issue of cultural identity formation can be even more complicated for individuals of Latino ethnicity, who are also of African descent—an issue that is of greater significance for the United States than for Latin and Caribbean nations (Brown, 1995; Comas-Diaz, 1996; Ramos, Jaccard, & Guilamo-Ramos, 2003).

Thus, the sense of "rootedness" and the cultural nature of one's community, whether explicit or implicit, have grounding effects on the lives of Latino youth. Feelings of connectedness are often disregarded in considering their development. Knowing who one is and how one sees oneself in the U.S. context is an important identifier of well-being for Latino youth (Montero-Sieburth & Batt, 2001).

The stereotypes of minority youth living in urban experience communities present additional challenges for underrepresented youth. For example, African American youth must deal with the double consciousness, presented first by DuBois (1969) and discussed by Dunbar (2002), of how African Americans are perceived, how they view themselves, and how they define themselves. The media, for example, often represents urban African American youth as super-predators, thugs, or deviant youth (Dorfman & Schiraldi, 2001; Dorfman & Woodruff, 1998; Dorfman, Woodruff, Chavez, & Wallack, 1997; Entman, 1992). The African American youth in urban neighborhoods must deal with these cultural stereotypes as they form their own racial identity.

Similarly, as Way (1998) noted, the myth concerning urban communities with significant population densities of underrepresented youth is that these communities have high rates of pregnancy, drug addiction, violence, welfare dependency, and fatherless homes. Such stereotypes are likely to lead programs for youth in these communities to focus excessively on prevention rather than promotion.

Moreover, anthropologists and educators have argued that minority youth experience an incongruent or asynchronous cultural experience as they interact with the most common practices in traditional U.S. institutions (Delpit, 1990; Irvine, 1991; McCarthy, 1990; Ogbu, 1993), precisely because these institutional practices reflect the cultural norms of the White European American culture. African American and Latino American youth have cultures that are distinct from those of European American middle-class youth.

Too often, the cultures of ethnic minority youth are viewed as inferior or "culturally deficient" rather than "culturally different" (Foley, 1991, p. 63). Consequently, the charge of social institutions and programs has often been to assimilate these youth into the mainstream culture. For these youth, the assimilative practices of programs and formal institutions (e.g., schools) represent a loss of their separate cultural and ethnic identities. Clark (1993) suggested that these youth experience cultural bereavement at the devaluing of their primary culture. She also suggested that their cultures need reinforcement from legitimating social institutions, such as school and community programs. Rights of passage programs, for example, provide cultural experiences including historical experiences that both facilitate the understanding and acceptance of one's own cultural strengths and direct participants to community engagement through service.

Historically, African American and Latino youth are seen as a collection of problems and liabilities rather than as assets in the process of becoming future parents, neighbors, and workers, who need maximum adult involvement, support, teaching, and encouragement to grow and become productive, contributing adults. The messages these youth receive are often coined in expressions such as *"Your language is not good," "Your background is insufficient," "You are the wrong color,"* or *"You don't fit."* Under these circumstances, it is not surprising that such students either leave school or simply give up.

In part, many of the perceptions held about this population of youth have been developed, nurtured, and perpetuated in public schools. African American and Latino youth have been disproportionately placed in special education and alternative school environments (Dunbar, 2002). They have been described as academic incompetents and social misfits (Dunbar, 2002). Hirschi suggested in 1969 that poor academic performance relates directly to disruptive behavior. Hence, devaluing a student's social and cultural capital creates a situation where youth disengage from teachers and from what schools represent. Schools subsequently become an affront to the quintessential fabric of who youth say they are and how they identify themselves. As a result, schools once thought of as safe havens—institutes for socializing children into mainstream culture and sites where the playing field has been leveled—are becoming instead a venue for active resistance. Hence, community-based social institutions are increasingly important in the lives of underrepresented youth from urban communities because they provide a context of individual and cultural identity. But what kinds of programs are appropriate? To answer this question, we begin by discussing how appropriate some of the assumptions underlying many positive youth development programs are for adolescents of color, particularly Latino adolescents.

ASSUMPTIONS RELATED TO COMMUNITY YOUTH DEVELOPMENT

One assumption of positive youth development is that integrated community supports are needed for developing individual empowerment. Such empowerment is assumed to enhance the adolescents' developmental outcomes. Another assumption is that creating supportive communities for young people and empowering them to engage actively in their own development, while contributing to the well-being of the larger community, will increase the likelihood of positive developmental outcomes because such experiences facilitate the acquisition of both an internal locus of control and competence in taking on responsibility.

On the one hand, there is little that one can say to refute these assumptions. On the other hand, one must ask whether this view of positive adolescent development supports the cultural meanings of the adolescent-to-adult transition in all groups. Stated somewhat differently, the positive youth development approach is premised on the notion that communities and adults must create structures that enable youth to achieve their individual potential through needed skills, values, and competencies. The development of these skills and competencies and the recognition of their value present some of the major cultural challenges that youth of color, most notably Latino and African American youth, must struggle against within their daily contexts. Are the cultural values of the adolescent-to-adult transition commensurate with the "developmental outcomes" that are inherent within a cultural model of adult lives in these communities? And are such transitions differentiated by group, from group to group, or context to context, or within groups?

Within this discourse, there is an inherent assumption that "power" and "knowledge" are owned by one constituency and can be successfully transmitted to others. This pedagogical framework is especially important to acknowledge when working within "marginalized" communities, where dimensions of learning and development are grounded in cultural epistemologies that are not always transparent to outsiders.

Similarly, this approach acknowledges the inherent abilities of individuals in the contexts in which they live and interact. Moreover, it acknowledges the person-in-environment approach (also viewed as developmental contextualism or human ecological approach) that recognizes the systemic interactions between an individual and the surrounding environments, institutions, and people with whom they choose to be (or not to be) engaged. The aim of a positive developmental approach, then, is to help youth become confident, competent, and civic-minded adults within both their own racial ethnic community and the larger society in which they interact. In short, this approach recognizes the inherent values of individuals and draws on individual and community strengths by: (a) building on capacities and competencies for creating sustainable opportunities known through scientific research, and (b) enabling an entire community to benefit from their ideas, talents, and energy, similar to the sociologists' idea of achieving social/cultural capital.

Ironically, this latter point is not necessarily a focus of youth development research. The work to date has focused primarily on interpersonal and intrapersonal attributes that predict "healthy and successful" outcomes (e.g., risk and protective factors, thriving indicators, or internal and external assets). Although this focus is critical, it misses the important dimension of understanding the cultural and community structures that support the developmental pathways of youth. In addition, it tends to overlook the strengths (or challenges) that are inherent to the cultural contexts of personal development.

So what should programming for youth of color look like? What kinds of programs might do a better job of incorporating the strengths and challenges inherent in the cultural contexts of personal development? Before attempting to answer these questions, we will discuss positive youth development more generally, considering both the limitations and the strengths of many programs for youth of color.

THE FOUNDATION FOR THE YELLOW BRICK ROAD

Programming Foundation

Many programs still focus too much on prevention and not enough on positive youth development. Helping youth develop life skills and values in preparation for the challenges of adolescence and the independence and responsibilities of adulthood is essential for youth development programs.

Such experiences include after-school education programs, leadership development, mentoring, youth clubs, sports and recreation activities, child welfare, community service activities, and structured out-of-school experiences. These programs offer opportunities for youth to focus on the issues that they care about in ways that provide more control over their own development of skills, knowledge, and dispositions. Youth have greater control because the activities often involve hands-on activities in small groups with more one-on-one contact between adults and youth than is possible in classroom settings with over 25 students. Effective programs also offer the chance to use the language and skills that youth bring to the program in positive and supportive ways, while providing opportunities to involve parents and other community members. Finally, successful positive youth development experiences provide high-quality, sustained engagement with young people as partners and resources, as well as healthy coaching and mentoring relationship experiences between youth and adults. These positive experiences are designed to meet the young people's developmental needs at every stage of their lives (Eccles & Gootman, 2002; Larson, 2002; Perkins, Borden & Villarruel, 2001).

When young people have access to safe and healthy youth development activities, they are less likely to become involved in the high-risk, unhealthy behaviors that can delay or derail their own development (Eccles & Gootman, 2002). But the cultural contexts in which youth are developing also need to be considered. Too often, programs, particularly those focused heavily on prevention rather than promotion, are divorced from the community and from family reinforcement and socialization factors that help youth develop.

Furthermore, Larson (2002) argued that contemporary youth development is inextricably linked to global and pluralistic issues, and is socially constructed as a product or by-product of larger societal forces. Formerly, youth development tended to be described locally and situationally. Yet with the worldwide demographic landscape changing due to migration, emigration, and immigration, and the diasporas of diverse groups, youth development has yet to assume transnational and global dimensions. Youth programs that build on these transnational approaches through mentoring, however, have offered unique insight into programmatic structures (Roffman, Suárez-Orozco, & Rhodes, 2003). Recognizing that population increases are already concentrated in regions of the developing world, such as Latin America, Southeast Asia, South Asia, the Middle East, and Africa, where populations are expected to double despite the AIDS epidemic (Larson, 2002; Lutz, Sanderson, & Scherbov, 2001), and that the mobility of such populations in search of a means to meet their economic needs will be fluid, it is critical that researchers examine the theoretical underpinnings and challenges of adapting models of community youth development for

underrepresented youth in transition. Such an examination requires delv-
ing into the philosophical, psychological, social, and cultural meanings underlying youth development.

Research Foundation

Until recently, researchers have focused on documenting both the barriers
to, and the impact of deficits on, the developmental pathways of youth of
color. This deficit perspective, as well as the associated stereotypes of minority youth growing up in urban communities, is reinforced by the media
through overrepresentation of negative stories and images about Latino
and African American youth (Dorfman & Schiraldi, 2001).

However, recent research, highlighting the unequal treatment of African
American and Latino youth within the juvenile justice system, underscores
the failure of researchers, practitioners, and policy professionals to understand the developmental pathways and challenges that youth of color con-
front in urban contexts (Dorfman & Schiraldi, 2001; Males & Macallair,
2000; Poe-Yamagata & Jones, 2000; Villarruel & Walker, 2002). Moreover,
ethnographic research has chronicled the realities of urban communities
and has shown that these neighborhoods can and do serve as contexts for individual achievement (Swanson, Spencer, Dell'Angelo, Harpalani, &
Spencer, 2002; Taylor et al., 2002a, 2002b) as well as causing youth to struggle with their daily and future realities and life changes (e.g., Canada, 1995;
Hersch, 1998; Taylor, 1989; Way, 1998).

Given the everyday challenges to which underrepresented youth are exposed, it is not surprising that the average number of positive developmental
outcomes reported for these youth are fewer than for their European American White counterparts (Scales, Benson, Leffert, & Blyth, 2000). But we
need to know more about both the positive and problematic aspects of the
communities in which these youth live. We also need to know more about the
skills and knowledge needed to succeed in both one's own community and
the larger majority community. For example, we need to know more about the
role of language, accents, and access to the cultural capital in order to navigate both one's own culture and the majority culture in the developmental
trajectories of these young people's lives. Moreover, we need to know what it
takes to challenge the barriers imposed by the majority culture.

For example, in a study of gender, ethnicity, and identity status among 7th
and 8th graders, Streitmatter (1993, cited in Swanson, Spencer, & Petersen,
1998) found that minority youth, especially females, demonstrated significantly more foreclosure than White youth. Streitmatter concluded that this
difference may reflect the willingness of the minority youth to accept the
perception that they have limited social access rather than either to challenge or explore other options. The willingness to challenge the stereotypes

and explore other options is critical to positive youth development for ado-lescents of color. It is difficult to succeed in this society without such attrib-utes, yet they are often ignored in studies of Latino and African American youth (Montero-Sieburth & Villarruel, 2000). Finally, and most impor-tantly, we need to know what types of structured after-school programs will facilitate the acquisition of the necessary skills and knowledge found to be critically important for these young people.

Even more obvious is the lack of attention to unique contextual factors that influence developmental processes (Garcia Coll, Lamberty, Jenkins, et al., 1996). Traditional comparative studies of race have focused on compari-sons of behavior between subordinate cultural versus dominant mainstream groups, framing the behavior of underrepresented minority youth as a prob-lem rather than as a difference. These designs have ignored intragroup vari-ability, neglecting individual differences among these groups as well as the sources of deviation from the norms of development within African Ameri-can and other populations (McLoyd, 1990). In addition, Dunbar (2002) noted that research based on a deficit orientation has also promoted the view within the resiliency literature that African American youth are less competent and more deviant than other groups. This deficit perspective fails to illustrate structural forces that negatively affect development in mi-nority youth. It also limits our ability to understand their resilient function-ing. Spencer and Markstrom-Adams (1990) stated:

> For many minority youth, transient models of self or identity development (a) ignore socioeconomic developmental processes, (b) assume homogeneity among group members, (c) overlook patterns of coping and adaptation, (d) fail to link unique ecosystem or multi-leveled environmental experiences with life course models (which integrate historical, sociocultural, biological and psychological components with behavioral response patterns), and as a consequence (e) ignore the opportunity of furthering or broadening the knowledge extant on risk and resilience for youth whose normative experi-ences require ongoing adaptive coping strategies as a function of race, ethnic-ity and/or color. (p. 304)

Consequently, existing research and subsequent programming is still skewed toward minorities living in poverty and urban communities. The re-search tells us very little about the normal growth and development of mi-nority children with diverse social backgrounds. Moreover, research that identifies the types of educational experiences necessary for the develop-ment of self-efficacy, academic achievement, positive coping skills, and re-siliency is scarce. We know very little about how to analyze and evaluate after-school programs in local communities, particularly ethnic, urban com-munities. Moreover, the perspective against which these programs are measured still tends to derive from middle-income White youth, which may not be relevant to urban youth.

Many minority children who are poor grow up in stable families where they are loved, well cared for, and given an opportunity to succeed. Their parents' ways of rearing may not be like that of their European American White counterparts, yet they may be like what Delgado-Gaitan (2002) terms "folk ways" (p. 28) of connecting and relating to youth. For example, whereas White European American adolescents may be told about sexual behavior through sex education classes, counselors, and the distribution of condoms, for some Latinos the use of *consejos* or sayings that carry a moral and implicit message of social behavior may be the way that parents communicate the same issues. Moll and Greenberg's (1992) research on community funds of knowledge demonstrates that Latino children in the Southwestern states of the United States learn issues outside of school that are often not considered by schools but are critical for their achievement. Yet such evidence tends to be scarce and more anecdotal than empirical and hence, unknown (Gonzalez, 1992).

Policy Foundation

Research on the plight of poor minority children and adolescents is strongly associated with swings in the political ideology of policymakers from right to center and then left. Sometimes these swings are stimulated by reports of significant declines in the quality of life for African American and Latino children (e.g., Bempechat, Graham, & Jimenez, 1999; Denner, Kirby, Coyle, & Brindis, 2001; Gillock & Reyes, 1999; Gutman & Eccles, 1999). Since minority studies are often undertaken when "poverty consciousness" is running high, little research has focused on the healthy development of African American and Latino youth. Studies of risk factors greatly outnumber studies of the well-being and success of ethnic minority youth.

BUILDING THE YELLOW BRICK ROAD

As our synthesis suggests, there is a demand, both scientific and practice-based, for education and training to be specifically oriented to the youth from underrepresented groups living in urban communities. On the one hand, today's education and training do very little to prepare a beginning youth development professional to work in socially isolated and disadvantaged neighborhoods. Thus, providing education and training in the understanding of cultural norms that exist within a *barrio, colonia,* ghetto, and urban neighborhood can assist these professionals to understand not only the worldview of underrepresented youth from urban communities, but also their distinct developmental pathways and challenges.

On the other hand, in order to implement a positive youth development framework in urban communities, one needs to be familiar with how underrepresented youth, who live in these environments, make sense of their daily lives and experiences. Making generalizations about socially isolated and disadvantaged neighborhoods, based on census data or other block-level statistics and/or superficial media accounts, runs the risk of creating biases and stereotypes about youth that devalue their capabilities. Stereotypes about community life are exaggerated through the media. What needs to be understood are the many ways in which living in a disadvantaged urban neighborhood can impact developing youth. If youth are not openly displaying direct effects from a stressful environment, one cannot assume that there is not stress or upheaval in their lives. Youth adjust to their circumstances in a variety of ways, at times using silence as a means of internally controlling their environment, while at other times, using oppositional behavior—cursing, shouting, name calling—as a way to call attention to their situation.

This behavior can best be addressed by creating programs that are intentionally designed to promote the positive development of the young participants. These programs must recognize the cultural, educational, and social needs of the young people participating in them. Thus, intentionally designed programs must carefully assess the environment within which these programs are placed, identifying adults who can provide an environment that is both physically and emotionally safe while allowing young people to build positive relationships with adults and peers. Moreover, young people need to be valued and given significant leadership roles within programs that are designed to provide them with the necessary skills for moving successfully into adult roles within their communities (Outley, 2000; Perkins & Borden, 2003; Walker, Marczak, Blyth, & Borden, chap. 18, this volume). Thus, these programs should be developed from a holistic perspective rather than a pathological (deficit) perspective. Barriers or risks do have to be overcome, but there should be a focus on fostering success rather than simply preventing failure. Resilience as a cultural and social factor can be identified through careful analysis, and the threshold levels at which these youth respond positively to their context can become known so that instructional materials, curriculum, and assessment are focused on the strengths of youth and not their weaknesses.

Models for Future Research

Models of resilience have long been used to examine the developmental pathways of urban youth of color. Central to this question is, "How do youth living in adverse environments overcome the odds to achieve positive developmental outcomes?" Drawing upon the early work of Rutter

(1987) and Werner and Smith (1992), researchers need to recognize that resilience results from a combination of an individual's institutional factors and environmental influences (a both/and proposition as opposed to an either/or proposition). For urban youth, this requires not only confronting the difficult situations in their own environments, but also adapting to behavioral, academic, and social changes while they manage the psychological and cultural stressors that affect their developmental trajectories (Borgenschneider, 1998).

Bempechat's (1998) research on achievement in learning and teaching outlines the three types of research needed for youth of color: (a) *retrospective studies* that focus on the recounting of successful adults who frame their current perspective on their experiences of the past—the caring teacher, parents, or member of the family or school; (b) *large scale surveys* of children and parents that identify a variety of home and school factors that help explain children's academic performance in broad strokes; and (c) *ethnographic studies* of the past 20 years in which family members are interviewed at length and in-depth and are observed over time. Although the research arising from these approaches has yielded extensive findings, many of these studies have ignored the importance of the role that culture and context play in influencing and guiding parents in the raising of their children.

This omission is a serious oversight in the field's efforts to understand how youth, particularly underrepresented youth, are influenced by the cultures through which they learn about the world, the languages by which they form symbolic meaning, and the ways they think about how to construct their daily worlds. Ironically, McLaughlin and her colleagues (McLaughlin, Irby, & Langman, 1994) have recognized the importance of "internal" and "external wizards" who can recognize the importance of these dimensions of youth and create unique learning opportunities for them in neighborhood and community-based programs. The ecocultural perspective espoused in the work of Cooper and her colleagues (e.g., Cooper, 1999; Cooper & Denner, 1998; Cooper, Jackson, Azmita, & Lopez, 1998) challenges researchers, practitioners, and policy professionals to recognize that individuals, families, and programs, seeking to facilitate the integration and meaning making of the cultural niches within a broader ecological context, are more conducive to the promotion of developmental pathways that contribute to positive outcomes for underrepresented youth. More specifically, they state that:

A key methodological implication of the ecocultural model lies in its formulating ecocultural dimensions as socially constructed by members of the community, thus including what could be considered subjective and objective qualities. This assumption challenges researchers to discover these socially constructed meanings through interviews with community members as well as with standardized measures. (Cooper et al., 1998, pp. 113–114)

In short, how parents and community institutions transmit and reinforce accepted norms and values, not only of youth but also of important learning outcomes, serves as an important lens through which youth from underrepresented communities learn to decipher symbols and meanings within contexts as well as to develop their own perspectives for establishing a discourse that later becomes the basis for their individual and collective learning. The significance of this view then is not the development of a new paradigmatic orientation, but rather the creation of a context where youth workers can work "in the hyphen" (i.e., between the multiple worlds of underrepresented youth).

Examples of how this can occur are exemplified in the work of Montero-Sieburth and Batt (2001), who synthesized current explanatory educational models of learning that have been developed primarily to explain the failures versus successes of underrepresented youth. Specifically, they argued that the glaring demands of providing education for all youth require that cultural and symbolic separation between socioeconomic classes as well as contextual variations (i.e., rural, suburban, urban) be narrowed. Moreover, they argued that it is necessary to deconstruct negative explanations of Latinos in favor of more resilient and successful examples of their own achievements. Although this may be viewed as a resiliency-based focus, the key point is that it builds on the developmental strengths and opportunities that exist within individuals, cultures, and communities. Thus, rather than focusing on interventions that attempt to "fix" or address "dysfunctions" within individuals, this approach emphasizes the need to create opportunities for families, schools, and communities to engage in collective actions that influence the engagement and achievement of youth. These activities can range from service learning, where youth are mentored by professionals while studying an issue in depth and where they are supported in learning from those experiences, to opportunities to explore what their communities are about and what perspectives can be found from different community members. These are ways in which academic experiences become self-explorations of identity and rootedness and hence of their own strengths.

Clearly, there is no yellow brick road; rather, the complexities of understanding underrepresented youth requires deconstruction of the negative layering that has taken place for lack of sound, contextually based research on the lives of these youth. How underrepresented youth are able to reinvent themselves against the odds, makes Dorothy's dream, instead of a yellow brick road, a reality.

ACKNOWLEDGMENT

Special thanks to Amy Griffin, Doctoral Student, Family and Child Ecology, Michigan State University, for her comments and reflections on earlier drafts of this chapter.

REFERENCES

Bempechat, J. (1998). *Against the odds: How "at-risk" students exceed expectations.* San Francisco: Jossey Bass.

Bempechat, J., Graham, S. E., & Jimenez, N. V. (1999). The socialization of achievement in poor minority students: A comparative study. *Journal of Cross Cultural Psychology, 30,* 139–158.

Borgenschneider, K. (1998). What youth need to succeed: The roots of resiliency. In *Wisconsin family impact seminars briefing report: Building resiliency and reducing risk: What youth need from families and communities to succeed* (pp. 1–16). Center for Excellence in Family Studies, School of Human Ecology, University of Wisconsin–Madison.

Brimhall, D., Reaney, L., & West, J. (1999). *Participation of kindergartners through third-graders in before- and after-school care. Statistics in brief* (ED 433 147). Washington, DC: U.S. Department of Education, Office of Educational Research and Improvement.

Brown, U. (1995). Black/White interracial young adults: Quest for a racial identity. *American Journal of Orthopsychiatry, 5,* 125–130.

Canada, G. (1995). *Fist, stick, knife, gun.* Boston: Beacon Press.

Capizzano, J., Tout, K., & Adams, G. (2000). *Child care patterns of school-age children with employed mothers* (Occasional Paper 41). The Urban Institute. Retrieved December 9, 2003, from http://www.urban.org

Catalano, R. F., Bergund, M. L., Ryan J. A. M., Lonczak, H. S., & Hawkins, J. D. (1999). *Positive youth development in the United States: Research findings on evaluations of positive youth development programs.* Washington, DC: U.S. Department of Health and Human Services, National Institute for Child Health and Human Development.

Clark, S. (1993). The schooling of culture and ethnic subordinate groups. *Comparative Education Review, 37,* 62–69.

Comas-Diaz, L. (1996). Latinegra: Menthal health issues of African Latinais. In M. Root (Ed.), *The multiracial experience* (pp. 167–190). Thousand Oaks, CA: Sage.

Cooper, C. R. (1999). Cultural perspectives on individuality and connectedness in adolescent development. In A. Masten (Ed.), *Minnesota symposia on child psychology: Culture and development* (pp. 135–158). Mahwah, NJ: Lawrence Erlbaum Associates.

Cooper, C. R., & Denner, J. (1998). Theories linking culture and psychology: Universal and community-specific processes. *Annual Review of Psychology, 49,* 559–584.

Cooper, C. R., Jackson, J. F., Azmita, M., & Lopez, E. (1998). Multiple selves, multiple worlds: Three useful strategies for research with ethnic minority youth on identity, relationships, and opportunity structures. In V. C. McLoyd & L. Steinberg (Eds.), *Studying minority adolescents: Conceptual, methodological, and theoretical issues* (pp. 111–125). Mahwah, NJ: Lawrence Erlbaum Associates.

David, T. B., & Weinstein, C. S. (1987). The built environment and children's development. In C. Weinstein & T. David (Eds.), *Spaces for children: The built environment and child development* (pp. 3–17). New York: Plenum.

Delgado-Gaitan, M. (2002). *New frontiers for youth development in the twenty-first century.* New York: Columbia University Press.

Delpit, L. (1990). The silenced dialogue: Power and pedagogy in educating other people's children. In N. M. Hidalgo, C. L. McDowell, & E. V. Siddle (Eds.), *Facing racism in education* (Reprint Series No. 21). Cambridge, MA: Harvard Educational Review.

Denner, J., Kirby, D., Coyle, K., & Brindis, C. (2001). The protective role of social capital and cultural norms in Latino communities: A study of adolescent births. *Hispanic Journal of Behavioral Sciences, 23,* 3–21.

Dorfman, L., & Schiraldi, V. (2001). *Off balance: Youth, race & crime in the news.* Washington, DC: Building Blocks for Youth.

Dorfman, L., & Woodruff, K. (1998). The roles of speakers in local television news stories on youth and violence. *Journal of Popular Film & Television, 26,* 80–85.

Dorfman, L., Woodruff, K., Chavez, V., & Wallack, L. (1997). Youth and violence on local television news in California. *American Journal of Public Health, 87,* 1311–1316.

DuBois, D. L., Neville, H. A., Parra, G. R., & Pugh-Lilly, A. O. (2002). Testing a new model of mentoring. *New Directions for Youth Development, 93,* 21–57.

DuBois, W. E. B. (1969). *The souls of Black folk.* New York: New American Library.

Dunbar, C. (2002). *Alternative schooling for African American youth: Does anyone know we're here?* New York: Peter Lang.

Eccles, J., & Gootman, J. A. (2002). *Community programs to promote youth development.* Committee on Community-Level Programs for Youth. Board on Children, Youth, and Families, Commission on Behavioral and Social Sciences Education, National Research Council and Institute of Medicine.

Entman, R. M. (1992). Blacks in the news: Television, modern racism, and cultural change. *Journalism Quarterly, 69,* 341–361.

Foley, D. E. (1991) Reconsidering anthropological explanations of ethnic school failures. *Anthropology and Education Quarterly, 22,* 61–83.

Garbarino, J. (1999). *Lost boys: Why our sons turn violent and how we can save them.* New York: Free Press.

Garcia Coll, C., Lamberty, G., Jenkins, R., McAdo, H. P., Crnic, K., Wasik, B. H., & Vásquez-García, H. (1996). An integrative model for the study of developmental competencies in minority children. *Child Development, 67,* 1891–1914.

Gillock, K. L., & Reyes, O. (1999). Stress, supports, and academic performance of urban, low-income, Mexican-American adolescents. *Journal of Youth and Adolescence, 28,* 259–283.

Gonzalez, N. E. (1992). Child language socialization in Tucson: United States Mexican households. (Doctoral dissertation, University of Arizona, 1992). *Dissertation Abstracts International, 53,* 1202.

Greenberg, M. T., Domitrovich, C., & Bumbarger, B. (1999). *Preventing mental disorders in school-age children: A review of the effectiveness of prevention programs.* University Park: Pennsylvania State University, Prevention Research Center.

Gutman, L. M., & Eccles, J. V. (1999). Financial strain, parenting behaviors, and adolescents' achievement: Testing model equivalence between African American and European American single- and two-parent families. *Child Development, 70,* 1464–1477.

Hawkins, J. D., Catalano, R. F., & Olsen, J. J. (1998). Community interventions to reduce risks and enhance protection against antisocial behavior. In D. W. Stoff, J. Breiling, & J. D. Mastgers (Eds.), *Handbook of antisocial behavior* (pp. 365–374). New York: Wiley.

Hersch, P. (1998). *A tribe apart: A journey into the heart of American adolescence.* New York: Ballantine Books.

Hirschi, T. (1969). *Causes of delinquency.* Los Angeles: University of California Press.

Irvine, J. (1991). *Black students and school failures: Policies practices, and prescriptions.* New York: Praeger.

Larson, R. (2002). Globalization, societal change, and new technologies: What this means for the future of adolescence. *Journal of Adolescent Research, 12,* 1–30.

Lutz, W., Sanderson, W., & Scherbov, S. (2001). The end of world population growth. *Nature, 412,* 543–545.

Males, M., & Macallair, D. (2000). *The color of justice: An analysis of juvenile adult court transfers in California.* Washington, DC: Building Blocks for Youth.

Marsh, H. W. (1992). Extracurricular activities: beneficial extension of the traditional curriculum or subversion of academic goals? *Journal of Educational Psychology, 84*(4), 553–562.

McCarthy, C. (1990). Rethinking liberal and radical perspectives on racial inequality in schooling. In N. M. Hidalgo, C. L. McDowell, & E. V. Siddle (Eds.), *Facing racism in education* (Reprint Series No. 21). Cambridge, MA: Harvard Educational Review.

McLaughlin, M. (2000). *Community counts: How youth organizations matter for youth development.* Washington, DC: Public Education Network.

McLoyd, V. (1990). The impact of economic hardship on Black families and children: Psychological distress, parenting, and socioemotional development. *Child Development, 61,* 311–346.

McLaughlin, M. W., Irby, M. A., & Langman J. (1994). *Urban sanctuaries: Neighborhood organizations in the lives and futures of inner-city youth.* San Francisco: Jossey-Bass.

Moll, L. C., & Greenberg, J. B. (1992). Creating zones of possibilities: Combining social contexts for instruction. In L. C. Moll (Ed.), *Vygotsky and education: Instructional implications and applications of sociohistorical psychology* (pp. 319–348). New York: Cambridge University Press.

Montero-Sieburth, M., & Batt, M. C. (2001). An overview of the educational models used to explain the academic achievement of Latino students: Implications for research and policies into the new millennium. In R. E. Slavin & M. Calderon (Eds.), *Effective programs for Latino students* (pp. 331–368). Mahwah, NJ: Lawrence Erlbaum Associates.

Montero-Sieburth, M., & Villarruel, F. A. (Eds.). (2000). *Making invisible Latino adolescents visible: A critical approach to Latino diversity.* New York: Falmer.

Oakes, J. M. (1997). Discovery through graphing. *The Science Teacher, 64*(1), 33–35.

Ogbu, J. (1993). Variability in minority school performance: A problem in search of an explanation. In E. Jacob & C. Jordan (Eds.), *Minority Education: Anthropological perspectives* (pp. 83–112). Norwood, NJ : Ablex.

Outley, C. W. (2000). *Kickin it: An investigation of leisure behavior among inner city African American children.* Unpublished doctoral dissertation, Texas A&M University, College Station.

Perkins, D. F., & Borden, L. M. (2003). Risk behaviors, risk factors, and resiliency among adolescents. In R. M. Lerner, M. A. Eastbrooks, & J. Mistry (Eds.), *Comprehensive handbook of psychology* (Vol. 6, pp. 373–394). New York: Wiley.

Perkins, D. F., Borden, L. M., & Villarruel, F. A. (2001). Community youth development: A plan for action. *School Community Journal, 11,* 39–56.

Poe-Yamagata, E., & Jones, M. (2000). *And justice for some: Differential treatment of minority youth in the justice system.* Washington, DC: Building Blocks for Youth.

Proshansky, H. (1978). The city and self-identity. *Environment and Behavior, 10,* 147–169.

Posner, J. K., & Vandell, D. L. (1994, April). Low-income children's after-school care: Are there beneficial effects of after-school programs? *Child Development, 65*(2), 440–456.

Quinn, J. (1999). Where needs meet opportunity: Youth development programs for early teens. In R. Behrman (Ed.), *The future of children: When school is out* (pp. 96–116). Washington, DC: The David and Lucile Packard Foundation.

Ramos, B., Jaccard, J., & Guilamo-Ramos, V. (2003). Dual ethnicity and depressive symptoms: Implications of being Black and Latino in the United States. *Hispanic Journal of Behavioral Sciences, 25,* 147–173.

Rhodes, J. E. (2002). *Stand by me: The risks and rewards of mentoring today's youth.* Cambridge, MA: Harvard University Press.

Rhodes, J. E., Grossman, J. B., & Resch, N. L. (2000). Agents of change: Pathways through which mentoring relationships influence adolescents' academic adjustment. *Child Development, 71,* 1662–1671.

Roffman, J. G., Suárez-Orozco, C., & Rhodes, J. (2003). Facilitating positive development in immigrant youth: The role of mentors and community organizations. In F. A. Villarruel, D. F. Perkins, L. M. Borden, & J. G. Keith (Eds.), *Community youth development: Programs, policies, and practices* (pp. 90–117). Thousand Oaks, CA: Sage.

Rutter, M. (1987). Psychosocial resilience and protective factors. *American Journal of Orthopsychiatry, 57,* 316–331.

Scales, P., Benson, P. L., Leffert, N., & Blyth, D. (2000). Contribution of developmental assets to the prediction of thriving among adolescents. *Applied Developmental Sciences, 4,* 27–46.

Schorr, L. B. (1988). *Within our reach: Breaking the cycle of disadvantage.* New York: Doubleday.

Spencer, M., & Markstrom-Adams, C. (1990). Identity processes among racial and ethnic minority children in America. *Child Development, 61,* 290–311.

Streitmatter, J. (1993). Gender differences in identity development: An examination of longitudinal data. *Adolescence, 28,* 55–66.

Swanson, D. P., Spencer, M. B., Dell'Angelo, T., Harpalani, V., & Spencer, T. R. (2002). Identity processes and the positive development of African Americans: An explanatory framework. *New Directions for Youth Development, 95,* 73–99.

Swanson, D. P., Spencer, M. B., & Petersen, A. E. (1998). Identity formation in adolescence. In K. Borman & B. Schneider (Eds.), *The adolescent years: Social influences and educational challenges. Ninety Seventh Yearbook of the National Society for the Study of Education* (pp. 18–41). Chicago: University of Chicago Press.

Taylor, C. S. (1989). *Dangerous society.* East Lansing: Michigan State University Press.

Taylor, C. S., Lerner, R. M., von Eye, A., Balsano, A. B., Dowling, E. M., Anderson, P. M., Bobek, D. L., & Bjelobrk, D. (2002a). Individual and ecological assets and positive developmental trajectories among gang and community-based organizations. *New Directions for Youth Development, 95,* 57–72.

Taylor, C. S., Lerner, R. M., von Eye, A., Balsano, A. B., Dowling, E. M., Anderson, P. M., Bobek, D. L., & Bjelobrk, D. (2002b). Stability of attributes of positive functioning and of developmental assets among African American adolescent male gang and community-based organization members. *New Directions for Youth Development, 95,* 35–55.

U.S. Department of Agriculture Cooperative State Research, Education, and Extension Service. (2000). *The next agenda—National 4-H Strategic Plan 2000.* Available from Alan Smith, National 4-H Program Leader Families, 4-H and Nutrition, Cooperative State Research, Education and Extension Service, USDA U.S. Dept. of Agriculture, Stop 2225, 1400 Independence Ave. SW, Washington, DC 20250-2225.

Villarruel, F. A., Perkins, D. F., Borden, L. M, & Keith, J. G. (Eds). (2003). *Community youth development: Program, policies, and practices.* Thousand Oaks, CA: Sage.

Villarruel, F. A., & Walker, N. E. (2002). *¿Dónde Está La Justicia?: A call to action on behalf of Latino and Latina youth in the U.S. justice system.* Washington, DC: Building Blocks for Youth.

Way, N. (1998). *Everyday courage: The lives and stories of urban teenagers*. New York: New York University Press.

Werner, E., & Smith, R. (1992). *Overcoming the odds: High risk children from birth to adulthood*. Ithaca, NY: Cornell University.

Wilson, W. J. (1996). *When work disappears: The world of the new urban poor*. New York: Knopf.

Zill, N., Nord, C. W., & Loomis, l. S. (1995). *Adolescent time use, risky behavior, and outcomes: An analysis of national data*. Rockville, MD: Westat.

7

Youth–Adult Research Collaborations: Bringing Youth Voice to the Research Process

Ben Kirshner
Jennifer O'Donoghue
Milbrey McLaughlin
Stanford University

As researchers seek to understand and design after-school learning environments, it is important that young people themselves be part of the inquiry process. Young people, in collaboration with adults, are well situated to design and carry out research about their schools, neighborhoods, and after-school programs. Such partnerships not only produce important findings and useful knowledge; they also support broader youth development goals by incorporating youth voice into program decision-making and by providing youth the opportunity to effect community change (Horsch, Little, Chase Smith, Goodyear, & Harris, 2002). Despite increasing evidence of the benefits of youth participation in community development and institutional change (Youniss et al, 2002; Zeldin, McDaniel, Topitzes, & Calvert, 2000), it is still uncommon for researchers to collaborate in the research process with youth themselves.

The purpose of this chapter is twofold. We first address a conceptual gap by offering a framework for understanding youth–adult research partnerships. We then use this framework to examine two research projects in which university researchers (ourselves included) collaborated with youth to examine their neighborhoods, schools, and after-school programs. We conclude with a discussion of the benefits, challenges, and implications of youth–adult research collaborations.

THEORIZING YOUTH–ADULT RESEARCH PARTNERSHIPS

Why Do We Need a Framework?

Methods such as participatory action research, empowerment evaluation, and inquiry-based reform have been designed to ease the tensions between researchers and practitioners and to improve understandings of local context and processes (Fetterman, 1996; Fullan, 1993; Rapoport, 1985). These techniques recognize the importance of local knowledge and expertise in formulating and answering research questions. However, these research methods have focused primarily on working with adult practitioners, program participants, and school personnel. Research methodology remains a domain in which young people's "competence and ability to participate is undervalued" (Hart, 1992, p. 17).

Although examples of youth–adult research partnerships are rare, a growing number of groups have engaged young people in the research process across a variety of contexts—from schools to community youth organizations to after-school programs (Fielding, 2001; Horsch et al., 2002; McLaughlin, Irby, & Langman, 2001; Meucci & Schwab, 1997; Penuel & Freeman, 1997; Schwab, 1997; Youth IMPACT, 2001). Studies of these projects highlight the benefits of working with young people in the research process, such as improved access to youth perspectives. However, they do not provide a framework for understanding what youth–adult research partnerships might look like or the relevant dimensions to consider in such efforts.[1] It is this gap in our understanding of youth involvement in research that we address here. Our framework highlights some of the tradeoffs that arise when involving youth in research in different ways and illustrates how research purposes influence decisions about how to collaborate with young people.

Framework for Understanding Youth–Adult Research Partnerships

Research with youth takes varied forms across multiple dimensions. Here we offer a framework through which to analyze our own work in or-

---

[1]Fielding (2001) developed a framework for conceptualizing student involvement in school improvement efforts that reflects the range of ways in which students can be engaged in research projects, from data sources to researchers. Fielding's framework serves as an important starting point in understanding how youth and school personnel can work together to improve schools. In focusing on the school setting, however, Fielding does not offer a more global framework for understanding youth–adult research partnerships that span neighborhoods and other contexts in youth's lives. Also, the relationship between an adult, university based researcher and a young person in a local community may be quite different from that between teachers and students in a school.

der to illuminate the benefits and challenges of working in partnership with youth researchers. Drawing from literature on research methodology and youth development, we develop a typology of strategies for conducting research with youth (see Table 7.1). This typology begins with the most familiar research strategies, those that involve youth as "informants."[2] These represent the most common approaches to studying youth development in after-school contexts and have played an invaluable role in building the knowledge base in this area (for a helpful review

TABLE 7.1

Framework for Understanding Research With Youth

	Youth as Research Informants	*Youth as Research Assistants*	*Youth as Research Partners*
Youth–Adult Relationship	Little to Some Interaction	Quasipartners	Full Partners
Youth Development	Limited	Basic Skills	Youth Development
Expertise/ Knowledge	Adult researchers are experts; decide what is important; create knowledge	Adults are experts on questions; youth not necessarily knowledge creators	Youth are experts on questions; local knowledge valued; youth generate knowledge with help of adults
Ownership	Situated primarily in research institutions	Attempts to share	Fully shared
Audience	Academic, policymaking, research audience; adults have control over data use and presentation	Mixed audience; youth may have some say in data use and presentation	Primarily local audience; may extend to others; shared control over data use and presentation
Ecological Validity	Varies from study to study	Improved	Improved

---

[2]A wide variety of approaches—from survey research to ethnography—fall under this category. The relationship between researchers and informants in ethnography, for example, is likely to be more developed than that in a survey design. Similarly, researchers within this category may develop techniques to support youth learning and development. Rather than explore the multiple distinctions within this category, however, we treat it broadly in order to distinguish it from approaches in which youth are more actively involved in the research process.

of this development research, see Eccles & Gootman, 2001; Roth, Brooks-Gunn, Murray, & Foster, 1998).

We focus on the difference between this approach, in which youth's role in the research *process* is largely to respond to adult inquiries, and more participatory research strategies, which involve young people as "research assistants" or as "research partners." This second distinction—between youth as assistants and as partners—is an important one; it clarifies the different types of collaborative research relationships adults can form with youth and the decisions and challenges that need to be addressed in implementing these strategies. Although we do not argue that such collaborative research should replace conventional methods of research about youth or after-school programming, we highlight the promise and challenge of this unfamiliar terrain. In the sections that follow, we outline the dimensions that give shape to these distinct research strategies.

Youth–Adult Relationship. One of the first dimensions that must be considered when conducting research about or with youth is the nature of the youth–adult relationship. What roles will youth have? What will the interaction between youth and adults look like? Most social science research that includes youth falls under the *youth as informants* category. In this case, adults determine the research relationship and the youth–adult interaction, which may vary from little interaction between an adult researcher and a youth respondent (e.g., filling in a survey) to greater interaction (e.g., in an adult-led focus group or interview).

Youth as research assistants and *youth as research partners* strategies require a mental changing of frames (Mitra, 2001) about the role of youth (and of adults) in the research process. For this approach to be successful, researchers need to redefine and reshape prevailing notions of youth and adult roles so that youth–adult interactions become more equal and more focused on shared decision-making and shared work (Camino, 2000). (Similarly, there has been a strong push within participatory action research and empowerment evaluation literature for increased collaboration and democratic partnership between researchers and local participants; e.g., Fetterman, 1996; Rapoport, 1985). Such partnerships recognize and draw on the strengths that adults and youth bring to the research process. Adults may share their expertise about research methods, for example, whereas youth contribute their knowledge about their schools and neighborhoods. Also, academic or policymaking audiences may be more accessible because of the connections of adult researchers, and youth involvement may bring greater legitimacy and relevance for practitioners and local community members. This type of collaborative partnership may be especially critical for youth in terms of decreasing the alienation of local people from the research and program planning process (Hart, 1992). Rather than assuming that the data collected by adult researchers can speak *for* youth, in partnership relationships young people are involved as active participants in the research process.

We frame our understanding of youth–adult partnerships as including both "quasi" and "full" partnership arrangements. In quasi-partnerships, youth are involved as research assistants, collecting and analyzing data in response to direction by adult researchers. Generally, youth in this arrangement do not lead the development of lines of inquiry. In full research partnerships, youth and adults work together to generate research questions and to collect and analyze data. These two levels reflect different partnership configurations that can arise as adults and youth negotiate their relationship with each other. They are also a function of research purpose and method. Research aimed at tallying the number of youth organizations in a community, for example, might not benefit from the involvement of youth. Research seeking to assess the value of these youth resources, however, might engage youth either in quasi or full partnerships.

Youth Development. Building the strength and capacity of local participants is an important feature of participatory action research and empowerment evaluation (Fawcett et al., 1996; Fetterman, 1996; Hart, 1992; Linney & Wandersman, 1996; Mayer, 1996; Rapoport, 1985). In translating this into research with youth, we have chosen to use the concept of *youth development*. Learning and development are central aspects of any participatory project with youth (Camino, 2000; Fielding, 2001; Hart, 1992). We divide this learning into two general types—skill development and more comprehensive youth development.

Skill development refers to technical research skills such as interviewing, conducting observations, writing up field notes, and analyzing data. Often, however, youth–adult research partnerships are more than just opportunities to master discrete skills. Youth development relates to supports and opportunities that foster more general themes of agency and persistence as well as communication, cooperation, and collective action. Research partnerships offer youth meaningful roles and responsibilities identified as central to youth development (Costello, Toles, Spielberger, & Wynn, 2000, Eccles & Gootman, 2001). In addition, these partnerships can stimulate empowering learning by allowing young people to understand problems and barriers to change and to develop strategies to overcome them (Hart, 1992). Although we make a conceptual distinction between basic skill development and youth development, the boundaries are not rigid and there is great interaction between them.

When youth are informants, youth development in the research process is limited as this is not often a primary goal of these strategies.[3] When work-

---

[3]We recognize that youth development is often a *goal* of research, no matter which of these strategies it employs, in that researchers aim to improve practice and thereby improve the developmental effectiveness of after-school programs. What we wish to emphasize here is the developmental nature of the actual *process* of research.

ing in collaboration with youth, as in the youth as research assistants and youth as research partners categories, youth development is often a focus of the research process, either implicitly or explicitly. In other words, although youth development may not be the stated purpose, youth are still likely to be exposed to powerful learning experiences. When youth act as research assistants, their training and work often focuses on data collection and perhaps analysis. This level of involvement may provide youth with basic skill development, but not necessarily more comprehensive developmental supports and opportunities. When youth are involved as full research partners, they are more likely to have transformative developmental experiences as they are more engaged in defining and coming to understand research problems, questions and findings, are placed in positions of greater responsibility, and have more participatory and nonhierarchical interactions with adults.

Expertise/Knowledge.   Conceptions of expertise and knowledge comprise the third dimension in our framework. Differences in expertise have been described as one of the "factors making for endemic tensions" in researcher–participant collaborations (Rapoport, 1985, p. 268). Variations in skills, expertise, and values may become institutionalized in training programs, which establish hierarchies of legitimate or credible knowledge that place scientific, theoretical, or academic knowledge above local or practical knowledge. This process is exacerbated in research on youth issues, as young people's knowledge and understandings are often undervalued or seen as invalid (Hart, 1992).[4]

In the youth as informants research strategies, expertise resides within adult researchers. Although they may focus their efforts on gaining information from youth or eliciting youth voice, adult researchers maintain the locus of control, determining what is important (e.g., by choosing research questions and designing survey instruments or interview protocols) and using data from youth to create knowledge. In addition, the primary aim of knowledge creation is often theoretical and intended to make a contribution to the scientific field, rather than having an immediate practical influence on program design or practice.

In the youth as research assistants strategy, expertise and knowledge is more mixed, but leans in the direction of adult researchers. Adults are still experts on what matters in terms of the research frame and questions;

---

[4]The valuing of local knowledge seems to be gaining more mainstream appeal, as evidenced by Lerner et al.'s (2000) discussion of the need to expand our ideas of what constitutes knowledge. They argue that scientific knowledge, historically the source of "basic knowledge," must be supplemented by community understandings of the relational interplay between knowledge and local context. Moreover, they maintain that knowledge is not just defined by "scientist-derived data," concluding that, "a learning collaboration between scholars and community members must become a part of the knowledge generation process" (p. 13). (See also Greeno et al., 1999, and Zeldin, 2000, for related discussions.)

however youth are seen as expert data collectors, knowing what contexts matter and how best to uncover information. While engaged in the data collection process in this way, youth researchers may or may not be seen as knowledge creators.

The youth as research partners strategy draws on the expertise and knowledge of young people and their communities. Youth are seen to have fuller contextual knowledge; they become experts, determining what questions are important as well as the appropriate data collection strategies. As analysts of data, young people become creators of new knowledge. In addition, the rationale for the research is determined in collaboration with youth. As a result, research will typically lead to the creation of practical knowledge that can contribute to meeting needs that are valued by youth themselves. As in other dimensions, the purpose of the research will strongly influence the types of knowledge and expertise desired and therefore the research relationship between adults and youth.

Ownership.   We define *ownership* as a phenomenon in which people care about the research activity, are engaged in it, take responsibility for the outcome, and, in most cases, literally "own" the data that has been collected. This concept helps distinguish conventional research from newer models of participatory action research with youth. In research traditions where youth are informants, ownership is situated primarily in research institutions. The youth themselves often have limited knowledge of the purpose of the research project, and thus have little incentive to care deeply about its results (even if the results may have long-term consequences that are quite relevant to their lives). In contrast, in research projects that collaborate with youth, shared ownership is a key goal, especially if the research partnership aims to benefit from the local expertise and unique insights of youth.

Community Youth Mapping (Academy for Educational Development, 2001) is one example of a research endeavor in which youth ownership is promoted. Youth mapping is a strategy that enables young people to work together and with adults to document the places and resources available to them and their families. Goals and strategies are developed locally, depending on the needs and priorities of the community. Examples of participatory action research also seek to share ownership with youth by collaborating on research design and implementation (see, e.g., Meucci & Schwab, 1997). In both of these cases, youth are not merely research assistants trained to collect data, but instead share responsibility for the direction and purpose of the project.

The degree to which authentically shared ownership is achieved depends on the relationship between youth and adult researchers. Attempts to share ownership with youth as research assistants tend to be one-sided because the youth themselves do not design the project. They may carry out research activities, but without being involved in research design, they may not care deeply about or understand the broader goals. In contrast, when working with youth as research partners, ownership is more likely to be fully shared because the research design itself is a collaborative endeavor.

Audience. The audience for and dissemination of research findings is another dimension that distinguishes research strategies, and it follows logically from distinctions about ownership. Traditionally, the audience for research on youth issues is found in academic, philanthropic, and policymaking communities, whether advancing theory or identifying implications for practice. In either case, consumers of the research are likely to be professionals who are familiar with the vocabulary and techniques of scholarly reporting. It is much less common for the audience of youth research to be youth themselves or residents of the communities where they live. This dimension, too, would be one that distinguishes working with youth as research partners from the other two research strategies. Although youth as research assistants may be more likely to have mixed audiences—including community members and university researchers—it is still motivated by the leadership and goals of adult researchers. By contrast, the goal for youth as research partners is more likely to reach a primarily local audience, comprised of youth, parents, youth workers, and teachers.

In addition, dissemination activities associated with each research strategy raise important questions: Who gets to use the data that is collected and how? Whose voice counts in relating the findings? Who speaks in the name of youth (Baksh-Soodeen, 2001)? Methods in which youth are informants typically speak to academic audiences; research findings are compiled and presented by adult researchers skilled in speaking to such audiences. When adults engage with youth as research assistants, youth may have limited involvement in determining how data is analyzed and presented. For example, they may be asked to do preliminary data analysis, but adults would produce the final results. In the youth as research partners strategy, youth are central to decisions around how the data is used and presented. Young people play a critical role in dissemination and opportunities are created for youth to speak for themselves through a variety of forms tailored to reach a more local programmatic and policymaking audience.

A youth program that we observed as part of a multisite study of afterschool centers provides one example of local audience and dissemination. A group of students identified sexual harassment as an issue that they wanted to change in their school. With the assistance of an adult facilitator, the students began a year-long project involving interviews with administrators, surveys of students, and research on school district policy. The results of their research were communicated to students in workshops at schools across the district and through a handbook given out to all students. The group succeeded in persuading the school board to revise its policies and procedures regarding sexual harassment. In sum, the findings, which were substantial, were channeled back to the constituency that was most affected by the problem. Although there was most likely theoretical significance to the research as well, what was most important to the youth activists was to make sure they reached the audience that would be most impacted by the study.[5]

Ecological Validity. Researchers of youth development have grown increasingly critical of methods and experiments that are isolated from the natural contexts in which youth lead their lives (Lerner, Fisher, & Weinberg, 2000; Zeldin, 2000). Many well-designed laboratory experiments and survey instruments are criticized for lacking *ecological validity*, referring to the extent to which research maintains the integrity of the real life situations it is designed to investigate (Cole, 1996). Do the environments in which the research takes place, and the variables in question, represent the everyday lived experience of people being studied—"the actual ecology of human development" (Lerner et al., 2000, p. 14)? Ethnography is one answer to this criticism; it represents an effort to understand the local realities and culturally specific meanings that contextualize youth's experiences (Burton, Obeidallah, & Allison, 1996).

Unlike ownership or audience, ecological validity is not a dimension that necessarily differentiates the three research strategies. After all, the job of skilled adult ethnographers is to gain insider knowledge through spending time in a particular setting and developing trusting relationships with the people there (Johnson, 1997). Even surveys and experimental tasks have the potential to reflect the lived experience of research informants (Cole, 1996). Nevertheless, collaborating with youth to conduct research has the potential to strengthen ecological validity in ways that adults may be unable to do alone. In work with youth as research assistants, youth can reach peers who are not readily accessible through familiar channels such as the school or after-school youth center. Also, youth researchers may have an easier time than adults seamlessly integrating themselves into an activity for observation.

Youth working as research assistants or partners also play a crucial role in interpreting data, helping to strengthen the ecological validity of interpretations. Youth perspective in analysis could help get at, for example, whether low levels of youth participation in an after-school program signal lack of youth interest in organized activities generally or the fact that the particular

---

[5]This example is discussed in greater depth in Sherman (2003).

offerings are not interesting to them and why. Or, in analyzing focus group or interview transcripts, youth researchers may draw on unique frames of reference that enable them to offer alternative, and perhaps more accurate, interpretations of the data. Furthermore, in work with youth as research partners, the research questions themselves are likely to reflect a true problem or puzzle in the community being studied, as reflected in the sexual harassment example mentioned.

Collaborating with youth participants in the communities being studied, then, can strengthen ecological validity. It is important to recognize, however, that youth participation does not guarantee ecological validity, as differences in social status, gender, race/ethnicity, and class are salient for youth as well. *Youth* as a category is not homogeneous, and it would be a mistake to assume that all youth share essential attributes.

These six dimensions provide a framework through which to explore the complexities involved in working with youth as researchers. The framework points to some of the possible benefits of youth–adult partnerships for research in after-school settings, such as transformative developmental opportunities for the youth researchers and strengthened ecological validity for the research enterprise. Such joint inquiries can gather information about what youth value about these settings and link researchers and community members in meaningful ways. The framework also raises important questions about the possible limitations or tradeoffs inherent in such collaborations. Decisions about which research strategy is most appropriate are closely connected to research purpose. It may be inappropriate, for example, to choose a youth as research partners strategy for a large-scale, multisite investigation aimed at drawing conclusions across sites rather than focusing specifically on local context and practice. In the following section, we present two cases in which university-based adult researchers worked with young people to conduct research on their neighborhoods, schools, and after-school programs. These cases help to illustrate further the rewards and challenges involved in developing youth–adult research collaborations.

YOUTH–ADULT RESEARCH COLLABORATION: EXAMPLES FROM PRACTICE

Program Profiles

The Youth Ethnographers Project: Evaluating After-School Contexts. The Youth Ethnographers Project (YEP) was one component of a qualitative evaluation of five after-school youth centers in a major west-coast city. YEP had its strategic roots in the "junior ethnographers" who assisted in Heath and McLaughlin's research on the operation and contribution of youth serving urban community based organizations (see McLaughlin, Irby,

& Langman, 1994/2001). In that research, approximately 10 young people who participated in the organizations in the study were hired to go places and ask questions that the adult research team could not. Youth were given brief training in the use of interview protocols and tape recorders and in how to prepare a research memo. Members of the research team living onsite supervised the youth and data were forwarded to Heath and McLaughlin at Stanford. The value of the junior ethnographers was considered primarily in terms of access. The data they provided from late-night meetings, road trips, and other settings inaccessible to the research team as well as data from formal interviews proved invaluable in constructing an understanding of program and neighborhood contexts. Although youth were data collectors, the adult researchers assumed primary responsibility for developing lines of inquiry and interpretation.

Similarly, YEP was developed to complement the efforts of adult researchers by adding a youth component to the larger evaluation project, which was designed to examine youth's experiences in after-school youth centers and the role the centers played in their daily lives. During the first part of the evaluation, adult researchers (ourselves included) relied on focus groups and case study interviews with youth as well as informal observations of the after-school program activities. The YEP aspect of the evaluation was added in the 9th month, with the hope that youth researchers would be well-situated to collect data and solicit perspectives that were otherwise unavailable to us. In addition, partnering with young people was consistent with the objectives of the study, which sought to highlight youth's opinions and experience. Further, we felt that working with youth researchers would provide us with corrective feedback about our research direction: Were we looking in the right places? Were we asking the right questions?

A total of 21 youth were selected to work as youth ethnographers in the five after-school program sites. They varied in age, gender, race, ethnicity, and class background. Overall, there were 13 middle-school students, 7 high-school students, and 1 college freshman (who worked as a mentor at one of the youth centers and lived in the neighborhood where it was located). All youth took part in a day-long training session that introduced them to the research goals of the broader evaluation and taught them interviewing and observation skills that they would use in their work. Research workshops emphasized a range of skills, both conceptual and technical. For example, although we wanted to be sure that youth could draw a conceptual distinction between description and interpretation—that is, "the room had a mural on the wall showing kids playing" versus "the room was pretty"—we also wanted to make sure that youth felt comfortable with basic procedures, such as asking permission to record an interview and operating a tape recorder.

The long-term direction of the YEP research was deliberately left open to allow for flexibility in responding to the interests and questions of the youth at each site and to local neighborhood and after-school contexts. For this reason, youth (and their adult coordinators) at the different sites worked fairly autonomously, focusing on different aspects of the research. For example, one site focused almost entirely on understanding after-school opportunities for youth in the neighborhood, whereas others looked at youth's experiences in school, or the reasons why some youth did not spend time at the after-school center.

The YEP project spanned 5 months, with site meetings every other week and cross-site meetings held twice throughout the project. Roughly 3 months were spent on data collection and the remainder was dedicated to data analysis. Youth read through interview transcripts and field notes and worked to cull themes from the data. Adult research coordinators wrote memos summarizing the main conclusions drawn by each team of youth ethnographers. These memos were then incorporated into the 2 years of data collected by adult researchers.

Youth Engaged in Leadership and Learning: Exploring Community Resources for Youth.   Youth Engaged in Leadership and Learning (YELL) is an after-school program based in the John W. Gardner Center for Youth and Their Communities (JGC) at Stanford University that trains young people to become researchers and advocates. Participants identify a problem they care about, gather evidence pertinent to that problem, and make recommendations based on their findings. It bears some similarity to participatory action research (Penuel & Freeman, 1997) as well as "youth mapping" programs that are aimed at training youth to identify resources and needs in their communities (Academy for Educational Development, 2001). Because it is responsive to youth's interests and concerns, the YELL curriculum is not limited to studying after-school environments, but instead can include community and school issues. Nevertheless, lessons from YELL are pertinent to our framework because it is an example of a youth–adult research partnership. This section discusses the YELL program's 2000-1 pilot year in Redwood City, a mixed-income city located near the Stanford University campus.[6]

The background for the YELL project in Redwood City is important: Redwood City was undergoing a multiyear effort to improve youth development resources and opportunities, and community leaders wanted input from youth themselves. In collaboration with the JGC, it was decided that YELL would be housed in a middle school, where JGC staff would recruit and train 8th graders (13 to 14 years old) for the project. One adult coordinator ran the project with the help of two undergraduate assistants and one graduate researcher.

---

[6]The collaboration between the university and Redwood City is ongoing. Cohorts of community youth researchers continue to be involved.

Program participants came from a cross-section of neighborhoods, which varied in terms of socioeconomic status and ethnicity. Of the 13 participants, 10 were Latino and 3 were European American. The program met twice a week after school for approximately 7 months. After initial trainings in various research methods, youth participants split into three research groups— video documentary, interviews, and survey. Each group collected and analyzed information about youth's experiences in their neighborhoods and schools. The research, however, was just the first step—upon completion of data analysis, the group worked to turn their findings into recommendations, which were presented to city government and school officials. In all, the youth researchers made four presentations to Redwood City agencies, including community groups, schoolteachers, and the city council. These presentations led to further opportunity for young people to participate in local decision-making bodies.

Assessing Youth–Adult Research Partnerships

These different projects offer a compelling contrast for our purposes in this chapter because they varied on several dimensions. On the whole, we characterize YEP's strategy as one of youth as research assistants and YELL's as youth as research partners, although of course there is some gray-area between these two designations. In examining the strengths and limitations of each of these projects, we do not suggest that one strategy is in all cases better than the other. Here we lay out two approaches as they played out in different settings to give a better sense of the options available to researchers who wish to include youth in the process.

Youth–Adult Relationship. Adults in these projects made an intentional effort to develop a different kind of relationship with youth than the typical one between researcher and informant. In both cases, there was an effort made to have youth help lead the process and, in this sense, act as partners of the adults. In YEP, we collaborated with youth in the process of doing research by asking them not just to carry out interviews, but also to develop protocols and give feedback about the study. Youth ethnographers' descriptions of the project acknowledged this effort to work together. In a representative example, one young person described the project as "a research project conducted by Stanford students who work together with students from various middle and high schools to gather information on a community center."

There was a similar collaborative approach in YELL, in which youth played an active role in shaping the direction of the research.

Nevertheless, it is more accurate to describe the youth–adult relationship in these projects as quasi-partnerships. In the case of YEP, this distinction stems from the genesis of the project: Adult researchers approached youth seeking their help in answering some of the research questions of a broader research study. YELL was different in that youth had much greater latitude in selecting their topic and making decisions about the direction of their work. Still, the project was initiated by adults who sought a youth perspective on resources available in Redwood City. Because YELL is ongoing, we may see it transform, as young people take on greater responsibilities for its leadership. For example, in its second year (2002–2003), four 9th-grade youth served as mentors and facilitators for the new cohort.

A second factor that complicated the relationship in both projects had to do with the fact that these programs were offered as employment opportunities to the youth. Although stipends were important as incentives for participation as well as recognition of legitimate work, they made the relationship between adults and youth sometimes appear to be like one typical of employer and employee. One result was that some participants thought of it primarily as a job. For example, one YEP participant wrote, "I think I did take this project very seriously because it was like a real job." Another wrote, "I enjoyed … bragging about having a job." Although the fact of having a job itself does not preclude a sense of partnership, it added an employer–employee dimension to the relationship that reinforced the power differentials between adults and youth.

These examples show that the goal of creating adult–youth partnerships can be complicated by the realities of actually running a project, with stipends, training, work expectations, and the like. Adults are required to manage a sensitive balance between treating youth as partners while also being guides and teachers.

Youth Development.   In YEP, where youth were treated more like research assistants, youth researchers showed improvement in their skills as interviewers and observers. They reported learning several basic research skills: interviewing, asking follow-up questions, and using a tape recorder. However, adult coordinators did not get a strong impression of more personal or transformative developmental changes.

At the same time, YEP demonstrates that the line between basic skills and youth development is quite blurry. For example, in a questionnaire administered to youth at the end of the project, youth ethnographers offered a range of responses to the question, "What have you gotten out of this experience?" Some responses focused on basic skills like learning to use a tape recorder or how to cash a check. Others focused on the content of their research, such as learning that "the Youth Center isn't a cheap scam acting like it's helping kids but really getting money for just sitting around" or "learning what people thought about school and their neighborhood." And still others described what they would take in a more personal way, linking it to career motivation or an understanding of the position of young people in society. Interpreting this range in responses is difficult because of the significant age differences of participants. Nevertheless, the diversity of responses reflects how permeable the category of *youth development* can be and shows that different individuals may draw different lessons from the same general experience.

Youth's perceptions of what they learned showed similar diversity in YELL. On one hand, participants talked about learning specific skills, such as public speaking, working with others, and conducting interviews. In addition, however, they discussed more intangible changes in their own personal maturity and in their sense of connection to community. For example, members talked about becoming less shy, developing better reputations among teachers because of their role as YELL participants, and gaining self-confidence relative to high-achieving students in the school. Several also described a new sense of connectedness to their neighborhoods and communities. In reflecting on the city council presentation, one youth said that it was "the first time I actually got my point across to other people." Another student talked about a newfound appreciation of her own neighborhood: "I never thought my community was … really fancy or anything, but since coming from some of my friend's neighborhoods, I think my neighborhood is pretty good." Others developed a new perception of inequalities in Redwood City:

> I didn't know that there's a really bad side of Redwood City. I never actually seen it up close … So I see it and I was just, like, whoa! I never knew it was like that … So now I think something has to be done about that. I don't think enough people know how it looks. So more people should know what else is going down.

Although this section does not offer a comprehensive analysis of youth's learning in these projects, these examples show some of the variety of insights and lessons that youth derived from their experiences and suggest the rich ways that youth can benefit from taking part in them.

Expertise/Knowledge. YEP and YELL were both based on the premise that youth have expert knowledge about the environments in which they spend their time. We reasoned that they would have insights and ideas that would not occur to outside researchers. In both projects, to ensure that their knowledge and expertise was utilized, youth were asked to design interview protocols, choose the location of their observations, and help analyze their data. Additionally, in both programs, youth were given a substantial amount of room to be creative in determining valid research topics. Facilitators wanted to see where youth would lead them and tried to foster this as much as possible. For example, in YEP, one youth ethnographer raised the issue of gentrification, even though it was not a topic included in the research questions. Her coordinator encouraged her to pursue this line of research, which resulted in interesting observations about the changing face of the neighborhood and the implications of this for youth.

Yet despite these efforts, the extent to which youth knowledge and expertise was tapped in YEP was limited by the project's design. The research questions preceded youth's involvement in the study, and, in this sense, efforts to empower local knowledge and expertise were inhibited by adult's control over basic components of the research process. Moreover, although youth were involved in some initial analysis of their data, this was folded into the larger analysis and meaning-making process of the adults, preventing young people from having a deeper role in knowledge creation. There were other constraints as well: Without in-depth training and ongoing support, it may have been difficult for some youth to see themselves as "experts" in the data analysis process.

YELL had greater success in engaging the full range of youth's knowledge and expertise. As mentioned earlier, YELL participants were expected to come up with not just the research protocols, but also the general research design and questions. Youth chose to address the question: "How can we make Redwood City better for youth?" One example of how YELL provided a forum for youth to articulate their knowledge can be seen in a video documentary that several of the participants created. The youth who made this video wanted to provide visual "proof" of the way things were in their neighborhoods. Unlike the YELL participants who used surveys and interviews for their research, it was less important to the videographers to make generalizations about all youth in West City, but instead to provide evidence of their own experiences and living conditions in their neighborhoods.

A brief description of the video gives a sense of the kinds of knowledge that youth articulated. To make this video, the group ventured out after school into different neighborhoods and taped images of places that they cared about. The first line of narration conveyed its central theme: "Redwood City is like two different cities." The video then cut to a two-part montage of neighborhood scenes, in which images of parks and new buildings were contrasted with images of litter, gang graffiti, and freeway obstruction walls (adjacent to low-income housing where some of the youth researchers lived). This theme of "two cities" was picked up throughout the video. A later segment showed a new technology office building from the road. The voiceover said, "We're driving down Silicon Valley. A couple blocks ago there were really bad houses and litter, but now look at all the clean brand new buildings."

In sum, the video expressed a perspective that Redwood City is really like two cities, in which one part has open parks, shiny new office buildings, and well-maintained roads, while the other is burdened by poorly maintained housing, gangs, and litter. By questioning a standard story of prosperity in Redwood City, the youth adopted roles not merely as data collectors, but as critical thinkers with a political message to communicate.

One potential drawback of this kind of expertise, however, is its aura of opinion and advocacy rather than detached social science. As a research document, the video did not make an effort to corroborate its stance by seeing if other youth in Redwood City felt the same way, but instead argued a particular position. Nevertheless, although the video offered a more subjective form of evidence than surveys or interviews, it was an example of the youth telling a story about something they were experts on—their own experience growing up in Redwood City.

Ownership.   Although "ownership" is a somewhat intangible dimension to analyze, it is possible to ascertain differences in ownership by looking at how youth participants talked about the project and their degree of engagement in it. In YEP, adult researchers tried to share ownership with youth, but the adults did not reach a point where they felt that ownership was fully shared. In an internal evaluation of the project, YEP coordinators felt that lack of ownership by youth was a major weakness of the project. For example, coordinators noticed that youth ethnographers seemed removed from the research questions and outcome of the study:

> I don't think that they felt a strong connection to the research questions or strong ownership of the project. It was more about "what do *you* want to know, what do *you* want to find out?" instead of, "*we* should ask this, or *we* should try to find out that."

> I'm not sure how much the youth felt that they determined the research questions, and so I'm not sure if they were really interested in the answers they were getting in the interviews.

The YELL facilitators also placed great importance on organizing the project so that youth would feel responsible for its outcomes and a sense of ownership over its direction and results. In general YELL was more successful in doing this. For example, youth participated in the analysis of findings and development of recommendations. Youth took responsibility for presenting the findings, and some extended these presentations by participating on city planning committees as well. Lastly, one of the messages that youth communicated—about inequities in the distribution of resources across parts of the city—is an indicator of their feeling of ownership over the message of the project.

It is important to point out that youth ownership carries risks as well. For example, the YELL researchers explored some topics that did not always correspond with questions of concern to community leaders or areas adults saw as actionable. Adults have an important role to play in guiding youth's focus to relevant domains for action, rather than leaving research topics completely open for youth to specify. At the same time, adults who invite youth to engage in this process should expect the unexpected and be prepared to respond to findings and recommendations that emerge.

Audience.   As suggested by the framework, our experiences with YEP and YELL varied in terms of their audiences and strategies for dissemination. In YEP, the audience was determined by adults, and more specifically by the sponsors of the evaluation. Because this audience, which included the community-wide initiative, its funders, its advisory council, and other stakeholders, was agreed upon even before the evaluation was begun, there was little room for youth to consider alternative arenas in which to share their findings. Nor were youth invited to determine strategies for dissemination. Moreover, as youth's findings were incorporated into the larger analysis conducted by adults, we did not provide a forum for young people to offer their own opinions about how the data they collected was used and/or presented.

YELL participants, on the other hand, selected their audience and carried out the presentations themselves, choosing to share with school teachers, the school board, and the city council. It was important to the YELL participants that they speak to city leaders because that is where they saw the greatest likelihood of getting results based on their recommendations. There are limitations, however, to seeking a local, community-based audience, because the impact of the work can remain restricted in scope. Therefore, rather than assume that local audiences are the end purpose of this kind of research, we recommend that such partnerships engage young people in thinking through the benefits of connecting with broader audiences as well.

Ecological Validity.   One of the strengths of YEP was its sensitivity to the settings youth move through in their daily lives. The advantages in this project were especially clear in youth's research on neighborhood contexts outside of the after-school youth center. Youth chose to observe places that would not have occurred to adults on the evaluation team or were inaccessible to them. By virtue of their familiarity with the routines and popular places in youth's lives, the youth ethnographers provided windows that were otherwise unavailable to adult researchers. For example, one youth chose to observe the field outside of her school where kids hang out in nonschool time, where they smoke and "let loose." This field represented an important space for young people, a place where, according to the youth ethnographer, they talk about their interests and worries about life. Another youth researcher documented his time spent after school hanging out at a local café that was popular with his peers because of its safe atmosphere (but that, needless to say, did not offer "programs" for youth).

In addition to access to physical spaces, youth ethnographers in YEP helped to raise issues that might not have surfaced otherwise. One YEP coordinator, who had been conducting focus groups and interviews at the site for almost a year, learned of racial tension in the neighborhood from youth ethnographers that she had not heard about before. The youth ethnographers' research led the coordinator to explore this more fully in her own research at the site. In addition to accessing new spaces and issues, data collected by youth helped to triangulate the conclusions drawn by adults. For example, a major theme that arose in the adults' work had to do with the after-school centers as "safe places." The youth ethnographers' work provided further evidence of this finding, showing that, in fact, youth used these same descriptors when talking about the after-school centers with their peers.

The context of the YELL project was quite different from YEP in that it was not nested in a larger research study. However, in the work with YELL youth, ecological validity was an important founding assumption. That is, the organizers based the project partly on the belief that youth would focus on problems and questions that were real and meaningful to other young people. This posed complications, however, when it came to Redwood City, because of the diversity of neighborhoods within it. In other words, when talking about validity, whose ecology is being assumed? Youth who came from neighborhoods where gangs were prevalent assumed that gangs would be an issue everywhere. And for those youth participants from more affluent neighborhoods (including gated communities), the local issues were different—there the salient problems focused more on overcoming boredom.

One result of this diversity was that some YELL participants had stronger convictions about the problems in Redwood City than was reflected in the survey findings, which drew from a sample of youth from all parts of Redwood City. These youth had to reconcile their initial beliefs about Redwood City with the results of their research. A second result was that the YELL participants came away with a richer sense of the range of Redwood City's diversity. Those from affluent neighborhoods reflected on new insights they had learned about living conditions in other neighborhoods, such as differences in city services in the two places. One youth from a working-class neighborhood reported his surprise to learn that some parts had gangs and others didn't, because, in his words, "I thought gangs were all over."

This issue perhaps points to the problems inherent in assuming a natural "ecological validity" for youth across ethnic and class lines. Instead, when undertaking research work with youth, it is important to be open to the multiple environments that youth navigate, and to be aware that ecological validity does not apply uniformly just because people share the same status as youth.

LIMITATIONS, BENEFITS AND IMPLICATIONS OF YOUTH–ADULT RESEARCH PARTNERSHIPS

Our experience working with youth as researchers—whether as assistants or partners—has taught us important lessons about the limitations and benefits of working with young people in the research process, as well as practical implications for policymakers. The framework and analysis just presented highlight some of these, grounding them in the tensions and complexities of real-world experience. In proposing the significance of youth–adult research partnerships in general, we do not want to suggest that collaborative research replace conventional research strategies. Instead, we suggest that different models can play an important complementary role in the research enterprise. Here we synthesize some of the lessons we learned, and look more closely at the implications of these types of research strategies for after-school contexts.

Limitations

Before initiating a youth–adult research partnership, there are important methodological, ethical, and practical considerations that should be addressed. From a methodological standpoint, research collaborations with youth (or community members in general) do not always follow the same standards of rigor that are expected in university-based research. Sampling is not always systematic, thereby making generalization to other settings more difficult. Also, youth informants might feel pressured to respond in certain ways to youthful peers who conduct interviews and focus groups.[7] Young people who are drawn to this kind of research project may be atypical, and therefore the youth perspective that one gets from this form of study may not reflect youth in general or even youth in the population studied. Also, more advanced analytic techniques, whether in ethnographic analysis or statistical methods, are not necessarily available to youth researchers. Finally, when community members (whether youth or adults) are involved in carrying out research, the possibility increases that interpretations of data may be biased toward community interests.

From the standpoint of advancing knowledge for a general audience, these methodological limitations should be considered when youth and adults engage in joint research. In our work with both YELL and YEP, it is

---

[7]This is not to suggest that bias does not also enter interactions between adult interviewers and youth.

true that specific local needs formed the basis for the work. The YELL participants had an explicit agenda of improving opportunities for youth in Redwood City. It is likely that some of the YEP researchers were biased by their desire to show their youth centers in a positive light. These issues arise in applied research that aims to have practical consequences for non-specialists. As is characteristic of other forms of "action" or "empowerment" research, this practical relevance is in fact a principle justification of the research endeavor. It is important to point out, however, that such efforts do not necessarily work at cross-purposes with the goal of doing valid research. In projects like this, therefore, it is important that youth and adult researchers pay careful attention to the distinction between evidence and speculation. As in other forms of social research, claims should be based on systematic data analysis.

This last point raises a second, practical limitation: Research partnerships require training, support, and sensitivity to the developmental levels of youth. Accomplished researchers spend years mastering the techniques associated with rigorous research, whether experimental, ethnographic, or otherwise. Youth do not necessarily become experts in these skills in the short time that they are trained, and research reports from these partnerships may not always hold up to the same standards that would be desired by policymakers or academic journals. In addition, efforts to train and support youth take time and resources, which adult researchers may not have. To be effective, collaborative research projects require knowledge of how to do rigorous research *and* how to run a youth program, a doubly difficult task. One way to alleviate this is to include experienced youth development practitioners on any collaborative research project.[8] It is also necessary to attend to the developmental levels of youth participants in structuring any research partnership. For example, during the YEP project, we learned that 12th graders thrived on levels of autonomy and independence that left 7th graders struggling. More important, however, than working with a uniform age group is accommodating youth's developmental needs. Middle-school students were capable of doing effective research; they just required more training, structure, and support from the coordinators than did the high-school seniors.

A third potential limitation to consider pertains to the ethics of research collaborations. These kinds of projects raise dilemmas about who will have control over where and how information will be used. For exam-

---

[8]This constraint posed particular challenges in the YEP project where we learned, over time, that to be successful we needed to provide a structured program for the youth ethnographers that included group-building, trust, and relationship development, in addition to the research activities themselves. For specific resources on strategies for organizing youth–adult research projects, see the following websites: John W. Gardner Center for Youth and Their Communities (gardnercenter.stanford.edu) and Youth in Focus (www.youthinfocus.net).

ple, we could imagine a situation where the information gathered by youth researchers is then used for other purposes, which the youth were not aware of when they were doing their fieldwork.[9] There is certainly this risk in a collaboration of this kind, and it is an ethical responsibility on the part of adult partners to ensure that youth researchers are informed of the purposes of and audiences for their work. This risk is alleviated somewhat in a full-partnership model, as youth have substantially greater control over audience selection and data use. It is also important to emphasize informed consent when youth ethnographers interview their peers and observe activities in informal settings.

Benefits

Despite these legitimate concerns, youth–adult research partnerships, when organized around adequate training and support for young people, represent a promising direction for the field. This is especially true for those researchers and policymakers who seek a deeper understanding of the experiences of youth and who wish to engage youth in building institutions that make a positive difference in their lives. We have identified benefits of youth–adult research collaborations that fall in three broad areas: those accruing to youth, to research, and to policies and practices that affect after-school and youth development contexts.

Youth development is a critical dimension of working with youth as researchers both in terms of learning basic skills and more holistic development. There were tangible benefits for participants of the YEP and YELL projects themselves. They learned new research skills, earned a stipend (for many of them this was their first experience receiving a paycheck), and developed new understandings of their communities, schools, and after-school centers. YELL participants also gained access to seats of power in their communities through presentations to city policymakers.

The quality of research findings can also be strengthened by youth involvement. Working with youth as researchers brings access to information and perspectives that adult researchers would not have on their own. In this way, it taps into new expertise and brings new perspectives into the process of meaning-making and knowledge creation. Further, youth are positioned to bring issues and concerns to the attention of outsiders (or even adults who are insiders) that might have otherwise gone unnoticed, or at least unexamined. In this way, youth's participation helps strengthen ecological validity by bringing an insider's view to after-school contexts and youth's experiences, and by reminding us not to assume homogeneity in young people's experience, needs, or interests.

---

[9]Joseph Kahne made helpful comments on this point.

After-school programs (and youth organizations more broadly) can also benefit from youth involvement in research and evaluation, which can be useful both as a source of feedback for programming and as a programming opportunity of its own. By including youth voice, collaborative projects heighten the likelihood that research findings will be relevant to the needs of both youth participants and program staff. In addition, youth–adult research partnerships comport with youth development philosophy by engaging youth as resources in work that is important to their communities. These kinds of research projects, for example, share certain key features of effective learning environments, such as cycles of practice, performance, and feedback (McLaughlin, 2000). The benefits are mutually reinforcing because as youth involvement in research strengthens programming and knowledge about after-school contexts, program offerings that engage youth in such research provide greater opportunity for positive youth development.

Implications

Not all collaborative research projects with youth need to or should aspire to the full partnership variety. After all, YEP, which we described as a quasi-partnership, was successful in meeting limited goals related to data collection for a larger evaluation and providing new learning opportunities for the youth. However, the full potential of working with youth as researchers is most likely to be realized in a model that embraces them as partners throughout the research process. This requires a combination of sharing ownership of the project with the youth and supporting youth leadership and development in the project. Practically, this means designing projects that: (a) involve youth in an early stage of research question development; (b) provide a steady, consistent, program structure; (c) utilize periodic cycles of data collection and analysis; (d) allow time and resources for youth development as well as meeting data collection needs; and (e) provide opportunities for engagement that are developmentally appropriate.

Policymakers also have a role to play in the development of youth–adult research partnerships. Funding streams, for example, should support youth research. However, more is needed than simply funding youth research projects; it also means creating the space for policymakers to "hear" youth and act on their research findings. In Redwood City, for example, YELL participants were able to find an audience in a receptive city government, and subsequently new roles were created for young people to sit on a variety of city planning committees. Youth IMPACT (2000), a youth evaluation project in San Francisco, is another example that shows how policymakers can legitimate youth's research efforts. After completing a citywide study of youth serving organizations, these youth evaluators developed criteria for program quality that community youth organizations receiving public funds are now required to meet.

Adult responsibility to create opportunities for youth input more often than not is overlooked. Yet our experience makes it clear that changes in adult roles in relation to youth, in the nature of the "tables" set for policymaking, and in expectations for using youth research must go along with changed youth roles in the community. Otherwise, policymakers risk launching yet another pro forma "youth commission" or "youth voice" project and, in the process, deepening youth's cynicism about the value adults attach to young people and their contributions.

ACKNOWLEDGMENT

We would like to thank the editors of this volume for their helpful comments on earlier drafts.

REFERENCES

Academy for Educational Development. (2001). *Community youth mapping.* Retrieved August 2, 2001, from http://www.aed.org/youth_development.html

Baksh-Soodeen, R. (2001). Lessons from the gender movement: Building a discipline to support practice. *CYD Journal, 2*(2), 61-64.

Burton, L. M., Obeidallah, D., & Allison, K. (1996). Ethnographic insights on social context and adolescent development among inter-city African-American teens. In R. Jessor, A. Colby, & R. Shweder (Eds.), *Ethnography and human development* (pp. 327–338). Chicago: University of Chicago Press.

Camino, L. A. (2000). Youth–adult partnerships: Entering new territory in community work and research. *Applied Development Science, 4*(3, Suppl.), 11–20.

Cole, M. (1996). *Cultural psychology: A once and future discipline.* Cambridge, MA: Harvard University Press.

Costello, J., Toles, M., Spielberger, J., & Wynn, J. (2000). History, ideology and structure shape the organizations that shape youth. In *Youth development: Issues, challenges, and directions* (pp. 185–231). Philadelphia: Public/Private Ventures.

Eccles, J., & Gootman, J. A. (Eds.). (2001). *Community programs to promote youth development.* Washington, DC: National Academy Press.

Fawcett, S. B., Paine-Andrews, A., Francisco, V. T., Schultz, J. A., Richter, K. P., Lewis, R. K., Harris, K. J., Williams, E. L., Berkley, J. Y., Lopez, C. M., & Fisher, J. L. (1996). Empowering community health initiatives through evaluation. In D. M. Fetterman, S. J. Kaftarian, & A. Wandersman (Eds.), *Empowerment evaluation: Knowledge and tools for self-assessment and accountability* (pp. 161–187). Thousand Oaks, CA: Sage.

Fetterman, D. M. (1996). Empowerment evaluation: An introduction to theory and practice. In D. M. Fetterman, S. J. Kaftarian, & A. Wandersman (Eds.), *Empowerment evaluation: Knowledge and tools for self-assessment and accountability* (pp. 3–46). Thousand Oaks, CA: Sage.

Fielding, M. (2001). Students as radical agents of change. *Journal of Educational Change, 2*(2), 123–141.

Fullan, M. (1993). Why teachers must become change agents. *Educational Leadership,* 50(6), 12–17.

Greeno, J. G., McDermott, R., Cole, K. A., Engle, R. A., Goldman, S., Knudsen, J., Lauman, B., & Linde, C. (1999). Research, reform, and aims in education: Modes of action in search of each other. In E. C. Lagemann & L. S. Shulman (Eds.), *Issues in education research: Problems and possibilities* (pp. 299–335). San Francisco, Jossey-Bass.

Hart, R. (1992). *Children's participation: From tokenism to citizenship.* Florence, Italy: UNICEF International Child Development Centre.

Horsch, K., Little, P. M. D., Chase Smith, J., Goodyear, L., & Harris, E. (2002, February). Youth involvement in evaluation and research. *Issues and Opportunities in Out-of-School Time Evaluation Briefs, 1,* 1–8. Cambridge, MA: Harvard Family Research Project.

Johnson, R. (1997). Examining the validity structure of qualitative research. *Education, 118*(2), 282–292.

Lerner, R. M., Fisher, C. B., & Weinberg, R. A. (2000). Toward a science for and of the people: Promoting civil society through the application of developmental science. *Child Development, 71*(1), 11–20.

Linney, J. A., & Wandersman, A. (1996). Empowering community groups with evalua-tion skills: The prevention plus III model. In D. M. Fetterman, S. J. Kaftarian, & A. Wandersman (Eds.), *Empowerment evaluation: Knowledge and tools for self-assessment and accountability* (pp. 259–276). Thousand Oaks, CA: Sage.

Mayer, S. E. (1996). Building community capacity with evaluation activities that em-power. In D. M. Fetterman, S. J. Kaftarian, & A. Wandersman (Eds.), *Empowerment evaluation: Knowledge and tools for self-assessment and accountability* (pp. 332–378). Thousand Oaks, CA: Sage.

McLaughlin, M. W. (2000). *Community counts: How youth organizations matter for youth development.* Washington, DC: Public Education Network.

McLaughlin, M. W., Irby, M. A., & Langman, J. (2001). *Urban sanctuaries: Neighborhood organizations in the lives and futures of inner-city youth.* San Francisco: Jossey-Bass. (Original work published 1994)

Meucci, S., & Schwab, M. (1997). Children and the environment: Young people's par-ticipation in social change. *Social Justice, 24*(3), 1-10.

Mitra, D. (2001). *Makin' it real: Involving youth in school reform.* Unpublished doctoral dissertation, Stanford University, Palo Alto, CA.

Penuel, W. R., & Freeman, T. (1997). Participatory action research in youth program-ming: A theory in use. *Child and Youth Care Forum, 26*(3), 175–185.

Rapoport, R. N. (Ed.). (1985). *Children, youth, and families: The action–research relation-ship.* Cambridge, England: Cambridge University Press.

Roth, J., Brooks-Gunn, J., Murray, L., & Foster, W. (1998). Promoting healthy adoles-cents: Synthesis of youth development program evaluations. *Journal of Research on Adolescence, 8*(4), 423–459.

Schwab, M. (1997). Sharing power: Participatory public health research with California teens. *Social Justice, 24*(3), 11–32.

Sherman, R.F. (2003). Building young people's public lives: One foundation's strategy. *New Directions for Youth Development, 96,* 65–82.

Youniss, J., Bales, S., Christmas-Best, V., Diversi, M., McLaughlin, M., Silbereisen, R. (2002). Youth civic engagement in the twenty-first century. *Journal of Research on Adolescence, 12*(1), 121–148.

Youth IMPACT. (2001). *Youth voices inspiring creative change.* San Francisco: Department of Children, Youth, and Their Families.

Zeldin, S. (2000). Integrating research and practice to understand and strengthen communities for adolescent development: An introduction to the special issue and current issues. *Applied Developmental Science, 4*(1), 2–10.

Zeldin, S., McDaniel, A. K., Topitzes, D., & Calvert, M. (2000). *Youth decision-making: A study on the impacts of youth on adults and organizations.* University of Wisconsin–Madison, in partnership with the Innovation Center for Community and Youth Development and the National 4-H Council.

II

Developmental Processes and Outcomes

8

Everybody's Gotta Give: Development of Initiative and Teamwork Within a Youth Program

Reed Larson
David Hansen
Kathrin Walker
University of Illinois, Urbana-Champaign

After the last bell rings, a typical high school classroom is transformed into a meeting place as youth begin arriving. These members of the Clarkston High School FFA chapter seat themselves on top of desks and begin several excited conversations, generating ideas for planning a Day Camp for 4th graders in the middle of the summer.[1] The youth's goal for the camp is to interest children in agriculture, partly with the hope that they will want to become FFA members when they reach high school. As the cascade of conversations goes on, the adult advisor interrupts to ask who is leading the meeting, and the youth in unison point to Susan. In the minutes that follow, youth continue to throw out ideas in spontaneous and rapid succession. Many of these ideas are wildy unrealistic, which adds to the humor, and despite occasional entreaties from Susan and others to "focus," their ideas flow for 45 minutes with little apparent or clear direction.

---

[1]The name of the high school and the names used for youth and adult leaders have been changed. The FFA, formerly called Future Farmers of America, is an after-school program for high school students in the United States, which is oriented toward preparing youth for careers in agriculture, food, fiber, and natural resource systems.

These youth are in the process of putting themselves into a tight spot. Shortly after this meeting, they recruited 20 children from the community to attend their camp for 2½ days in midsummer, only 2 months hence. Yet, although they are full of ideas, they face numerous hurdles in order to develop these ideas into workable shape. These youth are inexperienced in planning a large-scale event such as the day camp; they have little knowledge of how to coordinate the people and resources needed for such an event to occur; and several of these youth will encounter conflicts in their schedule or will lose interest as the hard work of preparation turns out to be less fun that spinning out ideas. How do these teenagers organize themselves, individually, and as a team, to make this camp happen? What are the crucial strategies for planning this type of event that they must learn along the way?

This chapter focuses on the development of we have called *initiative*, the capacity to direct cumulative effort over time toward achievement of a long-term goal (Larson, 2000). We are interested in understanding the constellation of knowledge, dispositions, and skills that youth must learn to carry out a project, such as creating the day camp. This capacity to carry out a plan of action, both individually and as a team, is of increasing importance in the rapidly changing world of the 21st century (Brandstädter & Lerner, 1999; Larson, 2000). Within the occupational sphere, automation has reduced the market value of rote and manual labor, and more jobs require abilities to think and act with a plan, to carry out "initiatives" either individually or collaboratively. In other spheres of life as well, the erosion of traditional norms has made daily life less codified, thus, individuals need the ability to deliberately shape their lives (Larson, Wilson, Broan, Furstenberg, & Verma, 2002). For communities, too, it is essential that their members possess capabilities for "social entrepreneurship" in order to maintain and extend the communities' values and goals (Frumkin, 2002; Gauvain, 1999). So there is reason to contend that the capabilities these FFA members must learn to successfully organize the day camp are critical ones.

In this chapter we describe our current qualitative research on initiative, using the creation of the day camp by these FFA youth as a case example for in-depth analysis. Our first objective is to begin to understand the development of initiative within the context of organized youth programs. What did these teenagers need to learn to organize this day camp? Our second objective is to understand how the adult leaders of youth programs support this development. What role can or should they play in facilitating preparations for an event like this day camp? Effective, youth-serving practitioners give teens responsibility and ownership (McLaughlin, 2000), but they also provide support and guidance so that the youths' efforts do not flounder (Camino & Zeldin, 2002)—in this case, so the camp does not "flop." How do adults balance these competing imperatives?

BACKGROUND:
DEVELOPMENTAL ANTECEDENTS OF INITIATIVE

The Capabilities of Children and Adolescents

A useful first step to understanding the development of initiative is to examine what is known about its antecedents in childhood. Research on children helps us think about the capabilities for planful action that they will bring into youth programs in adolescence. If we start with young children, Piaget (1954) demonstrated that their understanding of the world is limited in a number of ways that prevent them from exercising initiative. Among these constraints, they have little sense of future time as an arena for organizing their actions (Haith, 1997). They are, in a sense, trapped in the immediate world in front of them. But research shows that children gradually acquire abilities to plan actions and anticipate contingencies within a short-term future horizon. By age 5, children are capable of considering alternative courses of action and formulating a series of 5 to 6 steps toward reaching a short-term goal, such as building a tower from blocks. By late childhood, they are able to develop more elaborate sequences and plans that are flexible, take into account situational constraints, and include if–then contingencies (Gauvain, 1999; Gauvain & Perez, in press).

Even by adolescence, however, there remain limits to most young people's capabilities for carrying out longer term initiatives, limits that reflect lack of experience and cognitive tools. Youth at the outset of adolescence are typically not able to devise plans that involve long sequences of actions and include a large number of separate components and actors (Gauvain & Perez, in press). Even older adolescents often have limited abilities to coordinate the multiple abstract levels and systems that might be involved in reaching a long-term goal (Mascolo, Fisher, & Neimeyer, 1999); in fact many adults remain ineffective in implementing long-term plans (Gollwitzer, 1999). Another constraint is that teenagers are still developing abilities to understand emotions and use this knowledge to regulate their emotional states; thus, encounters with frustration, anxiety, and boredom can disrupt sustained attention to a long-term project (Larson, 1985).

These limits partly reflect the fact that adolescents are just starting to learn to use and manipulate abstract concepts. Teenagers' conception of future time is typically unelaborated (Nurmi, 1991), which may impair their ability to plan. They are only beginning to develop capabilities to think analytically about systems (Keating, 1980), emotional processes (Larson, Clore, & Wood, 1999), and the causal sequence among complex narrative events (Habermas & Bluck, 2000). Adolescents also are just gaining abilities for what cognitive psychologists call *metacognition*—the ability to "think about thinking." This means they have limited abilities to think strategically; to think about the planning process itself as an object of thought. In short, adolescents' internal tools for organizing a set of future interactions with a complex environment—as required for planning an event like the day camp—are at a nascent stage.

When we look at team projects with peers, other cognitive limitations are likely to affect adolescents' exercise of initiative. Piaget (1929, 1954) found that young children are cognitively egocentric, they assume that other people experience the world exactly as they do. In a planning task, they see collaborators as instruments of their own intentions, rather than as individuals who may have intentions of their own (Gauvain, 2001). Research shows that the abilities required to understand other people's points of view are formidable, and their development is a long process stretching through adolescence, if not further. Early teens begin to acquire the capacity to understand other people as centers of thought and feeling, but they do not always use it (Selman, 1980). Adolescents are prone to assume that others are thinking about the same information that they are (Elkind, 1967). This adolescent egocentrism may handicap them in understanding and anticipating the differing point of view and intentions of collaborators (which is hard enough for experienced adults), thus making coordination of work on a team more difficult.

The Role of Adults

What is important to know, however, is that children and adolescents are capable of functioning at a higher level of planfulness and initiative when they are assisted by others. When working in pairs, peers provide some degree of mutual assistance (Rogoff, 1998), despite the problem of egocentrism just discussed. However, research with 9- to 11-year-olds indicates that peers rarely verbalize longer term strategies to each other, but rather work on one step at a time and focus on completion of the immediate task. They do not share ideas about a larger plan of action. As a result, youth in peer collaboration situations do less well on a posttest planning task than youth who have worked with adults—who are much more likely to verbalize long-term strategies (Radziszewska & Rogoff, 1988, 1991).

Gauvain (1999) argued that, at least in Western culture, interactions with parents are the major context in which younger children develop abilities to formulate and carry out plans. In daily life, parents and children often engage in joint planning of activities for the child and the family, and parents often play a guiding role in these collaborations. Parents help children identify goals, determine steps to reach these goals, and monitor progress. Parents provide scaffolding; they structure, instruct, and model elements of the initiative process that children are not yet able to do on their own. Following the theories of Vygotsky (1978), this process of working together appears to help expand children's planning abilities; they gradually learn parts of the process that their parents are providing. Indeed, as they get older, children take on more of the tasks involved in joint planning with parents, such as organizing materials and contributing strategic information and ideas (Gauvain, 1999; Gauvain & Perez, in press).

How much children learn, of course, differs as a function of what parents do. Research by Gauvain and Huard (1999) suggested that too much or too little guidance from parents is associated with slower development of planning capabilities. Authoritarian parents were found to be more directive in planning discussions, whereas permissive parents more often left planning in children's hands. It was the authoritative parents who most often engaged their children in joint planning and most often used open-ended, nondirective, scaffolding techniques, like reminders and suggestions. Not surprisingly, when children in the research reached adolescence, those with authoritative parents made more contributions to joint family planning.

These findings about parents' role are important to our discussion of youth programs in a couple of ways. First, they suggest that, to support development of initiative, adult leaders need to find a middle ground between being too directive and too *laissez faire*. But this is easier said than done, and we need to ask what it really means in the everyday situations that adult leaders face. Second, although research indicates that parents provide support for development of planning skills in childhood, parents are less involved in adolescents' daily lives, and thus engage in less joint planning with them (Gauvain, 1999; Gauvain & Perez, in press). This creates a gap in opportunities for teenagers to continue developing their planning and initiative skills, a gap that might potentially be filled by good youth programs.

YOUTH PROGRAMS

Our interest in youth programs as contexts for the development of initiative emerged from our research in which adolescents carried pagers for one week and provided reports on their psychological states at random times when signaled by the pagers. We found across samples of hundreds of youth that, when teens were participating in extracurricular activities and other structured programs, they consistently reported both high motivation and engaged attention. This is a combination likely to provide optimal conditions for the development of self-directed action (Larson, 2000). We were also influenced by the finding of Heath (1998, 1999) that adolescents in highly effective youth programs start using new types of language. New members in these programs showed dramatic increases in their use of what-if questions, scenario building, conditionals, and other linguistic tools for planning and executing plans—what we call initiative. This led us to ask what internal changes in youths' thought processes underlie the increased used of these linguistic tools. What insights and new ways of thinking are related to the development of initiative?

Our first step to evaluating this prediction was to ask youth to tell us about their developmental experiences in these contexts. We conducted 10 focus groups with high-school students in which we asked them to describe what they were learning in youth programs (Dworkin, Larson, & Hansen, 2003). What struck us first was that these teens almost always portrayed themselves as the agents of their learning experiences within these contexts. These appeared to be contexts in which youth were "producers of their own development" (Lerner & Busch-Rossnagel, 1981; Silbereisen, Eyferth, & Rudinger, 1986). Among the types of development they described, these students readily identified a set of competencies they were learning that related to initiative. These included skills involving management of one's energies and resources: learning to set realistic goals, exert effort, manage time, and take responsibility. They also included skills related to working effectively in a team: learning communication skills, the giving and taking of feedback, and taking responsibility within a group.

It is important to ask, however, whether young people really have these learning experiences more often in youth programs than in other contexts? In a second study, we developed a survey that identified different types of learning experiences, including those related to initiative, and we asked a high-school sample to rate how often they had had each of these experiences in youth programs, in their classwork, and during time "hanging out with friends" (Hansen, Larson, & Dworkin, 2003). These teenagers reported having all of the learning experiences related to initiative and teamwork skills at significantly higher rates within youth programs than in these comparison activities. For example, 40% of teens involved in youth programs reported that they had "learned to consider obstacles when making plans" in that context; whereas only 21% reported this experience in a school class and only 29% reported it in their interactions with friends. These findings supported our thesis that youth programs may be a particularly fertile context for the development of initiative.

The next step for us is to observe, close up, how this development takes place. Our goal is to use intensive observation to begin developing theory and practical knowledge about how initiative is fostered within youth programs. To achieve this, we chose to look at high-quality programs where there was a high likelihood of observing the development of initiative in process.

AN INTENSIVE STUDY

We chose an FFA chapter as one of the sites for our research because the FFA organization stresses the development of initiative skills. The motto of the National FFA Organization is "*Learning to do, doing to learn*, earning to live, living to serve" [italics added]. Over the course of a year, FFA clubs and members within those clubs have the opportunity to participate in a wide range of activities and competitions that involve working toward a goal. In the months before and during our research, the FFA chapter we studied was involved in an agricultural mechanics contest, ran a community toy show, took part in a parliamentary procedure contest, planned their annual banquet, and competed in a poultry judging contest, as well as planning the day camp and several other activities. In some ways an FFA chapter might be seen as analogous to an urban neighborhood club where youth choose from a smorgasbord of activities. The difference is that FFA programs are located in schools and many of these activities involve competitions in which the chapter and participants vie for first, second, and third place rankings, and so forth, at the district and state levels.

We chose the Clarkston FFA chapter because it had a reputation for being very successful in these competitions. We also chose it because the agriculture teachers who were its advisors, Mr. Baker and Mr. Jensen, had strong reputations for caring about their students and making a difference in their lives. The Clarkston chapter had 77 members and was located in a rural, conglomerated high school of approximately 500 students. These members did not stand out as a self-selected group of high achievers and school leaders, as is the case with many high-school extracurricular activities (Holland & Andre, 1987). Some participants reported that there was a social stigma associated with being a member of FFA and several members saw themselves as social "outcasts." But the structure of the program provides many roles and ways for youth to fit in and contribute. The chapter had close to a dozen officer positions that provided leadership opportunities, as well as committees for each activity that allowed students to step into an activity of their choice.

We began the study in early April, when planning for the day camp was soon to get underway, and continued through mid-July, when the day camp was held. During the first 2 months, while school was in session, members were involved in a range of FFA activities, and our data included students' experiences in these activities. The idea of doing a summer day camp for 4th graders was originated by members 3 years before. This year, the adult advisors were experimenting with giving the youth more control over the development of the camp than they had in the 2 prior years. It was agreed between the advisors that Mr. Baker would take primary responsibility for supervising the day camp preparations and Mr. Jensen would help out as needed.

Our objective was to understand the functioning of the Clarkston FFA program and the development of the day camp from three points of view. First, over the 4 months, one or more of our staff members observed the chapter's activities on 13 different occasions (11 times by D. Hansen). Second, with input from the advisors, we chose 11 youths, most of them officers;

and one of our staff members was matched with each and conducted bi-weekly interviews with her or him over the 3½-month period. The interviews at the beginning, at midpoint, and at the end were conducted face-to-face; the other interviews were conducted by phone. The students included 3 seniors, 1 junior, 3 sophomores, and 4 freshmen (6 females and 5 males). Several of these students withdrew from FFA participation at the end of school in May, so we conducted final interviews with these youth at that time, and continued only with the 6 youth who were involved in planning the day camp. We completed a total of 74 youth interviews. Our third source of data was interviews with the two adult FFA advisors. D. Hansen and K. Walker were each paired with one of the advisors and interviewed them following the same biweekly schedule as used with the youth. A total of 15 advisor interviews were conducted.

In presenting this case study, we want to stress that it represents only one example of how the development of initiative occurs and is fostered. We start by providing a narrative description of what happened after that first day camp planning meeting, based primarily on the observers' notes. The two subsequent sections deal with the students' accounts of their learning experience and the role of the adult leaders in supporting the students' development of initiative skills. As a confirmatory step, we asked the two advisors of the program to read a close-to-final draft of this chapter and they reported that the account was "right on."

NARRATIVE DESCRIPTION: HOW THE YOUTH PLANNED THE DAY CAMP

Initial Brainstorming Phase: Fantasy and Fun

The meeting we described at the outset of the chapter initiated a phase of high enthusiasm. The free-flowing and enjoyable nature of this brainstorming phase crystallized members' ownership of the day camp, which was critical later on when the going got tougher. Over a sequence of three meetings, the members continued to throw out a wide range of ideas about activities they could do with the 4th graders. Most suggestions were built on topics such as plants, pets, or farm animals, for which they had developed expertise through prior FFA activities. The group quickly decided that one day of the camp would be focused on chickens, motivated no doubt by their success in tying for first place in the FFA state poultry judging contest. Many of their ideas for activities, however, were unrealistic, or deliberately funny. For example, someone joked that after doing activities with live chickens in the morning, they could make fried chicken with them in the afternoon.

During this initial phase, the students did not seem to want or need input from the adult advisors. One girl joked, "We'll let you know if we need any thing, we'll write you a note." The advisors played a convivial, background role and joined in the humor. After the group decided that the 3 days would be focused on chickens, plants, and dogs, Mr. Baker introjected a word play on the Wizard of Oz, "Chickens and plants and dogs, oh my!" In their interviews, the advisors reported restraining the desire to push the planning process forward, even though they could see how much work had to be done. They did encourage ideas they liked, for example, the proposal that members go to the grade school to actively publicize the day camp. The advisors also made occasional suggestions to support the students' planning. They encouraged the youth to narrow down their ideas, made sure that someone was documenting ideas on paper, helped youth assess the feasibility of ideas, and they began to offer the next steps for the development of ideas. At the third meeting, Mr. Baker suggested that the youth break into three planning committees having responsibility for each day of the camp, a suggestion they followed almost immediately.

Although this phase was productive in generating investment in the day camp and settling on the topics that would be the focus of each day, the amount of progress being made was slowing down. Several youth felt that, since they had decided on the topics, the planning was done and there was no need to meet further. Yet the task of developing the plan—designing specific activities for each day, making arrangements, and getting the necessary materials—was not yet addressed.

Middle Phase: Wheel Spinning

In the next phase, progress came to a near standstill, mired in tension and an inability to take things to the next step. The group continued to meet but it was the observer's impression that these meetings did not accomplish much that had not already been done. Part of the problem was that members failed to show up at meetings and failed to follow through on what they had agreed to do. About 10 to 12 youth were involved at this stage, but several meetings had only 4 to 6 members in attendance. School was ending and people got caught up in summer jobs and other activities, or just had difficulty arranging transportation to come in for meetings. At one meeting, for example, the girl who was writing the lesson plan for one committee did not show up, leaving the other two members frustrated. Strains and conflicts also emerged that immobilized work. One younger student had taken over the role of leader from Susan but he locked horns with an older member on the question of how long a camp session should be and, then, on whether the children should be split into smaller groups.

The preparation process also appeared to be hampered by members not being able to formulate what they needed to accomplish next. One student later reflected that they did not know what they were doing or what they had to do. The group tended to go over the same things it had in the previous meetings. For example, at each meeting, they talked about setting the schedule for the day camp in 15-minute increments, but they did not create a process for filling in those increments. Our observer felt they were using the meetings as a crutch, that is, "if we are meeting we must be making progress." Whether due to inexperience, cognitive limitations, interpersonal gridlock, or just a lack of felt urgency, the students seemed unable or unwilling to engage in future-oriented thinking. The observer wrote in his notes, "No where near being ready—the youth are no further along than they were at meetings 2 and 3!"

Aware that the process was stalling, the adult advisors began to take a more active role. Mr. Baker decided it would be helpful to teach the students how to construct a lesson plan, and then he suggested that the group set deadlines for the committees to have these lesson plans ready. When these deadlines were not met, Mr. Baker set new deadlines and invested his authority by saying he wanted to look at each of these plans. Mr. Baker also acted to resolve problems with the group process. He asked each person to take responsibility for getting the other members of their committee to the meetings. In addition, he began to make phone calls to the youth in leadership roles, checking up on their work and suggesting points about which they should be thinking.

Meetings during this phase had much less humor and more frequent expressions of strain. At each interview, we asked students to rate how much progress was being made on a scale from 1 to 10, and these ratings dipped during this middle phase. One student later said that the process "fell apart"; another that "it was frustrating going to meeting after meeting and not getting anything done." But some progress was being made. For example, the group working on chickens searched university Web sites for activities they could do with the children. The observer noted that when one of the students asked a question unrelated to the camp, the group admonished him to stay focused. Most importantly, as we will see when we turn to the youths' accounts, they were developing awareness of what the challenges were and what needed to be done, an awareness that kicked in during the final weeks of preparation.

The Serious Planning Phase: Student Leaders Step Forward

Only four youth showed up for the final planning meeting, 2 weeks prior to the day camp. But these were the four who were most invested and had assumed leadership roles. They had a clear sense of what to do and were committed to holding what they called a "working meeting." They got right down to business and focused on details of the day camp, intermittently working separately and as a unit. They ran through and set up the activities for each 15-minute period of the day camp. They completed mundane tasks, like creating name tags for the children and creating labels to identify chicken and dog anatomy. Several youth stayed for 3 to 4 hours, and some continued to work and meet with members of their committees until the weekend before the camp.

During this period, the youth appeared to work together seamlessly, setting aside past tensions between individuals. A student reported in her phone interview, "We worked really hard as a team. Everyone did their part and, if someone didn't, then another person was there to pick up the pieces and help things continue on." During this stage, the students readily accepted responsibility for whatever needed to be done.

The adult advisors, at this phase, worked closely with youth providing supports. At the final meeting, Mr. Baker offered specific suggestions on what they needed to accomplish. Both advisors helped youth find material and circulated among the groups responding to requests for help. Our observer noted that the advisors still "didn't *tell* the youth what to do!" They asked members for their permission to offer assistance. For example, one student was looking on the Internet for cartoon pictures of dogs to use for name tags, and she found one but did not like the size and way it printed. Mr. Baker politely asked her, "Can I help?" When she said "Yes," he sat down and showed her how to change the picture so it was the way she wanted it.

The Day Camp: Moment of Truth

After these last 2 weeks of intensive effort, the dates of the camp finally arrived, and the youth ran it successfully with only a few minor problems. Between 7 and 10 FFA youth showed up each day to supervise the 20 children. Members of each committee took responsibility for their day, and our observers noted that several of the youth did a superb job of executing their lesson plans, demonstrating a high level of preparedness and sensitivity to the children. On one day, Mr. Baker took over leading the sessions because the children became unruly; and a planned field trip to the animal shelter did not work out as anticipated because no one had made a key phone call. But overall, the day camp was a great success. The children appeared to have a good time learning about chickens, dogs, and plants. Nearly all the FFA members expressed satisfaction that it had gone well and that they had had a positive influence on the children.

WHAT THE YOUTH LEARNED

So what happened that allowed the youth to come together and make the camp successful? In the final interview conducted right after the day camp, and in bits and pieces throughout the period, the Clarkston FFA members in the study reported developing fundamental insights about how to accomplish a project like this. To understand this process of acquiring initiative skills, we turn now to analyzing the members' accounts of the day camp preparations. At every biweekly interview, we asked the students, among other things, what "challenges or obstacles" they faced, what means they were using to address these challenges, and what they were learning from their experiences. We then systematically analyzed their responses employing procedures of qualitative data analysis and grounded theory that are designed to identify underlying patterns and concepts within textual data (Strauss & Corbin, 1998; Taylor & Bogdan, 1998).

Challenges and Obstacles

The experiences of challenges appeared to be key. The learning youth described toward the end of the period appeared to be related to the types of challenges they identified during the middle phases of the day camp and in other FFA activities. Our analysis of their reported challenges and obstacles revealed several repeated themes, fitting into two categories. The first category was *instrumental challenges*: impediments to their work. The second was *interpersonal challenges*: obstacles in coordinating one's work with peers.

Many of the instrumental challenges had to do with mobilizing one's time and effort. A frequent response to our question about challenges and obstacles was: "Just getting it done," or, "Making sure I do my part." The youth reported experiencing conflicts with other activities in their lives and having difficulty finding the time, as well as difficulties in knowing how to do something or what to do next. The youth also reported encountering emotional and motivational obstacles to getting work done. These concerned experiences of stress, negative feelings, and lack of motivation. One girl reported her challenge to be: "Sleeping in. I need to get around that. And I get on the Internet a lot, I need to stop doing that and just get out there and do it [the FFA work]. I mean, I'm motivated, but when I'm sitting there at home and after a full week of school, on Saturday I'm so relaxed, I just don't feel like going out there." This youth, like others, was struggling with basic self-organizational issues.

Interpersonal challenges, related to working with peers, accounted for two thirds of the challenges and obstacles for the work on the day camp. Not surprisingly, these were reported most frequently during the middle phase. Attempting to coordinate the planning with her committee's day, one exasperated youth said, "They're driving me nuts, aahh," and at the next interview, "I have dates to get that stuff in and, if they're busy, then I'm gonna be like, oh crap." The students provided a litany of complaints about others not doing their part, not showing up, putting in little effort,

and just being difficult. The way youth phrased these interpersonal challenges ranged from those that simply blamed others—"It was Chris's meeting and he wasn't there; did he just forget?"—to those that recognized
other people's irresponsibility as part of the problem to be solved. For example, one girl described the challenge:

> Making sure that everybody does their part and we're not having to pick up af-
> ter someone else. You know, this person didn't call so and so to find out if we
> could do this, or this person didn't make sure they gave us a list of things they
> needed bought and now they don't have everything they need. Or just making
> sure that everything gets done right and gets done on time.

In this example, one can see that the formulation of the challenge—which
recognizes the flakiness of others—contains its solution. Indeed the challenges appeared to provide the germination for developmental change.

Insights Into Instrumentality

The members' reported learning experiences often appeared to stem from
the challenges concerned with mobilizing time and effort. A frequent category of these reports entailed *learning that achieving something requires concerted effort and discipline*. The youth reported learning to start early, to work
on the project every day, and that achieving a long-term goal "takes a lot of
self-discipline." They reported learning to more deliberately coordinate the
different competing parts of their lives. One girl said, "It's sort of a new idea
for me, this idea of knowing what you are doing a week before. Usually I'm
just day-by-day." It appeared to come as a major discovery to many of these
youth, that "If you work hard toward something, it will pay off in the long
run." This lesson at first seemed rudimentary to us, something one might associate with Erikson's (1950) preadolescent stage of "industry." But for
many youth, this lesson contained a higher order, metacognitive concept—
that one's time and effort can be organized strategically. The underlying developmental insight was that one's own time and effort are *quantities* that
one can manipulate, allocate, and invest. Excited by this insight, one member said he was now going to "turn attention toward other things that I like,
and work hard toward them." It appeared that future time had taken form
for these youth as an arena in which the deployment of effort could be pur-
posefully organized toward reaching a goal.

A related set of learning experiences appeared to arise from the challenges presented by emotional and motivational obstacles. The students reported learning to be less nervous, "not get stressed out," and control
negative feelings. These fit in the category, *learning to self-regulate internal
states*. One girl reported learning, "You just live with yourself. Even if you

don't wanna do it, you don't have a choice most of the time." After one only partially successful FFA competition, the same girl said, "We couldn't let our anger, disappointment, and stress take over and completely smash the project that had to be done." These lessons, too, reflect metacognitive insight: that strong emotions interfere with the investment of attention and with effective work. Although intangible and abstract, emotional and motivational states are entities that can, at least partly, be controlled. In order to make progress on a task, one has to stand above what you feel in the moment and think about the larger goal to be achieved. The challenges of carrying out a project, such as the day camp, involves understanding and learning to manage one's time, one's effort, and one's inner life.

One thing we expected but did not hear were insights on how to organize the steps of the planning process. Although the youth articulated abstract psychological concepts about self-management, they said little about logistic strategies for creating and executing an effective plan, for example, what steps should be taken early and late in carrying out a project like this and how the steps relate to each other. We do not know whether this is because youth did not learn these things, or they were not salient for them. They did, however, articulate developing this type of strategic thinking about collaborating with peers.

Insights Into Working as a Team

Over half of the students' reported learning experiences were related to the interpersonal challenges of working with other people. Our coding process yielded a set of categories that involved being more understanding of others, which we present followed by examples of each in individual quotes:

- *Accepting others' viewpoints.* "You [learn to] consider people's opinions and thoughts; you're patient with them, and you accept their beliefs."
- *Giving people space.* "If they're doing their job, but not doing it the way you want, you feel like you need to step back and sort of let them do it on their own." "You learn that if someone says something that you don't like, you kind of ignore them. I used to snap right back at them, and I've learned to kind of wait and then sit down and say, 'this is how I feel.'"
- *Recognizing individual differences.* "You have to know like some people they can handle a lot of criticism, but then [with] others you have to be more careful of their feelings. Like some of the guys you can just tell them, 'You better get this done otherwise you're gonna be kicked out,' but [with] some of the girls [you] are like, 'Could you please start working a little harder?'"
- *Working together.* "That one person can't do everything on their one, it's got to be a group effort to put something like this on." "Even

though we're fighting and arguing, we got back together, put everything behind us and came out with a great product."

These reports suggest advancement from an egocentric perspective,
which positions their own views and intentions at the center, to a more
sociocentric perspective, which is understanding of and gives weight to the
subjective realities and agency of other team members. This shift toward a
sociocentric orientation is effectively summarized by a freshman girl who
played a key role in the day camp: "When I first started, I was pretty intoler-
ant of just about anybody, but you know, I am sure that they're pretty intoler-
ant of me sometimes. So everybody's gotta give and everybody's just gotta
hold back just a little."

But giving and holding back did not mean total self-abnegation. The FFA
members also reported learning to be more confident and self-assertive in a
group context. On the one hand, a girl reported learning that "If someone is
a slacker, you still have to make them feel like they are doing something."
But she also learned that "Sometimes you gotta get your foot up their rear
and drag em in." A common theme among the students who stepped forward was to "not let peers' irresponsibility derail your work." One of these
student leaders reported learning, "You can't let other people affect you, and
make you negative; you just gotta be you; sometimes you've just gotta hold
your breath and do it." Another said, "I've never thought of this until now,
but you work as a team individually. It's kinda neat. You do a lot of stuff individually that you're doing, not for yourself, but for everyone else." So students described themselves as learning to listen and work with others, but
not at the cost of setting aside their own views, or letting the work be
dragged down by others' irresponsibility.

The Development of Initiative

What the youth were telling us, then, was that they were developing new
ways of thinking and acting that transcended the experience of the present moment and their own personal perspective. Out of their struggle with
the challenges of the task, they appeared to be acquiring a more elaborated view of time that included the future—the days ahead—as a field for
the strategic allocation of effort. They were developing a way of operating
that incorporated other people as independent centers of intentionality. It
appeared to us that they were gaining use of new abstract concepts—effort
as quantity, emotion, other people's intentions—that allowed them to coordinate multiple levels and systems of activity. Acquisition of these initiative skills may contribute to the findings of others that participation in
youth programs predicts later educational achievement (Eccles & Barber,
1999; Marsh, 1992) and adult occupational attainment (Glancy, Willits,

& Farrell, 1986). As a result of participation in FFA and the day camp planning, these youth appeared to be gradually acquiring skills of thinking and acting that made them more able to organize effort toward the achievement of long-term goals.

Before examining the adult leaders' role in supporting this learning, it is important to register appropriate cautions. The methods we used are those of theory building; further research is required to definitively test the processes of change suggested here. We have only studied one exceptional program, and our data come from a subset of youth who volunteered to organize the day camp. Even within this group, we observed variations between those youth in leadership roles—who most often articulated these advanced initiative insights—and those playing supportive roles, who were learning at levels that may prepare them to jump up to the advanced level the next year.

We also want to point out that there are additional dimensions to these developmental changes that we have not been able to cover in this limited space (Friedman & Scholnick, 1997). One is the role of brain development, a topic about which little is yet currently known.[2] Another is the role of confidence, perceived control, self-efficacy, and similar motivational constructs. Current research on planful action sees these motivational constructs in ways that are interrelated with what we have discussed: less as dispositional traits, and more as changeable beliefs about the efficacy of goal-directed action. Research shows that people who possess these beliefs—this confidence—act in more efficacious ways. In turn, experiencing success is likely to strengthen these beliefs, and lack of success may undermine this confidence (Skinner, 1997). In this vein, a number of the Clarkston youth preparing the day camp described gaining confidence as an important part of their learning experience. One additional observation was that this confidence was not just an individual quality, it was negotiated and shared within the group. Thus, the scaffolding that group members provided for each other's learning was not just in learning cognitive skills but also in building each others' confidence in their ability to succeed in this project—as well as in other projects in the future.

WHAT THE ADULT LEADERS DID

The students experienced this learning as coming from themselves. But Mr. Baker and Mr. Jensen played important, partly invisible, roles in facilitating

---

[2]Recent research shows that the frontal cortex of the brain, which plays an important role in self-regulation and planning, is still developing in adolescence (Gauvain, 2001). This may explain some of the limits in young people's initiative skills, but evidence consistently shows that brain growth and experience reciprocally influence each other (Shonkoff & Phillips, 2000). So the fact that this region of the brain is changing suggests that it may be particularly important to give youth opportunities to develop the capabilities located in this region.

it. The Clarkston advisors faced two objectives, which were not always compatible. They wanted to help youth to learn and they also wanted to be certain that the day camp was a success. The students' learning of initiative skills, as we have just seen, stemmed in great part from holding responsibility, from having ownership for the challenges of the preparation process. Yet, as began to happen midway through the planning, when youth hold sole responsibility, their work can stall or become disorganized, which can undermine their motivation and the success of the project. The horns of the paradox for adult leaders, then, are that if they take over control, youth will not learn, but if they give youth total control, things may get off track (see also Camino, 2000). By analyzing the data we obtained from the advisors, the youth, and our observations, it became apparent that Mr. Baker and Mr. Jensen had developed expertise in a number of techniques that helped them avoid both horns of this paradox and achieve both objectives. We describe four that were particularly effective in allowing the members to maintain ownership while keeping the preparation process on track.

One of these techniques was *following youths' lead*. In the interviews with the advisors, one of their repeated mantras was: "It's their camp." This technique was most apparent in the brainstorming phase, when they almost entirely stood aside and supported the students' development of ideas for the day camp. But the advisors continued to use this approach through to the final working meeting, when Mr. Baker was still asking members' permission before giving help. The students were very aware that responsibility for setting the direction for the camp and for other FFA activities was being given to them. As one youth said, "Rarely, rarely, rarely, do the advisors just say 'Here's how it's gonna be,' which is nice." Another said, "That's the neat thing about it, you're never really truly forced to do something. It's, 'do you wanna do this? Or, hey Mr. Baker, Mr. Jensen, I wanna do this.' And then they help you, they help you do it."

This technique builds students' ownership, but requires considerable restraint from the advisors. In the words of Mr. Baker, "By allowing them to come up with ideas, they *become* their ideas." However, giving youth this much authority—to potentially mess things up—is not easy. In the middle phase, our observer reported that *he* felt quite anxious that things were falling apart, an anxiety that Mr. Baker did not appear to share. We observed in other FFA activities that Mr. Baker was not adverse to letting youth fail, even when it meant that their program received a lower ranking in a competition. He viewed failure as an opportunity for youth to learn, and said that the adult advisors have to "check our egos at the door." Although the advisors progressively shifted to more assertive techniques in the middle phase—because letting the students fail was not an option for the day camp—they remained committed to following and supporting the directions set by the youth.

A second technique they used was *asking guiding questions*. In the early part of the planning process these were often questions that helped youth clarify suggestions or filter out ideas that were not likely to work, like "What would be the way to do it?" and "How feasible is a field trip?" Their questions directed the youth to evaluate whether a proposed activity would be appropriate, fun, interesting, approved by parents, and so on. In the middle and final phases, these questions became more focused on the preparation process, on strategies: "How can we find out everyone's schedule?," "How many practices will you need?," and "Who's going to be responsible for that?" The advisors posed these questions but did not offer their answers, although they may often have known good answers based on their past experience.

The advisors' described using this technique very intentionally. Mr. Baker said he used questioning to "Make them see where we need to be heading, and to let them come up with those directions." The virtue he saw in this technique was, "Even though we're bringing the questions up, it's still their idea and their project." In some cases, he pointed out, the youth come up with completely original ideas, for example, the suggestion of recruiting children for the camp through visits to their classrooms. Mr. Baker also described use of questions for a "debugging" process, where he and Mr. Jensen ask trouble-shooting questions and help the youth anticipate things that might go wrong with their plans. In some cases, the nature of the advisors' questions suggests an acceptable range of answers, nonetheless the youth were being given the responsibility for providing the answer—and also for following up on the answer. Questioning is a nonthreatening technique that, when used well, can provoke youth to think more deeply and strategically while keeping ownership with the youth.

What is most interesting is that we could see the youth internalize this questioning process. Toward the end of the day camp preparations, the observer recorded several youths beginning to pose these kinds of questions. In the final interview, one of the girls reported understanding exactly what the advisors were doing: "They are like, 'Where are you getting the tools, where you getting money, where you getting ... you know?' They do what they need to do to keep our heads on straight."

When it became clear that the youth were having difficulty structuring their work, the advisors deployed a third technique, *providing intermediate structures*. This included partial or mediating structures that helped organize the group, helped the students break their work into manageable steps, and provided realistic goals and deadlines. Mr. Baker's suggestion that they create committees for each day of the camp helped overcome the gridlock of everyone (or no one) being responsible for everything. One of the youth commented that this helped them "split up the responsibilities and come together as a team." When these committees got stuck, the advisors recommended that each should create a lesson plan, mapped out in 15-minute blocks. This framework was open enough that it still allowed the youth to fill in their own activity and feel a sense of ownership, but it provided a structure to help focus the members' planning. When needed, the advisors also provided conceptual structures to help the youth shape what should go in each block. As one student described: "There's like a verbal outline they told us, 'You're gonna wanna discuss this, this, and this, and you're gonna wanna have points, you know so they [the children] can go home and tell their parents, 'This is what I learned and this is what we did,' not 'This is what they told us.'"

The students appeared to welcome these intermediate structures as timely scaffolding. One boy said the advisors were making sure "that we are not trying to do something that is out of our power." The literature on youth organizations stresses the importance of providing challenge to youth (Gambone & Arbreton, 1997), but challenge that is beyond someone's skills creates anxiety (Csikszentmihalyi, 1975) and youth can feel betrayed if adults let them crash and burn in a situation that is beyond their abilities (Camino, 2000). These intermediate structures helped fit challenges to the limits in adolescents' initiative skills that we discussed at the beginning of the chapter. They helped youth divide up future time and the planning process into manageable chunks.

The fourth technique employed by the advisors was *monitoring to keep the youth on track*. In the early stages, this mainly took the form of observing and asking questions. As one student reported, "I think they're just watching over us right now and making sure we're getting it done, but they're letting us decide what we wanna do and make our own decisions." Another member said, "They kinda let us just take over, but they're there just in case." Monitoring sometimes took the form of behind-the-scenes support, done so as to be transparent to the students, such as verifying with a phone call that arrangements for the purchase of potted flowers had been made.

When the group was not progressing satisfactorily, the advisors intervened in more direct ways, as happened toward the end of the middle phase when they became more assertive in checking up on members' work. A student said, "We kind of ran around like chickens with our heads cut off for a while, but they got us back in line, got things organized." Although Mr. Baker has more of a laissez-faire approach to leadership, Mr. Jensen is a stronger advocate for intervention: "If things aren't coming together the way I think they should, eventually I'm going to step in and do whatever I have to do. You have to step in before it's too late to get something accomplished. Especially if we're dealing with public kinds of issues."

Over 8 years of working together, the two advisors have developed effective rapport, and both agreed that greater intervention was needed to get the day camp preparation on track.

This shift to greater adult control can be hazardous. When adults take over a project that was being run by youth, the youth can feel embarrassed, angry, and disempowered (Camino, 2000; Soep, 1997). When the FFA advisors became more assertive, it did threaten the sense of ownership for a couple of students. One reported:

> If they know something wasn't done, they'll call us in the morning to ask us "did you do this yet," "have you gotten this done yet?" We'll say "No" or we just won't answer the phone and they know that it hasn't been done. They'll do it themselves sometimes, then they get upset but it's what you get when you deal with high-schoolers [laughs].

What is interesting here is that this student was aware of the paradox the advisors were facing. She knew their intervention was needed but also expressed some bitterness at being pressured, at having authority taken away from her. Most students, however, accepted the advisors' assistance, indeed, they recognized that the advisors were helping them regain control. In the final interview, all, including this student, felt that it had been *their* [the students'] camp. In effect what the advisors had done was to shore up the weak points in the preparation process, so that the youth could maintain a sense of ownership *and* create a successful day camp. Their intervention maintained a channel for the students' exercise of agency, and it kept the youth in the envelope of working toward a successful camp.

Take Home Messages on Adult Leadership

The key to the advisors' use of these techniques, we believe, is that they were adjusted to the capabilities of the youth. As we have discussed, most adolescents' have a constrained sense of future time that limits their ability to plan, or feel urgency that things need to get done early. The intermediate structures the advisors created—such as setting deadlines for specific tasks to be done—were introduced when needed to help break future time into more tangible pieces, fitted to the abilities of these youth. Adolescents are also just beginning to be able to think about other people as centers of thought and feeling. Mr. Baker's suggestion that the work be divided into committees permitted the students to narrow their focus to thinking about and coordinating their actions with the thoughts and intentions of the smaller number of people in their group.

Each technique was deployed and adjusted according to what students could handle. For example, in a study of preadolescents in Little League teams, Heath and Langman (1994) described coaches' use of questioning to get the children simply to remember and rehearse the basic rules of the game. These FFA advisors posed questions at a more advanced level, which challenged youth to think about complex problems and come up with original solutions. As we have mentioned, we were struck by how little these youth talked about long-term strategies, about the *process* of preparation for the day camp. The questions the advisors used often pointed the youth toward strategic issues, and the intermediate structures they introduced provided strategic scaffolding. The leaders helped bridge skills that were in a developmental stage for these youth.

A lesson of our case study is that adult leaders who want to promote the development of initiative and teamwork need to keep the limited capabilities of youth in mind and be prepared to make adjustments to fit these capabilities. By allowing members to go the edge of the challenges they could handle, these two expert adult leaders provided optimal conditions for the youth to develop initiative skills. But adult leaders also need to be ready to provide intermediate structures and "shoring up," so that participants experience themselves in a channel of opportunities and challenges within their capability. They need to steer a course between supporting youth ownership and restrained intervention.

Of course, there are other techniques for maintaining this channel besides the four described here. Other adult leaders may balance control and youth ownership through different methods. Indeed, these two FFA advisors used additional techniques to support students' participation in the competitions that make up much of the chapter's activity. We observed that, as new opportunities arose, they had a special knack for fitting individual youth to specific challenges and roles. They spoke of looking for the "hook" that would get each individual involved, whether it be the student's skills in welding, a strong competitive drive, or interest in educating children. Another effective tool they used was cultivating a group culture that was passed from older to younger youth. This included a group spirit, ways of thinking, and aphorisms about how FFA members handled different situations. These techniques, we emphasize, may vary depending on the personality and style of the leader, as well as those of individual youth. As we have suggested, Mr. Baker and Mr. Jensen had somewhat different approaches, and one or the other was sometimes more successful for a given youth.

The techniques adult leaders use will also vary across different types of programs and program contexts. The position of these advisors as teachers at the school gave them leverage that adult leaders in community-based organizations do not have—they saw many of the FFA members every day in their agriculture classes, and it was undoubtedly easier to get students to stay after school for an activity than it is to get them to come to a community center. The advantage of being in a school was evident in the difficulties with "no shows" that emerged for the day camp planning once school was out. In addition, we have focused here on a collaborative project, but initiative development also can be supported in programs where students work toward individual goals, such as may happen in an arts or gymnastics program. We are now studying additional programs to understand the development of initiative, as well as other domains of growth across a range of programmatic and ecological contexts.

The essential ingredient of effective youth work, it is argued, is *intentionality* (Walker, Marczak, Blyth, & Bordon, chap. 18, this volume). Adult leaders need to be clear about their goals and develop a repertoire of methods for achieving these goals. When the goal is to promote development of initiative in youth, adults place themselves in what may sometimes seem like a paradoxical position of handing the intentionality over to the youth. But these beginning findings from our research shows that effective adult leaders develop methods for rising above this seeming paradox. They skillfully implement techniques that maintain a sense of ownership with the youth but also keep the youth in a channel of challenges, work, and growth that the youth can manage. Much evidence shows that, given the right support, young people can carry out quite remarkable projects (Heath & Smyth, 2000; Yates & Youniss, 1999). In so doing, they can develop important initiative skills for deliberately shaping their environment, a capability that is increasingly important to adults in the 21st century.

ACKNOWLEDGMENTS

We offer profuse thanks to Mr. Baker, Mr. Jensen, and the youth who shared their experiences with us, and to the William T. Grant Foundation for its support of this research.

REFERENCES

Brandstädter, J., & Lerner, R. M. (Eds.) (1999). *Action and self-development: Theory and research through the life span*. Thousand Oaks, CA: Sage.

Camino, L. A. (2000). Youth-adult partnerships: Entering new territory in community work and research. *Applied Developmental Science, 4*, 11–20.

Camino, L., & Zeldin, S. (2002). From periphery to center: Pathways for youth civic engagement in the day-to-day life of communities. *Applied Developmental Science, 6*, 213–220.

Csikszentmihalyi, M. (1975). *Beyond boredom and anxiety: The experience of play in work and games*. San Francisco: Jossey-Bass.

Dworkin, J. B., Larson, R., & Hansen, D. (2003). Adolescents' accounts of growth experiences in youth activities. *Journal of Youth and Adolescence, 32*, 17–26.

Eccles, J. S., & Barber, B. L. (1999). Student council, volunteering, basketball, or marching band: What kind of extracurricular involvement matters? *Journal of Adolescent Research, 14*, 10–43.

Elkind, D. (1967). Egocentrism in adolescence. *Child Development, 38*, 1025–1034.

Erikson, E. H. (1950). *Childhood and society*. New York: Norton.

Friedman, S. L., & Scholnick, E. K. (1997). An evolving "blueprint" for planning: Psychological requirements, task characteristics, and social-cultural influences. In S. L.

Friedman & E. K. Scholnick (Eds.), *The developmental psychology of planning: Why, how, and when to we plan?* (pp. 3–22). Mahwah, NJ: Lawrence Erlbaum Associates.

Frumkin, P. (2002). *On being nonprofit.* Cambridge: Harvard University Press.

Gambone, M. A., & Arbreton, A. J. A. (1997). *Safe havens: The contributions of youth organizations to healthy adolescent development.* Philadelphia, PA: Public/Private Ventures.

Gauvain, M. (1999). Everyday opportunities for the development of planning skills: Sociocultural and family influences. In A. Göncü (Ed.), *Children's engagement in the world: Sociocultural perspectives* (pp. 173–201). New York: Cambridge University Press.

Gauvain, M. (2001). *The social context of development.* New York: Guilford.

Gauvain, M., & Huard, R. D. (1999). Family interaction, parenting style, and the development of planning: A longitudinal analysis using archival data. *Journal of Family Psychology, 13,* 75–92.

Gauvain, M., & Perez, S. (in press). Not all hurried children are the same: Children's participation in planning their after-school activities. In J. E. Jacobs & P. Klaczynski (Eds.), *The development of judgment and decision-making in children and adolescents.* Mahwah, NJ: Lawrence Erlbaum Associates.

Glancy, M., Willits, F., & Farrell, P. (1986). Adolescent activities and adult success and happiness: Twenty-four years later. *Sociology and Social Research, 70,* 242–250.

Gollwitzer, P. M. (1999). Implementation intentions: Strong effects of simple plans. *American Psychologist, 54*(7), 493–503.

Habermas, T., & Bluck, S. (2000). Getting a life: The emergence of the life story in adolescence. *Psychological Bulletin, 126,* 748–769.

Haith, M. M. (1997). The development of future thinking as essential for the emergence of skill in planning. In S. L. Friedman & E. K. Scholnick (Eds.), *The developmental psychology of planning: Why, how, and when to we plan?* (pp. 25–42). Mahwah, NJ: Lawrence Erlbaum Associates.

Hansen, D., Larson, R., & Dworkin, J. (2003). What adolescents learn in organized youth activities: A survey of self-reported developmental experiences. *Journal of Research on Adolescence, 13,* 25–55.

Heath, S. B., & Langman, J. (1994). Shared thinking and the register of coaching. In D. Biber & E. Finegan (Eds.), *Sociolinguistic perspectives on register* (pp. 82–105). New York: Oxford University Press.

Heath, S. B. (1998). Working through language. In S. M. Hoyle & C. T. Adger (Eds.), *Kids talk: Strategic language use in later childhood* (pp. 217–240). New York: Oxford University Press.

Heath, S. B. (1999). Dimensions of language development: Lessons from older children. In A. S. Masten (Ed.), *Cultural processes in child development: The Minnesota symposium on child psychology* (Vol. 29, pp. 59–75). Mahwah, NJ: Lawrence Erlbaum Associates.

Heath, S. B., & Smyth, L. (2000). *Art show: Youth and community development.* Washington, DC: Partners for Livable Communities.

Holland, A., & Andre, T. (1987). Participation in extra-curricular activities in secondary school: What is known, what needs to be known? *Review of Educational Research, 57,* 437–466.

Keating, D. P. (1980). Thinking processes in adolescence. In J. Adelson (Ed.), *Handbook of adolescence* (pp. 211–246). New York: Wiley-Interscience.

Larson, R. (1985). Emotional scenarios in the writing process—an examination of young writers' affective experiences. In M. Rose (Ed.), *When the writer can't write: Studies of disruption in the composing process* (pp. 19–42). New York: Guilford.

Larson, R. (2000). Toward a psychology of positive youth development. *American Psychologist, 55*, 170–183.

Larson, R. (2002). Globalization, societal change, and new technologies: What they mean for the future of adolescence. *Journal of Research on Adolescence, 12*(1), 1–30.

Larson, R., Clore, G., & Wood, G. (1999). The emotions of romantic relationships: Do they wreak havoc on adolescents? In W. Furman, B. B. Brown, & C. Feiring (Eds.), *Romantic relationships in adolescence* (pp. 19–49), New York: Cambridge University Press.

Larson, R., Wilson, S., Brown, B. B., Furstenberg, F. F., & Verma, S. (2002). Changes in adolescents' interpersonal experiences: Are they being prepared for adult relationships in the 21st century? *Journal of Research on Adolescence, 12*(1), 31–68.

Lerner, R., & Busch-Rossnagel, N. (1981). *Individuals as producers of their development.* New York: Academic.

Marsh, H. W. (1992). Extracurricular activities: Beneficial extension of the traditional curriculum or subversion of academic goals? *Journal of Educational Psychology, 84*(4), 553–562.

Mascolo, M., Fisher, K., & Neimeyer, R. (1999). The dynamic codevelopment of intentionality, self, and social relations. In J. Brandstädter & R. M. Lerner (Eds.), *Action and self-development: Theory and research through the life span* (pp. 133–166). Thousand Oaks, CA: Sage.

McLaughlin, M. (2000). *Community counts: How youth organizations matter for youth development.* Washington, DC: Public Education Network.

Nurmi, J. (1991). How do adolescents see their future? A review of the development of future orientation and planning. *Developmental Review, 11*, 1–59.

Piaget, J. (1929). *The child's conception of the world.* Totowa, NJ: Littlefield, Adams, & Co.

Piaget, J. (1954). *Construction of reality in the child.* New York: Basic.

Radziszewska, B., & Rogoff, B. (1988). Influence of adult and peer collaborators on children's planning skills. *Developmental Psychology, 24*, 840–848.

Radziszewska, B., & Rogoff, B. (1991). Children's guided participation in planning imaginary errands with skilled adult or peer partners. *Developmental Psychology, 27*, 381–389..

Rogoff, B. (1998). Cognition as a collaborative process. In W. Damon, D. Kuhn, & R. Siegler (Eds.), *Handbook of child psychology* (5th ed., Vol. 2, pp. 679–744). New York: Wiley.

Selman, R. (1980). *The growth of interpersonal understanding.* New York: Academic.

Shonkoff, J. P., & Phillips, D. A. (Eds.). (2000). *Rethinking nature and nurture. From neurons to neighborhoods.* National Research Council. Washington, DC: National Academy Press.

Silbereisen, R. K., Eyferth, K., & Rudinger, G. (Eds.). (1996). *Development as action in context: Problem behavior and normal youth development.* New York: Springer-Verlag.

Skinner, E. A. (1997). Planning and perceived control. In S. L. Friedman & E. K. Scholnick (Eds.), *The developmental psychology of planing: Why, how, and when to we plan?* (pp. 263–284). Mahwah, NJ: Lawrence Erlbaum Associates.

Soep, E. (1997). Walking on water and knocking on doors. *New Designs for Youth Development, 13*(4), 32–35.

Strauss, A., & Corbin, J. (1998). *Basics of qualitative research: Techniques and procedures for developing grounded theory* (2nd ed.). Thousand Oaks, CA: Sage.

Taylor, S. J., & Bogdan, R. (1998). *Introduction to qualitative research methods: A guidebook and resource* (3rd ed.). New York: Wiley.

Vygotsky, L. S. (1978). *Mind and society.* Cambridge, MA: Harvard University Press.

Yates, M., & Youniss, J. (Eds.). (1999). *Roots of civic identity.* Cambridge, England: Cambridge University Press.

9

Benefits of Activity Participation: The Roles of Identity Affirmation and Peer Group Norm Sharing

Bonnie L. Barber
Margaret R. Stone
James E. Hunt
University of Arizona

Jacquelynne S. Eccles
University of Michigan

The importance of out-of-school time for healthy development has been stressed in recent reports by foundations and researchers (e.g., Carnegie Corporation, 1992; Eccles & Gootman, 2002; Eccles & Templeton, 2002; Larson, 2000). There is good evidence that participating in extracurricular activities is associated with both short- and long-term indicators of positive development during adolescence. Previous research, however, tells us less about the reasons for these associations. Scholars have suggested that activities can (a) help adolescents acquire both the educational credentials and the cognitive skills needed for adult work roles, (b) work through issues of personal and social identity, (c) acquire the interpersonal skills needed to form healthy social relationships and to succeed in the world of work, and (d) refine the emotional and behavioral skills needed to become fully functioning, independent adults.

In this chapter, we discuss two mechanisms that may help explain the connection between activities and positive development: identity pursuit and affirmation, and peer group norm-sharing. To explain the connection between activities and positive development, we have proposed a synergistic system connecting activity involvement with identity exploration and peer group composition (Barber, Eccles, & Stone, 2001; Eccles & Barber, 1999). In keeping with organismic principles (Cairns, 1996), and systems theory (Ford & Lerner, 1992), we think that such a system involves bidirectional transactions between subsystems operating at several levels. Individual level systems involving values, expectancies, and identities would thus interact reciprocally with social systems and subcultural systems of meaning and values. Specifically, we believe that enhanced outcomes result for adolescents who experience a confluence of activity participation, activity-based identity adoption, and a benign peer context. Previous research, including our own, has demonstrated the pervasive connections between each of these three factors and numerous outcomes. The story we unfold is mostly one of additive main effects, but we wanted, as well, to be sensitive to the possibility of contingencies between factors that would be suggested by possible interactions.

IDENTITY—THE ROLE OF SELF-BELIEFS IN ACTIVITY PARTICIPATION CHOICES

Researchers in leisure studies emphasize the importance of leisure activities that provide a forum in which to explore and express one's identity and passion (Kleiber, 1999). The activities adolescents choose can reflect core aspects of their self-beliefs. Over the past 20 years, Eccles and her colleagues have developed and tested a model of the motivational factors influencing achievement behaviors and goals, including educational choices and recreational activity participation (see Eccles, 1987; Eccles et al., 1983; Meece, Parsons, Kaczala, Goff, & Futterman, 1982). The model links achievement-related choices such as whether or not to participate in sports or activities directly to two sets of beliefs: the individual's expectations for success in, and sense of personal efficacy for, the various options, and the importance or value the individual attaches to the available options.

For example, consider activity participation decisions. The model predicts that people will be most likely to participate in activities that they think they can master and that they value. Expectations for success (and a sense of domain-specific, personal efficacy) depend on the confidence the individual has in his or her abilities and on estimations of the difficulty of the activity. These beliefs have been shaped over time by the individual's experiences and by a subjective interpretation of those experiences (e.g., does the person think that her or his successes are a consequence of high ability or lots of hard work?). Likewise, the value of a particular activity to the individual is assumed to be influenced by several factors. For example, does the adolescent enjoy doing the sport or activity? Does the activity validate the adolescent's identity? Is the activity seen as instrumental in meeting one of the individual's long- or short-range goals?

One additional feature of this model is important to highlight: the assumption that achievement-related decisions, such as the decision to try out for an organized sport team or to switch to the swim team rather than play baseball, are made within the context of a complex social reality that presents each individual with a wide variety of choices; each with both long range and immediate consequences. Consequently, the choice is often between two or more positive options or between two or more options that have both positive and negative components. For example, the decision to join the swim team is typically made in the context of other important decisions such as whether to play in the school band or get an after-school job, or whether to participate in an activity with one's best friend.

Over the last several years, we have been conducting longitudinal work to investigate how useful the model is in predicting involvement in sports, social activities, instrumental music, and academic subjects. The model works very well in each of these domains. It is especially powerful in predicting individual differences in voluntary leisure type activities like sports. The evidence supporting the power of expectancies and values as both direct effects and as mediators of gender differences in behavioral choices is quite strong. Using longitudinal data, we found that gender differences in expectation-related and value-related self-beliefs explained the gender difference in sports participation at both 10th and 12th grades (Eccles, Barber, & Jozefowicz, 1998). Males' greater participation in sports was explained by their self-beliefs. Males thought they were more able at sports, thought participating in sports was more useful, and enjoyed participating in sports more than females.

In addition to directing choices about selecting activities, self-beliefs predict persistence in activities. In our research, we have studied adolescents who were active in sports and who perceived themselves to be among the very best at sports in the 7th grade, and whose highly positive self-perceptions of sport competence were corroborated by the high ratings from their mothers or their teachers. Girls were underrepresented in the group of adolescents who labeled themselves as highly competent in sports (11% of all females and 30% of all males categorized as "Competent" based on their 7th-grade self and parent or teacher ratings). Gender differences in sport participation of even these talented adolescents increased over time. By the 10th grade, 30% of the Competent females were no longer involved in competitive sports at school, compared to only 13% of the Competent males. By the 12th grade, 46% of the Competent athletes had dropped out of organized sport activities; again this was more true for the females than the males (55% of females compared to 41% of males). We assessed the relation of an array of 10th grade psychological and contextual predictors with continued sports participation in the senior year of high school. Consistent with the Eccles expectancy-value model, 10th grade ratings of enjoyment, perceived importance, and self-concept of ability in sports predicted persistence in sports 2 years later for both males and females (Barber, Jacobson, Eccles, & Horn, 1997). We imagine that similar processes may operate in nonathletic youth programs. Those who enjoy and value program activities are more likely to maintain participation, whereas those who find the experience irrelevant, boring, or lacking in challenge may opt out.

EMERGING ADOLESCENT IDENTITIES

We concur with Erikson's (1963) notion that voluntary participation in discretionary activities stimulates assessment of one's talents, values, interests, and place in the social structure. More rigidly structured arenas of participation such as school, work, and church may provide less freedom to explore and express identity options than discretionary activities. Therefore, voluntary participation in discretionary extracurricular activities provides an opportunity for adolescents to be personally expressive and to communicate to both themselves and others that "This is who I am" or "This is what I believe I am meant to do." Eccles and colleagues refer to this aspect of activities as *attainment value*—the value of an activity to demonstrate to oneself and to others that one is the kind of person one most hopes to be. Eccles (1987), for example, argued that gender-role identity influences activity participation because activities vary in the extent to which they provide the opportunity to explore one's masculine or feminine self. Eccles and Barber (1999) argued that activities allow one both to express and to refine one's identities.

Sports provides a very good example of these processes. Engaging in sports allows one to demonstrate that one is an athlete or a "Jock" and to explore whether being an athlete or a Jock is a comfortable identity. The decision to engage in sports should be influenced by the extent to which one places high value on being athletic or being a Jock. Engaging in sports should also facilitate the internalization of an identity as an athlete or a Jock. To the extent that one both develops a Jock identity and engages in sports, one is likely to pick up other characteristics associated with the athletic peer culture in one's social world. We explored these hypotheses with our longitudinal Michigan Study of Life Transitions (MSALT) data.

Eccles and Barber (1999) showed different patterns of outcomes, depending on the type of activity adolescents were involved in and their social identity group. Both involvement in prosocial activities and having a

"Brain" identity were associated with low alcohol and drug use, higher self-esteem, and positive academic outcomes. These adolescents also had the most academically oriented peer group and the fewest friends who drank or used drugs. The Jocks were most involved in sports; the "Princesses" reported the highest rates of involvement in school spirit and governance activities. Both involvement in sports and school spirit activities and having a Jock or a Princess social identity were associated with a mixed pattern of outcomes: positive academic outcomes and high alcohol use. Not surprisingly, the majority of these adolescents' friends were both academically oriented and regularly drank alcohol. The "Criminals" were not generally engaged in organized extracurricular activities, were involved in risky behaviors such as alcohol and drug use, and had the highest proportion of friends who both drank and used drugs. The Criminals' most common activity was sports.

Youniss and Smollar (1985) argued that adolescents develop a social sense of self as well as an individual and autonomous sense of self during adolescence. In addition, Brown and colleagues have suggested that adolescents develop socially construed representations of their peers' identities, or "crowd" identities, which serve not only as preexisting, symbolic categories through which they can recognize potential friends or foes, tormenters, collaborators, or competitors (Brown, Mory, & Kinney, 1994) but also as public identities for themselves that are recognized and accepted by peers (Stone & Brown, 1998). These social identities have been linked to both positive and risky outcomes (Barber et al., 2001; Brown, Dolcini, & Leventhal, 1997), but we do not know whether self-perceptions of belonging to particular social crowds in high school might influence one's experiences in particular activities. Of central importance from a person–environment fit perspective, we do not know if those students who perceive themselves to be Jocks or Princesses are those who benefit most from participating in those activities that validate their self-images and foster integration into relevant social traditions such as sports or cheerleading. Our recent work focuses on these types of questions. We describe our findings in this chapter.

PEER GROUP NORMS

Activities help structure one's peer group; adolescents in extracurricular activities have more academic friends and fewer friends who skip school and use drugs than adolescents who do not participate in activities (Eccles & Barber, 1999). In turn, having more academic and less risky friends predicts other positive outcomes for adolescents. Conversely, being part of a peer network that includes a high proportion of youth who engage in, and encourage, risky behaviors predicts increased involvement in risky behaviors and decreased odds of completing high school and going on to college.

Some activities facilitate membership in positive peer networks; other activities facilitate membership in more problematic peer networks (Dishion, Poulin, & Burraston, 2001; Stattin, Kerr, Mahoney, Persson, & Magnusson, chap. 10, this volume). This confluence of peers and activity participation has also been described as a *leisure culture* (Eckert, 1989). The critical mediating role of peer affiliations in the link between extracurricular activities and youth outcomes has also been documented by Eder and Parker (1987), Kinney (1993), Mahoney and Cairns (1997), and Youniss, McLellan, Su, & Yates (1999). These researchers suggest that peer affiliations influence development, either positively or negatively, through the social norms associated with the peer group culture, through reduction in social alienation, and through acquisition of improved social skills. Such suggestions are quite consistent with what is believed to be true about peer influence more generally (e.g., Brown, 1990; Dishion et al., 2001; Kinney, 1993).

Together, peer group membership and activity involvement are also linked to identity exploration because both are linked to adolescents' sense of belonging to a particular type of peer group and having a particular activity-based persona (e.g., being a Jock or a Brain). The peer crowd prototypes associated with one's activities are potentially powerful influences on the content of one's emerging personal and social identities. For example, athletes are more likely than those who do not play sports to consider themselves to be Jocks (Eccles & Barber, 1999). In fact, attaining the typically favored male social identity of Jock may even require participation in several sports (Brown, 1990). Involvement in a sport also provides the opportunity to become integrated into the cultural milieu connected to being an athlete (Fine, 1987), thus increasing the likelihood of engaging in other behaviors associated with this leisure culture.

THE MICHIGAN STUDY
OF ADOLESCENT LIFE TRANSITIONS:
LINKS BETWEEN IDENTITY AND ACTIVITIES

MSALT began with a cohort of 6th graders drawn from 10 school districts in southeastern Michigan in 1984. We have followed approximately 1,800 of these youth through eight waves of data collection: two while they were in the 6th grade, two while they were in the 7th grade, one while they were in 10th grade, one while they were in 12th grade, one in 1992–1993 when most were 21 to 22 years old, and one in 1996–1997, when most were 25 to 26 years old. The vast majority are White and come from working and middle-class families. Many of the families worked in the automobile industry when we began the study and have been adversely affected by the changes in this industry over the last 10 to 15 years.

The data were collected via self-administered questionnaires completed either at school during regular school hours or at home. The 7th-grade waves were collected in the adolescents' math classrooms. The 10th- and 12th-grade waves were collected in a large common room—usually the lunchroom. The post high-school waves were completed at home using a mailed questionnaire. In addition, complete school records from Grade 5 to Grade 12 were collected for participants; these included grades, absences, and courses taken.

Measures of Activity Participation and Identity

Activity Involvement. At 10th grade, adolescents were provided with a list of 16 sports and 30 school and community clubs and organizations and asked to check all activities in which they participated. To measure sports participation, we asked: Do you compete in any of the following school teams (varsity, junior varsity, or other organized school program) *outside of PE?* Sports included in the checklist are listed in Table 9.1. To measure participation in nonsport activities, we asked: Do you participate in any of the following activities or clubs at school? Activities included in the checklist are listed in Table 9.2. We also asked about a range of activities outside of school: Do you participate in any of the following clubs or activities outside of school? Activities included in this checklist included: Scouts/Girls or Boys, Clubs/Ys, 4–H, Junior Achievement, Political campaign, Church groups, and Volunteer/service work. In order to understand patterns related to participation in various types of activities, we grouped the extracurricular activities into five categories: (a) *Prosocial Activities*—church group involvement and/or participation in volunteer and community service type activities; (b) *Team Sports*—participation on one or more school teams; (c) *Performing Arts*—participation in school band, drama, and/or dance; (d) *School Involvement*—participation in student government, pep club, and/or cheerleading; and (e) *Academic Clubs*—participation in debate, foreign language, math, or chess clubs, science fair, or tutoring in academic subjects.

Identity Group. *The Breakfast Club* (Hughes, 1985) was a prominent film when our study participants were in the 10th grade. We asked the participants to indicate which of five characters (the Princess, the Jock, the Brain, the Basket Case, or the Criminal) was most like them. We told them to ignore the gender of the character and base their selection on the type of person each character was. Twenty-eight percent selected the Jock identity, 40% the Princess, 12% the Brain, 11% the Basket Case, and 9% the Criminal. In this section, we summarize our findings of links between activity participation and self-identification into one of the five *Breakfast Club* character types.

TABLE 9.1

Percentage in Sports Activities Who Profess Each Social Identity for Each Gender (All Measured in 10th Grade)

Females	n	Princess	Jock	Brain	Basket Case	Criminal	Chi Square
Softball	94	43	**35**	9	7	6	54.898***
Basketball	55	38	**38**	13	7	4	37.812***
Volleyball	91	41	**30**	11	12	7	31.775***
Baseball	18	39	11	11	11	**28**	25.522***
Track/Cross-Country	63	52	**29**	14	5	0	23.394***
Football	16	50	13	6	6	**25**	17.979**
Soccer	19	37	**42**	11	5	5	16.019**
Cheerleading	66	71	12	6	9	2	7.372
Swimming/Diving	69	55	16	13	10	6	2.982
Tennis	53	58	17	11	11	2	2.271
Gymnastics	24	58	8	8	17	8	1.519
Any Sport	283	57	**22**	11	6	4	68.294***
Total Females	541	57	13	11	15	4	

Males	n	Princess	Jock	Brain	Basket Case	Criminal	Chi Square
Football	134	1	**78**	4	2	14	53.988***
Basketball	108	2	**81**	8	4	5	43.017***
Baseball	121	1	**78**	7	2	12	39.905***
Ice Hockey	37	0	**73**	3	3	22	11.659*
Wrestling	59	2	**73**	8	3	14	10.321*
Track/Cross-Country	66	3	70	14	5	9	7.370
Golf	37	0	65	24	3	8	4.697
Volleyball	21	5	62	5	5	24	4.090
Soccer	38	3	68	11	5	13	3.576
Tennis	35	3	63	23	0	11	3.515
Softball	11	0	64	9	0	27	2.915
Swimming/Diving	53	2	58	19	8	13	.756
Any Sport	280	2	**69**	*14*	5	*11*	73.237***
Total Males	400	3	55	20	7	16	

Note. Bold print highlights cells with percentages higher than would be expected by chance; italics highlights cells with lower percentages than expected.* $p < .05$. ** $p < .01$. *** $p < .001$. Activities with fewer than 10 participants within gender are not reported in table.

192

A series of chi-squared analyses revealed that social identities were differentially distributed across sports and activities (see Table 9.1). Not all athletes saw themselves as Jocks. Because sports was the most common activity, there were substantial numbers of sports team participants in each of the five *Breakfast Club* identity groups. Similar to their female nonathlete peers, female athletes often self-identified as Princesses (58% of gymnasts and 55% of swimmers) rather than Jocks (8% and 16%, respectively). The vast majority of cheerleaders saw themselves as Princesses (71%) rather than Jocks (12%). The highest proportion of female athletes who considered themselves to be Jocks participated in basketball, softball, soccer, volleyball, and track (see Table 9.1). A higher proportion of female Criminals than one would expect by chance was found in baseball and football. Overall, 22% of female athletes considered themselves to be Jocks, which is substantially higher than in the general female population (13%). Demonstrating remarkably high stability of participation for females with an identity linked to their sports involvement, 90% of the female Jocks were still playing sports 2 years later in Grade 12.

Male athletes frequently identified themselves as Jocks (69%); this was especially true for those who played basketball, football, baseball, ice hockey, and wrestling (see Table 9.1). These five sports also had the fewest participants who self-identified as Brains. Overall, male athletes were unlikely to label themselves as Brains (14% of athletes compared to 20% in the male population), with golf, tennis, and swimming being the only sports with substantial participation by Brains. There was moderate stability in sports play among the male Jocks, with 70% still playing sports in 12th grade.

Although the distribution of the five identities across the nonsport activities was less extreme, the patterns were what one would expect (see Table 9.2). Among the females, the Princesses were overrepresented in pep club and dance; the Brains were overrepresented in band and orchestra and underrepresented in dance. Among males, the Brains were overrepresented in foreign language clubs, math and science clubs, and band or orchestra; the Basket Cases and Princesses were overrepresented in drama. Although few males (3%) self-identified as Princesses, the male Princesses were also overrepresented in dance, foreign language club, and band.

We think that these data indicate an important variability across activities and sports. Not all extracurricular involvement is equivalent. In fact, even within the category of *sports*, the teams seem to vary considerably from each other in the types of students who participate, and the meanings attached to team membership. These differences are reflected in the identities of participants. One dimension that may be relevant for identity differences is the gender-appropriateness of the activity. Participation in gender-appropriate sports is linked to popularity, and better heterosocial status. For example, female gymnasts are rated by males as the most desirable athletes to date, and male football players are the most preferred dates

TABLE 9.2
Percentage of Females and Males in Activities
Who Profess Each Social Identity (All Measured in 10th Grade)

Females	n	Princess	Jock	Brain	Basket Case	Criminal	Chi Square
Dance	83	**75**	10	4	10	2	13.612**
Band/Orchestra	112	55	11	**17**	16	1	9.809*
Pep Club	71	**72**	11	8	8	0	9.776*
Foreign Language Club	70	66	4	14	14	1	8.307
Art	48	52	10	8	21	8	3.705
Student Government	65	65	14	8	12	2	3.174
Drama	78	56	9	12	21	3	3.174
Service Club	17	65	6	18	12	0	2.590
Math, Science Clubs	17	53	18	12	18	0	1.194
Any Organization	345	57	13	12	14	3	7.032
Total Females	541	57	13	11	16	4	

Males	n	Princess	Jock	Brain	Basket Case	Criminal	Chi Square
Drama	29	**14**	*24*	31	**21**	10	29.310***
Math, Science Clubs	26	*4*	*19*	**38**	8	**31**	15.120**
Band/Orchestra	52	**8**	*37*	**35**	8	13	14.647**
Foreign Language Club	19	**11**	*32*	**47**	5	5	14.625**
Dance	23	**13**	48	13	4	22	9.570*
Student Government	23	9	70	17	0	4	7.331
Service Club	12	8	33	33	8	17	3.344
Art	32	6	56	16	9	13	2.209
Any Organization	177	**5**	*44*	**27**	9	15	20.988***
Total Males	396	3	55	20	7	16	

Note. Bold print highlights cells with percentages higher than would be expected by chance; italics highlights cells with lower percentages than expected. * $p < .05$. ** $p < .01$. *** $p < .001$. Activities with fewer than 10 participants within gender are not reported in table.

for females (Holland & Andre, 1994). The Princess identity that accompanies gymnastics and cheerleading in our study is likely connected to more traditional gender role enactment and the typical body-type associated with those athletic activities. We are also interested in the social meaning of arts and performance activities like band and drama, which include the largest numbers of Basket Cases. Perhaps art is considered a more non-conformist activity, and marginalized youth may find a place for themselves in a performance art that would not be open to them in the more traditional activities of sports, cheerleading, or student government. Finally, some of the variability in identity across activities may reflect local or regional differences in values for different activities or sports—for example, wrestling may be the most popular and jocklike male sport in some regions, compared to football and basketball in our school districts. What does seem to be clear in these data is that we should expect differences in the benefits and risks that may accompany different activities.

As noted earlier, participation in activities has positive consequences for several aspects of adolescent functioning. Are these relations stronger if one's activities map well onto one's social identity? In keeping with our expectations regarding both additive and contingent effects, we used analyses of variance (ANOVA) to examine possible main and interactive effects of activity participation and identity group on outcomes. Although few interactions were significant, those that were supported the idea that consistency between one's identity and one's activities predicts better functioning than inconsistency. For example, those Jocks who were not involved in school sports had lower GPAs, $F (4, 829) = 3.2, p < .05; Ms = 213$ and 258, and felt more socially isolated, $F (4, 620) = 2.0, p < 1; Ms = 3.1$ and 2.9, than those who were (see Appendix for a description of measures). Similarly, those Princesses who were involved in school spirit activities reported higher levels of occupational identity formation in 10th grade than those who were not involved, $F (4, 893) = 2.8, p < .05; Ms = 6.0$ and 5.7. Based on these findings, we looked next at the consequences of dropping out of an activity that fit well with one's social identity. The clearest example of this connection in our data is in the domain of sports.

Negative Consequences of Dropping Out of Sports for the Jocks.   What are the consequences of dropping out of a highly valued activity such as sports that is also central to one's identity? Athletes who discontinue sports participation are likely to experience a reduction in the level of recognition they receive (e.g., praise from peers or coaches, or seeing their name in the school paper) for their participation in sports. In addition, these adolescents may have experienced the rejection associated with being cut from the team because they were not good enough. Both of these consequences are likely to undermine these athletes' self-concept of sports ability and this is what happened: Among our 10th grade athletes, those who discontinued sport participation by 12th grade started lower and declined in self-concept of sports ability, whereas those who continued to play were higher in 10th grade and increased by 12th grade (Hunt, 2002). These results suggest there is an identity affirming role of continued sports play in the domain of sports competence.

Dropping out of, versus continuing to play, sports also predicted changes in psychological adjustment from 10th to 12th grade. This association was complex, depending on both the value attached to sports in 10th grade and the participation in other extracurricular activities in 12th grade (Hunt, 2002). The continuing sport participants generally looked the best; they showed declines in depressed affect regardless of the value they placed on sports in 10th grade. The pattern was more complex for those adolescents who had dropped out of sports between 10th and 12th grade. For those sport dropouts who had placed high value on sports in 10th grade, depressed affect increased if they were not involved in any other extracurricular activity at 12th grade. In contrast, if they had replaced sports with another extracurricular activity in the 12th grade, they showed a decrease in depressed mood.

To further examine the value of sport to one's identity, we tested the convergence of sports play, activity participation, and Jock identity, and the three-way interaction was significant for depressed mood, $F(2, 318) = 5.17$, $p < .05$. The least positive changes in depressed mood from 10th to 12th grade were for those who did not see themselves as Jocks, but were still playing sports, and had no other activities, and for those who saw themselves as Jocks, were not playing, and had no other activities. The most positive changes, as with sports value, were for those who saw themselves as Jocks, and had taken up an activity after discontinuing sport play.

Dropping out of sports may also undermine attachment to school. Though a sense of belonging at school may result from a number of personal and social contextual factors, extracurricular activities are an especially likely path to attachment to one's school. They can facilitate connections in the school context that satisfy adolescents' developmental need for social relatedness, competence, and autonomy. Activities also contribute to one's identity as a valued member of the school community. Such links to school likely result in the findings that activity participants have higher academic focus (Marsh & Kleitman, 2002) and reduced likelihood of dropping out (Mahoney & Cairns, 1997). In our research, activity involvement predicts higher GPAs and future college attendance and greater school attachment, even after controlling for academic and social success (Eccles & Barber, 1999). This is particularly true for sports participation. Interestingly, discontinuing sports participation was not uniformly negative for our adolescents. The sports-school attachment link was particularly strong for those who highly valued sports (Barber, Jacobson, Horn, & Jacobs, 1997). For example, consistent with a person–environment fit framework, those students who placed a high value on sports in 10th grade and were no longer involved in sports in the 12th grade suffered the most dramatic decline in attachment to school. Those athletes who had not placed high value on sports in 10th grade and were no longer involved in sports in 12th grade did not experience this decline in school attachment (Barber et al., 1997). Thus, the extent to which sports were more central to one's identity influenced the connection between participation and school attachment.

Taken together, these findings suggest that one mechanism whereby sports and activities may have a positive influence is through their validation of identity. When activities confirm or support one's self-concept, they may promote psychological well-being and attachment to the school setting that provides the participation opportunities. When opportunities are withdrawn, unavailable to those who desire them, or a bad match to the interests of the adolescents, such support for identity exploration and affirmation are lacking. A second mechanism through which activities can influence positive development is through the social networks created through participation.

Activities as Peer Contexts

Activities link adolescents to certain types of peers and to changes in peer contexts. Adolescents who play on teams together or work together on projects or performances are likely to spend considerable amounts of "down time" together, developing new friendships; sharing experiences; discussing values, goals, and aspirations; and co-constructing activity-based peer cultures and identities (Brown, 1990; Youniss & Smollar, 1985).

We have examined the link between activity participation and the characteristics of one's friends at two time points during high school. At 10th and 12th grades, participants were asked about the proportion of their friends who were involved in risky behaviors and the proportion of their friends who were academically oriented. To assess the relative riskiness of their peer context, we asked them what proportion of their friends regularly drank alcohol, used drugs, and skipped school. To assess the relative academic orientation of their peers, we asked them what proportion of their friends planned to go to college and were doing well in school. Response options ranged from 1, *none*, to 5, *all*. We then computed a *risky peer context* variable and an *academic peer context* variable by deriving means for the risky and academic peer items. Next, each participant was coded as being in a relatively more risky or less risky peer context for each grade, depending on whether he or she had reported a proportion of peers above or below the mean proportion for that grade. We then classified our participants into four categories: (a) *consis-*

tently risky peer context, in a relatively more risky peer context at both 10th grade and 12th grade; (b) *increasingly risky peer context,* in a riskier peer context at 12th grade than at 10th grade; (c) *decreasingly risky peer context,* in a better peer context at 12th grade than at 10th grade; and (d) *consistently less risky peer context,* in a relatively less risky peer context at both grades. Analogous groups were created based on the variables computed at 10th and 12th grade for the relative academic orientation of participants' peer contexts.

We next conducted four sets of analyses. First, we assessed the differential distribution of peer context categories across five activity categories. Because the same adolescent can participate in more than one activity category, we ran separate chi-square analyses for each activity category. We conducted these analyses separately for females and males because particular types of activities are likely to have different meanings for each gender. Next, we assessed the peer context distributions for individual sports and activities. Third, we assessed the distribution of peer contexts across our five social identities. Finally, we assessed the relation of peer contexts to our major indicators of adolescent functioning in order to determine whether the characteristics of peer contexts were consistent with the types of outcomes associated with activity participation and activity-based social identities. Consistency in indicators of adolescent functioning across peer contexts, identities, and activities would support our hypothesis that the link between activity involvement and adolescent development reflects in part the synergistic influences of peer contexts, identity formation, and activity involvement.

More and Less Risky Peers.   For both females and males in prosocial activities, the distribution of risky high school peer contexts differed significantly from that expected by chance. In keeping with our consistency hypothesis, adolescents involved in prosocial activities were unusually likely to report being in a low risk peer context at both time points and particularly unlikely to report being in a high risk peer context at both time points (see Table 9.3). Looking within activity types, two specific activities were associated with being in increasingly risky peer contexts for males: football and swimming: Although 18% of males in general reported peer contexts that were increasingly risky, 29% of football players and 33% of swimmers did. Male football players were also underrepresented in consistently less risky peer contexts (26% vs. the marginal 36%) and decreasingly risky peer contexts (11% vs. 18%).

Interestingly and in contrast to the male swimmers, competitive swimming was associated with a relatively benign peer context for females, with 53% of female swimmers consistently reporting a less risky peer context (vs. the marginal 36%) and only 4% reporting increasingly risky peer contexts (vs. the marginal 14%). Females, but not males, in band or orchestra

TABLE 9.3
**Percentage of Students in Peer Contexts of Varying Riskiness
and Academic Orientation in Each Extracurricular Activity Type**

	n	Less Risky	Getting Better	Getting Worse	Consistently Risky	Chi Square
Females						
Activity Type						
Prosocial Activities	122	**46**	25	18	*11*	21.514***
Any Sport	188	39	23	13	26	
Performing Arts	188	37	22	**18**	22	7.244tr
School Involvement	102	35	22	18	26	
Academic Club	72	40	24	17	19	
All females	409	36	25	14	25	
Males						
Activity Type						
Prosocial Activities	52	**60**	14	14	*14*	16.984**
Any Sport	181	33	17	20	30	
Performing Arts	62	42	18	18	23	
School Involvement	26	58	8	12	23	6.612tr
Academic Club	30	40	17	7	37	
All males	273	35	19	18	29	

	n	Never Academic	Getting Less Academic	Getting More Academic	Consistently Academic	Chi Square
Females						
Activity Type						
Prosocial Activities	122	*21*	11	24	44	8.429*
Any Sport	188	23	12	*15*	50	25.566***
Performing Arts	188	27	11	22	40	
School Involvement	102	*17*	12	24	**48**	13.700**
Academic Club	72	*21*	6	21	53	11.680**
All females	410	31	11	20	38	

(continued on next page)

TABLE 9.3 (continued)

	n	Never Academic	Getting Less Academic	Getting More Academic	Consistently Academic	Chi Square
Males						
Activity Type						
Prosocial Activities	52	*19*	19	15	**46**	8.864*
Any Sport	181	32	17	20	30	
Performing Arts	62	23	11	24	**42**	6.079
School Involvement	26	15	27	19	39	
Academic Club	30	*10*	27	27	**37**	7.871*
All males	274	31	16	22	31	

Note. Bold print highlights cells with percentages higher than would be expected by chance; italics highlights cells with lower percentages than expected. * $p < .05$. ** $p < .01$. *** $p < .001$.

were unusually likely to report being in increasingly risky peer contexts (22% vs. the marginal 14%).

Our next analyses revealed connections between risky peer contexts and our most prominent activity-based social identity. Male Jocks were over-represented in increasingly risky peer contexts (23% vs. the marginal 18%) and underrepresented in decreasingly risky peer contexts (14% vs. 19%). In contrast, female Jocks were under-represented in increasingly risky peer contexts (4% vs. 14%).

The relative riskiness of one's peer context was also associated with academic and substance use outcomes. Adolescents reporting the riskiest peer context pattern had higher rates of drinking, getting drunk, and marijuana use at age 18 than all other groups (contrasts significant at $p < .001$), after controlling for gender. They had lower high-school GPAs at age 18 than those in the consistently less risky peer context pattern ($p < .001$), even after controlling for ability, socioeconomic status (SES), and gender (see Table 9.4 for means).

More importantly for this chapter, there was a significant interaction between risky peer context and participation in school involvement activities for years of schooling achieved by age 24, $F(3, 435) = 3.305, p < 05$: Consistent with our hypotheses, students who reported both risky peer contexts

TABLE 9.4
**Ms for Academic Outcomes and 12th-Grade Substance
Use Outcomes With MANCOVA Results**

	More Risky	Getting Worse	Getting Better	Less Risky	F
High School GPA	263.9	272.9	276.0	295.4	10.037***
Years of Schooling	14.9	14.9	14.7	15.2	2.280
Drinking Frequency	5.5	4.3	3.2	2.7	51.225***
Frequency of Getting Drunk	5.2	3.8	2.8	2.3	82.488***
Marijuana Use Frequency	2.9	1.8	1.3	1.2	38.579***
	Never Academic	Getting Less Academic	Getting More Academic	Consistently Academic	F
High School GPA	262.6	274.8	287.9	285.5	6.531***
Years of Schooling	14.5	14.9	14.8	15.4	10.054***
Drinking Frequency	4.1	4.2	3.6	3.6	1.874
Frequency of Getting Drunk	3.6	3.9	3.4	3.2	2.252
Marijuana Use Frequency	2.1	1.8	1.7	1.5	2.788*

Note. Ms have been adjusted for covariates; academic outcomes adjusted for ability, SES, and gender; substance use outcomes adjusted for gender. * $p < .05$. ** $p < .01$. *** $p < .001$.

and noninvolvement in school spirit and governance activities completed approximately 1 year less of schooling on average (14.7 years) than those in risky peer contexts who had participated in school involvement activities (15.6 years). Thus, the positive impact of school involvement activities was accentuated for participants in the riskier contexts.

We next conducted analyses to assess the operation of synergy effects on substance use outcomes for Jocks, hypothesizing that individuals would be at more risk if they were in both sports and more risky peer contexts than if they were in sports but not in risky peer contexts. Repeated measures multivariate analyses of variance (MANOVAs) encompassing within-subject time effects provided support for our synergy hypothesis, revealing that athletes with a Jock identity and consistently having riskier friends (i.e., those exhibiting a confluence of identity, activity, and risky peers) had higher levels of drinking overall across the two waves than those who had less risky friends at either wave, $F(3, 24) = 3.619, p < .01$ for females and $F(3, 58) = 5.165, p < .01$ for males. Furthermore, significant interactions between time and peer context for Jocks, $F(3, 58) = 5.856, p < .05$ for males and $F(1, 26) = 8.283, p < .01$ for females, indicated that having an increasingly risky peer group was associated with comparatively large increases in drinking frequency.

More and Less Academic Peers. Adolescents' distribution across the four academic peer contexts supported hypotheses based on the link between activity contexts and academic achievement (see Table 9.3). Over-representation in consistently academic peer contexts and/or under-representation in consistently less academic peer contexts was revealed for females in prosocial, sports, school involvement, and academic club activities and for males in prosocial, performing arts, and academic club activities.

Examination of individual activities within activity types revealed that participation in softball (60%), swimming (51%), basketball (52%), volley-ball (55%), pep club (49%), service clubs (78%), student government (56%), debate and forensics (80%), and foreign language clubs (53%) pre-dicted overrepresentation in the most academic peer context pattern for girls (marginal rate, 38%). For boys, participation in tennis (53%) and band or orchestra (50%) predicted the most academic peer context pattern (mar-ginal rate for males, 31%).

Analyses regarding the distribution of more and less academic peer con-text patterns within *Breakfast Club* identities indicated significant differ-ences for females, $\chi^2 (3, N = 333) = 24.09 \, p < .05$. Again as predicted by the relation of identities to academic outcomes, the female Jocks were overrepresented in consistently academic peer contexts (53% compared to the marginal 39%) but male Jocks were not. Follow-up contrast analysis of percentages of academically oriented friends at each wave revealed that fe-male Jocks had a higher proportion of academically oriented friends than male Jocks did in 12th grade, $F(1, 191) = 7.29, p < .01; Ms = 4.0$ and 3.7 or approximately 75% and 68% .

Thus, the likelihood of having a relatively benign or a relatively risky peer context varies systematically across identities and activities. We have found, as well, that outcomes can be contingent on particular synergistic or asyn-chronous patterns of activity, identity, and peer context. For example, look-ing specifically at our male and female Jocks, we found that those who went on to college and who completed a college degree by age 24 were more likely than expected to report being in consistently academic peer contexts $\chi^2 (3, N = 133) = 12.68, p < .01$ for college attendance and $\chi^2 (3, N = 112) = 10.03, p < .05$ for degree completion. Three quarters of Jocks who reported consistently academic peer contexts went on to college and one half had completed a degree by age 24. In contrast, only 40% of the Jocks who had reported being in consistently nonacademic peer contexts went to college after high school, and only 17% had completed a degree by age 24. Logistic regression analyses that partialed out the effects of ability, SES, and gender confirmed that the likelihood of college attendance and college completion was significantly greater for those Jocks who were in consistently academic peer contexts than for those in consistently nonacademic peer contexts, χ^2 (1, $N = 114$) $= 7.61$, $p < .01$ and χ^2 (1, $N = 100$) $= 7.01$, $p < .01$, respectively. Importantly for our hypotheses, an analysis of covariance (ANCOVA) on completed years of schooling (controlling for ability, SES, and gender) also revealed a significant effect for academic peer context, $F(3, 99) = 3.58$, $p < .05$. Contrasts indicated that those Jocks who were in consistently more academic peer contexts had completed approximately one more year of schooling than those in consistently less academic peer contexts (15.4 years vs. 14.5 years; contrast significant at $p < .01$).

Exposure to more versus less academic peers was associated with high school GPA and years of schooling for our sample as a whole. Having more academic peers at both 10th and 12th grades predicted better educational outcomes than having fewer academic peers at one or both waves (see Table 9.4). More importantly for this chapter, an interaction between sports activities and academic peer context, $F(3, 436) = 3.071$, $p < .05$, indicated that for athletes, better educational attainment accrued for individuals who were exposed to a relatively more academic peer context either at 10th grade or at 12th grade, or both (approximately 15.5 years vs. 14.6 years). For nonathletes, better educational outcomes were contingent on being in an academic peer context at both waves (15.5 vs. approximately 14.3). In other words, nonathletes completed fewer years of schooling than athletes unless they had consistently academic peers.

Academic peer contexts were also associated with 12th-grade marijuana use and frequency of getting drunk (see Table 9.4). Individuals consistently in relatively academic peer contexts reported less frequent marijuana use than those consistently in less academic peer contexts in their senior year (contrast significant at $p < .01$).

SYNERGIES AND DEVELOPMENT DURING ADOLESCENCE

Our findings suggest that activity involvement may indeed provide opportunities for adolescents to define and publicly express identity (Barber et al., 2001; Brown, 1990; Eccles & Barber, 1999). Peer crowd identities, often forged through activity participation, may represent an important way in which agency is expressed by individuals as they commit to the patterns that will characterize their adult lives.

Activities also appear to provide peer group niches in which adolescents may do the work of co-constructing values and identities (Youniss & Smollar, 1985). Our findings suggest that the characteristics of our participants' peer contexts reflected both their social identities and their activity involvement. For example, those athletes who also considered themselves to be Jocks hung around with a mixed group of peers—peers who were academically oriented and peers who consumed large amounts of alcohol. Consequently, it is not a surprise that these adolescents also had high educational outcomes and consumed large amounts of alcohol.

We are interested in the workings of these synergies but do not expect to document firm causal conclusions about the relations among components of the system as a whole. We believe that the ordering of the relations among activity participation, identity pursuit and affirmation, peer group norm sharing, and developmental changes in academic and psychosocial functioning during adolescence is, in fact, quite fluid and bidirectional. Similarly, Cairns (1996) suggested that continuity and change depend on the collaboration of systems at the level of individuals, dyads, social networks, subcultures, that regulatory constraints are correlated, and that they collaborate to organize behavior in directions that are contingent upon context. Our findings are consistent with this emphasis on the collaboration and contingency of regulatory constraints. We found strong evidence that these domains of adolescent life are correlated—leading to the increased likelihood that specific individuals will either be exposed to the confluence of their characteristics or will not be exposed to any of their characteristics. Whether this confluence begins with selection and ends with socialization or begins with socialization and ends with the joint effects of selection and mutual socialization is less interesting to us than the processes that underlie the confluence itself. In fact, we consider sorting out selection influences from the influences of social experience to be a futile effort in naturalistic, longitudinal studies. We have done everything we can by controlling for their position on the outcome measures prior to the point at which we assessed participation. However, because we think selection and social experience work together as a fluid, synergistic system to influence developmental trajectories, the "unique" or net influence of either selection or socialization becomes meaningless.

We believe that our results reflect Cairns's (1996) notion of *sociogenesis*— the transactional processes wherein individuals and their social environments collaborate to effect continuity and change in development. Adolescent selves and values are not created in a vacuum and they must be constructed rather than bequeathed from parents or genetic endowment. However, rather than a prepackaged youth culture to which all adolescents subscribe, we, like others, believe that there are various subcultures or prototypic identity groups within the social milieu of the high school, at least in North American secondary schools (Brown, 1990; Stone & Brown, 1999). Each group has well-defined, distinctive characteristics and lifestyles, and many of them are associated with particular extracurricular activities. Research centering on extracurricular activities (Eccles & Barber, 1999; Eckert, 1989; Fine, 1987; Youniss, Yates, & Su, 1997) suggests that crowds are part of a larger contextual system—including personality and personal identity, activity choices, co-participants, and the cultural features of particular activities—that influences individuals' pathways through adolescence.

But we must ask how this contextual system actually influences development. Youniss and Smollar (1985) described a process of *consensual validation,* wherein individuals collectively work out their views on identities, issues, and activities. We think that it is through such processes that high-school students decide collectively whether it is "cool" or not to aspire to a college degree or a construction job, to cut class, to participate in classroom discussions, or to go out for football. Discussions regarding alcohol, marijuana, or the science fair are, we believe, different depending not just on whether they take place at a cafeteria table peopled by students who participate in extracurricular activities or not, but also on the activity in which the students participate. Because there is a strong association between hanging out with substance-using peers and the likelihood of using substances oneself (Brown et al., 1997; Curran, Stice, & Chassin, 1997; Hawkins, Catalano, & Miller, 1992), the views promoted in particular peer contexts are of extreme importance in determining adolescent risk behavior. The attitudes of friends regarding academics are also an extremely important influence on adolescents' own attitudes and achievement (Fuligni, Eccles, & Barber, 1995; Sage & Kinderman, 1999).

FINAL CONCLUSION

Why then do 10th-grade activities have such lasting predictive effects? Previous theory and research suggest that crowd identities may reflect personality dispositions and values that predate the adolescent years and that adolescents *choose* crowds to a certain extent. However, it also appears that adolescents can be *assigned* to crowds by peers in recognition of their behavioral choices and personalities (Brown, 1989, 1990). Perhaps adolescents make use of the formal activities and the informal social organization of the high school to negotiate and formalize their identities. The patterns of behavior expressed, solidified, and formalized first in high school organized activities may carry forward, providing both continuity in connection to others with similar values and backgrounds, and the ongoing validation of the social identity established in adolescence. In this sample, the adolescents who are active in high school clubs and organizations and who do volunteer work are most likely to continue their activity participation patterns in young adulthood (Raymore, Barber, Eccles, & Godbey, 1999). Therefore, our results may reflect not only the benefits of participation during adolescence, but also the enduring impact of a continuing synergistic relationship between activity involvement and social identity across the transition to adulthood.

Making diverse clubs and activities available to a wide range of students is important. At a time when identity formation is a central concern, the opportunity to embed one's identity in multiple extracurricular contexts and to experience multiple competencies facilitates attachment to school and adjustment. Beyond the identity exploration possibilities, activity participation is also linked to affiliation with peers who are academically focused. It is this synergistic system that adolescents can benefit from when varied opportunities are available for participation.

ACKNOWLEDGMENTS

The Michigan Study of Life Transitions has been funded by grants from NICHD, NIMH, NSF, the Spencer Foundation, and the William T. Grant Foundation to Jacquelynne Eccles and to Bonnie Barber. We wish also to thank the following people for their contributions over the years to this project: Carol Midgley, Allan Wigfield, David Reuman, Harriet Feldlaufer, Douglas Mac Iver, Janis Jacobs, Constance Flanagan, Christy Miller Buchanan, Andrew Fuligni, Deborah Josefowicz, Pam Frome, Lisa Colarossi, Amy Arbreton, Laurie Meschke, Kim Updegraff, Kristen Jacobson, Miriam Linver, Mina Vida, and Sun-A Lee.

APPENDIX

Additional Measures

Psychological Adjustment.   Participants responded to a set of items about psychological adjustment at Waves 5 and 6. The seven-point items began with "How often do you ..." and responses ranged from 1, *never* to 7, *daily*. Self-esteem was measured with 3 items (Cronbach alphas = .77 at Wave 5 and .80 at Wave 6) including "feel sure about yourself," "feel satisfied with who you are," and "feel good about yourself." Depressed mood was measured with 3 items: (Cronbach alphas = .60 at Wave 5 and .66 at Wave 6) that included "feel unhappy sad or depressed?," "lose your appetite or eat a lot when you get upset?," and "feel that difficulties are piling up so high that you can't overcome them?" Social isolation was measured using a single item: "feel lonely?" Although the three psychological adjustment scales were significantly correlated between

Wave 5 and Wave 6, the correlations were not high (less than .48 for all 3 scales) indicating that these mood state variables had adequate variability to consider changes from Wave 5 to Wave 6.

Value of Sports and Self-Concept of Sports Ability. The value participants placed on sports was assessed using a 2-item scale at Wave 5 (*alpha* = .70). These items were "How much do you enjoy playing sports?" (1, *a little* to 7, *a lot*) and "For me, being good at sports is ..." (1, *not at all important* to 7, *very important*). A dichotomous score was computed for low- and high-sports value for further analysis. To create the split, anyone with a score of 6 or above was coded as having a higher value for sports, and those who scored below 6 were coded as having a lower value for sports. Self-concept of sports ability was assessed using a 2-item scale at Waves 5 and 6 (*alphas* = .80 and .84, respectively). The items in the scale were "How good at sports are you?" (1, *not at all* to 7, *very good*) and "If you were to rank all the students your age from the worst to the best in sports, where would you put yourself?" (1, *the worst* to 7, *the best*).

Occupational Identity. Occupational identity was measured with three items (*alpha* = .79) following a question asking about the kind of job participants would like to have in adulthood. These items included "How sure are you that this is the kind of job you would like?" (1, *not at all* to 7, *very sure*) and "How much have you thought about this choice?" (1, *a little* to 7, *a lot*).

Family Demographics. We included mother's education as a measure of family socioeconomic status. This variable was collected from mothers at the first wave when the adolescents were in the 6th grade. Mothers indicated on a 9-point ordinal scale their highest level of education with 1, *grade school*, 3, *high-school diploma*, 6, *college degree*, and 9, *PhD or other advanced professional degree like an MD*. We collapsed this scale into a 4-point ordinal scale with 1, *less than high-school diploma* (10% of sample overall), 2, *high-school diploma or GED* (40%), 3, *some postsecondary* (30%), and 4, *bachelor's degree or more* (20%).

Academic Aptitude. We collected the verbal and numerical ability subscores (percentile rankings) on the Differential Aptitude Test (DAT; The Psychological Corporation, 1981) from 9th-grade school records.

REFERENCES

Barber, B. L., Eccles, J. S., & Stone, M. R. (2001). Whatever happened to the jock, the brain, and the princes? Young adult pathways linked to adolescent activity involvement and social identity. *Journal of Adolescent Research, 16*, 429–455.

Barber, B. L., Jacobson, K. C, Eccles, J. S., & Horn, M. C. (1997, April). *"I don't want to play any more": When do talented adolescents drop out of competitive athletics?* Paper presented at the biennial meeting of the Society for Research on Child Development, Washington, DC.

Barber, B. L., Jacobson, K. C, Horn, M. C., & Jacobs, S. L. (1997, August). *Social and individual factors that predict adolescents' school attachment during high school.* Paper presented at the seventh European Association for Research on Learning and Instruction (EARLI) Conference, Athens, Greece.

Brown, B. B. (1989). The role of peer groups in adolescents' adjustment to secondary school. In T. J. Berndt & G. W. Ladd (Eds.), *Peer relationships in child development* (pp. 188–215). New York: Wiley.

Brown, B. B. (1990). Peer groups and peer cultures. In S. S. Feldman & G. R. Elliott (Eds.), *At the threshold: The developing adolescent* (pp. 171–196). Cambridge, MA: Harvard University Press.

Brown, B. B., Dolcini, M. M., & Leventhal, A. (1997). Transformations in peer relationships at adolescence: Implications for health-related behavior. In J. Schulenberg, J. L. Maggs, & K. Hurrelmann (Eds.), *Health risks and developmental transitions during adolescence* (pp. 161–189). New York: Cambridge University Press.

Brown, B. B., Mory, M. S., & Kinney, D. (1994). Casting adolescent crowd in a relational perspective: Caricature, channel, and context. In R. Montemayor, G. R. Adams, & T. P. Gullota (Eds.), *Advances in adolescent development: Vol. 5. Personal relationships during adolescence* (pp. 123–167). Newbury Park, CA: Sage.

Cairns, R. B. (1996). Socialization and sociogenesis. In D. Magnusson (Ed.), *The lifespan development of individuals: Behavioral, neurobiological, and psychosocial perspectives: A synthesis* (pp. 277–295). New York: Cambridge University Press.

Carnegie Corporation. (1992). *A matter of time: Risk and opportunity in the out-of-school hours.* New York: Author.

Curran, P. J., Stice, E., Chassin, L. (1997). The relation between adolescent alcohol use and peer alcohol use: A longitudinal random coefficients model. *Journal of Consulting and Clinical Psychology, 65*(1), 130–140.

Dishion, T. J., Poulin, F., & Burraston, B. (2001). Peer group dynamics associated with iatrogenic effects in group interventions with high-risk young adolescents. In D. W. Nangle, & C. A. Erdley (Eds.), *The role of friendship in psychological adjustment.* (pp. 79–92). San Francisco, CA: Jossey-Bass/Pfeiffer.

Eccles, J. S. (1987). Gender roles and women's achievement-related decisions. *Psychology of Women Quarterly, 11,* 135–172.

Eccles, J. S., Adler, T. F., Futterman, R., Goff, S. B., Kaczala, C. M., Meece, J. L., & Midgley, C. (1983). Expectancies, values, and academic behaviors. In J. T. Spence (Ed.), *Achievement and achievement motives: Psychological and sociological approaches* (pp. 75–146). San Francisco: W. H. Freeman.

Eccles, J. S., & Barber, B. L. (1999). Student council, volunteering, basketball, or marching band: What kind of extracurricular involvement matters? *Journal of Adolescent Research, 14,* 10–43.

Eccles, J. S., Barber, B. L., & Jozefowicz, D. (1998). Linking gender to educational, occupational, and recreational choices: Applying the Eccles et al. model of achievement-related choices. In W. B. Swann, J. H. Langlois, & L. C. Gilbert (Eds.), *Sexism and stereotypes in modern society: The gender science of Janet Taylor Spence* (pp. 153–192). Washington, DC: American Psychological Association.

Eccles, J. S., & Gootman, J. A. (2001). *Community programs to promote youth development.* Washington, DC: National Academy Press.

Eccles, J. S., & Templeton, J. (2002). Extracurricular and other after-school activities for youth. *Review of Research in Education, 26,* 113–180.

Eckert, P. (1989). *Jocks and burnouts: Social categories and identity in the high school.* New York: Teachers College Press.

Eder, D., & Parker, S. (1987). The cultural production and reproduction of gender: The effect of extracurricular activities on peer-group culture. *Sociology of Education, 60*(3), 200–213.

Erikson, E. H. (1963). *Childhood and society.* New York: Norton.

Fine, G. A. (1987). *With the boys: Little League baseball and preadolescent culture.* Chicago: University of Chicago Press.

Ford, D. H., & Lerner, R. M. (1992). *Developmental systems theory.* Newbury Park, CA: Sage.

Fuligni, A. J., Eccles, J. S., & Barber, B. (1995). The long term effects of seventh grade ability grouping in mathematics. *Journal of Early Adolescence, 15,* 58–89.

Hawkins, J.D., Catalano, R. F., & Miller, J. Y. (1992). Risk and protective factors for alcohol and other drug problems in adolescence and early adulthood: Implications for substance abuse prevention. *Psychological Bulletin, 112*(1), 64–105.

Holland, A., & Andre, T. (1994). Prestige ratings of high school extracurricular activities. *High School Journal, 78*(2), 62–72.

Hughes, J. (Writer/Director). (1985). *The breakfast club* [Motion picture]. United States: Universal Pictures.

Hunt, J. E. (2002). *High school sports as a protective factor: What happens to athletes who stop playing.* Unpublished master's thesis, University of Arizona, Tucson.

Kinney, D. A. (1993). From nerds to normals: The recovery of identity among adolescents from middle school to high school. *Sociology of Education 66*(1), 21–40.

Kleiber, D. (1999). *Leisure experience and human development: A dialectical approach.* New York: Basic Books.

Larson, R. W. (2000). Toward a psychology of positive youth development. *American Psychologist, 55,* 170–183.

Mahoney, J. L., & Cairns, R. B. (1997). Do extracurricular activities protect against early school dropout? *Developmental Psychology, 33,* 241–253.

Marsh, H., & Kleitman, S. (2002). Extracurricular school activities: The good, the bad, and the non-linear. *Harvard Educational Review, 72*(4), 464–514.

Meece, J. L., Parsons, J. E., Kaczala, C. M., Goff, S. B., & Futterman, R. (1982). Sex differences in math achievement: Toward a model of academic choice. *Psychological Bulletin, 91,* 324–348.

The Psychological Corporation. (1981). *Differential Aptitude Test* (4th ed., Form VNW). San Antonio, TX: Harcourt Brace.

Raymore, L. A., Barber, B. L., Eccles, J. S., & Godbey, G. C. (1999). Leisure behavior pattern stability during the transition from adolescence to young adulthood. *Journal of Youth and Adolescence, 28,* 79–103.

Sage, N., & Kinderman, T. (1999). Peer networks, behavior contingencies, and children's engagement in the classroom. *Merrill-Palmer Quarterly, 45,* 143–171.

Stone, M. R., & Brown, B. B. (1998). In the eye of the beholder: Adolescents' perceptions of peer crowd stereotypes. In R. Muuss (Ed.), *Adolescent behavior and society: A book of readings* (5th ed., pp. 158–169). Boston: McGraw-Hill.

Stone, M. R., & Brown, B. B. (1999). Identity claims and projections: Descriptions of self and crowds in secondary school. In J. A. McLellan & M. J. Pugh (Eds.), *New directions for child development: 84. The role of peer groups in adolescent social identity: Exploring the importance of stability and change* (pp. 7–20). San Francisco: Jossey-Bass.

Youniss, J., McLellan, J. A., Su, Y., & Yates, M. (1999). The role of community service in identity development: Normative, unconventional, and deviant orientations. *Journal of Adolescent Research, 14*(2), 248–261.

Youniss, J., & Smollar, J. (1985). *Adolescent relations with mothers, fathers, and friends.* Chicago: University of Chicago Press.

Youniss, J., Yates, M., & Su, Y. (1997). Social integration: Community service and marijuana use in high school seniors. *Journal of Adolescent Research Special Issue: Adolescent Socialization in Context: Connection, Regulation, and Autonomy in Multiple Contexts, 12*(2), 245–262.

10

Explaining Why a Leisure Context Is Bad for Some Girls and Not for Others

Håkan Stattin
Margaret Kerr
Örebro University, Sweden

Joseph Mahoney
Yale University

Andreas Persson
Örebro University, Sweden

David Magnusson
Stockholm University, Sweden

As youth move through adolescence, they spend progressively more time away from home and away from the supervision and influence of their parents. They have considerable latitude to choose their leisure settings, and this is a source of concern for many parents. Studies show that well-adjusted adolescents are more actively involved in structured leisure time activities and settings such as organized sports, hobbies, religious activities, music, theater, art, and politics, whereas less well-adjusted adolescents are more likely to hang out on the streets and at public drinking places (Cochran & Bo, 1987). These activities seem to facilitate the development of adjustment problems and antisocial behavior (e.g., Agnew & Peterson, 1989;

Hirschi, 1969; McCord, 1978; Osgood, Wilson, O'Malley, Bachman, & Johnston, 1996; Shannahan & Flaherty, 2001).

In most European and North American communities, adults have tried to provide recreation opportunities for youth who have not chosen structured activities. Often, recreation centers exist where adults are present, but do not direct the activities, and the aim is to coax at-risk adolescents off the streets and into semisupervised situations. In Sweden, such youth centers are government-supported and available in most communities to adolescents 13 years old and older. Typically, they open every evening around dinnertime and close as late as 11:30 p.m. They usually offer pool, ping-pong, video games, darts, TV, music, and coffee. Adults are present at these centers, but they do not direct the youth's activities or place any demands on them.

As a group, youth who attend these centers regularly are more antisocial and have more antisocial friends than those who do not attend (Mahoney & Stattin, 2000). They have more conflicted relationships with their parents, and their parents know little about their activities. More detailed studies of boys suggest that troubled boys gravitate to these centers. Boys with multiple problems at age 10 were most likely to attend the youth centers at age 13 (Mahoney, Stattin, & D. Magnusson, 2001). But, problems also intensified for boys who attended the centers, whether they had more or fewer problems before attending. After controlling for prior demographics, family factors, and social–academic competence, boys who attended the centers at age 13 had higher rates of criminal offenses up to age 30 than boys who did not go to the centers. Although other explanations are possible, the findings are consistent with the idea that socialization into criminal activity is taking place among boys at these centers. In this study, we look at whether the same is true for girls who attend the centers, and we extend the bases for inferring socialization effects by looking at the friends' characteristics of girls who attend the centers, and exactly what they do with those friends.

Like other gathering places, the youth centers offer many opportunities for meeting others and forming relationships. However, two features of the youth centers increase the likelihood that these relationships could spell problems for girls, and would lead us to predict that youth center attendance should be linked to problem behavior among girls. One is that the youth centers are not age-graded as many organized activities tend to be. This means that young adolescent girls are exposed to older peers, who are at an age when normbreaking is much increased. The other is that these youth centers tend to have a concentration of poorly adjusted adolescents (cf. Dishion, McCord, & Poulin, 1999; Patterson, 1993). This combination of factors means that young adolescent girls will be more exposed to older peers who are engaging in more normbreaking activities. To mention one likely scenario, girls who attend the centers could make friends with same-age or older girls who are engaging in normbreaking behavior, and they might quite naturally enter into these activities as well. Another likely scenario is that girls who attend the centers become involved with older boyfriends and start spending time with and being influenced by those boys and their friends. Thus, there are reasons to expect that girls who attend the youth centers will tend to get drawn into antisocial behavior by the more antisocial peers who populate the centers.

An alternative idea, however, is that center attendance and the characteristics of peers at the youth centers are relatively unimportant, but that heavy peer involvement, per se, should lead to higher normbreaking. Heavy involvement with peers has been linked to more normbreaking in past studies, ostensibly because heavy peer involvement signals a rejection of adult values and influences (P. Cohen & J. Cohen, 1996; Stattin & Kerr, 2002). This suggests that the girls who get involved in a wide variety of peer relationships with friends or boyfriends, particularly older boyfriends, should be more likely than other girls to engage in normbreaking, regardless of whether they attend the centers or not. They might be more likely to attend the youth centers because they can meet many youths there, but youth center attendance should be less important than peer involvement in explaining their normbreaking. In this chapter, we test these two alternative ideas using data from a childhood-to-midlife longitudinal study.

GIRLS' PARTICIPATION IN YOUTH CENTERS: A LONGITUDINAL STUDY

The longitudinal data used in this study have been used previously to show that boys' participation in youth centers is linked to registered offending (Mahoney & Stattin, 2000; Mahoney et al., 2001). Registered offending among girls was less frequent (9% of girls and 38% of boys were registered by age 30). Therefore, in this study we concentrate on self-reported normbreaking, which shows sufficient variability. First, we look at whether youth center attendance is linked to normbreaking in girls as it was to criminality in boys. We rule out the explanation that aggressive girls or girls from troubled homes were more likely to attend the centers and that these factors rather than their center attendance explain their normbreaking. Then, we test the two alternatives already described: heavy peer involvement and advanced social behavior through heterosexual relationships. We evaluate these factors as mediators and moderators of the link between center attendance and normbreaking. In a final step, we test our major conclusions using as the outcome measure registered offending, rather than self-reported normbreaking.

METHOD

Participants and Procedures

The participants were from a prospective, longitudinal investigation that began in 1965. The longitudinal study, Individual Development and Adaptation (IDA; D. Magnusson, 1988; D. Magnusson, Dunér, & Zetterblom, 1975), started with all 3rd graders in a city of about 100,000 (512 girls). The students participated again in the 6th grade and 8th grade. Their parents and teachers also provided information. This sample is representative of the Swedish population, generally, on factors such as registered offending (Stattin, D. Magnusson, & Reichel, 1989).

Primary Measures

Youth Center Participation.   When participants in the IDA cohort were 13 years old, they reported how often they attended the youth centers. Participation was coded on a 5-point scale ranging from *no participation,* to *participation every evening of the week.* For some of the analyses reported here, we collapsed the scale into a 3-point indicator of the frequency of youth center participation: 0, *no participation;* 1, *sporadic participation* (participation 1 to 4 times a month); and 2, *frequent participation* (participation 2 to 7 times a week). Eleven percent (58/523) of the 13-year-old girls in this sample attended the centers frequently, 15% (79/523) attended sporadically, and as many as 74% (386/523) never attended.

Normbreaking.   The normbreaking scale is from a self-report instrument administered when the girls were 15 years old. The girls were asked how often they had shoplifted; gotten drunk; forged someone's signature; stolen things or money; smoked hashish; vandalized property; avoided paying at the movies, cafés, and so on; run away from home; hit somebody; teased or tormented someone; or loitered on the streets at night. Youth responded to each of the questions on a 5-point scale ranging from 1 *(never)* to 5 *(10 or more times).* The alpha reliability for this scale was .81.

RESULTS AND DISCUSSION

Is Youth Center Attendance Linked to Normbreaking in Girls?

We ask, first, whether youth center attendance is linked to normbreaking in girls as it was to registered criminality in boys from the same sample. The answer is "yes." The more often the girls attended youth recreation centers at age 13, the more normbreaking they reported at age 15 (standardized scores

= −.13, .16, and .60 for girls who never, occasionally, and often attended, respectively). These differences were statistically significant, $F (2, 430) = 11.76, p < .001$. There are a number of possible explanations for this relation, however, and we tested several.

Prior Behavior and Family Factors as Explanations. One obvious explanation for the relationship between center attendance and normbreaking that must be ruled out is that already-problematic girls or girls with problem family situations chose to go to the youth centers more often than well-adjusted girls did, and those pre-existing factors rather than their youth center experiences explain their higher levels of normbreaking. To test this, we examined some potential precursors that we had used in earlier investigations of boys (Mahoney et al., 2001). They included age 10 teachers' ratings of (a) aggression; (b) hyperactivity (a combined measure of motor restlessness and poor concentration); (c) poor school motivation; (d) peers' ratings of popularity; (e) national achievement test scores in Swedish and mathematics; (f) parents' reports of concern about the youth's behaviors; (g) family SES; and (h) family status (intact or not). If these factors explain the link between center attendance and normbreaking, then they should be strongly predictive of center attendance, and they should eliminate the link between center attendance and normbreaking when entered along with center attendance as predictors of normbreaking.

First, do these factors predict center attendance? Taken together, the model explained a small, but statistically significant proportion of the variance in age-13 center attendance, Model $F (7, 381) = 2.15, p = .031; R^2 = .06$. Family SES, however, was the only significant individual predictor, $\beta = −.13, t = −2.45, p = .015$. None of the behavior measures (aggression, hyperactivity, achievement, or peer preference) predicted youth center involvement. Thus, although girls from poorer families tended to go to the youth centers more than those from wealthier families, girls with behavior problems such as aggression or hyperactivity were not more likely to go to the centers. Thus, the explanation that the early problem girls are the ones who start to visit the centers does not receive strong support.

As the next step, we tested whether these factors explained why girls who attend the centers did more normbreaking later on. We used these same age-10 predictors to explain age-15 normbreaking (Step 1) and then entered center attendance (Step 2). If the family and behavioral predictors explain the link between center attendance and normbreaking, then center attendance should not significantly predict normbreaking when entered in the model with the family and behavioral predictors. (Entered alone, youth center attendance was a highly significant predictor of normbreaking, $\beta = .24, t = 5.03, p < .001$.) Of the behavior and family factors entered in Step 1, only family status significantly predicted later normbreaking, $\beta = .12$, $t = 2.37$, $p = .019$. In Step 2, family status remained significant ($\beta = .11$, $t = 2.18$, $p = .03$), but center attendance was a significant predictor independent of that ($\beta = .22$, $t = 4.18$, $p < .001$). Thus, center attendance predicted later normbreaking independently of these potential precursors. There was a slight change (change in $\beta = .02$) when these factors were controlled, but the change was slight enough that these factors cannot be considered as explaining why the girls who go to the youth centers are higher in normbreaking.

We conducted a similar analysis controlling for behavior and family measures collected at age 13. None of these factors predicted youth center attendance. Further, although family status ($\beta = -.14$, $t = -2.85$, $p = .005$) and school achievement ($\beta = .15$, $t = 2.5$, $p = .013$) were significant predictors of normbreaking with all these behavior and family factors controlled, center attendance still had a unique predictive role for later normbreaking ($\beta = .20$, $t = 4.13$, $p < .001$). (Again, note that the reduction in the β for youth center attendance was only .04.) Thus, frequency of center attendance seems to be a risk factor for later normbreaking behavior independent of other prior and concurrent risk factors.

One Explanation: Heavy Peer Involvement

Peer Involvement as a Mediator of the Link Between Youth Center Attendance and Normbreaking. One idea about the role of peer involvement is that heavy involvement with peers comes as a consequence of spending a lot of time at the youth center where many youth congregate and the directive role of adults is minimal. Because of heavy involvement with a peer group and little involvement with adults or others outside of the peer group, youth might lose perspective about, or tend to disregard, society outside of the peer culture and feel relatively disinhibited about breaking the norms of society. Thus, according to this idea, girls who start going to the centers might become heavily involved in a peer culture that excludes conventional adult values and prohibitions against normbreaking.

The girls in this study answered several questions that we used as indicators of their involvement with peers rather than family: "How many peers do you have that you are together with really often after school?" "How many evenings per week do you usually meet your peers?" and "How many evenings per week do you usually spend at home?" (reversed). The interitem correlation for these three measures was .34. The range was .27 to .40.

At first blush, the explanation seems promising that heavy peer involvement mediates the link between center attendance and normbreaking. Youth center attendance correlated significantly with all three measures of peer involvement: meeting peers after school ($r = .26$, $p < .001$); evenings meeting peers ($r = .26$, $p < .001$); evenings not home ($r = .24$, $p < .001$).

So, girls who visited youth recreation centers did seem to have been more involved with peers and less often at home than other girls. Additionally, two of the three peer-involvement measures correlated significantly with later normbreaking at age 15: evenings spent with peers ($r = .20, p < .001$) and evenings away from home ($r = .27, p < .001$). However, if heavy peer involvement is the mediating factor, then controlling for peer involvement should eliminate the relation between normbreaking and center attendance. As shown in Table 10.1, it does not. With peer involvement controlled in a hierarchical regression analysis, youth center attendance at age 13 still uniquely predicts normbreaking at age 15 ($\beta = .18, p < .001$). (The beta was .24 when youth center attendance was entered alone.) Thus, the mediating explanation—that girls who attended the centers became heavily involved with peers and peer involvement produced an increase in their normbreaking behaviors over time—is not strongly supported by the data.

Peer Involvement as a Moderator of the Link Between Youth Center Attendance and Normbreaking. Another explanation rests on the idea that the youth centers do not necessarily produce peer involvement. Peer involvement will occur in varying degrees inside and outside of the youth centers. The problem arises when girls become heavily involved with peers who might draw them into normbreaking activities, and those peers are overrepresented at the youth centers. Thus, center involvement should lead to more normbreaking only if a girl is heavily involved with peers.

To examine this, we first summed the three z-transformed peer involvement measures, which were intercorrelated at the .34 level. Next, we performed a multiple-regression analysis with normbreaking behavior at age 15 as the dependent variable, and peer involvement and center attendance as the two age-13 predictors. Both of these measures significantly predicted normbreaking behavior 2 years later when entered alone ($\beta s = .16$ and $.20$, $ps < .001$, for center attendance and peer involvement, respectively). However, when the interaction between frequency of center attendance and peer involvement was entered in the equation, it was significant ($\beta = .12, p = .02$), peer involvement remained significant ($\beta = .19, p < .001$), and the predictive utility of center attendance was considerably reduced ($\beta = .10, p = .07$). A graphical description of the interaction, reported in Fig. 10.1, shows that peer involvement does, indeed, moderate the relation between center attendance and normbreaking. Center attendance is visibly linked to normbreaking for girls who are heavily peer involved and much less so for those who are not. Thus, heavy peer involvement with youth at the center is one explanation why the youth center environment can be bad for some girls and not for others.

TABLE 10.1
Hierarchical Regression of Peer and Center Attendance Predictors of Normbreaking at Age 15

Variables in the Model	B	SE	Standardized B	t-value	P value
Step 1. Peer orientation at age 13					
Number of after-school peers	–.00	.02	–.01	–0.26	.797
Evenings/week spent with peers	.03	.01	.11	2.16	.031
Evenings/away from home	.06	.01	.23	4.43	< .001

Note. Model F (4, 430) = 13.14, p < .001; R^2 = .11.

Step 2. Add youth recreation attendance at age 13					
How many peers do you have?	–.02	.02	–.05	–0.89	.373
How often do you meet peers?	.02	.01	.09	1.72	.087
How often are you away from home?	.05	.01	.21	3.99	< .001
Youth recreation center attendance	.08	.02	.18	3.64	< .001

Note. Model F (4, 430) = 13.14, p < .001; R^2 = .11.

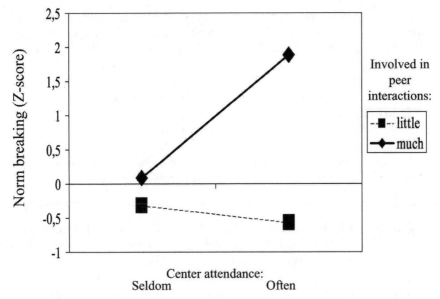

FIG. 10.1.   The interaction between youth center attendance and peer interactions at age 13 as predictors of normbreaking at age 15.

Another Explanation: "Advanced" Social Behavior Through Heterosexual Relations

On average, boys are more involved in delinquency than are girls. To the extent that peers socialize female adolescents into normbreaking, relationships with boys should be something of a risk factor for normbreaking. In several studies we have documented a strong association between heterosexual relations and normbreaking among girls (Stattin & Magnusson, 1990) and shown that heterosexual relationships largely explain why early maturing girls are more normbreaking than later maturing girls (Gustafson, Stattin, & D. Magnusson, 1989; D. Magnusson, Stattin, & Allen, 1986; Stattin, Gustafson, & D. Magnusson, 1989; Stattin & C. Magnusson, 1996; Stattin & D. Magnusson, 1989, 1990). In interpreting these findings, we suggested that the early-developing girls formed relationships with older boys, and these associations channeled them into social situations where more drinking, drug use, and norm-breaking behaviors were taking place than in the younger, predominantly female friendship groups. Applying a similar chain of logic here, one could reason that the youth centers give girls exposure to older boys, but also boys who are more involved in normbreaking. This suggests two possibilities. One is that the youth center, by providing a meeting place, makes it more likely that girls will get involved with boys and then be drawn into advanced social behavior, according to the hypothesis outlined. Thus, according to this interpretation, heterosexual relationships are the mediating mechanism connecting girls' center attendance with their normbreaking behavior. Another possibility is that center attendance is not an instigating factor for heterosexual relations, but if girls go to the youth centers *and also* become involved with boys, then they should be at highest risk for normbreaking, again according to the advanced social behavior hypothesis. In this case, heterosexual relationships are a moderator of the link between center attendance and normbreaking. In other words, we should find an interaction between center attendance and heterosexual relationships in predicting girls' normbreaking.

Measures of Heterosexual Relationships. We examined different aspects of girls' involvement in heterosexual relationships at age 15. Girls were asked, "Are you popular among boys?" "Do you consider yourself more sexually experienced than your age mates?" "Do you have a steady boyfriend?" and "Have you had sexual intercourse?" Responses were rated on 3- or 5-point scales.

All these age-15 measures were significantly correlated with age-15 normbreaking (range between .24 and .46; all of them significant at the p < .001 level). In addition, age-13 center attendance was significantly, albeit moderately, correlated with several of these age-15 measures: having had sexual intercourse, having steady relations, and perceiving oneself as more sexually experienced than peers (rs = .15 to .19, ps < .01). Thus, it is reasonable to examine the possible mediating or moderating roles of heterosexual relationships.

Heterosexual Relationships as a Mediator. Is the development of heterosexual relationships a mediating mechanism to explain why early youth center attendance is related to later normbreaking? We examined this with the two regression equations shown in Table 10.2. First, we regressed normbreaking behavior at age 15 on the different aspects of heterosexual relations at the same age, and indeed there were strong associations. The four measures of heterosexual relations accounted for 27% of the variance in the normbreaking measure. Apparently, heterosexual relations are closely linked to normbreaking among 15-year-old girls. Of the different measures, having had sexual intercourse and considering oneself as sexually more experienced than other girls were unique, significant predictors of normbreaking at age 15. However, if these relationships mediate the link between center attendance and normbreaking, then center attendance, when added to this equation, should not be a significant predictor. Nevertheless, as shown in Table 10.2, center attendance is a significant predictor inde-

TABLE 10.2

Hierarchical Regression of Heterosexual Relations at Age 15 and Age 13 Center Attendance Predictors of Normbreaking at Age 15

Variables in the Model	B	SE	Standardized	t-value	p value
Popular among boys	.07	.05	.07	1.44	.149
Sexually experienced	.15	.05	.15	2.96	.003
Steady relationship	.06	.05	.06	1.14	.254
Sexual intercourse	.31	.05	.31	6.10	< .001
Youth center attendance	.12	.07	.14	3.27	.001

Note. Model F (5, 415) = 30.06, $p < .001$; $R^2 = .27$.

pendent of all these measures of heterosexual relationships. Thus, even though the girls who attended the youth centers were more involved in heterosexual relationships, and heterosexual relationships are linked to normbreaking, heterosexual relationships do not fully explain why youth center attendance at age 13 is related to later normbreaking.

Heterosexual Relationships as a Moderator. Girls who attended the youth centers were more involved in heterosexual relationships, but the correlations, although significant, were modest, at best. This suggests that the girls who attend the youth centers are a heterogeneous group in terms of heterosexual relationships; some are involved in relationships with boys and some are not. If the development of relationships with boys is the risk factor for normbreaking, then the girls who enter these centers and do not establish heterosexual relationships should not show future problem behavior. Normbreaking should be concentrated on the girls who enter these centers *and* develop intimate relationships with boys.

To test this idea, we looked for an interaction between center attendance and heterosexual relationships in predicting normbreaking behavior at age 15. The interaction would indicate that the relation between center attendance and normbreaking depends upon whether girls are involved in close relationships with boys. As the measure of heterosexual relationships, we used a mean of the four separate measures. We entered that composite measure as a predictor together with frequency of center attendance at age 13 and the interaction between center attendance and sexual intercourse. If heterosexual relationships are a moderator, then the interaction should be significant.

As reported in Table 10.3, the moderating hypothesis does find support. First, center attendance at age 13 was not a significant unique predictor of normbreaking, independent of heterosexual relations and the interaction between heterosexual relations and center attendance. Thus, center attendance in itself is not a strong risk factor for later normbreaking—only if heterosexual relationships are involved. Second, heterosexual relationships was a significant unique predictor, thus suggesting that establishing heterosexual relationships early, whether this occurs in the center context or not, is a risk factor for normbreaking in midadolescence. Third, and most important, the strongest predictor was the interaction term, and this suggests that the relation between heterosexual relationships and normbreaking depends on how frequently girls attend the youth centers.

To understand how youth center attendance moderates the relation between heterosexual relationships and normbreaking, we solved the regression equation for high and low values of center attendance and heterosexual relationships and plotted the predicted points. The graph, which appears in Fig. 10.2, shows that frequent attendance is only a risk factor for later normbreaking behavior if girls develop relationships with boys. The predicted normbreaking score for girls who attended the centers frequently and were heavily involved in heterosexual relationships was more than 2 standard deviations above the mean; it was at the mean for the girls who attended the centers frequently but were not involved in heterosexual relationships. Figure 10.2 also shows that involvement with boys is a risk factor for the girls who seldom visit these centers, as well as for those who often visit them, but less of a risk. Thus these findings provide another explanation why the youth center context is bad for some girls and not for others. These findings are also consistent with the explanation that, because boys tend to be more involved in normbreaking than girls, relationships with boys is a risk factor in general. But, because boys who attend the youth centers are more involved in normbreaking than boys who do not, relationships with such boys is a particular risk factor.

Registered Offenses as the Outcome. In a final step, we tested whether the same interaction between center attendance and heterosexual involvement would emerge if, instead of self-reported normbreaking, we used registered criminal offenses, a more serious measure of normbreaking. We used stepwise logistic regression, and predicted registered criminality as a dichotomous variable (registered vs. not registered) from center attendance at age 13, heterosexual involvement at age 15, and the interaction between the two. Center attendance and heterosexual involvement were continuous variables.

As mentioned earlier, the frequency of registered criminality among these girls was low. In Sweden, crimes are registered with the social welfare authorities for youths up to age 15; thereafter they are registered with the police (see Stattin

TABLE 10.3

Multiple Regression Predicting Normbreaking Behavior at Age 15
From Heterosexual Relations and Youth Recreation Center Attendance

Variables in the Model	B	SE	Standardized B	t-value	p value
Step 1 Main effects of center attendance and peer association at age 13[a]					
Center attendance	.09	.03	.16	3.30	.001
Peer interaction	.11	.03	.20	3.98	< .001
Step 2 Add the interaction between center attendance and peer association at age 13[b]					
Center attendance	.06	.03	.10	1.81	.073
Peer interaction	.11	.03	.19	3.89	< .001
Interaction C × P	.05	.02	.12	2.27	.024

[a]Model $F (2, 425) = 20.04$, $p < .001$; $R^2 = .09$.
[b]Model $F (3, 424) = 15.21$, $p < .001$; $R^2 = .10$.

223

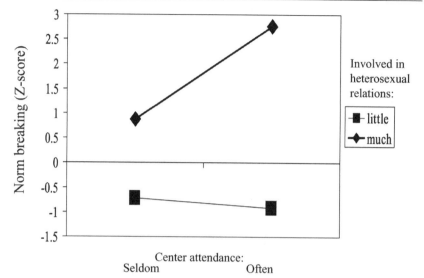

FIG. 10.2.   The interaction between youth center attendance and heterosexual relations as predictors of normbreaking at age 15.

& Magnusson, 1991). We included all registered crimes up to age 35 to define
girls as registered or not registered. Thirty-one (7%) of the 427 girls with complete data for the independent measures were registered at least once.

The findings were similar to those using normbreaking as the outcome.
The interaction term was significant (Wald = 8.69, p = .003), but there
were no unique effects of heterosexual relations at age 15 or center attendance at age 13. Figure 10.3 shows a graphical depiction of the interaction.
Criminality was high for the girls who often visited the youth centers in early
adolescence *and* were most involved in relationships with boys in middle adolescence. Twenty-five percent of these girls were registered for some offense
up to age 35. This was a considerably higher proportion than for any other
group. Thus, the findings that we have reported here are not limited to minor normbreaking during adolescence. They apply also to registered criminality in adolescence and later into adulthood. Girls who visited youth
centers frequently and were involved in heterosexual relationships in middle adolescence were overrepresented among registered criminals.

CRITICAL MISSING LINKS: A CROSS-SECTIONAL STUDY

The explanations that we have given of the moderating effects of peer involvement and heterosexual relationships rest on a couple of assumptions.
One is that girls who have relationships with boys actually do more

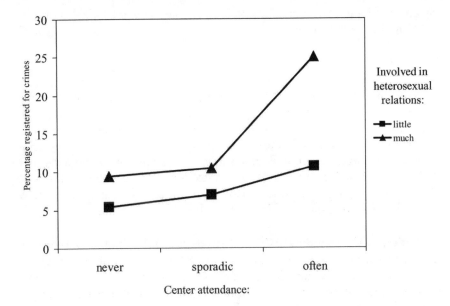

FIG. 10.3.   The interaction between youth center attendance at age 13 and heterosexual relations at age 15 as predictors of registered delinquency up to age 35.

normbreaking with those boys than girls do with their same-sex friends. Another is that girls do more normbreaking with the same-sex friends that they
meet at the youth centers than with those they meet elsewhere. As of yet,
we have not presented any evidence that these assumptions are valid, but
such evidence is critically important. Unless these phenomena can be
shown, our explanations of the moderating effects are only speculative.
Therefore, in this section, we use data from another study to fill in these
missing links in the explanations.

METHOD

Sample and Procedures

As part of a community-based study that started in 2001, involving all the
children and adolescents from 10 to 18 years of age ($N = 3,100$) in a town in
central Sweden with a population of about 36,000, the youths filled out
questionnaires during an ordinary school day. The teachers passed out the
questionnaires and gave the instructions. When the students finished, they
slipped their completed questionnaires through a slot into a sealed box.
They were assured that no one but the researchers would open the box, and
that their responses would be kept confidential. For this study, we focused

on girls in Grade 7 through Grade 9, because they were most likely to be attending the youth centers.

Measures

Very Important Persons.   The youth gave information about the very
important persons (VIPs) in their lives. We defined a VIP as "someone you
talk with, hang out with, and do things together with." We explained that a
VIP might be a friend, a sibling, or a boyfriend or girlfriend, but it could not
be a parent or another adult. Four hundred of these girls (86%) named other
girls as their first VIPs, and 65 (14%) named boys. Because these VIPs were
also in the study and we had asked about center attendance, we knew how
often the girls themselves and their friends visited the centers.

Activities With the First VIP.   We asked the girls which activities they
did with their first, or most important, VIP. We asked how often during the
last month they had studied together; watched TV/videos; played hooky;
shoplifted; used the computer, Internet, or played TV videogames; gotten
drunk; kept secrets from parents; talked about illegal things; went out looking for boys; and done illegal things other than shoplifting. The girls answered on a 3-point scale: 0 *(no)*, 1 *(once during the last month)*, and 2 *(several
times during the last month)*.

RESULTS AND DISCUSSION

Do Girls Do More Normbreaking
With Boys Than With Other Girls?

First we examined whether the girls who mentioned a boy as their first VIP
reported doing more normbreaking activities during a normal month with
that VIP than did girls who reported another girl as their first VIP. The results, which appear in Table 10.4, suggest that the answer is "yes"; girls do
more normbreaking with boys than with other girls. The girls who mentioned a boy as their first VIP had drunk alcohol together, kept secrets from
their parents together, talked about things that are illegal together, and
done other things for which they could get caught by the police, more frequently during the last month than the girls who mentioned a girl as their
VIP. Also, the girls who mentioned a boy as their first VIP had more frequently watched TV/videos, but considerably less often had been out looking for boys. Note that the girls whose primary VIP was a boy did not differ
from other girls in doing activities together that are not considered as
normbreaking behavior (studied together; talked on the phone or chatted;
or used the computer, Internet, or played TV videogames). Thus, the as-

TABLE 10.4

**Different Kinds of Activities During the Last Month
With One's First Very Important Person (VIP) Among Girls
Who Had a Female or a Male as the First VIP**

Activities with the first VIP during the last month	The VIP is		F	p
	Female (N = 388)	Male (N = 65)	(Df = 1, 452)	
Studied	.64	.69	.16	.693
Watched TV/videos	1.42	1.69	7.08	.008
Played hooky	.20	.35	3.70	.055
Talked on the phone/chatted	1.72	1.68	.30	.585
Shoplifted	.08	.07	.06	.799
Used the computer, Internet or played TV videogames	1.12	1.26	1.28	.260
Drank alcohol until you were drunk	.30	.70	20.10	< .001
Kept secrets from parents	.72	.98	4.71	.031
Talked about things that are illegal	.53	.92	11.25	.001
Went out looking for boys	1.14	.47	30.46	< .001
Did other things, apart from shoplifting, for which one could get caught	.17	.48	15.96	< .001

sumption that we made earlier—that associations with boys involve more normbreaking than associations with girls do—finds support in these data.

Do Girls Do More Normbreaking With Girlfriends Who Are Youth Center Goers Than With Those Who Are Not?

Considering only girls who named another girl as their first VIP, we first examined the association between the girls' own youth center attendance and the center attendance of the first VIP. The correlation was substantial, $r = .53$, $p < .001$. Thus, if a girl seldom attended the centers, her first VIP also seldom attended the centers, but if she attended the centers often, the likelihood was high that her female VIP also attended the centers often. For instance, for girls who never visited the centers, only 11% of the VIPs attended sporadically or often; for girls who visited the centers sporadically, 46% or their first female VIPs attended sporadically or often; and for girls who attended often, as many as 70% of their first VIPs also visited the centers sporadically or often. Thus, girls who attend the youth centers tended to have friends who attend the centers also.

The question, then, is whether girls do more normbreaking with friends who attend the centers than with those who do not. We compared the activities that the girls had done with their first VIP the last month, dividing the VIPs into three groups—never, sporadically, or often visiting the centers (VIP reports). The findings are reported in Table 10.5. Significant differences existed for 3 of the 11 activities. When female VIPs were center attendees, girls had shoplifted, been drunk together, and talked about illegal things more often during the last month than when female VIPs were not center attendees.

As a final analysis, we examined the interaction between girls' own attendance and the first VIP's attendance in predicting frequency of shoplifting, getting drunk, and talking about illegal things. For shoplifting and getting drunk, the strongest predictor was the interaction term. In both cases, shoplifting and getting drunk were most frequent among the girls who often visited the centers and whose female VIP also often visited the centers. None of the three predictors were significant in the case of talking about illegal things (but in a model without the interaction term, the girls' own center attendance was a significant predictor). In short, then, girls do seem to do more normbreaking with girlfriends who are youth center goers than with those who are not, and that is especially true if the girls are themselves youth center attendees. Thus, the assumptions that we made in explaining the moderating effects of peer involvement and heterosexual relationships—that girls who have relationships with boys actually do more normbreaking with those boys, and that girls do more normbreaking with the same-sex friends that they meet at the youth centers than with those they meet elsewhere—seem to be valid assumptions.

GENERAL DISCUSSION

In most Western societies, adults have tried to provide recreation opportunities for youth who might otherwise be hanging out on the streets or getting into trouble. In some countries this is done on the community level, perhaps by giving youth access to pool tables at the local YMCA or other facilities. In other countries, the efforts are more centralized. The thinking, however, seems to be fairly universal: It is better for youth to be hanging out

TABLE 10.5
Different Kinds of Activities During the Last Month With One's First Very Important Person (VIP) Among Girls Whose First Female VIP Never, Sporadically, or Often Attended the Centers

Activities with the first VIP during the last month	The female VIP attend the centers			F $(Df = 2, 264)$	p
	Never $(N = 213)$	Sporadically $(N = 33)$	Often $(N = 19)$		
Studied	.65	.69	1.00	1.59	.206
Watched TV/videos	1.37	1.67	1.67	2.91	.056
Played hooky	.20	.24	.42	1.35	.261
Talked on the phone/chatted	1.78	1.67	1.89	0.95	.386
Shoplifted	.06	.09	.39	6.91	.001
Used the computer, Internet or played TV videogames	1.07	1.18	1.11	0.22	.806
Drank alcohol until you were drunk	.22	.36	.84	9.45	< .001
Kept secrets from parents	.75	.67	1.11	1.59	.207
Talked about things that are illegal	.45	.65	1.00	4.25	.015
Went out looking for boys	1.27	1.00	1.53	2.41	.092
Did other things, apart from shoplifting, for which one could get caught	.17	.18	.44	2.05	.131

in a place where adults are present and can at least observe what the youth are doing than to be out on the streets doing whatever they like without any kind of supervision. Our past studies of boys suggest that hanging out at a youth center results in increases in problem behavior over time; it is not protective (Mahoney et al., 2001).

The present study shows that the same is true for girls. The more often girls attend the community youth recreation centers, the more likely they are to be engaging in what we term *normbreaking*—doing things such as getting drunk, shoplifting, forging a signature, smoking hashish, vandalizing property, running away from home, fighting or harassing someone, for example—both concurrently and 2 years later. This does not seem to be because they were more aggressive or hyperactive before they started going to the centers, and it does not seem to be because these are girls from bad family situations, and they would be engaging in normbreaking because their parents are being negligent about socializing them, regardless of where they spend their free time. There is some evidence that economic disadvantage is a reason for going to the youth centers to begin with, but it does little to explain the link between center attendance and later normbreaking.

What does seem to explain that link is socialization by normbreaking peers at the center—girlfriends and boyfriends. The evidence supports the idea that the friends who attend the youth centers are high on normbreaking, and the more involved girls are with these friends, the more normbreaking they do. The evidence also supports the idea that girls who get involved with boys adjust to the boys' more frequent normbreaking, and if those boys are the more antisocial boys who tend to populate the youth centers, this will be especially problematic.

We tested a couple of theoretical explanations that were not born out by the data. One was that youth centers encourage or produce such intensive involvement with peers that the norms of conventional society begin to fade in importance compared with the norms and values of the peer group. Because of this, inhibitions against breaking the norms of conventional society are reduced. If this were a good theoretical explanation, then peer involvement should have emerged as a mediator of the relation between center attendance and normbreaking, but it did not. Another idea that did not find support was that the centers serve as meeting places, making heterosexual contacts and relationships more likely, and through these relationships, girls who go the centers end up being drawn into more normbreaking. If this were a good theoretical explanation, then heterosexual relationships should have emerged as a mediator of the relation between center attendance and normbreaking, but they did not. Both of these are mediating hypotheses, suggesting that if not for center attendance, girls would not become heavily involved with peers or become involved in heterosexual relationships and that it is these involvements that explain why center attendance is related to normbreaking. This would suggest that the youth centers are problematic in and of themselves, but we do not see evidence for that. On the contrary, our results suggest that heavy peer involvement or heterosexual relationships can happen inside or outside of the youth centers. The problems seem to be linked to the particular peers who tend to congregate at the youth centers.

The theoretical explanations that were born out by the data, however, were moderating explanations. Although center attendance, peer interactions, heterosexual relations, and what the girls do together with peers in everyday life are all associated with later normbreaking in separate analyses, we argue that how they interact with each other is most important for understanding normbreaking. The results confirm our ideas. Youth recreation centers are not negative in and of themselves for later social adjustment problems. They are for some girls, and it is the girls who become heavily involved with peers or who develop intimate relationships with boys. These peer and opposite sex relations seem to play a less important role for later normbreaking activities for the girls who do not visit the centers early.

We suggested that whether a leisure setting influences adjustment in a positive or negative fashion depends much on the individuals who participate in the setting. When the participants are predominantly normbreaking youths, the likelihood of developing future normbreaking for girls who choose to spend their time at these settings increases. We have not argued that these settings have a bad influence on all girls, but they may have negative developmental consequences for some of the female participants. The primary hypothesis that we advanced is that leisure settings that are overrepresented by deviant youths will be associated with increased normbreaking behavior through peer socialization for some girls. The girls who visit these centers and develop strong peer associations or opposite sex relations with boys who are presumably more normbreaking than other boys are more likely themselves to develop normbreaking behavior. Our results support this proposal and advance the existing literature on this topic (e.g., R. B. Cairns & B. D. Cairns, 1994; Coie, Terry, Lenox, Lochman, & Hyman, 1995; Patterson, Reid, & Dishion, 1992). Because the youth centers become available to children at an age when peer influence is particularly salient (i.e., early adolescence), the influence of engagement with deviant peers may be especially likely to introduce or augment behavior patterns of a negative, antisocial sort.

One potential limitation of this study is that the girls who participated were adolescents in the 1970s. One could question whether the results apply to adolescent girls today. We think that they do. One reason for our confidence is that the cross-sectional study we reported in this chapter was done in 2001. Currently, then, girls do more normbreaking with boys and with girls who go to the centers, and these are the phenomena underlying our arguments about the longitudinal results. A second reason for our confidence is that the structure, activities, and participants at the centers are not much different today from 30 years ago. Most communities in Sweden have several youth centers, as before. The national agenda ensures that commonalities exist in the centers' goals and activities, and the organization and guiding philosophy of the centers has not changed much during the last 30 years. The overall philosophy is the same; namely, that youth should be allowed to develop their own interests; attendance and activity participation is voluntary; and adults at the centers should not impose demands on the adolescents (i.e., there should not be any formal requirements or evaluations of the participants). This context, then, is set up to provide the same kinds of experiences for youth today as before. Thus, there are good reasons to believe that these results apply to girls today.

In this study, we have suggested a peer socialization explanation for the findings—girls who go to the youth centers are socialized into normbreaking behavior by the other girls and the boys they meet there. We have used longitudinal data to try to rule out alternative explanations such as family background and prior behavior problems, and the peer socialization explanation still looks like the best one.

The question, however, is what youth center and community leaders should do to try to keep this socialization from happening. To answer this question, another type of research is needed—research that looks at what happens when changes are made. The results of this study suggest some changes that could be tried. One would be to reduce the age spread in the activities at the centers. If older peers are primarily responsible for the harmful socialization effects, then keeping the activities more age-graded might help. Another possibility is to try to change the normative value system in the centers by recruiting as additional center participants better adjusted youth who would not normally attend. Adding some more organized activities or instructions at the centers might help attract these youths. Past research has shown that even the best intended interventions can backfire, however (e.g., Dishion et al., 1999), so sweeping policy changes should be avoided. We suggest small-scale intervention studies with prudent evaluations of the consequences.

In most European and North American communities, adults try to provide meaningful recreation opportunities for youths who do not want to go into sports, hobbies, religious activities, music, theater, art, and politics. They do this with the best of intentions—to provide youth with opportunities to stay off the streets and out of trouble in the evenings. This study and our earlier studies (Mahoney et al., 2001) show that being off the streets and in the company of adults does not necessarily mean being out of trouble. The unfortunate thing is that it has taken 30 years to come to this conclusion.

Perhaps the clearest message from this research is that policymakers, youth workers, and researchers should work together more closely.

REFERENCES

Agnew, R., & Peterson, D. M. (1989). Leisure and delinquency. *Social problems, 36,* 332–350.

Cairns, R. B., & Cairns, B. D. (1994). *Lifelines and risks: Pathways of youth in our time.* New York: Cambridge University Press.

Cochran, M. M., & Bo, I. (1987). *Connections between the social networks, family involvement and behavior of adolescent males in Norway.* University of Rogaland (No. 75).

Cohen, P., & Cohen, J. (1996). *Life values and adolescent mental health.* Mahwah, NJ: Lawrence Erlbaum Associates.

Coie, J. D., Terry, R., Lenox, K. F., Lochman, J. E., & Hyman, C. (1995). Childhood peer rejection and aggression as predictors of stable patterns of adolescent disorder. *Development and Psychopathology, 7,* 697–713.

Dishion, T. J., McCord, J., & Poulin, F. (1999). When interventions harm: Peer groups and problem behavior. *American Psychologist, 54,* 755–764.

Gustafson, S. B., Stattin, H., & Magnusson, D. (1989). Aspects of the development of a career versus homemaking orientation among females: The longitudinal influence of educational motivation and peers. *Journal of Research on Adolescence, 2,* 241–259.

Hirschi, T. (1969). *Causes of delinquency.* Berkeley: University of California Press.

Magnusson, D. (1988). *Individual development from an interactional perspective: A longitudinal study.* Hillsdale, NJ: Lawrence Erlbaum Associates.

Magnusson, D., Dunér, A., & Zetterblom, G. (1975). *Adjustment: A longitudinal study.* New York: Wiley.

Magnusson, D., Stattin, H., & Allen, V. (1986). Differential maturation among girls and its relation to social adjustment: A longitudinal perspective. In P. Baltes, D. Featherman, & R. Lerner (Eds.), *Life span development* (Vol. 7, pp. 134–172). New York: Academic Press.

Mahoney, J. L., & Stattin, H. (2000). Leisure time activities and adolescent anti-social behavior: The role of structure and social context. *Journal of Adolescence, 23,* 113–127.

Mahoney, J. L., Stattin, H., & Magnusson, D. (2001). Youth leisure activity participation and individual adjustment: The Swedish youth recreation center. *International Journal of Behavioral Development, 509–520.*

McCord, J. (1978). A 30-year follow-up of treatment effects. *American Psychologist, 33,* 284–289.

Osgood, D. W., Wilson, J. K., O'Malley, P. M., Bachman, J. G., & Johnston, L. D. (1996). Routine activities and individual deviant behavior. *American Sociological Review, 61,* 635–655.

Patterson, G. R. (1993). Orderly change in a stable world: The antisocial trait as chinera. *Journal of Consulting and Clinical Psychology, 61,* 911–919.

Patterson, G. R., Reid, J. B., Dishion, T. J. (1992). *A social learning approach: Vol. 4. Antisocial boys.* Eugene, OR: Castalia.

Shannahan, M. J., & Flaherty, B. P. (2001). Dynamic patterns of time use in adolescence. *Child Development, 72,* 385–401.

Stattin, H., Gustafson, S. B., & Magnusson, D. (1989). Peer influences on adolescent drinking: A social transition perspective. *Journal of Early Adolescence, 9*, 227–246.

Stattin, H., & Kerr, M. (2002). Adolescents' values matter. In J.-E. Nurmi (Ed.), *Navigating through adolescence: European perspectives* (pp. 21–58). *The Michigan State University Series on Families and Child Development*. New York: Routledge Farmer.

Stattin, H., & Magnusson, C. (1996). Leaving home at early age among females: Antecedents, adolescent adjustment and future life implications. In J. A. Graber & J. S. Dubas (Eds.), *Leaving home: Understanding the transition to adulthood. New Directions for Child Development, 71*, 53–69.

Stattin, H., & Magnusson, D. (1989). Social transition in adolescence: A biosocial perspective. In A. de Ribaupierre (Ed.), *Transition mechanisms in child development: The longitudinal perspective* (pp. 147–190). Cambridge: Cambridge University Press.

Stattin, H., & Magnusson, D. (1990). *Pubertal maturation in female development*. Hillsdale, NJ: Lawrence Erlbaum Associates.

Stattin, H., & Magnusson, D. (1991). Stability and change in criminal behavior up to age 30: Findings from a prospective, longitudinal study in Sweden. *British Journal of Criminology, 31*, 327–346.

Stattin, H., Magnusson, D., & Reichel, H. (1989). Criminal activity at different ages. A study based on a Swedish longitudinal research population. *British Journal of Criminology, 29*, 368–385.

11

Activity Choices in Middle Childhood: The Roles of Gender, Self-Beliefs, and Parents' Influence

Janis E. Jacobs
Margaret K. Vernon
Pennsylvania State University

Jacquelynne Eccles
University of Michigan

Many parents enroll their children in organized activities or encourage participation in individual activities because they believe that such involvement is good for them or builds confidence. In addition, parents may select specific activities based on their perceptions of what is appropriate for girls or boys. For example, they are more likely to enroll their daughters in art or ballet and to enroll their sons in Little League. Beyond anecdotal evidence shared between parents, does participation in organized activities have an impact on children's attitudes or self-beliefs? Do the kinds of activities or the amount of participation matter? Finally, how is participation in gender-differentiated activities related to later attitudes and beliefs?

Recent research has documented the positive benefits of involvement in extracurricular activities for adolescents, linking activity involvement to positive social, emotional, and academic outcomes (e.g., Eccles & Barber, 1999; Mahoney & Cairns, 1997), and to later positive social outcomes such as more prestigious occupations, civic engagement, voting, and volunteering in one's community (e.g., Youniss, McLellan, Su, & Yates,

1999). In addition, adolescents who are involved with extracurricular activities are less likely to become involved in problem behaviors (e.g., Eccles & Barber, 1999; Mahoney, 2001). Although the literature relating activity involvement with positive outcomes has primarily focused on the period of adolescence, a few studies suggest that individuals who are involved with extracurricular activities in middle childhood also have more positive psychosocial and academic outcomes (e.g., McHale, Crouter, & Tucker, 2001; Posner & Vandell, 1999).

If, as suggested by previous research, involvement in extracurricular activities is related to positive developmental outcomes, it is important to understand why children choose to become involved and stay involved in particular types of activities. If we are to encourage children to become involved in activities at young ages, it is also critical to understand the correlates of activity choice and sustained involvement. For example, we know that children prefer activities that are congruent with their gender (McHale, Crouter, & Tucker, 1999); however, very little is known about the role gender may play in the kinds, types, or breadth of activities children choose during middle childhood. In addition, although theoretical links between self-perceptions and activity choices have been made (e.g., Eccles et al., 1983), we have much to learn about the ways in which early extracurricular involvement may impact the development of self-perceptions, activity interest, or long-term engagement in activities during middle childhood.

The goal of this chapter is to begin to explore these issues, both conceptually and empirically. We begin by briefly reviewing the links between positive outcomes and extracurricular activities during both adolescence and middle childhood, and then turn to some of the factors that may be related to early activity choice, including self-concept, task values, and long-term involvement in specific activities. We also explore some of the ways in which extracurricular activities during this age period may vary by gender, including type of activity, number of activities, time spent on various activities, and dispersion of involvement. Finally, we provide some empirical evidence related to gender differences in extracurricular activities and relations to later outcomes.

FACTORS RELATED TO ACTIVITY CHOICES
IN MIDDLE CHILDHOOD

Although extracurricular involvement has been associated with various outcomes, very little is known about the types and amounts of activities in which children are involved during middle childhood, and how children develop preferences for various kinds of activities. Involvement in extracurricular activities develops within the contexts of children's lives, thus, we believe that it is important to consider the motivational factors that lead children to choose one set of activities over another. For example, children are unlikely to remain involved in activities that they do not value or those in which they feel incompetent or unsupported. In addition, they are apt to become involved in activities that match their gender-typed beliefs about what a boy or a girl should do rather than those that do not. By the same token, involvement in extra-curricular activities is likely to help shape values and self-competence over time, and these beliefs, in turn, may reinforce the desire to continue participating. We expect a variety of factors to be related to activity involvement in middle childhood, including task values, self-perceptions, gender, and parental support. Each of these factors is now reviewed briefly.

Task Values

According to some of the modern expectancy-value theories (e.g., Eccles et al., 1983; Feather, 1988; Wigfield & Eccles, 1992), an individual's values for particular goals and tasks can help explain *why* a child chooses one activity over another. Two types of values that are likely to play a role in extracurricular activity choices are attainment value and intrinsic value. We define *attainment value* as the personal importance of doing well on the task, and link it to the relevance of engaging in a task for confirming or disconfirming salient aspects of one's self-beliefs (see Eccles, 1987). *Intrinsic value* is the enjoyment the individual gets from performing the activity, or the interest the individual has in the subject. We have found that values are closely linked to how children and adolescents choose to spend their time. For example, even after controlling for prior performance levels, task values predict involvement in sport activities, as well as course plans and enrollment decisions in mathematics, physics, and English (Eccles & Harold, 1991; Eccles & Wigfield, 1995). Others also have found that interest or intrinsic value is highly related to involvement in sports (Garton & Pratt, 1987); that fun or enjoyment is the most often reported reason for continued involvement in sports (Wankel & Berger, 1990); and that adolescents choose leisure activities that they consider intrinsically motivating and challenging (Larson, 2000).

In addition, values for leisure activities may change, as children get older. For example, in a longitudinal study of changes in children's values, we found declines across the elementary school years for valuing of music and sports (Wigfield et al., 1997). Wigfield and Eccles (1992) suggested that during the early elementary school grades, the subjective value of a task may be primarily characterized by children's interests in the task, thus, young children's choices of different activities may stem from their interests in those activities. At young ages, interests may shift fairly rapidly, so that children may try many different activities for a short time before deciding which activities they enjoy the most. During the early and middle elementary school grades, children's sense of the usefulness of different activities, especially for future goals, may not be very clear, and so this component may only be understood later. If such a shift in values for the same activity occurs, it would be tantamount to engaging in a task due to the intrinsic value of the task (interest) in childhood, but staying engaged over time due to utility values (perceived usefulness).

Self-Perceptions of Competence

A second part of our model is perceptions of competence or self-concept. This is the part of the self-system that is typically thought of as "earned" based on competence and interests, and the competence component is often labeled *self-competence* or *self-esteem*. According to numerous theories (e.g., attribution theory, self-efficacy theory, self-worth theory) children are more motivated to select increasingly challenging tasks when they believe that they have the ability to accomplish a particular task (e.g., Bandura, 1994). Thus, the child who feels competent at playing the clarinet in middle childhood is likely to be motivated to continue to play music and to push on to greater heights (e.g., trying out for a competitive music ensemble or trying more difficult passages of music).

We have found that self-competence beliefs are related to achievement in a variety of domains, even after controlling for previous achievement or ability (e.g., Eccles, 1987; Eccles, Adler, & Meece, 1984; Eccles, Wigfield, Harold, & Blumenfeld, 1993). In addition, Harter (1998) has suggested that self-esteem and motivation are enhanced when one values those activities at which one is competent. This suggests that the relations between individuals' subjective task values and competence perceptions will be important for understanding how children choose to allot their leisure time among different activities. According to Harter (1998), the ability to form congruent hierarchies of task values and competence beliefs should lead to higher self-esteem and continuing motivation, whereas incongruent hierarchies of beliefs will lead to negative self-esteem and lowered motivation. For example, individuals may cope with being incompetent in baseball by lowering the value they attach to it and by enhancing the value they attach to another sport or another activity domain. Several studies have provided support for the close links between self-concept and values (Jacobs, Lanza, Osgood, Eccles, & Wigfield, 2002; Harter, 1990). This work suggests that children's values for various leisure activities are likely to change as they refine their perceptions of self-competence, increasing the value they attach to some activities while decreasing the value they attach to others. These attitudinal changes, of course, are related to the fact that their actual competence is likely to be increasing if they spend more time on the specific activities that are valued.

Gender

Our previous research has revealed gender-typed differences for attitudes about sports, social activities, English, and music (e.g., Eccles et al., 1993; Jacobs et al., 2002) across a variety of age groups. In addition, children prefer activities that are congruent with their gender and also participate in gender-typed activities more often than in gender atypical activities. Interestingly, during middle childhood, activity preferences are more gender typed than either children's gender role attitudes or their gender-typed personality qualities (McHale et al., 1999). Girls spend more time outside the home in organized activities, taking lessons, doing academic activities, engaging in outdoor play and socializing, whereas boys spend more time outside the home in unorganized activities (McHale et al., 2001; Posner & Vandell, 1999) and in team sports (Eccles & Barber, 1999; Larson & Verma, 1999; McHale et al., 2001).

In addition, the gender of siblings and parents has been implicated in children's activity choices, with male sibling dyads engaged in more male gender-typed activities than any other group (Stoneman, Brody, & MacKinnon, 1986), and children involved in more activities that fathers than mothers endorse (McHale et al., 1999). It appears that one of the main ways in which children express gender identity is by participating in and valuing gender-appropriate activities; however, very little is known about how gender may play a role in the amount, types, or breadth of activities in which children are involved at different ages.

Parental Encouragement

Although children may become interested in some types of activities without any adult input, most activities that are available to children during middle childhood are the result of socialization on the part of parents,[1] teachers, or other adults. This is especially true for organized activities that some researchers suggest are most beneficial (Larson, 2000). Over the years, numerous studies have linked parenting practices to children's achievement motivation (see Eccles, Wigfield, & Schiefele, 1998, for a review); however, few researchers have focused on how parents motivate, encourage, and support their children as they participate in a variety of activities.

---

[1]It is important to note that we use the term *parents* in this review of the literature, although in later sections of the chapter our data examines only mothers' influence, and mothers and fathers may affect patterns of activity involvement in different ways.

We have developed a model of parental influence on achievement motivation in a variety of contexts (Eccles et al., 1983) that includes several ways in which parents influence their children: (a) by the general social–emotional climate they offer and by their general childrearing beliefs; (b) by providing specific experiences for the child (e.g., enrollment in lessons, involvement in church activities); (c) by modeling involvement in valued activities; and (d) by communicating their perceptions of the child's abilities and expectations for performance. The environment, role modeling, and messages that parents provide regarding the value they attach to various activities are expected to influence children's motivation to pursue any particular activity. Over time, children make their own decisions and have their own values for particular activities and integrate these beliefs into their self-systems.

We have tested and found support for each of the four components of parent influence for achievement in a variety of domains, including both in-school and out-of-school activities (e.g., see Jacobs & Eccles, 2000, for a summary). In this chapter, however, we focus only on the ways in which the experiences parents provide for their children are influenced by their perceptions of their children's abilities and interests and parents' valuing of the activity domain (e.g., sports, music, math, science). We know from our previous work that parents' perceptions of their children's abilities, their expectations for their children's success, and their gender stereotypes predict children's self-perceptions of competence and their actual achievement, even after previous indicators of achievement are controlled (e.g., Jacobs, 1991; Jacobs & Eccles, 1992). In this way, parents appear to play the role of "interpreters of reality" for their children (Eccles, Adler, & Kaczala, 1982). Although little work has been done to relate these same factors to children's involvement in activities, in one study, parents were more likely to provide extra sports experiences for their children if they believed that the children were interested in the activity and had sports ability (Fredericks, 1999). We expect parents' beliefs about their children's abilities as well as their own values to be highly related to the opportunities they provide for their children. In addition, parents also may be more likely to provide experiences for their children that fit existing expectations for gender-appropriate activities (e.g., enrolling their daughters in dance lessons and their sons in peewee football).

OUR RECENT RESEARCH ON ACTIVITY PARTICIPATION DURING MIDDLE CHILDHOOD

We have briefly reviewed the factors that we believe play a major role in children's activity choices during middle childhood, providing evidence from our previous work for an expectancy-value model of activity choice that includes the importance of individual identity markers (such as gender) and socializers (such as parents). We turn now to an examination of recent data that addresses our hypotheses about the importance of these factors during the middle childhood years. We examined gender differences in Grade 1 through Grade 6 children's leisure participation by types of activities, number of activities, and breadth of activities. In addition, we related activity participation in middle childhood to later value and perceived competence in various activity domains. Finally, we examined the effect of concentration in one activity type in middle childhood and its relation to later value and perceived competence in the same type of activity.

Participants and Design

The analyses reported here used data that were collected as part of the Childhood and Beyond (CAB) study, a longitudinal project employing a cohort-sequential design. Data were collected from three cohorts of children and their parents between 1989 and 1999; beginning when Cohort 1 was in kindergarten, Cohort 2 was in Grade 1, and Cohort 3 was in Grade 3. Data for the analyses reported here were collected from children when they were in early middle childhood (Grade 1, Grade 2, and Grade 4); again when they were in late middle childhood (Grade 3, Grade 4, and Grade 6); and finally, when children were in adolescence (Grade 7, Grade 8, and Grade 10). Children attended 10 public, elementary schools in four middle-class school districts in the suburbs of a large midwestern city. Activity participation, children's activity-related values, and self-concept data used in the analyses reported here were collected via questionnaires answered during school class time by approximately 500 children (50% female). Data about number, type, and frequency of activities, as well as mothers' values about activities were collected from the same children's mothers via mailed questionnaires during this same time period.

GENDER DIFFERENCES AND LONGITUDINAL TRENDS IN ACTIVITY PARTICIPATION

Children's activity participation was assessed by asking mothers to list the specific activities in which their child was involved and to describe how much time and how frequently the child participated. Mothers' reports of children's activity participation were used because we believe that mothers' reports are likely to be more reliable than children's reports during the early elementary school years.

We then assigned each individual activity listed by mothers to one of the following categories: (a) *team sports* (e.g., basketball, soccer); (b) *individual sports* (e.g., tennis, gymnastics, swimming, karate); (c) *academic activities* (e.g., creative writing, homework, math enrichment); (d) *music/drama orga-*

nized activities (e.g., playing a musical instrument, vocal music lessons, or choir, dance, drama); (e) *hobbies* (e.g., crafts, model making, collections); (f) *group activities* (e.g., church groups, scouting, day-camp, community programs). Based on these assignments, we computed the total number of activities in which children participated across categories, the number of activities in each category for each child and the total number of categories for each child as a way to compare overall level of activity and variety of activity involvement.

As can be seen in Fig. 11.1, older children participate in activities slightly more than younger children; and this age difference is apparent for both girls and boys. Repeated measures ANCOVAs were conducted that included gender as a between-subjects variable and activity participation at three time points as a within-subjects variable (cohort was also included as a covariate to control for the effects of age at time one). These analyses revealed significant differences by grade, with children involved in significantly more activities as they got older, $F\ (2,\ 276) = 2.86, p < .05$; however, the number of hours of activity involvement did not differ significantly with age. Interestingly, no significant differences were found between girls and boys, although the trend was clearly one of girls having slightly higher involvement in extracurricular activities at all ages during this time period. In addition, no significant differences between boys' and girls' total amount of time spent on extracurricular activities was found.

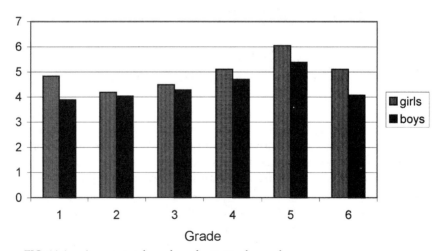

FIG. 11.1.   Average total number of activities by gender.

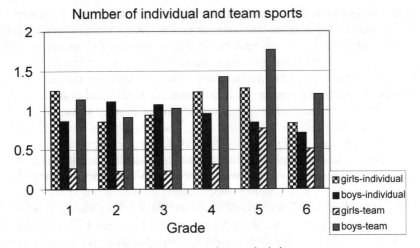

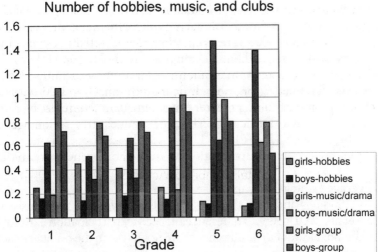

FIG. 11.2. Average number of activities in each category by gender.

A quick glance at Fig. 11.2, however, suggests that although boys and girls may be participating in similar numbers of activities, their involvement in any particular category of activity is *not* similar. As expected, boys participated in significantly more team sports than girls, $F(1, 277) = 112.44, p < .001$. Girls' participation was significantly higher than boys, however, for individual sports, $F(1, 277) = 6.72, p < .01$, hobbies, $F(1, 277) = 6.07, p < .05$, music/drama activities, $F(1, 277) = 66.12, p < .001$, and organized group activities, $F(1, 277) = 5.31, p < .05$.

The fact that girls and boys are participating in almost the same number of activities, but that girls are more involved in almost every category of activities suggests that the major gender difference in activity involvement during middle childhood is the dispersion of activities rather than the total number (or total amount of time spent). We investigated this hypothesis by examining several measures of dispersion. We created a *total category* variable, a *homogeneity index*[2] and three proportion variables: *proportion of activities in team sports* (number of team sports/total number of activities), the *proportion of activities in individual sports* (number of individual sports/total number of activities), and the *proportion of activities in music/drama* (number of music/drama activities/total number of activities).

We next examined each of these variables to assess any gender differences. Not surprisingly, girls were involved in more activity categories than boys, F (1, 277) = 5.69, p < .05. When we examined the proportion of activities in team sports, individual sports, and music/drama out of total number of activities, we found that boys were involved in a larger proportion of team sports than girls, F (1, 277) = 126.66, p < .001. In addition, girls were involved in a greater proportion of individual sports than boys, F (1, 277) = 4.93, p < .05. In addition, girls spent a greater proportion of their total activities in music/drama than boys, F (1, 277) = 59.30, p < .001. The proportion of total activities spent in team sports, individual sports, and music/drama is illustrated in Fig. 11.3.

Finally, the homogeneity index allowed us to capture the individual proportions just described in a single index, ranging from .04 to 1.00, with numbers closer to one indicating greater homogeneity. It is interesting to note that children's activity participation became significantly less homogeneous after the first wave, F (2, 276) = 4.11, p < .05. In addition, this measure revealed that boys' activity participation was more homogeneous than that of girls, F (1, 277) = 12.33, p < .001 (girls' average homogeneity index = .33; boys' average homogeneity index = .40).

These findings indicate that, as has been suggested previously (e.g., McHale et al., 2001), gender differences in activity participation exist in middle childhood. However, the differences are not found in the number of activities in which girls and boys participate, but in the types of activities. Boys are participating primarily in team sports, whereas girls participate in a more diverse array of activities that include team sports, as well as individual sports, music/drama, hobbies, and clubs. In addition, these gender differences in dispersion of activities begin early and continue through middle childhood.

RELATIONS BETWEEN ACTIVITY PARTICIPATION, PERCEIVED COMPETENCE, AND TASK VALUES

Although we can describe the pattern of activity involvement and how it differs by gender, if we are to comprehend why children choose to be in-

---

[2]The homogeneity ratio was calculated as follows: [(number of team sports/total number of activities)^2 + (number of individual sports/total number of activities)^2 + (number of academic activities/total number of activities)^2 + (number of hobbies/total number of activities)^2 + (number of music/drama activities/total number of activities)^2 + (number of group activities/total number of activities)^2].

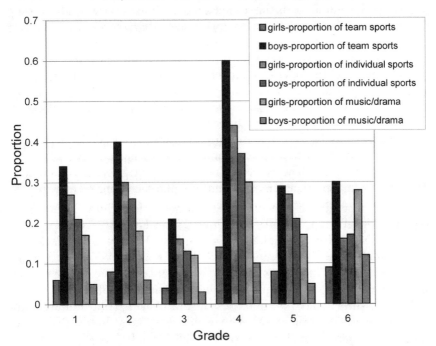

FIG. 11.3. Proportion of total activities spent in team sport, individual sports, and music/drama by gender.

volved in one activity versus another in middle childhood we need to examine some of the correlates of particular activity choices. The research reviewed earlier indicates that activity involvement is valuable for children; therefore, it is important to understand the ways in which their beliefs and those of their parents may be related to such involvement. The Eccles expectancy-value model suggests that perceived competence, task values, and parents' attitudes and behaviors may each contribute to the activity choices that children make. Our earlier empirical work has typically focused on academic choices rather than on extracurricular choices, but we believe that the same relations are likely to be found for activity involvement. In short, children are unlikely to choose to spend time on activities that they do not value or at which they feel incompetent. In addition, time spent on activities in any given domain is likely to lead to higher values and perceptions of competence over time for similar activities.

To test these relations for extracurricular activities during middle childhood, we assessed the impact of activity participation during middle childhood on later (early adolescence) task values and self-perceptions of ability in two domains—sports and the arts. Children's self-perceptions of ability and task values were assessed when children were in Grade 1, Grade 2, and Grade 4 and again when they were in Grade 3, Grade 4, and Grade 6, using 7-point Likert-type scales. Self-concept of music ability was measured with a 5-item scale ($\alpha = .74 - .94$) containing questions such as "How good are you at playing a musical instrument?" Sports self-concept was assessed with a 5-item scale ($\alpha = .84 - .94$) with items such as "How good at sports are you?" A 3-item scale ($\alpha = .86 - .93$) was used to assess music values (e.g., How important is being good at music to you?). Sports value was assessed with a 4-item scale ($\alpha = .58 - .92$), using similar measures.

We began by looking simply at the relations between earlier domain-specific values and self-perceptions of competence and later activity participation within the same domain (controlling for gender because we already know that participation in these activities varies by gender). Interestingly, we found that sports self-concept and values at Grade 1, Grade 2, and Grade 4 each predicted team sports participation 2 years later (self-competence: $b = .27, p < .001, R^2 = .24$; values: ($b = .15; p < .01, R^2 = .20$), but neither sports values nor self-competence predicted later participation in individual sports. Likewise, music values and self-competence at wave 2 were not significantly related to participation in music activities 2 years later.

We were surprised to find that these results provided only minimal support for our expectation that prior self-concept and values would be related to later participation in a variety of activities. Indeed, these findings suggest that early domain-specific perceptions of competence and values are *not* necessarily related to later activity participation; the relations appear to depend on the specific activities. In the case of team sports, the relationships may be due to the fact that children in this country begin to be involved in team sports at young ages, thus, they may have formulated both self-perceptions and values by early in middle childhood and these are related to continued involvement. These domain-differences may be a result of the availability of particular activities at early ages (e.g., team sports) or knowledge about the activities (e.g., watching older siblings play soccer or baseball).

Activity Self-Perceptions of Competence

We next turned the tables and examined the effects of participation in activities on later domain-specific values and perceptions of competence. Specifically, we examined the relations between activity participation in Grade 3, Grade 4, and Grade 6 on perceived competence in music and sports and value for music and sports in early adolescence (Grade 7, Grade 8, and Grade 10). We used blockwise regressions to do this, entering gender as the first block, and prior (Grade 1, Grade 2, and Grade 4) self-perceptions or values in the specific domain (sports or arts) in the second block as a control. The number of activities in which the child participated in the particular activity domain was entered in Block 3. For example, if the outcome variable was sports self-concept in adolescence, gender was entered in the first block, sports self-concept in early middle childhood (Grade 1, Grade 2, and Grade 4) was entered in the second block, and participation in sports (team and individual were run separately) in late middle childhood (Grade 3, Grade 4, and Grade 6) was entered in Block 3.

We found that in the areas of team sports and music, individuals who participated in more domain-specific activities in late middle childhood had significantly higher self-perceptions of competence in that domain in early adolescence, even after controlling for gender and prior self-perceptions in the same domain (team sports: $b = .21, p < .001$; music: $b = .24, p < .001$). The same pattern was not found for individual sports. In addition, we found main effects for gender in the expected direction for each domain (team sports: $b = .30; p < .001$; individual sports: $b = .30, p < .001$; music: $b = -.21, p < .001$). Overall, the combination of variables accounted for 26% of the variance in self-perceptions of competence in team sports, 24% in individual sports, and 14% in music. Thus, activity involvement in later middle childhood is related to self-perceptions of ability 4 years later; however, as in our earlier analyses, it appears that the relations between activity involvement and self-perceptions are activity-specific.

Activity Values. The same analysis strategy was used to test the role of gender, prior values, and activity participation in predicting later domain-specific values. We found that individuals who participated in more domain-specific activities had significantly higher values for those particular activities, even after controlling for gender and prior values (team sports: $b = .30, p < .001$; individual sports: $b = .13, p < .05$; music: $b = .22, p < .001$). Once again, main effects for gender in the expected direction were found for all activity values (team sports: $b = .28, p < .001$; individual sports: $b = .28, p < .001$; music: $b = -.17, p < .01$). Overall, the combination of variables was able to account for 22% of the variance in task values for team sports, 16% in individual sports, and 9% in music.

The impact of activity concentration on self-perceptions of ability was tested using the same block-wise regression method. We measured concentration of activities as described earlier (an individual's number of domain-specific activities divided by the total number of activities reported by that individual); thus, ratios closer to 1.0 show greater concentration of activities. We found that those who had higher concentrations of activities in one domain in Wave 4 had higher self-perceptions of their abilities 4 years later (team sports: $b = .22, p < .001, R^2 = .27$; individual sports: $b = .13, p < .05, R^2 = .25$; music: $b = .22, p < .001; R^2 = .12$). Main effects for gender were also found (team sports: $b = .33$, $p < .001$; individual sports: $b = .33$, $p < .001$; music: $b = -.22$, $p < .001$).

These analyses provide support for two important points that we raised in our earlier review. First, prior values and self-perceptions are related to later sports team participation over a 2-year period in middle childhood; however, the relationship was not found in other activity domains. This suggests that values and self-perceptions in some areas may not be very well developed due to lack of experience with the activity or for other reasons. Second, activity participation during middle childhood (number of activities and concentration) is related to values and self-perceptions 4 years later, even after controlling for prior values and self-perceptions. Indeed, the links between activity participation and self-beliefs span middle childhood into adolescence.

RELATIONS BETWEEN MOTHERS' PERCEPTIONS OF CHILDREN'S COMPETENCE, TASK VALUES, AND CHILDREN'S ACTIVITY PARTICIPATION

Another important component of our previous work and of the Eccles' model is the role of socializers in children's activity choices (see Jacobs & Eccles, 2000, for a longer review). As we suggested earlier, children are more likely to become involved in activities that their parents value (especially at the youngest ages), and they are more likely to stay involved in activities that their parents encourage and support. We provide some evidence for that perspective from mothers of the same middle school children that we have been describing.

Mothers' values were assessed via questionnaire during the same time in which children's data were gathered, by asking, "How important is it to you that (child) does well in sports/music?" Answers were given on a 1 to 7 response scale; 1 *(Not at all important)*, 7 *(Very important)*. Mothers' perceptions of their children's abilities in each domain were assessed by asking, "How good is your child in sports/music?" Mothers responded on a 1 to 7 response scale: 1 *(Not good at all)*, 7 *(Very good)*.

We again used blockwise regressions, with gender entered in the first block, children's self-perceptions of ability in a given activity domain in the second block (as a control for prior ability), and mothers' ratings of the importance of the activity domain in the third block (each of these predictors was measured when the children were in Grade 1, Grade 2, and Grade 4). We examined the effects of these predictors on children's activity participation, self-perceptions of ability, and value for that activity in Grade 3, Grade 4, and Grade 6. We found that mothers' beliefs about the importance of participation in domain-specific activities were significantly related to later participation in team sports ($b = .18$, $p <$

.001, $R^2 = .30$) and in music/drama activities ($b = .19, p < .001, R^2 = .15$), even after controlling for gender and children's prior abilities. As before, main effects for gender were found (team sports: $b = .44, p < .001$; music: $b = -.34, p < .001$).

We conducted a similar set of analyses with the same predictors, but with children's self-perceptions of ability and values for the particular activity domains as dependent variables. We found that mothers' earlier ratings of the importance of the activity domain were significantly related to their children's later self-perceptions of ability in the same domain (sports: $b = .17, p < .001, R^2 = .33$; music: $b = .20, p < .001, R^2 = .13$), even after controlling for prior perceptions of ability. Main effects were again found for gender in sports only ($b = .41, p < .001$). Similarly, we found that mothers' ratings of the importance of domain-specific activities were significantly related to their children's valuing of the same activities 2 years later (sports: $b = .14, p < .010, R^2 = .23$; music: $b = .13, p < .05, R^2 = .08$). Main effects for gender were also found for sports only ($b = .19, p < .001$).

The previous analysis indicated a significant relationship between mothers' and children's values for sports and music, after controlling for a variety of other factors. To directly test the differences between their values, we conducted a repeated-measures ANOVA with mothers' and child's value for sports and music at Wave 2 (Grade 1, Grade 2, and Grade 4) and again 2 years later, including gender as an independent variable and cohort as a covariate. We found that mothers valued sports significantly less than children at both Wave 2, $F(1, 451) = 140.89, p < .001$, and Wave 4, $F(1, 375) = 25.16, p < .001$. Mothers also valued music significantly less than their children at Wave 3, $F(1, 439) = 3.97, p < .05$; however, at Wave 4, mothers valued music significantly more than their children, $F(1, 366) = 31.14, p < .001$. In addition, boys and mothers of boys valued sports significantly more than girls or mothers of girls at both waves and the gender effect was reversed for music at both waves.

In summary, these results suggest a very consistent pattern that is not unlike many of our earlier findings about the importance of parents' beliefs for their children's academic self-perceptions and values (e.g., Jacobs, 1991; Jacobs & Eccles, 1992; Parsons, Adler, & Kaczala, 1982). It is clear that if mothers believe that particular activities are important, their children are more likely to participate in those activities as well as to value the activities themselves. In addition, children whose mothers value particular activities feel more self-competent in those domains (probably as a result of greater participation). Importantly, these relationships were observed over a period of 2 years and across Grade 1 through Grade 6. It also is clear that mothers' and children's values and participation are gender-typed, with higher participation and valuing of the arts for girls and of sports for boys.

CONCLUSIONS

We began this chapter by discussing previous research that has consistently linked activity involvement with positive outcomes for adolescents, and to a lesser extent, for children in middle childhood. Although those findings suggest that extracurricular activities are valuable, more information is needed about different patterns of activity involvement and the psychosocial factors that may be linked to such involvement if we, as parents and professionals, are to create conditions that will maximize the benefits of activity involvement. In order to do this, we need to know much more about what contributes to activity choice and sustains children's involvement over time. Using the Eccles' model, we highlighted four factors that might be expected to contribute to activity choice during this developmental period: gender, self-perceptions of ability at a given activity, activity value or importance, and parental support for the activity. We presented support for each of these potential contributors from our previous research that is largely on academic achievement, and then provided corroborating evidence from our study of children's activity choices in middle childhood and adolescence.

What can we conclude? Not surprisingly, gender differences in activity participation begin early and continue throughout middle childhood. Although girls and boys participate in the same numbers of activities, they participate in different activities and girls try a wider variety of activities. Boys are involved in a large number of activities that fall into the category of *team sports*. Although girls participate in team sports, they are participating in them less frequently than boys, giving girls more time to explore a wide variety of activities, as evidenced by their greater participation in individual sports, arts activities, hobbies, and clubs. We tried to capture this differential dispersion of activity involvement by calculating a homogeneity index; counting the number of categories in which a child was involved, and creating scores for the proportion of activity involvement in each category. No matter how we calculated it, the picture was the same—boys' activity participation was significantly more homogeneous than that of girls. During middle childhood, boys are already limiting the types of activities in which they are involved.

Does this difference in dispersion of activities matter in the long run? Although it is not possible to answer that question completely from the analyses presented here, we found that self-perceptions of competence and values during adolescence are clearly linked to earlier activity participation during middle childhood (number of activities and concentration), even after controlling for prior values and self-perceptions. Our previous work indicates that boys have significantly higher self-perceptions of competence in sports than do girls at all ages (Jacobs et al., 2002), and that, on average, these beliefs decline over time for both boys and girls. A potential explanation for this finding is boys' greater concentration of activities in the sports arena.

This point leads to another major conclusion that we can draw from our previous work, as well as the data presented—activity participation is highly related to later self-perceptions of competence and values. This relationship holds across 4 years and across a variety of domains, even after prior domain-specific values and competence are controlled. This highlights the importance of early activity participation for constructing a set of self-beliefs and values that may determine whether or not the child stays engaged in the activity or chooses other similar activities. Early values and self-perceptions did not predict later participation in activities; however, except in the area of team sports. These findings were somewhat of a surprise, because we have typically found relations in that direction. This may have been due to the young ages at which we tested these links; children in the early elementary grades may not yet have enough experience with many activities to have strongly differentiated values and self-perceptions.

The role of parents is also important. Although children may excel in one area or another and prefer one type of activity instead of another, they are not able to become involved in organized activities without some adult's help during middle childhood, and this help is most likely to come from a parent. The fact that more boys end up in team sports and girls in individual sports is related to the opportunities available and the choices made by parents, as much as it is to children's preferences in the early grades. We found that children are more likely to participate in activities, as well as value the activities if mothers believe that those particular activities are important. Children whose mothers value particular activities also feel more self-competent in those domains. Although we did not test the role of fathers in the analyses presented here, our previous studies have shown the influence of fathers' attitudes on children's achievement to be similar to that of mothers (e.g., Eccles, et al., 1983; Jacobs, 1991). It is also important to note that, although parents play a pivotal role in influencing activity choices, children may be influenced by other adults in their lives (e.g., teachers, coaches, or club leaders). In addition, siblings and friends are likely to influence children's decisions to participate in particular activities.

The current results are consistent with the Eccles' model of parent socialization for achievement and with our earlier findings about the importance of parents' beliefs for their children's academic self-perceptions and values (e.g., Jacobs, 1991; Jacobs & Eccles, 1992; Parsons et al., 1982). The ties between parents' values and the choices they make for their children's involvement in extracurricular activities are apt to be even stronger than for academic achievement because extracurricular activities are completely optional. Parents are unlikely to pay for lessons, buy equipment, or encourage their children to participate in activities that they find objectionable or that do not coincide with their perceptions of what is appropriate for their child's gender, social class, or age. This may explain why few boys are enrolled in dance classes or art lessons, options that many parents may not consider for their sons and that some parents may find inappropriate for males.

Parents are most likely to encourage activities that they value and do what they can to get their children interested in pursuing them. It is important to remember that parents' roles may shift as their children mature, from providing exposure, opportunities, and role modeling in the early phases of activity choice to providing encouragement and guidance for activities that their children choose at later points in development. As children get older, parents may begin to "react" to children's ideas about activity involvement rather than to initiate all aspects of involvement (see Jacobs & Eccles, 2000, for longer description of this process). As we suggested earlier, children may or may not stay involved in the activities that they sample during middle childhood for a variety of reasons. They may lose interest, feel less competent as competition becomes stronger, or decide to spend more time on just one or two activities. We found that the number of activities and types of activities children are participating in declines to some extent during late middle childhood; however, the hours of extra-curricular participation do not. This suggests that children may be refining their likes and dislikes and spending more time on those activities that have value to them. It is clearly a very complex process, one that takes place over time and across many interactions. We are continuing to explore the processes that underlie both continuity and change across time in varied settings and across activities.

ACKNOWLEDGMENT

This research was supported by Grant HD17553 from the National Institute for Child Health and Human Development to Jacquelynne S. Eccles, Allan Wigfield, Phyllis Blumenfeld, and Rena Harold.

REFERENCES

Bandura, A. (1994). *Self-efficacy: The exercise of control.* New York: W. H. Freeman.

Eccles, J. S. (1987). Gender roles and women's achievement-related decisions. *Psychology of Women Quarterly, 11,* 135–172.

Eccles, J., Adler, T. F., Futterman, R., Goff, S. B., Kaczala, C. M., Meece, J. L., & Midgley, C. (1983). Expectancies, values, and academic behaviors. In J. T. Spence (Ed.), *Achievement and achievement motivation* (pp. 75–146). San Francisco, CA: W. H. Freeman.

Eccles, J. S., Adler, T. F., & Meece, J. L. (1984). Sex differences in achievement: A test of alternative theories. *Journal of Personality and Social Psychology, 46,* 26–43.

Eccles, J. S., & Barber, B. L. (1999). Student council, volunteering, basketball, or marching band: What kind of extracurricular involvement matters? *Journal of Youth and Adolescence, 6*(3), 281–294.

Eccles, J. S., & Harold, R. D. (1991). Gender differences in sport involvement: Applying the Eccles' expectancy-value model. *Journal of Applied Sport Psychology, 3*, 7–35.

Eccles, J. S., & Wigfield, A. (1995). In the mind of the achiever: The structure of adolescents' academic achievement related-beliefs and self-perceptions. *Personality and Social Psychology Bulletin, 21*, 215–225.

Eccles, J. S., Wigfield, A., Harold, R., & Blumenfeld, P. (1993). Age and gender differences in children's achievement self-perceptions during the elementary school years. *Child Development, 64*, 830–847.

Eccles, J. S., Wigfield, A., & Schiefele, U. (1998). Motivation to succeed. In W. Damon (Series Ed.) & N. Eisenberg (Vol. Ed.), *Handbook of child psychology: Social, emotional, and personality development* (pp. 105–107). New York: Wiley.

Feather, N. T. (1988). Values, valences, and course enrollment: testing the role of personal values within an expectancy—value framework. *Journal of Educational Psychology, 80*, 381–391.

Fredericks, J. (1999). *"Girl-friendly" family contexts: Socialization into math and sports*. Unpublished doctoral dissertation, University of Michigan, Ann Arbor.

Garton, A. F., & Pratt, C. (1987). Participation and interest in leisure activities by adolescent schoolchildren. *Journal of Adolescence, 10*(4), 341–351.

Harter, S. (1990). Causes, correlates, and the functional role of global self-worth: A life-span perspective. In J. Kolligan & R. Sternberg (Eds.), *Perceptions of competence and incompetence across the life span* (pp. 43–70). New York: Springer-Verlag.

Harter, S. (1998). The development of the self. In W. Damon (Series Ed.) & N. Eisenberg (Vol. Ed.), *Handbook of child psychology: Social, emotional, and personality development* (pp. 553–617). New York: Wiley.

Jacobs, J. E. (1991). The influence of gender stereotypes on parent and child math attitudes: Differences across grade-levels. *Journal of Educational Psychology, 83*, 518–527.

Jacobs, J. E., & Eccles, J. S. (1992). The influence of parent stereotypes on parent and child ability beliefs in three domains. *Journal of Personality and Social Psychology, 63*, 932–944.

Jacobs, J. E., & Eccles, J. S. (2000). Parents, task values, and real life achievement choices. In C. Sansone & J. Harackiewicz (Eds.), *Intrinsic motivation* (pp. 408–433). San Diego, CA: Academic.

Jacobs, J. E., Lanza, S., Osgood, D. W., Eccles, J. S., & Wigfield, A. (2002). Changes in children's self-competence and values: Gender and domain differences across grades one through twelve. *Child Development, 73*(2), 509–527.

Larson, R. (2000). Toward a psychology of positive youth development. *American Psychologist, 55*(1), 170–183.

Larson, R., & Verma, S. (1999). How children and adolescents spend time across the world: Work, play, and developmental opportunities. *Psychological Bulletin, 125*(6), 701–736.

Mahoney, J. L. (2001, April). *After-school activities in the community: What helps and what hurts?* Paper presented at the 2001 biennial meeting of the Society for Research in Child Development, Minneapolis, MN.

Mahoney, J. L., & Cairns, R. B. (1997). Do extracurricular activities protect against early school dropout? *Developmental Psychology, 33*(2), 241–253.

McHale, S. M., Crouter, A. C., & Tucker, C. J. (1999). Family context and gender role socialization in middle childhood: Comparing girls to boys and sisters to brothers. *Child Development, 59*(2), 990–1004.

McHale, S. M., Crouter, A. C., & Tucker, C. J. (2001). Free-time activities in middle childhood: Links with adjustment in early adolescence. *Child Development, 72*(6), 1764–1778.

Parsons, J. E., Adler, T. F., & Kaczala, C. M. (1982). Socialization of achievement attitudes and beliefs: Parental influences. *Child Development, 53,* 322–339.

Posner, J. K., & Vandell, L. (1999). After-school activities and the development of
low-income urban children: A longitudinal study. *Developmental Psychology, 35*(3),
868–879.

Stoneman, Z., Brody, G. H., & MacKinnon, C. E. (1986). Same-sex and cross-sex siblings: Activity choices, roles, behavior, and gender stereotypes. *Sex Roles, 15*(9–10),
495–511.

Wankel, L. M., & Berger, B. G. (1990). The psychological and social benefits of sport and
physical activity. *Journal of Leisure Research, 22*(2), 167–182.

Wigfield, A., & Eccles, J. (1992). The development of achievement task values: A theoretical analysis. *Developmental Review, 12,* 265–310.

Wigfield, A., Eccles, J. S., Yoon, K. S., Harold, R. D., Arbreton, A. J., Freedman-Doan,
C., & Blumenfeld, P. C. (1997). Change in children's competence beliefs and subjective task values across the elementary school years: A 3-year study. *Journal of Educational Psychology, 89,* 451–469.

Youniss, J., McLellan, J. A., Su, Y., & Yates, M. (1999). The role of community service in
identity development: Normative, unconventional, and deviant orientations. *Journal of Adolescent Research, 14*(2), 248–261.

12

Youth Music Engagement in Diverse Contexts

Susan A. O'Neill
Keele University, Staffordshire, UK

Musical activities are a major part of the life and culture of young people over the course of their development. Even prior to birth, the fetus is able to hear and respond to music (e.g., Hepper, 1991; Lecanuet, 1996; Trevarthen, 1999–2000). The nonverbal communication that occurs in early infancy between caregiver and infant contains musical parameters that express emotions, needs, and mental states (Papoušek, 1996), and this form of communication exists in every culture (Trehub, Schellenberg, & Hill, 1997). Musical enculturation is experienced by all young people to some extent through exposure to informal learning practices and music making from an early age. Young children progress through a series of phases in their early musical development without any formal instruction. These phases consist of "babbling songs" based on experimentation with pitch and contour, approximate imitations of songs heard in their environment, followed by careful listening and copying of songs (Hargreaves, 1986). This practice of learning by listening and copying also has a long tradition in folk and traditional music, and is the most often used method in the self-education of popular musicians and many others who engage in informal music making.

During the past 100 years, many societies around the world have developed structured music programs for young people (cf. Campbell, 1991; Hargreaves & North, 2001). Formal educational practices within different countries and/or nationalities often co-exist (although at times uneasily) with other informal cultural traditions and popular culture (Green, 2001). There are opportunities for many young people to participate in music programs from early childhood through to higher education in young adulthood. The majority of youth participation in music takes place in outside or after-school contexts, often with little help from musically trained educators or direct supervision by adults. For example, adolescents spend more of their leisure time listening to music than any other activity with perhaps the exception of watching television (Brown, Campbell, & Fischer, 1986; Fitzgerald, Joseph, Hayes, & O'Regan, 1995; North, Hargreaves, & O'Neill, 2000). Larson, Kubey, and Colletti (1989) found that youth experienced greater psychological engagement when listening to music than when watching television. Researchers have stressed the benefits of youth participation in musical activities that take place in isolation, often in the solitude of a young person's own bedroom (Larson & Kleiber, 1993; North et al., 2000), as well as those that take place in social situations (Eccles & Barber, 1999; Tarrant, North, & Hargreaves, 2000).

Young people's musical engagement in contemporary society is multifaceted, diverse, and heterogeneous. As such, the impact of musical involvement is not direct but interdependent on the situation in which it occurs. Past investigations into young people's participation in music have focused primarily on formal instrumental music training that was developed in Western cultures and is sometimes referred to as the "classical *conservatoire*" tradition. This type of training emphasizes the acquisition of performance skills that require the accurate reproduction of printed music notation, usually classical music, although other musical styles such as jazz, folk, and popular music are increasingly subjected to similar types of formal training. Other characteristics include the mastery of a common core set of pieces that are progressively graded according to levels of technical difficulty, structured teaching methods that are taught by specialists, and some form of evaluative achievement or competition. These educational practices have contributed to a sense of musical "elitism" toward formal training that does not exist in many non-western cultures.

Increasingly, researchers are turning their attention to more diverse and informal forms of youth involvement in music. These activities are commonly (but not always) associated with leisure activities, informal learning practices, unstructured or unsupervised settings, and often the involvement of "close-knit" social groups. Informal musical engagement is more likely to occur outside school, at home or at local community or youth centers. Kleiber's (1999) description of the two main characteristics of leisure activities are important components of informal musical engagement, as follows: (a) it occurs in a context that is relatively free, providing opportunities for self-expression, and (b) the development of the activity can be at least partially self-directed. Both informal music listening and music making can be considered within this broad framework.

In considering these issues, the first section of this chapter provides an overview of research that highlights the importance of music activities for youth development that occurs in both formal and informal contexts. The vast majority of this research is situated in the United States, Canada, and the United Kingdom. In some cases, researchers have argued for the merits of musical engagement within a "multi-arts" perspective that does not distinguish between different arts activities (e.g., music, drama, dance, visual arts). The rationale for this is based on the notion that all arts activities are potentially beneficial. However, music activities have received far more attention mainly because of the high profile and advocacy that exists among music practitioners and educators, who are well-organized both in terms of policy and curriculum issues. This chapter does not include an examination of specific musical skill-based competencies. For reviews on the development of musical skills, the reader may refer to other sources (Deliège & Sloboda, 1996; Parncutt & McPherson, 2002). Rather, the focus here is on the broader benefits that youth derive from engagement in music activities, beginning in the first section with a review of academic, social, and psychological outcomes.

The second section reports findings from a recent study my colleagues and I conducted in the United Kingdom (O'Neill, 2002c, 2003). The study examined young people's music participation before and after the transition from elementary to secondary school. We know from previous research findings and government reports that the largest decline in young people's involvement in musical activities (with the exception of listening to music) takes place following this transition. Therefore, we focused our research on the motivational and social factors that influence children's decisions to sustain or give up playing a musical instrument. Our findings provide some indication of how we might best sustain youth interest and involvement in instrumental music programs. The chapter concludes with some directions for future research.

THE IMPORTANCE OF YOUTH ENGAGEMENT IN MUSIC

There are two broad theoretical perspectives on the importance of musical engagement for positive youth development. The first focuses on the specific and unique contribution that structured music programs make in terms of cultivating various nonmusical competencies. It is argued that these outcomes transpire either directly or through the nature and quality of the educational and/or social settings in which they occur. For example, arts participation has been linked over time to positive academic outcomes and higher levels of creative thinking (Burton, Horowitz, & Abeles, 2000; van Well, Linssen, Kort, & Jansen, 1996). Recent comprehensive reviews provide excellent summaries and evaluations of a large body of empirical research that has examined a diverse range of positive outcomes associated with active arts participation (Deasy, 2002; Winner & Cooper, 2000; Wolf, 2001). Musical activities such as learning to play an instrument as part of a structured music program feature predominately in these reviews.

The second perspective focuses more broadly on how musical activities build and perpetuate "cultural capital" within a society. According to Winner (2000),

> The two most important reasons for studying the arts are to enable our children to be able to appreciate some of the greatest feats humans have ever achieved (e.g., a painting by Rembrandt, a play by Shakespeare, a dance choreographed by Ballanchine, a sonata by Mozart) and to give our children sufficient skill in an art form so that they can express themselves in this art form. (p. 29)

Winner and Hetland (2000) argued that a distinction needs to be made between the core justifications for teaching the arts versus the bonus reasons (such as enhanced learning in nonarts disciplines) that may or may not occur. In Western countries in particular, basic academic skills are valued and the arts are considered at best a complement to the key curriculum and at worst just an extra activity or even a break for young people from their more important educational needs. When school budgets are inadequate, arts programs are typically the first to be trimmed down or cut altogether. It is therefore not surprising that many arts educators have welcomed studies that demonstrate the academic, social, and psychological value and positive benefits of arts programs for youth in order to justify their continued existence. However, there is controversy and debate about whether arts programs should have to justify their existence on these terms. For example, Winner (2000) argued that math educators are not expected to show that math skills transfer to better musical skills. The following section begins with an overview of the effects of music programs on cognitive and academic outcomes, followed by a discussion of other social and psychological outcomes associated with youth involvement in music.

Cognitive Outcomes and Academic Achievement

In 1993, a small-scale laboratory study of college students was published in *Nature* (Rauscher, Shaw, & Ky, 1993). The researchers claimed that participants who listened to 10 minutes of Mozart before completing a spatial ability task requiring mental rotation improved significantly compared to those groups who had 10 minutes of silence, or who had 10 minutes of a verbal relaxation tape. This result has become known as the *Mozart effect*. The intense media interest that followed this study led to a large number of replication studies with mixed results (for a review, see Hetland, 2000). It also led to an intense public and political interest—with arts advocates using it as a justification that music programs are indeed valuable. Some states in America began to hand out free music tapes to mothers of all newborns in the hope that it would help babies to grow up smarter. But none of these claims were justified by the research. The effect was found with adults, not children or infants, it was limited to a specific form of spatial reasoning, and it was temporary—no reliable lasting effects have been found to date.

Since this time, a number of researchers have presented evidence to suggest that the skills learned in instrumental music lessons facilitate the skills learned in mathematics (e.g., Graziano, Peterson, & Shaw, 1999; Rauscher et al., 1997). Vaughn (2000) conducted three meta-analyses investigating the relationship between music and mathematics. The studies included in the analyses involved mainly elementary and secondary school children. The results indicated a modest positive association between voluntary study of music and mathematics achievement. However, much of the research to date has been criticized for not being sufficiently rigorous to draw conclusions about the unique, direct effects of arts participation on young people's academic achievement or cognitive development. For example, Costa-Giomi (1999) found an association between music lessons and spatial ability only for the highly motivated music students. (For a detailed discussion of motivational issues in the development of music performance skills, see O'Neill & McPherson, 2002.) Many of the studies reporting an effect of music participation on school achievement used correlational designs making causal conclusions problematic. Other shortcomings range from small sample sizes and lack of longitudinal studies to lack of randomized experiments and small effect sizes. As such, the hypothesis that music training enhances mathematics achievement has yet to be subjected to the kind of rigorous testing that would support such claims with any degree of certainty.

Another problematic issue with studies that focus on the transfer effects of music participation to nonmusical outcomes is the absence of theories that could explain why some youth experience positive outcomes from engagement in music programs specifically. It has been suggested that being involved in any structured, after-school program that takes place in a safe and supportive environment is useful in promoting positive youth development, and that constructive leisure activities promote skills associated with self-regulation, planfulness, self-efficacy, and initiative (Larson, 2000). Others predict beneficial outcomes because participation in such activities provide youth with opportunities to contribute to the well-being of their community, to belong to socially recognized and valued groups, and to establish supportive social networks of peers and adults (Eccles & Gootman, 2002; Eccles & Templeton, 2002). Musical activities are just one of many extracurricular or after-school activities found to be associated with positive outcomes such as lower rates of school dropout, higher academic achievement, and reduced risk of problem behaviors (Eccles & Barber, 1999).

Although many young people have opportunities to participate in a variety of different constructive activities during their after-school time, the vast majority say that music is an important part of their life and has influenced how they think about important issues (Leming, 1987; North et al., 2000). It is therefore reasonable to suggest that musical activities, when combined with the components of successful youth development programs, are likely to attract young people and result in positive outcomes. More research is necessary to establish the magnitude of any direct or indirect effects of musical involvement on other nonmusical outcomes. However, in considering these issues further, the remainder of this section provides a brief overview of some of the key areas where musical involvement plays an important role in young people's lives.

Youth Identity

Musical activities provide a forum for young people to define and express their identity (Fredricks et al., 2002; see also MacDonald, Hargreaves, & Miell, 2002; O'Neill, 2002b; O'Neill, Ivaldi, & Fox, 2002). Young people have been described as using music "as a badge" in terms of their identification with peers and subcultural groups (Frith, 1981). For example, in the United States, wearing a band or choir jacket during high school is often a source of pride that symbolizes identification and belonging for many young people. There is increasing evidence to suggest that music functions within youth subcultures as a way of defining the self (North et al., 2000), creating collective energy and excitement (Weinstein, 1985), and bringing about a sense of solidarity and subcultural consciousness (see also Epstein, 1995; Martin, 1979). The type of music one listens to or plays is associated with particular beliefs, values, images, and behaviors. Although there is a common assumption that adolescents' musical tastes might be predictive of problem or negative behaviors, the evidence suggests that this is not the case (e.g., for behavioral problems or delinquency, see Epstein & Pratto, 1990; Epstein, Pratto, & Skipper, 1990; for drug use and suicidal risk, see Lacourse, Claes, & Villeneuve, 2001). Nevertheless, music can be a powerful social, cultural, and national symbol that serves particular functions in the socialization and enculturation of young people, particularly in terms of defining themselves as belonging to a particular group and separating their group from other groups (Folkestad, 2002).

Emotion and Communicative Functions

Music is an important way in which young people express their emotions. In a study of over 2,000 adolescents in England, North et al. (2000) found that participants reported both listening to music and playing a musical instrument as important in terms of fulfilling their emotional needs. Music is used as a means of creating, enhancing, sustaining, and changing subjective, cognitive, bodily, and self-conceptual states such as calming down, getting into the right mood, or venting strong emotions (Sloboda & O'Neill, 2001). Young people exhibit considerable awareness of the music they need to hear or play in different situations and at different times, often working as disc jockeys to themselves (DeNora, 1999).

Music also serves a social function in sharing or communicating emotions to others. This does not mean that music is simply used to express some internal, private feeling or state, nor that it simply "acts upon" individuals, like a stimulus. Rather, it is used as a resource for the identification work of "knowing how one feels." It is part of the construction of emotion itself through the way in which individuals orient to it, interpret it, and use it to elaborate, "fill in" or "fill out," to themselves and others, an emotional feeling or display. For example, DeNora (1999) described a student who repeatedly played at full volume a song from Radiohead entitled "We Hope You Choke!" not only as a way of diffusing her anger against her boyfriend's parents when she lived with them over the summer holidays, but also as a way of communicating her anger to them. In other words, the display of anger or irritation described by the girl expressed a judgment of the moral quality of some other person's actions. Such a display was also an act of protest directed toward the boyfriend's parents. Music provided one means by which this display was acted out on an interpersonal level. Young people use music as a means of self-expression, while exerting considerable control over the musical choices they make. The issue of agency and individuality are also linked to musical activities and situations where young people describe the private, solitary contexts where emotional work can be accomplished with the help of music.

Family, Community, and Religious Music Making

Historically, music has been an important part of the social activities of families, communities, and religion. Blacking (1976) described the music making in many non-Western communities as a habitual activity from early childhood that involves the entire population, making it difficult to find a nonmusical person. However, in Western countries, as technology has advanced and families and communities have diversified, communal music making has declined. Recorded music has replaced live music making in many contexts. Despite this overall decline, there is still great diversity in the opportunities for youth engagement with music, and these differences are associated with the beliefs and values shared by socioeconomic, ethnic, racial, cultural, and national groups. This diversity makes it difficult to study the specific benefits of family and community music making on youth development. However, according to Folkestad (2002), "global youth culture and its music, because it is the same regardless of the national, ethnic or cultural heritage of the context in which it operates, might have a non-segregating and uniting function" (p. 160). This notion is certainly worthy of consideration, particularly among researchers who are interested in cross-cultural, ethnic, and racial differences in youth musical involvement.

There is tremendous diversity in the music programs available for youth from different countries and nationalities. Youth centers in many communities provide opportunities for musical activities that facilitate communal music making. Additionally, youth centers may use music in the background to enhance the time youth spend doing other activities. One area that provides an increasing forum for youth music participation in the United States takes place during sports activities, particularly the marching band. During football games, for example, an unofficial competition often takes place between bands from rival schools during intermissions. According to Radocy (2001), the strong emphasis that is placed on music competition in American schools can lead some music educators to put the accolades and recognition that are obtained for the school by doing well in competitive settings above the musical knowledge, understanding, and attitudes of young people. Additionally, the focus on competition may result in musical opportunities being offered only to those individuals who demonstrate the highest levels of performance skill. This contrasts sharply with some of the noncompetitive forms of communal music making that take place in the United Kingdom. For example, there is a strong tradition of brass bands in the north of England where older members of the band group mentor younger members. Also, in Scotland, Ireland, and Wales, a tradition of playing folk music takes place in many communities and involves individuals from all ages and all levels of ability.

Music is also featured in the practices and traditions of many religious groups and organizations, for example, singing in gospel or church choirs. Few studies have considered the role of religion in young people's involvement in music, although there is some evidence that there may be psychological as well as social benefits (e.g., Hill & Argyle, 1998; Kincheloe, 1985). Overall, we still know little about the different social contexts in which young people engage in music during after-school hours, particularly when musical activities take place outside of educational institutions. What we do know is that the contexts associated with youth communal music making within families, communities, and religious groups are an important way in which the beliefs and values associated with those groups are transmitted and perpetuated.

Friendships, Peer Groups, and Stereotypes

The role of peers in continuing adolescents' motivation for instrumental music, drama, choir, and sports activities was the focus of a recent study based on in-depth interviews with talented adolescents and their parents (Patrick et al., 1999). More than half of the adolescents reported that their involvement in the activity provided them with an important opportunity to make friends, and that this enhanced their enjoyment of, and commitment to, the activity. This pattern of results was found across all the activities examined. However, only for arts activities did the adolescents' report negative reactions from peers. Howe and Sloboda (1992) found similar results in England among young people attending a specialist music school. Many of the young musicians, age 10 to 17 years old, reported that they experienced some pronounced problems with their peer relationships prior to attending the specialist music school. These problems included loss of popularity and increased bullying, and were so severe that some of the young people contemplated giving up instrumental music altogether. Many of the participants said they valued the opportunity afforded to them at a specialist music school that provided an environment where they were with like-minded peers who shared a commitment to musical engagement (see further, O'Neill, 1997).

Friendships based on shared musical tastes are particularly important during adolescence. Many forms of musical learning take place through interaction with friends, siblings, and other peers. The contexts in which musical groups are formed varies greatly; however, there is some evidence to suggest that the formation of informal bands or musical groups is more common and happens earlier among boys than girls (Clawson, 1999). There may be a protective factor for boys in establishing a male band in terms of helping them maintain their masculine identity in the face of stereotypes associated with youth musical involvement. A number of studies have indicated that gender-stereotyped beliefs about musical activities create self-imposed boundaries for many young people (see O'Neill, 1997, 2002a). There is considerable social pressure from peers to avoid gender inappropriate activities and not cross over traditional gender lines.

In England, there are roughly twice as many girls learning to play instruments than boys, and girls achieve a higher percentage of passes than boys in music examinations (Department of Education and Science, 1991). Colley, Comber, and Hargreaves (1994) found that 11- to 13-year-olds considered music at school to be a "feminine" subject. Findings from a study of 7- to 10-year-old children in the United States indicated that girls reported more competence beliefs and values for instrumental music than boys (Eccles, Wigfield, Harold, & Blumenfeld, 1993). According to the researchers, "[instrumental music] is the only instance we know about in which the gender-role differentiated beliefs and self-perceptions in childhood are opposite to the gender differences in participation one observes in the adult world" (p. 845). Musical instrument preferences have also been found to be strongly related to young people's gender-typed beliefs (e.g., Abeles & Porter, 1978; Delzell & Leppla, 1992; Harrison & O'Neill, 2000; O'Neill & Boulton, 1996). For example, in a recent study (Harrison & O'Neill, 2003), we found that girls were learning the majority of instruments they thought were appropriate for girls (e.g., flute, violin), and boys were playing the majority of instruments they thought were appropriate for boys (e.g., guitar, drums). We found that both girls and boys thought that a child of the same gender as themselves would be liked less and bullied more by other children if she or he played an instrument that was viewed as gender inappropriate (O'Neill, 1997). One determinant of a child's success in instrumental music may be the selection of an instrument for study (Fortney, Boyle, & DeCarbo, 1993). It is important, therefore, that children do not add to the difficulty of playing an instrument by imposing boundaries on their potential success by avoiding or declining the opportunity to play certain instruments on the basis of gender-stereotyped associations.

However, musical engagement involving peer groups provides opportunities that not only reinforce stereotypes but also challenge them. For example, in the context of a community center with a youth leader, Green (1997) described an incident where a group of girls were playing electric and percussion instruments to create their own rap music. The boys at the center first referred to the girls' music as "rubbish" and made derogatory personal remarks about the girls who were involved. However, the girls persisted and eventually the boys heard a finished number and found themselves listening more closely and being convinced of the value of the music the girls played. According to Green, not only were the boys challenged to reevaluate their initial assumptions, the girls who were actively involved in the music making were able to gain direct experience of new possibilities that challenged traditional gendered musical roles. More research is needed that examines the role of peers in the development of young people's musical engagement, particularly in relation to the extent that peers help sustain youth involvement and the specific benefits associated with peer support. This issue is considered further in the next section, which focuses on the factors that help sustain youth involvement in music following the transition to high school.

YOUTH MUSIC PARTICIPATION BEFORE AND AFTER THE TRANSITION TO SECONDARY SCHOOL

As children grow and develop, they engage in musical activities that are part of the institutions and traditions of their sociocultural environments. Although many children have the opportunity to engage in structured music programs, as they approach adolescence, many drop out. By late adolescence, most have abandoned these activities altogether (Harland, Kinder, & Hartley, 1995). There is also evidence to suggest that young children have very positive beliefs about musical activities but that these beliefs show a marked decline following the transition to secondary school, and this downward trend continues throughout adolescence (Wigfield et al., 1997). In order to further our understanding of this decline, my colleagues and I recently conducted a 2-year longitudinal study that focused on the transition that young people make from elementary to secondary school (O'Neill, 2002c, 2003).

The Study

Our research was based in the United Kingdom and involved approximately 1,500 youth, their parents, friends, and teachers. Three waves of data collection began in 1999 in the northwest region of England. Wave 1 took place at the end of Year 6 (final year of elementary school, age 10 to age 11 years), Wave 2 was collected at the start of Year 7 (first year of secondary school; age 11 to12 years), and Wave 3 took place at the end of Year 7. This enabled an examination of the transition from elementary to secondary school and whether there was an immediate effect on music participation following the change to secondary school compared to the effect found by the end of the first year of secondary school. The majority of the sample were White European, although 26% were from other ethnic/racial backgrounds (mostly Indian and Pakistani). Participants completed questionnaires during all three waves of data collection that included measures of musical involvement, motivation for engagement in instrumental music, as well as the perceived social support they received from parents, peers, and teachers. Our aim was to focus on the children's own views, because the way they viewed their involvement in musical activities was likely to have the largest impact on their motivation and future participation.

Characteristics of the Sample

Our sample has several unique features. First, the recruitment of participants was designed to follow the maximum number of children who were making the transition to one of 11 secondary schools. The schools were selected to cover a range of neighborhoods, including rural, farm-based neighborhoods, middle-class suburban neighborhoods, and low-income urban neighborhoods. The schools were also selected to cover a range of music provision both in terms of quality and quantity (based on government school inspection reports and local authority information about each school's provision). The main feeder elementary schools ($n = 43$) participated in the first wave of data collection (10 of the elementary schools were also evaluated for the quantity and quality of their music provision by a government school inspector). All of the children that made the transition to one of the 11 secondary schools were followed in subsequent waves of the study (approximately 1,000). Attrition only resulted when children went to a high school other than the 11 selected schools, or when the family moved to another area.

Another unique feature of this data set is the educational context. Music has been part of a national curriculum in England and Wales since 1993, and is a required subject for all students from age 5 to 14 years. Classroom teachers who are not necessarily music specialists teach the music curriculum in elementary schools; music specialist teachers are more common in secondary schools. A key component of the music curriculum is performance, and all young people are expected to gain some degree of proficiency at producing music. This is not always in the form of instrumental music lessons, although playing instruments such as the recorder and electronic keyboards, as well as singing, are common features of many music programs. As such, the results from our study need to be interpreted within this context. In the United States, music classes are often required during elementary school, but are usually an elective subject in junior high and high school. Despite these educational differences, the decline in children's music participation following the transition to secondary school has been documented in both countries (Wigfield, O'Neill, & Eccles, 1999).

Evidence for the Decline in Music Participation

Although the largest part of our research was devoted to playing musical instruments, we also asked children about their involvement in listening to music, dancing to music, singing, and using a computer to make music in both formal (at school) and informal (outside school) contexts. Children reported a decline in their participation for all of these musical activities immediately following the transition to secondary school, and this decline continued throughout the first year of secondary school. A notable exception was found for listening to music, which showed an overall increase particularly in after-school contexts. The number of youth playing instruments showed a marked decline in both formal and informal contexts. Less than 35% of young people who played instruments during elementary school remained playing by the end of their first year of secondary school. Girls were more likely than boys to continue (48% as opposed to 35%). Gender differences were most significant among children playing traditionally "masculine" instruments. The number of girls playing these instruments hardly declined from elementary to secondary school. There was a massive decline, however, in boys playing these instruments. The decline was most marked for trumpet, drums, and acoustic guitar. The curious and initially paradoxical finding is, therefore, that boys who start traditionally "feminine" or "neutral" instruments at elementary school level are more likely to continue with them than boys who start traditionally masculine instruments. However, on reflection it may be that boys taking up feminine instruments at elementary school have accumulated considerable motivation and support to challenge gender stereotypes, leading to greater long-term commitment (O'Neill, 2002c, 2003).

Factors That Sustain Involvement in Instrumental Music

In our study, several factors differentiated youth who continued playing instruments from those who gave up following the transition to secondary school. We examined the main responses of 426 children who played instruments during the last year of elementary school. They were divided into two groups according to whether they continued playing ($n = 240$) or gave up playing ($n = 186$) during their first year of secondary school. The results of t tests indicated a number of statistically significant differences between the two groups. Descriptive summaries of the main results are presented here. We found that continuers were more likely to have played an instrument for more than 1 year while they were at elementary school. Starting an instrument younger, and having played an instrument for longer, appears to act as a protective factor in terms of continued interest and commitment toward the instrument at high school. If a child does not learn to play an instrument early on, then the increasing musical skills required to become involved in a musical group may limit an individual's opportunities for participation. In other words, an individual may not have acquired a sufficient degree of proficiency on an instrument to be considered good enough to join a musical group at high school.

Both groups emphasized the importance of being able to choose their own musical instruments, music, and musical activities. However, continuers were more self-directed and autonomous than "gave ups." Those who gave up reported feeling that they had fewer opportunities to take responsibility for various aspects of their musical involvement, particularly following the transition. One can sense the frustration that this might cause as young people reach a point in their development where they seek to establish a greater sense of independence and control over the choices they make. There was often a mismatch between the instruments young people wanted to learn to play and the instruments they actually played. Those who were most likely to continue reported valuing the instruments they played and identified positively with adult role models who played similar instruments.

We found that participants with more positive motivational beliefs and values were more likely to continue playing following the transition to secondary school. Those who continued had greater confidence in their own ability, and valued playing an instrument more than those who gave up.

Continuers reported more positive experiences in terms of overcoming the challenges associated with learning an instrument, and believed that hard work would yield improvements more than gave ups. Continuers had more close associates who played instruments and had been involved in more performance groups. However, what appeared to be important was not so much winning competitions, but rather having the sense of structured goals to work toward that were viewed as a challenge or opportunity to improve skills and not just as an opportunity to display competence.

The most differential source of perceived social support came from parents. Continuers were far more likely to view their parents as valuing and supportive of their involvement in music. Siblings' and friends' direct support showed little difference between groups, although it helped if friends believed that all young people have the potential to learn to play an instrument. The support received from teachers made less difference than the support received from parents, although it helped if teachers were able to communicate a belief in the child's ability and chose music that the child liked (O'Neill, 2002c, 2003).

FUTURE DIRECTIONS

In light of the many positive outcomes associated with youth participation in music, the reasons why so many young people abandon playing instruments, particularly following the transition to secondary school, is certainly an area worthy of further research. The most frequently offered explanations for young people's declining music participation tend to focus on the social and educational changes that take place following the transition in terms of societal expectations, friendship patterns, institutional structures, and teaching practices. Another explanation that is gaining increasing attention among developmental psychologists suggests that the negative beliefs and behaviors that are apparent following the transition to high school result from a mismatch between the needs of children approaching early adolescence and the opportunities afforded them by their social and educational environments (see, e.g., Eccles, Lord, & Buchanan, 1996; Eccles, Lord, & Roeser, 1996; Eccles, Lord, Roeser, Barber, & Hermandez Jozefowicz, 1997). This suggests the need to examine the changing nature of the educational and social environments experienced by youth engaged in musical activities. Although not always mutually exclusive, there are important differences in the characteristics, approaches, networks, attitudes, and values associated with youth musical involvement in formal and informal contexts. Some music programs may not be providing the kinds of activities that are valued by, and acceptable to, many young people. It is therefore important to identify the characteristics of successful music programs if we are to understand fully how we might best sustain young people's interest and involvement. In this way, we might be able to reduce the decline in young people's music making, particularly during early adolescence when music becomes an increasingly important part of everyday life.

For the most part, researchers have focused on the outcomes associated with musical involvement and achievement (i.e., what influence do musical activities exert on development?). As Brown (1988) pointed out, far less attention has been paid to the processes associated with how extracurricular activities enhance or impede specified, desired outcomes (i.e., what are the processes by which musical activities exert an influence?). In order to address this latter issue, more attention needs to be focused on the individual differences associated with young people's musical engagement, as well as the role of socializing agents, learning practices, and sociocultural settings. Among music educators and youth development policymakers, there is little consensus about the objectives of, and approach to, providing musical opportunities to young people. And among developmental psychologists, there is little acknowledgment of the diversity of contexts and approaches involved in young people's musical engagement. Any meaningful account of the processes associated with youth involvement in music and the ways in which they impact on development must take into account both the objectives and the diversity of contexts and approaches that characterize youth engagement in musical activities.

Unlike many other activities that young people are involved in, they have considerable autonomy in the way they engage in music activities, both as consumers and performers. Therefore, an understanding of their role as active agents in the construction of their musical lives can shed considerable light on how young people make decisions and come to make sense of the world. Such decisions and forms of understanding are a key component in the transition that all young people make from recipients of formal or structured educational contexts to active constructors of their own skills and knowledge. As such, we need to consider not only the musical opportunities that are made available to young people, but also the extent to which these opportunities are likely to be accepted by them in engaging and meaningful ways at different stages of their development.

REFERENCES

Abeles, H. F., & Porter, S. Y. (1978). The sex-stereotyping of musical instruments. *Journal of Research in Music Education, 26,* 65–75.

Blacking, J. (1976). *How musical is man?* London: Faber.

Brown, B. B. (1988). The vital agenda for research on extracurricular influences: A reply to Holland and Andre. *Review of Educational Research, 58*(1), 107–111.

Brown, J. D., Campbell, K., & Fischer, L. (1986). American adolescents and music videos: Why do they watch? *Gazette, 37,* 19–32.

Burton, J. M., Horowitz, R., & Abeles, H. (2000). Learning in and through the arts: The question of transfer. *Studies in Art Education, 41,* 228–257.

Campbell, P. S. (1991). *Lessons from the world: A cross-cultural guide to music teaching and learning.* New York: Schirmer Books.

Clawson, M. A. (1999). Masculinity and skill acquisition in the adolescent rock band. *Popular Music, 18*(1), 99–115.

Colley, A., Comber, C., & Hargreaves, D. J. (1994). Gender effects in school subject preferences: A research note. *Educational Studies, 20*(1), 13–18.

Costa-Giomi, E. (1999). The effects of three years of piano instruction on children's cognitive development. *Journal of Research in Music Education, 47,* 198–212.

Deasy, R. J. (Ed.). (2002). *Critical links: Learning in the arts and student academic and social development.* Washington, DC: Arts Education Partnership.

Deliège, I., & Sloboda, J. A. (Eds.). (1996). *Musical beginnings: Origins and development of musical competence.* Oxford, UK: Oxford University Press.

Delzell, J. K., & Leppla, D. A. (1992). Gender association of musical instruments and preferences of fourth-grade students for selected instruments. *Journal of Research in Music Education, 40,* 93–103.

DeNora, T. (1999). Music as a technology of the self. *Poetics, 27,* 31–56.

Department of Education and Science. (1991). *Music for ages 5 to 14: Proposals of the Secretary of State for Education and Science and Secretary of State for Wales.*

Eccles, J. S., & Barber, B. L. (1999). Student council, volunteering, basketball, or marching band: What kind of extracurricular involvement matters? *Journal of Adolescent Research, 14*(1), 10–43.

Eccles, J. S., & Gootman, J. (Eds.). (2002). *Community programs to promote youth development.* Washington, DC: National Academy Press.

Eccles, J., Lord, S., & Buchanan, C. M. (1996). School transitions in early adolescence: What are we doing to our young people? In J. L. Graber, J. Brooks-Gunn, & A. C. Peterson (Eds.), *Transitions through adolescence: Interpersonal domains and contexts* (pp. 251–284). Mahwah, NJ: Lawrence Erlbaum Associates.

Eccles, J., Lord, S., & Roeser, R. (1996). Round holes, square pegs, rocky roads, and sore feet: The impact of stage-environment fit on young adolescents' experiences in schools and families. In S. L. Toth & D. Cicchetti (Eds.), *Adolescence: Opportunities and challenges* (Vol. 7, pp 49–93). Rochester, NY: University of Rochester Press.

Eccles, J., Lord, S., Roeser, R., Barber, B., & Hermandez Jozefowicz, D. (1997). The association of school transitions in early adolescence with developmental trajectories through high school. In J. Schulenberg, J. I. Maggs, & K. Hurrelmann (Ed.), *Health risks and developmental transitions during adolescence* (pp. 283–321). New York: Cambridge University Press.

Eccles, J. S., & Templeton, J. (2002). Extracurricular and other after-school activities for youth. In W. G. Secada (Ed.), *Review of Research in Education* (Vol. 26, pp. 113–180). Washington, DC: American Educational Research Association.

Eccles, J., Wigfield, A., Harold, R. D., & Blumenfeld, P. (1993). Age and gender differences in children's self- and task perceptions during elementary school. *Child Development, 64,* 830–847.

Epstein, J. S. (Ed.). (1995). *Adolescents and their music.* New York: Garland.

Epstein, J. S., & Pratto, D. J. (1990). Heavy metal rock music, juvenile delinquency, and satanic identification. *Popular Music and Society, 14*(4), 67–76.

Epstein, J. S., Pratto, D. J., & Skipper, J. K. (1990). Teenagers, behavioral problems, and preferences for heavy metal and rap music: A case study of a southern middle school. *Deviant Behavior, 11,* 381–394.

Fitzgerald, M., Joseph, A. P., Hayes, M., & O'Regan, M. (1995). Leisure activities of adolescent schoolchildren. *Journal of Adolescence, 18,* 349–358.

Folkestad, G. (2002). National identity and music. In R. A. R. MacDonald, D. J. Hargreaves, & D. Miell (Eds.), *Musical identities* (pp. 151–162). Oxford: Oxford University Press.

Fortney, P. M., Boyle, J. D., & DeCarbo, N. J. (1993). A study of middle school band students' instrument choices. *Journal of Research in Music Education, 41*(1), 28–39.

Fredricks, J. A., Alfeld-Liro, C., Hruda, L. Z., Eccles, J. S., Patrick, H., & Ryan, A. M. (2002). A qualitative exploration of adolescents' commitment to athletics and the arts. *Journal of Adolescent Research, 17*(1), 68–97.

Frith, S. (1981). *Sound effects.* New York: Pantheon.

Graziano, A., Peterson, M., & Shaw, G. L. (1999). Enhanced learning of proportional math through music training and spatial-temporal training. *Neurological Research, 21,* 139–152.

Green, L. (1997). *Music, gender, education.* Cambridge: Cambridge University Press.

Green, L. (2001). *How popular musicians learn: A way ahead for music education.* Aldershot, Hants, England: Ashgate.

Hargreaves, D. J. (1986). *The developmental psychology of music.* Cambridge: Cambridge University Press.

Hargreaves, D. J., & North, A. C. (Eds.). (2001). *Musical development and learning: The international perspective.* London: Continuum.

Harland, J., Kinder, K., & Hartley, K. (1995). *Arts in their view: A study of youth participation in the arts.* Slough, Berkshire, England: National Foundation for Educational Research.

Harrison, A. C., & O'Neill, S. A. (2000). Children's gender-typed preferences for musical instruments: An intervention study. *Psychology of Music, 28*(1), 81–97.

Harrison, A. C., & O'Neill, S. A. (2003). Preferences and children's use of gender-stereotyped knowledge about musical instruments: Making judgments about other children's preferences. *Sex Roles, 49,* 389–400.

Hepper, P. G. (1991). An examination of fetal learning before and after birth. *The Irish Journal of Psychology, 12*(2), 95–107.

Hetland, L. (2000). Listening to music enhances spatial-temporal reasoning: Evidence for the "Mozart effect." *Journal of Aesthetic Education, 34*(3–4), 105–148.

Hill, P., & Argyle, M. (1998). Music and religious experiences and their relationship to happiness. *Journal of Personality and Individual Differences, 25*(1), 91–102.

Howe, M. J. A., & Sloboda, J. A. (1992). Problems experienced by talented young musicians as a result of the failure of other children to value musical accomplishments. *Gifted Education, 8,* 16–18.

Kincheloe, J. L. (1985). The use of music to engender emotion and control behavior in church, politics, and school. *Creative Child and Adult Quarterly, 10*(3), 187–196.

Kleiber, D. (1999). *A dialectical interpretation: Leisure experience and human development.* New York: Basic Books.

Lacourse, E., Claes, M., & Villeneuve, M. (2001). Heavy metal music and adolescent suicidal risk. *Journal of Youth and Adolescence, 30*(3), 321–332.

Larson, R. (2000). Toward a psychology of positive youth development. *American Psychologist, 55*, 170–183.

Larson, R., & Kleiber, D. (1993). Daily experience of adolescents. In P. Tolan & B. Cohler (Eds.), *Handbook of clinical research and practice with adolescents* (pp. 125–145). New York: Wiley.

Larson, R., Kubey, R., & Colletti, J. (1989). Changing chords: Early adolescent media choices and shifting investments in family and friends. *Journal of Youth and Adolescence, 18*, 583–600.

Lecanuet, J.-P. (1996). Prenatal auditory experience. In I. Deliège & J. A. Sloboda (Eds.), *Musical beginnings: Origins and development of musical competence* (pp. 3–34). Oxford, UK: Oxford University Press.

Leming, J. (1987). Rock music and the socialisation of moral values in early adolescence. *Youth and Society, 18*, 363–383.

MacDonald, R. A. R., Hargreaves, D. J., & Miell, D. (Eds.). (2002). *Musical identities.* Oxford, UK: Oxford University Press.

Martin, B. (1979). The socialization of disorder: Symbolism in rock music. *Sociological Analysis, 40*(2), 87–124.

North, A. C., Hargreaves, D. J., & O'Neill, S. A. (2000). The importance of music to adolescents. *British Journal of Educational Psychology, 70*(1), 255–272.

O'Neill, S. A. (1997). Gender and music. In D. J. Hargreaves & A. C. North (Eds.), *The social psychology of music* (pp. 46–63). Oxford, UK: Oxford University Press.

O'Neill, S. A. (2002a). Crossing the divide: Feminist perspectives on gender and music. *Feminism and Psychology, 12*(2), 133–136.

O'Neill, S. A. (2002b). The self-identity of young musicians. In R. A. R. MacDonald, D. J. Hargreaves, & D. Miell (Eds.), *Musical identities* (pp. 79–96). Oxford, UK: Oxford University Press.

O'Neill, S. A. (2002c). *Young people and music participation project: Practitioner report and summary of findings.* Retrieved from http://www.keele.ac.uk/depts/ps/ESRC

O'Neill, S. A. (2003). *Motivation and young people's participation in music: A longitudinal analysis.* Manuscript in preparation.

O'Neill, S. A., & Boulton, M. J. (1996). Boys' and girls' preferences for musical instruments: A function of gender? *Psychology of Music, 24*(2), 171–183.

O'Neill, S. A., Ivaldi, A., & Fox, C. (2002). Exploring the identity and subjectivity of 'talented' adolescent girls. *Feminism and Psychology, 12*(2), 153–159.

O'Neill, S. A., & McPherson, G. E. (2002). Motivation. In R. Parncutt & G. E. McPherson (Eds.), *The science and psychology of music performance: Creative strategies for teaching and learning* (pp. 31–46). Oxford, UK: Oxford University Press.

Papoušek, M. (1996). Intuitive parenting: A hidden source of musical stimulation in infancy. In I. Deliège & J. A. Sloboda (Eds.), *Musical beginnings: Origins and development of musical competence* (pp. 88–112). Oxford, UK: Oxford University Press.

Parncutt, R., & McPherson, G. (Eds.). (2002). *The science and psychology of music performance: Creative strategies for teaching and learning.* Oxford, UK: Oxford University Press.

Patrick, H., Ryan, A. M., Alfeld-Liro, C., Fredricks, J. A., Hruda, L. Z., & Eccles, J. S. (1999). Adolescents' commitment to developing talent: The role of peers in continuing motivation for sports and the arts. *Journal of Youth and Adolescence, 28*(6), 741–763.

Radocy, R. E. (2001). North America. In D. J. Hargreaves & A. C. North (Eds.), *Musical development and learning: The international perspective* (pp. 120–133). London: Continuum.

Rauscher, F. H., Shaw, G. L., & Ky, K. N. (1993). Music and spatial task performance. *Nature, 365,* 611.

Rauscher, F. H., Shaw, G. L., Levine, L., Wright, E., Dennis, W., & Newcomb, R. (1997). Music training causes long-term development of preschool children's spatial–temporal reasoning. *19*(2–8).

Sloboda, J. A., & O'Neill, S. A. (2001). Emotions in everyday listening to music. In P. Juslin & J. Sloboda (Eds.), *Music and emotion: Theory and research* (pp. 413–429). Oxford, UK: Oxford University Press.

Tarrant, M., North, A. C., & Hargreaves, D. J. (2000). English and American adolescents' reasons for listening to music. *Psychology of Music, 28*(2), 166–173.

Trehub, S., Schellenberg, G., & Hill, D. (1997). The origins of music perception and cognition: A developmental perspective. In I. Deliège & J. A. Sloboda (Eds.), *Perception and cognition of music* (pp. 103–128). Hove, England: Psychology Press.

Trevarthen, C. (1999–2000). Musicality and the intrinsic motive pulse: Evidence from human psychobiology and infant communication. *Musicae Scientiae* [Special Issue] *Rhythm, musical narrative, and origins of human communication,* 155–215.

van Well, F., Linssen, J., Kort, T., & Jansen, E. (1996). Ethnicity and youth cultural participation in the Netherlands. *Journal of Leisure Research, 28,* 85–95.

Vaughn, K. (2000). Music and mathematics: Modest support for the oft-claimed relationship. *Journal of Aesthetic Education, 34*(3–4), 149–166.

Weinstein, D. (1985). Rock: Youth and its music. *Popular Music and Society, 9*(3), 2–15.

Wigfield, A., Eccles, J. S., Yoon, K. S., Harold, R. D., Arbreton, A. J. A., Freedman-Doan, C., & Blumenfeld, P. C. (1997). Change in children's competence beliefs and subjective task values across the elementary school years: A 3-year study. *Journal of Educational Psychology, 89*(3), 451–469.

Wigfield, A., O'Neill, S. A., & Eccles, J. S. (1999, April). *Children's achievement values in different domains: Developmental and cultural differences.* Paper presented at the Bienniel Meeting of the Society for Research in Child Development, Albuquerque, NM.

Winner, E. (2000, August). *The relationship between arts and academic achievement: No evidence (yet) for a causal relationship.* Paper presented at Beyond the Soundbite: What the research actually shows about arts education and academic outcomes, The J. Paul Getty Trust, Los Angeles, CA.

Winner, E., & Cooper, M. (2000). Mute those claims: No evidence (yet) for a causal link between arts study and academic achievement. *Journal of Aesthetic Education, 34*(3–4), 11–75.

Winner, E., & Hetland, L. (2000). The arts in education: Evaluating the evidence for a causal link. *Journal of Aesthetic Education, 34*(3–4), 3–10.

Wolf, D. P. (2001). *A summary report from the Arts Effects Project* [Rep. prepared for the John S. and James L. Knight Foundation]. Cambridge, MA: Harvard University Press.

13

Participation in Sport: A Developmental Glimpse at Emotion

Tara K. Scanlan
University of California at Los Angeles

Megan L. Babkes
University of Northern Colorado

Lawrence A. Scanlan
University of California at Los Angeles

Consider the following young athlete:

Jeniqua is a 13-year-old junior elite gymnast who is ranked 5th in the country for her competitive level. She is 4'6" tall, weighs 72 pounds, and has only just started showing signs of puberty—she has some secondary sex characteristics, but has not started menstruating. Jeniqua is very bright, skipped a grade in elementary school and gets straight As in her coursework. Although she has many fellow gymnastics friends, she does not have a social network outside of athletics and does not participate in the social functions of other "normal" girls her age. She also still relies on the adults in her life for decisions and as a basis for her self-perceptions.

As we will see when we review the emotional response literature later in this chapter, competitive sport offers a rich emotional context with many potential sources of stress and enjoyment. We also know from previous research that the sources of these emotional responses organize

275

into three categories: *intrapersonal, situational,* and *significant others.* If we examine Jeniqua, we might see that she experiences a certain amount of stress from being a perfectionist (intrapersonal), participating in championship meets (situational), and dealing with negative social evaluation from her coach (significant others). However, she derives considerable enjoyment from learning new gymnastics skills (intrapersonal), winning (situational), and from the friendships she has established through participation (significant others).

The competitive sport domain also offers a robust developmental research environment because four important developmental components—social, cognitive, motor, and physical—all play critical roles in the sport experience. Jeniqua provides an exemplar snapshot of the different levels of development for each component. Her lack of ability to make independent choices and dependence on adults for decision making demonstrate lower social development, whereas her success academically indicates greater cognitive maturity. Her ranking and talent in gymnastics expose advanced motor development, whereas the fact that she has not gone through puberty shows a lack of physical development.

At a future time, Jeniqua will have progressed developmentally on each of these components, although advancement in some will be greater than in others. Thus, as chronological age increases, we anticipate seeing a regularly changing profile among the four developmental components. With these changes in profile, we expect that the nature of the emotional response, as well as the influence of specific intrapersonal, situational, and significant other sources, will likely differ.

This chapter focuses on athletes' emotional responses to competitive sport participation including developmental influences and implications for after school activity programs. We have four specific goals: (a) to elucidate the developmental components of the sport context; (b) to establish a thorough conceptual and empirical foundation of the extant stress and enjoyment research; (c) to build on this foundation to offer directions for the study of emotional responses developmentally; and (d) to use our understanding of emotional responses to suggest ways to structure after school sport programs.

We formally define *sport* as an "institutionalized competitive activity involving two or more opponents and stressing physical exertion by serious competitors who represent or are part of formally organized associations" (Nixon, 1984, p. 13). Participation in competitive team and individual sports occurs both in and out of school. Team activities such as basketball, softball, and soccer; and individual sports such as gymnastics, ice skating, and wrestling can be pursued at any age level from youth to adult and at any skill level from novice to elite. In this chapter, we present data covering these ranges of age and skill.

EMOTIONAL RESPONSES

The systematic examination of emotional responses from a developmental perspective requires a conceptual model to provide the structure necessary to organize the existing literature and stimulate future investigations. The model illustrated in Fig. 13.1 arranges the sources of emotional responses, the four developmental components of sport participation, and developmental progression as a cube. Sources of stress and enjoyment occupy the vertical axis. The four developmental components—social, cognitive, motor, and physical—complete the horizontal axis, while depth represents developmental progression or maturation. The developmental data to fully populate the cells in the figure do not yet exist.

Although limited developmental data exist, a significant understanding of the nature and sources of stress and enjoyment in sport derived from previous research provides a solid knowledge base. Similar to many of the other major issues in sport psychology, the approach to investigations of emotional responses in competitive sport focus first on "getting the constructs under control" before extending in new directions. Operational definitions for stress and enjoyment exist, as do validated measures, established methodologies, and articulated motivational consequences. Importantly, for the current discussion, a consistent, coherent, replicated, and generalizable set of findings have emerged that may now be applied to developmental questions.

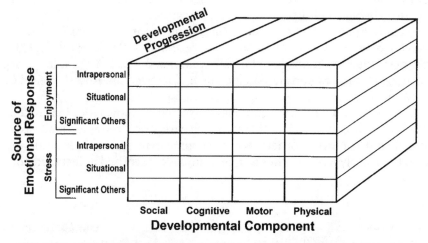

FIG. 13.1.   Research model for the developmental examination of emotional responses. The face of the cube shows the combinations of the sources for the two emotional responses, stress and enjoyment, and the four developmental components present in the sport setting: social, cognitive, motor, and physical.

Many of the same sources surface regardless of sample population, competitive level, gender, team versus individual sport contexts, age, and research methodology.

Further, where differences have been found, the conflicting studies have generally used different methodologies and asked different questions, precluding direct comparisons. For example, an effect may emerge using an open-ended interview but not be found using a survey method simply because the corresponding question was not asked. The existing results do suggest that more similarities than differences may exist developmentally. However, new empirical data will be required to determine if during developmental progression: (a) sources of stress and enjoyment remain the same, (b) sources remain the same but change in relative importance, (c) all or most sources change, or (d) some sources change and some do not.

Figure 13.2 shows how athletes' perceptions of the sport experience can lead to emotional responses, which in turn, influence motivational consequences. Perceptions lead to either the negative emotional response of stress or the positive response of enjoyment, or both. A negative emotional response can lead to a reduction in the desirability of the activity and negative motivational consequences. Conversely, a positive emotional response can increase the desirability of the activity and results in positive motivational consequences. Specifically, continued stress can lead to avoidance behaviors (Gould, Greenleaf, & Krane, 2002) such as dropout or burnout (Gould & Dieffenbach, 1999; Smith, 1986), whereas the feeling of enjoyment can lead to participation (Brustad, Babkes, & Smith, 2001; Weiss & Petlichkoff, 1989), persistence, desire to exert effort, perceptions of higher effort expended (T. K. Scanlan, Stein, & Ravizza, 1989), and commitment, that is, the desire and determination to persist in an endeavor over time (Carpenter & T. K. Scanlan, 1998; Carpenter, T. K. Scanlan, Simons, & Lobel 1993; T. K. Scanlan, 2000; T. K. Scanlan, Carpenter, Schmidt, Simons, & Keeler, 1993; T. K. Scanlan, Russell, Beals, & L. A. Scanlan, 2003; T. K. Scanlan & Simons, 1992).

As noted previously, the sources of stress and enjoyment identified in the literature can be organized into three categories: intrapersonal, situational, and significant others. A given source may operate independently or interactively with another source. Sources categorized as intrapersonal

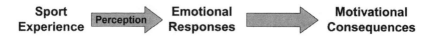

FIG. 13.2.   Emotional responses result from the athlete's perception of the sport experience that, in turn, leads to motivational consequences.

relate to athletes' personality dispositions, cognitions, and psychological states. The situational category includes events that commonly occur in the competitive sport context such as social evaluation, and victory or defeat. The significant others category incorporates sources that relate to the influences of parents, coaches, peers, fans and the community on an athletes' sport participation.

Historically, the study of stress proceeded enjoyment and we present the literatures in that order. Both reviews include construct definitions and a synopsis of the breadth of the research including sample populations, variables, and research methodologies.

STRESS

Definition and Measurement of Stress

Competitive sport can be stressful to some participants because of its inherent achievement elements including the very public demonstration, testing, and evaluation of athletic ability (T. K. Scanlan, 2002). The construct of *stress* has historically been defined as an individual's appraisal of a situation as too taxing or exceeding one's resources and, thus, endangering his or her sense of well-being (Lazarus, 1966). In competitive sport, this sense of feeling threatened occurs when the athlete perceives an imbalance between the performance demands and his or her capabilities to meet those demands under conditions where the consequences of failure are thought to be important (Martens, 1977). Note that the athlete's *perception* of an imbalance, along with the anticipation of negative consequences, not objective reality, yields the negative emotional response. The perceived consequences include unfavorable social evaluation of physical competence from significant people to the athlete such as coaches, parents, peers, fans, and spectators (T. K. Scanlan, 2002).

Stress responses to competitive sport have, for the most part, been measured in the form of state anxiety (T. K. Scanlan, 1984). *State anxiety* involves assessments of feelings of apprehension, tension, and autonomic nervous system activation that occur as immediate, "right now" reactions to situations that are perceived as threatening to one's self-esteem (Spielberger, 1966). State anxiety can be measured along behavioral, physiological, and psychological dimensions. Behavioral measures include nervous laughter, being jittery, losing one's appetite, and insomnia. Physiological measures include increases in heart rate, respiration, galvanic skin responses, and palmar sweating. Psychological measures include state anxiety and other in-depth assessments of negative cognitions and feelings.

Psychological measures of competitive sport stress generally vary depending on whether the research used a quantitative or qualitative methodology.

Quantitative investigations have typically employed one of a few well-validated measures of state anxiety such as the State Anxiety Inventory for Children (SAIC; Spielberger, 1973), the Competitive State Anxiety Inventory (CSAI; Martens, Burton, Rivkin, & Simon, 1980), or the Competitive State Anxiety Inventory–2 (CSAI-2; Martens, Burton, Vealey, Bump, & Smith, 1990). Each of these inventories includes multiple items that produce a single indicator of stress level. Characteristically, they are used to assess state anxiety before, during, or after competition.

Qualitative approaches have used in-depth interviews to gain a broader and deeper understanding of the sources of stress. These studies specifically define stress for the participant and have typically used definitions such as "negative emotions, feelings, or thoughts" (Cohn, 1990; Gould, Eklund, & Jackson, 1991, Gould, Jackson, & Finch, 1993; T. K. Scanlan, Stein, & Ravizza, 1991) or "taxing or exceeding resources" (Gould, Eklund, & Jackson, 1993; Gould, Finch, & Jackson, 1993). These interviews also allowed discussion of less transitory sources of stress that pervaded the careers of elite athletes. They pertain not only to competitions, but also to the larger sport context such as events and interactions occurring during practices and off the field of play. Consistent with the qualitative research, we use the term stress rather than state anxiety throughout the following sections because it better conveys the emotional character of the response in lay terms.

Breadth of Stress Literature

The sources of stress have been investigated using a broad range of population samples, experimental settings, and research methodologies, yielding highly consistent findings that demonstrate the robust and generalizable nature (external validity) of the results. Populations include males and females from youth sport, collegiate, adult recreational, and elite athletic samples including both individual and team sports. In addition, laboratory experiments have been conducted with general student body members from elementary school through collegiate levels. Quantitative methods have been used in studies conducted in both laboratory and naturalistic sport settings. Qualitative interviews have provided the voice of the athlete to plum the depth of their experience and have made a significant contribution to the knowledge base in two ways: (a) identification of new sources not previously known, and (b) the emergence of a substantially deeper understanding of stress sources (T. K. Scanlan & Simons, 1992). Table 13.1 provides research reference citations organized by research methodology, sample population, sport type, and measurement method.

The several research methodologies used to develop this literature strengthen the validity of the findings. Initial research on sources of stress used a controlled laboratory environment, which allowed high internal va-

TABLE 13.1
Sport Stress Reference Citations Arranged by Research Methodology, Sample Population, Sport Type, and Measure

Research Methodology

Laboratory experiments

Martens & Gill, 1976	Scanlan, 1975, 1977, 1978

Quantitative/survey

Bray, Martin, & Widemeyer, 2000	Kroll, 1979
Feltz, Lirgg, & Albrecht, 1992	Pensgaard & Roberts, 2000
Gould, Horn, & Spreemann, 1983	Pierce & Stratton, 1981
Gould & Weinberg, 1985	Scanlan & Lewthwaite, 1984
Griffin, 1972	Scanlan & Passer, 1978, 1979
Johnson, 1949	Simon & Martens, 1979

Qualitative/interview

Cohn, 1990	Gould, Jackson, & Finch, 1993
Gould, Eklund, & Jackson, 1991, 1993	Scanlan, Stein, & Ravizza, 1991
Gould, Finch, & Jackson, 1993	

Sample Population

Males

Bray, Martin, & Widemeyer, 2000	Kroll, 1979
Cohn, 1990	Martens & Gill, 1976
Feltz, Lirgg, & Albrecht, 1992	Pensgaard & Roberts, 2000
Gould, Eklund, & Jackson, 1991, 1993	Pierce & Stratton, 1981
Gould, Finch, & Jackson, 1993	Scanlan, 1975, 1977, 1978
Gould, Horn, & Spreemann, 1983	Scanlan & Lewthwaite, 1984
Gould, Jackson, & Finch, 1993	Scanlan & Passer, 1978
Gould & Weinberg, 1985	Scanlan, Stein, & Ravizza, 1991
Griffin, 1972	Simon & Martens, 1979
Johnson, 1949	

Females

Bray, Martin, & Widemeyer, 2000	Martens & Gill, 1976
Feltz, Lirgg, & Albrecht, 1992	Pensgaard & Roberts, 2000
Gould, Finch, & Jackson, 1993	Pierce & Stratton, 1981
Gould, Jackson, & Finch, 1993	Scanlan & Passer, 1979
Griffin, 1972	Scanlan, Stein, & Ravizza, 1991

(continued on next page)

TABLE 13.1 (*continued*)

Youth sport

Bray, Martin, & Widemeyer, 2000   Scanlan, 1975, 1977

Cohn, 1990   Scanlan & Lewthwaite, 1984

Griffin, 1972   Scanlan & Passer, 1978, 1979

Martens & Gill, 1976   Simon & Martens, 1979

Pierce & Stratton, 1981

Collegiate and adult

Gould & Weinberg, 1985   Kroll, 1979

Johnson, 1949   Scanlan, 1978

Elite

Feltz, Lirgg, & Albrecht, 1992   Gould, Jackson, & Finch, 1993

Gould, Eklund, & Jackson, 1991, 1993   Pensgaard & Roberts, 2000

Gould, Finch, & Jackson, 1993   Scanlan, Stein, & Ravizza, 1991

Gould, Horn, & Spreemann, 1983

Sport Type

Individual

Bray, Martin, & Widemeyer, 2000   Johnson, 1949

Cohn, 1990   Kroll, 1979

Feltz, Lirgg, & Albrecht, 1992   Martens & Gill, 1976

Gould, Eklund, & Jackson, 1991, 1993   Pensgaard & Roberts, 2000

Gould, Finch, & Jackson, 1993   Scanlan, 1975, 1977, 1978

Gould, Horn, & Spreemann, 1983   Scanlan & Lewthwaite, 1984

Gould, Jackson, & Finch, 1993   Scanlan, Stein, & Ravizza, 1991

Gould & Weinberg, 1985   Simon & Martens, 1979

Griffin, 1972

Team

Pensgaard & Roberts, 2000   Scanlan & Passer, 1978, 1979

Pierce & Stratton, 1981

Measure

Competitive trait anxiety

Feltz, Lirgg, & Albrecht, 1992   Martens & Gill, 1976

Gould, Horn, & Spreemann, 1983   Scanlan, 1975, 1977, 1978

Gould & Weinberg, 1985   Scanlan & Passer, 1978, 1979

Griffin, 1972

State anxiety

Bray, Martin, & Widemeyer, 2000   Scanlan, 1975, 1977, 1978

Johnson, 1949	Scanlan & Passer, 1978, 1979
Kroll, 1979	Simon & Martens, 1979
Martens & Gill, 1976	Scanlan & Lewthwaite, 1984
Stress	
Cohn, 1990	Gould, Jackson, & Finch, 1993
Gould, Eklund, & Jackson, 1991, 1993	Pensgaard & Roberts, 2000
Gould, Finch, & Jackson, 1993	Pierce & Stratton, 1981
Gould, Horn, & Spreemann, 1983	Scanlan, Stein, & Ravizza, 1991

lidity by making it possible to clearly establish causal relationships between sources of stress and the resulting emotional response. The laboratory findings were then replicated in the real-life arena of youth sport, thereby, demonstrating the ecological validity of the results. *Ecological validity* is a special form of external validity that indicates how well findings generalize to the real world. More recent studies have complemented and elaborated on the previous survey methods with interview and panel discussion techniques to provide further ecological validity to the body of knowledge.

Review of Stress Literature

Table 13.2 identifies the sources of competitive stress using the three major categories outlined earlier: intrapersonal, situational, and significant others. The following paragraphs review the sources of stress using these three categories to show how each one tips the balance to create the negative emotional response experienced by some athletes.

Intrapersonal Sources of Stress

Stable and transitory intrapersonal sources of stress, which typically reflect perceptions of inadequacy, have been identified in the literature. Specific sources include athletes' personality dispositions; cognitions and worries related to failure, competition, and training; performance expectancies; negative feelings; physical and mental difficulties; and commitment concerns revealed among elite athletes.

Personality Dispositions.   Self-esteem and Competitive Trait Anxiety (CTA) represent two stable personality dispositions that significantly influence stress. *Self-esteem,* defined as the general evaluative attitude about one's own capability, success, and self-worth (Coopersmith, 1967), predicts precompetitive stress in boys and girls involved in soccer. Youth with low

TABLE 13.2
Sources of Stress

Source Type	Examples From Research
Intrapersonal sources	
Personality dispositions	Low self-esteem
	High competitive trait anxiety (CTA)
Cognitions and worries	Fear of failure
	Making mistakes
	Lack of success in competition
	Athletic inadequacy
	Lack of competitive readiness
	Potential problems during competition
	Self-doubts about talent
	Perfectionism
Performance expectations	Low team performance expectancies
	Low personal performance expectancies
Negative feelings	Lack of fun
	Guilt related to potentially hurting opponents
Physical or mental difficulties	Coping with injury
	Maintaining physical fitness
	Weight control
	Dealing with sore muscles
	Fear of getting hurt
	Not being mentally ready to compete
Elite level commitment concerns	Personal costs
	Low commitment to skating
Situational sources	
Contextual elements	Sport type
	High importance of competition
	Playing a particularly difficult shot

	Performance-oriented motivational climate
Competition outcome	Win, loss, tie, margin of victory or defeat
Hassles within the larger sport context	Political bureaucracy
	Financial demands and costs
	Time demands and costs
	Accommodations, facilities, food, and transportation at away competitions

Significant other sources

Performance expectations, Evaluation and feedback	Parental pressure to participate
	Parental and coach expectations to perform well
	Striving to meet parental expectations
	Negative performance feedback from parents, coaches, and teammates
	Social evaluation of general and performance-specific ability
Interaction of elite level performers	Communication problems with others
	Lack of social support
	Interpersonal conflict
	Psychological warfare

self-esteem experience greater precompetitive stress than youth with high self-esteem (T. K. Scanlan & Passer, 1978, 1979). CTA is a personality disposition reflecting the tendency to perceive competitive situations as threatening to self-esteem (Martens, 1977) and, in contrast to the transitory nature of state anxiety, it represents a more chronic perception that evolves over time. Those high-CTA participants experience higher stress (state anxiety) in a competitive situation than low-CTA participants.

CTA consistently emerges as an influential predictor of stress in both laboratory and field studies investigating individual and team sport participants. Results from laboratory experiments revealed that college males (T. K. Scanlan, 1978) and boys (T. K. Scanlan, 1975, 1977) with high CTA reported greater stress than did their low CTA cohorts prior to competition. Martens and Gill (1976) found that CTA was a source of precompetition stress for both boys and girls and found even greater differences during the middle of the competition. Scanlan and colleagues (T. K. Scanlan & Lewthwaite, 1984; T. K. Scanlan & Passer, 1978, 1979) replicated the laboratory findings in the field setting with young wrestlers and male and female soccer players. CTA also has been found to be a source of stress for young elite distance runners (Feltz, Lirgg, & Albrecht, 1992), junior elite wrestlers (Gould, Horn, & Spreemann, 1983), and adult sport participants (Kroll, 1979).

Cognitions and Worries. Athletes from various age and competitive levels cite their worries about failure and making mistakes in competition as sources of stress. At lower competitive levels, young and adult athletes indicated that thoughts about not performing well, making mistakes, and prematch concerns about failure were stressors (Gould & Weinberg, 1985; Kroll, 1979; Pierce & Stratton, 1981; T. K. Scanlan & Lewthwaite, 1984). Young elite athletes have consistently reported that a fear of failure and thoughts about athletic inadequacy were sources of stress (Feltz et al., 1992; Gould et al., 1983). Similarly, predictors of stress for older elite and Olympic level athletes include worries about failure, competitive readiness, and encountering potential problems during competition (Gould, Eklund, et al., 1991, 1993; Gould, Finch, et al., 1993). In T. K. Scanlan et al. (1991), elite level skaters identified self-doubts regarding their skating talent and having a perfectionist attitude related to their athletic involvement as stressors. Self-doubts about talent reflected low levels of self-confidence, whereas perfectionism consisted of their need to skate flawlessly and accept no less from themselves.

Performance Expectations. Low expectations of team and personal ability to perform well in competition cause stress for athletes. T. K. Scanlan and Passer (1978, 1979) found that male and female youth soccer players who reported lower team expectancies experienced higher precompetition stress than their peers who maintained higher performance expectations. For boys, low personal performance expectations also led to higher stress prior to competition. T. K. Scanlan and Lewthwaite (1984) found the same results with young male wrestlers, and Cohn (1990) found an analogous result with male high-school golfers.

Negative Feelings. Two negative feelings, lack of fun and guilt attached to injuring opponents, are also intrapersonal sources of stress. Results from two studies (T. K. Scanlan & Passer 1978, 1979), as well as follow-up research (T. K. Scanlan & Lewthwaite, 1984), revealed that a lack of fun during competition predicted postcompetitive stress for young male and female athletes, regardless of game outcome. Negative feelings associated with guilt about potentially hurting opponents were found to be a source of stress for adult participants (Kroll, 1979).

Physical and Mental Difficulties. Physical and mental difficulties have been reported as sources of stress by adult and elite level athletes (Gould & Weinberg, 1985; Gould et al., 1983; Kroll, 1979; T. K. Scanlan et al., 1991) but have not been assessed with youth performers. Physical difficulties included coping with injury, maintaining physical fitness, fighting weight, and dealing with sore muscles. Mental difficulties consisted of the fear of getting hurt and not being mentally ready to compete.

Commitment Concerns at the Elite Level. Finally, elite athletes identify stress factors related to the personal cost and commitment associated with the long duration and high intensity of their involvement (T. K. Scanlan et al., 1991). Personal costs focused on feelings of having lost one's sense of self-worth, identity, or social support due to the high level of sport involvement, whereas commitment concerns referred to an ongoing evaluation of whether or not to continue with competitive skating.

Situational Sources of Stress

Two general categories of situational stressors have been identified in the sport environment. The first involves contextual elements such as the type of sport, importance of the competition, and motivational climate. The second category includes events that commonly occur either (a) during competitions, with the most significant being competition outcome, and (b) hassles within the larger sport context such as political, financial, time, and travel demands.

Contextual Elements. The nature of the athletic context can induce stress. The sport type, whether individual or team, was one of the first sources of competitive stress investigated (Griffin, 1972; Johnson, 1949; Simon & Martens, 1979). Findings revealed that stress was higher in young participants who competed in individual sports. Furthermore, participation in individual contact sports such as wrestling was associated with higher stress than noncontact, individual sports such as swimming. Elite athletes find playing in championship meets or competitions to be stressful (Gould et al., 1983) and that the importance of an event further contributes to stress (T. K. Scanlan et al., 1991). Similarly, male high-school golfers felt that playing particularly difficult shots induced higher stress (Cohn, 1990). Finally, motivational climate contributed to the stress experienced by Norwegian Olympic athletes (Pensgaard & Roberts, 2000). A performance-oriented climate, one with an emphasis on normative standards and social comparison, produced higher levels of stress than a mastery-oriented climate where the coach emphasizes skill mastery and the importance of effort.

Competition Outcome.   A lost game, match, or competition predicts stress for athletes regardless of competitive level, age, or environment. Early laboratory experiments showed that losing was associated with higher levels of stress for elementary school boys and girls (Martens & Gill, 1976; T. K. Scanlan, 1975, 1977) and college males (T. K. Scanlan, 1978). These findings were replicated in the natural field setting with youth soccer players of both genders (T. K. Scanlan & Passer, 1978, 1979), with male wrestlers (T. K. Scanlan & Lewthwaite, 1984), and in interviews with elite athletes (Gould, Jackson, et al., 1993; T. K. Scanlan et al., 1991).

Two sets of findings show athlete's sensitivity even to gradations of the particular outcome. First, losing a soccer game by a close margin produced greater stress for young boys than losing games by a larger margin (T. K. Scanlan & Passer, 1978). Second, a "tied" competition outcome was not a neutral experience. Findings from a laboratory experiment with boys (T. K. Scanlan, 1975) and field research with young female soccer players (T. K. Scanlan & Passer, 1979) revealed that postcompetition stress following a "tie" fell between the levels associated with a win and a loss (T. K. Scanlan, 1977).

Hassles Within the Larger Sport Context.   Adult and elite level athletes consistently report that other aspects of competitive sport involvement, such as the political bureaucracy, the financial and time demands, as well as the accommodations, food, transportation, and facilities while traveling are sources of stress. Dealing with politics was explained in more detail as the lack of control over decisions made and dealing with unfair judging (Feltz et al., 1992; Gould, Finch, et al., 1993; Kroll, 1979; T. K. Scanlan et al., 1991). Scanlan and colleagues found that receiving biased judging, not getting support from the national sport governing body, and having a coach who is a poor politician all contributed to higher stress for elite figure skaters. These same athletes, as well as Olympic wrestlers and skaters interviewed by Gould and colleagues (Gould, Eklund, et al., 1991, 1993; Gould, Finch, et al., 1993), indicated that the financial drain associated with the sport and the time commitment necessary for practice, were significant sources of stress.

Significant Other Sources of Stress

The public nature of achievement in sport can lead to athletes perceiving significant others as stressors. Coaches, parents, and peers can create this negative affect through their expectations for participation and performance, their evaluation, and their negative feedback. Additionally, elite athletes find problems pertaining to communication, social support, conflict, and psychological warfare to be stressful.

Performance Expectations, Evaluation, and Feedback.   Research on sources of competitive stress conducted with children, adolescents, adults, and elite athletes of all ages has repeatedly demonstrated that perceptions of negative interactions with coaches, parents, teammates, and peers predict a negative emotional response. Early on, T. K. Scanlan & Lewthwaite (1984) found that perceived parental pressure to wrestle, and worries about receiving negative performance evaluations from parents and coaches were significant sources of prematch stress for the young athletes they surveyed. In subsequent studies, athletes from youth sport to elite levels have reported that striving to meet parental and coach expectations, negative performance evaluations, and precompetition worries related to receiving negative feedback were stressors (Bray, Martin, & Widemeyer, 2000; Cohn, 1990; Gould, Jackson, et al., 1993; Gould & Weinberg, 1985; Pierce & Stratton, 1981; T. K. Scanlan et al., 1991). Additionally, recent research has revealed that young competitive skiers who report more concerns about what their fellow competitors and friends think of their general skiing ability, as opposed to evaluation of specific performances, had higher levels of stress (Bray et al., 2000).

Interaction of Elite Performers With Others.   Interviews conducted with elite athletes have revealed other stressful negative interactions. Specifically, Olympic wrestlers and figure skaters cited coach and teammate communication problems and a lack of general social support as predictors of negative emotion (Gould, Eklund, et al., 1991, 1993; Gould, Finch, et al., 1993). *Interpersonal conflict,* defined as discord between oneself and parents, coaches or skating peers; and psychological warfare or "mind games" used by opponents and their parents, were also identified to be stressors (T. K. Scanlan et al., 1991).

Conclusions on Sources of Stress

Diverse sources of competitive stress exist for athletes with results demonstrating that a number of the same intrapersonal, situational, and significant other sources exist across the various ages, competitive levels, sports examined, and laboratory and natural field settings. As noted in the introduction, new empirical data will be required to determine if these results remain the same over developmental progression. Additionally, where sources have only been identified with a single group, we do not currently know if the results may be explained by methodological differences or if particular groups experience unique sources of stress. For example, sources associated with long-term commitment, high competitive levels, and extensive training are likely more common to elite athletes than lower level competitors.

ENJOYMENT

The positive emotional response of enjoyment is one of the cornerstones of motivation (T. K. Scanlan & Simons, 1992) and is central to most theories explaining *why* athletes choose to maintain participation and exert effort in the physical domain (see Weiss & Ferrer-Caja, 2002). Today, most major sport motivation theories have an enjoyment component including achievement goal theory (Nicholls, 1989), self-determination theory (Deci & Ryan, 1985), competence motivation theory (Harter, 1978, 1981), expectancy value theory (Eccles et al., 1983), and the sport commitment model (T. K. Scanlan, 2000; T. K. Scanlan, Carpenter, Schmidt, et al., 1993; T. K. Scanlan, Russell, Beals, & L. A. Scanlan, 2003).

Definition and Measurement of Enjoyment

Many aspects of athletic involvement are considered to be enjoyable to athletes of all ages, competitive levels, and sports. *Sport enjoyment* may be defined as "a positive affective response to the sport experience that reflects generalized feelings such as pleasure, liking and fun" (T. K. Scanlan & Simons, 1992, p. 202). Viewed as a positive emotional response experienced in athletic contexts, it falls between the generalized construct of global positive affect and specific emotions such as excitement.

Work by Scanlan and associates (T. K. Scanlan, Simons, Carpenter, Schmidt, & Keeler, 1993) unified several of the enjoyment measures used historically and demonstrated the workings of a single underlying construct. Historically, surveys used items focused on enjoyment (Brustad, 1988; Wankel & Kreisel, 1985a, 1985b), liking (Brustad, 1988; T. K. Scanlan & Lewthwaite, 1986), and fun (Harris, 1984; T. K. Scanlan & Lewthwaite, 1986; Wankel & Sefton, 1989). However, without evidence that these several measures were tapping the same construct, the interpretation of results among studies was problematic (Kendzierski & DeCarlo, 1991). As part of the development of the Sport Commitment Model, T. K. Scanlan and colleagues (T. K. Scanlan, Simons, et al., 1993) investigated 25 measurement items that potentially predicated commitment including four descriptors of enjoyment derived by adding "happy" and "enjoy" to the "liking" and "fun" items from T. K. Scanlan and Lewthwaite (1986). Factor analytic results indicated that the four enjoyment measures all loaded on the enjoyment component of the Model. The findings strengthen previous research by demonstrating that the enjoyment, fun, liking, and being happy items used throughout the literature reflect the same construct, thereby providing the necessary validity for their use as measures of enjoyment.

Breadth of Enjoyment Literature

Similar to the stress literature, sport enjoyment research has studied positive emotional responses using quantitative and qualitative methodological approaches, diverse samples and sport types, and different time references. Extending the stress research, male and female inner-city populations with diverse ethnicity, including participants who were of African American, Asian, White, and Hispanic descent have been studied. Studies have focused on sources of sport enjoyment from youth sport participants to elite athletes involved in team and individual sports. The ages of the athletes participating in these studies ranged from as young as 7 years old (Wankel & Kreisel, 1985a, 1985b) to world class athletes in their 20s (T. K. Scanlan, Stein, et al., 1989). Researchers have examined predictors of enjoyment related to (a) specific points in time, including before or after a game, and (b) periods of time, such as over an entire season or during the most competitive years of an athlete's career. For complete reviews of this research, see T. K. Scanlan and Simons (1992) and T. K. Scanlan, Carpenter, Lobel, and Simons (1993). Table 13.3 provides a complete list of references arranged by research methodology, sample population, sport type, and time frame.

Investigations of the sources of enjoyment in sport have been approached using both quantitative and qualitative methods. As we have seen with stress, the mixture of methods employed has served to establish a solid foundation for our understanding of the nature and meaning of this construct. The initial studies focused on sources of enjoyment with large samples of children and used primarily quantitative methods such as surveys and questionnaires (Brustad, 1988; T. K. Scanlan, Carpenter, Lobel, et al., 1993; T. K. Scanlan & Lewthwaite, 1986; Wankel & Kreisel, 1985a; Wankel & Sefton, 1989). The findings from these studies were critical to establishing the external validity needed to make broad conclusions about what youth consider fun and likable about involvement in athletics. Subsequent research employed a more inductive, qualitative approach (T. K. Scanlan, Ravizza, & Stein, 1989, T. K. Scanlan, Stein, et al., 1989), in the form of in-depth interviews with world-class athletes. As noted earlier in the review of stress, the opportunity for elite athletes to speak about their sources of enjoyment and elaborate on the meaning of those experiences identified many new sources and contributed breadth, depth, and personal meaning to the existing literature (T. K. Scanlan & Simons, 1992).

Review of Enjoyment Literature

As with the stress literature, we examine sources of enjoyment using three major categories: intrapersonal, situational, and significant others. Table 13.4 lists the specific sources in each of the three categories. At the end of

TABLE 13.3
Sport Enjoyment Reference Citations Arranged by Research Methodology, Sample Population, Sport Type, and Time Frame

Research Methodology

Quantitative/survey

Averill & Power, 1995	Scanlan, Carpenter, Lobel, & Simons, 1993
Babkes & Weiss, 1999	Scanlan & Lewthwaite, 1986
Brustad, 1988	Stephens, 1998
Chalip, Csikszentmihalyi, Kleiber, & Larson, 1984	Wankel & Kreisel, 1985a
Leff & Hoyle, 1995	Wankel & Sefton, 1989
Passer & Scanlan, 1980	

Qualitative/interview

Csikszentmihalyi, 1975	Wankel & Kreisel, 1985b
Harris, 1984	Weiss, Smith, & Theeboom, 1996
Scanlan, Stein, & Ravizza, 1989	

Sample Population

Males

Averill & Power, 1995	Scanlan, Carpenter, Lobel, & Simons, 1993
Babkes & Weiss, 1999	Scanlan & Lewthwaite, 1986
Brustad, 1988	Scanlan, Stein, & Ravizza, 1989
Chalip, Csikszentmihalyi, Kleiber, & Larson, 1984	Stephens, 1998
Csikszentmihalyi, 1975	Wankel & Kreisel, 1985a, 1985b
Harris, 1984	Wankel & Sefton, 1989
Leff & Hoyle, 1995	Weiss, Smith, & Theeboom, 1996
Passer & Scanlan, 1980	

Females

Babkes & Weiss, 1999	Scanlan, Carpenter, Lobel, & Simons, 1993
Brustad, 1988	Scanlan, Stein, & Ravizza, 1989
Chalip, Csikszentmihalyi, Kleiber, & Larson, 1984	Stephens, 1998
Harris, 1984	Wankel & Sefton, 1989
Leff & Hoyle, 1995	Weiss, Smith, & Theeboom, 1996

Passer & Scanlan, 1980

Youth sport

Averill & Power, 1995

Babkes & Weiss, 1999

Brustad, 1988

Chalip, Csikszentmihalyi, Kleiber, & Larson, 1984

Csikszentmihalyi, 1975

Harris, 1984

Leff & Hoyle, 1995

Passer & Scanlan, 1980

Scanlan, Carpenter, Lobel, & Simons, 1993

Scanlan & Lewthwaite, 1986

Stephens, 1998

Wankel & Kreisel, 1985a, 1985b

Wankel & Sefton, 1989

Weiss, Smith, & Theeboom, 1996

Ethnically diverse, inner-city

Leff & Hoyle, 1995

Scanlan, Carpenter, Lobel, & Simons, 1993

Elite

Scanlan, Stein, & Ravizza, 1989

Sport Type

Individual

Chalip, Csikszentmihalyi, Kleiber, & Larson, 1984

Leff & Hoyle, 1995

Scanlan & Lewthwaite, 1986

Scanlan, Stein, & Ravizza, 1989

Weiss, Smith, & Theeboom, 1996

Team

Averill & Power, 1995

Babkes & Weiss, 1999

Brustad, 1988

Chalip, Csikszentmihalyi, Kleiber, & Larson, 1984

Csikszentmihalyi, 1975

Passer & Scanlan, 1980

Scanlan, Carpenter, Lobel, & Simons, 1993

Stephens, 1998

Harris, 1984

Wankel & Kreisel, 1985a, 1985b

Wankel & Sefton, 1989

Weiss, Smith, & Theeboom, 1996

Time Frame

Before and after game

Chalip, Csikszentmihalyi, Kleiber, & Larson, 1984

Passer & Scanlan, 1980

Wankel & Sefton, 1989

(continued on next page)

TABLE 13.3 (continued)

Season-long

Brustad, 1988   Scanlan & Lewthwaite, 1986

Scanlan, Carpenter, Lobel, & Simons,
1993

Most competitive years

Scanlan, Stein, & Ravizza, 1989

Overall (positive emotion in general)

Averill & Power, 1995   Leff & Hoyle, 1995

Babkes & Weiss, 1999   Stephens, 1998

Csikszentmihalyi, 1975   Wankel & Kreisel, 1985a, 1985b

Harris, 1984   Weiss, Smith, & Theeboom, 1996

this section, we offer an argument for partially consolidating the currently separate participation motivation and sport enjoyment literatures.

Intrapersonal Sources of Enjoyment

Intrapersonal sources of enjoyment include perceived ability and the sense of being special, mastery, motivational goal orientation, personal movement experiences, and personal coping and emotional release through sport. Literature on each is reviewed in the following paragraphs.

Perceived Ability and the Sense of Being Special.   Perceptions of high sport ability or competence are a salient source of enjoyment for youth sport participants involved in team and individual sports as well as elite level athletes (Brustad, 1988; Chalip, Csikszentmihalyi, Kleiber, & Larson, 1984; Csikszentmihalyi, 1975; Harris, 1984; T. K. Scanlan & Lewthwaite, 1986; T. K. Scanlan, Stein, et al., 1989; Wankel & Kreisel, 1985a, 1985b, Wankel & Sefton, 1989). For example, young male wrestlers who had higher self-perceptions of their wrestling ability reported greater season-long enjoyment (T. K. Scanlan & Lewthwaite, 1986). Perceived competence emerged as a prominent theme in the interviews with elite skaters and reflected two enjoyment sources: successfully demonstrating skills and the performing aspects of achievement (T. K. Scanlan, Stein, et al., 1989). Performance achievement was defined as the social achievement related to performing, such as the ability to use performance techniques and one's skating talent to control audience reactions, or to ex-

TABLE 13.4
Sources of Enjoyment

Source Type	Examples From Research
Intrapersonal sources	
Perceived ability and the sense of being special	High perceived competence
	Performance achievement
Mastery	Learning new skills
	Practicing skills
	Doing skills
	Developing and improving skills
	Exerting effort
	Preference for challenge
	Perfecting skills
Motivational goal orientation	Self-referenced success criteria
Personal movement experiences	Movement sensations
	Self-expression/creativity
	Athleticism
	Flow/peak experiences
	Excitement of game
	Being highly active
Coping and emotional release	Escape from personal and family problems
Situational sources	
Competitive outcomes and processes	Win/loss
	Opportunity to compare/measure skills against others
	Competitive achievement
Social recognition and opportunities	Extrinsic rewards (trophies, ribbons, etc.)
	Standing ovations
	Fame, prestige, glamour, media coverage
	Travel and seeing other places
Significant other sources	
Positive perceptions of adult influence	Low parental pressure to participate
	Parental and coach performance satisfaction
	Fewer parental negative reactions to performance
	Parental and coach sport involvement and support
	Realistic parental performance expectancies
	Making family and coach proud and giving them pleasure through talent
Social interactions with teammates	Team interactions/support and peers
	Companionship/making friends/affiliation

perience audience interaction and sharing. Finally, skaters at the highest echelon of their sport revealed that feeling special due to being so highly talented was a source of enjoyment (T. K. Scanlan, Stein, et al., 1989)

Mastery. Other factors related to competence, including the process and outcomes of engaging in mastery emerge as sources of enjoyment for all groups of athletes. Mastery through learning, practice, use, and improvement of skills results in enjoyment (Csikszentmihalyi, 1975; Gill, Gross, & Huddleston, 1985; Sapp & Haubenstricker, 1978; T. K. Scanlan, Carpenter, Lobel, et al., 1993; T. K. Scanlan, Stein, et al., 1989; Wankel & Kreisel, 1985a, 1985b). Survey research conducted with youth sport and adult participants suggests that they derive enjoyment from putting in the effort to learn new skills and improve existing ones (Csikszentmihalyi, 1975; T. K. Scanlan, Carpenter, Lobel, et al., 1993; Wankel & Kreisel, 1985a, 1985b).

The opportunity to engage in mastery development through optimally challenging situations also has been associated with enjoyment in sport. Wankel and Sefton (1989) found that experiencing challenge was important to having fun during a season for team sport participants of both genders. Harris (1984) found that young male baseball players desired more challenge and more chances to display their competence, and that when these opportunities were provided, they experienced more fun. Brustad's (1988) study produced similar results with young male and female basketball players. Chalip and colleagues (1984) showed that greater perceived challenge, or tests of competence, result in greater enjoyment for those in physical education class, informal sport situations, and organized sport. Finally, interviews with elite athletes demonstrate that they also derive enjoyment from both the processes and outcomes of conquering and perfecting difficult tasks (T. K. Scanlan, Stein, et al., 1989).

The emergence of mastery as a significant predictor of enjoyment contradicts a common misconception known as the "Pizza Parlor Phenomenon" (T. K. Scanlan, Carpenter, Lobel, et al., 1993, p. 282). The error stems from the mistaken belief that athletes only experience enjoyment *after* the hard practice, when they can affiliate with teammates at the local pizza parlor. In fact, athletes experience fun during the processes of practicing and mastering sport skills. Although this conclusion seems obvious, we encourage the reader to listen for the Pizza Parlor Phenomena in future conversations and observe how it so commonly plays out.

Motivational Goal Orientation. An athlete's motivational goal orientation determines how they define success in the athletic arena. Those who report higher levels of task orientation and define success by self-referenced criteria such as effort, exertion, and mastery, experience higher sport enjoyment (Fox, Goudas, Biddle, Duda, & Armstrong, 1994; Stephens, 1998).

Personal Movement Experiences.   Other intrapersonal sources of enjoyment include experiences derived from the act of movement or "doing the sport" such as movement sensations, self-expression, feeling athletic, having flow experiences or experiencing excitement (Csikszentmihalyi, 1975; T. K. Scanlan, Stein, et al., 1989). T. K. Scanlan and colleagues found four sources associated with the act of skating: (a) movement sensations including exhilaration and feelings of freedom; (b) self-expression; (c) athleticism related to the physically strenuous nature of the sport; and (d) flow or peak experiences described as effortless performance "producing an intense, memorable, and seemingly sensory experience" (T. K. Scanlan, Stein, et al., 1989, p. 79). Simply the opportunity to be highly active also has been cited as a reason for enjoying sport (Harris, 1984, Wankel & Sefton, 1989).

Coping and Emotional Release.   Finally, athletes find enjoyment in using their sport to escape or cope with difficult non-sport issues such as a troubled home life (T. K. Scanlan, Stein, et al., 1989). Moreover, they enjoy the emotional release resulting from physical activity (Csikszentmihalyi, 1975).

Situational Sources of Enjoyment

Situational factors pertain to sources of enjoyment inherent in the competitive sport context. Competitive outcomes, the achievement processes related to those outcomes, recognition, and opportunities associated with competitive sport have emerged as sources of enjoyment.

Competitive Outcomes and Processes.   Regardless of gender or sport type, favorable competitive outcomes lead to both postgame and general sport enjoyment. In some of the earliest work on the impact of competitive sport on children, Passer and T. K. Scanlan (1980) found that young athletes experienced more enjoyment when they won a game than when they lost. Subsequent research found that the amount of fun experienced by children during a game or a match was inversely related to their postcompetition stress, regardless of winning or losing (T. K. Scanlan & Lewthwaite, 1984; T. K. Scanlan & Passer, 1978, 1979). In youth sport research that focused on general sport enjoyment rather than game-specific emotions, male team sport participants ranked winning as a predictor of enjoyment, but lower in importance than intrinsic or social factors (Wankel & Kreisel, 1985a). In a follow-up study conducted with male and female youth sport participants examining sources of overall enjoyment in sport, findings again revealed that youth who had a winning season reported more fun than their peers who had a losing record (Wankel & Sefton, 1989). Elite skaters also identified winning or placing to be enjoyable (T. K. Scanlan, Stein, et al., 1989).

Sources of enjoyment for youth and elite sport athletes also are linked to the process of competition in sport. Engaging in competition and having the opportunity to compare one's skills against others were enjoyment predictors for young males involved in team sports (Csikszentmihalyi, 1975; Wankel & Kreisel, 1985a). Similarly, interviews conducted with elite athletes found that performing better than other skaters in practice was a source of enjoyment (T. K. Scanlan, Stein, et al., 1989).

Social Recognition and Travel Opportunities. Youth, recreational, and elite athletes experience enjoyment resulting from social recognition of competitive success, such as receiving ribbons and trophies (Csikszentmihalyi, 1975; Wankel & Kreisel, 1985a). In addition to these tangible rewards, elite skaters talked about how performance recognition received from an audience, in the form of a standing ovation for example, and achievement recognition, such as fame, prestige, glamour, and media coverage, were very enjoyable (T. K. Scanlan, Stein, et al., 1989). Moreover, the opportunity to travel to various sport venues and experience different places and cultures were also sources of enjoyment for these elite athletes.

Significant Other Sources of Enjoyment

In the review of stress, we saw that significant others can cause stress when their interactions and feedback are perceived to be negative. With enjoyment, we find the opposite situation; enjoyment results from the positive perceptions of interactions and feedback with coaches, parents, and peers.

Positive Perceptions of Adult Influence. The literature shows that youth sport and elite level athletes identify perceived positive parental and coach interactions and reactions as sources of enjoyment. Compared to their less fortunate cohorts, wrestlers experienced greater seasonal enjoyment when they perceived (a) lower parental pressure to participate in wrestling, (b) greater parent and coach satisfaction with their wrestling performance, (c) fewer negative performance reactions from their mothers, and (d) higher levels of parent and coach involvement and support (T. K. Scanlan & Lewthwaite, 1986). Similarly, perceived parental pressure, negative performance reactions, and high performance expectations have been associated with lower enjoyment in several recent studies with youth participants (Averill & Power, 1995; Babkes & Weiss, 1999; Brustad, 1988; Leff & Hoyle, 1995). At the elite level, we see similar significant other enjoyment themes emerge. Skaters found enjoyment in bringing pleasure or pride to their families and coaches through their personal skating talent (T. K. Scanlan, Stein, et al., 1989).

T. K. Scanlan and colleagues (T. K. Scanlan, Carpenter, Lobel, et al., 1993) found both consistent and conflicting results with the other literature when studying a diverse sample of inner-city youth athletes. Consistent with other research, positive perceptions of coach support and performance appraisals were significant sources of enjoyment. The interesting contrast requiring further research attention was that no parental influence factors were found to predict enjoyment for these youth.

Positive Social Interactions With Teammates and Peers.   At all competitive levels, affiliation aspects of sport participation are pervasive sources of enjoyment for athletes. Positive interactions related to being on a team, interacting with teammates, building friendships, and social support are consistently identified as very enjoyable aspects of athletic involvement (Csikszentmihalyi 1975; T. K. Scanlan, Carpenter, Lobel, et al., 1993; Wankel & Kreisel, 1985a, 1985b). The companionship and pleasant play associations identified as key aspects of sport friendships also have been found to be salient sources of enjoyment for young athletes (Weiss, Smith, & Theeboom, 1996).

Consolidating the Participation Motivation and Sport Enjoyment Literatures

Although participation motivation has been treated as a separate literature, significant commonalities exist between it and sport enjoyment, suggesting that a partial consolidation of the two would be beneficial. Participation motivation research provides important descriptive data into the reasons athletes participate in sport; however, it gives little insight as to why these reasons or "participation motives" create motivation. Typically, athletes are asked to rank, in order of importance, their major reasons for participating. Reasons given include enjoyment or fun, affiliation, challenge of competition, excitement of competition, fitness, and mastery related motives such as learning skills and improving skills (Gill et al., 1985; Gould, Feltz, & Weiss, 1985; Longhurst & Spink, 1987; Petlichkoff, 1996; Sapp & Haubenstricker, 1978; Weiss & Petlichkoff, 1989).

A remarkable similarity exists between the participation motivation and sport enjoyment literatures. In addition to the characteristic identification of enjoyment or fun as one of the most important motives for participation, many of the other participation motives have been shown to be factors that make sport enjoyable (see Table 13.4). By reframing these enjoyment-related participation motives, we can provide theoretical coherence to the knowledge base and gain better insight into the underlying mechanisms that create the motivational consequences. Specifically, these sources result in enjoyment and it is this positive affective response that creates the desire to participate (Fig. 13.2). This approach has an advantage when structuring after-school programs because it tells us what makes the experience fun, which directly addresses the issue of how to facilitate participation. Many, but not all, participation motives have an enjoyment parallel and can benefit from this approach. The others should remain as independent motives.

Conclusions on Sources of Enjoyment

As with stress, the intrapersonal, situational, and significant other sources of enjoyment remain common across many different groups of athletes. The consistency across groups for both the stress and enjoyment literatures demonstrates a significant understanding of the underlying constructs and provides a strong foundation for the extension of emotional response research to the study of developmental components and progression.

STRATEGIES FOR EXAMINING EMOTIONAL RESPONSES DEVELOPMENTALLY

We now consider strategies to examine stress and enjoyment as individuals change within the social, cognitive, motor, and physical components of development using the research model described at the beginning of the chapter and depicted in Fig. 13.1. We have chosen three strategies that we believe provide the breadth of data necessary, combined with efficient data collection. They are: (a) integrate existing developmental research with the sources of emotional responses reviewed in this chapter, (b) use a longitudinal approach to examine stress and enjoyment among the four developmental components, and (c) study stress and enjoyment responses between groups with similar profiles determined by examining developmental progression metrics for each of the four developmental components.

The first strategy does not examine all of the combinations of developmental components and developmental progression suggested by our research model. Rather, it takes advantage of existing research on specific developmental components to efficiently incorporate emotional responses and their sources. The second and third strategies consider all of the conditions included in our research model and offer alternative approaches to systematically obtaining the data.

Regardless of the specific research strategy selected, the stress and enjoyment findings make it abundantly clear that a combination of quantitative and qualitative methods must be employed to fully appreciate the concepts underlying emotional responses. These mixed-method approaches may be accomplished together in a single study (T. K. Scanlan, Russell, Wilson, & L. A. Scanlan, 2003) or as shown in this chapter, separately, as part of a line of research. The power of quantitative measures combined with the depth of interpretation available from qualitative interviews and related methods will enable the developmental extension of emotional responses.

Integrate Research Domains

The first study direction integrates established developmental lines of research with the sources of stress and enjoyment reviewed in this chapter to build on the broad base of existing knowledge. Two particularly attractive candidates for concurrent investigation are: (a) changes in an individual's ability to make distinctions between ability and effort (Fry & Duda, 1997; Nicholls, 1978); and (b) age-related differences in sources of competence information (Horn, Glenn, & Wentzell, 1993; Horn & Hasbrook, 1986, 1987; Horn & Weiss, 1991).

Integrating the findings on children's development of the concept of *ability* with our understanding of the sources of stress and enjoyment can provide early insight into emotional responses in the cognitive component. Research has shown that as children develop cognitively, they begin to make clearer distinctions between effort and ability. Young children equate outcome with effort leading to high-perceived competence and, as we have seen in the review of the enjoyment literature, experience high enjoyment. However, at older ages, ability and effort can be differentiated, requiring that one play well in addition to playing hard, to maintain perceptions of high competence and a continuing experience of enjoyment. Failing to play well could result in stress from feelings of failure. By combining these two areas, we can begin to understand how the development of children's conceptions of ability and effort impact their enjoyment and stress in athletic participation.

The second combination integrates research on developmental changes in sources of competence information with our sources of stress and enjoyment. The literature on the saliency of significant others as sources of competence information suggests a shift from adult-centered to peer-centered social evaluation as children develop into adolescence (Horn & Hasbrook, 1986, 1987; Horn et al., 1993; Horn & Weiss, 1991). Our reviews of stress and enjoyment demonstrated that coaches, parents, and peers all contribute significantly to athletes' emotional responses. Although the overall emotional responses may remain the same, the social evaluation literature suggests that the relative importance of coaches, parents, and peers as specific sources may change as the child matures. Combining the two areas allows an important first step to understanding how emotional responses vary with developmental progression in the social component.

Longitudinal

An obvious developmental approach would be to use a traditional longitudinal study of stress and enjoyment, and their sources, assessed for each developmental component to provide the desired breadth of data, including interactions among the variables. Clearly, this approach requires significant data collection over an extended period of time and most likely would require a collaborative effort among several researchers. One would start with a diverse and relatively large sample of young athletes and would measure them at various points in time as they develop throughout the life span. At each measurement point, studies similar to those reviewed previously would examine stress and enjoyment and their sources. In parallel, measures of progression on each of the four developmental components would be obtained so that all of the cells shown in Fig. 13.1 would eventually be included. The established quantitative measures currently used for each developmental component would be augmented with qualitative measures and combined with mixed-method measures of emotional responses and their sources. This approach provides the necessary data to fully understand how development impacts emotional responses and their sources. As a simple example, taking periodical physical measures of developmental indicators such as height, weight, and emergence of secondary sex characteristics, along with emotional response assessments, would facilitate examinations of the relationship between changes in physical development and sport-related affect.

Developmental Profiles

Our third approach identifies groups with similar developmental profiles to provide the breadth of data desired. As with the longitudinal approach, mixed-method measures of emotional responses and their sources combined with measures of progression in each of the four developmental components would be gathered. However, rather than collecting data on the same sample over time, measures would be taken for a particular population and cluster analytic techniques would then be used to identify groups of individuals with similar levels of developmental progression for each of the four components of our research model (S. P. Reise, personal communication, March 2001). For example, data collected from a large group of 12-year-old male and female competitive swimmers might yield two profiles. One profile might describe athletes very far along in motor and physical progression, but with limited progress in the social and cognitive components. The second profile group might include individuals with high progression levels in the cognitive, motor, and social components but lagging in physical development. Analysis of the emotional responses and their sources for these two example groups, combined with data from other identified profiles, allows the breadth of data necessary to understand emotional responses developmentally. Similar to the longitudinal, this approach allows assessment of potential interactions among the four developmental components and identifies only naturally occurring profiles.

CONCLUSION

Stress and enjoyment, the predominate emotional responses in sport, have well developed and integrated literatures that reflect the solid understanding we can use as a foundation for future examinations of developmental influences. Competitive sport offers a rich developmental context that encompasses social, cognitive, motor, and physical components and provides an ideal venue for the study of emotional responses. Furthermore, because of the motivational consequences of stress and enjoyment, understanding the relationships between the sources of these emotional responses and developmental progression has important practical implications. When we know the relevant sources as a function of developmental progression, we will have the knowledge to structure sport programs in ways to optimize the experience for participants throughout their lives.

Although we do not yet have an understanding of the developmental progression of emotional responses, we can suggest ways to structure after-school sport activities to encourage continued participation based on our current knowledge. The literature clearly shows the positive motivational consequences of enjoyment and the negative consequences of stress. A program structure that provides the largest number of enjoyment sources while minimizing the sources of stress can be expected to attract youth and keep them positively involved.

The many and highly diverse sources of enjoyment makes it particularly easy to tap a number of them to captivate participants and motivate them over the long haul. Because of their diversity, sources may be achievement or nonachievement orientated and can be either intrinsic or extrinsic (T. K. Scanlan & Lewthwaite, 1986). Incorporating numerous sources contributes to both the immediate and the long-term attractiveness of an activity by allowing the relative importance of specific sources to go up or down without significantly changing the overall perception of the activity as enjoyable. In some cases, normal day-to-day variability accounts for the changes while in others, the changes may be more permanent and result from developmental progression. In the absence of specific data on these effects, structuring an activity to include the largest number of sources increases the likelihood of continued participation.

The specifics of the particular after-school activity will influence which of the intrapersonal, situational, and significant other sources of enjoyment may most easily be emphasized. Table 13.4 provides a summary of the enjoyment sources available in sport and many can and should be applicable to other after-school activities. The text summarizes the effect of each source and Table 13.3 conveniently cross-references enjoyment sources and the original research citations to aid access to the source data. Similarly, Table 13.2 lists the sources of stress to be avoided to the greatest extent possible.

An interesting parallel exists between the enjoyment sources discussed here and some of the positive developmental features of after school programs discussed by Eccles and Gootman (2002). In chapter 4, they draw on the existing developmental literature to identify eight characteristics or features of after-school programs that can be expected to lead to positive youth development. Of the eight features discussed, one half have characteristics similar to the sources of enjoyment listed in Table 13.4. For example, the feature, "Support for Efficacy and Mattering," characterized as "... Practice that includes enabling, responsibility granting, and meaningful challenge ..." (p. 90) has a direct parallel in the mastery subcategory of intrapersonal sources of enjoyment. Similarly, the program feature, "Supportive Relationships," described as "... closeness; connectedness; caring; support; guidance ..." (p. 90) has characteristics very similar to the significant other source of enjoyment. The remaining two, "Opportunities to Belong," and "Opportunities for Skill Building," have similar counterparts among the sources of sport enjoyment. These parallels reinforce the importance of structuring programs to include as many sources of enjoyment as possible.

Now let us revisit Jeniqua to see what effects 3 years has had on her development and her emotional responses:

> Jeniqua is now 16 years old. She started menstruating, grew 6 inches, and gained 20 pounds in the last year. Although Jeniqua has begun to adjust to her growth spurt, her ability to learn new gymnastics skills seems to have reached a plateau for several months. She is still excelling in her schoolwork and has a date to the junior prom. Her peers have become increasingly more important to her decision making and she has started to base her self-perceptions more on previous experiences than on the input of her coach or parents.

Although Jeniqua used to experience low stress and high enjoyment associated with her gymnastics, changes in her social, cognitive, motor, and physical development have impacted her emotional responses to participation. Three years after we first met her, Jeniqua's cognitive ability remains high but she has experienced significant changes in her physical and social development while her motor development has progressed less dramatically. In fact, her motor development has reached a plateau. Because of these changes, she is no longer experiencing as much success in competition and reports higher levels of stress due to worries about failure. However, Jeniqua still finds gymnastics enjoyable enough to compensate for her increased stress. As she continues to progress in each of the developmental compo-nents, her emotional responses will continue to fluctuate. What impact will further changes in her social, cognitive, motor, or physical development have on the stress and enjoyment she experiences in athletics? What effect will these changes have on her motivation to continue in gymnastics? Only future study will tell.

ACKNOWLEDGMENTS

This chapter has been funded, in part, from the following sources: UCLA Blyth Hedge Trust, Various Donors Fund, and Parker Elderly Housing Corporation.

REFERENCES

Averill, P. M., & Power, T. G. (1995). Parental attitudes and children's experiences in soccer: Correlates of effort and enjoyment. *International Journal of Behavioral Development, 18*, 263–276.

Babkes, M. L., & Weiss, M. R. (1999). Parental influence on children's cognitive and af-fective responses to competitive soccer participation. *Pediatric Exercise Science, 11*, 44–62.

Bray, S. R., Martin, K. A., & Widemeyer, W. N. (2000). The relationship between evaluative concerns and sport competition state anxiety among youth skiers. *Journal of Sport Sciences, 18*, 353–361.

Brustad, R. J. (1988). Affective responses in competitive youth sport: The influence of intrapersonal and socialization factors. *Journal of Sport and Exercise Psychology, 10*, 307–321.

Brustad, R. J., Babkes, M. L., & Smith, A. L. (2001). Youth in sport: Psychological con-siderations. In R. N. Singer, H. A. Hausenblas, & C. M. Janelle (Eds.), *Handbook of sport psychology* (2nd ed., pp. 604–635). New York: Wiley.

Carpenter, P. J., & Scanlan, T. K. (1998). Changes over time in the determinance of sport commitment. *Pediatric Exercise Science , 10*, 356–365.

Carpenter, P. J., Scanlan, T. K., Simons, J. P., & Lobel, M. (1993). A test of the Sport Commitment Model using structural equation modeling. *Journal of Sport and Exercise Psychology, 15*, 119–133.

Chalip, L., Csikszentmihalyi, M., Kleiber, D., & Larson, R. (1984). Variations of experi-ence in formal and informal sport. *Research Quarterly for Exercise and Sport, 55*, 109–116.

Cohn, P. J. (1990). An exploratory study on sources of stress and athlete burnout in youth golf. *The Sport Psychologist, 4*, 95–106.

Coopersmith, S. (1967). *The antecedents of self-esteem.* San Francisco: Freeman.

Csikszentmihalyi, M. (1975). *Beyond boredom and anxiety.* San Francisco: Jossey-Bass.

Deci, E. L., & Ryan, R. M. (1985). *Intrinsic motivation and self-determination in human be-havior.* New York: Plenum.

Eccles, J., Adler, T. F., Futterman, R., Goff, S. B., Kaczala, C. M, Meece, J. L., & Midgley, C. (1983). In J. Spence & R. Helmreich (Eds.), *Achievement and achievement motives: Psychological and sociological approaches* (pp. 75–146). San Francisco: Freeman.

Eccles, J., & Gootman, J. A. (Eds.). (2002). *Community programs to promote youth development*. Washington, DC: National Academy Press.

Feltz, D. L., Lirgg, C. D., & Albrecht, R. R. (1992). Psychological implications of competitive running in elite young middle distance runners: A longitudinal analysis. *The Sport Psychologist, 6*, 128–138.

Fox, K. M., Goudas, M., Biddle, S., Duda, J., & Armstrong, N. (1994). Children's task and ego profiles in sport. *British Journal of Educational Psychology, 64*, 253–261.

Fry, M. D., & Duda, J. L. (1997). A developmental examination of children's understanding of effort and ability in the physical and academic domains. *Research Quarterly for Exercise and Sport, 68*, 331–344.

Gill, D. L., Gross, J. B., & Huddleston, S. (1985). Participation motivation in youth sports. *International Journal of Sports Psychology, 14*, 1–14.

Gould, D., & Dieffenbach, K. (1999). Psychological issues in youth sports: Competitive anxiety, overtraining, and burnout. In R. M. Malina (Ed.), *Organized sport in the lives of children and adolescents*. Michigan Youth Sport Institute Conference Proceedings, May 23–26.

Gould, D., Eklund, R. C., & Jackson, S. A. (1991). 1988 U. S. Olympic wrestling excellence: I. Mental preparation, precompetitive cognition and affect. *The Sport Psychologist, 6*, 358–362.

Gould, D., Eklund, R. C., & Jackson, S. A. (1993). Coping strategies used by U. S. Olympic wrestlers. *Research Quarterly for Exercise and Sport, 64*, 83–93.

Gould, D., Feltz, D., & Weiss, M. R. (1985). Motives for participating in competitive youth swimming. *International Journal of Sport Psychology, 16*, 126–140.

Gould, D., Finch, L. M., & Jackson, S. A. (1993). Coping strategies used by national champion figure skaters. *Research Quarterly for Exercise and Sport, 64*, 453–468.

Gould, D., Greenleaf, C., & Krane, V. (2002). Arousal-anxiety and sport behavior. In T. Horn (Ed.), *Advances in sport psychology* (pp. 207–241). Champaign, IL: Human Kinetics.

Gould, D., Horn, T., & Spreemann, J. (1983). Sources of stress in junior elite wrestlers. *Journal of Sport Psychology, 5*, 159–171.

Gould, D., Jackson, S. A., & Finch, L. M. (1993). Sources of stress in national champion figure skaters. *Journal of Sport and Exercise Psychology, 15*, 134–159.

Gould, D., & Weinberg, R. (1985). Sources of worry in successful and less successful intercollegiate wrestlers. *Journal of Sport Behavior, 8*, 115–127.

Griffin, M. R. (1972). An analysis of state and trait anxiety experienced in sports competition at different age levels. *Foil (Spring)*, 58–64.

Harris, J. C. (1984). Interpreting youth baseball: Players' understandings of fun and excitement, danger and boredom. *Research Quarterly for Exercise and Sport, 55*, 379–382.

Harter, S. (1978). Effectance motivation reconsidered. *Human Development, 21*, 34–64.

Harter, S. (1981). A model of intrinsic mastery motivation in children: Individual differences and developmental change. In W. A. Collins (Ed.), *Minnesota symposium on child psychology* (Vol. 14, pp. 215–255). Hillsdale, NJ: Lawrence Erlbaum Associates.

Horn, T. S., Glenn, S. D., & Wentzell, A. B. (1993). Sources of underlying personal ability judgments in high school athletes. *Pediatric Exercise Science, 5*, 263–274.

Horn, T. S., & Hasbrook, C. A. (1986). Informational components influencing children's perceptions of their physical competence. In M. R. Weiss & D. Gould (Eds.), *Sport for children and youths* (pp. 81–88). Champaign, IL: Human Kinetics.

Horn, T. S., & Hasbrook, C. A. (1987). Psychological characteristics and the criteria children use for self-evaluation. *Journal of Sport and Exercise Psychology, 9*, 208–221.

Horn, T. S., & Weiss, M. R. (1991). A developmental analysis of children's self-ability judgments in the physical domain. *Pediatric Exercise Science, 3,* 310–326.

Johnson, W. R. (1949). A study of emotion revealed in two types of athletic contests. *Research Quarterly, 20,* 72–79.

Kendzierski, D., & DeCarlo, K. J. (1991). Physical activity enjoyment scale–2 validation studies. *Journal of Sport and Exercise Psychology, 13,* 50–64.

Kroll, W. (1979). The stress of high performance athletics. In P. Klavora & J. V. Daniel (Eds.), *Coach, athlete and sport psychologists* (pp. 211–219). Champaign, IL: Human Kinetics.

Lazarus, R. S. (1966). *Psychological stress and the coping process.* New York: McGraw-Hill.

Leff, S. S., & Hoyle, R. H. (1995). Young athletes' perceptions of parental support and pressure. *Journal of Youth and Adolescence, 24,* 187–203.

Longhurst, K., & Spink, K. S. (1987). Participation motivation of Australian children involved in organized sport. *Canadian Journal of Sport Sciences, 12,* 24–30.

Martens, R. (1977). *Sport Competition Anxiety Test.* Champaign, IL: Human Kinetics.

Martens, R., Burton, D., Rivkin, F., & Simon, J. (1980). Reliability and validity of the Competitive State Anxiety Inventory (CSAI). In C. H. Nadeau, W. R. Halliwell, K. M. Newell, & G. C. Roberts (Eds.), *Psychology of motor behavior and sport–1979* (pp. 91–99). Champaign, IL: Human Kinetics.

Martens, R., Burton, D., Vealey, R. S., Bump, L. A., & Smith, D. E. (1990). Development and validation of the Competitive State Anxiety Inventory-2. In R. Martens, R. S. Vealey, & D. Burton (Eds.), *Competitive anxiety in sport* (pp. 117–190). Champaign, IL: Human Kinetics.

Martens, R., & Gill, D. (1976). State anxiety among successful and unsuccessful competitors who differ in competitive trait anxiety. *Research Quarterly, 47,* 698–708.

Nicholls, J. G. (1978). The development of the concepts of effort and ability, perception of academic attainment, and the understanding that difficult tasks require more ability. *Child Development, 49,* 800–814.

Nicholls, J. G. (1989). *The competitive ethos and democratic education.* Cambridge: Harvard University Press.

Nixon, H. (1984). *Sport and the American dream.* New York: Leisure Press.

Passer, M. W., & Scanlan, T. K. (1980). The impact of game outcome on the postcompetition affect and performance evaluations of young athletes. In C. H. Nadeau, W. R. Halliwell, K. M. Newell, & G. C. Roberts (Eds.), *Psychology of motor behavior and sport–1979* (pp. 100–111). Champaign, IL: Human Kinetics.

Pensgaard, A. M, & Roberts, G. C. (2000). The relationship between motivational climate, perceived ability and sources of distress among elite athletes. *Journal of Sport Sciences, 18,* 191–200.

Petlichkoff, L. M. (1996). The dropout dilemma in sport. In O. Bar-Or (Ed.), *Encyclopaedia of sports medicine: The child and adolescent athlete* (Vol. 6, pp. 418–430). Oxford, England: Blackwell Scientific.

Pierce, W. J., & Stratton, R. K. (1981). Perceived sources of stress in youth sport participants. In G. C. Roberts & D. M. Landers (Eds.), *Psychology of motor behavior and sport–1980* (pp. 116–134). Champaign, IL: Human Kinetics.

Sapp, M., & Haubenstricker, J. (1978, April). *Motivation for joining and reasons for not continuing in youth sports programs in Michigan.* Paper presented at AAHPERD Conference, Kansas City.

Scanlan, T. K. (1975). *The effects of competition trait anxiety and success-failure on the perception of threat in a competitive situation.* Unpublished doctoral dissertation, University of Illinois, Urbana-Champaign.

Scanlan, T. K. (1977). The effects of success–failure on the perception of threat in a competitive situation. *Research Quarterly, 48*, 144–153.

Scanlan, T. K. (1978). Perceptions and responses of high- and low- competitive trait anxious males to competition. *Research Quarterly, 49*, 520–527.

Scanlan, T. K. (1984). Competitive stress and the child athlete. In J. M. Silva III & R. S. Weinberg (Eds.), *Psychological foundations of sport* (pp. 118–129). Champaign, IL: Human Kinetics.

Scanlan, T. K. (2000, April). *Presenting a new interview methodology designed to test, modify, and expand theory using the Sport Commitment Model as an exemplar.* Paper presented at the symposium on Achievement Motivation and Engagement in Different Domains at the British Psychological Society, Winchester, England.

Scanlan, T. K. (2002). Social evaluation and the competition process: A developmental perspective. In F. L. Smoll & R. E. Smith (Eds.), *Children and youth in sport: A biopsychosocial perspective* (2nd ed., pp. 393–407). Dubuque, IA: Kendall/Hunt.

Scanlan, T. K., Carpenter, P. J., Lobel, M., & Simons, J. P. (1993). Sources of sport enjoyment for youth sport athletes. *Pediatric Exercise Science, 5*, 275–285.

Scanlan, T. K., Carpenter, P. J., Schmidt, G. W., Simons, J. P., & Keeler, B. (1993). An introduction to the Sport Commitment Model. *Journal of Sport and Exercise Psychology, 15*, 1–15.

Scanlan, T. K., & Lewthwaite, R. (1984). Social psychological aspects of competition for male youth sport participants: I. Predictors of competitive stress. *Journal of Sport Psychology, 6*, 208–226.

Scanlan, T. K., & Lewthwaite, R. (1986). Social psychological aspects of the competitive sport experience for male youth sport participants: IV. Predictors of enjoyment. *Journal of Sport Psychology, 8*, 25–35.

Scanlan, T. K., & Passer, M. W. (1978). Factors related to competitive stress among male youth sport participants. *Medicine and Science in Sports, 10*, 103–108.

Scanlan, T. K., & Passer, M. W. (1979). Sources of competitive stress in young female athletes. *Journal of Sport Psychology, 1*, 151–159.

Scanlan, T. K., Ravizza, K., & Stein, G. L. (1989). An in-depth study of former elite figure skaters: I. Introduction to the project. *Journal of Sport and Exercise Psychology, 11*, 54–64.

Scanlan, T. K., Russell, D. G., Beals, K. P., & Scanlan, L. A. (2003). Project on Elite Athlete Commitment (PEAK): II. A direct test and expansion of the Sport Commitment Model with elite amateur sportsmen. *Journal of Sport and Exercise Psychology, 25*, 377–401.

Scanlan, T. K., Russell, D. G., Wilson, N. C., & Scanlan, L. A. (2003). Project on Elite Athlete Commitment (PEAK): I. Introduction and methodology. *Journal of Sport and Exercise Psychology, 25*, 360–376.

Scanlan, T. K., & Simons, J. P. (1992). The construct of sport enjoyment. In G. C. Roberts (Ed.), *Motivation in sport and exercise* (pp. 199–215). Champaign, IL: Human Kinetics.

Scanlan, T. K., Simons, J. P., Carpenter, P. J., Schmidt, G. W., & Keeler, B. (1993). The Sport Commitment Model: Measurement development for the youth sport domain. *Journal of Sport and Exercise Psychology, 15*, 16–38.

Scanlan, T. K., Stein, G. L., & Ravizza, K. (1989). An in-depth study of former elite figure skaters: II: Sources of enjoyment. *Journal of Sport and Exercise Psychology, 11*, 65–83.

Scanlan, T. K., Stein, G. L., & Ravizza, K. (1991). An in-depth study of former elite figure skaters: III. Sources of stress. *Journal of Sport and Exercise Psychology, 13*, 103–108.

Simon, J. A., & Martens, R. (1979). Children's anxiety in sport and nonsport evaluative activities. *Journal of Sport Psychology, 1*, 160–169.

Smith, R. E. (1986). Toward a cognitive-affective model of burnout. *Journal of Sport Psychology, 8*, 36–50.

Spielberger, C. D. (1966). *Anxiety and behavior.* New York: Academic Press.

Spielberger, C.D. (1973). *Preliminary test manual for the State-Trait Anxiety Inventory for Children ("How I feel questionnaire").* Palo Alto, CA: Consulting Psychologists Press.

Stephens, D. E. (1998). The relationship of goal orientation and perceived ability to enjoyment and value in youth sport. *Pediatric Exercise Science, 10*, 236–247.

Wankel, L. M., & Kreisel, P. S. J. (1985a). Factors underlying enjoyment of youth sports: Sport and age group comparisons. *Journal of Sport Psychology, 7*, 51–64.

Wankel, L. M., & Kreisel, P. S. J. (1985b). Methodological considerations in youth sport motivation research: A comparison of open-ended and paired comparison approaches. *Journal of Sport Psychology, 7*, 65–74.

Wankel, L. M., & Sefton, J. M. (1989). A season-long investigation of fun in youth sports. *Journal of Sport and Exercise Psychology, 11*, 355–366.

Weiss, M. R., & Ferrer-Caja, E. (2002). Motivational orientations and sport behavior. In T. S. Horn (Ed.), *Advances in sport psychology* (2nd ed., pp. 101–183). Champaign, IL: Human Kinetics.

Weiss, M. R., & Petlichkoff, L. M. (1989). Children's motivation for participation in and withdrawal from sport: Identifying the missing links. *Pediatric Exercise Science, 1*, 195–211.

Weiss, M. R., Smith, A. L., & Theeboom, M. (1996). "That's what friends are for": Children's and teenagers' perceptions of peer relationship in the sport domain. *Journal of Sport and Exercise Psychology, 18*, 347–379.

14

After-School Sport for Children: Implications of a Task-Involving Motivational Climate

Joan L. Duda
Nikos Ntoumanis
The University of Birmingham, UK

It could be argued that youth sport is one of the most pervasive and popular activities engaging girls and boys in their free time in contemporary American society. *Youth sports* are those involving young people between the ages of 6 to 18 years that are adult organized and/or supervised. After-school youth sports encompass extracurricular (interscholastic) athletic activities, agency-sponsored community sports (e.g., Little League), club sports, and recreational sport programs organized by recreation departments.

Less than 20 years ago, it was estimated that 25 million out of approximately 47 million youngsters participated in some type of organized/supervised youth sport in the United States. Today, participation estimates suggest that 47 million boys and girls (from what census data indicate to be a population of close to 52 million) have joined, at one point or another, an after-school sport program (Ewing & Seefeldt, 2002). Although more boys still engage in after-school sport than girls, the greater involvement of females in sport over the past 20 years has certainly contributed to the observed increase in overall participation percentages. With respect to other issues of diversity, the world of after-school sport is multiracial and multiethnic, with young people from various cultural backgrounds represented among participants. Females of color, however, have been found to be particularly underrepresented in both interscholastic and agency-sponsored youth sport programs (Ewing & Seefeldt, 2002).

311

Only about 14% of all children and adolescents who participate in sport in the United States are members of interscholastic athletic teams (which take place before or after classes but within the school setting). The largest number of youth participants are engaged in an agency-sponsored sport program. Indicating a potential growing significance of after-school sport in young people's lives, this increase in engagement in organized, community sport programs in recent years is coupled with a decreased involvement in spontaneous, unsupervised, free-play types of activities (Ewing & Seefeldt, 2002). One cannot help but wonder about the possible implications of such differential trends for how youngsters are now being socialized via their experiences in the physical domain. Moreover, as those who are more physically able are more likely to feel at home in organized sport programs (perhaps due to their more competitive features; Roberts, 1984), the ramifications of the enhanced attractiveness of after-school sport activities (in contrast to the seemingly diminished appeal of informal physical activities and games) for the development and long-term involvement of *all* children has yet to be determined.

IMPORTANCE OF AFTER-SCHOOL SPORT IN AMERICAN CULTURE

There is no question that sport is considered to be a valued achievement domain among U.S. youth and in society at large. Further, to be known within one's peer networks as a good athlete is a central contributor to social status, especially in the case of boys. It is believed that involvement in organized sport activities allows young people to learn (in a presumed "safe" environment) many of life's lessons and develop desired attributes within the mainstream society (Smoll & Smith, 2002). Engagement in after-school sport programs is supposed to promote boys' and girls' moral functioning, self-discipline, ability to work with others, and capacity to compete and effectively cope with success as well as failure.

There are those who argue for reducing the opportunity for physical activity within a youngster's day (particularly during her or his school day) because they assume that the academic progress of girls and boys is reduced when children or adolescents spend more time in physical education or after-school sport. However, although the positive associations that have emerged to date are weak and there are uncertainties regarding cause–effect, evidence does suggest that sport participation (or quality physical education curricular offerings) does not necessarily diminish academic performance and is sometimes associated with greater classroom achievement (Lindner, 1999; Shephard, 1997). It has been suggested that any positive interdependencies between sport/physical activity engagement and academic accomplishment is probably a result of indirect effects of participation on young people's self esteem and physical health (Barnett, Smoll, & Smith, 1992; Tremblay, Inman, & Willms, 2000; Whitehead & Corbin, 1997).

One purported aim of after-school sport involvement is the promotion of children's and adolescents' fitness and health and their adoption of an active lifestyle (Smoll & Smith, 2002). Active youth are less likely to smoke than their inactive peers and more likely to have a lower body-mass index (Tremblay et al., 2000). In contrast, sedentary behavior during childhood and adolescence has been linked to a number of risk factors for cardiovascular disease and the etiology of Type II diabetes (e.g., obesity, hypertension, elevated blood lipids; Gutin et al., 1994; Raitakari et al., 1994). Although there is a dearth of longitudinal, methodologically sound studies on this issue, it is assumed that active boys and girls will be more likely to grow into active men and women—especially if their engagement in sport and physical activity is enjoyable and competence-enhancing (Trudeau, Laurencelle, Tremblay, Rajic, & Shephard, 1998).

AFTER-SCHOOL SPORT:
WONDROUS POSSIBILITIES OR LOST PROMISE?

A perusal of the extensive literature on the psychological and physical implications of youth sport participation, however, quickly calls any uncritical and unwavering advocating of such involvement into question (Gould & Weiss, 1987; Smoll & Smith, 2002). As Martens (1978) pointed out a number of years ago, there can be joy but also sadness in young people's sport pursuits. For example, at times, engagement in after-school sport appears to contribute to character building whereas, in other instances, youth sport seems to be developing "characters" with heightened aggressive tendencies and lower sportspersonship (Shields & Bredemeier, 1995). For many youngsters, the sport experience brings considerable enjoyment (Scanlan & Simons, 1992) whereas for others, involvement in after-school sport activities is plagued by debilitating anxiety (Scanlan, 1984).

THEORETICAL FRAMEWORK:
THE IMPLICATIONS OF ACHIEVEMENT GOALS

In essence, the existent literature centered on the psychological implications of after-school sport involvement for young people suggests that arguing that youth sport is good *or* bad is very simplistic. The answer to such debates, it seems, is "It depends!" That is, the potential consequences of involvement in after-school sport seem to be a function of how the psychological environment in that context is structured and the manner in which young athletes process that environment.

One theoretical framework that can foster understanding of differential interpretations of and responses to after-school sport among young people is achievement goal theory (AGT; Ames, 1992; Dweck, 1999; Nicholls, 1989). Over the past 10 years, AGT has become a predominant conceptualization employed by motivation psychologists to investigate the meaning and ramifications of youth sport activities (Duda, 2001; Roberts, 2001; Treasure, 2001). In short, this theory focuses on the antecedents and motivational consequences of task and ego goals.

Concepts of Task and Ego Involvement

It is generally held that the achievement goal framework is applicable to settings in which perceptions of competence are relevant to achievement striving (Nicholls, 1989). A plethora of studies, stemming from a variety of models of motivation, have indicated that one's level of perceived ability is salient in athletic settings, including the particular context of youth sport (Roberts, 1984, 2001). AGT assumes that, besides perceptions of ability, it is critical to consider how individuals judge their level of competence (Nicholls, 1984, 1989). Nicholls (1984), in particular, proposed that there are two major ways of judging ability, which, in turn, underpin task versus ego achievement goals. When in a state of task involvement (i.e., when focused on a task goal), young athletes process their ability in a self-referenced manner: They feel competent and, therefore, successful with respect to goal accomplishment when realizing learning, personal improvement, task mastery, and/or doing one's best. When ego-involved, a young sport participant would feel a sense of (high) competence and subsequent subjective success when she or he exhibited superior ability compared to others by either outperforming others or performing equivalently but with less effort. Central to the predictions emanating from AGT is the premise that these states of task and ego involvement entail qualitatively different ways of experiencing achievement endeavors such as after-school sport (Duda & Hall, 2001). This is because the concerns of a task- versus ego-involved young athlete are dissimilar (i.e., developing and improving one's competence versus displaying or proving one's ability).

AGT (Ames, 1992; Dweck, 1999; Nicholls, 1989) also assumes that a focus on task-involved goals will correspond to adaptive achievement patterns (e.g., exerting effort in training and competitions, maintaining one's involvement in sport, performing optimally given one's level of sport ability), regardless of whether youngsters are confident of their athletic abilities or question their competence. At least with respect to short-term, achievement-related indices (see Duda, 2001, for further discussion of this issue), an emphasis on ego-involved goals is expected to link to positive cognitions, emotions, and behaviors. When an ego-goal focus is coupled with perceptions of low ability, however, maladaptive achievement patterns in after-school programs are hypothesized (e.g., not giving one's best effort, performance impairment, dropping out of a sport). Overall, these predictions emanating from AGT have been supported in research conducted in youth sport settings (see Duda, 1996, 2001; Roberts, 2001, for reviews of this literature).

Individual Differences

One factor that is presumed to impact whether it is more or less likely that someone engaging in sport is more or less task- and/or ego-involved is their dispositional goal orientation (Nicholls, 1989). Sport participants are assumed to vary with respect to their degree of task and ego orientation. Instruments, such as the Task and Ego Orientation in Sport Questionnaire (TEOSQ; Duda, 1989; Duda & Nicholls, 1992) and the Perceptions of Success Questionnaire (POSQ; Roberts, Treasure, & Balague, 1998), have been developed to tap individual differences in the criteria underlying subjective success in the sport domain. In general, in any typical after-school sport program, we would find youngsters who are high in both orientations, high in one orientation and low in the other, or low in both orientations (Duda, 2001; Duda & Whitehead, 1998). Being low task- and low ego-oriented implies that an individual is *not* particularly interested in demonstrating competence in sport—whether that competence is self- or other-referenced (Duda, 2001). Thus, we would not expect to find many low task and low ego orientation children and adolescents participating in organized, competitive sport programs. If such young people are currently engaged in after-school sport, we would predict that their participation will not be long-standing.

THE MOTIVATIONAL CLIMATE

Children's and adolescents' dispositional goal orientations do not develop in a vacuum. Achievement goal theorists (e.g., Ames, 1992; Nicholls, 1989) assume that the social psychological environments that surround young people "give out messages" that make them more or less concerned about improving and/or developing (as reflected in an emphasis on task goals) or proving/protecting (as reflected in an emphasis on ego goals) their level of competence. Ames (1992), in particular, spearheaded the conceptualization and our appreciation of the consequences of situationally emphasized goals or what Ames referred to as the *motivational climate*. In Ames's view, these climates created by significant others (such as teachers, coaches) can be more or less task- and/or ego-involving (which Ames refers to as a *mastery* or *performance* climate, respectively). Perceived motivational climates, or prevailing psychological atmospheres, are held to be multifaceted and encompass such situational structures as (a) the standards of and criteria underlying evaluation and the manner in which that evaluation is carried out, (b) the bases of recognition and the way in which individuals are recognized, (c) the source(s) of decision making and authority, (d) the presentation and structuring of tasks, and (e) the manner in which individuals are grouped and the type of individual-to-individual and individual-to-group interactions that are reinforced.

Research on achievement goals in sport has examined the motivational climate created by mainly two influential social agents, coaches and parents. With regard to the perceived climate created by coaches, Newton, Duda, and Yin (2000) proposed a hierarchical multidimensional model and instrument (Perceived Motivational Climate in Sport Questionnaire-2; PMCSQ–2) to assess perceptions of task- and ego-involving climates. At the apex of this model are two higher order factors measuring task- and ego-involving climates, each of these underpinned by three lower order factors. The lower order factors of the task-involving climate are cooperative learning, coaches' emphasis on athletes' effort and/or improvement, and athletes' feeling that everybody has an important role on the team. With respect to the ego-involving climate, the underlying facets of the psychological environment are intrateam member rivalry, unequal recognition by the coach, and athletes' punishment for mistakes. Considering evidence exists regarding the validity and reliability of the PMCSQ–2 but it is important to examine its psychometric validity with children and adolescents only.

Parents also play an important influential role in youth sport by fostering and encouraging task- or ego-involving criteria for success. Duda and Hom (1993) showed that children's goal orientations were significantly related to those of their parents. Furthermore, White (1996) reported that the task orientation of junior female volleyball players was significantly predicted by a perceived task-involving parental climate, whereas a perceived parental ego-involving climate predicted players' ego orientation. However, one should bear in mind that such correlational findings cannot establish causal links nor can they rule out the possibility that parental climate and athletes' goal orientations correlate because they are caused by common extraneous variables (e.g., media influence).

Coaches and parents are not the only contributors to the motivational climate manifested in after-school youth sport. Peers, sport heroes (Carr, Weigand, & Jones, 2000), and the media also transmit task- and ego-involving criteria for success. Therefore, it is important to broaden the scope of research on the psychological environment surrounding young athletes and examine the impact of other significant social agents, as well as their comparative influence, across different age and gender groups.

IMPLICATIONS OF GOAL ORIENTATIONS IN YOUTH SPORT

Studies of children and adolescent sport participants have provided strong support for Nicholls' (1989) theorizing regarding the cognitive, affective, and behavioral concomitants of task- and ego-goal orientations in achievement contexts. We now summarize research examining the interplay between dispositional goals and young people's: (a) beliefs about the determinants of success, (b) views about the nature of ability, (c) perceptions of the purposes of sport involvement, (d) positive and negative affective responses, (e) achievement strategies, (f) extent of physical activity engagement and physical and/or sport skill development, and (g) moral functioning and aggressive tendencies.

Beliefs About the Causes of Success

Task orientation in sport predicts more adaptive beliefs about success than ego orientation: *Task orientation* is associated with the belief that success requires high effort and collaboration with peers. In contrast, *ego orientation* is often unrelated to effort beliefs and positively related to the belief that success is the outcome of high normative ability, deception, and impressing the coach and significant others. This pattern of associations between sport-related goals and beliefs has been observed in children (e.g., Duda, Fox, Biddle, & Armstrong, 1992), adolescents (e.g., Hom, Duda, & Miller, 1993; Lochbaum & Roberts, 1993; Treasure & Roberts, 1994) and young people from non-Western cultures (e.g., Biddle, Akande, Vlachopoulos, & Fox, 1996).

The motivational implications of manifesting different belief systems are important. A belief that effort is a precursor of success can help children with both high- and low-perceived competence to realize their full athletic potential. In contrast, the belief that normative ability is a determinant of success would not be conducive to long-term motivation because children have little or no control over their athletic ability (Roberts, 2001). Ability beliefs may lead children who are not physically talented to conclude that it is not worth trying hard to learn and improve sport skills as they are not "naturally gifted." Some children questioning their competence but still wanting to achieve normatively based success (e.g., being the winner) may engage in deceptive strategies and the moral overtones of this option are obvious. However, even the youngsters who try to cheat and impress their way through sport will probably end up dropping out because at the early stages of sport participation, hard work and persistence are important prerequisites for building solid sport skill foundations necessary to a successful future career.

Normative ability beliefs can prove maladaptive even for highly competent children (Roberts, 2001) who may feel complacent and not try hard to maximize their athletic potential. Furthermore, an emphasis on ability beliefs could be particularly detrimental to those who experience early biological maturation. These athletes are in an advantageous position (e.g., taller, stronger) over other children and may experience success early that will make them feel satisfied and confident. However, early maturers who hold normative ability beliefs maybe more prone to experiencing disappointment and lack of confidence in subsequent years when late maturers "catch-up."

Beliefs About the Nature of Sport Ability

Task and ego achievement goals also relate to children's theories about the nature of their physical ability. For example, Sarrazin et al. (1996) adapted Dweck's (1999) work on theories of intelligence to sport. Sarrazin et al. postulated that some children may view physical ability as a fixed entity that cannot be changed through effort, whereas other children may view their physical ability as a dynamic and malleable quality. Using a sample of 11- to 12-year-old British children, Sarrazin et al. found that theories of sport ability were related as predicted to achievement goals: More than one half of the children with an incremental belief of physical ability chose a task-involving goal over an easy ego-involving goal or a difficult ego-involving goal. In contrast, more than one half of the children with a fixed view of physical ability chose one of the two ego-involving goals over the task-involving goal. In a sample of French adolescents, Sarrazin et al. found that task orientation correlated with beliefs that sport ability is incremental, unstable, and the product of learning. In contrast, ego orientation correlated with the belief that sport ability is a gift as well as with the belief that sport ability generalizes across different sports.

Clearly, divergent personal theories regarding the nature of physical ability can have different implications for children's motivation. A belief that physical ability is a natural "gift" that is not changeable through effort may undermine the value of hard training for both high- and low-perceived competent children. In contrast, a belief that physical ability is changeable through effort and learning may help low-perceived competent children to achieve some level of success, and high competent children to advance to higher competitive levels. Unfortunately, there is no empirical evidence in sport to substantiate these arguments despite their importance for program design.

Beliefs About the Purposes of Sport Participation

A last set of beliefs investigated by achievement goal research refers to what children perceive should be the main purposes of sport participation. Consonant with research in academic settings (e.g., Nicholls, Patashnick, & Nolen, 1985), sport researchers have shown that task orientation is related to the belief that sports participation should foster cooperation, the value of striving for mastery, skill development, and lifetime health. In contrast, ego orientation is positively related to beliefs that sport should enhance social status, self-importance and career mobility, and is negatively related to the view that sport should foster good citizenship (e.g., see Duda, 1989; Treasure & Roberts, 1994). Thus, task-oriented people appear to focus more on the intrinsic and prosocial aspects of sport involvement whereas ego-oriented people have a "what is in it for me" extrinsic approach to sport participation (Duda, 1996).

In conclusion, a convincing amount of evidence shows that achievement goals in youth sport are related, as predicted by Nicholls (1989), to beliefs about sport success, the nature of sport ability and the purposes of sport participation. Studies are needed that: (a) examine the role of parents, coaches, peers and the media in socializing these beliefs, and determine whether these socializing influences vary depending on the age, gender, and other important personal characteristics of young people; and (b) how strongly these beliefs predict young athletes' achievement strategies and affective responses. Although no direct evidence exists to answer this question, there is abundant indirect correlational evidence linking achievement goals with different behavioral and affective indicators of sport participation. This evidence is reviewed next.

Positive and Negative Affect

Researchers interested in emotion and sport participation have focused mainly on enjoyment, satisfaction, anxiety, tension, and boredom. In Nicholls's (1989) view, task orientation is more conducive to the experience of positive emotions in achievement contexts than ego orientation. This is because individuals high in task orientation strive for such achievable goals as personal improvement rather than the less controllable goals of outperforming others. Individuals with high ego orientation should experience positive affect only when they do better than others. Thus, ego-oriented young athletes may become bored or disinterested in situations where they are not given the opportunity to demonstrate their superiority. Similarly, high ego-oriented individuals who question the adequacy of their ability and are fearful of social evaluation are likely to experience tension and anxiety because their self-worth is under threat (Duda & Hall, 2000).

Mostly, research findings in youth sport support these predictions, although the moderating role of perceived competence has not been tested. For example, Duda and Nicholls (1992) reported that task orientation was positively correlated with high school students' satisfaction and negatively with their boredom in sport. Ego orientation was unrelated to these two types of affect. Similarly, in Fox, Goudas, Biddle, Duda, and Armstrong (1994), children with high task orientation experienced higher levels of enjoyment than children with low task orientation. Finally, in a recent meta-analysis of research on achievement goals and affect in sport, Ntoumanis and Biddle (1999a) clearly showed that task orientation is much more strongly related to enjoyable and satisfying experiences in sport than ego orientation. Perhaps the low relation between ego orientation and satisfaction can be attributed to the fact that research has not differentiated between different *types* of satisfaction. Because task and ego orientation relate to different criteria for success, individuals with high ego orientation should feel satisfied when they do better than others. Indeed, in a study of 11-, 13-, and 15-year-olds, Treasure and Roberts (1994) showed that satisfaction for high ego-oriented athletes was derived from winning and the social approval resulting from outperforming others. For high task-oriented athletes, satisfaction was derived from mastery experiences (e.g., learning new skills) and the social approval resulting from high effort and mastery.

Anxiety has been the focal point of research examining the negative affective concomitants of goal orientations in sport. Most findings in this area are based on studies with adults, but a study of junior fencers by Hall and Kerr (1997) showed that for low perceived ability fencers, ego orientation is positively related to cognitive anxiety 2 days, 1 day, and 30 minutes before a fencing tournament. In the same sample, task orientation was negatively related to cognitive anxiety 1 day and 1 hour before the tournament. Some evidence exists in adult sport (e.g., Ntoumanis, Biddle, & Haddock, 1999) to show that certain coping strategies may explain the relation between goal orientations and affect. It would be interesting to determine whether this is the case in youth sport in view of the fact that coping strategies are still developing (Compas, Malcarne, & Banez, 1992). Intervention studies could be designed to teach children how to cope in ego-involving sport situations (e.g., use of rationalization instead of venting of emotions when their ability is challenged) and to reduce negative affect.

Achievement Strategies, Extent of Physical Activity Involvement, and Skill Development

Individuals with high task orientation should feel competent when they try hard and learn new skills. In contrast, those with high ego orientation should feel competent only when they demonstrate high normative ability (Nicholls, 1989). Therefore, one would expect that young athletes with high task orientation should be more committed to practice and learning, and in general should employ more adaptive achievement strategies than those with high ego orientation. Empirical findings in youth sport settings support these hypotheses. For example, Lochbaum and Roberts (1993), using a sample of high-school athletes, showed that high task orientation was positively related to self-reported use of skill development strategies (e.g., extra practice) and high effort in competition, and was negatively related to practice avoidance. In contrast, ego orientation was positively related to practice avoidance and demonstration of normative competence. Other studies have shown that persistence in youth sport is positively related to task orientation and negatively related to ego orientation (e.g., Andree & Whitehead, 1996; Duda, 1989). Furthermore, research has shown that task orientation relates more strongly to moderate-to-vigorous physical activity than ego orientation (e.g., Dempsey, Kimiecik, & Horn, 1993; Kimiecik, Horn, & Shurin, 1996; Tzetzis, Goudas, Kourtessis, & Zisi, 2002; Wang, Chatzisarantis, Spray, & Biddle, 2002). In sum, the predicted relations between young peoples' achievement goals and their strategies in practice and competition, as well as the extent of their involvement in physical activity emerge regularly in cross-sectional and nonexperimental studies.

More recent experimental evidence by Cury and colleagues corroborates the association of task orientation with adaptive learning strategies and skill development in physical education courses. In two experiments with adolescent French students engaged in a basketball dribbling task, Cury, Biddle, Sarrazin, and Famose (1997) showed that under conditions of free-choice behavior, as well as following failure, students characterized by high ego orientation, low task orientation, and low perceived competence spent the least amount of time practicing the dribbling task than students with high levels of task orientation and/or perceived competence. Cury and Sarrazin (1998) also examined the learning strategies adopted by French adolescent boys under three experimental conditions involving climbing tasks and basketball skills. Again, results showed that the high ego/low task/low perceived competence group did not display adaptive learning strategies because they selected very easy or very difficult tasks, spent less time practicing during a free-choice period, and did not choose information that would facilitate skill development. Similar findings were also reported by Cury, Famose, and Sarrazin (1997). In this study, French boys with a high ego orientation, low task orientation, and high perceived competence sought normative feedback to compare their performance to that of others, but were not interested in informational feedback that would facilitate their learning of basketball dribbling. More strikingly, high ego/low task-oriented boys with low perceived competence rejected any kind of feedback. In total, the results of the experimental studies by Cury and associates indicate that variations in achievement goals (and indirectly beliefs about success) can predict differences in learning strategies and type of feedback sought. Such work underlines the importance of identifying children with low perceptions of normative competence and intervening to alter their achievement strategies.

Moral Functioning and Aggressive Tendencies

Nicholls (1989) argued that there is an association between achievement goals and the perceived legitimacy of certain behaviors leading to goal accomplishment. A preoccupation with outplaying others and demonstrating superiority (i.e., epitomizing someone with high ego orientation) is likely to lead to a lack of concern about fairness and the welfare of the opponent, and to the belief that cheating and aggression are justifiable means to achieve success in competitive settings. In contrast, by emphasizing learning, cooperation, and personal improvement, task orientation should relate to prosocial attitudes and sportspersonship behavior. Research in youth sport supports these predictions. For example, Duda, Olson, and Templin (1991) found that high-school basketball players with high task orientation were less likely to perceive cheating as legitimate and were more likely to endorse sportspersonship behavior than those high in ego orientation. The latter reported that they were more inclined to engage in intentionally aggressive acts to win a game. J. G. H. Dunn and J. C. Dunn (1999), in a study of elite Canadian male youth hockey players, found that high ego orientation was positively related to approval of aggressive behaviors, whereas high task orientation was positively associated with respect for social conventions, respect of personal commitment to participation, and respect for rules and officials. In their goal profile analysis (i.e., comparing groups with high–high, low–low, high–low and low–high levels of task and ego orientations), J. G. H. Dunn and J. C. Dunn (1999) also showed that athletes with the low task orientation and/or high ego orientation profile reported the lowest levels of sportspersonship and the highest levels of aggression. In contrast, the athletes with the high task/low ego orientation profile reported the highest levels of sportspersonship.

Lee, Whitehead, Ntoumanis, and Hatzigeorgiadis (2001) investigated the links between achievement goals and morality from the perspective of values. According to this approach, the underlying motivation to behave in a prosocial or antisocial manner essentially reflects the value system of an individual. Lee et al. (2001) proposed that values guide attitudes and behaviors in achievement situations and that the influence of values on attitudes may be mediated through goal orientations. In a sample of 549 young British sport participants, valuing competence predicted respect for commitment to sport participation and respect for social conventions. This path was mediated largely by task orientation. In contrast, valuing status predicted cheating and gamesmanship (a British term for unacceptable but legitimate behavior such as unsettling the opposition) and this path was partly mediated by ego orientation. Lastly, sociomoral values (e.g., trying to be fair) had a direct positive influence on prosocial attitudes (commitment to participation and respect for rules and conventions) and a direct negative effect on antisocial attitudes (cheating and gamesmanship).

In sum, research in sport settings disputes a commonly held assumption by many educationalists and sport lovers that sport builds character and facilitates prosocial and moral behavior. In fact, what young athletes aim to achieve from their game determines how they play it (Nicholls, 1989). Moral functioning in sport is promoted when athletes are less preoccupied with winning and demonstrating superiority and are more concerned with learning, cooperation, and personal progress. Given the high levels of cheating and aggression in youth sport reported in the academic and popular press, it is surprising that there are no published intervention studies designed to promote morality by emphasizing task-oriented criteria for success.

IMPLICATIONS OF MOTIVATIONAL CLIMATE IN YOUTH SPORT

AGT research has shown that perceptions of the motivational climate created by significant others has important influences on young people's motivated behavior and the quality of their achievement experiences (Ntoumanis & Biddle, 1999b). In this section, we discuss the relation of the major dimensions of the motivational climate in youth sport with various cognitive, behavioral, and affective variables.

Cognitive, Behavioral, and Affective Concomitants of Motivational Climate

Treasure and Roberts (1998) examined how motivational climate and goal orientations relate to beliefs about success and sources of satisfaction in a sample of female basketball summer campers. A perceived task-involving climate was associated with the belief that success results from high effort, whereas a perceived ego-involving climate was related to the belief that success stems from normative ability and deception. Similar findings were reported by Seifriz, Duda, and Chi (1992) with high school male basketball players. In terms of sources of satisfaction, Treasure and Roberts (1998) found that those in a perceived task-involving climate reported that they derived satisfaction from mastery experiences and social approval, whereas those in a perceived ego-involving climate gained satisfaction from winning. Goudas (1998) also reported positive correlations between a task-involving climate and ratings of enjoyment and self-reported effort in a sample of 100 Greek adolescent male basketball players. Ego-involving climate was unrelated to these ratings. Variations in perceptions of motivational climate also have implications for aggressive behavior in sport. Stephens and Bredemeier (1996) showed that girls who reported that they were likely to aggress against an opponent were also likely to perceive their coach as placing greater importance on ego-oriented goals. This work and related studies (Guivernau & Duda, 2002) underline the need for intervening and promoting a task-involving climate and diminishing ego-involving environments in youth sport.

One of the most vivid accounts of the nature and consequences of an ego-involving climate in youth sport was depicted in a case study of a former elite female gymnast (Krane, Greenleaf, & Snow, 1997). Often at an elite level, coaches, sport administrators, and parents place young children under extreme pressures to win, disregarding the long-term impact such demands might have. The motivational climate described by the gymnast in the Krane et al. (1997) study was one which placed constant emphasis on social comparison, external feedback and rewards, and the need for superiority and perfection. The gymnast refused to listen to medical advice in order to prepare for competitions, practiced and competed while seriously injured, employed unhealthy eating practices, and overtrained. Eventually, her frustration from being unable to realize her ego-involving goals led her to drop out of gymnastics.

INTERACTIVE EFFECTS OF GOAL ORIENTATIONS AND MOTIVATIONAL CLIMATE

A fundamental precept of achievement goal theory is that dispositional goal orientations and perceptions of motivational climate interact to predict behavior, cognition, and affect in achievement situations (Nicholls, 1989). Recently this hypothesis is beginning to be tested. For example, in a sample of junior female volleyball players, Newton and Duda (1999), found that task orientation and perceptions of a task-involving climate interacted to predict effort beliefs. In essence, they found that a high task-involving climate buffered the detrimental effect on effort beliefs resulting from a low task orientation. This buffering did not occur under a low task-involving climate. In contrast, when task orientation was high, variations in the task-involving climate did not result in noteworthy differences in effort beliefs between high and low levels of task orientation. A very similar interaction between task orientation and task-involving climate in predicting mastery experiences in sport (e.g., learning, challenge) was reported by Treasure and Roberts (1998). These authors also found a significant interplay between ego orientation and perceptions of an ego-involving climate in predicting ability beliefs. Specifically, when ego orientation was low, there were no differences in ability beliefs under a perceived high and a low ego-involving climate. In contrast, when ego orientation was high, a high perceived ego-involving climate predicted stronger ability beliefs compared to a low perceived ego-involving climate.

MODIFYING THE MOTIVATIONAL CLIMATE

Previous work in sport psychology on the implications and modification of coaching behaviors in youth sport settings has shown that the degree of reinforcements, instruction, and punishments provided by the coach impacts young athletes' attitudes toward the sport, their coach, and teammates, persistence in the activity, and self-esteem (see Smoll & Smith, 2002). This line of work, which led to the development and testing of Smith and Smoll's Mediational Model of Leadership, has demonstrated that it is the young athletes' perceptions of what their coach does more than the coaches' actual behaviors that best predict the athletes' responses and self perceptions. Coaches who are seen as providing a bountiful amount of instruction and encouragement and exhibiting limited punitive behaviors have athletes who are more pleased with their sport experience and themselves. When such research has provided the foundation for coach education programs (Smoll & Smith, 2002), experimental examinations of such efforts in youth sport have indicated that it is possible "to teach old dogs new tricks!": The behaviors of the coach can and do change with training.

To date, limited work has pulled from the achievement goal framework in designing intervention programs and testing ensuing modifications of the motivational climate in after-school settings. In attempting to manipulate the psychological environment, these investigations have borrowed from Epstein's (1989) TARGET principles as a guideline. With respect to family interactions, Epstein identified six environmental structures that have implications for variations in motivational processes among students; that is, the design of the Task, the source of Authority, the nature of the Recognition provided, aspects of Grouping, how students are Evaluated, and the pace or Timing of instruction. The research that has been done (Theeboom, DeKnop, & Weiss, 1995; Treasure, 1993) has provided evidence for the efficacy of reengineering the coach-created youth sport environment so that it is more task-involving. Moreover, the results of such manipulation efforts, in terms of the affective, cognitive, and behavioral responses of youngsters, are consistent with the tenets of AGT (Ames, 1992; Dweck, 1999; Nicholls, 1989). More of such intervention studies in real-world, after-school sport programs are needed, especially applied investigations that specifically test the environment—cognitive and affective mechanisms—behavior links embedded in the achievement goal framework. As the research conducted so far has entailed short-term manipulations of the climate (e.g., across 10 sessions in the Treasure, 1993, study and 3 weeks in the Theeboom et al., 1995, investigation), more long-term, longitudinal work is also warranted.

CONCLUSION

Contemporary participation data make it clear that involvement in after-school sport among children and adolescents provides a major leisure outlet for young people in the United States. Many youngsters are engaged and many hours are spent running, jumping, kicking, batting, swimming in gyms and pools, on fields and courts. The potential ramifications of such participation for girls' and boys' physical, cognitive, emotional, and social development are impressive. The central premise of this chapter is that the implications of youth sport engagement can be "good," "bad," and, most disturbingly, even "ugly," depending on the ways in which children and adolescents interpret and find meaning in such activities. The literature also suggests that variability in such interpretations and meanings is a function of the achievement goals being emphasized by the youngsters themselves and the achievement goals encouraged in the social environments in which they interact. All in all, sport investigations over the past 10 years point to the wisdom of strengthening the task orientation of girls and boys and doing all that is possible to make after-school youth sport programs task-involving.

REFERENCES

Ames, C. (1992). Classrooms, goal structures, and student motivation. *Journal of Educational Psychology, 84*, 261–274.

Andree, K. V., & Whitehead, J. (1995). The interactive effect of perceived ability and dispositional or situational achievement goals on intrinsic motivation in young athletes. *Journal of Sport and Exercise Psychology, 17* (Suppl.), S7.

Barnett, N., Smoll, F. L., & Smith, R. E. (1992). Effects of enhancing coach–athlete relationships on youth sport attrition. *The Sport Psychologist, 6*, 111–128.

Biddle, S. J. H., Akande, A., Vlachopoulos, S., & Fox, K. (1996). Towards an understanding of children's motivation for physical activity: Achievement goal orientations, beliefs about sport success, and sport emotion in Zimbabwean children. *Psychology and Health, 12*, 49–55.

Carr, S., Weigand, D. A, & Jones, J. (2000). The relative influence of parents, peers, and sport heroes on the goal orientations of children and adolescents in sport. *Journal of Sport Pedagogy, 6*, 34–56.

Compas, B. E., Malcarne, V. L., & Banez, G. A. (1992). Coping with psychosocial stress: A developmental perspective. In B. N. Carpenter (Ed.), *Personal coping: Theory, research, and application* (pp. 47–63). Westport, CT: Praeger.

Cury, F., Biddle, S. J. H., Sarrazin, P., & Famose, J.P. (1997). Achievement goals and perceived ability predict investment in learning a sport task. *British Journal of Educational Psychology, 67*, 293–309.

Cury, F., Famose, J. P., & Sarrazin, P. (1997). Achievement goal theory and active search for information in a sport task. In R. Lidor & M. Bar-Eli (Eds.), *Innovations in sport psychology: Linking theory and practice. Proceedings of the IX World Congress in Sport Psy-*

chology: Part I (pp. 218–220). Netanya, Israel: Ministry of Education, Culture and Sport.

Cury, F., & Sarrazin, P. (1998). Achievement motivation and learning behaviours in sport tasks. *Journal of Sport and Exercise Psychology, 20* (Suppl.), S11.

Dempsey, J. M., Kimiecik, J. C., & Horn, T. S. (1993). Parental influence on children's moderate to vigorous physical activity participation: An expectancy-value approach. *Pediatric Exercise Science, 5,* 151–167.

Duda, J. L. (1989). Relationship between task and ego orientation and the perceived purpose of sport among high-school athletes. *Journal of Sport and Exercise Psychology, 11,* 318–335.

Duda, J. L. (1996). Maximizing motivation in sport and physical education among children and adolescents: The case for greater task involvement. *Quest, 48,* 290–302.

Duda, J. L. (2001). Achievement goal research in sport: Pushing the boundaries and clarifying some misunderstandings. In G. C. Roberts (Ed.), *Advances in motivation in sport and exercise* (pp. 129–182). Champaign, IL: Human Kinetics.

Duda, J. L., Fox, K., Biddle, S. J. H., & Armstrong, N. (1992). Children's achievement goals and beliefs about success in sport. *British Journal of Educational Psychology, 62,* 313–323.

Duda, J. L., & Hall, H. K. (2001). Achievement goal theory in sport: Recent extensions and future directions. In R.N. Singer, H. Hausenblas, & C. Janelle (Eds.), *Handbook of sport psychology* (2nd ed., pp. 417–443). New York: Wiley.

Duda, J. L., & Hom, H. L. (1993). Interdependencies between the perceived and self-reported goal orientations of young athletes and their parents. *Pediatric Exercise Science, 5,* 234–241.

Duda, J. L., & Nicholls, J. G. (1992). Dimensions of achievement motivation in schoolwork and sport. *Journal of Educational Psychology, 84,* 290–299.

Duda, J. L., Olson, L. K., & Templin, T. J. (1991). The relationship of task and ego orientation to sportsmanship attitudes and the perceived legitimacy of injurious acts. *Research Quarterly for Exercise and Sport, 62,* 79–87.

Duda, J. L., & Whitehead, J. (1998). Measurement of goal perspectives in the physical domain. In J. L. Duda (Ed.), *Advances in sport and exercise psychology measurement* (pp. 21–48). Morgantown, WV: Fitness Information Technology.

Dunn, J. G. H., & Dunn, J. C. (1999). Goal orientations, perceptions of aggression, and sportspersonship in elite youth male ice hockey players. *The Sport Psychologist, 13,* 183–200.

Dweck, C. S. (1999). *Self-theories: Their role in motivation, personality, and development.* Philadelphia: Psychology Press.

Epstein, J. (1989). Family structures and student motivation: A developmental perspective. In C. Ames & R. Ames (Eds.), *Research on motivation in education* (Vol. 3, pp. 259–295). New York: Academic Press.

Ewing, M. E., & Seefeldt, V. (2002). Patterns of participation in American agency-sponsored youth sports. In F. L. Smoll & R. E. Smith (Eds.), *Children and youth in sport: A biopsychological perspective* (2nd ed., pp. 39–60). Dubuque, IA: Kendall/Hunt.

Fox, K., Goudas, M., Biddle, S., Duda, J., & Armstrong, N. (1994). Children's task and ego goal profiles in sport. *British Journal of Educational Psychology, 64,* 253–261.

Goudas, M. (1998). Motivational climate and intrinsic motivation of young basketball players. *Perceptual and Motor Skills, 86,* 323–327.

Gould, D., & Weiss, M. (Eds.). (1987). *Advances in pediatric sport sciences (Vol. 2).* Champaign, IL: Human Kinetics.

Guivernau, M., & Duda, J. L. (2002). The relationship of the moral atmosphere to aggressive tendencies in young soccer players. *Journal of Moral Education, 31*(1), 45–62.

Gutin, B., Islam, S., Manos, T., Cucuzzo, N., Smith, C., & Stachura, M.E. (1994). Relation of percentage of body fat and maximal aerobic capacity to risk factors for atherosclerosis and diabetes in Black and White seven- to eleven-year-old-children. *Journal of Pediatrics, 125*, 847–852.

Hall, H. K., & Kerr, A. W. (1997). Motivational antecedents of precompetitive anxiety in youth sport. *The Sport Psychologist, 11*, 24–42.

Hom, H. L., Duda, J. L., & Miller, A. (1993). Correlates of goal orientations among young athletes. *Pediatric Exercise Science, 5*, 168–176.

Kimiecik, J. C., Horn, T. S., & Shurrin, C. S. (1996). Relationships among children's beliefs, perceptions of their parents' beliefs and their moderate-to-vigorous physical activity. *Research Quarterly for Exercise and Sport, 67*, 324–336.

Krane, V., Greenleaf, C. A., & Snow, J. (1997). Reaching for gold and the price of glory: A motivational case study of an elite gymnast. *The Sport Psychologist, 11*, 53–71.

Lee, M., Whitehead, J., Ntoumanis, N., & Hatzigeorgiadis, A. (2001). Goal orientations as mediators of the influence of values on sporting attitudes in young athletes. In A. Papaioannou, M. Goudas, & Y. Theodorakis (Eds.), *In the dawn of the new millennium: Programme and proceedings on the 10 World Congress of Sport Psychology* (Vol. 2, pp. 193–194). Thessaloniki, Greece: Christodoulidi Publications.

Lindner, K. J. (1999). Sport participation and perceived academic performance of school children and youth. *Pediatric Exercise Sciences, 11*, 129–143.

Lochbaum, M. R., & Roberts, G. C. (1993). Goal orientations and perceptions of the sport experience. *Journal of Sport and Exercise Psychology, 15*, 160–171.

Martens, R. (1978). *Joy and sadness in children's sports.* Champaign, IL: Human Kinetics.

Newton, M., & Duda, J. L. (1999). The interaction of motivational climate, dispositional goal orientations, and perceived ability in predicting indices of motivation. *International Journal of Sport Psychology, 30*, 63–82.

Newton, M. L., Duda, J. L., & Yin, Z. (2000). Examination of the psychometric properties of the Perceived Motivational Climate in Sport Questionnaire-2 in a sample of female athletes. *Journal of Sports Sciences, 18*, 275–290.

Nicholls, J. G. (1984). Achievement motivation: Conceptions of ability, subjective experience task choice, and performance. *Psychological Review, 91*, 328–346.

Nicholls, J. G. (1989). *The competitive ethos and democratic education.* Cambridge, MA: Harvard University Press.

Nicholls, J. G., Patashnick, M., & Nolen, S. B. (1985). Adolescents' theories of education. *Journal of Educational Psychology, 77*, 683–692.

Ntoumanis, N., & Biddle, S. J. H. (1999a). Affect and achievement goals in physical activity: A meta-analysis. *Scandinavian Journal of Medicine and Science in Sport (Special Issue: European perspectives in sport motivation research), 9*, 315–332.

Ntoumanis, N., & Biddle, S. J. H. (1999b). A review of motivational climate in physical activity. *Journal of Sport Sciences, 17*, 643–665.

Ntoumanis, N., &. Biddle, S. J. H., & Haddock, G. (1999). The mediating role of coping strategies on the relationship between achievement motivation and affect in sport. *Anxiety, Stress, and Coping: An International Journal, 12*, 299–327.

Raitakar, O. T., Porkka, K. V., Taimela, S., Telema, R., Rasanen, L., & Viikari, S. A. (1994). Effects of persistent physical inactivity on coronary risk factors in children and young and adults. *American Journal of Epidemiology, 140*, 195–205.

Roberts, G. C. (1984). Toward a new theory of motivation in sport: The role of perceived ability. In J. Silva & R. Weinberg (Eds.), *Psychological foundations of sport* (pp. 214–228). Champaign, IL: Human Kinetics.

Roberts, G. C. (2001). Understanding the dynamics of motivation in physical activity: The influence of achievement goals on motivational processes. In G. C. Roberts (Ed.), *Advances in motivation in sport and exercise* (pp. 1–50). Champaign, IL: Human Kinetics.

Roberts, G. C., Treasure, D. C., & Balague, G. (1998). Achievement goals in sport: The development and validation of the Perception of Success Questionnaire. *Journal of Sports Sciences, 16,* 337–347.

Sarrazin, P., Biddle, S., Famose, J. P., Cury, F., Fox, K., & Durand, M. (1996). Goal orientations and conceptions of the nature of sport ability in children: A social cognitive perspective. *British Journal of Social Psychology, 35,* 399–414.

Scanlan, T. K. (1984). Competitive stress and the child athlete. In J. M. Silva & R. S. Weinberg (Eds.), *Psychological foundations of sport* (pp. 118–129). Champaign, IL: Human Kinetics.

Scanlan, T. K., & Simons, J. P. (1992). The construct of sport enjoyment. In G. C. Roberts (Ed.), *Motivation in sport and exercise* (pp. 199–215). Champaign, IL: Human Kinetics.

Seifriz, J. J., Duda, J. L., & Chi, L. (1992). The relationship of perceived motivational climate to intrinsic motivation and beliefs about success in basketball. *Journal of Sport and Exercise Psychology, 14,* 375–391.

Shephard, R. J. (1997). Curricular physical activity and academic performance. *Pediatric Exercise Science, 9,* 113–126.

Shields, D. L. L., & Bredemeier, B. J. L. (1995). *Character development and physical activity.* Champaign, IL: Human Kinetics.

Smoll, F. L., & Smith, R. E. (2002). Coaching behavior research and intervention in youth sports. In F. L. Smoll & R. E. Smith (Eds.), *Children and youth in sport: A biopsychological perspective* (2nd ed., pp. 211–234). Dubuque, IA: Kendall/Hunt.

Stephens, D., & Bredemeier, B. J. (1996). Moral atmosphere and judgments about aggression in girls' soccer: Relationships among moral and motivational variables. *Journal of Sport and Exercise Psychology, 18,* 174–193.

Theeboom, M., DeKnop, P., & Weiss, M. R. (1995). Motivational climate, psychological responses, and motor skill development in children's sport: A field-based intervention study. *Journal of Sport and Exercise Psychology, 17,* 294–311.

Treasure, D. C. (1993). *A social-cognitive approach to understanding children's achievement behavior, cognitions, and affect in competitive sport.* Unpublished doctoral dissertation, University of Illinois.

Treasure, D. C., & Roberts, G. C. (1994). Cognitive and affective concomitants of task and ego goal orientations during the middle school years. *Journal of Sport and Exercise Psychology, 16,* 15–28.

Treasure, D.C., & Roberts, G. C. (1998). Relationships between children's achievement goal orientations, perceptions of the motivational climate, beliefs about success, and sources of satisfaction in basketball. *International Journal of Sport Psychology, 29,* 211–230.

Tremblay, M. S., Inman, J. W., & Willms, J. D. (2000). The relationship between physical activity, self-esteem, and academic achievement in 12-year-old children. *Pediatric Exercise Science, 12,* 312–323.

Trudeau, F., Laurencelle, L., Tremblay, J., Rajic, A. M., & Shephard, R. J. (1998). A long-term follow-up of participants in the Trois-Rivieres semi-longitudinal study of growth and development. *Pediatric Exercise Science, 10,* 366–377.

Tzetzis, G., Goudas, M., Kourtessis, T., & Zisi, V. (2002). The relation of goal orientations to physical activity in physical education. *European Physical Education Review, 8,* 177–188.

Wang, C. K. J., Chatzisarantis, N. L. D., Spray, C. M., & Biddle, S. J. H. (2002). Achievement goal profiles in school physical education: Differences in self-determination, sport ability beliefs and physical activity. *British Journal of Educational Psychology, 72,* 433–445.

White, S. A. (1996). Goal orientation and perceptions of the motivational climate initiated by parents. *Pediatric Exercise Science, 8,* 122–129.

Whitehead, J. R., & Corbin, C. B. (1997). Self-esteem in children and youth: The role of sport and physical education. In K. R. Fox (Ed.), *The physical self: From motivation to well-being* (pp. 175–204). Champaign, IL: Human Kinetics.

15

Community Service
and Identity Formation
in Adolescents

Hugh McIntosh
Edward Metz
James Youniss
The Catholic University of America

The physical and hormonal changes that come with adolescence essentially demand that young people take a long, intense look in the mirror and ask, "Who am I?" In addition to changes in the way they look and feel, teenagers develop increased cognitive abilities that allow them to see and understand the world in new ways, capabilities that may ultimately compel them to ask, "Where do I belong?" Answers to such questions provide the opportunity for young people to develop a new sense of identity that can be quite different from the self they knew in childhood. Although it continually changes over the life span, identity is likely to undergo a particularly rigorous "renovation" during adolescence. Indeed, according to Erikson (1968), developing a clear idea of who one is and how one fits into the culture of a particular time and place is the chief developmental task of adolescence. Without that development, youth may fail to achieve their potential as they move into adulthood. Or if the task is accomplished in socially unacceptable ways, adolescents may develop a negative, rather than a positive, identity. Either outcome represents a loss to the community, as well as to the individual.

Theory and research both suggest that community service can support adolescents' development as they go through this process of identity reformulation. The basic theoretical argument for this idea was articulated by

331

Erikson (1968), who believed that identity is central to all stages and changes throughout the life span but that its most critical period of development occurs during adolescence. The stage for identity formation is set during the earlier school-age years (6 to 12 years of age) when the individual develops the capacity for *industry*, the ability to achieve chosen goals through one's own efforts. During adolescence, the individual looks beyond his or her personal experience to find a worthwhile ideology—an ethnic or religious tradition, a political cause, an economic system—with which to identify that provides "a convincing world image" (p. 31). Such an ideology helps the adolescent simplify and organize the myriad experiences of everyday life, creating the opportunity to use his or her skills (industry) in the collective effort to pursue the goals of the ideology.

Building on these ideas, Youniss and Yates (1997) proposed that Erikson's developmental theory provides a useful way to understand how community service influences the formation of a prosocial identity during adolescence. They suggested that when adolescents take on community service, they usually do so under the auspices of adults or organizations that model or openly espouse the norms and values (ideology) of a particular social cause. Equipped with this ideological rationale and plan for action, the adolescents can use their recently developed capacities to correct social wrongs and experience themselves as taking on responsibility for the well-being of society. By committing to and working for such an ideology, adolescents come to see where and how they can fit into the world in a positive, rewarding way. Through this process, social identity is formed, clarified, and strengthened in ways that last throughout life.

Empirical research offers other evidence of a link between community service and identity formation. Based on their review of 44 studies of community service published from 1952 to 1994, Yates and Youniss (1996) concluded that community service enhances identity formation in three developmental areas: (a) agency (self-directedness, self-competence, self-understanding), (b) social relatedness (family and peer relationships and institutional affiliations), and (c) moral–political awareness (moral feelings and reasoning, and civic activism). The studies reviewed indicated that students who participate in service come to like themselves more and to have feelings of inner-directedness and self-competence, as well as more self-confidence. They tend to feel more competent to help others, have a greater sense of social relatedness, and experience less alienation and more social connection than before. They often develop greater tolerance and openness toward others. Service was associated with increased prosocial behaviors, such as giving blood and helping in the community, as well as decreased antisocial behaviors, such as truancy and school misbehavior (see also Eccles & Barber, 1999). It was also associated with stronger moral attitudes about helping others (see also the review by Andersen, 1998). The reviewers found that service can evoke strong moral feelings or strong feelings of care about the plight of others. A subsequent review by Youniss, McLellan, and Yates (1997) found further studies that link service during youth to increased civic participation even 25 years later in adulthood.

More recent research on community service has concentrated on elaborating the processes through which it might influence identity formation. Yates and Youniss (1998), for instance, looked at how political commitments developed through participation in community service might influence identity formation. Their investigation involved a case study of 160 middle-class students who were participating in a mandatory, year-long, service-learning program during 11th grade at an urban, predominantly (95%) Black Catholic high school. Over the year, all students worked at least four times in a downtown soup kitchen for the homeless and attended a religion course on social justice. Data were collected through questionnaires, student essays, small-group discussions, and observations in the classroom and at the soup kitchen. Engagement in this intense service stimulated students to rethink their notions about others, to reflect on social problems, and to reconsider their own responsibility to society. Many of the students emerged from the program with a stronger sense of social responsibility and personal agency, as well as a commitment to act politically for social change. A survey of 117 alumni who had participated in the program 3, 5, or 10 years previously indicated that 32% were currently doing voluntary community service. Many of these alumni linked their current stances on social issues to their prior participation in the service-learning course.

The general process thought to be at work in community service is that of connecting youth with normative adult society. Coleman (1961) observed that modern industrialized societies have developed separate cultures that belong specifically to youth and exclude adults. Given the influence of youth activities in patterning identities that last well into adulthood (Youniss et al., 1997), the importance of community service in orienting young persons toward the prosocial ideologies of normative society becomes more apparent. In a study of 13,000 youth in a nationally representative survey of high-school seniors, Youniss, McLellan, Su, and Yates (1999) found that participation in community service was associated with young persons' integration into adult normative society. Specifically, the study found that frequency of participation in community service and/or civic affairs was strongly and positively correlated with participation in normative activities (voting, participating in a political campaign, attending religious services, etc.) and negatively related to deviance (smoking marijuana). Participation in community service and/or civic affairs in all instances was a stronger predictor than gender, ethnicity, family structure, socioeconomic status, or any other measure. Perhaps most important, community service and/or civic affairs participation also strongly predicted involvement in unconventional political activities such as boycotting or demonstrating for a cause. Thus, the authors concluded, community service does not merely lead to acquiescence to the norms and values of adult society; rather, it stimulates many youth to challenge the status quo and to try to change society for the better.

In considering the influence of community service on identity formation, potentially confounding factors need to be considered. Metz, McLellan, and Youniss (2003) found in a 9-month study of 428 students in a public high school that doing any type of voluntary community service predicted intentions to perform community service in the future. However, they also found that students who did social-cause types of community service showed significant increases in social concern and intentions to become involved in unconventional civic activities, compared with those involved in standard service. Standard types of service included tutoring other students at school, coaching local Little League teams, doing administrative tasks (data entry, filing), and performing manual labor (raking leaves, shoveling snow). Social-cause service, by contrast, placed volunteers in direct contact with the needy (persons in homeless shelters, the elderly in nursing homes, handicapped children in Special Olympics) or involved volunteers in causes to remedy specific social problems such as hunger, drug abuse, drunk driving, and racial intolerance. It appears, then, that social-cause types of service more closely approximate the community service mediated developmental process outlined by Youniss and Yates (1997).

In addition, youth with certain characteristics tend to get involved with community service more frequently than other youth. The studies reviewed by Andersen (1998) and Yates and Youniss (1996) showed that such youth tend to be active and intense, have a strong sense of competence and control over their lives, and enjoy doing service, as well as helping others. They often have parents who are involved in service (see also Fletcher, Elder, & Mekos, 2000), and they are frequently affiliated with community institutions such as a church, 4-H, or other youth clubs. Using national data on more than 3,000 high-school seniors, Youniss, Yates, and Su (1997) found that females participated in community service more than males and that youth with highly educated parents were more involved in service than other youth. The theoretically more interesting finding, however, was that youth who participated more in adult-endorsed youth activities (school, sports, and creative leisure activities) and in normative adult institutions (religious and political) participated more frequently in community service than did youth more oriented toward fun activities (being with friends, going to bars, parties, or rock concerts) or who were disengaged. However, youth the researchers classified as all-around with high participation in fun activities, as well as adult-endorsed activities, showed the highest rates of participation in community service. Overall, these findings indicated that youth already well integrated into adult society tend more frequently than other youth to volunteer for community service. But the finding that all-around youth had the highest rates of participation in community service indicates that many participants in community service also have strong characteristics of autonomy, as well as social integration.

Some evidence suggests that self-selection into community service and the beneficial effects of service participation may constitute a positive feedback cycle that builds identity. In a 3-year study (Grade 10 through Grade 12) of 294 Catholic high-school students whose schools required them to do 75 hours of community service, Youniss and Reis (2002) found that youth who consistently had a clear sense of identity participated in challenging social-cause types of service in 10th grade more frequently than those who consistently scored low on identity clarity. In turn, youth who participated in challenging service in both 10th and 12th grade increased in identity clarity over the study, while those who did challenging service in 10th grade but switched to relatively less demanding standard service in 12th grade showed no change in identity clarity scores. The investigators interpreted these results to suggest that youth with a relatively clear sense of identity early in adolescence tend to engage in more challenging types of community service and, as a result, develop even clearer identity.

The gist of the research on community service over the past 50 years suggests that during adolescence, participation in community service has a beneficial effect on identity development. But other influences may dampen or enhance those effects. In a follow-up study of their sample, Reis and Youniss (2004) asked whether the quality of relationships with mothers and friends might explain the drop in identity clarity observed in one group of students (20% of total) in their earlier study. Compared with the rest of the students in the study, those who declined in identity clarity showed a lack of improvement in communication with their mothers. They also showed continuing conflicts with their peers over the 3 years of the study; for other youth, the rates of peer conflict decreased. Taken together, the results of these two studies suggest that although community service can have positive effects on identity development, these developmental benefits need to be considered in the context of other factors, such as negative social relationships that may counterbalance those positive effects.

THE CURRENT STUDY

In this chapter, we look more closely at the process of identity clarification as it unfolds during the high-school years. Focusing on Erikson's (1968) ideas that connect industry to identity, we expected that community service activities would play a key role in shaping and clarifying identity because such activities provide concrete ways to assess one's achievement along with an ideology that places achievement within a social and historical context. Such experiences give the identity process grounding on which adolescents can give meaning and direction to their actions and their lives. We therefore look at factors associated with identity clarity and expect that service and other youth activities will increase in importance as the adolescents progress through high school. We hypothesize that over time, adolescent identities will depend more on school- and community-based activities and less on background factors such as personality and parents as the larger reference for identity expands to society and history as Erikson postulated. Thus, although our primary goal is to explore the relation between identity clarification and participation in community service activities, we also look at other possible influences on identity development such as religious orientation, personality characteristics, peer attitudes toward school, parental volunteering, extracurricular activities, and background factors such as gender, ethnicity, and socioeconomic status of the family (Larson, 1994; Yates & Youniss, 1996; Youniss & Smollar, 1985).

We use the findings from a 3-year study of community service at a suburban middle-class public high school near Boston to explore these issues. In 1997, this high school enacted a 40-hour community service requirement for graduation. Participants in our study were from the class of 2001, the first in the school to graduate with the new community service requirement. In October 1998 (Time 1), when they were in the 10th grade, 235 members of the class of 2001 completed the questionnaire. One hundred seventy-three of them (74%) also completed questionnaires each May in 1999 (Time 2), 2000 (Time 4), and 2001 (Time 6). Questions pertained to the quantity, quality, and type of community service they performed. *Community service* was defined as activities students did to fulfill service requirements for graduation or that students did voluntarily not for school credit. The service activities that students reported were similar in type to those found by Metz et al. (2003).

The questionnaires also probed other aspects of the students' lives such as school, peer crowd, family, personality, extracurricular activities, post-high-school plans, deviant behaviors (theft, drinking alcohol, smoking marijuana), social and political concerns, and individual beliefs about morality and religion, as well as their demographic profiles.

In this chapter, our main dependent measure is a set of 11 items designed to measure clarity of identity (see Table 15.1). The participants were asked to indicate the degree to which each statement described how they felt on a 5-point scale ranging from *strongly disagree* to *strongly agree*. Cronbach's alpha in this scale ranged across waves from .83 to .86. Because only statements 1, 2, 4, 5, 10, and 11 were used in the Time 4 survey, this subset of statements was used in some analyses. This smaller scale yielded alphas from .72 to .78.

Students were also asked how frequently they participated in 10 different leisure activities: reading books, magazines, or newspapers; creative

TABLE 15.1
Statements for Assessing Identity Clarity

1. I have a clear idea of what I want to be.

2. I've got my life together.

3. I like myself and I am proud of what I stand for.

4. I can't decide what to do with my life.

5. I find that I have to keep up a front when I am with others.

6. I don't know what kind of person I am.

7. I don't really feel involved.

8. The important things are clear to me.

9. I feel mixed up.

10. I don't really know who I am.

11. I change my opinion about myself a lot.

Note.   From "From Trust to Intimacy: A New Inventory for Examining Erikson's Stages of Psychosocial Development," by D. Rosenthal, R. Gurney, and S. Moore, 1981, *Journal of Youth and Adolescence, 10*(6), p. 536–537. Copyright © 1981 by Kluwer Academic/Plenum Publishers. Adapted with permission.

writing or arts and crafts; school music or performing arts; school govern-ment; school clubs; school newspaper or yearbook; sports in general, exer-cise, or athletics; school athletic teams; parties or other social affairs; and taverns, bars, or nightclubs. Students could chose from 5 responses rang-ing from *never* to *daily*. We wanted to collapse response categories in order to have meaningful group sizes, but we also wanted to maintain at least three groups so that we could test for quadratic relationships between some predictors and identity clarity. We therefore set a minimal *n* size of 20 and, where possible, collapsed response categories into three groups, which we tested for linear and quadratic relationships using contrast codes in the fashion described by Judd and McClelland (1989). Where distribu-tion of responses did not permit trichotomization, we collapsed the re-sponse categories into two groups, either *high* versus *low* or *yes* versus *no*, depending on the particular distribution.

We used several measures to assess the influence of peers, parents, and re-ligion. The peers question asked whether the student's peers enjoyed school and tried hard, whether they were positive about school, were neutral about it, or hated it. To maintain an n size of at least 20, we collapsed the latter two categories and nonresponders into one group, leaving three categories for the *peer attitudes toward school* variable: enjoy, positive, and neutral/hate/no response. We created a parental variable asking whether the student's parent had done any volunteer work during the previous year. We also used a question asking how important religion is to the student. Response categories were *very, pretty, a little,* and *not at all.* We collapsed the first three categories into a *yes* group and designated the latter as a *no* group.

To control for self-selection based on personality differences, the larger study included a set of 33 phrases adapted from Barber's (1998) adolescence version of the "big five" adult personality traits: active, neurotic, difficult, introverted, and conscientious. Students were asked to indicate how well each of the phrases applied to themselves, using a 5-point scale ranging from *hardly at all like me* to *very much like me.* Examples of these phrases include physically active, fearful, messy, easily irritated or mad, and full of life.

To check for influences of other background characteristics of the students, we assessed gender, race/ethnicity, and socioeconomic status, as well as GPA. Because the student population is about 75% White with no large minority groups, we collapsed race/ethnicity responses into *White* and *non-White* categories. We used mother's education as an indicator of socioeconomic status, collapsing responses into three categories (*less than a 4-year degree, 4-year degree,* and *professional degree*) and testing them for linear and quadratic effects.

We conducted three sets of analyses, the first of which explored how identity clarity changed over time. In a second analysis, we asked which factors might predict identity clarity, whether predictive factors might differ between males and females, and whether the mix of predictive factors differed between Time 1 (fall of 10th grade) and Time 6 (spring of 12th grade). In the third analysis, we divided the sample into four groups, based on gains or losses in students' identity clarity scores from Time 1 (high vs. low) to Time 6: those with high identity clarity at Time 1 who gained more by Time 6 (high gain), those with high identity clarity at Time 1 who either lost clarity or gained none by Time 6 (high loss), those with low identity clarity at Time 1 who gained more by Time 6 (low gain), and those with low identity clarity at Time 1 who lost clarity or gained none by Time 6 (low loss).[1] The two pairs of identity clar-

---

[1]To create these groups, students were first divided into high and low groups, using the median identity clarity score at Time 1 as the cut point. Students who tied for the median score were randomly assigned to high or low categories to form approximately equal groups (high, n = 87, and low, n = 86). Identity clarity difference scores (score at Time 6 minus score at Time 1) were calculated, and students with difference scores greater than 0 were assigned to a "gain" group (high gain, n = 31, and low gain, n = 56), while those with difference scores equal to or less than 0 were assigned to a "loss" group (high loss, n = 56, and low loss, n = 30).

ity groups (high gain/high loss and low gain/low loss) showed different patterns of identity development over time. The two high groups showed roughly similar patterns, but with the high-gain group increasing more sharply than the high-loss group at Time 6. By contrast, the two low groups showed a nearly symmetrical pattern, with the low-gain group steadily rising over time and the low-loss group steadily declining. We then looked for differences among these groups in terms of various predictors.

Changes in Identity Clarity Over Time

To test whether identity becomes clearer over the course of high school, we calculated mean identity clarity scores at Time 1, Time 2, Time 4, and Time 6 for 6 identity clarity questions for those students who answered these questions at all four times ($N = 136$), as well as separate calculations for males ($n = 46$) and females ($n = 90$). The results of this analysis are presented in Fig. 15.1. They indicate no overall gain in identity clarity over the 3 years of the study; rather, scores declined between Time 1 and Time 4 before rising sharply between Time 4 and Time 6. Although this pattern was essentially the same for males and females, the average identity clarity score for males was higher than that for females at all four times.

By asking adolescents how clearly they perceive who they are and what is important to them, we obtained a reasonable estimate of how far along these youths are in the in the process of identity reformulation. In our sample, this measure showed that the change in clarity did not change linearly, but followed a path that declined over the middle high-school years before turning up sharply in the 12th grade. The dip is striking, particularly because it is

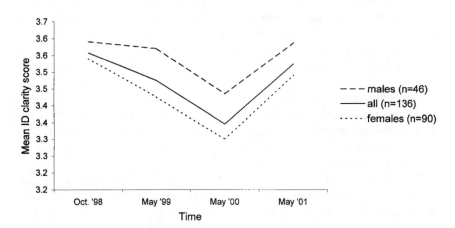

FIG. 15.1.   Identity clarity by gender.

similar for males and females. Although several explanations are possible, we suggest that the dip may represent a time of transition between a secure identity based primarily on home and family, to one founded more on new interests and friends at school and in the community. Another interpretation is that in this population of students with highly educated parents (76% of mothers had a 4-year-college or advanced degree), the dip may represent the growing uncertainty of where to attend college, followed in 12th grade by the sudden clarity associated with finding out. It may also be that both factors contribute to the dip. It is worth noting that in our unpublished work involving two Catholic high schools, we have evidence of a similar V-shaped trajectory in one high school sample but not in the other. Our interpretation, therefore, is speculative but in accord with theory and present data.

Factors Associated With Identity Clarity

To test whether predictors of identity clarity change over the course of high school, and whether community service, other youth activities, and peers become increasingly important predictors, we regressed identity clarity at Time 1 and Time 6 on our set of predictor variables for the full sample ($N = 173$), as well as separately for males ($n = 73$) and females ($n = 100$).

At Time 1, identity clarity was positively predicted by ethnicity, two personality factors (active and conscientious), and positive peer attitude toward school, and negatively predicted by neurotic personality and leisure reading habits (see Table 15.2). At Time 6, however, out of this list of predictors, only neurotic personality still predicted identity clarity. New predictors of identity at Time 6 included both required and voluntary community service participation, as well as having friends who enjoy school, participating in sports, exercise, or athletics, and going to parties or other social affairs. The negative quadratic relation between the latter and identity clarity indicates that youth who participated moderately in social activities had higher identity clarity than those who participated at either higher or lower rates. These youth, we suspect, are similar to the all-round youth identified by Youniss et al. (1997). Taken together, these results illustrate the growing importance of community service and leisure activities as predictors of identity development over the high-school years in this sample. Although these findings do not indicate causality, they are consistent with other research showing positive developmental benefits associated with participation in community service (Andersen, 1998).

The change in the relation between identity clarity and its predictors over time is also evident in R^2 data from the hierarchical regressions. Personality factors, for example, accounted for 62% of R^2 at Time 1 but less than one half that amount (28%) at Time 6 (Table 15.3). Community service and leisure activities, on the other hand, accounted for only 22% of R^2 at Time 1

TABLE 15.2
Regressions of Identity Clarity in Fall of 10th Grade and Spring of 12th Grade

| | Fall, 10th grade | | | | | | | | | Spring, 12th grade | | | | | | | | |
| | All | | | Male | | | Female | | | All | | | Male | | | Female | | |
Variable[a]	b	β	r	b	β	r	b	β	r	b	β	r	b	β	r	b	β	r
Gender																		
Male vs. female	−.013	−.020	.006	—	—	—	—	—	—	.036	.055	.076	—	—	—	—	—	—
Mother's education																		
Linear	−.015	−.017	.026	.049	.057	.015	−.038	−.042	.036	.034	.039	.024	−.044	−.053	−.070	−.015	−.017	.118
Quadratic	.048	.108	.149	.035	.075	.146	.087	.199	.152 *	.041	.094	.107	−.069	−.151	−.122	.102	.241	.275
Ethnicity																		
White vs. non-White	.131	.164	.081 *	.088	.103	.128	.182	.239	.047 *	.009	.012	.105	−.190	−.231	.063	−.009	−.013	.128
GPA	−.026	−.022	.019	.146	.138	.072	−.240	−.166	−.034	.184	.169	.139	.230	.227	.189	.098	.078	.142
Personality																		
Active	.332	.209	.246 *	.399	.256	.290 *	.011	.007	.210	−.027	−.018	.102	.024	.016	−.023	.224	.149	.206
Introverted	−.030	−.044	−.180	.086	.115	−.012	−.105	−.155	−.312	−.005	−.007	−.067	−.138	−.188	−.122	.093	.139	−.060
Conscientious	.159	.275	.276 **	.141	.254	.287 **	.095	.153	.280	.065	.115	.094	.067	.122	.166	.022	.036	.059
Neurotic	−.328	−.380	−.331 ***	−.386	−.381	−.201 ***	−.384	−.464	−.437 ***	−.319	−.372	−.271 ***	−.143	−.145	−.356	−.323	−.390	−.195 **
Difficult	.020	.020	−.099	.086	.083	−.133	.183	.193	−.074	.068	.070	−.088	−.178	−.174	−.366	.262	.284	.126
Parent volunteers																		
Yes vs. no	.021	.031	.117	.078	.117	.140	.039	.059	.099	−.049	−.074	.037	−.123	−.183	.081	.000	−.001	−.001

(continued on next page)

341

TABLE 15.2 (continued)

Variable[a]	Fall, 10th grade									Spring, 12th grade								
	All			Male			Female			All			Male			Female		
	b	β	r	b	β	r	b	β	r	b	β	r	b	β	r	b	β	r
Religion is important																		
Yes vs. no	-.060	-.076	-.034	-.056	-.071	-.020	-.090	-.114	-.044	-.008	-.010	.026	-.150	-.175	.135	-.019	-.024	-.068
Peers' school attitude																		
Enjoy vs. positive, others[b]	.043	.067	.174	.084	.121	.137	.093	.150	.202	.107	.209	.172	.201 *	.367	.239	.075	.156	.133
Positive vs. others[b]	.126	.175	.243 *	-.034	-.047	.079	.338	.452	.391 ***	-.108	-.145	.019	-.240 *	-.319	-.073	-.050	-.066	.128
Leisure activities																		
Read books, etc.																		
Linear	-.180	-.198	-.043 *	-.233	-.262	-.170	-.160	-.167	.067	.027	.031	.055	.223	.258	.126	-.142	-.168	.001
Quadratic	.029	.058	.025	-.054	-.113	-.121	.104	.202	.152	-.044	-.091	-.094	-.013	-.026	-.210	.061	.128	.001
Creative writing, arts/crafts																		
Linear	.082	.099	.089	-.007	-.009	.089	.271	.290	.098 **	-.008	-.010	-.017	.027	.035	-.149	-.001	-.002	.129
Quadratic	.046	.095	.069	.084	.165	.143	-.044	-.093	.012	.069	.145	.102	.036	.072	.112	.039	.086	.087
School performing arts																		
Linear	.074	.103	.055	-.066	-.094	-.064	.052	.069	.157	-.028	-.036	.074	.077	.097	-.069	-.002	-.003	.183
Quadratic	.022	.034	.079	.115	.157	.042	-.027	-.045	.103	.024	.048	.042	.041	.080	.167	.001	.001	-.060
School government																		
Yes vs. no	.021	.025	.045	-.142	-.172	-.093	.093	.106	.161	.093	.135	.138	.081	.117	.114	.126	.181	.149

School clubs																		
Linear	-.085	-.105	.020	-.124	-.157	.059	-.134	-.159	-.010	-.083	-.099	.102	-.143	-.174	.097	-.028	-.033	.124
Quadratic	.026	.055	.051	-.055	-.109	-.119	.087	.191	.172*	-.059	-.131	-.089	-.038	-.081	-.005	-.104	-.240	-.161
School paper/yearbook																		
Yes vs. no	.060	.072	.034	.159	.174	-.007	.100	.124	.064	.103	.158	.135	.004	.006	.070	.113	.176	.184
Sports/exercise/athletics																		
High vs. low	-.123	-.168	-.059	-.248	-.342	-.073	-.005	-.007	-.048	.144	.214	.132	-.091	-.134	.144	.220	.331	.129*
School athletic teams																		
Linear	-.010	-.012	-.026	-.063	-.078	-.004	.070	.088	-.043	-.076	-.104	.019	.317	.413	.238	-.151	-.217	-.155
Quadratic	.013	.023	.071	.013	.025	.168	-.070	-.110	-.019	-.054	-.098	.082	.000	.000	.291	-.099	-.171	-.098
Parties/social affairs																		
Linear	.016	.017	.009	.149	.154	.027	-.028	-.029	-.004	.095	.090	.044	-.090	-.088	.061	.043	.039	.031
Quadratic	-.025	-.056	-.021	.035	.072	.045	-.030	-.067	-.072	-.097	-.221	-.205*	-.196	-.441*	-.354*	-.010	-.022	-.093
Taverns, bars, nightclubs																		
Yes vs. no	-.025	-.036	.020	.018	.027	.012	.015	.021	.026	-.089	-.133	-.053	-.105	-.152	-.109	-.016	-.025	-.013
Community service																		
Required (yes vs. no)	.088	.129	.168	.128	.189	.125	.057	.083	.203	.125	.174	.055*	.094	.125	.060	.056	.081	.046
Voluntary (yes vs. no)	-.050	-.071	.037	.033	.043	.101	-.130	-.192	-.006	.149	.228	.157*	.207	.312	.184	.123	.184	.167
R^2			.418			.454			.680			.360			.637			.456
N			157			68			89			158			69			89

[a]Code values for male, White, yes, and high = 1; code values for female, non-White, no, and low = -1. [b]Others = neutral/hate/no response. *$p < .05$, **$p < .01$, ***$p < .001$.

TABLE 15.3
R^2 Values for Hierarchical Regressions

	Time 1						Time 6					
	All		Males		Females		All		Males		Females	
Background[a]	.030	(7.2)	.043	(9.5)	.029	(4.3)	.050	(13.9)	.066	(10.4)	.106	(23.2)
Personality	.259	(62.0)	.232	(51.1)	.365	(53.7)	.102	(28.3)	.178	(27.9)	.141	(30.9)
Parents, Religion	.005	(1.2)	.006	(1.3)	.006	(.9)	.009	(2.5)	.040	(6.3)	.002	(.4)
Peer attitudes	.034	(8.1)	.001	(.2)	.138	(20.3)	.042	(11.7)	.082	(12.9)	.041	(9.0)
Leisure activities	.076	(18.2)	.152	(33.5)	.118	(17.4)	.103	(28.6)	.239	(37.5)	.143	(31.4)
Community service	.014	(3.3)	.020	(4.4)	.024	(3.5)	.054	(15.0)	.032	(5.0)	.023	(5.0)

Note. Numbers in parentheses are percentages. Column percentages may not sum to 100 due to rounding.

[a]Background factors include gender, mother's education, ethnicity, and GPA. Gender is omitted from analyses for males and females.

but twice that amount (44%) at Time 6. The amount of R^2 explained by community service increased more than fourfold over the course of the study, from 3.3% at Time 1 to 15% at Time 6. Some of this increase may be explained by the larger numbers of students participating in community service at Time 6. Between Time 1 and Time 6, the number of students doing required service increased from 101 to 125, and the number doing voluntary service rose from 55 to 99. But these changes seem too small to completely explain the fourfold increase in R^2 associated with community service.

Overall, these results support the idea that adolescents go through a transition from a home-based identity to one based more on relationships in school and community. The findings in Table 15.2 suggest that many factors are linked to identity clarity and that the mix and importance of these factors change over the course of high school. Early in the high-school years (Time 1), background factors such as personality are more strongly associated with identity clarification than they are late in the high-school years (Time 6). By contrast, youth activities and other community-based influences show relatively less association early in the high-school years but much stronger relationships later in high school. In particular, these findings suggest that community service, whether required or voluntary, is strongly and positively associated with this process.

Our study indicates that both required and voluntary service may be beneficial to students in terms of identity clarity (Table 15.2). These results are consistent with those of McLellan and Youniss (2003), who, in their study of students from two Catholic high schools, report finding that both required and voluntary service can benefit identity development in adolescents. They concluded that although the motivations for participation in required and voluntary service are different, the developmental outcomes depend more on the type of service performed (i.e., social, cause, teach/coach, or functionary) than on the system (required or voluntary) through which the service is performed. The reason for this is that service type is often associated with the sponsor of service so that, for example, students who do service under the auspices of a cause-based organization would be confronted with more challenging service than, say, students who tutor peers or coach younger children's athletic games. The lack of distinction between required and voluntary service follows from this same factor; that is, a student doing required service for a cause-based organization and one doing voluntary service would both be exposed to the same prosocial ideology. The key is not whether service was done freely or not; the key is exposure to the rationale of the sponsoring organization.

Our findings suggest possible gender differences in the associations between community service participation and identity clarity, but the reasons for these differences are unclear (Table 15.2). At Time 6, participation in voluntary community service predicted marginally higher identity clarity for males ($b = .207, p < .10$) but not for females. One possible explanation is that males with high identity clarity self-select into voluntary service. This is consistent with the finding of Youniss and Reis (2002) that youth with high identity clarity become involved in community service at higher rates than those with low identity clarity. If this is the case, however, why do females with high identity clarity not also self-select into voluntary community service at similarly high rates? A possible explanation is that identity clarity may have less association with female involvement in community service. If females develop a sense of caring much earlier than boys, as suggested by the work of Gilligan (1982), then a measure of caring might reveal an association between caring and community service among females (and possibly among males). Thus, females high in caring may show positive associations with participation in community service, no matter their level of identity clarity. Similarly, if there is less association among females between service participation and identity clarity, this would also explain why participation in voluntary community service would influence identity clarity in males to a greater extent than in females at Time 6, if indeed, there is causality in that direction.

Another explanation for this gender difference may lie in the way identity clarity is measured. Our study found that males, on average, had higher identity clarity than females at all times during the study (Fig. 15.1). Rosenthal, Gurney, and Moore (1981) found similar differences in their initial study using the identity clarity measure employed here. They proposed that the gender differences in the findings may be due to the fact that items in the measure deal with feelings of self-esteem and well-being. Females, they suggested, may be more willing than males to report problems in these areas. The researchers also suggested that in the present climate of social change, female roles may be less clear than male roles, and that this confusion may extend for a longer period than for males. Either prospect would conceivably contribute to lower identity scores for females during the period of identity formation, although score averages ought to be the same for both sexes.

The regression results also show an intriguing gender difference in the associations between peer attitudes toward school and identity clarity. At Time 1, having friends who are positive about school is highly associated with identity clarity for females but not at all for males (Table 15.2). At Time 6, however, peer attitudes toward school are completely unpredictive for females, whereas for boys having friends who enjoy school or who feel positively about it predicts identity clarity (although the associations are in opposite directions). The R^2 data for males and females reflect these findings. In males, peer attitudes explain a much larger proportion of R^2 at Time 6 (13%) than at Time 1 (less than 1%), whereas the reverse is true for females (Table 15.3). Larson and Richards (1994) noted that peer influence peaks in early adolescence. Our findings suggest that this peak may occur earlier for females than males, at least in terms of predicting identity clarity.

It is also interesting that for males, having peers who enjoy school positively predicted identity clarity, whereas having peers who were merely positive about school negatively predicted identity clarity. Thus, although the youth literature supports the contention that peers are particularly influential during adolescence, our data underscore the point that peer influence may have a positive or negative influence on identity formation. Again, however, we would emphasize that these results show only associations, and further studies will be necessary to clarify directions of causality.

Differences Among Identity Clarity Groups

As in Youniss and Reis (2002), we looked at change in identity clarity among four distinct groups of students, based on their identity clarity scores at Time 1 (high–low) and on whether they gained or lost clarity by Time 6 (gain–loss). To look for group differences among our predictor variables, we conducted a series of t tests, first comparing the high-identity clarity group with the low-identity clarity group and then comparing the two subsets (gain vs. loss) in each of these groups.

A comparison of high- and low-identity clarity youth indicates significant differences between the two groups (Table 15.4). In general, those with high identity clarity tended to have more positive personalities, to have friends with more positive attitudes toward school, and to participate more frequently in extracurricular activities, both at Time 1 and Time 6. Interestingly, considering the aims of our study, there was no difference between high- and low-identity clarity youth in their frequency of participation in either required or voluntary service at either time.

Among high-identity clarity youth, the "gain" students participated more frequently in required community service at Time 1 than did the "loss" students (Table 15.5). There was, however, no difference in community service participation between the two groups at Time 6. This finding was not surprising. We have suggested that community service provides a rich developmental context, and we would expect those who participate in it early in high school to show developmental benefits, such as increased clarity, over time. Although our finding does not demonstrate causality, it lends support to the contention of Youniss and Reis (2002) that high-identity clarity youth who choose to participate in challenging community service activities early in high school reap the developmental advantages of that challenge over the course of high school.

Among the results for low-identity clarity youth, we found nothing that offered a theoretically reasonable explanation for why some of them gained identity clarity between 10th and 12th grade while others lost identity clar-

TABLE 15.4
Identity Clarity Groups (High vs. Low)

Variable	Time 1	Time 6
	t	t
Active personality	2.921**	na
Conscientious personality	2.827**	na
Neurotic personality	−3.856***	na
Peer attitude toward school:		
Enjoy vs. Positive, neutral/hate/no response	2.274	2.843**
Positive vs. Neutral/hate/no response	3.626***	—
Reads books, magazines, newspapers (linear)	—	2.332*
Participation in school music or performing arts (linear)	—	2.379*
Participation in school music or performing arts (quadratic)	2.497*	—

Note. All Ns ≥ 82. na = not applicable: personality factors were measured only at Time 1.
*p < .05.

TABLE 15.5
High-Identity Clarity Groups (Gain vs. Loss)

Variable	Time 1	Time 6
	t	t
Participation in school clubs (quadratic)	2.063*	—
Does creative writing or arts and crafts (quadratic)	—	3.031**
Participation in community service: required (yes vs. no)	2.070*	—

Note. All Ns ≥ 30.
*p < .05, **p < .01.

ity (Table 15.6). For low-gain students, we expected to see positive associations with community service; instead, we found none. One explanation for this lack of findings may be that in dividing our sample into four groups ranging in size from 30 to 56, we greatly reduced the power to detect significant results. Another possible explanation is that factors other than community service may be more strongly associated with identity clarity in youth who have low-identity clarity than in those with high-identity clarity. Reis and Youniss (2004) found that youth who lost identity clarity between 10th and 12th grade showed no improvement in communication with their mothers and persistent conflict with their friends during the study, compared with youth who showed no loss of identity clarity during that time. These findings suggest that gains in identity formation associated with participation in community service might be offset by losses in identity development associated with poor relations with parents and peers.

CONCLUSION

Identity development is a life-long process, but in adolescence it passes through a particularly intense phase. As youth push out from the home and family that have supplied much of their identity during childhood, they begin to explore new sources of identity at school and in the community. If this process is successful, some emerge from adolescence with a clearer, more individuated idea of who they are and how they fit into the world. The findings presented in this chapter suggest that community service and other types of positive youth activities are associated with this important transition, along with other factors such as peers and personality.

The emerging literature on the role of activities outside of the academic curriculum is forcing the field to catch up with its own acknowledgment of the multiple worlds that are involved in the transition to adulthood. Adolescence is not a final state but a step in the transition to individuated adult-

TABLE 15.6
Low-Identity Clarity Groups (Gain vs. Loss)

Variable	Time 1 t	Time 6 t
Participation in school clubs (quadratic)	—	−2.509*

Note.   All Ns ≥ 29.
*$p < .05$.

hood (Grotevant, 1999). Activities apart from the academic curriculum play an obvious role in the development of real-world skills and in connecting young people to the societal context in which they must live. Recent research has helped to emphasize the importance of institutions—peer groups, athletic teams, churches, community-based youth organizations, and so forth—which provide young people with experiences that, via behavior and norms, help integrate them into adult society (e.g., Fletcher et al., 2000). The importance of these venues for experiencing life is beginning to be addressed by policymakers who now recognize that, in addition to lives at home and school, young people have a life in "after school" hours that may be critical to their development and that merits serious attention (e.g., Eccles & Gootman, 2001; Pittman, Diversi, & Ferber, 2001).

In keeping with this expanding view of the environment that affects adolescent development, we want to emphasize that community service is but one aspect, albeit a critical one, in connecting youth to society. One of the central roles it can play is as a port of entry (Raskoff & Sundeen, 1999) into the world of ideologies that offer youth an interpretative frame for understanding their own behavior and envisioning the direction society ought to take. Service introduces young people to these ongoing ideologies and gives them the opportunity to experience themselves as participants in them. It is this function that most obviously contributes to identity formation as Erikson (1968) pictured the process, whereby youth would be offered compelling rationales for taking moral and political stands that make life worth living. In this view, identity is found not so much by turning inward and asking "Who am I?" Rather, it is forged by looking outward, asking "Where do I belong?" and finding one's place in history.

REFERENCES

Andersen, S. (1998). *Service learning: A national strategy for youth development*. Retrieved May 21, 2002, from http://www.gwu.edu/~ccps/pop_svc.html

Barber, B. K. (1998). *Adolescent personality inventory (big five)*. Unpublished manuscript.

Coleman, J. (1961). *The adolescent society*. New York: Free Press.

Eccles, J. S., & Barber, B. L. (1999). Student council, volunteering, basketball, or marching band: What kind of extracurricular involvement matters? *Journal of Adolescent Research, 14*(1), 10–43.

Eccles, J. S., & Gootman, J. A. (Eds.). (2001). *Community programs to promote youth development*. Washington, DC: National Academy Press.

Erikson, E. (1968). *Identity: Youth and crisis*. New York: Norton.

Fletcher, A., Elder, G. H., Jr., & Mekos, D. (2000). Parental influence on adolescent involvement in community activities. *Journal of Research on Adolescence, 10*(1), 29–48.

Gilligan, C. (1982). *In a different voice: Psychological theory and women's development*. Cambridge, MA: Harvard University Press.

Grotevant, H. D. (1998). Adolescent development in family contexts. In W. Damon (Series Ed.) & N. Eisenberg (Vol. Ed.), *Handbook of child psychology: Vol. 3. Social, emotional, and personality development* (5th ed., pp. 1097–1149). New York: Wiley.

Judd, C. M., & McClelland, G. H. (1989). *Data analysis: A model comparison approach.* San Diego, CA: Harcourt Brace Jovanovich.

Larson, R. (1994). Youth organizations, hobbies, and sports as developmental contexts. In R. K. Silbereisen & E. Todt (Eds.), *Adolescence in context: The interplay of family, school, peers, and work in adjustment* (pp. 44–65). New York: Springer Verlag.

Larson, R., & Richards, M. (1994). *Divergent realities.* New York: Basic Books.

McLellan, J., & Youniss, J. (2003). Two systems of youth service: Determinants of voluntary and required youth community service. *Journal of Youth and Adolescence, 32*(1), 47–58.

Metz, E., McLellan, J., & Youniss, J. (2003). Types of voluntary service and adolescents' civic development. *Journal of Adolescent Research, 18*(1), 1–16.

Pittman, K., Diversi, M., & Ferber, T. (2002). Social policy supports for adolescence in the twenty-first century: Framing questions. *Journal of Research on Adolescence, 12*(1), 149–158.

Raskoff, S., & Sundeen, R. A. (1999). Community service programs in high schools. *Law and Contemporary Problems, 62*(4), 73–111.

Reis, O., & Youniss, J. (2004). Patterns in identity change and development in relationships with mothers and friends. *Journal of Adolescent Research, 19*(1), 31–44.

Rosenthal, D., Gurney, R., & Moore, S. (1981). From trust to intimacy: A new inventory for examining Erikson's stages of psychosocial development. *Journal of Youth and Adolescence, 10*(6), 525–537.

Yates, M., & Youniss, J. (1996). A developmental perspective on community service in adolescence. *Social Development, 5*(1), 85–111.

Yates, M., & Youniss, J. (1998). Community service and political identity development in adolescence. *Journal of Social Issues, 54*(3), 495–512.

Youniss, J., McLellan, J., Su, Y., & Yates, M. (1999). The role of community service in identity development: Normative, unconventional, and deviant orientations. *Journal of Adolescent Research, 14*(2), 249–262.

Youniss, J., McLellan, J., & Yates, M. (1997). What we know about engendering civic identity. *American Behavioral Scientist, 40*(5), 620–631.

Youniss, J., & Reis, O. (2002). Identity development and social engagement in American youth. In H. Uhlendorff & H. Oswald (Eds.), *Wege zum Selbst* [Paths to the self] (pp. 249–260). Stuttgart, Germany: Lucius.

Youniss, J., & Smollar, J. (1985). *Adolescent relations with mothers, fathers, and friends.* Chicago: University of Chicago Press.

Youniss, J., & Yates, M. (1997). *Community service and social responsibility in youth.* Chicago: University of Chicago Press.

Youniss, J., Yates, M., & Su, Y. (1997). Community service and marijuana use in high school seniors. *Journal of Adolescent Research, 12*(2), 245–262.

16

The Present and Future of Research on Activity Settings as Developmental Contexts

Jacquelynne S. Eccles
University of Michigan

In chapter 1, we foreshadowed what this book would be about and summarized why people might want to understand organized activities as developmental contexts. We began by defining *organized activities* as activities "characterized by structure, adult supervision, and an emphasis on skill-building" (p. 4) and pointed out that participation in such activities is often voluntary and heavily dependent on access. We discussed the hypothesis that participating in such organized activities should facilitate the attainment of age-appropriate competencies, which in turn should "allow an individual to take advantage of personal and environmental resources that promote positive functioning in the present, reduce the risk for developing problem behaviors, and increase the likelihood for healthy adjustment in the future" (p. 6). We also provided a brief review of the evidence to support this hypothesis and discussed the characteristics of programs likely to moderate the impact of participation on development as well as the opportunities for, and barriers to, participation that influence access.

In this chapter, I discuss the major themes that emerged in chapter 2 through chapter 15, focusing on theoretical and methodological issues, and make suggestions for where this field of study should go in the future. I organize my comments about the theoretical themes around three broad questions: Who gets into organized activities? Who stays in these activities? And what are the consequences of participating in organized activities? I organize my comments about methodology around the relevance of different methods for addressing various theoretical and applied questions.

THEORETICAL THEMES

Who Participates?

This question has two parts: Who gets into and who continues to participate in organized activities? I address the first part now. The authors of several of the chapters discussed many reasons why individuals might choose to participate in various organized activities. Common reasons included learning new skills, developing existing skills, competing with members of other organized teams or groups, exploring and solidifying one's personal identities, being with one's friends, having fun, filling time, escaping alternative bad situations, and gaining skills needed for unrelated short- and long-term goals.

At a most basic level, several authors stressed the utility of activity participation for being with one's friends and spending time doing things that are enjoyable. This theme is particularly salient in the chapters by O'Neill (chap. 12), by Stattin et al. (chap. 10), and by Scanlan et al. (chap. 13). In their discussion of the motivational consequences of various types of coaching patterns, Duda and Ntoumanis (chap. 14) also make it clear that participating in organized sports can be fun. These chapters provide excellent examples of the ways in which activity participation can facilitate a range of positive emotional experiences—from just the good feelings associated with spending quality time with one's friends to the intense emotional and cognitive state of flow. Undoubtedly, this opportunity is the reason why many youth participate in organized activities. Unfortunately, these positive emotional experiences are not always obtained and sometimes experiences with one's friends can have negative consequences for development. I discuss this more later.

The link between activity participation and identity formation and consolidation is stressed in the chapters by Barber et al. (chap. 9), Jacobs et al. (chap. 11), McIntosh et al. (chap. 15), and O'Neill (chap. 12). Each of these authors pointed out that participating in specific activities helps one explore related identities (e.g., being a jock, or a civic-minded person, or a musician, or a feminine or masculine person). If one discovers a good fit of a specific identity with one's experiences of the demands and opportunities associated with the related activity domain, then one is likely to continue both participating in the activity and consolidating the parts of one's identities associated with that activity. In addition, McIntosh et al. (chap. 15) provide evidence that participating in service activities helps in the more general process of identity exploration and consolidation.

Some organized activities, particularly sports and competitive arts and music activities, provide an arena for competition. Some individuals participate in these activities because these activities provide the opportunity for the individuals to develop their own skills to the high levels necessary to compete against others in valued domains. This basis for participating in organized activities and the consequences and correlates of such participation is discussed extensively by Duda and Ntoumanis (chap. 14) and by Scanlan et al. (chap. 13). As these authors point out, engaging in activities for competitive reasons can produce either positive or quite negative emotional responses at the individual level and either positive or quite negative interaction patterns between peer and between the youth and either their parents or their coaches and teachers. Even more importantly, highly competitive situations likely produce a complex mix of positive and negative emotional reactions and interpersonal relationships. We are just beginning to understand the situational and personal factors that influence this mix.

The authors of several chapters also discuss the fact that children and adolescents are not always the initiators of participation. Parents play a big role in getting and keeping their children in activities. Parents do this for many reasons. Jacobs et al. (chap. 11) discuss how parents' gender role stereotypes could lead them to put their sons and daughters into different types of activities either because they want their children to learn gender-role-appropriate skills or because they assume their children have gender-role stereotypic abilities and interests. Both Duda and Ntoumanis (chap. 14) and Scanlan et al. (chap. 13) discuss how parents enroll their children in sports for different reasons and that these reasons have a substantial impact on their children's experiences while doing the activity as well as on the children's own motivation for participating. Finally, Casey et al. (chap. 4) discuss the need of parents to find safe places for the children during the after-school hours and how welfare reform policies provided the funds for some parents to fulfill this need. In some neighborhoods, parents feel safe taking their children to organized activities settings; in other neighborhoods, parents may see the community centers and organized activities as dangerous and a risk for their children's development.

At a more macrolevel, one needs to consider access issues. Not all young people have equal access to organized activities. Kleiber and Powell (chap. 2) discuss the historical changes in both the availability and the reasons for organized, out-of-school activity settings. They conclude that we are now in a period in which there is substantial support for such activity settings because our society is convinced that formal programs can reduce the prevalence of problem behaviors, can promote positive youth development, and can increase school achievement. Nonetheless, as both Pedersen and

Seidman (chap. 5), and Villarruel et al. (chap. 6) stress, there is still great inequity in access to high quality, culturally appropriate, organized activities. Casey et al. (chap. 4) reiterate this theme in their discussion of why the adolescents in the welfare reform programs are not participating at high rates in organized activities. Finally, several of the authors, including Kirshner et al. (chap 7), Osgood et al. (chap. 3), and Pedersen and Seidman (chap. 5), point out that the opportunities for participation in organized community-based activities is lower for adolescents than for preteens. In addition, the number of slots for participation in some types of extracurricular school-based activities (e.g., sports) decline and become more competitive over the high-school years. All of these factors make it quite difficult for some youth who would like to participate in organized activities to actually have this opportunity.

The second part of the question "Who participates?" relates to the issue of who *continues* to participate. Many of the factors just discussed as reasons for starting to participate also help explain who continues to participate. But few studies have actually directly addressed this question. Presumably, youth will continue to participate if doing so is important, enjoyable, and not too emotionally, psychologically, behaviorally, or financially costly. Some aspects of each of these factors are discussed in various chapters. Casey et al. (chap. 4), for example, discuss the possibility that older adolescents do not participate because they need or want to work for pay instead. In their discussions of the motivational processes involved in sport participation and the importance of the quality of the experience, both Duda and Ntoumanis (chap. 14) and Scanlan et al. (chap. 13) offer several suggestions for types of emotional and competence-related experiences that would either facilitate continued participation or drive participants away. The impact of the quality of the experience on continued participation is also discussed by O'Neill (chap. 12). McIntosh et al. (chap. 15), O'Neill (chap. 12), Villarruel et al. (chap. 6), and Kirshner et al. (chap. 7) also discuss the critical role of a sense of connectedness as a powerful reason for continued participation.

The importance of person–environment fit and identity consolidation are discussed extensively by Barber et al. (chap. 9), McIntosh et al. (chap. 15), O'Neill (chap. 12), and Villaruel et al. (chap. 6). Each of these authors stress the fact the people will enjoy most activity settings that provide the kinds of experiences most valued by the individuals; for example, activities that allow individuals to perfect those skills that they value or that people close to them value. Often such activities are closely linked to the individuals' emerging value system as well as the individuals' emerging personal and social identities. Good person-environment fit can also reflect the opportunity to spend time doing things that the individual enjoys and in which the individual gets to experience a sense of flow. Finally, good person–environmental fit can emerge from a good developmental fit with individual's increasing maturity. We know that young people often drop out of organized activities as they move into adolescence. Many reasons have been offered ranging from lack of opportunities to participate to the need to do other things with one's time (which I discuss in this chapter). One likely reason that has received relatively little attention except in the work by McLaughlin and her colleagues (Kirshner et al., chap. 7), and Eccles and her colleagues (Barber et al., chap. 9) is the possible failure of organized programs to provide the kinds of roles that adolescents might find challenging and respectful of their increasing maturity and expertise. McLaughlin (2000) provided extensive examples of organized programs that allow youth to play increasing leadership and teaching roles as they mature in the programs. Such increases are examples of what Eccles and her colleagues have labeled *Stage–Environment Fit* (Eccles et al., 1993), by which they meant activities that fit well with the developmental needs of the participants and that change in ways that reflect the changing developmental needs and strengths of the participants. More studies focused on why youth leave programs are needed to test these many hypotheses.

One related influence on continued participation is not discussed in any great detail except by Casey et al. (chap. 4). This is the psychological and behavioral costs of continued participation. Individuals do not have the time or energy to participate in an unlimited number of organized activities. They must make choices among available options. We understand relatively little about the determinants of these choices. As Casey et al. (chap. 4) point out, the need to work for pay during the out-of-school hours may lead some youth to drop out of organized activities. Similarly, the increasing competitiveness of some types of organized activities may require youth to focus on one particular activity and drop out of other activities. Increasing social pressures to behave in ways appropriate to one's gender or one's cultural group may lead youth to narrow their participation to activities that fit well with these roles or other socially prescribed roles. The needs of one's family may require some youth to drop out of organized activities that either are considered luxuries that the family cannot afford or that take time away from other activities considered critical for the family's well-being. I could provide additional examples but we do not have sufficient space for greater elaboration. What is important is that more work is needed on the personal and social factors that either facilitate continued participation or precipitate discontinuing one's participation in either specific organized activities or more generally in the whole range of organized volunteer activities themselves. Such work needs to consider the kinds of structural barriers discussed by Kleiber and Powell (chap. 2), Pedersen and Seidman (chap. 5), and Villarruel et al. (chap. 6), as well as the many more psychological factors discussed in the majority of the chapters.

Consequences of Participation

What are the consequences of participating in organized activities? This question is important to both policymakers and basic researchers; the former to make wise funding decisions, the latter to advance our understanding of human development. Policymakers often ask the question in its most general form: Does participation in some activity setting affect some loosely selected set of positive youth outcomes like school grades or avoidance of problem behavior or increases in prosocial behaviors or character traits? The underlying question is whether there are sufficient benefits of the program to warrant the dollars spent on the program. Typically, the question is answered through some form of program evaluation.

As I discuss later, such a general approach has limited utility either for future program development or for increasing our understanding of the impact of organized activities on human development. As the studies in this book show, one needs to be much more specific about both the outcomes and the nature of the experience at the activity setting before one can learn very much about the impact of participation in structured activities on development. There are now numerous studies documenting a link between participation and developmental outcomes using both longitudinal survey type designs and experimental treatment designs. We summarize some of these findings in chapter 1. There is also increasing evidence that both the quality and the nature of the experience matters. Certainly this one of the key findings across the chapters in this book; the results clearly show that the developmental consequences of participating in organized activities depend on the nature of the experience. In addition, when tested, the developmental consequences often depend on characteristics of the participants as well. Program evaluation studies need to take this fact into account if the studies are to inform program development and wise programming decisions. In chapter 1, we summarize the characteristics of general programs that are likely to matter for program effects. I discuss the relevance of the findings reported in this book for these characteristics later.

Both applied and basic developmental scientists are also interested in consequences of participation in organized activities. But because the kinds of developmental scientists represented in this book are interested in understanding the nature of socialization and development in organized activity settings (see also Eccles & Templeton, 2002; Larson, 2000), we typically look at programs in much more nuanced and specific ways than policymakers and funders. For both qualitatively and quantitatively oriented developmental researchers, a theoretical framework linking specific experiences to specific outcomes is critical—either as the grounded product of intensive qualitative work or as the overarching guide for more prospective quantitative studies. In addition, the most informative work also clearly articulates the mechanisms proposed to underlie the associations between these two specific sets of constructs.

The chapters in this book provide several excellent examples of the beginnings of such in-depth theorizing. For instance, consider the chapters on sport. The authors of both of these chapters (Duda & Ntoumanis, chap. 14; Scanlan et al., chap. 13) lay out a clear theoretical framework that links specific experiences in organized sport programs to specific psychological and behavioral consequences for the participants. Furthermore, they specify the experiential and personal characteristics linked to both positive and negative consequences for the participants. On one hand, coaching practices that create a task-focused motivational climate create more enjoyment, greater persistence, and better skill learning than coaching practices that create an ego-focused motivational climate. On the other hand, both Duda and Ntoumanis (chap. 14) and Scanlan et al. (chap. 13) discuss how participating in some types of organized sport programs can be quite anxiety provoking and psychologically painful, depending on characteristics of both the participants and their families, as well as characteristics of the coaches and the athletic program.

The importance of specific characteristics of the activity settings is also stressed by Stattin et al. (chap. 10). They report evidence showing that participation in certain types of activity centers with particular types of peers can lead some adolescents into increased problem behaviors. These findings resonate with issues discussed by Osgood et al. (chap. 3), who summarize evidence that spending lots of time with peers in unstructured settings leads to increases in problem behavior. The activity centers studied by Stattin et al. had very little structure and thus were likely to increase the probability of being recruited into a peer group that engages in the kinds of activities that will increase the "situational motivation" of the participants to take part in normbreaking behaviors.

Clearly the answer to question, "What are the consequences of participating in organized activities?" is "it depends." We are just beginning to understand exactly what "it" depends on. To move forward, we need well-articulated theories that specify, at a minimum, the links from (a) the characteristics of the activity setting to the behaviors of the adults and peers in that setting, (b) the behaviors of the adults and peers in the setting to changes in the participants, and (c) changes in the proposed mediating characteristics of participants to changes in the "outcome" characteristics of the participants. One can elaborate and add theoretical links depending on one's intellectual discipline and the level of question being asked by the study. For example, more sociological and/or anthropological developmental scientists and policymakers might well want to know the links between larger societal characteristics and both the characteristics and the availability of activity settings. Systems theorists might want to know which organization characteristics facilitate a community center having all high-quality programs rather than a mix of high- and low-quality experiences for its participants. Evaluations of community centers provide evidence that the quality of experiences often vary across activities within a center (Eccles & Gootman, 2001). We need theories to guide research on the impact of such local diversity on the participants. Chapter 2 through chapter 15 provide examples of the beginnings of both the building and testing of such theories.

What Matters?

Several themes about what matters emerge in chapter 2 through chapter 15. One important factor is the very essence of structured programs—the presence of adult supervision over structured activities. Osgood et al. (chap. 3) summarize the evidence that extensive periods of time in unstructured activities with peers are linked with higher levels of problem behaviors. According to Stattin et al. (chap. 10) high involvement with risky peers at "organized" centers with limited adult supervision and limited structured activities also predicts increased levels of nonnormative and problem behaviors. It is likely that the relative lack of structure and adult supervision in these centers contributes to this finding.

Closely related to the issue of adult supervision are the characteristics of developmentally appropriate levels of structure and positive relationships with adults. Both of these characteristics are well illustrated in the chapters by Larson et al. (chap. 10) and by Kirshner et al. (chap. 7). Larson et al. provide a very complete picture of what developmentally appropriate levels of structure look like in action. Their chapter also illustrates the close connections between providing appropriate levels of structure, high-quality instruction, and the formation of close bonds between adolescents and the adult supervisors in organized activity settings. Kirshner et al. illustrate further the ways in which appropriate levels of structure and high-quality instruction can empower youth to be active participants in the research activity itself.

Although the role of close relationships with adult mentors is not a specific focus in chapters 2 through chapter 15, the presences of highly involved adult supervisors, who are also not overcontrolling, should increase the likelihood of participants developing close relationships with adults who might then serve as mentors. The specific power of mentorship relationships is discussed by Rhodes and Spencer (chap. 19) in the final set of chapters.

Another important factor in several chapters is the nature of the other participants and the individuals' peer group. Osgood et al. (chap. 3) provides strong evidence of the negative power of peers in the absence of organized activities. Stattin et al. (chap. 10) illustrate the power of the peers whom youth meet and associate with in organized centers. Similarly, Barber et al. (chap. 9) illustrate the fact that both the negative and positive outcomes of participating in organized extracurricular activities are mediated by the nature of one's peer group. Finally, Petersen and Seidman (chap. 5) argue that exposure to risky peers could be one reason why participating in some types of organized activities increases problem and antisocial behaviors. They also suggest that presence of prosocial peers might help explain the relation between participation in organized religious activities and positive youth development.

The importance of the quality of the instruction and the opportunities to experience a sense of efficacy and optimal motivation is explicated best in the two sport chapters (Duda & Ntoumanis, chap. 14; Scanlan et al., chap. 13), O'Neill (chap. 12) on music, Kirshner et al. (chap. 7) on bringing youth to the research process, and Larson et al. (chap. 8) on the association of participation with developing initiative. The relevance of these characteristics for skill development is stressed by several authors. The relevance of the opportunities to experience a sense of efficacy for understanding the lower participation rates of adolescents in organized programs is also discussed by Casey et al. (chap. 4). Finally, the chapters by McIntosh et al. (chap. 15), Kirshner et al. (chap. 7), and Larson et al. (chap. 8) also illustrate the importance of a related program characteristic—provision of opportunities to make a meaningful difference—that is, to matter.

Both McIntosh et al. (chap. 15) and Barber et al. (chap. 9) discuss and demonstrate empirically the role that participating in organized activities can play in identity formation and consolidation. These authors argue that providing an opportunity to explore one's identities may be one of the most important characteristics of organized activity settings for adolescents.

Finally, several of the authors discuss the important role that participating in organized activities can play in building individuals' connectness to both social institutions and prosocial groups. Both O'Neill (chap. 12) and Barber et al. (chap. 9) discuss the role that participating in the musical and sports programs at school can play to increase school engagement and school attachment. McIntosh et al.(chap. 15) make the same claims for the role of service activities in the school. Larson et al. (chap. 8) discuss a similar phenomenon for organizations such as the National Future Farmers of America. Finally, Pedersen and Seidman (chap. 5) suggest that the association between participation in organized religious activities and positive youth development may be mediated in part by a sense of connectedness to prosocial institutions and prosocial peer groups.

In summary, the results reported in chapter 2 through chapter 15 confirm the importance of the program characteristics outlined in chapter 1 for positive youth development. Some of the findings, however, remain at a quite general level despite the fact that the authors offer many quite specific hypotheses regarding the likely mechanisms underlying these associations. The next generation of studies needs to focus more on the specifics.

METHODOLOGICAL THEMES AND ISSUES

Looking across the new and reviewed studies and the studies in the chapters in this book, I was struck by the variety in the design features represented. The studies reported or reviewed used methods ranging from (a) in-depth ethnographic studies of small local programs, (b) cross-sectional and longitudinal survey-type studies of youth development across a diverse set of contexts, (c) large- and small-scale experimental program evaluations, (d) descriptive studies of programs considered to be effective by the communities in which they reside, and (e) meta-analyses of both published and nonpublished reports. The new studies reported in chapter 2 through chapter 15 focused mostly on local programs housed in schools or community-based youth centers or programs, or on longitudinal studies of populations of youth who reported their involvement in such extracurricular or community-based programs. This range of research designs reflects both the goals of the researchers, funders, and policymakers, and the current state of our knowledge. The field associated with the scientific study of organized activities as developmental contexts is very new. Research focused on the domain of organized sport is probably the most mature and even it is still in its childhood. Research focused on other domains of organized activities is even less mature. Yet policymakers are calling for advice on which programs to fund. The range of designs represented in this book reflect the tension between doing carefully designed, theoretically driven work that might inform program development and the demand of policymakers to determine if specific programs work or not. I say more about this later.

The studies throughout this book also vary in the types of participants studied and the outcomes assessed. The heterogeneity in the outcomes is particularly striking—ranging from increases in academic achievement, school engagement, mental health, and life skills to decreases in, or avoidance of, such problematic outcomes as teen pregnancy, alcohol and drug use and/or abuse, and involvement in delinquent and violent behaviors. This range represents both the growing importance of the promotive orientations inherent in both positive psychology and positive youth development and the continuing concerns with preventing problem behaviors in our young people. The diversity in the range across studies, however, makes it difficult to compare across studies. What is needed are studies with more comprehensive sets of developmental indicators of the young people's functioning across the multiple domains thought to be influenced by participating in organized activities. It is clear from just the studies in this book that experiences in organized activities are likely to have many different effects on the participants and that these effects depend on multiple characteristics of the activity settings themselves. We would know a lot more if we regularly measured multiple aspects of both the contexts themselves and the developmental functioning of the participants.

The range of populations included in the studies reported in this book is wider than often represented in books published in North America; it includes populations from Sweden and England, as well as populations from both urban and more suburban communities in the United States. A couple of chapters also include youth of color growing up in quite poor urban communities. Nonetheless, the heterogeneity is still not as diverse as it should be given the diversity of youth across the world potentially being influenced by the presence or absence of high quality organized activity settings. The authors have done as much as they can with the studies available to them. Nonetheless, as pointed out so well by Villarruel et al. (chap. 6) and by Pedersen and Seidman (chap. 5), we need studies that examine the issues raised in all of the chapters on the many understudied populations of youth in the United States. There is even a greater need for more studies of youth from different cultures and different regions of the world (Larson & Verma, 1999). The variations in the findings across the populations included in the chapters make it clear that the both the benefits and the costs of participation in different types of organized activities varies across different types of young people. Understanding these variations is essential both for our understanding of the dynamics that govern the influence of these activity experiences and settings on human development and for the design of appropriate organized activities for the many different types of youth in this country.

Now let me turn to a more specific discussion of the methods used along with suggestions for future research.

Qualitative Studies

Larson et al. (chap. 8) illustrate the power of qualitative studies to generate new hypotheses and to help us understand the mechanisms underlying program effects. Larson argues that qualitative studies are essential for theory building, particularly in a field that is still quite new. The importance of the qualitative work by McLaughlin and Heath, reviewed to some extent by Kirshner et al. (chap. 7), is another example of the power of qualitative research and mixed-method research to move our understanding forward (see also McLaughlin, 2000). A variety of techniques are used in these qualitative studies, including techniques that involve the youth themselves as active researchers. Other techniques include the experience-sampling techniques developed by Larson and colleagues, focus groups, participant observation, ethnography, neighborhood mapping, and intensive qualitative interviews with both participants and the adult in the program as supervisors, leaders, teachers, coaches, mentors, and parents.

Quantitative Survey and Longitudinal Studies

Many of the studies reviewed in these chapters relied on either cross-sectional or longitudinal survey-type methods that link participation in organized activities to a variety of different individual level outcomes—typically, indicators of school achievement and engagement, mental health, social development, and involvement in several different types of problem behaviors. The primary goal of such studies is to describe the relation between participation and other individual-level indicators of youth development. Few of the reviewed studies, outside of the field of sports psychology, directly measured characteristics of the programs themselves, making it difficult to know which aspects of the activity setting were responsible for the developmental changes in the participants. Nonetheless, this basic descriptive work is a necessary first step toward firm inferential conclusions.

The reports of several new studies with new analyses in several of the chapters and the work reported in the two sport chapters illustrate what is gained when we focus more directly on the characteristics of the activity settings themselves and when we specify more specifically the mechanisms that might underlie the relation between participating in organized activities and developmental changes in the participants. In these studies, the researchers measured the hypothesized mediators of participation on individual change and then used causal modeling techniques to test these hypo- theses. Such analytic designs tell us more about the plausible "causes" of the any longitudinal changes that might be associated with participation in the activity. For example, in several of the chapters, the researchers used complex analytic strategies with longitudinal studies to test specific hypotheses about the mechanism that might underlie the relations obtained between participation in various types of organized activities and activity settings and both positive and negative developmental outcomes (e.g., the tests of mediation and moderation used in the chapters by Stattin et al., chap. 10, Osgood et al., chap. 3, and Barber et al., chap. 9).

Others used similar methods to test hypotheses regarding individual differences in the impact of particular experiences on developmental changes. As evident in Jacobs et al. (chap. 11), Pedersen and Seidman (chap. 5), McIntosh et al. (chap. 15), Sttatin et al. (chap. 10), Barber et al. (chap. 9), Duda and Ntoumanis (chap. 14), and Scanlan et al. (chap. 13), youth who participate in activities differ among themselves in many ways, ranging from demographic and social characteristics of their families and communities and their own gender to more psychological characteristics such as their identity clarity, achievement goals, initial levels of competence, and the characteristics of their friends and peer group. The results of these new studies demonstrate that the relations of various contextual characteristics of organized activities with a wide variety of developmental changes vary in systematic and theoretically interesting ways across participants.

However, even the more sophisticated longitudinal studies of activities and activities settings are subject to selection concerns. As evident in the chapters by Jacobs et al. (chap. 11), Pedersen and Seidman (chap. 5), McIntosh et al. (chap. 15), and Osgood et al. (chap. 3), youth who participate in various types of activity settings are often fundamentally different than youth who do not. In part, this is a necessary consequence of the fact that participation in these settings or programs is typically voluntary. Nonetheless, these differences make causal inferences about participation effects difficult. Osgood et al. (chap. 3) discuss the utility of fixed effect models as one solution to this problem. Alternatively, because one major concern related to selection effects focuses on the likelihood that associations reflect the impact of unmeasured third variables, some of the longitudinal studies included the most obvious third variables likely to provide an alternative explanation for longitudinal changes. Although this is not evident in the chapters in this book, economists and sociologists are increasingly using instrumental variable techniques to help control for selection effects (Foster & McLanahan, 1996).

Selection issues are also a theoretical concern. As pointed out by Barber et al. (chap. 9), some developmental scientists believe that development is a dynamic, synergistic process. Both choosing to participate in an activity and participating are integral to this process—making it difficult, and perhaps inappropriate, to try to separate the influence of those characteristics that lead to participation from the influence of participating itself. Longitudinal fixed effects models are likely the best strategy to capture the inherent complexity of these developmental processes. Person-centered approaches also offer great promise for investigating such complex synergistic systems. Recent efforts to use more person-centered approaches is proliferating, with much of it being done by authors in this book (e.g., the work by Barber et al., chap. 9, this volume; Bartko & Eccles, 2003; Larson et al., chap. 8, this volume; Mahoney, 2000; Stattin and colleagues, chap. 10, this volume, as well as a new volume by Bergman, Magnusson, & El-Khouri, 2003).

Experimental and Quasi-Experimental Evaluation Studies

Randomized trial experimental studies are often considered to be the best way to test causal hypotheses regarding the impact of experiences on development. With the exception of some of the studies summarized in the two chapters on sports and the randomized welfare reform experiments discussed by Casey et al. (chap. 4), few of the studies reported in chapter 2 through chapter 15 used experimental or quasi-experimental designs. These three chapters clearly illustrate the power of the experimental method for allowing definitive causal inferences. For example, the work summarized in Duda and Ntoumanis (chap. 14) and Scanlan et al. (chap. 13) provides excellent examples of the use of the experimental method to test specific hypotheses about the effects of different types of coaching strategies on young people's experiences in organized sport contexts as well as on the developmental consequences of such experiences. Some of these studies also illustrate the importance of the interaction between contextual characteristics and individual entry level characteristics in determining the likely consequences of participating in organized, competitive sport programs. Finally, some of the studies summarized in these two chapters illustrate the usefulness of training interventions to change the behavior of coaches, thereby changing the experiences of the youth participants. Together these types of studies illustrate the power of a well-development theoretical system to generate well-designed experimental studies to allow the strongest form of causal inference.

The work reviewed by McIntosh et al. (chap. 15) on community service programs also includes experimental studies that demonstrate the effectiveness of this experience on such positive youth developmental outcomes as increased identity clarity, school grades, and commitment to civic engagement in the future, as well as lowered rates of teen pregnancy. However, even in these activity domains, the range of outcomes, experiences, and contextual characteristics assessed and studied is quite limited.

Finally, the work reported by Casey et al. (chap. 4) illustrates a very interesting use of randomized trial policy evaluations. The families in these studies were randomly assigned to either a specific welfare-to-work program or a control group that did not receive the program's package of supports. These families were then studied over time. Information was gathered on both the types of organized activities in which the children participated and a wide array of indicators of development that could be used as outcome variables. The design allowed a definitive conclusion about whether the program had any impact on the participation rates of the children. Then coupling this feature of the design with its longitudinal survey properties, Casey et al. (chap. 4) were able to use the kinds of causal modeling techniques discussed earlier to test hypotheses regarding the impact of participation on the development of these children.

An Alternative View of Best Research Practices

Although experimental and quasi-experimental methods are often considered to be the "gold standard" of research, they can be quite expensive and difficult to implement. In addition, they may not always be the best method to study the impact of participation in organized activities on human development. In my opinion and in the opinion of many of authors in this book, the best methods for studying the impact of organized activity experiences on human development depend on several factors. Most importantly, the best method depends on the question being asked. The best method also depends on the nature of the "thing" being studied. Studies of organized activities can focus several different levels: For example, they could focus on individual activities such a basketball program or a planning activity in a local chapter of the National Future Farmers of America. Alternatively, they could focus on evaluating or studying the impact of participating in the undefined activities at specific centers such as the youth centers in Sweden. Finally, they could focus on evaluating the general impact of participating in a type of organization that exists in many communities (e.g., participating in Boy Scouts, Girl Scouts, or in Boys' Club or Girls' Club). Clearly, organizations such as the youth centers in Sweden and Boys' and Girls' Clubs in the United States contain a wide variety of programs and activities and likely vary in the quality of programming across as well as within sites. The best method of study depends on which of these levels one wants to study as well as the specific questions one wants to answer.

The most comprehensive theories about participation effects typically focus on either the specific nature of the programs or the activities themselves. Most of the chapters in the first two-thirds of this book deal with organized activities at either the individual level or the activity level and most focus on what is going on within those settings that might influence the development of the participants. In addition, most experimental and quasi-experimental studies and program evaluation focus on this level for two major reasons: (a) Programs and activities are simple enough to allow for explicit theories regarding the nature of the impact of the proposed experience on youth development, and (b) programs and activities are small enough to make random assignment to the treatment and control groups possible.

But even studying and evaluating programs within organizations can be quite difficult. Most organized, nonacademic programs are voluntary. Although parents may try to insist that their children attend, their ability to enforce their desires on their children declines as their children move into and through adolescence. In addition, many community organizations for youth include a diverse array of programs from which youth select. Often their selections vary from week to week or day to day, making each individual youth's experiences at the organization quite unique. Furthermore, the quality of their experiences from day to day and from activity to activity within the same center likely varies to a great extent.

Each of these program and organizational characteristics has implications for the experimental study of the impact of participation in organized activities on development. For example, the voluntary nature of many organized programs creates a problem with selection bias at both the entry and continued participation level. The voluntary nature of joining and attending some types of organized programs can lead to sporadic attendance and high rates of dropping out. Consequently researchers are faced with uncontrolled factors that influence attendance. In this case, rigid adherence to random assignment classification in analyzing one's results is likely to underestimate the programs impact for those participants who are actually exposed to it over an extended period of time.

Similarly, the diverse nature of many organized programs for youth makes exact specification of the treatment problematic. Because individuals can select which parts of the program to attend and how often, the researchers often know little about each individual's exposure to various aspects of the center's programming. Such variation makes it difficult to determine which aspects of the programming are responsible for which developmental outcomes. Finally, the evolving nature of many successful organized programs poses problems for the experimental study of "program effects." Experimental methods usually assume a static linear system. Nonexperimental research on youth programs suggests that the most highly respected and well-attended programs are dynamic—shifting, for example, in response to seasonal activity structures, changing clientele, changing staff, and information derived from ongoing reflective practice and self-evaluation, as well as from the youth themselves (McLaughlin, 2000; McLaughlin, Irby, & Langman, 1994).

Given these concerns, it is not surprising then that some of most careful studies of extracurricular and other organized youth development programs use either nonexperimental methods or mixed methods in which small experiments are embedded as part of an action research agenda. Also not surprisingly, some of the strongest experimental evaluations of organized programs for youth have been conducted on school-based programs often offered during the regular school hours. Such approaches come close to the new theory-based models of program evaluation (e.g., Connell, Gambone, & Smith, 2000; Reynolds, 1998). Given this relation, I want to end this chapter with a brief discussion of this approach to studying the impact of such things as organized activities on human development because of its relevance to designing the next generation of basic studies of the impact of participation in organized out-of-school activities on human development.

Theory-based evaluation acknowledges the importance of substantive theory, quantitative assessment, and causal modeling, but it does not require experimental or even quasi-experimental design. Instead it focuses on causal modeling derived from a well-specified theory of change. First, the researchers, usually in collaboration with the program developers, work out a comprehensive model of change that specifies all of the relations (both mediated and moderated relations) among the various contextual characteristics and youth "outcome" characteristics. Often these theoretical models include several layers of hypothesized relations between different aspects of the context as well as between different aspects of the context and youth outcomes. The models lay out a predicted sequence of contextual changes that must occur before one is likely to see changes in youth outcomes. Thus these models propose which contextual features must change first in order to produce changes in other contextual features as well as which contextual features are likely to influence change on which specific youth outcome measures. Finally, these models sometimes specify how characteristics of the youth themselves, as well as of the program personnel, are likely to affect the relations outlined in the general model. For example, the most comprehensive of such models hypothesize differential effectiveness of program characteristics for various groups of youth and program personnel.

Measures are developed and then collected on all of the causal links between contextual or program characteristics and outcome variables. In the best of such designs, these measures are collected over time so that the hypothesized mediational and moderational relations can be tested as the program is implemented. The researchers then use the data collected from these measures to do causal analyses, typically using sophisticated longitudinal data analytic techniques. If the causal modeling analyses indicate that the obtained data are consistent with what the program theory predicts, then the researchers are willing to conclude that the theory is valid and the program is successful for the reasons outlined in the theory.

Very few of the studies reported in the chapters in this book and more generally in the youth program evaluation field use this approach at any more than a superficial level. I believe that we will learn much more about impact of participation in organized activities on human development when we systematically use comprehensive theory-based approaches in both experimental and nonexperimental, longitudinal designs. Finally, to adequately use this approach, it is also essential that we compare the fit of our data with competing theoretical models in order to demonstrate that the model we favor does a better job at explaining the relations obtained than competing theoretical models. Without these comparisons, we really cannot conclude that our model provides the best explanation for the relations obtained.

CONCLUSION

As we move deeper into understanding the impact of out-of-school activities, we will be confronted with the need for greater complexity in our models. This is most evident in the progress that has been made in the sport domain. Like work on school engagement, lots of work has gone into understanding the dynamics of youth sport engagement. This is evident in the chapters by Duda and Ntoumanis (chap. 14) and by Scanlan et al. (chap. 13). The questions being asked in these chapters go beyond those being asked in the other chapters, where the focus is on simpler issues, such as does participation relate to one aspect of positive development such as grades or identity and on a few of the most obvious possible mediators. But as is clear in the sport chapters and is beginning to be clear in some of the other chapters, understanding the impact of participating in any type of activity raises many questions dealing with who participates, how long they participate, why do they participate, what they learn while participating, who continues, and how is opportunity to participate influenced by sociocultural and other more macrolevel forces. How do we design experiences to optimize outcomes and what should we be trying to optimize in these experiences? At one level, we want to know if programs work. But work for what end? At a higher level, we want to test fundamental theories about skill acquisition, human motivation, interpersonal interactions, and the impact of social experiences on motivation and engagement and skill acquisition. These questions require different types of studies and different theoretical perspectives.

The chapters in the final section of this book take a slightly different look at organized activities as developmental contexts. They focus on the broader function of community-based programs. As pointed out by Kleiber and Powell (chap. 2), both the public and policymakers now see organized activities as an important part of the services for children and families in the United States. When done well, organized activities can provide a service to working parents, engage youth positively in school and community, promote positive youth development, and bring cohesion across communities, organizations, and families. Some youth advocates think these types of community programs are our hope for the future (see Eccles & Gootman, 2001; Pittman, 1991; Pittman, Tolman, & Yohalem, chap. 17, this volume; Pittman, Yohalem, & Tolman, 2003; Quinn, 1999). The chapters in the last section discuss these issues with great clarity and provide a framework for policymakers interested in creating and supporting community-based programming for youth. The evidence reviewed in chapter 2 through chapter 15 certainly provides empirical support for the likely benefits of such efforts.

ACKNOWLEDGMENTS

I would like to thank my many colleagues and friends who have helped me understand the role that organized activities play in children's and adolescents' lives. These include, but are not limited to, Bonnie Barber, Margaret Stone, Robert Roeser, Jan Jacobs, Phyllis Blumenfeld, Jenifer Fredricks, Corinne Alfeld-Liro, Reed Larson, Joe Mahoney, Milbrey McLaughlin,

Shirley Bryce Heath, Wayne Osgood, Constance Flannagan, Jim Youniss, Hakan Stattin, Jackie Goodnow, Cathy Cooper, and Barrie Thorne.

REFERENCES

Bartko, W. T., & Eccles, J. S. (2003). Adolescent participation in structured and unstructured activities: A person-oriented analysis. *Journal of Youth and Adolescence, 32,* 233–241.

Bergman, L. R., Magnusson, D., & El-Khouri, B. M. (2003). *Studying individual development in a interindividual context: A person-oriented approach.* Mahwah, NJ: Lawrence Erlbaum Associates.

Connell, J. P., Gambone, M. A., & Smith, T. J. (2000). Youth development in community settings: Challenges to our field and our approach. In P. P. Ventures (Ed.), *Youth development: Issues, challenges and directions* (pp. 281–300). Philadelphia, PA: Public/Private Ventures.

Eccles, J. S., & Gootman, J. A. (2001). *Community programs to promote youth development.* Washington, DC: National Academy Press.

Eccles, J. S., Midgley, C., Wigfield, A., Buchanan, C. M., Reuman, D., Flanagan, C., & MacIver, D. (1993). Development during adolescence: The impact of stage–environment fit on adolescents' experiences in schools and families. *American Psychologist, 48,* 90–101.

Eccles, J. S., & Templeton, J. (2002). Extracurricular and other after-school activities for youth. *Review of Research in Education, 26,* 113–180.

Foster, E. M., & McLanahan, S. (1996). An illustration of the use of instrumental variables: Do neighborhood conditions affect a young person's chance of finishing high school. *Psychological Methods, 1,* 249–260.

Larson, R. W. (2000). Toward a psychology of positive youth development. *American Psychologist, 55,* 170–183.

Larson, R. W., & Verma, S. (1999). How children and adolescents spend time across the world: Work, play, and developmental opportunities. *Psychological Bulletin, 125,* 701–736.

Mahoney, J. L. (2000). Participation in school extracurricular activities as a moderator in the development of antisocial patterns. *Child Development, 71,* 502–516.

McLaughlin, M. W. (2000). *Community counts: How youth organizations matter for youth development.* Washington, DC: Public Education Network.

McLaughlin, M. W., Irby, M. A., & Langman, J. (1994). *Urban sanctuaries: Neighborhood organizations in the lives and future of inner-city youth.* San Francisco: Jossey-Bass.

Pittman, K. (1991). *Promoting youth development: Strengthening the role of youth serving and community organizations.* Washington, DC: USDA Extension Service.

Pittman, K., Yohalem, N., & Tolman, J. (Eds.). (Spring, 2003). When, where, what, and how youth learn: Blurring school and community boundaries. *New Directions in Youth Development.* San Francisco: Jossey-Bass.

Quinn, J. (1999). Where need meets opportunity: Youth development programs for early teens. In R. Behrman (Ed.), *The future of children: When school is out* (pp. 96–116). Washington, DC: The David and Lucile Packard Foundation.

Reynolds, A. J. (1998). Confirmatory program evaluation: A method for strengthening causal inference. *American Journal of Evaluation, 19,* 203–221.

III

Integrating Research, Practice, and Policy

17

Developing a Comprehensive Agenda for the Out-of-School Hours: Lessons and Challenges Across Cities

Karen Pittman
Joel Tolman
Nicole Yohalem
The Forum for Youth Investment, Washington, DC

Over the last ten years, national attention to programs in the out-of-school hours has increased dramatically. With new urgency, individuals at all levels of decision making are calling for safe spaces between the hours of 3 p.m. and 6 p.m., extended opportunities for academic learning, meaningful linkages between school and community, additional services for young people at risk, and improved supports for families with two working parents. Accompanying these calls are significant shifts in public will, public policy, philanthropy, and research.

This chapter summarizes these shifts by describing the current context in which discussions of out-of-school time are occurring. We then lay out a broad vision for thinking about the out-of-school hours, one that revolves around expanded opportunities for learning and development for young people across the developmental trajectory. Finally, the remainder of the chapter addresses how the efforts of a handful of cities across the nation map against this broad vision of out-of-school time. We identify common tasks communities grapple with as they work to improve the local opportunity landscape for young people, and provide concrete examples of how individuals in these communities are addressing these tasks. We draw heavily on our experiences implementing the Greater Resources for After-School Programming project (GRASP), as well as the publications that documented that work (Tolman, Pittman, Yohalem, Thomases, & Trammel, 2002).[1]

THE CONTEXT: A NEW NATIONAL URGENCY

Public will is growing. The public provides a clear mandate for after-school programming, declaring overwhelming support in national polls. For instance, in 2001, 94% of voters polled—up 6% from the previous year—believed that there is a need for some type of organized activity or place where children can go after school every day that provides opportunities to learn. Sixty-seven percent said they were willing to pay $100 in additional state taxes each year to expand after-school programs, up 5% from the previous year (Afterschool Alliance, 2001).

New public dollars are available. A small federal community schools initiative—the 21st Century Community Learning Centers program (21st CCLCs)—has been transformed over the past several years into a billion dollar public–private partnership targeting money for school-based, after-school programs in communities across the country. When combined with other public funding streams—the Child Care and Development Fund and Temporary Assistance to Needy Families (TANF) in particular—this represents an unprecedented federal investment in school-age child care and out-of-school programs. The devolution of 21st CCLCs to the states as part of the federal No Child Left Behind legislation has caused many states to raise after-school on their policy agendas, as well. With the support of the Charles Steward Mott Foundation, a number have begun to develop comprehensive state strategies for after-school funding that move well beyond federal mandates. Thus, even in a funding climate marked by budget deficits, after-school programming remains a priority—marked in California, for instance, by the passage of a major ballot initiative and new forays into high-school after-school funding.

New private dollars are flowing. 21st CCLCs dollars are accompanied by new investments from national and local foundations. A scan of private foundation grant making reveals some important trends. Investments are still categorical—outcome-specific (academic and, to a lesser extent, civic and vocational), time-specific (after school) and age-specific. Foundations like C.S. Mott are once again looking toward major public institutions

---

[1] The Forum for Youth Investment is a national organization committed to increasing the quality and quantity of youth investment and involvement by promoting a "big picture" approach to planning, research, advocacy and policy development among the broad range of organizations that help communities invest in youth. The GRASP project, described in more detail in this chapter, typifies the documentation and capacity building work of the Forum.

(parks, schools, libraries) as delivery systems for out-of-school programming, after mixed success in building the infrastructure of community-based providers. At the same time, foundations are recognizing increased investments in out-of-school time as a way to advance long-standing commitments—the Carnegie Corporation, the Annenberg Foundation, and others with school reform; the C. S. Mott Foundation with community schools; and the Open Society Institute with an urban renewal focus (Pittman, 2000). It also appears that a growing number of foundations—The Wallace-Reader's Digest Funds[2] and Irvine Foundations, for instance—are demonstrating renewed or sustained willingness to make place-based, out-of-school investments (Forum for Youth Investment, 2002, Summer).

New research is fueling the movement. Research on out-of-school programs—called for by "A Matter of Time," the Carnegie Council on Adolescent Development's landmark 1992 report on out-of-school opportunities—is coming into its own. The work of institutions like the Chapin Hall Center for Children, Stanford University's John Gardner Center for Youth and Their Communities, and the MacArthur Task Force on Middle Childhood are focusing new attention on out-of-school programming. The evaluation of the 21st CCLCs program is one of a number of major national evaluation efforts shedding new light on the impact and status of programming. The Harvard Family Research Project (2000) has identified major out-of-school "evaluations to watch" and has observed enough momentum to justify the creation of an online database of out-of-school time program evaluations. Perhaps most important, the National Research Council and Institute of Medicine (2002) issued "Community Programs to Promote Youth Development," a comprehensive research review that marshals existing data to underscore the critical role of community-based programs in young people's learning and development.

These forces have created a long overdue opportunity to build a solid infrastructure for supports during the out-of-school hours. However, it is unclear whether they are sufficiently powerful to knit together a patchwork delivery system weakened by two persistent challenges: fragmentation and insufficient funding. Diverse funding sources, each with its own target population and outcome focus, have created a patchwork system of services. Much of the funding for elementary-age children comes through the child-care door. Funding for middle-school youth is often provided in the name of supervision, problem prevention, and remediation. Funding for older youth tends to be attached to prevention, remediation, diversion, and employment efforts (Newman, Smith, & Murphy, 1999).

Inadequate and unstable funding has compounded the fragmentation problem. Programs trying to deliver a broad base of out-of-school opportuni-

---

[2]The Wallace-Reader's Digest Funds changed their name to The Wallace Foundation in 2003.

ties for young people have not only had to cobble funding together across multiple funding streams; they have had to do this on an annual basis, responding to an unpredictable set of external opportunities and priorities. The result has been a lack of investment in infrastructure. Few programs have gone to scale. Even fewer communities have a comprehensive plan for developing services and supports to meet the needs of young residents.

Fragmentation and inadequate funding are serious challenges. But narrow visions may be the most serious threats to capitalizing on the enormous public and political will focused on out-of-school time.

THE VISION: EXPANDED OPPORTUNITIES FOR LEARNING AND DEVELOPMENT

What would expanded opportunities for learning and development look like, in the context of the everyday lives of individual children and youth? Where would these opportunities take place? How would they connect with schools and families? How would those opportunities look different across the developmental trajectory? Our vision, depicted through fictional snapshots of two young people we call Samantha and Delonte, looks something like this:

At age 10, Samantha, like many others her age, looks forward to the end of the school day. It's not that she doesn't like school; in fact, her after lunch class has gotten much more interesting since the staff of a local museum and an arts program started coming in to work with her teacher, Ms. Ellis, toward the end of the day. But Samantha does look forward to the afternoons. She knows the routine, and likes it. Tuesdays and Thursdays, student tutors from her neighborhood high school come to her school to work with her on reading and writing. Wednesday, she and several other students visit the retirement community nearby the school, where they're creating a collection of stories about the experiences of older community members. Mondays and Fridays, she chooses between an arts workshop and a nature walk in a local park, both led by organizations in the community. Whatever day it is, she knows that she's going to spend her afternoon with an adult who knows her well, in a place she feels safe, doing something where she gets to move around and do something interesting. Her parents know, too, that the programs are flexible enough to work with the changes in their work schedule.

At 17, Delonte is an articulate speaker and a talented performer, almost always wearing a warm smile. Though slow to admit it, he is enjoying his first semester as a high-school senior. In his Monday morning meeting with his advisor, conversations about the play he is reading in his literature seminar, his performance the following weekend with a local youth-led theater company, and his college applications flow seamlessly together. His advisor and his drama coach are usually the ones who help him connect the pieces—school work, out-of-school activities, his dreams for the future—though increasingly, he's learning to make those connections for himself.

There are certainly a lot of things to connect. Monday afternoon he gets to experience college firsthand in a dual enrollment class. On Tuesday, his after-school leadership club visits with the candidates running for open school board seats; he is able to use his communication skills to interview two of the candidates and will be working with his friend, Steve, during the next week to prepare a brochure summarizing where each candidate stands on issues youth care about. Wednesday and Thursday are his busiest days—he goes to the local YMCA to teach dance after school, followed by play rehearsals. By Friday, he is grateful to have an afternoon off to spend with friends, and to pull the pieces of his week together before the play goes on that weekend.

Integrated, developmentally appropriate, engaging experiences like those we imagine for Samantha and Delonte do not occur coincidentally. Ensuring that all children and young people have the opportunities and supports they need requires a great deal.

It requires the development a sufficient quantity of programs and opportunities, provided at a high level of quality, that are connected with one another to ensure K–12 continuity. This, in turn, requires sufficient capacity and resources—facilities that are safe and supportive, funds that do not dry up, organizations with the strength to build outstanding opportunities. Ensuring adequate resources and capacity depends on a broad climate of support that includes leadership, vision, demand from the public, and shared accountability. Together, all of this demands parents, schools, community organizations, city governments, advocates, young people themselves, and dozens of other stakeholders working in concert. But again, the most basic need is for a clearer picture of what young people need and can do.

Naming and Framing the Developmental Imperative

If we are going to make progress in providing the supports that young people need during the out-of-school hours, we first need a shared sense of what we are talking about. Over the last 20 years, youth advocates have made solid progress in advancing three critical concepts that have now gained widespread acceptance. These three concepts help define what we mean by "the developmental imperative":

Young people need and deserve supports throughout their waking hours. In early childhood the charge is clear. Infants and young children need constant care and attention. Leaving them alone for several hours is seen as negligence. As young people grow, they reach an age when they should have time by themselves. Still, out of sight does not mean out of mind. Parents work hard to ensure that their children have safe places to go and supportive people to be with. Children and youth are influenced at all hours of the day.

Young people deserve early and sustained investments throughout the first 20 years of life. Although research suggests that some ages witness particularly crucial stages of development, all ages are critical. Investing in early childhood is necessary but not sufficient; there is no way to sufficiently "inoculate" children so they will be immune to later developmental challenges and tasks (Pittman, Irby, Tolman, Yohalem, & Ferber, 2002). Development is ongoing, and does not stop because program funds run out or because young people reach a certain age.

Young people need investments to help them achieve a broad range of outcomes. For young people, academic success is critical, but it is not enough. Although they may not use these terms, young people and their families realize that becoming fully prepared for adulthood also requires vocational, physical, emotional, social, and civic development.

It is the basic logic of these three statements that makes them powerful. From the time that young people are small until they are fully grown, they wake up every morning looking for things to do, people to talk to, and places to be and explore. The more intentional communities and governments are about helping families provide these people, places, and possibilities—not only in the preschool years but throughout childhood and adolescence—the better the child and youth outcomes.

The Cube: A Simple Way to Frame the Vision

Take these three ideas—*times, ages, outcomes*—and make them the axes of a cube see Fig. 17.1). Creating a cube defines a space to be filled—a space for which all who touch the lives of young people, either directly or indirectly, share responsibility.

With the cube in hand, we can begin to tell interesting stories about the ways we support young people. Take early childhood, for instance. A concerted effort by foundations, researchers, and advocates over the past 10 years has bolstered common sense. Young children need a range of opportunities and services throughout their waking hours that address a variety of developmental needs. Public funding for early childhood supports is far from adequate. Yet there is a broad understanding that young children need this range of supports (National Association of Child Advocates, 2000). As children move out of their early years, schools become the dominant institution in their lives. But schools tend to focus on only a subset of the competency areas (primarily academic), hours of the day (primarily 8 a.m. to 3 p.m.) and ages (primarily age 5 to age 18).

This relatively narrow role of schools presents two constant challenges: First, advocates, researchers, and educators need to consider how schools can aid in youth development more broadly—how, for instance, schools can intentionally aid young people's social and emotional development, or help them take on roles as capable citizens. Second, we also need to recognize that schools cannot do everything in the limited hours in which they work

WHAT FILLS THE SPACE?

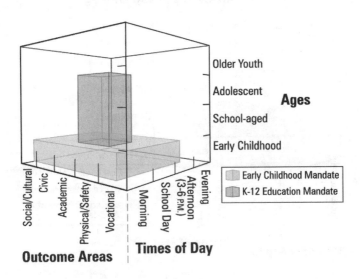

FIG. 17.1. What fills the space?

with students. What is the "gel" that surrounds schools? How do we think about the space surrounding the school day as a whole?

Unfortunately, the current national discussion of "out-of-school time" focuses primarily on the goal of creating more after-school programs. Many of the largest funding streams and programs are focused on the hours directly after the school day, students primarily in elementary school (and, increasingly, middle school), and outcomes directly related to academic competence and physical safety. During other hours, funding and programming are considerably less robust (see Fig. 17.2). Young people have few options during their mornings, evenings, weekends, and summers. Opportunities and supports tend to phase out as young people leave early adolescence. Perhaps most importantly, those services, opportunities, and supports that are available lack coherence, connection, and continuity. Even in neighborhoods and cities where much is going on outside of school hours, little is being done to link programming into a continuous, intentional web of support (Tolman et al., 2002).

THE REALITY: AN UNEVEN COMMITMENT

How typical are the experiences of Samantha and Delonte? How are communities doing in relation to the idea of a broader picture of out-of-school time?

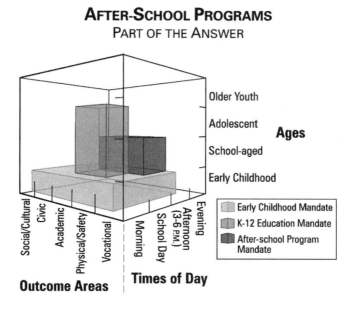

FIG. 17.2.   After-school programs—part of the answer.

Unfortunately, the reality is fairly grim. Some hours are empty. Some age groups have remarkably few opportunities. Some important outcomes are consistently neglected. The experiences of four cities involved in the GRASP project confirm these generalizations and underscore particularly critical gaps in the supports available to young people when they are not in school.

The GRASP Project

Recognizing the critical role of community-level change in moving an out-of-school time agenda, the Forum for Youth Investment began the GRASP project with support from the Charles Stewart Mott Foundation. Through GRASP, the Forum helped four cities—Chicago, Kansas City, Little Rock, and Sacramento—assess their current work and deepen community discussions about the out-of-school opportunities that should be available to young people. GRASP had three closely connected goals:

1. *To develop tools that broaden local and national conversations from after-school programs to out-of-school opportunities.* The Forum embarked on the project believing that after-school programs are critical, but only part of the bigger picture of what young people are doing throughout their waking hours, from early childhood through late adolescence, to achieve a

range of positive outcomes. We worked with communities to understand and use this bigger picture.

2. *To partner with several cities to take a snapshot of their out-of-school landscapes.* GRASP was an effort to map local activities and document local stories—aiming to both inform national policy and support other communities as they make new commitments to out-of-school programming. Rather than collecting the data and writing case studies ourselves, the Forum offered resources to local agencies to marshal existing information and fill gaps with new data collection efforts when necessary in order to create a rough picture of the programming available to young people. City partners also profiled innovative initiatives and identified the most important tasks and challenges facing their efforts.

3. *To engage communities in a time-limited planning process, using better information to rally stakeholders and make better decisions about the out-of-school hours.* GRASP also acted as a light community organizing process. Although the process varied across the cities, Forum staff generally traveled to each city twice to participate in a series of meetings, bringing together a range of public and private players to participate in a "big picture" discussion, share the results of data collection, and discuss challenges and opportunities facing the city. Out of these meetings and the relationships that the GRASP process facilitated emerged a number of new commitments, partnerships, and possible steps forward. While its goals were broad, GRASP was a time-limited, focused project. It was not a long-term technical assistance effort. Nor was it a major research or evaluation endeavor. It was an opportunity to support local planning, to test some new ways of thinking and to understand how the after-school movement is playing out in particular places.

Across the four cities involved in the GRASP project, several clear patterns related to young people and out-of-school time emerged:

During many times of the day, in many communities and neighborhoods, there is little or nothing for young people to do. Findings from "A Matter of Time" were important in raising awareness about adolescent time use. "... about 40 percent of young people's waking hours are discretionary—not committed to other activities ... Many young adolescents spend virtually all of this discretionary time without companionship or supervision from responsible adults" (Carnegie Council on Adolescent Development, 1992, p. 28). Although the after-school movement has created opportunities during some of this discretionary time, during other hours—weekends, evenings, summers—young people continue to have few options and opportunities. In Sacramento, for example, 87% of organizations reported running programs Monday through Friday, while only 13% operated on the weekend. In Little Rock, no program surveyed reported that it operated 7 days a week during the school year, and only one indicated that it is open 6 days a week (Tolman et al., 2002). Yet all of young people's waking hours—not just those directly after school—represent an opportunity for learning and development.

The number of organized opportunities for young people in the out-of-school hours actually decreases as they grow older. A three-community study by Public/Private Ventures found that while two thirds of 13- to 15-year-olds report that they had constructive things to do in their out-of-school hours, only one half of 16- to 17-year-olds and one third of 18- to 19-year-olds report being engaged. Despite the lack of opportunities, young people reported they were looking for things to do and asking for more adult interaction (Sipe & Ma [with Gambone], 1998). In Little Rock, although the number of programs that serve middle- and high-school youth is larger than the number open to younger children, the largest programs tend to focus on the elementary grades and therefore the actual number of spaces available inside of programs for older youth decreases (Tolman et al., 2002). Nationally, more than one half of teens wish there were more community or neighborhood-based programs available after school, and two thirds of those surveyed said they would participate in such programs if they were available (YMCA of the USA, 2001).

Investments in academics and in problem prevention outstrip commitments to other youth outcomes. The amount that communities invest in young people's preparation and participation pales in comparison to dollars spent on prevention and punishment (Newman et al., 1999). By adolescence, especially late adolescence, funding for youth programs outside of school often comes into communities almost exclusively attached to mandates to prevent or address problems and punish delinquents (Coleman Advocates for Children and Youth, 1994). Even the expansion of dollars for after-school programming is attributable to the strong link made to crime reduction and academic remediation (Forum for Youth Investment, 2002). Simultaneously, concern about academic achievement overshadows interest in other areas of development. It is absolutely critical that young people develop the cognitive skills needed to function in the 21st century, but there is ample evidence that (a) academic success is connected to physical, vocational, civic, emotional, and social development (National Research Council, 2002); and (b) interest in building academic skills can often be fostered by focusing on the strengths or interests young people have in other areas (Melaville, Shah, & Blank, 2002). Yet some outcomes—civic outcomes in particular—are being crowded out or overlooked in many after-school and out-of-school programs (Tolman et al., 2002).

Tackling Challenges at the Community Level

If this reality is to improve significantly, it will almost certainly be because of shifts in the opportunity landscape at the community level. Communities are where the "rubber hits the road," where supports and opportunities are or are not available, where young people are or are not being fully prepared for adult life and fully engaged in meaningful work, learning, and contribution. Communities are also where innovative responses to persistent challenges bubble to the surface. Moreover, communities are where diverse agendas, funding streams, policy realities and societal forces join to shape young people's pathways through development.

Like young people's own growth, the process by which cities come to support young people is a developmental one. Localities face a common set of "tasks" in which they must progress in order to grow a mature system of out-of-school supports. As with youth development, attention to all of the developmental tasks is critical. The communities involved in the GRASP Project came to the out-of-school issue from remarkably different starting points. Yet when the Forum asked individuals in very different cities what it would take to provide meaningful out-of-school opportunities for all young people, a remarkably consistent set of tasks emerged. Although no list is definitive or complete, reflecting on city level conversations that took place during the GRASP project, we now identify nine specific tasks that cluster into three broad challenges.

Challenge 1: Creating a Strong Base of High-Quality Programs

For out-of-school programs to support learning and development, they must embody a vision of quality rooted in what we know about development. Just as critical as quality of individual programs is the availability of a sufficient quantity of programs as well as continuity within and across programs. Access to a coherent web of supports is a critical factor in young people's development. Three tasks are essential to achieving this.

Defining and Delivering Quality. As cities make substantial investments in providing out-of-school opportunities at scale, an increasing number are ready for serious discussions about how to ensure that programs are of high quality—that is, that they live up to high standards of practice and deliver on the outcomes that they claim they will achieve. This is a particularly ripe moment for cities to embark on the process of defining quality standards. There is growing consensus among those who study and evaluate program quality about the features of effective programs.[3] At the same time, the new report from the National Research Council (2002), "Community Programs to Promote Youth Development," clearly defines the features of environments that support young people's development.

Cities that build on these strong foundations and define standards that reflect what research says about youth development move a long way toward building out-of-school program quality. Further, communities that want their standards to last and reflect local needs are involving a range of stakeholders in their development. In Kansas City, for example, young people and providers drove the process. In Chicago, funders, community-based organizations and city government are all at the table. Nearly all of the resulting standards address a set of central issues related to organizational capacity, program characteristics, staffing, health and safety, and family involvement. The existing standards speak less frequently (with notable exceptions) to the importance of meaningful youth engagement in programs or involving community members and resources in programs.

City Snapshot: Building Quality Standards for Teen Programs in Kansas City

A growing number of cities are beginning to develop standards documents relevant to adolescents—requiring a different process and different content than when standards have been developed for elementary school-age programs. One critical difference: Young people must be at the table for the standards to be relevant to their needs and experiences. YouthNet of Greater Kansas City, a network of youth-serving organizations with a history as a capacity building intermediary, was among the first to take on the challenge of developing teen-program standards. The process involved the development of teen surveys distributed in schools, brainstorming sessions on what makes a good program, and the review of national program resources on teens. Based on information collected, a draft of teen standards was created. This draft was disseminated to agency representatives and teenagers for their input and review. YouthNet believes that by involving both youth and agency members, it has created not only a quality assessment tool of the standards of teen programs, but also a philosophical shift—because of the participation of youth in the process.

Although the standards discussion can come to dominate the quality discussion, holding programs accountable requires a significant investment in capacity building support. Such investments have been shown to pay off, as in the San Francisco Bay Area, where a year-long investment in organizational improvement resulted in programs that much more frequently deliver critical supports and opportunities to young people (see City Snapshot on p. 389).

---

[3]A February 2002 meeting hosted by the Forum for Youth Investment, High/Scope Educational Research Foundation, and Youth Development Strategies Inc., brought together a range of experts on youth program quality to identify the emerging common ground across assessment tools, models, and approaches.

Holding programs accountable also requires assessment and evaluation capacity—currently limited in most communities. Although a handful of national organizations are beginning to support small-scale evaluation work, there is much more capacity-building to be done in this area.

Ensuring Quantity. Ensuring that an adequate number of out-of-school opportunities is available is a major issue for most communities, but quantity also speaks to a subtler set of concerns that often determine access and use. Increasing quantity means not only increasing the sheer number of slots, but expanding the hours (beyond 3 p.m. to 6 p.m. into evenings, weekends, and summers), expanding geography to underserved and isolated neighborhoods and schools, increasing the range of settings in order to draw on a broad array of participants in communities, and increasing outreach to underserved populations—those academically, physically, or socially at risk, those in vulnerable families, teens, and out-of-school youth.

Creating Continuity. Looking at out-of-school programs from a developmental perspective also affirms the importance of continuity—across ages, across times of day, and across the settings in which young people find themselves. Continuity involves linking to the range of other supports and opportunities present in a community—realizing, in short, a vision of after-school programs as bridges that connect various aspects of young people's lives, or what Noam, Biancarosa, and Dechausay (2002) called "intermediary environments." Out-of-school programs are part of a web of supports for young people's learning and development, and can serve a critical role in building connections and continuity across that range of learning experiences (see City Snapshot below).

City Snapshot: Building a Ladder of Participation in Chicago

"I would want to build a ladder of opportunity for kids—across places and times and ways of contributing. We should provide opportunities for youth that move from participation, to contribution, to access to internships and meaningful first jobs (Forum for Youth Investment, 2002, Summer)." Wynn (2002), a researcher at the Chapin Hall Center for Children in Chicago, explains the big idea behind After School Matters—a new public–private partnership in Chicago aiming to reach half of the city's high school-aged young people with quality out-of-school programs by the year 2012. The core of After School Matters is a set of sports, arts, writing, and technology programs operated by clusters of schools, parks, and libraries, and based on a successful arts apprenticeship model pioneered by Gallery 37. But creating the sort of continuity that

Wynn (2000) and others imagine requires weaving together a variety of strategies to support this core program. Wynn describes one—a way for young people to recognize and reflect on their experiences:

> Whether taking care of siblings or painting and repairing a house over the summer, they ought to get recognition for that ... We're creating a Web-enabled portfolio and resume builder that's meant to engage kids in a highly supportive coaching process ... that recognizes what kids do across the spectrum of their out-of-school lives—this is what I do at home, in the community, through service learning, internships and jobs. It will be a personal record for any 13- to 21-year-old that will capture what they've done, and the knowledge, skills and personal qualities they've demonstrated in the process (p. 4).

Realizing this vision of continuity requires addressing a number of questions. Are programs connected to young people's experiences before they attend (during the school day) and afterward (evenings with families, or perhaps other programs for older youth)? Do they reach down to the environments where young people spent time at younger ages, and up to the environments where young people find themselves when they "age out"? Do they create a "ladder of opportunity," in the words of Joan Wynn, within their programs—ensuring a progression of experiences and leadership opportunities over time? Do they create intentional links to other places where young people spend their time? Do they, in short, add up to part of a larger whole, across time, ages, and settings?

Challenge 2: Building a City Level Infrastructure

Investments in capacity are needed at the program and city levels—in quality staffing, program standards, and organizational horsepower—strategies aligned with what it takes to support youth development and learning. This capacity requires additional resources, financial and physical, that are aligned with developmental realities, sustained over time, and sufficient to support quality programming.

Building Capacity. Program level capacity means adequate, stable, well-trained staff and well-run programs and organizations. It is important to ask if staff and organizational development efforts are consistently aligned with a picture of quality that puts young people's development at the center, and is linked to ongoing assessments of how well programs are responding to those developmental needs. A range of perennial staffing challenges—high turnover, in particular—take on heightened importance when viewed through a developmental lens. Retention challenges, often conceived primarily as a logistical and training issue, are paramount when continuity, positive adult relationships, and stable environments are understood as critical program elements. Recent work by researchers Michelle Gambone and Jim Connell, in partnership with Community Network for Youth Development (CNYD), has linked a number of such organizational and staff capacity issues with their list of key supports and opportunities—for instance, low staff to student ratios are a key indicator of whether it's possible to have caring adult relationships (see City Snapshot below).

City Snapshot: Using Standards to Build Capacity in San Francisco

A unique collaboration between researchers Michelle Gambone and Jim Connell, a local intermediary called Community Network for Youth Development, San Francisco Bay Area community-based organizations, and local funders is proving that some things do work to improve program quality. The eight participating organizations agreed to take part in an intentional effort to provide the basic supports and opportunities that young people need: caring relationships, challenging experiences, high expectations, and the like.

The process takes place over the course of a full year. Woven throughout is an exploration of the Youth Development Framework for Practice as a model against which youth workers and organizational leaders reflect on their current practice. There are seven steps to the assessment process:

1. *Survey Youth.* Simple surveys give agencies a baseline measurement for the degree to which youth experience the key supports and opportunities within their program.
2. *Share the Data.* Sharing the data with youth and staff provides an opportunity for discussion about what the program is doing well and what needs improvement.
3. *Assess Organizational Practices.* Assessing practices helps an organization identify what they are doing well and what can be improved and then set priorities for improvement strategies.
4. *Determine Resources.* Identify time, people, spaces, and funds needed to implement the strategy.
5. *Set Targets for Improvement.* Set goals for increasing the number of youth having an optimal experience and decreasing the number of youth having an insufficient experience.
6. *Implement Improvement Strategies and Assess Their Impact.* Put plans for improvement into action and periodically check in with youth and staff to get feedback and make refinements.

> 7. *Readminister the Youth Survey.* After 1 year, survey youth again and
> begin a new cycle of program improvement.
>
> Data from the first round of surveys indicated that many organizations
> were not providing as many of the supports and opportunities as they
> wanted to. In response, CNYD, in collaboration with Gambone, worked
> with the organizations to increase their capacity to deliver supports and
> opportunities. One year later, youth rated their organizations at higher
> levels—sometimes markedly so—across many of the categories.

Identifying Resources.   Even in the context of growing public and private investments throughout the second half of the 1990s, in no city are
funds sufficient to reach all young people with quality out-of-school opportunities. With an economic slowdown putting the brakes on private and
public investments, and world events shifting funders' attention, cities are
struggling against retrenchment and struggling to make ends meet.

Working within the context of scarce resources, each GRASP city has
cobbled together a diverse set of investments and policies in order to provide
programming and build the infrastructure to support that programming.
This local entrepreneurship has resulted in significant innovations: dedicated resource streams, novel use of TANF dollars, and investments that
combine desegregation dollars, 21st CCLC funds, private investments, and
local public funds into a coherent whole (Langford, 2001; Tolman et al.,
2002). But such creativity has also resulted in uneven investments, missed
opportunities, and idiosyncratic programming. Many cities simply do not
know what resources they could tap into (e.g., Workforce Investment Act
dollars and prevention resources are underutilized). And few communities
have a sense of how the multiple investments—parks dollars, programs run
out of the mayor's office, and foundation investments, among many others—add up or align. Several themes emerge from an examination of the
multiple funding streams converging on out-of-school programming:

- Categorical funding continues to be a key obstacle to alignment and
  innovation.
- Public investments are essential to meeting the demand for programming, and private investments cannot hope to compensate for public
  disinvestment.
- Private foundation dollars are critical in supporting innovation, infrastructure, and young people who fall through the cracks.
- Few cities are fully leveraging the range of federal funding streams
  that could be used to support out-of-school programming.

Transportation and facilities are two specific resource challenges cities face as they attempt to build systems to support children and youth during the out-of-school hours. GRASP participants told stories of parks facilities that go unused because of insufficient funds for maintenance and staffing. Others indicated that gentrification and demographic shifts have moved young people out of neighborhoods where facilities are located—creating a construction and transportation headache. Most cities are trying to overcome the infrastructure and political challenges that come with opening up school buildings and other public facilities outside their normal hours of operation. Most are barely putting together a combination of public transportation—sometimes almost nonexistent in midsized cities—and school buses that are already stretched to the limits. Furthermore, all agreed that some facilities—churches and museums, for instance—are not yet playing the role they might.

City stakeholders also told stories of innovation in the face of transportation and facilities challenges. They spoke of cities converting vacant school buildings into community centers, young people leading advocacy efforts for reduced bus fares, organizations coordinating the use of a range of community facilities—including churches and businesses—with the aim of having spaces open to young people on every block. Through a combination of such efforts, some cities are beginning to make real progress on the facilities and transportation front (see City Snapshot below).

City Snapshot: Re-Creating Recreation in Detroit

In the early 1990s, few of Detroit's young people were showing up to the city's recreational centers and after-school programs—just as increasingly compelling research demonstrated that engagement in such programming helped young people avoid problem behaviors and achieve positive outcomes. One principle cause of low participation, according to research commissioned by the Skillman Foundation: The city's recreation infrastructure was in disrepair. Changes in the city's demographics meant that recreation centers were not available in many of the communities with the most young people. Many facilities were built prior to 1960 and required substantial investments in maintenance. Young people complained about stopped-up toilets and graffiti in locker rooms. A lack of indoor facilities meant that programs during the winter were particularly scarce (Skillman Foundation, 1995).

Responding to these findings, Skillman collaborated with other funders to create a unique public–private partnership—the Youth

Sports and Recreation Commission—to support facilities improvement and a variety of other infrastructure-building efforts. Because of a major up-front investment in research and relationship-building between city government and private foundations, the effort has shown impressive results. By 1999, the Commission helped raise funds to renovate 33 parks, spearheaded the major recapitalization of four recreation centers, and built significant support for broader use of school facilities (Davis, 1999).

Challenge 3: Creating a Climate Conducive to Action and Investment

Sustained demand—supported by diverse, engaged constituencies, including young people themselves—makes investments in out-of-school programs possible. Leadership—individual and organizational, from a range of sectors—complements this grassroots demand. Systems of accountability—information and data systems, ways of monitoring and encouraging progress toward common standards and goals—are also part of a climate that supports opportunities for development and learning.

Sustaining Public Will. When Traub (2000) of *The New York Times* wrote that "parents should be more worried about how youth spend their time outside of school than inside of school" (p. 52), his words matched the tenor and tone of public sentiment around the country. The media's continued warnings about unsupervised youth, policymakers' weariness with the pace of school reform, and families' growing challenges in addressing the needs of their children for supervision and stimulation are the conditions that set the stage for a national after-school movement. Public will is remarkably strong, as illustrated by the polling data mentioned in the beginning of this chapter.

The challenge for cities, then, is not primarily to build general commitment. Their task, instead, is to focus, leverage, sustain and mobilize the strong but often vague commitment that already exists.

- *Focus.* Perhaps the most critical challenge facing advocates is to broaden public will—now strongly behind after-school programs— to support opportunities throughout young people's development and waking hours, focusing on civic, vocational, social, and physical development as well as academic achievement. At the same time, advocates should be careful not to reinforce widespread negative perceptions of youth as they build the case for out-of-school investments.

- *Leverage.* By aligning inside advocacy strategies (building support among elected officials, building capacity inside government to move an agenda) and outside strategies (grassroots youth and citizen engagement), advocates can create the context for real change. Advocates can also learn to leverage communities' existing commitments—to school reform or civil rights, for instance—to fuel public will for out-of-school programming.
- *Sustain.* In the context of national crises and other front-burner issues, it would be easy for the momentum of the after-school movement to fade as quickly as it has grown. The goal of advocates should be to build the same consistent, lasting support for out-of-school opportunities that public education now appreciates.
- *Mobilize.* Advocacy is not, in the end, about commitment and awareness; it is about participation and action. The growing number of organizing efforts rallying around out-of-school issues points the way—build the power of young people, community members, and community-based organizations, and support for out-of-school opportunities will be secure in the long haul.

A variety of organizations and constituencies play roles in building this commitment. Parent and community organizing efforts, local education funds, child advocacy organizations, and agency alliances are all natural starting points for the sort of engagement described. Young people themselves are perhaps the most powerful advocates for investments in development and learning and have been critical to successful campaigns for program quality standards, better facilities, accessible transportation, and increased investments in programming in cities around the country (Tolman et al., 2002).

Building Information Systems. Effective city-level systems for mapping and tracking activities during the out-of-school hours are few and far between. In many cities, only the roughest estimates of the number of programs, or number of dollars invested, are available. Obtaining information about the quality of programs—the degree to which the programs support young people's development and learning—is much more difficult. Most cities lack both the research "horsepower" necessary to build credible information systems, and the systems for ensuring that programs are held accountable based on existing information. At the same time, robust information systems are critical for parents and young people seeking quality programs, for public institutions and foundations making funding decisions, for program providers and planners trying to improve the quality of their work, and for advocates trying to build public will for increased and re-directed investments (see City Snapshot on p. 394).

City Snapshot: Chicago's Chapin Hall Center for Children

Most cities have limited research horsepower relevant to out-of-school programming. But incorporating a research presence in a city's program development, implementation and evaluation can add to the information and ideas available at every stage. Chicago has had the benefit of such a research presence in the form of Chapin Hall Center for Children at the University of Chicago.

In the late 1980s, Chapin Hall researchers developed a framework for reconfiguring services and supports for children and youth. The Chicago Community Trust adopted this framework for a major initiative in 1990, committing $30 million over 10 years. Researchers provided technical assistance to seven organizations as they implemented the framework, documenting the progress and problems of the initiative.

In the mid-1990s, Chapin Hall researchers were commissioned by the Wallace-Reader's Digest Funds to evaluate the Making the Most of Out-of-School Time (MOST) initiative in three cities—Boston, Seattle and Chicago. The outside view provided by Chapin Hall researchers was particularly useful in looking across institutional jurisdictions to create a more systematic approach to out-of-school services in each of the participating cities. Chapin Hall's MOST evaluation continues to provide guidance to other cities that are trying to implement a systems approach to improving program quality and access.

Currently, Chapin Hall is working with the After School Matters initiative in Chicago. Working with the program developers early on, researchers are developing a dual-purpose research agenda to run in parallel with the program. The aim of this applied research is to directly inform the operation of the program and, at the same time, to address basic issues of interest to the constituencies involved in youth development in the out-of-school hours.

Engaging Local Leaders.   Municipal and community leaders—whether they gained their position through election, appointment, or more organic community processes—have been critical in moving out-of-school agendas in cities around the country. Roles range from vocal supporter, to consistent funder, to initiator of new departments and initiatives, to coalition and consensus builder. In addition to top-level elected and civic leaders, city agencies and their directors, community organization and intermediary leaders, members of the business community and neighborhood organizers can all help focus public attention and community resources on out-of-school issues. Neighborhood-level coordinating and leadership bodies, whether informal or formal, are just as critical as mayoral support in moving toward high-quality supports for young people. Wherever the leadership comes from, the capacity to move resources, broker connections, bring people around a common table, and enact strategy is critical.

> It takes a multifaceted approach. There is no easy formula—you need to have all the pistons running at the same time. Juggling all the balls simultaneously creates the tidal wave. You need to create the wave then catch it. Align politics and grassroots advocacy. Set up a department focused on all kids. Promote youth voice. Build communities and their nonprofits. Create a cadre of like-minded individuals throughout the bureaucracies. (Forum for Youth Investment, Summer 2002).
>
> Debbie Alvarez-Rodriguez
> City of San Francisco
> (p. 3)

Sharpening the Vision. Increasing support for out-of-school development and learning opportunities will require shifts in leadership, demand, and accountability. But the linchpin, in our opinion, is the vision—especially when it comes to linking development and academic achievement. Getting a foothold on expanding opportunities in the out-of-school hours will require crafting a fundamentally new vision of what learning is, when and where it happens, and how and by whom it is intentionally supported and monitored. Although there is broad public agreement that something should be happening in the out-of-school hours, ideas about what should be happening still need sharpening.

CONCLUSION

As is the case with human development, these basic challenges are interdependent and complementary. And as it is with human development, the development of out-of-school time systems is uneven. There are perhaps a handful of cities nationally with somewhat "mature" infrastructures, a second tier that are asking the right questions but still struggling to find the answers, and another set that have not begun nurturing the development of an out-of-school time system. Cities ahead in addressing some tasks are far behind in others, and progress toward one task does not guarantee equal progress in others. As one moves away from major cities to suburbs and particularly to rural areas, the likelihood of encountering a mature system decreases.

Together, these trends, challenges and stories present a daunting picture. Communities—even those who have demonstrated the most commitment and innovation—have a great deal of work ahead. However, the landscape is promising. A groundswell of activity has resulted in genuine progress on many of the critical tasks in a number of communities. Viable solutions and strategies are being incubated and field-tested. When linked to public and private investments, a coherent national support structure, and local commitment, these community-based innovations can begin to spread and take root, increasing and enhancing opportunities for young people during out-of-school time.

REFERENCES

Afterschool Alliance. (2001, July/August). *Afterschool alert poll report number 4: A report on findings of a nationwide poll of registered voters on afterschool programs*. Washington, DC: Author.

Carnegie Council on Adolescent Development. (1992). *A matter of time: Risk & opportunity in the nonschool hours*. Report of the Task Force on Youth Development and Community Programs. New York: Carnegie Corporation.

Coleman Advocates for Children and Youth. (1994). *Follow the money: An analysis of how San Francisco spends its money on youth, showing how funding policies affect youth development programs*. San Francisco, CA: Author.

Davis, L. (1999, September 29). Commission goes to bat for youths in Hamtramck, Detroit, Highland Park. *The Detroit News*, p. 7.

Forum for Youth Investment. (2002, Summer). Out-of-school opportunities: City-level responses. *FYI Newsletter*. Washington, DC: Author.

Harvard Family Research Project. (2000, Fall). Evaluations to watch. *Evaluation Exchange*. Cambridge, MA: Harvard Family Research Project.

Langford, B. H. (2001). *State legislative investments in school-age children and youth*. Washington, DC: The Finance Project.

Melaville, A., Shah, P., & Blank, M. (2002). *Linkages to learning*. Washington, DC: Coalition for Community Schools.

National Association of Child Advocates. (2000, December). *Making investments in young children: What the research on early care and education tells us*. Washington, DC: Author.

National Research Council and Institute of Medicine. (2002). *Community programs to promote youth development* [Research review]. Committee on community-level programs for youth (J. Eccles & J. A. Gootman, Eds.). Board on Children, Youth and Families, Division of Behavioral and Social Sciences and Education. Washington, DC: National Academies Press.

Newman, R. P., Smith, S. M., Murphy, R. (1999). *A matter of money: The cost and financing of youth development*. Washington, DC: Center for Youth Development and Policy Research, Academy for Educational Development.

Noam, G., Biancarosa, G., & Dechausay, N. (2002). *Learning beyond school: Developing the field of afterschool education.* Cambridge, MA: The Program in Afterschool Education and Research, Harvard Graduate School of Education.

Pittman, K. (2000). *Recent trends in foundation funding and interest in youth issues* [Written on behalf of the W. K. Kellogg Foundation]. Washington, DC: The Forum for Youth Investment.

Pittman, K., Irby, M., Tolman, J., Yohalem, N., & Ferber, T. (2002). *Preventing problems, promoting development, encouraging engagement: Competing priorities or inseparable goals?* Washington, DC: The Forum for Youth Investment.

Sipe, C., & Ma, P. (with Gambone, M.). (1998). *Support for youth: A profile of three communities.* Philadelphia: Public/Private Ventures.

Skillman Foundation. (1995, April). *Re-creating recreation in Detroit, Hamtramck and Highland Park.* Detroit: Author.

Tolman, J., Pittman, K., Yohalem, N., Thomases, J., & Trammel, M. (2002). *Moving an out-of-school agenda: Lessons and challenges across cities.* A publication of the Greater Resources for After-School Programming (GRASP) Project. Washington, DC: The Forum for Youth Investment.

Traub, J. (2000, January 16). Schools are not the answer. *New York Times Magazine*, p. 52.

Wynn, J. R. (2000, February). *The role of local intermediary organizations in the youth development field.* Chicago: Chapin Hall Center for Children at the University of Chicago.

YMCA of the USA. (2001). *After school for America's teens: A national survey of teen attitudes and behaviors in the hours after school.* Chicago: Author.

18

Designing Youth Development Programs: Toward a Theory of Developmental Intentionality

Joyce Walker
Mary Marczak
Dale Blyth
University of Minnesota

Lynne Borden
University of Arizona

How can community-based youth programs promote and achieve desired developmental outcomes for adolescents? Youth organizations operating under the banner of positive youth development have not traditionally anchored answers to such questions in empirical research or theory-driven models. The field of youth development has been grounded primarily in practical understandings of youth played out in a loose system of nontheoretically driven practices that relied heavily on organizational tradition and the common wisdom of the time. Recent analysis (Benson & Saito, 2001; Eccles & Gootman, 2002) suggests the field is now ready to use the evidence of research and theory, as well as best practice experience, to define its goals, outcomes, and program strategies. The theory of developmental intentionality responds to this readiness with a framework informed by research, theory, and practice. The framework captures the dynamic relationship between developmental outcomes, youth engagement, and intentionality in the philosophy, design, and delivery of program supports and opportunities for young people.

The theory of *developmental intentionality* focuses on the design and daily implementation of effective learning opportunities for young people. First, it holds that programs are most effective when attention to long-term developmental outcomes for adolescents permeates every aspect of the program; thus, intentionality is given center stage both in the design of learning opportunities and in the philosophy guiding youth worker interaction with youth. This attention should be directed not on shaping youth, but on shaping learning opportunities that help youth shape themselves. Following from this, a second precept of the theory is that youth are most likely to achieve desired developmental outcomes when they are actively engaged in their own learning and development. The program goals may originate from the organization and the youth workers, but young people need to be active collaborators in selecting strategies and defining the specific learning opportunities in order to create and sustain youth engagement. A third precept of the theory is that youth engagement results from a good fit between young people and the learning opportunities they take part in. Both the philosophy and the design of youth programs need to give special attention to creating this fit. These three precepts are made manifest when youth workers anchor their professional practice in what we call an ethos of positive youth development and when they use this ethos to shape learning opportunities in informed and purposeful ways.

This chapter lays out the basic components of this developing theory. First, we present the three precepts; then, we present six principles fundamental to an operational ethos of positive youth development. Next we describe how three essential components of successful learning opportunities—the relationships, the activities, and the contextual connections—set the stage for engagement and good fit when intentionally planned and implemented. Finally, we provide an illustration that shows the implementation of the theory within a youth program, and we conclude with a discussion of the implications of the theory for research and practice.

Advanced from a position bridging research and practice, the theory emerges from discussions among the authors around ongoing work. It is informed by our different academic disciplines in developmental psychology, sociology, family development, and adult education. It reflects our collaborative and individual professional experiences with quantitative and qualitative empirical studies of adolescents, the education and training of youth workers, leadership in national youth organizations, evaluation of youth programs, board and foundation consultation, and reflective practice and technical assistance with youth-serving organizations. We each work at the nexus of research and practice to help individuals and communities frame how they think about youth development and to translate research into application and program practice. These different perspectives, nonetheless, share an underlying philosophy that values the everyday life of young people, and a view that youth are resources to get engaged in their own learning and development (Roth & Brooks-Gunn, 2000).

Community-based youth programs are the focus because they offer choice and flexibility, and they present powerful venues for intentional development and learning. Such organizations are often small, flexible, and mission-focused. Often they serve relatively small numbers of youth. These organizations have programs with the flexibility to design approaches locally, provide content with high youth appeal, hire responsive staff and volunteers, and incorporate youth-sensitive strategies to create safe places. Youth participation is voluntary, and the youth-program fit can be intentionally shaped to better meet youth and community needs.

Some definitions are in order. First, the theory of developmental intentionality evolved from work with out-of-school time programs for young people in roughly the second decade of life; thus, it applies principally to youth roughly 8 to 18 years old and to opportunities that extend beyond the classroom to after-school hours, evenings, weekends, and summers. Second, the terms *youth development opportunities, learning opportunities,* and *youth programs* are used interchangeably to describe a structured series of activities or events that go together in some deliberate fashion, have reasonable duration or occur on a regular basis, and provide some level of adult participation and guidance. Third, the terms *practitioner* and *youth worker* are used interchangeably and include direct service staff and volunteers as well as supervisors and agency executives who design programs and organizations where youth are. Last, although the chapter does not address specific developmental outcomes for youth, the concept of *intentionality* is seen as a way to frame how a variety of positive developmental outcomes could be better reached through sound strategies to engage youth in their own learning and development. The goal is to be purposeful about identified outcomes and strategies in order to achieve those outcomes that help young people develop into caring, competent, contributing, confident, and connected individuals.

AN EMERGING THEORY OF DEVELOPMENTAL INTENTIONALITY

The theory of developmental intentionality is built around three key precepts—intentionality, engagement, and goodness of fit. In this section, each precept is introduced and their interrelationships defined.

Intentionality

Intentionality is the major precept. Deliberate, strategic decisions to create opportunities that maximize developmental outcomes are the responsibility of the youth worker and the youth organization. When youth workers put in place a series of goals, plans, and actions to achieve identified outcomes and when they can influence or adjust the program's implementation in order to maximize youth–program fit and stimulate engagement, they are being intentional. When youth development opportunities are intentional in conception, design, planning, and implementation, youth workers and young people can articulate a shared sense of purpose and explicit goals whether it is to encourage young people to master a musical instrument, make sound moral decisions, explore careers in science, or stimulate civic participation. Intention is not intended to suggest rigidity or inflexibility, but rather thoughtfulness and responsiveness with purpose. Whether youth are served prepared snacks or learn to prepare their own depends on the program goals and intended outcomes. In an independent living program, they might cook; at music camp, they probably would not. The fundamental hypothesis is that intentionality in community-based youth programs is essential to achieving immediate program goals and longer term developmental outcomes on more than a random basis.

The traditional lore of the youth development field suggests that somehow youth can be molded and shaped if they come to programs and cooperate. Time after time, however, young people have demonstrated that they come in all different shapes and sizes and want to be active determiners of their own shape! The theory of developmental intentionality moves the "shaping" away from something done to the young person and places it more properly within the realm of intentionality where deliberate constructs of program supports and opportunities are designed for and with youth. It is the learning opportunities, not the youth, that are intentionally shaped. Furthermore, the theory proposes that the chances of optimal attainment of developmental outcomes for adolescents are increased when (a) the organization and individual youth workers operate with an intentional ethos of positive youth development and (b) programs offer learning opportunities characterized by intentional relationships, activities, and contextual connections.

In reality, intentionality is given little attention in most youth development programs. In local, often independent, youth organizations, intentionality in program goals, activities, strategies, and priorities is not a given nor can one assume an ethos of positive youth development. In everyday practice, it would not be unusual to find an after-school opportunity for new immigrant young people that is not intentionally linked to ongoing programs, has no concerted outreach to family members, has no systematic input from the youth, has older teen leaders with little understanding of the immigrant experience, and relies on the practice of rote learning. Thoughtful alignment with and balancing of the principles of the youth development ethos and the dimensions of the learning opportunities allow an endless variety of program possibilities while maintaining the framework of intentionality.

Intentionality to promote positive development is not dependent on a checklist of program features. Rather, it relies on a thoughtful mix of evidence-based and best practice information crafted artfully in advance and at the scene of the action, with young people present and participating. This knowing how to put it together—the *art of intentional balance*—is not well understood and deserves the attention of researchers as well as professional development experts. It is regularly compared to jazz improvisation, with the suggestion that a youth worker must be both a learned, practiced, and intentional artist with an intuitive barometer sensitive to the changing tenor of the group and capable of stepping into the action and contributing to its success. Intentional program design relies on research-based knowledge of topics such as adolescent development and effective program strategies combined with the experiences of best practice and everyday life in the community. The intentional balance relies on thoughtful advance work as well as situational adaptation.

Engagement

The precept of engagement is central to the theory of developmental intentionality. At the most basic level, *engagement* refers to the extent to which young people are focused on and excited about the activities they are participating in at a particular point in time and space. It means more than mere participation and less than some optimal sense of flow that might be achieved. It can also refer in the broader sense to a youth being engaged in an ongoing interrelated set of experiences. For young people in out-of-school time settings, engagement is defined by their willingness to take part, become motivated and challenged by learning opportunities, experience some success, feel a sense of belonging, and a desire to stay involved for a significant period of time. When a young person stays engaged for an extended period of time, the chance of optimizing the achievement of developmental outcomes increases. Little is known about actual "dosage"—the length of time or intensity of engagement—but practical wisdom suggests intermittent or short-term participation is not sufficient to influence developmental outcomes in optimal ways. Participation throughout an intentionally designed series of learning opportunities that have a beginning and an end seems like a minimum. This might be 1 year of weekly 4-H club work culminating in a county fair demonstration, 2 weeks of residential camp, a 3-month preparation for a public theatrical event, a season of sports participation, or the 8 weeks of design, planning, and sponsorship of a special event.

Goodness of Fit

The third precept is the *goodness of fit* between the young person's needs
and the program's learning opportunities. In essence, the theory argues
that intentionality increases the probability of a good fit between the
youth and the program. The better the fit, the higher the probability of engagement. Thus, engagement is the result of good fit between the young
person and the intentionally designed youth program. Greater engagement leads to a greater probability of achieving desired developmental
and learning outcomes. When a program is well aligned to an individual's
needs and to a group's needs, it creates a force for increased engagement.
This theory builds on the program–youth fit while acknowledging the
group nature of most community-based youth programs, where the dynamic is between and among a number of adults and young people in a
group setting. Goodness of fit can be enhanced developmentally by socializing youth to the benefits of participation.

   In summary, the theory of developmental intentionality first argues that
engagement is the key to helping youth programs successfully impact developmental and learning outcomes. Youth who become engaged are more
likely to stay engaged, and longer term engagement leads to better outcomes. Second, the theory states that programs can be intentional about
both the operational ethos that permeates their work and the types of learning opportunities they design and implement. This intentionality focuses on
building that ethos and operating the learning opportunities in specific ways
that are discussed in the next section. Finally, this intentionality is deliberately focused on increasing the goodness of fit between the program and the
youth. As fit is maximized through intentionality, engagement increases. In
the end, this theory is simply laying out the operational principles and program components for which intentionality will make the biggest difference
in improving the impact of out-of-school programs.

AN ETHOS OF POSITIVE YOUTH DEVELOPMENT:
SIX PRINCIPLES TO GUIDE INTENTIONALITY

The ethos of positive youth development is a pervasive attitude, an essential spirit, a philosophy, and a way of working. The term *ethos of positive youth development* helps explain the extent to which the setting and
approaches used in an organization or by a youth worker are framed by an
underlying philosophy consisting of six principles of youth development.
As such, an *ethos* represents a fundamental commitment to how one
works with youth—a commitment that permeates how one thinks and
how one operates. Such an ethos is one way in which intentionality

works to create a better fit between the youth's needs and the program's learning opportunities.

Van Manen (1991) used the word *tact* instead of *ethos* to describe "a mindful orientation to our being and acting with children" (p. 149). People and programs imbued with an ethos of positive youth development stand out because they see possibilities, not pathology. Their practice builds on strengths, creates opportunities, offers supports, and rewards signs of healthy development. Youth workers invested in this philosophical way of being and relating in the world exhibit an authentic interest in the welfare of young people, respecting their role in their own development. In this theory, an ethos of positive youth development actively grows out of six basic principles of practice.

1. *Learning opportunities designed to address the basic developmental needs of adolescents authentically draw in and engage young people.* To be responsive to basic adolescent developmental needs, programs must keep young people conceptually and actively at the center of their vision. Konopka (1973) suggested eight basic requirements for healthy growth and development that Resnick (2000) contended hold up across different times and cultures: (a) Feel sense of safety and structure; (b) experience active participation, membership, and belonging; (c) develop self-worth through meaningful contribution; (d) experiment to discover self; (e) develop significant quality relationships with peers and adults; (f) discuss conflicting values and form their own; (g) feel the pride of competence and mastery; and (h) expand their capacity to enjoy life and know success is possible.

2. *Choice and flexibility provide important ways for young people to have a voice in their learning and development.* Young people are more likely to seize a voice in their own learning and development when opportunities provide choice and flexibility (Belle, 1999; McLaughlin, 2000). Participation in out-of-school time programs is voluntary for most adolescents. Developmentally responsive programs offer young people choices regarding their level of participation, their leadership roles, and their ways of contributing. Theater experiences are good examples, as they provide roles for stagehands, walk-ons, lead performers, supporting roles, costume makers, set designers, musicians, artists, and many others. The variety of roles youth play and their progressive involvement in sequential activities is important. Choice opens the door for a young person to engage with interesting combinations of people, places, and possibilities. Program choice and flexibility foster ownership, membership, and leadership, opening the way for the risk and energy required for the challenges of human development.

3. *Learning and development are enhanced when young people are engaged in active co-creation with adults and other youth.* Both youth and adults are resources to be tapped, each with important contributions to make (Camino,

2000; Finn & Checkoway, 1998; Noam, 2001; Youniss et al., 2002). Noam (2001) found that inviting "checked out" youth in urban neighborhoods to be co-creators of their own development is central to reengaging and reconnecting the most disconnected youth. Co-creation, shared leadership, and youth–adult partnerships are often touted and seldom done consistently and well in practice. The concept presents huge practical challenges in arenas where adults run the organizations, time is at a premium, program intention is unclear, and many question the value of involving youth. Our society commonly embraces a "do for" or "do to" approach to young people, valuing the accomplishment more than the developmental process. It is easy for adults to take over the bake sale when (despite a goal that youth learn responsibility and accountability) it is deemed more important to raise money than to allow the young people to work their way through the ups and downs of planning and pulling off a fundraiser.

4. *Young people benefit when opportunities for development and learning are grounded in their everyday life.* John Dewey (1938) and other progressive educators of the early 20th century based their philosophy and practice in the real-world experience of young people in the belief that learning and human development are processes of living, not simply preparation for a future life. In this sense, living and learning are not separate but are dimensions of life experience that mutually inform each other. Programs gain power to influence development when they are attentive to personal context, are community-based, and respectful of community values, traditions and culture. Service learning is one popular strategy to create learning opportunities that link young people to contributions in their everyday world. Whereas generosity and service to others have intrinsic value, service learning programs explicitly link what a person does and what a person learns in the doing. By involving youth participants in front-end planning and ongoing reflection, service learning programs can intentionally structure the experience of actively contributing to one's community and make a connection to the lessons individual young people learn from the experience.

5. *Young people benefit when their learning opportunities are conceived as a cohesive whole rather than constructed out of a series of fragmented events and activities.* Studies of successful programs conclude that programs addressing a wide range of positive youth development objectives had a higher level of effectiveness and tended to produce more positive youth outcomes in a wider variety of domains than approaches that targeted specific behaviors or skills to avoid specific behaviors (Catalano, Berglund, Ryan, Lonczak, & Hawkins, 1999; Quinn, 2001). Impacting positive development does not require targeting specific youth subgroups or precise negative behaviors (Roth, Brooks-Gunn, Murray, & Foster, 1998). Youth-serving organizations and community programs have considerable freedom to plan an integrated series of learning opportunities focused to foster selected developmental outcomes. Researchers

(McLaughlin, Irby, & Langman, 1994; Vandell & Shumow, 1999) indicated that community programs and opportunities are effective in meeting the developmental needs of young people because they can quickly shift, modify, and transform their way of working to better fit the changing circumstances, strengths, and needs of youth in a given community context.

6. *Young people benefit when structured supports and opportunities are guided by an asset-based approach.* People and programs designed to build assets stand out and look different. Programs and staff infused with a value system and thought process committed to building assets work from a position that all young people have the potential and possibility to contribute to their own learning and development. All have a mix of risk and protective factors in their lives, and it is more productive to concentrate on building assets than it is patching up deficits (Benson, 1997). Positive youth developers see what is normal about young people rather than what is wrong with them, and they focus on building strengths, creating opportunities, offering supports, and rewarding signs of healthy development.

It is both possible and necessary to assess each of the six principles that make up the youth development ethos of an organization and a youth worker's philosophy and such work is critical to testing this theory. In this theory, however, a complete positive ethos emerges only when all six values are present in sufficient strength. Empirical work is needed to test the interrelationships of these six principles, the power of each one (and all together) for enhancing engagement. It is also important to examine the consequences for youth workers and youth when the organizational ethos and the youth worker's ethos are inconsistent. For example, we would hypothesize that youth workers whose philosophical stance is more positive in orientation than their organization's ethos will be more likely to leave or be frustrated than when the reverse is true. For instance, a youth pastor committed to positive youth development principles like co-creation and cohesive programming is likely to feel frustrated and unsupported in a congregation that expects adults to plan and lead a variety of youth activities interspersed with traditional events like sponsoring a pancake breakfast and taking a ski trip. On the other hand, an inspired congregation motivated by an ethos of positive youth development can coach and encourage a less experienced or less developmentally minded youth worker to join in their way of being with young people.

INTENTIONALLY SHAPING
THE LEARNING OPPORTUNITY

If the ethos is the belief system inspiring the youth work, the multiple, sequential, integrated learning opportunities are the essence of what we commonly call the program. Emerging literature (Blum & Rinehart, 2001; Eccles & Gootman, 2002; Larson, 2000; Mahoney, 2000) suggests that young people benefit developmentally when they are engaged in out-of-school supports and opportunities that have certain characteristics. We focus here on three key components of successful learning opportunities: relationships, activities, and contextual connections. This means being intentional about maximizing (a) relationships that are respectful and caring; (b) activities incorporating safe, stimulating environments, relevant subject matter content, and appropriate pedagogical methodology; and (c) contextual connections responsive to factors like race, gender, culture, class and socioeconomic status in the lives of the participants. These three components of the learning opportunity, when intentionally designed, aligned, and implemented, should dramatically increase the goodness of fit between what a program offers and what a young person needs. When that fit is optimized, as noted, engagement is more likely to occur. When one or more components are not intentional, that component will reduce the goodness of fit and hence the probability of the youth's engagement. This dynamic combination, intentionally conceived and woven into the program with purposeful continuity, sequence, and integration (Tyler, 1949), has the potential to stir a powerful synergy of human interaction and engagement in learning. What is essentially new in each of these components, and what allows for greater intentionality, is that there is a growing research literature that better defines what each should look like in action.

Relationships

From a practice perspective, many say, "It's *all* about relationships!" The fundamental role respectful, caring relationships among adults and young people play in the synergy between the youth and the program experience is obvious in quality programs (Rhodes, 2002; Roth et al., 1998). Successful youth workers (McLaughlin et al., 1994) exhibit a highly relational stance in their work as they focus on youth and their potential, are authentic in their relationships, and believe their work makes a difference to others as they give back to the community. Their approach emphasizes the mutual trust, valuing, mattering, and respect inherent in growing, changing relationships.

Adults involved as leaders, advisors, coaches, program managers, resource developers, and direct-line youth workers in community youth programs generally express a passion for the work and for young people (Madzey-Akale & Walker, 2000). At their best, these adults take a partnership role as co-learners and co-creators with youth (Morrow & Styles, 1995). If supported to embrace a core set of values that sees young people as resources and their own roles as facilitators of positive learning and development, they can learn to share power and negotiate with young people as well as know how and when to set limits. The relationships they form can be a powerful force for positive development (Finn & Checkoway, 1998). On the other hand, adults who come to "fix kids" have less impact than those who come to meet young people "where they are" (Morrow & Styles, 1995). If they are unreasonably critical, controlling, cynical, judgmental, or prejudiced, these adults can do more harm than good. In the recruitment, selection, training, and ongoing support for the adult leadership, it is important for organizations to place caring and respect at the top of the list of qualifications to work with youth.

Activities

Community-based youth programs provide nonformal learning opportunities (LaBelle, 1981), operating with intention but without the systematized structures and processes of the formal school and with more focused program structure than the conversational "being present" stance of informal community educators (Jeffs & Smith, 1996). These nonformal learning programs, in concept, work with clear purpose to create high-quality, intentional learning experiences responsive to youth interests and developmental needs, employing varied, flexible approaches within the parameters of the organizational mission that forms the core of the program. Jeffs and Smith (1996) believed that nonformal learning opportunities benefit from a negotiated curriculum mutually determined by the adults and the young people involved. This approach takes the power to chose, edit, and control delivery of programs and activities out of the exclusive domain of agency personnel; nevertheless, increasing numbers of youth workers and organizations are recognizing the benefits of involving young people in the design, planning, delivery, and evaluation of programs. This theory argues that the degree to which the activities in the learning opportunity are appropriately challenging is critical for success.

Activities typically build on the *what*, the *where* and the *how*: the subject matter content, the environment, and the pedagogical methodology. Tyler (1949) used the term *learning experience* to describe the interaction between the learner and the elements of the learning opportunity with which the learner can interact. In this theory, the program activity is the most visible aspect of the learning opportunity and the spot where most young people begin their interaction.

Five principles that have historically guided the design of learning experiences (Tyler, 1949) stress that young people need challenging opportunities to (a) solve problems and practice doing relevant work, (b) feel satisfaction in the learning process, (c) take on tasks within the range of what it is possible to accomplish, (d) explore many avenues for engaging in the learning, and (e) engage in learning experiences that create opportunities for many different learning outcomes, depending on the learner. The dynamic between the environment, the subject matter content, and the pedagogical approach to learning stimulate the transformative process of development. Learning and development is enhanced when they compliment and build on each other.

The Subject Matter Content.   Generally subject matter is what brings youth in the door. The program content is the vehicle to excite young people and draw them in—an opportunity for development, not the end in itself. Youth come to play ball, tap dance, paint murals, go camping, plant a garden, sing in a choir, shoot pool, or study entomology. They come for biking, soccer, theater, music, rockets, outdoor skills, friendship groups, and bodybuilding. They come for individual lessons and for group membership. There is no limit to their taste in topics, interests, exploration, and learning. And when youth encounter exciting content in stimulating settings sparked by innovative hands-on learning strategies, they get engaged. The challenge for programs is how to decide what is offered, what form the learning experiences take, and what role young people play in shaping their own learning and development. Increasingly, the pressures to provide "more school after school" in response to mandates for improved academic achievement compete with program models stressing a youth-driven curriculum. Intentional science-based, experiential learning opportunities emphasizing developmental outcomes that complement the school curriculum are an alternative to more science worksheets after school. Heath and Roach (1998) documented patterns of success among young people in arts programs, relating their experiences to significant feelings of satisfaction with self and increased probability of continuing education after high school. They indicated that the arts expose young people to a greater range, degree, and frequency of risk, provide opportunities for individual identity development within a group, and demand high levels of responsibility for risks and consequences. There needs to be more study of whether one kind of subject matter has more potential for stimulating developmental outcomes than another content area.

The Environment.   Because community youth programs take place in so many diverse settings and spaces, youth workers do not have an easy success formula for managing the environment. Programs may take place in gymnasiums, churches, schools, community centers, parks, homes, malls, libraries, and corner lots; on the other hand, they may be at sports training facilities, retreat centers, or camps. In the case of a cyber camp, the environment can be a home-based Internet site providing virtual experiences spanning time and distance. The environment is often equated with the "delivery method" and carries subtle signals about what goes on when organizations describe their work as club, camp, after school, school enrichment, or site-based. Intentionality in the choice and use of different environments is important for the creation of integrated, congruent activities that foster learning and development.

Eccles and Gootman (2002) described the features of contexts that promote development; many of the features they cited are highly influenced by the environment. For example, crossing the street to attend a program may mean going from one gang territory to another, making safety an issue for an intentional youth worker. These authors also point out the interactive aspect of youth in the environment, noting that experiences arise from the young person's impact on the setting and the setting's influence on the young person. A key feature of a positive developmental environment is one where there is coordination, cohesion, and information flow between different systems (Eccles & Gootman, 2002).

The Pedagogical Method.   Carlson (1998) called for a youth-driven model that incorporates "self-efficacy, involvement, and high levels of perceived control in order to make learning meaningful. The self-directed learner is motivated by choice, intrinsic reward, a sense of discovery, and a 'flow' experience" (p. 45). This youth-driven model does not lessen the importance of intentionality on the part of those planning the experiences, but it does acknowledge that the interactions and reactions of the young person ultimately determine what is experienced and learned.

An optimal pedagogical choice is *experiential learning,* an approach that puts an emphasis on active exploration followed by critical reflection. Experiential learning happens in a very hands-on way, building on processes of discovery, experimentation, trial and error, generalization, and application (A. Kolb & D. A. Kolb, 2001). Typically the learning process incorporates the reality of possible failure and rewards young people who engage in risk to discover and learn. Developing the processes for critical investigation, reflection, and reassessment is as important as getting it right the first time.

Contextual Connections

In this theory, *contextual connections* include settings such as schools, neighborhoods, and workplaces; people such as family members, peers, teachers, and neighbors; and social forces such as culture, spirituality, gender roles, and socioeconomic status. Youth workers acknowledge that programs do not exist in isolation when they are intentionally responsive to the contextual connections of youth in their programs. Experiences, relationships, and forces outside the program influence whether and how young people engage and experience learning opportunities. Although ecological forces such as culture, race, and spirituality are abstract in concept, they are present in the lived experience of young people, often expressed through action, art, literature, and song. These contextual connections in everyday life are significant insofar as young people attach meaning to them, and meaning-making plays an important role in how young people's everyday life affects their learning and development. The theory of developmental intentionality begins to build the link between the science of the ecological nature of youth development and the practice of building learning opportunities for young people (Bogenschneider, 1996).

To be contextually responsive, adults are encouraged to take deliberate measures to understand and gain insights into the world these youth participants experience every day. Adults can explore the lived experiences of youth by visiting the physical and social landscapes of young people; observing youth interaction with friends, family and others; experiencing their rituals; reading their favorite books and magazines; watching their favorite shows and movies; and asking youth about their values, aspirations, hopes and dreams. Halpern and colleagues (Halpern, Baker, & Mollard, 2000) noted that staffs successful in working with youth in high-risk environments were attentive to what young people were wearing on a day-to-day basis. If they were wearing the same thing, it usually indicated that they were not going home at night.

Responsiveness requires that adults not only seek to understand the family–community context but also intentionally incorporate these insights as they plan opportunities and engage with youth. Programs youth identified as the best places to be (McLaughlin, 2000) were embedded in the community and reflected deep knowledge of the place, the situations, and the families of the youth who took part. They were culturally connected and acceptable to the families of the youth, and they were staffed to reflect the ethnic, racial, and cultural character of the community, not necessarily by being identical, but by being committed, respectful, and empathetic.

The complexity of youth development and its reciprocal relationship with contextual connections have implications. Meaningful collaborations with the community and the neighborhood are essential (Bogenschneider, 1996). Youth workers are challenged to value and learn from the experiences and discourses of diverse youth. A youth program intentionally responsive and connected to context has the potential to help young people increase multicultural understanding, navigate across diverse cultures, connect to community, build quality relationships with others, and value differences—outcomes desirable for the young people in programs and desirable for the programs themselves.

ILLUSTRATING INTENTIONALITY
TO GENERATE ENGAGEMENT

A youth organization with a clear mission, defined goals, and a guiding ethos of youth development is fertile ground for creating quality learning opportunities that engage youth and enhance the likelihood of outcomes. Here youth workers understand the standards for success and have values to guide the decisions of daily work. In practice, youth workers would manipulate the elements of the model to maximize youth engagement. Questions that might inform a scenario for intentional program development might go something like this.

What is the organizational mission? Are there youth needs in the community that can benefit from your program efforts? What developmental outcomes do you want to promote? What do you want to be intentional about?

Mayata, a youth worker with a local chapter of a national youth organization, has learned of an increase in serious fighting by middle-school girls who are fighting over boys as they try to find a way to belong. She decides to address their basic need to belong and to feel pride in mastery of positive new skills. She sets a goal to strengthen a sense of belonging, pride and social competence in a group of middle-school girls at risk for fighting. She decides to get the girls intentionally involved in a summer camp experience with activities focused on team building and mastery of outdoor living skills.

How do you get started? How do you respond to contextual connections? Can you do it alone or do you partner? How do you involve the families of the girls? How do you build on the everyday life experiences of the girls?

Mayata establishes a partnership with a small, after-school, academic enrichment program for Latino–Chicano youth and their families. The director there agrees to help identify 12 to 15 middle-school girls in the neighborhood and nominate them for participation in the program based on an identified asset they exhibit. Further, she agrees to host a meeting for the families of the prospective participants to build support for the program. At this meeting, it becomes clear that the families are not interested in having their daughters go away to camp for a week. They exhibit a reserved distrust of the national youth organization, but are willing to stay involved based on the enthusiasm of the after-school program staff. At the end of the meeting, all agree to support a program of learning opportunities based around the city's lakes and public parks 1 day a week for 12 weeks.

How do you co-create with the girls? How do you design the activities? How do you stimulate youth voice and youth creativity? How do you set reasonable expectations? How do you foster caring, respectful relationships?

Invitations are extended, and the 13 girls begin meeting at the after-school program site to plan their program. They form teams and draw up a wish list: sailing lessons, swimming lessons, canoeing, parasailing, fishing, picnics, jogging around the lakes, and an overnight! They begin to develop ground rules for themselves that include "We can all be winners." Meanwhile, Mayata identifies two Spanish-speaking high-school seniors interested in working as "big sisters." Fun trust-building activities are a part of every planning meeting, and group reflections become part of the routine.

How do you shape the learning methodology? Create a safe and supportive environment? How do you document success?

Building on a connection with an organizational board member, Mayata arranges to use the library space in an urban church within walking distance of the two city lakes as the weekly meeting space. She is drawn to the clean, quiet, spacious environment that feels safe and "club-like." She sets to work planning ways to get the girls involved in hands-on learning that emphasizes risk-taking and nonlinear ways of solving problems. She believes this methodology will develop intuition, trust of self, and appreciation of the strengths of others. She asks the girls how they want to keep their families informed of their activities; they decide to use photographs and disposable cameras to record their accomplishments and relationships. Mayata also works through the university department of leisure and recreational studies to identify four college students willing to volunteer 2 to 3 days as instructors for the sailing and swimming lessons—and the parasailing adventure.

The scenario pictured briefly here does not address the multitude of questions about things like finances, parental permission slips, insurance, volunteer recruitment, follow-up after the summer, and program evaluation. But it suggests the kinds of questions a youth worker is provoked to consider when working with developmental intentionality.

This youth worker begins from a position firmly embracing an ethos of positive youth development. She intentionally plans ways to build relationships and to responsively consider the values and concerns of the families and communities of the youth involved. Finally, in designing the learning experience, a setting that is conducive is selected, interesting subject matter is included, and appropriate learning methods are considered. Because the goal is to stimulate the engagement of young people in their own development and learning, their choices, roles, options, and needs weigh into the equation. Striking the balance between all the options for intentional action given the circumstances and the youth at hand draws upon the magic, the artistry, the science, and the craft of youth work.

IMPLICATIONS FOR RESEARCH AND PRACTICE

The emerging theory of developmental intentionality put forth in this chapter is designed to more fully frame the ways intentionality would operate, the key concepts involved, and the principles and values underlying its genesis and use. The theory has many practical applications. It is intended to create a common ground between academics and youth workers, provoke questions, and stimulate the generation and use of evidence to strengthen the youth development field. It has implications for the education and training of youth workers as well as for youth program design and delivery. It can also provide a framework for research and program evaluation questions related to the connection between youth programs and developmental outcomes. This section briefly examines some of the implications of such a theory for research and practice.

Explicitly and implicitly, the theory presents a range of testable hypotheses that need systematic, empirical examination. Because the theory is built on practitioner wisdom as well as emerging empirical evidence, the question of whether greater intentionality of philosophy (ethos) and program design of learning opportunities actually leads to greater engagement and impact is paramount. It is possible, for example, that an overly conscious focus on the elements of intentionality could detract from the spontaneous aspect of successful youth work that engages young people. Thus, too much intentionality may constrain rather then release the creativity in finding the right balance for optimal engagement. It is also possible that helping youth workers understand the critical elements of intentionality in a quality, engaging, high-impact learning experience will help them incorporate such elements in more natural ways throughout all their interactions with youth.

Developing a series of possible hypotheses around the type of training and support that can effectively increase youth worker intentionality is also worth testing. To what extent does having an explicit model integrating the design of activities, contextual connections, and relationships help or confuse youth workers in various settings? Does the responsibility for intentionality reside most effectively with front-line youth workers or with the organizational staff who supervise implementation? Does creating an ethos of positive youth development or a culture of learning in this arena increase the depth of intentionality in practice better than a focus on managing activities and improving specific youth worker skills? What happens when youth workers focus on maximizing fit and engagement rather than planning activities?

Even before such hypothesis testing is the need for basic research on how to measure the presence and strength of the ethos in an organization or a youth worker, the intentionality of learning opportunities, levels of engagement, and the goodness of fit. Must intentionality be visible to the young person or is it sufficient to see intentional patterns in the practice of a youth worker? Does intentionality need to be conscious or can it be intuitive? The theory suggests that engagement is fostered through an intentional weaving of relationships, activities, and contextual connections.

Research is needed to better understand what optimal engagement in developmentally intentional learning opportunities really looks like in scholarly and practical terms. There is also a need to understand how such engagement builds on itself over time and both within and across opportunities. The theory reveals the complexity of trying to influence engagement and to get new effects by combining different elements (e.g., the production of greater challenge by combining caring relationships with rich learning experiences in ways that stretch the learner). Just as important are questions about which types of outcomes (both learning and developmental) are most dependent on engagement. One could hypothesize that social–psychological outcomes and those that involve higher order thinking are more dependent on engagement than, say, knowledge acquisition.

For practitioners, likely questions might include: How would a youth worker recognize engagement in any given situation? What aspects of relationships, learning experiences, and contextual responsiveness promote optimal engagement? What can a youth worker do to maximize this dynamic or to make corrections when things go awry? How do we assess whether engagement is taking place, understand why it is or is not happening, and know what to do about it? Similarly, those who train youth workers might want to know how best to develop an underlying ethos of positive youth development and build practitioners who are able to intentionally implement, deliberately deliver, and reflectively review their work using this framework.

The differential utility of different forms of intentionality also deserves study. Is intentionality in one of the three precepts more or less important for certain outcomes or for work with certain audiences? For example, do disengaged youth who lack experience with trusting relationships benefit from greater intentionality around relationships initially? Are youth with high degrees of trusting and caring relationships impacted more significantly by opportunities with intentionally high degrees of challenge in the learning experiences? Do youth benefit differentially when their cultural experiences are intentionally highlighted to promote engagement? Is this more critical for youth from nondominate cultures? What are the reasons differential engagement might occur and how can program staff address it?

In conclusion, this chapter has begun to put forward a more explicit theory of how youth development programs during out-of-school time can engage youth and make a difference in their learning and development. It has identified the important concept of an intentional ethos of positive development as a factor in practitioner and organizational success. It has begun to operationalize the concept of intentional learning opportunities based upon the interplay among caring relationships, challenging activities, and ecologically contextual connections. It has delineated the importance of engaging youth by creating a better youth–program fit and the ways that might lead to greater impacts. The focus on out-of-school time opportunities that rely on attracting youth as voluntary participants has driven the theory to focus on connecting youth and getting them engaged. By putting engagement at the center of youth development programs, the theory hopefully provides insights into both what needs to be studied more thoroughly and how that might create more effective practice.

ACKNOWLEDGMENTS

The authors wish to acknowledge conceptual contributions to the ethos discussion by Michael Baizerman, Lisa Kimball, and other faculty members in the Youth Development Leadership Masters of Education Program at the University of Minnesota.

REFERENCES

Belle, D. (1999). *The after-school lives of children: Alone and with others while parents work.* Mahwah, NJ: Lawrence Erlbaum Associates.

Benson, P. (1997). *All kids are our kids: What communities must do to raise caring and responsible children and adolescents.* San Francisco: Jossey-Bass.

Benson, P., & Saito, R. (2001). The scientific foundations of youth development. In *Youth Development: Issues, challenges and directions* (pp. 125–148). Philadelphia: Public/Private Ventures.

Blum, R. W., & Rinehart, P. M. (2001). *Reducing the risk: Connections that make a difference in the lives of youth.* Minneapolis: University of Minnesota, Division of General Pediatrics and Adolescent Health.

Bogenschneider, K. (1996). An ecological risk/protective theory for building prevention programs, policies, and community capacity to support youth. *Family Relations: Journal of Applied Family and Child Studies, 45*(2), 127–138.

Camino, L. (2000). Putting youth–adult partnerships to work for community change: Lessons from volunteers across the country. *CYD Journal, 1*(4), 27–31.

Carlson, S. (1998, Winter). Learning by doing and the youth-driven model. In S. Carlson (Ed.), *The center: Today's 4-H connects youth to the world* (pp. 44–47). St. Paul: University of Minnesota, Center for 4-H Youth Development.

Catalano, R. F., Berglund, M. L., Ryan, J. A., Lonczak, H. S., & Hawkins, J. D. (1999). *Positive youth development in the United States: Research findings on evaluations of positive youth development programs.* Seattle: University of Washington School of Social Work.

Dewey, J. (1938). *Experience and education.* New York: Macmillan.

Eccles, J. S., & Gootman, J. A. (Eds.). (2002). *Community programs to promote youth development: Committee on Community-Level Programs for Youth.* Washington, DC: National Academy Press.

Finn, J. L., & Checkoway, B. (1998). Young people as competent community builders: A challenge to social work. *Social Work, 43*(4), 335–345.

Halpern, R., Baker, G., & Mollard, W. (2000). Youth programs as alternative spaces to be: A study of neighborhood youth programs in Chicago's West Town. *Youth and Society, 31*(4), 469–506.

Heath, S. B., & Roach, A. (1998). *The arts in the nonschool hours: Strategic opportunities for meeting the education, civic learning, and job-training goals of America's youth.* Briefing materials for President's Committee on the Arts and the Humanities.

Jeffs, T., & Smith, M. (1996). *Informal education—Conversation, democracy and learning.* Derby, England: Education Now Publishing.

Kolb, A., & Kolb, D. A. (2001). *Experiential learning theory bibliography 1971–2001*. Boston, MA: McBer. Retrieved February 2003 from http://trgmcber.haygroup.com/products/learning/bibliography.htm

Konopka, G. (1973). Requirements for healthy development of adolescent youth. *Adolescence, 8*(31), 2–25.

LaBelle, T. (1981, October). An introduction to the nonformal education of children and youth. *Comparative Education Review, 25*(3), 313–329.

Larson, R. W. (2000). Toward a psychology of positive youth development. *American Psychologist, 55*, 170–183.

Madzey-Akale, J., & Walker, J. (2000). *Training needs and professional development interests of Twin Cities youth workers*. Minneapolis: University of Minnesota, Center for 4-H Youth Development.

Mahoney, J. L. (2000). School extracurricular activity participation as a moderator in development of antisocial patterns. *Child Development, 71*(2), 502–516.

McLaughlin, M. (2000). *Community counts: How youth organizations matter for youth development*. Washington, DC: Public Education Network.

McLaughlin, M., Irby, M., & Langman, J. (1994). *Urban sanctuaries: Neighborhood organizations in the lives and futures of inner-city youth*. San Francisco: Jossey Bass.

Morrow, K. V., & Styles, M. B. (1995). *Building relationships with youth in program settings: A study of Big Brothers/Big Sisters*. Philadelphia: Public/Private Ventures.

Noam, G. G. (2001, May). *Afterschool time: Toward a theory of collaborations*. Paper presented at the biennial Urban Seminar Series on Children's Mental Health and Safety: Out of School Time, John F. Kennedy School of Government, Harvard University, Cambridge, MA. Retrieved from http://www.ksg.harvard.edu/urbanpoverty/Sitepages/UrbanSeminar/OutofSchool/harvard_225.pdf

Quinn, J. (2001, Spring). Harvard Family Research Project: A conversation with Jane Quinn. *The Evaluation Exchange, 7*(2), 8–9.

Resnick, M. D. (2000). Protective factors, resiliency, and healthy youth development. *Adolescent Medicine: State of the Art Reviews, 11*(1), 157–164.

Rhodes, J. (2002). *Stand by me: The risks and rewards of mentoring today's youth*. Cambridge, MA: Harvard University Press.

Roth, J., & Brooks-Gunn, J. (2000). What do adolescents need for healthy development: Implications for youth policy. *Social Policy Report, 14*(2). Ann Arbor, MI: The Society for Research in Child Development.

Roth, J., Brooks-Gunn, J., Murray, L., & Foster, W. (1998). Promoting healthy adolescents: Synthesis of youth development program evaluations. *Journal of Research on Adolescence, 8*(4), 423–459.

Tyler, R. W. (1949). *Basic principles of curriculum and instruction*. Chicago: The University of Chicago Press.

Vandell, D., & Shumow, L. (1999). After-school childcare programs. *The Future of Children: When School Is Out, 9*(2), 64–80.

Van Manen, M. (1991). *The tact of teaching: The meaning of pedagogical thoughtfulness*. Albany: State University of New York Press.

Youniss, J., Bales, S., Christmas-Best, V., Diversi, M., McLaughlin, M., & Silbereisen, R. (2002). Youth civic engagement in the twenty-first century. *Journal of Research on Adolescence, 12*(1), 121–148.

19

Someone to Watch Over Me: Mentoring Programs in the After-School Lives of Children and Adolescents

Jean Rhodes
University of Massachusetts, Boston

Renee Spencer
Boston University

An estimated 2.5 million American youth have an adult volunteer involved in their lives—a number that is rising rapidly. Despite the current popularity of mentoring, important questions about its effectiveness remain unresolved. In this chapter, we outline current knowledge about mentoring relationships, including a synthesis of our own and others' research on the topic. Many of our findings on mentoring are based on secondary analysis of data from the national evaluation of Big Brothers Big Sisters of America (Grossman & Tierney, 1998). We also draw on conclusions from a recent qualitative study of mentoring (Spencer, 2002). In synthesizing these findings, we intend to bring both complexity and words of caution to discussions about the role of mentoring programs in after-school lives of youth.

BACKGROUND

Most of us know of instances in which a caring relationship with a nonparent adult has helped a child or adolescent to overcome a very difficult life situation. For example, here is how Shadow, a vibrant 16-year-old Latina girl, described herself at the time when she was first matched with her volunteer mentor, Sophie. "I didn't care about anything. Or anybody. I didn't think nobody cared about me, so I just did anything I wanted." Shadow had been failing most of her classes and was increasingly getting into trouble in school and at home when her father decided to get her involved in the Big Sister program. Although it took almost a year for the relationship with her Big Sister, Sophie, to develop, Shadow grew to know that she could count on Sophie to listen to the details of her daily life, give her advice on how not to let what Shadow called her "attitude" get in the way of her doing well in school, or simply go with her to see the latest movie.

Sophie described the first year of their match as "exhausting" at times, in part because Shadow rarely said much and gave Sophie little indication of how she felt about her or their relationship. When Shadow provided an opening by sharing a particularly poor report card with her, Sophie responded by conveying both the ways that she had noted Shadow's capabilities and confidence that she could do better. Sophie challenged Shadow to bring her grades up and got involved by contacting her teachers and keeping track of Shadow's progress. Sophie also provided comfort when Shadow was angry with her parents or a friend. In Shadow's words, "I can get an attitude, and … then calm down and get back to my work."

Although she and her family continued to struggle with poverty and serious disputes, Shadow's schoolwork began to improve. She recently received an award acknowledging the significant improvement in her school performance and she described herself as happy. Her relationship with Sophie seemed to be shoring her up, helping her to feel that she "can really accomplish" things if she "puts [her] mind to it." Shadow's weekly outings with Sophie and regular phone calls have provided ongoing opportunities for Shadow to talk about what was on her mind and to figure out what to do when faced with new problems.

The story of Shadow and Sophie's relationship converges with emerging research literature, which suggests that supportive older adults—teachers, neighbors, extended family members, or volunteers—contribute to positive outcomes for youth living in high-risk circumstances (Rhodes, 2002). For example, in one recent study, those youth who had natural mentors (i.e., not forged through mentoring programs) were significantly less likely other youth to take part in a range of high-risk behaviors (Beier, Rosenfeld, Spitalny, Zanksy, & Bontempo, 2000). Similarly, in a study of 770 low-income urban adolescents, Zimmerman, Bingenheimer, and Notaro (2002) found that youth who had natural mentors had more favorable attitudes toward school and were less likely to use alcohol, smoke marijuana, and become delinquent than those without mentors.

THE LOSS OF NATURAL MENTORS

Unfortunately, many contemporary youth do not readily find supportive nonparent adults available in their communities. Changing family and marital patterns, crowded schools, and less cohesive communities have dramatically reduced the likelihood of caring adults becoming natural mentors for youth (Furstenberg, 1994; Putnam, 2000). The entry of many more women into the workforce over the past 30 years has changed American family life dramatically, and the public response to these changes has been insufficient. Many schools do not offer youth enough after-school alternatives to hanging out on street corners or staying in unsupervised homes. In today's families, fewer parents, particularly mothers, can provide transportation or serve as leaders in after-school clubs and organizations. Increasing class sizes have resulted in more students per teacher and a reduced availability of school-sponsored extracurricular activities has resulted in fewer informal connections between youth and committed teachers, coaches, and counselors. The extracurricular activities that do exist within communities have become increasingly age-segregated—a trend that further restricts opportunities for intergenerational contact (Kleiber, 1999). Many adolescents fill their nonschool hours with part-time jobs where their supervisors are not much older than they are (Darling, Hamilton, & Hames, 2003). Still other youth spend their after-school hours in unstructured, unsupervised environments (Belle, 1999).

Adults recognize the need for close, one-to-one relationships with youth but rarely take the time to form such ties. In a recent Gallup survey, 75% of adults reported that it was "very important" to have meaningful conversations with children and youth outside the family, but fewer than 35% reported actually doing so (Scales, Benson, Roehlkepartain, 2001). Policymakers are starting to address teenagers' need for adult supervision with affordable school and community-based programs; however, this response has not kept pace with demand. The existing public infrastructure to address after-school needs is an inadequate patchwork of unevenly distributed programs with underpaid staff and high employee turnover (Seligson, 1999).

Middle-class parents have, to a certain extent, purchased after-school supervision for their children by paying for programs, sitters, athletic clubs, music lessons, summer camps, and even psychotherapy. However, the 20% of U.S. children and teenagers who live in poverty have fewer options for adult contact. For them, the loss of adult helpers within the community is having much more serious consequences. But, in general, all American adolescents are experiencing fewer opportunities for informal interactions with adults than previous generations of teenagers had (Eccles & Gootman, 2002).

The Growth in Mentoring

Mentoring programs are being increasingly advocated as a means of redress-ing the decreased availability of adult support and guidance in the lives of youth (Grossman & Tierney, 1998; Rhodes, 2002). The best-known youth mentoring organization, Big Brothers Big Sisters of America, has more than 500 agencies, located in all 50 states, and more than 4,500 other mentoring initiatives have been established at the local, state, and organizational level. Much of the recent growth of mentoring programs can be attributed to pub-lic awareness of the difficult circumstances of disadvantaged youth and me-dia coverage that has highlighted the importance of adult involvement in young people's lives. There is also an increasing awareness that youth are most likely to engage in problematic behavior during unsupervised af-ter-school hours. Welfare reform, which moved low-income single mothers into the workforce, has put greater pressure on the comparatively few super-vised after-school programs for low-income, school-age children. As a re-sult, community leaders are increasingly appreciative of the role that volunteer mentors can play in supporting youth (Seligson, 1999).

Additional momentum comes from shifts in the philosophical orienta-tion of researchers and practitioners in the youth service sector. In particu-lar, there has been a growing emphasis on the promotion of positive youth development as opposed to the prevention of specific disorders (Larson, 2000; Lerner, 2000; Pittman, Ferber, & Irby, 2001). Instead of focusing on youth's problems, these researchers have attempted to identify "develop-mental assets," that is, competencies and resources within young people's lives that enhance their chances of positive development. In a nationwide study of youth, the Minnesota-based Search Institute found that the higher the number of such developmental assets present in a young person's life, the lower the rate of risk-taking behaviors. These researchers identified 40 developmental assets that are conducive to adolescents' healthy develop-ment; those assets include "support from three or more other adults" and "adult role models" (Benson, 1997, p. 17). Long-established organizations such as the YMCA, Boys and Girls Clubs of America, and Big Brothers Big Sisters are seen as exemplars of this youth-development model (Roth, Brooks-Gunn, Murray, & Foster, 1998).

EVALUATING MENTORING

A small but increasing number of well-designed studies do suggest that mentoring programs can positively influence emotional, behavioral, and academic outcomes (Cave & Quint, 1990; Davidson & Redner, 1988; DuBois & Neville, 1997; McPartland & Nettles, 1991; Taylor et al., 1999). Perhaps the most influential study of mentoring thus far is the evaluation of

Big Brothers Big Sisters of America, which was conducted by researchers at Public/Private Ventures in Philadelphia (Grossman & Tierney, 1998). This study included over a 1,000 youth who applied to one of eight urban Big Brothers Big Sisters programs. The youth were randomly assigned either to a group who would receive mentors during the study (the treatment group) or to a group who would be placed on the 18-month waiting list (the control group). Eighteen months later, the two groups were compared on various outcomes. Although youth in both groups showed decrements in academic, social–emotional, and behavioral functioning over time, the youth in the group that received mentoring declined more slowly than the youth in the control group. Effects varied considerably, depending on the characteristics of the individuals involved and the relationships formed. The challenge for researchers is to distinguish between effective and ineffective mentoring relationships and to understand the circumstances that give rise to each.

To address this challenge, DuBois, Holloway, Valentine, and Cooper (2002) used meta-analysis of 55 evaluations of youth mentoring programs. The researchers first identified relevant studies, and then summarized the results of each study and calculated effect sizes across the entire group of studies. They found favorable effects of mentoring programs across fairly diverse programs, including both programs in which mentoring was provided alone and those in conjunction with other services. However, the researchers noted that the magnitude of these positive effects on the average youth participating in a mentoring program was quite modest (.13). Larger effect sizes were found in programs where youth had, at the onset, more favorable life circumstances and better psychological and social functioning. Strong effects also emerged for youth who had more frequent contact with their mentors, who felt some emotional closeness to them, and whose mentoring relationships lasted longer. In general, program practices that increased relationship longevity (i.e., training for mentors, structured activities for mentors and youth, high expectations for frequency of contact, greater support and involvement from parents, and monitoring of overall program implementation) led to stronger positive effects.

Such practices, which enhance a program's ability to not only match mentors and youth but to sustain those matches, converge with the beneficial practices identified by other researchers (Herrera, Sipe, & McClanahan, 2000). Unfortunately, creating enduring relationships is not necessarily the priority in many mentoring programs. Although some pairs meet regularly for years, many mentoring relationships are short-lived. According to some estimates, one half of all volunteer mentoring relationships dissolve within only a few months (Freedman, 1993). Relationship dissolutions occur for a wide variety of reasons, many of which are not the mentor's responsibility. Graduations, illnesses, or parental remarriages also can affect adolescents' eligibility for mentoring programs or present impediments to regular meetings with a mentor (Sipe, 1996). Yet mentoring volunteers sometimes quit because of fear of failure or because of a perceived lack of effort or appreciation on the part of the young people with whom they have been paired. Many youth enter mentoring programs with histories of inconsistent and difficult relationships, and initial suspicions come across as indifference, defiance, and resistance. With competing demands for their time, many mentors do not persevere when the initial rewards are low.

Because a personal relationship is at the heart of mentoring, volunteers' inconsistencies and terminations can touch on youth's vulnerabilities in ways that other, less personal youth programs do not. Many adolescents participating in the programs come from single-parent homes; for some programs, that is an eligibility requirement. Such youth and may have already experienced a loss of regular contact with their noncustodial parent and may feel particularly vulnerable to (and responsible for) problems in subsequent relationships with adults (Wallerstein, 1988). If youth have begun to value the mentoring relationship and to identify with their mentors, they may feel profound disappointment if the relationship does not progress. Such feelings of rejection and disappointment can lead to a variety of negative emotional, behavioral, and academic outcomes (Downey & Feldman, 1996).

Analyzing data from the national Big Brothers Big Sisters study, Grossman and Rhodes (2002) found that the effects of mentor relationships varied with their duration. Mentored youth were categorized into three groups, depending on how long their mentoring relationships had lasted: less than 6 months, 6 to just under 12 months, and 12 months or more. Youth who were in matches that terminated within the first 3 months experienced significantly larger drops in feelings of self-worth and lower perceived scholastic competence than youth who did not receive any mentoring at all. On the other hand, youth who were in matches that lasted more than 12 months reported significantly higher levels of self-worth, social acceptance, and scholastic competence than the controls. Along similar lines, Slicker and Palmer (1993) found that students who were "effectively mentored" (as measured by the quality and length of the relationship) had better academic outcomes than controls, but those whose mentoring relationships terminated prematurely experienced a significant decline in self-concept when compared with the students who were not mentored.

Taken together, these findings suggest that, when the tool of change is a personal relationship, everyone involved should proceed carefully. As mentioned, however, not all mentoring programs are sensitive to this need. Moving youth off long waiting lists can sometimes take priority over creating high-quality matches that have a good chance of enduring. In one survey of 700 representative mentoring programs, fewer than one half provided volunteers with 2 or more hours of training, and 22% offered no training at all (Sipe & Roder, 1999). A follow-up study with this sample of mentoring programs found that those mentors who attended fewer than 2 hours of prematch orientation or training reported the lowest levels of satisfaction with their matches, and those who attended 6 or more hours of training reported having the strongest relationships (Herrera et al., 2000).

After the initial orientation and training, support to mentors tends to diminish even further. In their survey of mentoring programs, Sipe and Roder (1999) found that the median ratio of mentors to paid staff was 20:1 and that only one third of these programs contacted mentors more than once a month. Similarly, DuBois et al.'s (2002) meta-analysis of more than 50 mentoring programs revealed that fewer than 25% provided ongoing training for mentors once relationships had been established; however, the effectiveness of mentoring programs was determined in large part by the level of their commitment to the longevity of mentoring relationships. It may be the case that program staff, working under the assumption that mentoring programs are inherently beneficial to youth, so they put their limited resources into creating new matches rather than sustaining matches that have been made. Funding agencies reinforce this tendency; they often use the number of new matches, rather than their sustainability, as the measure of a program's efficacy.

Understanding Mentoring

In addition to comparing programs and outcomes, a deeper understanding of the underlying processes that govern mentoring relationships is needed. In general, mentoring appears to affect youth through three interrelated processes: (a) by enhancing their social skills and emotional well-being; (b) by improving their cognitive skills through instruction and conversation; and (c) by providing potential role models and advocates (Rhodes, 2002). The effectiveness of each of these three processes is generally affected by the quality and longevity of the relationships that are established between the young people and their mentors. In the following section, we briefly describe these processes.

ENHANCING SOCIAL AND EMOTIONAL DEVELOPMENT

A frequent observation among mentors and parents is that close connections with mentors can foster improvements in adolescents' relationships with others, especially their parents. Through consistently warm and accepting interactions with their mentors, youth can start to recognize the benefits of close relationships and open themselves to the people around them, particularly their parents. In some cases, mentors can serve as alternative or secondary attachment figures, helping youth to realign their conceptions of themselves in relation to other people. In other cases, mentors may act as sounding boards, providing models for effective communication and helping adolescents to better understand, express, and control both their positive and negative emotions (Pianta, 1999). Rhodes, Grossman, and Resch (2000) researched some of these social and emotional processes. Mentoring relationships led to improvements in adolescents' perceptions of their relationships with their parents (i.e., higher levels of intimacy, communication, and trust). Those improvements, in turn, led to positive changes in adolescents' sense of self-worth, scholastic competence, and scholastic achievement.

Improvements in adolescents' sense of self-worth can also be understood as an internalization of their mentors' positive appraisals of them. The sociologist Charles Horton Cooley, writing about the "looking glass self" around the turn of the 20th century, theorized that significant others become social mirrors into which adolescents look to form opinions of themselves. Those opinions are then integrated into the adolescents' sense of self-worth. George Herbert Mead and others built on this theory, suggesting that individuals try to imagine how they are perceived from the perspective of significant others. Thus, adolescents might project themselves into the role of their mentors and appraise situations and themselves from the mentors' standpoint. In this sense, adolescents' views of themselves are partially a "reflected appraisal" of others' judgments of them (Blumer, 1980). If a mentor views a youth positively, that can start to change the youth's view of herself and can even start to change the way she thinks parents, peers, teachers, and others view her. In such cases, a mentor's positive appraisal can gradually become incorporated into the adolescent's stable sense of self. This self-appraisal process is facilitated by the growing capacity of adolescents to understand the world from the perspective of others and to view themselves from that point of view.

This process of improved close relationships and self-concept is exemplified in the relationship between 12-year-old Leigh and her Big Sister Jules. Leigh's long-term relationship with Jules had become particularly important to her since her mother remarried and her maternal relationship had begun to shift. Leigh felt that her mother "just didn't have time" for her anymore because so much of her attention was now directed at her new spouse. Leigh felt she could talk to Jules about "anything," even "feeling pushed away" by her family. Jules also thought that it had been particularly important during this time that Leigh had someone "outside the family," a "very good friend to talk to that doesn't judge a lot." Leigh saw a link between being able to "spill everything out" with Jules and her sense of competence and confidence. Although having Jules to confide in did not take away the pain of the distance in Leigh's relationship with her mother, the mentoring relationship did help

Leigh to stay connected with her own feelings of sadness and anger rather than turning them inward on herself or directing them at others in negative or destructive ways. It also helped to preserve closeness between Leigh and her mother, as Leigh began to reinterpret her mother's actions through a less hurtful and rejecting lens. In fact, Jules actually helped Leigh to understand her mother's perspective, and the conflicting roles that her mother was being forced to play. Jules, who had herself gotten married since first being matched with Leigh, also demonstrated how the addition of a new person to her life did not inevitably diminish her preexisting relationships.

This story lends support to the possibility that connections with mentors can, indeed, facilitate changes in adolescents' self-perceptions and in their close relationships. Those changes, in turn, can have important effects on developmental outcomes.

IMPROVING COGNITIVE SKILLS
THROUGH MEANINGFUL CONVERSATION

Adolescence is a time of significant cognitive growth, when youth become both more self-reflective and more self-aware. Social interactions—particularly conversations—play an important role in improving these mental abilities. Vygotsky (1978) described adolescents' zone of proximal development—a level of functioning that is beyond what a young person reaches when problem-solving on his or her own but within the range of what he or she can do while working under adult guidance or with more capable peers (see also Rogoff, 1990). This research has important implications for mentoring programs. Conversations in which mentors listen to, attempt to understand, and show respect for what adolescents have to say can provide adolescents with opportunities to think more clearly and critically about the world, to stay in touch with feelings and thoughts, and to express themselves more fully. Given the complex transitions that other close relationships undergo in adolescence and the opportunities provided by adolescents' growing capacity for understanding and reflection, nonparent adults such as mentors may be uniquely positioned to engage youth in substantive, reflective conversations (Darling et al., 2003).

Opportunities for authentic conversation are particularly important for adolescents, who often hide their feelings from their parents, teachers, and others in their efforts to efforts to gain some autonomy (Darling et al., 2003). Again, qualitative reports hint at this possibility. For 17-year-old Elizabeth, one of the most important aspects of her 8-year relationship with her Big Sister, Tiffany, has been having someone she could talk with about her daily struggles. Reflecting on herself at the time she first met Tiffany, Elizabeth described herself as a "terrible kid." She elaborated by explaining that "I wouldn't let kids touch me, talk to me, say 'hi' to me or nothing ... I didn't like teachers, I'd give them attitudes and stuff. Yell at them and stuff." With her family plagued by poverty and violence, Elizabeth had lost hope in the possibility of positive connections with others. Over time, Elizabeth and Tiffany fell into a familiar pattern of going places together and talking. Elizabeth said that with Tiffany she had "opened up more" in response to Tiffany asking her questions and helping her to solve her problems. Elizabeth found it made her "feel good" to talk with Tiffany about problems—"sorting it out and stuff," in Elizabeth's words. Her conversations with Tiffany helped Elizabeth to develop new ways of dealing with the difficulties in her life. When struggling with a situation, she would turn to Tiffany, who she said would "think about it and help me solve and stuff." Elizabeth contrasted the problem-solving help from Tiffany—who, for example, has helped Elizabeth strategize about dealing with conflict in a friendship—with the more general, less helpful advice she tended to receive from others.

ROLE MODELING AND SHAPING

The social and cognitive changes of adolescents just described tend to be accompanied by profound changes in behaviors and expectations for the future. These changes often occur through the process of role modeling, in which mentors exemplify desired knowledge, skills, and behavior. Many lower income youth, in particular, have limited personal contact with positive role models outside the immediate family and believe that their opportunities for success are restricted (Blechman, 1992). Even among middle-class young adolescents, adult occupations and skills can seem obscure and inaccessible (Larson, 2000)]. Mentors can serve as concrete models of success for youth, demonstrating qualities that adolescents might wish to emulate, and providing training and information about the steps necessary to achieve various goals. By observing and comparing their own performance and that of their mentors, adolescents can begin to adopt new behaviors. This modeling process is thought to be reinforced through mentors' support, feedback, and encouragement (Kemper, 1968).

Even when mentors do not serve as direct models, they can be influential. They can, for example, teach new skills and help adolescents to select more socially desirable or higher achieving peer groups. Similarly, they can advocate on behalf of their protégés, opening doors to new opportunities and helping them to establish and make use of connections in the community, such as Little League, neighborhood associations, religious programs, and parent–teacher organizations. These sources of support, encouragement, and trust make up the "social capital" of a community, and the denser the networks, the better for young people. Social capital has been associated with school success above and beyond the contribution of family income, parents' education, or household composition. Mentors can help youth who might otherwise be adrift to make these important connections with other caring, cooperating adults within their own community (Putnam, 2000).

For 12-year-old T. K., his mentor Frank, provided this sort of modeling. T. K.'s mother decided to have her son participate in the Big Brother program when she began working the afternoon and evening shift in her new job as a fast-food restaurant manager. T. K's mentor, Frank, began checking in with him about his homework, asking if there was anything they needed to work on before they went out to do some other type of activity. When T. K. had a large project assigned to him in one of his classes, Frank became involved from beginning to end, helping T. K. with the initial research, offering guidance on how to write the report and, finally, attending the class when T. K. gave presentations Over the course of the almost 2 years they had known one another, T. K. has become more organized in his studies and is generally paying more attention in his classes—improvements that were beginning to be reflected in his grades.

T. K., the new kid in school the year before, had also been singled out for teasing. The conflicts with his peers began seeping into his relationships with his teachers and he began getting into trouble for misconduct. T. K. discussed his difficulties with Frank and found himself continuously drawing on his advice—"I remember all the things he told me," T. K. said. He had learned from Frank how to "stay away from people" who have a "problem" with him and if such a person approaches him to "just walk away, don't listen, ignore them." Saying that he was "coming up" in his school, T. K. was "meeting new people every day." T. K. imagined that he would be "going behind Frank's footsteps" in his future in that he planned to do well in school so that he could attend college. He hoped to be successful in his work, supportive of his wife, and a help to kids, perhaps by becoming a Big Brother himself.

WHICH RELATIONSHIPS ENHANCE DEVELOPMENT?

These relationships exemplify some of the key elements associated with successful mentoring relationships. Each of these pairs got together weekly, particularly during the first year of the match. The adults made, and kept, a 1-year commitment to the child. Although the intention was to promote the child's social, emotional, and cognitive development, the initial focus of these matches was on building a personal relationship and simply spending time together, engaging in activities that both participants enjoyed. It was then, in the context of a close relationship, that opportunities for the adult to offer support, guidance, and assistance emerged and were effectively acted on.

As we have discussed, programs vary widely in the amount and kind of support that they offer to the matches they establish. Frank, the Big Brother of T. K., offers an example of the kinds of challenges that mentors often find themselves facing. Over the course of the mentoring relationship with T. K., Frank had at times served as a sounding board for T. K.'s mother when she was wrestling with a decision regarding her son. One time in particular, T. K.'s mother asked Frank to intervene in a disciplinary decision the school made in response to T. K. spreading a false rumor about one of his classmates. Ambivalent about whether and how he should become involved in this situation, Frank called a match supervisor at the Big Brother Association, who responded by saying that the organization had dealt with school situations such as this one before and would be happy to offer T. K.'s mother the support she needed.

Cases such as this one remind us of the context within which mentoring relationships develop and, subsequently, may thrive, weaken over time, or even become potentially destructive in some way. They also serve as a reminder of the importance of careful mentor recruitment, training, and support. For example, efforts should be made to more accurately describe the benefits a volunteer can expect and the commitment that is required. Some marketing strategies exaggerate the potential benefits of mentoring while downplaying the degree of commitment necessary to achieve these gains. Once recruited, volunteers should be screened by program staff who are sensitive to any circumstances and characteristics that might put volunteers at risk for early termination. Drawing on data from the national evaluation of Big Brothers Big Sisters, Grossman and Rhodes (2002) identified several factors among youth that are predictive of early termination. For example, matches involving older adolescents are more likely to terminate than were matches with 10- to 12-year-olds. This is not surprising, because older adolescents tend to be more peer-oriented than their younger counterparts and less responsive to structured programs. Relationships with adolescents who had sustained abuse or had been referred for psychological treatment or educational remediation were also less likely to remain intact. These youth may present challenges that overwhelm mentors' capacity or willingness to help. Several characteristics of mentors were also predictive of the duration of a mentoring relationship. For example, matches involving volunteers with higher incomes tended to last longer than those involving volunteers with lower incomes. Higher income mentors probably have greater flexibility in their work schedules and could more readily afford amenities such as childcare and personal transportation that make sustained contact more convenient. Marriage was also a risk factor for early termination. Married volunteers in their mid- to late 20s were far more likely than average to terminate each month whereas, unmarried volunteers in that age range were far less likely to terminate. Although we did not specifically ask about volunteers' families, the competing demands of small children among the married group may have left them with neither the time nor flexibility to sustain contact with potentially troubled youth.

In addition to screening out or perhaps enhancing support to volunteers who may have difficulty making the necessary commitment, it might also be helpful to tap into pools of volunteers who are at lower risk for termination. Some programs have recognized the enormous volunteer potential that exists among retired adults, for example. Older adults have more time to devote to this pursuit and are ideally positioned to provide the level of personal attention and emotional support that many youth need (Taylor & Bressler, 2000). At the same time, efforts should be made to facilitate the volunteer efforts of working parents and other adults. A lack of time is not the only impediment to sustained volunteering. For many potential volunteers, a related issue is lack of money. Particularly among people on fixed incomes, such as students and elders, the costs of volunteering may be prohibitive. Transportation vouchers, onsite childcare, and corporate donations, if taken to a national scale, could sharply reduce the financial burdens of mentoring and give many more people an incentive to volunteer.

Of course, not all youth are suited for being mentored. Mentoring is not a substitute for professional treatment among youth who already have serious emotional or behavioral problems, nor can it inoculate all youth against developing these problems. Findings from DuBois' meta-analysis suggest that mentoring programs are not as effective with adolescents who are struggling with severe difficulties. At the other end, however, well-adjusted middle-class youth tend to derive relatively fewer benefits when compared with youth who are facing some degree of difficulty in their lives (Grossman & Johnson, 1998). Youth who fall in the middle of the continuum of functioning appear most likely to benefit. Furthermore, family and cultural influences (e.g., values regarding elders or outsiders) may render certain youth less likely to respond to one-on-one mentoring than others (Taylor & Bressler, 2000).

After screening and matching take place, the next challenge for program staff is to help mentors and youth foster a strong bond. A small but growing number of studies provide some insight into how close relationships are formed. Herrera et al. (2000), for example, examined the predictors of mentoring relationship quality, interviewing 669 volunteers who were in one-on-one matches in community and school-based programs. The strongest contributing factor to all measures of relationship quality was the extent to which the youth and mentors engaged in social activities (e.g., having lunch, just hanging out together). Other relationship factors that predicted closeness were engaging in academic activities, meeting more than 10 hours per month, and joint decision making. Four program practices also predicted strong relationships: making matches based on similar interests; providing more than 6 hours of volunteer training; offering postmatch training and support; and reasonably intensive screening. Grossman and Johnson (1998) found stronger beneficial effects among pairs who interacted more frequently and in which mentors sought the input of the youth and took a more open, less judgmental stance with them. Additionally, Hendry, Roberts, Glendinning, and Coleman (1992) found that the mentors' capacity to refrain from harsh judgment, effectively cope with difficulties, and express optimism and confidence made important contributions to the mentoring relationships. These findings have implications for the selection and training of volunteer mentors. Effective relationships emerge, it seems, through a combination of shared activity, structure, and emotional support—a mix calibrated in response to the needs of the particular adolescent and the stage of the relationship.

In addition to paying more attention to recruiting, matching, and building close relationships, there is a need to take a long-term perspective in evaluating outcomes. Evaluation strategies are needed that capture the full range of program effects, including those that may be masked by the wide variation across programs and within the treatment groups. Additionally, systematic comparisons of programs that vary in type, intensity, supervision, training, matching, and length should be conducted in order to provide a sound basis for comparisons and decision making in the field.

Because such decisions are rarely made in the absence of cost consideration, more detailed cost-benefit analyses are needed. Such analyses might help convince policymakers of both the costs of taking a haphazard approach to mentoring and the benefits of a generous, sustained investment. *Cost-effectiveness analyses,* which combine cost data with outcome data, can provide a foundation for such efforts (McCartney & Rosenthal, 2000). For example, Fountain and Arbreton (1998) determined that although there was considerable variation, the median cost of a one-on-one relationship was just over $1,000 per year, and that programs typically leverage volunteer time and donated goods and services that essentially match every dollar in the budget. Obviously there is no way to put a dollar estimate onto all of the problems that are prevented or all of the doors that are opened as a result of having or being a mentor. But even crude estimates can help shape policy debates. Such estimates would also help to situate mentoring on a continuum of intensity in youth programming.

In addition to comparing programs and specifying relative costs and benefits, theory-driven evaluation strategies should continue to be conducted that delve into the subtle changes that mentoring can bring about. Within this context, it is important to examine the ways in which mentoring relationships are both like and unlike the emotional frameworks developed through parent–child relationships. Attention to contextual factors, such as family histories, school climate, and demographic characteristics might help to explain variations in adolescents' experiences in mentoring relationships.

As mentoring programs assume an increasingly important role in our society, we need to improve our understanding of the ways in which they work—and do not work. With a deep, clear and academically rigorous understanding of mentoring, we can use mentoring programs to more effectively foster healthy transitions from adolescence through adulthood.

REFERENCES

Beier, S. R., Rosenfeld, W. D., Spitalny, K. C., Zanksy, S. M., & Bontempo, A. N. (2000). The potential role of an adult mentor in influencing high-risk behaviors in adolescents. *Archives of Pediatric Medicine, 154*, 327–331.

Belle, D. (1999). *The after-school lives of children: Alone and with others while parents work.* Mahwah, NJ: Lawrence Erlbaum Associates.

Benson, P. L. (1997). *All kids are our kids: What communities must do to raise caring and responsible children and adolescents.* San Francisco: Jossey-Bass.

Blechman, E. A. (1992). Mentors for high-risk minority youth: From effective communication to bicultural competence. *Journal of Clinical Child Psychology, 21*(2), 160–169.

Blumer, H. (1980). *Symbolic interactionism: Perspective and method.* Berkeley: University of California Press.

Cave, G., & Quint, J. (1990). *Career beginnings impact evaluation: Findings from a program for disadvantaged high school students.* New York: Manpower Demonstrations Research Corporation.

Darling, N., Hamilton, S. F., & Hames, K. (2003). Relationships outside the family: Unrelated adults. In G. Adams & M. Berzonsky (Eds.), *Blackwell handbook of adolescence* (pp. 349–370). Oxford, UK: Blackwell.

Davidson, W. S., & Redner, R. (1988). The prevention of juvenile delinquency: Diversion from the juvenile justice system. In R. H. Price, E. L. Cowen, R. P. Lorion, & E. J. Ramos-McKay (Eds.), *Fourteen ounces of prevention: theory, research, and prevention* (pp. 123–137). New York: Pergamon.

Downey, G., & Feldman, S. I. (1996). The implications of rejection sensitivity for intimate relationships. *Journal of Personality and Social Psychology* 6(70), 1327–1343.

DuBois, D. L., Holloway, B. E, Valentine, J. C., & Cooper, H. (2002). Effectiveness of mentoring programs for youth: A meta-analytic review. *American Journal of Community Psychology, 30*(2), 157–197.

DuBois, D. L., & Neville, H. A. (1997). Youth mentoring: Investigation of relationship characteristics and perceived benefits. *Journal of Community Psychology, 25*, 227–234.

Eccles, J., & Gootman, J. A. (Eds.). (2000). *Community programs to promote youth development.* Washington, DC: National Academy of Sciences.

Fountain, D. L., & Arbreton, A. (1998). The costs of mentoring. In J. B. Grossman (Ed.), *Contemporary issues in mentoring* (pp. 66–83). Philadelphia: Public/Private Ventures.

Freedman, M. (1993). *The kindness of strangers: Adult mentors, urban youth, and the new volunteerism.* San Francisco: Jossey-Bass.

Furstenberg, F. F. (1994). How families manage risk and opportunity in dangerous neighborhoods. In W. J. Wilson (Ed.), *Sociology and the Public agenda* (pp. 213–258). Newbury Park, CA: Sage.

Grossman, J. B., & Johnson, A. (1998). *Assessing the effectiveness of mentoring programs.* In J. B. Grossman (Ed.), *Contemporary issues in mentoring.* Philadelphia: Public/Private Ventures.

Grossman, J. B., & Rhodes, J. E. (2002). The test of time: Predictors and effects of duration in youth mentoring programs. *American Journal of Community Psychology, 30*(2), 199–219.

Grossman, J. B., & Tierney, J. P. (1998). Does mentoring work? An impact study of the Big Brothers/Big Sisters. *Evaluation Review, 22,* 403–426.

Hendry, L. B., Roberts, W., Glendinning, A., & Coleman, J. C. (1992). Adolescents' perceptions of significant individuals in their lives. *Journal of Adolescence, 15,* 255–220.

Herrera, C., Sipe, C. L., & McClanahan, W. S. (2000). *Mentoring school-age children: Relationship development in community-based and school-based programs.* Philadelphia: Public/Private Ventures; Arlington, VA: The National Mentoring Partnership.

Kemper, T. (1968). Reference groups, socialization, and achievement. *American Sociological Review, 33,* 31–45.

Kleiber, D. A. (1999). *Leisure experiences and human development: A dialectical interpretation.* New York: Basic Books.

Larson, R. W. (2000). Toward a psychology of positive youth development. *American Psychologist, 55,* 170–183.

Lerner, R. M. (2000). Developing civil society through the promotion of positive youth development. *Journal of Developmental and Behavioral Pediatrics, 21,* 48–49.

McCartney, K., & Rosenthal, R. (2000). Effect size, practical importance, and social policy for children. *Child Development, 71,* 173–180.

McPartland, J. M., & Nettles, S. M. (1991). Using community adults as advocates or mentors for at-risk middle school students: A two-year evaluation of project RAISE. *American Journal of Education, 99,* 568–586.

Pianta, R. C. (1999). *Enhancing relationships between children and teachers.* Washington, DC: American Psychological Association.

Pittman, K., Ferber, T., & Irby, M. (2001). *Unfinished business: Further reflections on a decade of promoting youth development.* Takoma Park, MD: International Youth Foundation.

Putnam, R. D. (2000). *Bowling alone: The collapse and revival of American community.* New York: Simon & Schuster.

Rhodes, J. (2002). *Stand by me: The risks and rewards of mentoring today's youth.* Cambridge, MA: Harvard University Press.

Rhodes, J. E., Grossman, J. B., & Resch, N. R. (2000). Agents of change: Pathways through which mentoring relationships influence adolescents' academic adjustment. *Child Development, 71*(6), 1662–1671.

Rogoff, B. (1990). *Apprenticeship in thinking: Cognitive development in social context.* New York: Oxford University Press.

Roth, J., Brooks-Gunn, J., Murray, L., & Foster, W. (1998). Promoting healthy adolescents: Synthesis of youth development program evaluations. *Journal of Research on Adolescence, 8*(4), 423–459.

Scales, P. C., Benson, P. L., & Roehlkepartain, E. C. (2001). *Grading grown-ups: American adults report on their real relationships with kids.* Minneapolis: Lutheran Brotherhood and Search Institute.

Seligson, E. (1999). The policy climate for school-age childcare. *The Future of Children, 9*(2), 145–159.

Sipe, C. L. (1996). *Mentoring: A synthesis of P/PV's research.* Philadelphia: Public/Private Ventures.

Sipe, C. L., & Roder, A. E. (1999). *Mentoring school-age children: A classification of programs.* Philadelphia: Public/Private Ventures.

Slicker, E. K., & Palmer, D. J. (1993). Mentoring at-risk school students: Evaluation of a school based program. *School Counselor, 40,* 327–334.

Spencer, R. (2002). *Hanging out and growing strong: A qualitative study of relationships with adults that foster resilience in adolescence.* Unpublished doctoral dissertation, Harvard University Graduate School of Education, Cambridge, MA.

Taylor, A. S., & Bressler, J. (2000). *Mentoring across generations: Partnerships for positive youth development.* New York: Kluwer.

Taylor, A. S., LoSciuto, L., Fox, M., Hilbert, S. M., Sonkowsky, M., & Tierney, J. P. (1999). The mentoring factor: Evaluation of the across ages intergenerational approach to drug abuse prevention. *Child and Youth Services, 20*(1–2), 77–99.

Vygotsky, L. S. (1978). *Mind in society.* Cambridge, MA: Harvard University Press.

Wallerstein, J. S. (1988). Children of divorce: Stress and developmental tasks. In N. Garmezy & M. Rutter (Eds.), *Stress, coping and development in children* (pp. 265–302). Baltimore: Johns Hopkins University Press.

Zimmerman, M. A., Bingenheimer, J. B., & Notaro, P. C. (2002). Natural mentors and adolescent resiliency: A study with urban youth. *American Journal of Community Psychology, 30*(2), 221–243.

20

After-School Programs for Low-Income Children: Differences in Program Quality

Deborah Lowe Vandell
University of Wisconsin–Madison

Lee Shumow
Northern Illinois University

Jill Posner
University of Wisconsin–Madison

Interest in after-school programs is at an all-time high. In 1991, approximately 1.7 million children were enrolled in 49,500 before- and/or after-school programs (Seppanen, Love, de Vries, & Bernstein, 1993). By 1997, 6.8 million children of employed mothers were reported to attend programs before and/or after school (Capizzano, Tout, & Adams, 2000). Fully two thirds of the principals in one recent national survey reported that their individual schools or school districts offered after-school programs (Belden Russonello & Stewart, 2001). Funding for after-school programs also has increased substantially. For example, the 21st Century Community Learning Centers (21st CCLCs), a federally funded initiative to support after-school programs in schools serving low-income children has grown from $40 million in 1997 to $1 billion in 2001 (Grossman, Walker, & Raley, 2001). Even so, the increased funding has not kept pace with interest from school districts in offering after-school programs. In 2000, 2,252 applications were submitted to the U.S. Department of Education to establish school-based after-school programs, but funds were available to support only 310 of these applications (C. J. Mitchell, personal communication, October 21, 2002).

This growth of programs has been sparked by a number of factors, including the child-care needs of working parents, concerns about behavioral problems when children are unsupervised, concerns about low academic achievement, and the posited benefits of voluntary structured activities (Larner, Zippiroli, & Behrman, 1999; Larson, 2000). Needs for after-school programs are seen as particularly acute for children from low-income families who face mandated work requirements as part of welfare reform and who cannot afford fee-based after-school lessons and enrichment activities. Youth advocates and policymakers have turned to after-school programs as a way of addressing these multiple concerns.

The research evidence regarding the effects of after-school programs on child developmental outcomes, however, is mixed. Although some studies (Fashola, 2002; Posner & Vandell, 1994) found programs to be associated positively with children's social competencies and academic achievement, others (Marshall et al., 1997; Pettit, Laird, Bates, & Dodge, 1997) have found no effects, and some (Mahoney, Stattin, & Magnusson, 2001; Vandell & Corasaniti, 1988) have even found negative effects. Several factors, including differences in program quality (Vandell & Posner, 1999), have been posited to contribute to these discrepant findings.

In a recent report for the National Research Council and Institute of Medicine, the Committee on Community-Level Programs for Youth (Eccles & Gootman, 2002) identified eight features of high quality programs that meet the developmental needs of adolescents. These programs are characterized by: (a) physical and psychological safety, (b) appropriate structure, (c) supportive relationships with adults and peers, (d) opportunities to belong to the group, (e) positive social norms, (f) support for efficacy and mattering, (g) opportunities for skill building, and (h) integration of family, school, and community. For the most part, however, researchers have not systematically studied the impact of variations in these quality features on school-age children.

In this chapter, we examine in some detail two after-school programs—Child Haven and Hamilton School After-School Program (program names are pseudonyms). The programs made an informative case study because they differed in many of the features outlined by Eccles and Gootman. Although the programs were located in the same city in relatively close proximity and both served low-income children, the programs were miles apart in other respects. By describing the children's experiences at the two programs, we can better understand the ways in which high-quality after-school programs can support children's development and the ways in which poor quality programs may fail to support development. Our second goal is to ascertain if the effects of program quality were more evident for children who have had a history of substantial behavior problems. Based on research that has indicated that "difficult" children are more susceptible to environmental effects (Belsky, 1997), we posited that the effects of program quality would be greater for children who have substantial behavioral problems than for children who had few behavior problems.

AN OVERVIEW OF THE TWO PROGRAMS

Both Child Haven and Hamilton were located in the heart of an inner city. Dilapidated housing and poverty characterized both neighborhoods. There were few activities and resources available for children in these neighborhoods save the after-school programs. Police statistics revealed some of the highest violent crime rates in the city. The local schools were always locked and identification was required before obtaining access to the buildings. Teachers' parking lots were protected by 10-foot high chain-link fences topped with barbed wire. An incident that occurred one day while we were at Hamilton exemplified the danger in these neighborhoods. During lunch recess, a teacher spotted a man waving a gun on the school playground. Teachers and aides quickly moved children inside the building and told them to stay away from windows until the police arrived. Immediately following this incident, one of us talked with a large, popular boy in our study. The boy's outward appearance—a confident walk, a fashionable haircut, and hip clothes—belied the fear evident in his hushed voice. When asked to think about and concentrate on a place he felt safe, he said, "There is nowhere I ever feel safe." After-school programs could serve a particularly important function for children who live in such circumstances. Beyond children's basic safety needs, after-school programs can provide opportunities to participate in skill-building activities and access to supportive adults.

Our information about the two after-school programs was collected over a 3-year period. Program directors were interviewed face to face or by telephone each year. The questions were open-ended and provided directors an opportunity to describe the philosophy of the programs and their approach to meeting the needs of the children being served. Directors also gave information about (a) program origins, auspices, and fees; (b) program enrollment and staffing; (c) staff support and training; (d) available space for different kinds of activities; (e) safety, health, and nutrition practices; (f) typical schedules and activities; (g) parent contact; and (h) ideas for improvements. Interviews were taped and later transcribed. Qualitative information regarding specific themes (history, program goals, organization of daily activities, links with school and family) was written up in narrative form shortly after the interviews.

We also conducted multiple structured observations at the programs. The observation format consisted of 20-minute time samples that focused on individual children's experiences. These time samples alternated between 30-second observation and 30-second recording intervals (20 observation intervals per cycle). Three sets of behaviors were scored: (a) an individual child's level of involvement in program activities (active, passive, unoccupied); (b) the quality of the program staff's interaction with the selected child (positive, neutral, or negative); and (c) the behavior management techniques used by the program staff (facilitates prosocial and positive solutions, uses negative behavior management strategies). At the conclusion of each 20-minute time sample cycle, observers used 4-point scales to rate: (a) emotional climate, (b) staff ability to stimulate children's development, and (c) the degree of child autonomy permitted in the program. Interrater agreement, which was monitored throughout the study, was assessed for 25% of the observations. Cohen's kappa for the time sample codes averaged .93. Cohen's kappa for the overall program ratings was .77 for *affective climate*, .87 for *stimulates development*, and .89 for *program flexibility*.

THE PROGRAM AT CHILD HAVEN

Operated by a nonprofit agency that was a member of a coalition to provide services for inner-city children, Child Haven was located in a well-maintained and spacious community center. Substantial opportunities for skill building were available in the gym, a roller-skating room, a lounge for homework or rest, and a number of activity rooms including a kitchen and crafts workshop. Two hundred forty children were on the roster, although each day the program limited the number of children to the first 70 to sign in because of staffing reasons.

The director of the Child Haven program talked with us at length about the philosophy of empowerment and the purpose of the center. She had an elaborated view of the program goals as well as ideas about how to implement them. Her explanations regarding the philosophy of the organization and the expectations for staff were explicit. She knew most children by name and was an active, hands-on manager. She often was visible during the afternoon, supervising staff and substituting for those who were absent. We learned that she preferred not to take phone calls or to schedule meetings while the children were present.

According to the director, a primary program goal was to provide children with strong emotional support. The Child Haven staff was typically positive in their approaches to behavior management. The director described the children as "growing up at Child Haven," and it was true that many of the teen assistants had attended the after-school program or the summer day camp as youngsters.

The director and staff were selected for their demonstrated commitment to children at risk. The orientation and supervision of staff was comprehensive and included a continually updated survival guide. There was ongoing training, which was incorporated into the weekly staff meetings. At the weekly meetings, staff discussed children's changing life circumstances. In this way, staff often knew when children were experiencing stressful situations at home. Staff took the opportunity to attend workshops and lectures. Perhaps as a result of the professional climate created by the director, none of the full-time professional staff left the program during the year.

The staff–child ratio at Child Haven was difficult to determine because there often were volunteers from the community, interns from the local colleges, and teenage aides participating. During our numerous observations at the center, there were usually two adults present (one staff member and one other adult) per group of 7 to 10 children, although the official child–staff ratio was 10:1.

There was a strong link between the programs and the children's families. Parents usually picked up their children and they had regular informal interactions with caregivers. Staff seemed attuned to children's families and often were aware of changes in the family circumstances. The link also was manifested in the "exchange" area that was located in the Child Haven lobby. Foodstuffs and used clothing were set on a table for parents to share. Parents were expected to reciprocate by donating outgrown clothing or surplus food from their households, and they did. Thus, instrumental aid was provided to families in a manner that emphasized empowerment and community spirit, and preserved their dignity. Further evidence of the commitment to empowerment was evident in the way children held "membership" in the organization. The yearly membership fee was $5 dollars, paid in 25-cent installments each day the child attended until the total was achieved.

The organizational format of the program activities underwent a series of changes during our 3-year study. During the first year when the study children were in Grade 3, the program structure and organization was child-determined, with children able to move freely from one activity station to another during the afternoon. In evaluating the program after a month or so, staff felt that this flexibility resulted in a chaotic atmosphere that was deleterious for the children who they believed required more stability and structure. The staff also believed that the open recreational approach was inappropriate because it did not foster commitment and responsibility between each child and the program. After struggling with these issues, the program evolved to a point where it successfully combined small stable groups of children and staff with some degree of child-selected activities. A routine was established whereby children were assigned to a stable group for the first 1 to 2 hours of the afternoon and then, at 4:30 p.m. staff were assigned to areas and children were allowed to choose between the available activities.

A second change in the program format occurred when the study children were in Grade 5. Prior to that time, children attended the program 1 day a week with their "social group." Staff, however, believed that the children would benefit from more regular contact at the program and began planning for a more extensive after-school program. When the children were in Grade 5, the program was reorganized so that children could attend up to 5 days per week.

A typical afternoon began when children walked several blocks together from a nearby elementary school to Child Haven, to find their social group and group leader in the gym. They spent 1½ hours with their group, generally engaging in one or two activities, including an additional 20 minutes in the snack room. Children helped to plan the program activities. While we were there, we saw children involved in many different activities including making donuts and tacos, creating silk-screened tee shirts, and learning complicated gymnastic moves. Between 4:30 p.m. and 5:30 p.m., children could then choose to participate in any activity being offered in the different rooms (indoor skating, crafts, pool, or pinball). There was a quiet lounge for homework, but this was not a very popular option.

Although Child Haven was located in a dangerous neighborhood, the staff occasionally took the children outside. One beautiful day, for instance, we observed the staff and children roller-skating around the block. It was evident that the staff did not minimize the danger because the children were closely supervised. The willingness to take the children outside may reflect, in part, the good connection between the program and the community. For example, teens from the neighborhood participated in the program as aides. They received training to work as staff and were considered to be important role models for the younger children. Most of the teens also had attended Child Haven as youngsters, prompting the director to remark, "They grew up here." In addition, Child Haven conducted job-training programs for adults in the community.

Thus, children who attended Child Haven experienced many of the program features identified by Eccles and Gootman (2002) as necessary to meet the developmental needs of youth. Children were physically and psychologically safe. The director and staff worked to create an appropriate structure. Children had supportive relationships with adults and peers, opportunities to belong, and exposure to positive social norms. There were numerous opportunities for the children to build skills. Finally, the program was integrated with the families and the community.

THE PROGRAM AT HAMILTON SCHOOL

The Hamilton After-School Program was a large, extended-day program serving about 530 children at an elementary school (85% of the student body). The program, which was offered free of charge to all children who attended the elementary school, was developed as part of a magnet school option that was designed to draw children from all over the city. The stated goal of the program was to provide children with opportunities to develop or strengthen talents in such areas as music, dance, drama, and art, and more advanced experiential opportunities in science, literature, and mathematics. As was the case at Child Haven, lessons and enrichment experiences in these domains were not typically within the financial means in the community. In other respects, the after-school program at Hamilton was quite different than the program at Child Haven.

Unlike Child Haven, the program director at Hamilton was only minimally involved in her program's day-to-day operations. Her management style was bureaucratic. She spent most of her time doing paperwork and scheduling. Although she indicated that she actively supervised the program, we rarely saw her outside of the school office and never saw her in a classroom during our numerous visits to Hamilton. The director also lacked a clear and articulated vision of the program goals. She had little to say about the program except that its purpose was to provide enrichment opportunities. She knew little about the theory of multiple intelligences on which the program was supposed to have been based. She was not able to describe the basic concepts of the theory nor did she seem to know what implementing it in an after-school program might entail.

Staff received little training or supervision from the director or the school principal. Regular staff meetings were held, but there was minimal supervision of the staff in the theme rooms. With one or two exceptions, the program staff at Hamilton was highly restrictive and punitive. We regularly observed children being yelled at and humiliated by teachers and staff. One of the teachers, for example, required children who broke classroom rules (such as talking out of turn or being out of seat without permission) to stand in the corner on one foot for several minutes. If the teacher saw a raised foot touch the ground, more time was added to the punishment.

Unlike the program at Child Haven, there were only minimal connections between home and the program at Hamilton. Most of the children who attended Hamilton were bused home, and the policy was for communication between parents and staff to flow through the director. If parents visited the school, they encountered an unfriendly institutional atmosphere in Hamilton's large central office. There also was a lack of connection with the community and neighborhood. We never observed children who attended the Hamilton program participate in outdoor activities, even on the nicest days.

The daily operations at Hamilton were very school-like in their structure. The bell rang at 2:15 p.m. and the children proceeded to the classroom in which their chosen theme was offered. The first theme ended at 3:10 p.m., the second theme ended at 4:45 p.m., and the third theme ended at 5:45 p.m.. A snack was provided in the cafeteria during the second theme class. With the exception of the sports program held in the gym, and dance and drama, which were in an open space in the basement, the theme rooms looked like classrooms and themes were organized like formal courses. Children were required to participate and follow the lessons of the day or they were punished. Children received grades in the themes, which were sent home with each report card.

Theme 1 was supervised and planned by the child's regular classroom teacher, and all children in the class participated. Theme 2 and Theme 3 were developed and taught by the after-school staff who were specialists in different areas (drama, dance, music, art). Children and their parents had the opportunity to select different themes four times a year, with 9 weeks devoted to each theme. Children were permitted to repeat themes during the year but could not change classes once they were registered. The offerings included arts, games, sports, music, creative writing, computers, dance, drama, science, and sewing. In addition, homework help and remedial reading and math help were provided for children who needed extra academic help.

In contrast to Child Haven, Hamilton lacked many of the features of positive settings, which were identified by Eccles and Gootman (2002) as important for high-quality programs. The structure was overly rigid and did little to develop a sense of efficacy in the children. The staff was not supportive and did not model or establish positive social norms. The children were not given opportunities to belong, and the program was not integrated with family or community. The one area in which Hamilton appeared strong, at least on paper, was the content of the themes, which suggested wonderful opportunities for skill building, one feature of high-quality programs identified by Eccles and Gootman (2002). Unfortunately, the activities at Hamilton were presented in such a rigid and punitive manner that little skill building actually occurred. Although the activities had the potential to develop skills in a variety of areas, the activities were implemented in a way that did not capitalize on this potential.

CHILDREN IN THE CASE STUDY

Next, we consider the experiences of individual children at these two programs. In our effort to understand program effects, we observed children who had substantial behavior problems as well as children who had relatively few behavior problems. We selected the children from questionnaires and interviews completed by the person who had primary custody for the child (typically the mother, but sometimes a grandmother, aunt, or father) when the children were in Grade 3. Based on the reports of behavior problems in Grade 3, we selected five children from each program for this case study. Two third graders (one boy and one girl) at each program were reported by their mothers to have substantial behavioral problems on the 28-item Behavior Problem Index (Peterson & Zill, 1986). Three third graders (two boys and one girl at each program) were reported to have relatively few behavior problems. In each case, a child at Child Haven was matched with a counterpart in the Hamilton program on gender, race, family structure, subsidized lunch status, and scores on the Behavior Problem Index. Pseudonyms are used to protect the confidentiality of the children. We were interested in studying children with substantial behavior problems as well as children with few behavior problems because we expected the effects of program quality to be more apparent for the children with pre-existing behavior problems. In particular, we expected the high-quality program to be particularly beneficial for children with behavior problems and the low-quality program to be particularly problematic for these children.

Two Grade 3 girls were reported by their mothers (and were confirmed by their teachers and the staff at the after-school programs) to have substantial behavior problems, especially in their interactions with peers. Lucretia had attended the program at Child Haven since she was in nursery school. As a third grader, Lucretia lived with her mother. At the end of Grade 4, Lucretia's grandmother obtained temporary custody of her because her mother was unable to care for her. The other children at Child Haven had an approach-avoidance style relationship with Lucretia. She often started out as the leader of a group of girls in the roller skating room, but eventually the other children moved away or argued with her. Lucretia was friendly to adults. One day when we were there with a camera, she presented herself with a smile and asserted that we needed to take her picture.

Tamika, one of the girls who attended Hamilton, was similarly reported by her mother to have numerous behavioral problems in Grade 3, particularly in her relations with peers. Tamika's family background was similar to Lucretia's in that she lived with a single parent and two younger siblings. Tamika's family moved several times during the study period, although it also should be noted that her mother was stably employed. Tamika was a very attractive girl but she was considered to be excessively bossy by the other children at the after-school program and at the school. Her keen intelligence was evident one day when a group of approximately 18 students was playing a strategy game (Match) in which players were progressively eliminated. Tamika won every round and took particular pleasure in beating the boys in the room. Fiercely assertive and brazen, Tamika often tried to garner the attention of teachers.

The two boys who were reported by their mothers in Grade 3 to have substantial behavioral problems were receiving therapeutic treatment in Grade 5 because of behavioral adjustment problems that interfered with their school and family functioning. Josh, the boy who attended Child Haven, spent the second half of Grade 5 in an alternative program for emotionally troubled children. Drew, who attended Hamilton, was admitted to the children's unit of the county mental health facility for a month of treatment following a serious crisis at home and concomitant outbursts at school. When he was released from the hospital near the end of Grade 5, his psychiatric support team recommended his transfer to a new school so that he might have a "fresh start." At that time, he withdrew from the after-school program at Hamilton.

The children identified by their mothers as having relatively few problem behaviors in Grade 3, although not without challenges in their lives, appeared to be negotiating school more effectively than those just described. Charity went to Child Haven after school. She was active in her church and had one particularly close girlfriend with whom she participated in many activities. Charity's father was deceased and her mother remarried when Charity was in Grade 4. Charity reported having good relationships with her mother and stepfather.

Barbara, who attended the program at Hamilton, was similar in several respects to Charity. Like Charity, her mother was a single mother when Barbara was in Grade 3. Barbara also had an especially close girlfriend who attended the school and after-school program. Like Charity, Barbara regularly attended church. Barbara was a child who was often chosen by the teachers to go on errands or be given some extra responsibility.

Two boys at each program were identified in Grade 3 as having relatively few behavioral problems. Sherrod and William attended Child Haven. Both boys had difficult family situations. Sherrod lived with his mother and his father, who was disabled, and four brothers. Sherrod's mother was an alcoholic and had some particularly severe binges when he was in Grade 5. The staff at Child Haven was aware of these problems and seemed especially sensitive to him when his mother was drinking heavily. William lived with his mother, stepfather, and two younger siblings. William's family moved three times over the course of the study, although always in the neighborhood. Both families received public assistance.

Both boys were athletic and spent more time in the gym than in passive after-school activities. Sherrod excelled in gymnastics. Without any formal instruction, he could do back and front flips and other complicated stunts that he and his friends invented. Both he and William enjoyed playing basketball and skating during the choice period. Although they were in the same age group and attended the same school, they were not close friends. Sherrod was more outgoing and social, whereas William was quieter and less peer-oriented. As the oldest boy in his family, William looked out for his younger sister and brother. On a number of occasions, we noted how responsive he was to his younger siblings who also attended Child Haven, looking for lost items and comforting his sister one day when she fell down and bruised her knee.

The final two boys were Dante and Lincoln. These boys attended the after-school program at Hamilton and were reported by their families to have relatively few behavioral problems in Grade 3. Dante lived with his aunt and uncle. Lincoln lived with his grandmother and adult uncle. Dante's aunt received public assistance and Lincoln's grandmother managed on her Social Security income. Dante was a well-behaved and good-humored boy. The teacher reported that Dante's aunt was involved in the child's education and usually attended school programs for parents. Lincoln's classroom teacher reported that his grandmother provided him with little academic support and never attended school programs even though she lived very near the school. This is not surprising; early in the study, we discovered that Lincoln's grandmother could not read or write. Both boys selected sports (basketball) as their first activity choice at the Hamilton after-school program. Both boys participated in play production, computers, and board games as after-school themes in Grade 5.

OBSERVATIONS OF CHILDREN'S EXPERIENCES AT TWO PROGRAMS

Table 20.1 presents a summary of our observations of these 10 children's experiences at the Child Haven and Hamilton. Each child was observed on multiple occasions. The proportions of 20-second time sampled intervals in which the specified behaviors occurred for the case study children are recorded on the table. As can be seen from the summary, the children at Child Haven spent more time actively engaged in program activities than did the children at Hamilton (85% of the time vs. 68% of the time). In addition, the children at Child Haven were more likely to have positive interactions with program staff (13% of the intervals vs. 3%) and less likely to experience negative interactions with program staff (1% of the intervals vs. 13%) than their counterparts at Hamilton. Children received far more negative behavior management at Hamilton than at Child Haven (33% of the intervals vs. 6%). Children in the two programs did not differ significantly in the proportions of intervals in which staff facilitated prosocial behaviors (16% at Child Haven and 11% at Hamilton).

The program ratings that were made at the end of each observation tell a similar story. These ratings can be seen in the bottom half of Table 20.1.

TABLE 20.1

Comparisons of Children's Experiences at Child Haven and Hamilton

	Child Haven		Hamilton		
Time Sample Counts	M Proportion intervals	(SD)	M Proportion intervals	(SD)	T
Child actively involved	.85	(.16)	.68	(.11)	2.43*
Staff positive interaction	.13	(.10)	.03	(.06)	2.79*
Staff negative interaction	.01	(.02)	.13	(.03)	−14.14*
Staff facilitates prosocial behavior	.16	(.04)	.11	(.08)	NS
Staff negative management	.06	(.05)	.33	(.21)	−2.39*
Program Ratings (4-point scales)					
Positive climate	3.1	(.3)	2.3	(.5)	2.75*
Stimulation	2.6	(.3)	2.1	(.1)	NS
Flexibility	3.3	(.4)	2.1	(.9)	4.07*

Note. Related sample *t*-test. Standard deviations are in parentheses.

Consistent with the differences in positive and negative interactions that were recorded on the time sample observations, observers rated the emotional climate at Child Haven to be more positive than the emotional climate at Hamilton (3.1 vs. 2.3). Program structure was rated as providing children with more flexibility and autonomy at Child Haven (3.3 vs. 2.1). Staff in the two programs did not differ significantly in their attempts to cognitively or academically stimulate the children.

Although the children at Child Haven had more positive experiences overall than did the children at Hamilton, variations in the children's experiences at the two programs were observed. Table 20.2 presents summaries of the experiences of the individual children. As shown on the table, staff members at Hamilton were particularly negative in their interactions with children who had behavior problems, whereas staff members at Child Haven responded to these demands with increased positive attention. This pattern was especially apparent for boys, but was also evident for girls.

TABLE 20.2
**Individual Children's Experiences at Child Haven and Hamilton
Reported as Proportion of Observation Intervals**

Child Haven	Josh: High Problems	Sherrod: Low Problems	William: Low Problems	Lucretia: High Problems	Charity: Low Problems
Child actively involved	.62	.96	.74	.88	.94
Staff positive interaction	.22	.21	.01	.04	.06
Staff negative interaction	.0	.0	.12	.04	.0
Staff facilitates prosocial behaviors	.15	.21	.19	.16	.11
Staff negative management	.0	.05	.05	.06	.11
Hamilton	Drew: High Problems	Dante: Low Problems	Lincoln: Low Problems	Tamika: High Problems	Barbara: Low Problems
Child actively involved	.63	.33	.50	.55	.80
Staff positive interaction	.12	.12	.01	.01	.0
Staff negative interaction	.13	.15	.01	.16	.10
Staff facilitates prosocial behaviors	.17	.27	.08	.06	.03
Staff negative management	.55	.44	.15	.39	.33

Note. The designation of high and low behavioral problems was based on mothers' responses to the Behavior Problems Index at Grade 3.

To illustrate, Drew, the boy with substantial behavioral problems who attended the Hamilton program, experienced more negative management than any other child in the study (55% of his observation intervals). Likewise, Tamika—the girl with substantial behavior problems who attended the Hamilton program—received more negative behavior management (39% of her observation intervals) and more negative interactions (16% of her observation intervals) than Barbara, whose mother reported that she had fewer behavior problems (33% and 10%, respectively). Lincoln, a boy with few problematic behaviors, was the only child who managed to escape extensive negative management and negative interactions from the staff at

Hamilton, although it must be noted that he still did not receive much positive attention or prosocial guidance.

A different pattern of experience was observed at Child Haven. Although the staff at Child Haven directed very little negative attention to any of the children, the staff appeared particularly sensitive and positive to those children with the greatest needs. As shown in Table 20.2, staff was very responsive to Josh's needs. He received considerable positive attention from staff and no negative interactions were recorded. Staff also appeared sensitive to Sherrod's special needs stemming from his mother's alcoholism. He received high levels of positive interactions and prosocial guidance, no negative interactions, and very little negative management. Similarly, Lucretia, the girl whose mother reported substantial behavioral problems, received a higher proportion of prosocial experiences from staff than did Charity, who exhibited fewer problem behaviors. Interestingly, negative interactions with staff at Child Haven were most frequent for William, a boy reported by his teachers to get along well with adults and peers. These interactions occurred in the context of his participation in sports activities in which the young male coaches did some yelling at the players.

AFTER-SCHOOL PROGRAMS AND CHILD FUNCTIONING

Next, we examined measures of child functioning in Grade 3 and Grade 5 to ascertain if there were changes in child functioning over time for the children at Child Haven and Hamilton. Proponents of after-school programs have argued that after-school programs can have beneficial effects on children's social and academic development. There have been, however, few longitudinal studies of children who attend programs that were of varying quality.

Our measure of academic functioning was the children's yearly average for reading and math report card grades that were scored on a 5-point scale ($1 = F$ and $5 = A$). Our measures of social functioning were the classroom teachers' reports of the children's peer relationships and work habits. The measure of peer relationships was composed of 11 items that were rated on a 5-point scale (Cronbach alpha = .91). Sample items were *this child teases other children,* which was reflected or reversed coded, and *this child is helpful to other children.* The measure of work habits was composed of 7 items that were rated using 5-point scales (Cronbach alpha = .91). Sample items include: *quits working on tasks when problems arise* (reflected or reverse scored) and *works well without the help of an adult.* Higher ratings designated more competent functioning.

Table 20.3 shows the mean performance and the individual scores for the 10 case-study children in the three aspects of child functioning at Grade 3 and at Grade 5. An examination of the mean scores at the two ages

TABLE 20.3
Child Social and Academic Functioning in Grade 3 and Grade 5

| | Report Card Grades | | | | Work Habits Rating | | | | Peer Relations Rating | | | |
| | Child Haven | | Hamilton | | Child Haven | | Hamilton | | Child Haven | | Hamilton | |
	3rd	5th	3rd	5th	3rd	5th	3rd	5th	3rd	5th	3rd	5th
Sherrod & Dante Low Problems	3.3	2.0	3.5	3.7	3.5	3.3	4.2	4.9	3.6	3.6	4.7	4.0
Josh & Drew High Problems	2.9	2.9	4.2	3.3	3.3	2.7	4.0	4.2	2.8	3.2	3.7	3.8
William & Lincoln Low Problems	2.6	2.3	3.3	1.8	3.3	3.4	3.5	1.4	2.8	4.1	2.8	1.9
Charity & Barbara Low Problems	3.7	3.7	3.6	3.7	3.3	3.7	4.3	4.1	4.1	4.4	4.7	4.5
Lucretia & Tamika High Problems	2.5	4.2	4.4	3.7	1.3	2.6	4.5	3.6	2.2	2.2	3.5	3.2
M	3.0	3.0	3.7	3.2	3.0	3.1	4.1	3.6	3.1	3.5	3.9	3.5

Note. The pseudonym for the child enrolled at Child Haven appears first and is followed by the pseudonym for the comparable child enrolled at Hamilton. All scores are based on 5-point ratings, in which a 5 designates more competent behaviors and were reported by classroom teachers.

reveals a similar pattern for the three areas. The children's peer relationships, report card grades, and work habits generally decreased from Grade 3 to Grade 5 for the children enrolled at the after-school program at Hamilton, whereas the overall performance of children at Child Haven remained the same or improved from Grade 3 to Grade 5. The interaction between program and grade was significant for peer relationships, $F(1, 8)$ = 5.46, $p < .05$, despite the small sample and limited statistical power. This pattern of results is consistent with the proposition that Child Haven served as a support children's academic and social functioning whereas Hamilton failed to support child functioning.

The examination of the functioning of individual children who attended the two programs also supports this proposition. Two children who attended Hamilton—Tamika and Lincoln—had the largest declines in functioning between Grade 3 and Grade 5. Both children had relatively stable home circumstances between Grade 3 and Grade 5, leading us to speculate that their experiences at the after-school program may have contributed to their poorer functioning over time. As shown in Table 20.2, Tamika had many negative interactions with the program staff. Lincoln had fewer negative interactions than other children at Hamilton, but still experienced more periods of negative behavior management than any child observed at Child Haven. Drew, the boy with substantial behavior problems in Grade 3 and the recipient of many negative interactions with program staff, also had a substantial decline in his academic grades in this period. The improvements in peer relations and work habits between Grade 3 and Grade 5 must be viewed cautiously because he had only been in the Grade 5 class for only a few weeks at the end of the year after hospitalization. The new teacher failed to rate many items because of insufficient information.

As indicated in Table 20.3, four of the children who attended Child Haven showed improved functioning between third and fifth grades. In the cases of Lucretia and Charity, their functioning in Grade 5 may well reflect improvements in their family circumstances coupled with positive experiences at Child Haven. One of the children at Child Haven, Sherrod, had a sharp decrease in grades and work habits from Grade 3 to Grade 5, even though he was the recipient of considerable positive attention at Child Haven. We suspect that the declines in grades and work habits occurred in response to his mothers' serious alcohol problems, and we wonder if his functioning would have been even more undermined without the positive attention received at Child Haven.

An alternative explanation for the improved functioning of the children at Child Haven is that their elementary school was better than the Hamilton School; we think, however, that this possibility is unlikely. The elementary school had limited financial resources and generally low performance; Hamilton School, a magnet school in the district, had many more resources and more experienced teachers.

CONCLUSIONS

The aim of this case study was to provide a starting point for identifying the conditions under which after-school programs can support (or fail to support) child development. We identified a number of ways in which Child Haven and Hamilton differed. The quality of staff–child relationships appeared particularly important. The supportive interactions and positive behavior management evident at Child Haven reflected the staff's ability to meet the needs of children. Program planning and activities also contributed to quality care. Children experienced continuity in peer group and staff support on one hand and the opportunity to select favorite and high-interest activities on the other hand. The program simultaneously provided children the opportunity for autonomy and support. The child- and community-centered philosophy, staff characteristics (e.g., commitment, training, and background), and age-appropriate activities provided by Child Haven were other important elements in this successful program. Finally, Child Haven's director had a clear vision of the overall goals and a deep understanding of the developmental needs and life circumstances of children at risk. These characteristics, her expertise at implementation, and her ability to communicate and support her staff were essential ingredients of program quality and underscore the importance of leadership. Our observations at Child Haven were heartening in that they demonstrate the feasibility of a high-quality program in an inner-city neighborhood. Moreover, the elements that made Child Haven exemplary can be replicated with moderate funds and strong commitment to children and families.

In contrast, our observations at Hamilton were disheartening. The children at Hamilton experienced many negative and punitive interactions with staff and had few positive or supportive experiences. The children at Hamilton were relatively unengaged in program activities even though these drama, music, and sports activities were initially selected by the children and would seem, on the surface, to be the sorts of activities that children would enjoy and find meaningful. We suspect that several factors contributed to the failure of the program at Hamilton. The director was not actively involved in the day-to-day operations of the program and she failed to provide the staff with the training and supervision that they desperately needed. There also was a poor connection between the program at Hamilton and parents. There was little effort to engage the parents or the school in the after-school program. If anything, parents were actively discouraged from becoming involved in the program.

The families of the children at both programs were struggling against challenging circumstances that could affect their children's development. Nevertheless, as we saw, when staff members understood family situations they were better able to provide emotional support and instrumental assistance to the children in their care. We felt this to be a critical component of the positive climate at Child Haven and this component was lacking at Hamilton.

Our case study also found some evidence of differences in child functioning over time related to attendance at Hamilton and Child Haven. In particular, we saw an improvement in peer relations for children who attended Child Haven and a decline in the quality of peer relations for children who attended Hamilton.

Several recommendations relevant for policy are suggested by this 3-year case study. For one, it appears that simply providing an after-school program, without attention to quality, is not enough to facilitate children's development. Although we saw indications that high-quality programs may promote children's development, we also saw evidence that poor-quality programs may impede development. The case study also found that the features of a high-quality program serving school-age children were similar to the features of high-quality programs for adolescents (see Eccles & Gootman, 2002). For both age groups, supportive relations between staff and children appear to be paramount, and programs need to be psychologically and physically safe environments. High-quality programs for both school-age children and adolescents need to provide ample opportunities for skill building, efficacy, and mattering. Programs need to have an appropriate amount of structure and organization so that they are neither chaotic nor overly rigid.

Our observations and interviews suggest that the program director may be an essential element in creating and sustaining high-quality programs. A leader who has an elaborated understanding of child development, defines serving children's emotional needs as the purpose of the program, has respect for staff, children, and the community, as well as an involved hands-on style can make a real difference in enacting those qualities at the program level. A second critical element in sustaining program quality is the selection, training, and retention of knowledgeable and caring program staff. Importantly, Child Haven stands as an example of how one program meets these standards.

At the current time, it is not possible to state whether the program at Hamilton or the program at Child Haven is more typical of the quality of after-school programs in the United States because, to date, there has been no nationally representative study that has assessed program quality. Such a study, repeated at regular intervals, is needed to determine the overall quality of programs in the United States. From our ongoing observations of after-school programs in other projects (Pierce, Hamm, & Vandell, 1999; Vandell & Pierce, 2001), however, we believe that exemplary programs are relatively rare and that many programs fail to achieve the quality indicators delineated by Eccles and Gootman (2002). It also should be noted that the program at Hamilton exemplifies one type of poor quality program. Its program staff was highly controlling and punitive, but other components of the program (stable funding, physical facilities that could support a variety of activities, and diverse activities that had the potential of engaging youth and of building skills) were not problematic. Other programs that we have observed struggle with unstable funding sources, high staff turnover, limited physical facilities, and a dearth of age-appropriate activities. And, some poor quality programs are chaotic, which may be more detrimental than those that are overcontrolled. Clearly, additional research is needed to evaluate the full range of programs and to determine which models are most or least effective. In the meantime, we hope that this case study proves useful to researchers, educators, and after-school program staff as an illustration of some of the variability in quality of programs serving low-income children.

REFERENCES

Belden Russonello & Stewart. (2001, August). *Principals and after-school programs: A survey of preK–8 principals* (Report). Washington, DC: Author.

Belsky, J. (1997). Variation in susceptibility to environmental influence: An evolutionary argument. *Psychological Inquiry, 8,* 182–186.

Capizzano, J., Tout, K., & Adams, G. (2000). *Child care patterns of school-age children with employed mothers* (Occasional paper 41). Washington, DC: The Urban Institute. Available at http://www.urban.org

Eccles, J., & Gootman, J. (2002). *Community programs to promote youth development.* Washington, DC: National Academy Press.

Fashola, O. S. (2002). *Building effective afterschool programs.* Thousand Oaks, CA: Corwin Press.

Grossman, J. B., Walker, K., & Raley, R. (2001). *Challenges and opportunities in after-school programs: Lessons for policymakers and funders.* Philadelphia: Public/Private Ventures.

Larner, M. B., Zippiroli, L., & Behrman, R. E. (1999). When school is out: Analysis and recommendations. *The Future of Children, 9,* 4–20.

Larson, R. (2000). Toward a psychology of positive youth development. *American Psychologist, 55,* 170-183.

Mahoney, J. L., Stattin, H., & Magnusson, D. (2001). Youth recreation center participation and criminal offending: A 20-year longitudinal study of Swedish boys. *International Journal of Behavioral Development, 25,* 509–520.

Marshall, N. L., Garcia-Coll, C., Marx, F., McCartney, K., Keefe, N., & Ruh, J. (1997). After-school time and children's behavioral adjustment. *Merrill-Palmer Quarterly, 43*(3), 497–514.

Peterson, J. L., & Zill, N. (1986). Marital disruption, parent–child relationship, and behavioral problems in children. *Journal of Marriage and the Family, 48,* 295–307.

Pettit, G. S., Laird, R. D., Bates, J. E., & Dodge, K. A. (1997). Patterns of after-school care in middle childhood: Risk factors and developmental outcomes. *Merrill-Palmer Quarterly, 43,* 515–538.

Pierce, K. M., Hamm, J. V., & Vandell, D. L. (1999). Experiences in after-school programs and children's adjustment in first-grade classrooms. *Child Development, 70,* 756–767.

Posner, J. K., & Vandell, D. L. (1994). Low-income children's after-school care: Are there beneficial effects of after-school programs? *Child Development, 65,* 440–456.

Seppanen, P. S., Love, J. M., deVries, D. K., & Bernstein, L. (1993). *National study of before- and after-school programs* (Final Report). Washington, DC: U.S. Department of Education.

Vandell, D. L., & Corasaniti, M. A. (1988). The relation between third graders' after-school care and social, academic, and emotional functioning. *Child Development, 59,* 868–875.

Vandell, D. L., & Pierce, K. M. (2001, April). *Experiences in after-school programs and child well-being.* Paper presented as part of a symposium at the meetings of the Society for Research in Child Development, Minneapolis, MN.

Vandell, D. L., & Posner, J. K. (1999). Conceptualization and measurement of children's after-school environments. In S. L. Friedman & T. D. Wachs (Eds.), *Assessment of the environment across the lifespan* (pp. 167–199). Washington, DC: American Psychological Association.

21

After-School Programs, Antisocial Behavior, and Positive Youth Development: An Exploration of the Relationship Between Program Implementation and Changes in Youth Behavior

Stephanie A. Gerstenblith
Caliber Associates, Fairfax, VA

David A. Soulé
Denise C. Gottfredson
Shaoli Lu
Melissa A. Kellstrom
Shannon C. Womer
Sean L. Bryner
University of Maryland

Recently, after-school programs have received national attention because of their potential to promote positive youth development and reduce the risks associated with being unsupervised after school, before parents or guardians return home from work. Although some research has addressed the potential benefits of after-school programs, relatively little has addressed the value of

457

high-quality program implementation and its relation to improving youth outcomes. The main goal of this chapter is to discuss the importance of the quality and quantity of program implementation in the development of after-school programs. In this chapter, examples from a recent evaluation of the Maryland After School Community Grant Program (MASCGP) is used to describe the relationship between program characteristics, such as program structure and type of activities offered and changes in youth behaviors. This study is not intended to assess the effectiveness of after-school programs, but rather to describe potentially important features of after-school programs as a guide to future program development.

This chapter is divided into four main sections. The first section reviews the relevant literature related to after-school programs and discusses the evidence relating program involvement to improved outcomes. The second section discusses the importance of measuring implementation quantity and quality. The third section presents the findings from the MASCGP evaluation, highlighting the relation between the level of program implementation and changes in youth behaviors. The final section presents conclusions and implications for program development.

UNDERLYING ASSUMPTIONS OF AFTER-SCHOOL PROGRAMS

Evidence suggests that the way young people spend their out-of-school time influences their development and well-being. This book has highlighted the many potential benefits of effective after-school programming. As millions of American children are dismissed from school each day, the potential for children to commit or become the victim of crime increases. Many after-school advocates believe that structured postschool activities may reduce problem behavior by providing constructive alternatives to misbehavior at a time when many youth are given the freedom to dictate their own activities. At the same time, it is suggested that the opportunity for children to develop their academic and social skills may be missed due to the lack of a structured and supervised environment. In this chapter, we discuss the relevance of program implementation to these outcomes.

The first major assumption of after-school programs is that they can provide positive, constructive alternatives for youth, which can reduce the incidence of undesired behaviors (e.g., Hirschi, 1969). Yet, the evidence relating involvement in extracurricular activities to the subsequent reduction in delinquent behavior is mixed. Survey research has shown that greater involvement can decrease delinquent behavior among high risk youths (Mahoney, 2000). Yet involvement has also shown to be unrelated to (G. D. Gottfredson, 1984), or related to increases in delinquent behavior (Polakowski, 1994) and substance use (Carlini-Cotrim & Aparecida de

Carvalho, 1993). Although these researchers did not specifically discuss the importance of involvement in after-school programs as a mediating factor in reducing problem behavior, their findings do suggest that factors other than involvement are important to our understanding of the elevated risks of being unsupervised during the after-school hours.

Analyses of the MASCGP initiative during the 1999–2000 school year suggest that after-school program participation may reduce delinquent behavior, but not simply by decreasing time spent unsupervised or by increasing involvement in constructive activities (D. C. Gottfredson, Weisman, Soulé, Womer, & Lu, in press). Rather, the findings suggest that after-school program participation decreases delinquent behavior primarily by decreasing peer drug models and increasing intentions not to use drugs. These findings suggest we should not be satisfied with merely decreasing youths' idle time, but rather we must further explore the type and quality of extracurricular involvement available to today's youth.

After-school programs may also influence a youth's well-being by reducing risk factors for problem behaviors and enhancing attitudes, values, and skills. Recent research has shown that similar factors often predict both positive (e.g. success in school) and negative (e.g. delinquency) outcomes for youth (Catalano, Berglund, Ryan, Lonczak, & Hawkins, 1998). Examples of activities that address these factors include tutoring, positive adult mentors, and structured social skills training. A structured after-school environment may allow children to enhance academic lessons learned during regular school hours, and build relationships with positive, caring adults (National Research Council and Institute of Medicine, 2002; U.S. Departments of Education and Justice, 2000). After-school programs can also help youth develop social skills and learn to get along with their peers (Posner & Vandell, 1994; Tierney, Grossman, & Resch, 1995). These programs, if well implemented, have the potential to increase youths' academic performance, instill a belief system that supports conventional social norms, and increase social competency skills, all of which relate to decreases in a variety of problem behaviors (Bachman, 1975; Jessor, 1976; Jessor, Chase, & Donovan, 1980; Kandel, Kessler, & Margulies, 1978; Wills & Shifman, 1985). To the extent that these factors can be manipulated by after-school programs, these programs may be successful at reducing problem behaviors and promoting positive youth development.

IMPORTANCE OF MEASURING QUANTITY AND QUALITY OF IMPLEMENTATION

Reviews of the effectiveness of preventive interventions summarizing research over the past 20 to 30 years show clearly that some forms of preventive activities reduce some forms of problem behavior (Botvin, Baker,

Dusenbury, Tortu, & Botvin, 1990; D. C. Gottfredson & Wilson, 2003; D. C. Gottfredson, G. D. Gottfredson, & Skroban, 1996; D. C. Gottfredson, Wilson, & Najaka, 2002; Hawkins, Arthur, & Catalano, 1995; Howell, Krisberg, Hawkins, & Wilson, 1995; Lipsey & Derzon, 1998; Tobler & Stratton, 1997). The growing research base has led to a rapid increase in the use of research findings by government and private organizations. Emerging evidence suggests, however, that when implemented in more typical settings and under more realistic conditions, programs are generally not as effective as they were in the original research settings. Instead, a great deal of variability is observed in the quantity and quality of programming actually delivered after training in research-based models. Botvin et al. (1990), for example, showed that the percentage of Life Skills Training materials covered in actual implementation varied from 27% to 97% across classrooms whose teachers had received training, with an average of 68%. This research also showed that when the program is delivered with greater fidelity to the program model, more positive effects are found. Similarly, in their report on prevention programs implemented as part of the U.S. Department of Education's Safe and Drug-Free Schools and Communities Program, Silvia and Thorne (1997) found that the level of implementation of these programs varied considerably across both schools and classrooms. Teachers reported that they had received insufficient training, were not comfortable with the material or teaching methods recommended, and that prevention-related material was of low priority.

A recent study of programs intended to prevent problem behaviors in a nationally representative sample of U.S. schools (D. C. Gottfredson & G. D. Gottfredson, 2002) found that the quality of implementation of school-based prevention practices is mixed. For example, only one half of the prevention curricula and one fourth of the school-based mentoring programs came close to providing the number of sessions offered in the originally studied programs. Only 47% to 78% of programs (depending on the type of program) lasted for longer than 1 month. In addition, programs operating during the after-school hours were significantly less likely to use practices that had been shown in prior research to be effective for reducing problem behaviors,[1] and were less intensive than programs operating at other times (G. D. Gottfredson et al., 2000). These results suggest that the quality of implementation of after-school programs, like prevention programs more generally, is likely to be extremely variable, and that this variability in implementation quality is likely to determine the ultimate effectiveness of these programs for achieving their desired outcomes. It is therefore crucial that after-school program managers be clear about the quantity and quality

---

[1]In this study, the practices reported for the after-school programs were compared with a set of practices that had been shown to be effective in research on school-based prevention programs.

of services they intend to provide, develop data systems to measure these "implementation standards," and use data feedback on the actual level of implementation to strengthen their programs.

MARYLAND AFTER-SCHOOL COMMUNITY GRANT PROGRAM

Throughout this chapter, we use findings from the 2000–2001 MASCGP evaluation to provide examples of the relation between program implementation and youth outcomes. MASCGP was initiated in 1997 by the Governor's Office of Crime Control and Prevention (GOCCP) with the intent of increasing the quantity and quality of after-school programming for elementary and middle school youth in Maryland. The MASCGP goals and objectives are listed in Table 21.1. The two main goals of the initiative were to reduce delinquency and drug use among after-school program participants in part by meeting the six objectives, which included reducing the number of unsupervised after-school hours and addressing a set of youth developmental aspects and risk factors. The objectives were developed based on risk and protective factors related to drug use and delinquency. The program components were then selected based on effective practices shown in research to influence the risk and protective factors reflected in the MASCGP objectives. Academic and social skills training components were developed based on findings that tutoring increased academic performance and reduced problem behavior (Cohen, J. A. Kulik, & C. C. Kulik, 1982; Coie & Krehbiel, 1984) and social competence promotion programs increased academic performance and reduced drug use and problem behavior (Botvin et al., 1990; Bry, 1982; Bry & George, 1979; Rotheram, 1982). In an attempt to increase attendance in the programs and promote attachments between participants and program staff, a recreation component was added in 1998. Following the selection of the program components, the program monitors from GOCCP, the University of Maryland evaluators, and the MASCGP program directors collectively developed implementation standards for the general administration of the after-school programs and individual program components. Examples of the MASCGP implementation standards are listed in Appendix A.

During each year of the program, the University of Maryland evaluators conducted both outcome and process evaluations using instruments developed specifically to measure the implementation standards and goals and objectives of the MASCGP initiative. The evaluators conducted regular implementation feedback sessions with the project directors and GOCCP monitors, encouraging the program staff to use the information to strengthen their programs. This feedback motivated GOCCP to provide training and technical assistance in areas including

TABLE 21.1
Goals and Objectives of the Maryland After-School
Community Grant Program

Goals
1. **Decrease levels of self-reported delinquency** for Maryland adolescents participating in the Maryland After-School Community Grant Program by June 2001.
2. **Decrease levels of self-reported drug use** for Maryland adolescents participating in the Maryland After-School Community Grant Program by June 2001.

Objectives
1. **Decrease number of unsupervised after-school hours** for Maryland adolescents participating in the Maryland After-School Community Grant Program by June 2001.
2. **Increase attachments to pro-social adults** for Maryland adolescents participating in the Maryland After-School Community Grant Program by June 2001.
3. **Increase involvement and investment in constructive activities** for Maryland adolescents participating in the Maryland After-School Community Grant Program by June 2001.
4. **Increase academic performance** for Maryland adolescents participating in the Maryland After-School Community Grant Program by June 2001.
5. **Increase beliefs against substances use and illegal behaviors** for Maryland adolescents participating in the Maryland After-School Community Grant Program by June 2001.
6. **Improve social skills** for Maryland adolescents participating in the Maryland After-School Community Grant Program by June 2001.

Source. Maryland After School Community Grant Program: Program Development and Evaluation Workbook.

research-based social skills programs, tutoring, and behavior management. It also guided the elimination of certain implementation standards found unrelated to youth outcomes.

In 1999–2000, those MASCGP programs that reported the use of structured social competency skill programming in areas including self-control, stress management, responsible decision making, social problem solving, and communication skills were most effective at reducing delinquent behavior among after-school program participants compared to a comparison group (D. C. Gottfredson et al., in press). In particular, those programs that placed a high emphasis on social skills instruction and practice were most effective at influencing those mediating factors, such as attitudes about drug use and association with drug-using peers, which are strongly related to delinquent behavior. These findings suggest that the type of programming provided by the MASCGP during the 1999–2000 school year was important for addressing the goals of the initiative and were the impetus for an expanded exploration of program implementation in subsequent evaluations. The MASCGP example provides preliminary evidence that after-school programs can influence levels of problem behavior by providing structured character development and social skills activities.

The evaluations described in this chapter were conducted during the 2000–2001 school year in the 21 MASCGP programs that were funded that year. The outcome evaluation conducted during the 2000–2001 school year involved a pre–post design, which consisted of surveying the youth participants at the beginning (September, 2000) and end of the school year (March and April, 2001), and collecting school records from the previous and current school years. This evaluation measured the changes exhibited in the youth's behaviors and attitudes across the school year. Pre–post designs are not ideal for assessing program effects because change from pre- to post- for program participants cannot be compared with change for a similar comparison or control group not exposed to the after-school program. Using these designs, it is not possible to determine whether changes exhibited from the beginning to the end of the school year are due to participation in the after-school program or to some other reason(s), including maturation. However, the design does at least show whether relevant attitudes and behaviors changed in the desired direction and the magnitude of that change. A pre–post design also permits investigation of program and youth characteristics related to change in youth behavior and attitudes.

The process evaluation collected data on the quality of the programs and the amount of services provided to the participants. One of the purposes of this data collection effort was to link the pre–post changes observed in the youth over the school year to the quality and quantity of program implementation.

MEASURES OF PROGRAM IMPLEMENTATION

The data collection instruments used to measure program implementation in the MASCGP programs were improved and expanded over the 4 years of the project. Initially, only data collection logs completed by program staff were required for the process evaluation, but as a means of improving and expanding the amount and detail of the data obtained on each program, observations and program director interviews were added during the 2000–2001 school year.

An evaluation manual, including logs and forms to be completed by program staff, was produced by the University of Maryland evaluators. Logs developed based on the implementation standards collect administrative data as well as information on each of the GOCCP-mandated program components (academics, recreation, and social skills). Logs were completed by the program staff on a daily basis and returned to University of Maryland evaluators each month for keypunching and analysis. A reproduction of the After-School Attendance and Daily Activities Log is included in Appendix B. The daily activities log includes daily student-level information on program attendance and the amount of time spent in academics, recreation, and structured social skills activities. The log also allows for the computation of a student–staff ratio during the academics component.

Observers from the University of Maryland measured program characteristics, including the structure of program components, youth engagement rates, social climate, and behavior management. Structured observation forms were completed by the evaluators at each site visit. Eight observations were completed at each program by the University of Maryland evaluators between December 2000 and March 2001. Example questions from the observation forms are included in Appendix C.

Interviews of each of the program directors were completed by an evaluator at the end of the year. The directors were asked about the populations their programs served, the staff in their program, and details about the program components. Example interview questions, based on questions from the National Study of Delinquency Prevention in Schools (Gottfredson et al., 2000) are included in Appendix D.

DESCRIPTION OF THE AFTER-SCHOOL PROGRAM SAMPLE

In September 2000, pretest surveys were administered to 486 youth who had previously registered to participate in the MASCGP programs and returned signed parental consent forms. At the end of the year, 83% (402) of pretested youth were posttested.

Registration forms provided information on the gender, race, and age of the participants. Nearly half (46%) of the youth sample was male. The sample was 82% non-White (71% Black or African American, 11% other races); the average age of the participants was 10.45 years. Twenty-seven percent of the sample was in Grade 4, 31% in Grade 5, 22% in Grade 6, 12% in Grade 7, and 8% in Grade 8.

Measures of Pre–Post Change

The purpose of the outcome evaluation was to measure change across the school year on youth participation in delinquency and drug use, as well as a variety of risk and protective factors for these problem behaviors. Risk factors are attitudes, beliefs, behaviors, and other characteristics that increase the likelihood youth will participate in problem behaviors such as delinquency and drug use; protective factors (or assets) are attitudes, beliefs, behaviors, and other characteristics that decrease the chances youth will participate in problem behaviors.

The design of the 2000-2001 outcome evaluation of the MASCGP programs involved pretesting all program participants prior to (or very early in) their participation in the after-school programs and posttesting all program participants, including those who dropped out of the programs during the school year, at the end of the program year. Pretests were administered in September 2000 and posttests were administered in April and May, 2001. Students completed a revised version of the What About You? survey (G, D, Gottfredson, 1991).

The What About You? survey measures students' attachment to school, rebellious and delinquent behavior, drug use, attitudes about drug use, peer relationships, parental supervision, commitment to education, and belief in rules. Additional items were added to the survey from the Social Skills Rating System Elementary Level Student Form (Gresham & Elliott, 1990), which measured students' social skills, and from the Communities That Care Youth Survey (Arthur, Pollard, Hawkins, & Catalano, 1995), which measured students' attachment to prosocial adults. Further items were added to measure unsupervised after-school time and involvement in constructive activities. Items from the survey were combined into scales to measure specific behaviors. Low base rates of after-school violent and property crime and after school drug use resulted in low reliabilities ranging between .17 and .37. Reliabilities on the remaining scales ranged from .52 to .87.

In addition to administering the What About You? survey, pre- and posttesting included the collection of school records (attendance and school grades). School records for the 1999–2000 school year were collected during the fall of 2000, and school records for 2000–2001 were collected in the late spring of 2001.[2]

Program Characteristics Related to Pre–Post Changes in Youth Behavior

Without a control or comparison group, it is impossible to determine whether the pre–post changes exhibited by the youth were due to their involvement in the after-school programs. However, we are able to determine whether certain aspects of the programs are related to changes in youth behavior and attitudes. In this section, we present graphs that illustrate the as-

---

[2]Complete attendance data (pre- and post-) was received for 53% of pretested youth, and complete grades (pre- and post-) were received for 60% of pretested youth.

sociation between the pre–post changes observed in the youth over the school year and the quality and quantity of program implementation.

Figure 21.1 shows that in programs rated by observers (see Appendix C) as having more efficient procedures, higher levels of behavior management, and higher levels of overall structure, students' reports of rebellious behavior increased[3] less from pre- to post-test.

Figure 21.2 shows that overall structure within programs was related to gains in children's intentions not to use drugs.

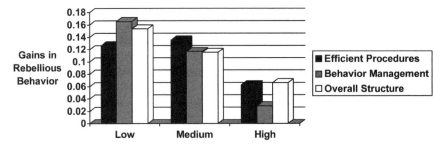

FIG. 21.1. Gains in rebellious behavior by program procedures, behavior management, and overall program structure. ($p < .05$ for efficient procedures and overall structure; $p < .01$ for behavior management. Gain scores represent the difference between pre- and posttest on a scale that ranges from 0 to 2.)

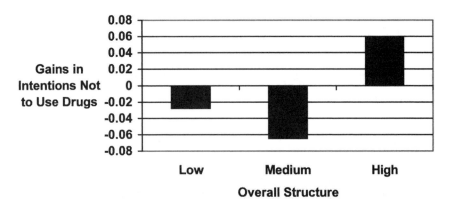

FIG. 21.2. Gains in intentions not to use drugs by overall program structure. ($p < .05$. Gain scores represent the difference between pre- and posttest on a scale that ranges from 0 to 1.)

---

[3]Increases in measures of problem behaviors are expected in this age range.

Programs implemented various social skills curricula. The programs were required to provide social skills training for 1½ hours per week, but programs varied in the amount of time spent in social skills training. Figure 21.3 and Fig. 21.4 illustrate that an emphasis on social skills in after-school programs is related to positive academic outcomes (GPA and attendance). As shown on Fig. 21.3, the number of social skills lessons completed by the program participants, as reported by the program directors in the interviews, was related to improvements in GPAs. Participation in more than 30 lessons (the cut-off used to define the *high* category) predicted increases in GPA; all other participants showed a decrease in GPA.

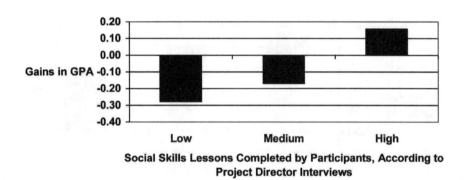

FIG. 21.3. Gains in GPA by social skills lessons completed. ($p < .01$. Gain scores represent the difference between pre- and posttest on a scale that ranges from 0 to 4.)

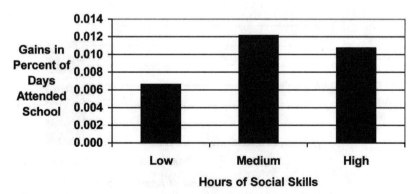

FIG. 21.4. Gains in percent days attended school by weekly hours of social skills. ($p < .01$. Gain scores represent the difference between pre- and posttest on a scale that ranges from 0 to 1.)

As shown on Fig. 21.4, the number of social skills lesson hours provided (according to program logs) predicted increased school attendance. Providing more than 1 hour of social skills per week predicted increases in school attendance.

The academic component of the after-school programs mainly consisted of homework assistance, rather than structured tutoring. Programs were required to offer at least 1½ hours of educational activities per week. Figure 21.5 and Fig. 21.6 illustrate the finding that the academics component of after-school programs was related to desirable outcomes for elementary youth. Figure 21.5 shows that the number of hours youth were involved in academics per week predicted significantly lower last year variety in drug use for elementary school youth. The relationship was not significant for mid-

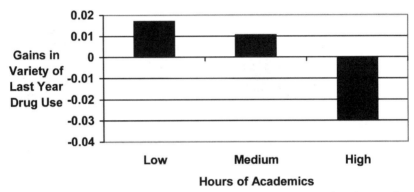

FIG. 21.5.   Gains in variety of last year drug use by weekly hours of academics, elementary participants. ($p < .01$ for elementary school youth only. Gain scores represent the difference between pre- and posttest on a scale that ranges from 0 to 2.)

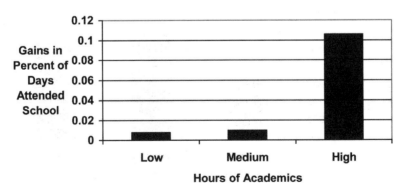

FIG. 21.6.   Gains in percent of days attended school by weekly hours of academics, elementary participants. ($p < .05$ for elementary school youth only. Gain scores represent the difference between pre- and posttest on a scale that ranges from 0 to 1.)

dle-school youth. More than 2.33 hours of academics per week predicted decreases in the variety of drug use by elementary school participants.

Figure 21.6 shows that more than 3 hours of academics per week predicted increases in the school attendance of elementary school participants.

All MASCGP programs offered educational or cultural enrichment activities (including field trips, club, or family activities) and sports. Nearly all programs included arts and crafts and performing arts, approximately one half of the programs provided wilderness or challenge activities and nearly one third of MASCGP programs included an entrepreneurship component. Observation records showed that the majority of the programs provided fairly structured recreational activities. Figure 21.7 shows that the percentage of time spent in recreation significantly predicted increases in delinquent behavior, after-school violent crime, and peer drug models for middle-school participants. During each site visit, observers recorded the amount of time spent in each activity. The percentages of time spent in recreation were averaged across all observations for each program.[4] Participants in programs that devoted up to 43% of program time (on average) to recreation (*low* category) showed either no change or decreased involvement in delinquent behavior. Participants in programs with 44% to 68% of program time concentrated on recreation showed slight increases in delinquent behavior for middle school youth. Additionally, participants in programs with high percentages of time spent in recreation showed significant increases in their reports of having peer drug models and being involved in

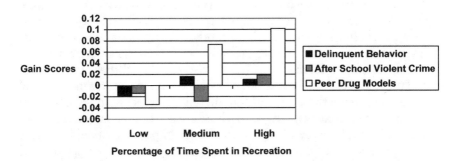

FIG. 21.7.   Gains in delinquent behavior, after-school violent crime, and peer drug models by percentage of time spent in recreation, middle school participants. ($p < .05$ for middle-school youth only, for all three outcome measures. Gain scores represent the difference between pre-and posttest on scales that range from 0 to 1.)

---

[4]Categories for percentages of time spent in recreation include: low (21% to 43%); medium (44% to 57%), and high (60% to 68%).

after-school violent crime. The relationships were significant for middle-school participants, but not for elementary school participants.

CONCLUSIONS AND IMPLICATIONS

Maryland's Governor's Office of Crime Control and Prevention initiated the MASCGP in response to a growing need for quality after-school programming for middle and elementary youth in Maryland. The evaluators were actively involved in the development and evaluation of the MASCGP programs from the start of the initiative. The academic and social skills training program components were selected based on research findings indicating the practices were effective at influencing the risk and protective factors targeted by MASCGP. Recreation activities were added to the programs to increase attendance and promote attachments between participants and staff. Ongoing evaluation and feedback activities throughout the project allowed for continual information sharing between evaluators and staff in an effort toward program improvement. During the project, the evaluation findings were utilized to strengthen programs, initiate training and technical assistance on program delivery and components, and modify implementation standards.

Aspects of program content and other program parameters found to be related to pre–post changes observed in youth over the 2000–2001 school year were presented in this chapter. The findings provide some useful guidelines for after-school program planners interested in developing effective models for after-school programs.

The findings suggest that program planners should consider adopting skill-building activities such as social skills training and academic activities. Social skills and academic activities were related to positive changes in youth behavior, including improved grades, attendance, and lower rates of drug use. A review of the research on extracurricular and after-school activities conducted by Eccles and Templeton (2002) also concluded that activities designed to build social and academic skills were common features in successful programs. Although these types of activities may not seem captivating for after-school program participants, with a little creativity, both program components can be made enjoyable for youth. Program planners should consider adopting research-based social skills programming that can be implemented in the after-school program setting. At the end of the 2000–2001 school year, the Maryland Governor's Office held a social skills fair to showcase research-based social skills programs that could be implemented in the after school setting. Programs that have been adopted in the after-school programs include Lions-Quest Skills for Adolescence and Working Toward Peace (www.quest.edu), Peacemakers Program (www.applewoodcenters.org/peacemakers.htm), Second Step (www.cfchildren.org/default.html), and All Stars (www.tanglewood.net). Based on the findings presented here, program schedules should allow for at least 1 hour per week of social skills instruction and/or practice, and if possible, at least 30 lessons should be provided over the course of a school year.

Recreation is a key component for attracting youth to programs. However, our findings suggest that program planners should be careful when planning the recreation components of their after-school programs. More than 2.6 hours per week of recreation was related to increases in delinquent behavior, violent crime, and peer drug models for MASCGP participants. We must caution, however, that all recreational activities, including sports, field trips, arts and crafts, and other activities, were combined into one category for these analyses, which makes it difficult for us to draw conclusions about specific activities. It is possible that alternative explanations may account for these findings, such as participants who may have selected programs based on the specific type and amount of recreational activities provided. Programs should be creative in planning their recreation time to be fun, yet also involve structured activities and sufficient supervision, as it appears that program participants seem to be learning from their delinquent peers during recreation time. Academics and social skills activities can be combined with recreational activities in order to maintain program attractiveness, while addressing the key components in after-school programs that are likely to result in positive youth outcomes.

Just as schools with efficient procedures and structure have been found to have positive student outcomes, our findings indicate that participants in after-school programs with these qualities experience reductions in rebellious behavior and increases in intentions not to use drugs. In concordance with Mahoney and Stattin (2000), the MASCGP results indicate that participation in activities described as highly structured is linked to smaller increases in antisocial behavior. Accordingly, program planners should focus efforts on increasing the structure of all program components and procedures by planning specific activities well in advance and confirming that they include explicit delivery plans. Additionally, increasing the efficiency of program procedures should be a priority. This can be done by following a daily schedule that is posted on the wall, using a bell or announcing transitions over a loudspeaker, minimizing dead time between activities by requiring youth to go directly to the next component, and holding routine opening activities such as taking attendance, and closing activities such as clean-up and sign-out. To maintain efficiency, it is important that youth always know where they are supposed to be and what they are supposed to be doing.

Use of a behavior management system in the MASCGP programs was related to slower increases over time in the rebellious behaviors of participants. High-quality behavior management systems include those that: (a) are specific about what behavior is expected for different activities and/or procedures, (b) are consistently applied by staff members, (c) post rules and consequences for students to see, (d) include an immediate response to misbehavior, and (e) include positive and negative consequences for appropriate and inappropriate behavior, respectively. Programs could consider developing program rules in collaboration with the participants, to increase youth buy-in. To maintain consistency in the use of discipline across all staff, behavior management training should be included as part of staff training at the beginning of the program year.

One of the limitations of existing evaluations of after-school and other extracurricular programs is the lack of attention to program implementation. This chapter illustrated the importance of high-quality program implementation in after-school programs as relates to youth out- comes. Program planners' consideration of the program features that are related to youth development, including social skills training, academic activities, structure, efficiency, and behavior management systems will increase the quality of after-school programs and their promise for fostering positive youth development.

ACKNOWLEDGMENTS

This project was supported by Grant No. ASPI–2001–0031 from the Maryland Governor's Office of Crime Control and Prevention with federal funds from the Bureau of Justice Assistance, Office of Justice Programs, U.S. Department of Justice. Points of view or opinions contained within this document are those of the authors and do not necessarily represent the official position or policies of the U.S. Department of Justice.

APPENDIX A:
EXAMPLE MASCGP IMPLEMENTATION STANDARDS

- A core group of 20 students participates regularly.
- 100% of core students attend 80% of all sessions every month.
- Every instance of nonattendance for core participants is checked.
- An assessment of educational needs will be made for 100% of students.
- An individual academic plan will be developed for 100% of students based on the assessment of educational need.
- Every core student will participate in a structured educational activity for an average of at least 1½ hours per week.
- Every core student will participate in a structured social skill and character development activity for an average of at least 1½ hours per week.

MARYLAND AFTER-SCHOOL COMMUNITY GRANT PROGRAM AFTER-SCHOOL ATTENDANCE AND ACTIVITIES LOG

Program_____

Date:_____

Students	Academic Achievement Activities			Recreation	Structured Social Skills
	Attendance Code	# Minutes	# Students including present student	# Staff	Total minutes spent in recreation activities	Total minutes spent in structured social skills

Instructions: Complete this log daily. **Attendance Codes:** P: days present; E: excused absence; U: unexcused absence; W: withdrawn. **Academic Achievement Activities:** Fill in the number of minutes, students and staff involved in academic activities. **Recreation:** Fill in the total minutes dedicated to any recreational activities. **Structured Social Skills:** Fill in the total minutes dedicated to the instruction and/or practice of *specific* social skills. At the end of the month, return all logs to your program evaluator: 2220 LeFrak Hall, College Park, MD 20742.

APPENDIX C:
EXAMPLE QUESTIONS FROM OBSERVATION FORMS

Discipline Management System

1. Rules/Behavior Management
   - (a) Are there clear expectations for the students' behavior?   Yes   No
   - (b) Are the expectations communicated to the students?   Yes   No
   - (c) Are the children who misbehave segregated from the group?   Yes   No
   - (d) Is good behavior rewarded?   Yes   No
   - (e) Is there consistency in managing students behavior?   Yes   No
   - (f) Is there effective monitoring of students' behavior?   Yes   No
   - (g) How often is there an immediate response to misbehavior?   Never   Sometimes   Often

2. Type of discipline management observed being used during the program (Mark all that apply)
   - ☐ Verbal reprimand
   - ☐ Time out/Separation from group
   - ☐ Demerits
   - ☐ Loss of privilege
   - ☐ Phone call to parents
   - ☐ Other (*specify*)
   _____
   _____

3. How many incidences of physical or blatant verbal defiance/misbehavior occurred during the program? _____

Program Structure

1. The degree of structure observed for this program can best be described as …
   - ☐ No plan or structure for activities, program activities completely improvised.
   - ☐ Had idea of topic/activities to be covered but had no lesson plan developed, some improvisation.
   - ☐ Had general plan that served as guide, poor use of transitions, a lot of dead time.
   - ☐ Had topics and activities planned but had some problems with delivery.
   - ☐ Extremely well-structured, had lesson plan that was scripted and in specific order, all activities planned in advance.

Procedures

1. Is the daily schedule efficient?   Yes   No
2. Is the daily schedule followed?   Yes   No
3. Are there efficient transitions between activities?   Yes   No
4. Are the opening and closing procedures efficient and orderly?   Yes   No

APPENDIX D: EXAMPLE QUESTIONS
FROM PROGRAM DIRECTOR INTERVIEW[5]

Program Goals

1. What are the goals of your program?
2. What are you trying to accomplish?

Program Population

3. What populations does your after school program serve? (Check all that apply.)
   - ☐ No special group is served.
   - ☐ Boys are served.
   - ☐ Girls are served.
   - ☐ Interested participants or volunteers are served.
   - ☐ A particular grade level or grade levels is/are served.
   - ☐ Youth who are school leaders or good citizens in school are served.
   - ☐ Youth at elevated risk of problem behavior such as drug use, dropout, or delinquency are served.
   - ☐ Youth who have been or are about to be expelled from school are served.
   - ☐ Gang members are served.

Program Staff

4. Regarding the organization chart of your after-school program, what are the roles of program staff? How many people are in each role?
5. How many people have left during this school year in each position?
6. How many have you added?
7. Have you had any difficulties finding and keeping qualified people to work in your program? (Mark one.)
   - ☐ Yes
   - ☐ No
8. If so, what difficulties?
9. What obstacles to recruiting the best staff have you experienced?

General Program Difficulties

10. What are the most significant difficulties you have faced in delivering this program?

---

[5]Based on questions from the National Study of Delinquency Prevention in Schools (G. D. Gottfredson et al., 2000).

REFERENCES

Arthur, M., Pollard, J., Hawkins, J. D., & Catalano, R. (1995). *Communities that care youth survey.* Seattle, WA: Developmental Research and Programs.

Bachman, J. G. (1975). *Youth in transition. Documentation manual* (Vol. 2). Ann Arbor: University of Michigan Institute for Social Research.

Botvin, G. J., Baker, E., Dusenbury, L., Tortu, S., & Botvin, E. M. (1990). Preventing adolescent drug abuse through a multi-modal cognitive–behavioral approach: Results of a 3-year study. *Journal of Consulting and Clinical Psychology, 58,* 437–446.

Bry, B. H. (1982). Reducing the incidence of adolescent problems through preventive intervention: One and five-year follow-up. *American Journal of Community Psychology, 10,* 265–276.

Bry, B. H., & George, F. E. (1979). Evaluating and improving prevention programs: A strategy from drug abuse. *Evaluation and Program Planning, 2,* 127–104.

Carlini-Cotrim, B., & Aparecida de Carvalho, V. (1993). Extracurricular activities: Are they an effective strategy against drug consumption? *Journal of Drug Education, 23,* 97–104.

Catalano, R. F., Berglund, M. L., Ryan, J. A., Lonczak, H. S., & Hawkins, J. D. (1998). *Positive youth development in the United States: Research findings on evaluations of positive youth development programs.* Washington, DC: U.S. Department of Health and Human Services and National Institute for Child Health and Human Development.

Cohen, P. A., Kulik, J. A., & Kulik, C. C. (1982). Educational outcomes of tutoring: A meta-analysis of findings. *American Educational Research Journal, 19,* 237–248.

Coie, J. D., & Krehbiel, G. (1984). Effects of academic tutoring on the social status of low-achieving, socially rejected children. *Child Development, 55,* 1465–1478.

Eccles, J. S., & Templeton, J. (2002). Extracurricular and other after-school activities for youth. In W. S. Secada (Ed.), *Review of educational research* (Vol. 26, pp. 113–180). Washington, DC: American Educational Research Association Press.

Gottfredson, D. C., & Gottfredson, G. D. (2002). Quality of school-based prevention programs: Results from a national survey. *Journal of Research in Crime and Delinquency, 39*(1), 3–35.

Gottfredson, D. C., Gottfredson, G. D., & Skroban, S. (1996). A multimodel school-based prevention demonstration. *Journal of Adolescent Research, 11,* 97–115.

Gottfredson, D. C., Weisman, S. A., Soulé, D. A., Womer, S. C., & Lu, S. (in press). *Do after school programs reduce delinquency? Prevention Science.*

Gottfredson, D.C., & Wilson, D. B. (2003). Characteristics of effective school-based substance abuse prevention. *Prevention Science, 4,* 27–38.

Gottfredson, D. C., Wilson, D. B., & Najaka, S. S. (2002). School-based crime prevention. In L. W. Sherman, D., P. Farrington, B. C. Welsh, & D. L. MacKenzie (Eds.), *Evidence-based crime prevention* (pp. 56–164). New York: Routledge.

Gottfredson, G. D. (1984). *The effective school battery: User's manual.* Odessa, FL: Psychological Assessment Resources.

Gottfredson, G. D. (1991). *What about you?* Ellicott City, MD: Gottfredson Associates.

Gottfredson, G. D. Gottfredson, D. C., Czeh, E. R., Cantor, D., Crosse, S. B., & Hantman, I. (2000). *A national study of delinquency prevention in school final report.* Ellicott City, MD: Gottfredson Associates.

Gresham, F., & Elliott, S. (1990). *Social skills rating system.* Circle Pines, MN: American Guidance Service.

Hawkins, J. D., Arthur, M. W., & Catalano, R. F. (1995). Preventing substance abuse. In M. Tonry & D. Farrington (Eds.), *Building a safer society: Strategic approaches to crime prevention*. Chicago: University of Chicago Press.

Hirschi, T. (1969). *Causes of delinquency*. Berkeley: University of California Press.

Howell, J. C., Krisberg, B., Hawkins, J. D., & Wilson, J. J. (1995). *A sourcebook: Serious, violent, and chronic juvenile offenders*. Thousand Oaks, CA: Sage.

Jessor, R. (1976). Predicting time of onset of marijuana use: A development study of high school youths. *Journal of Consulting Psychology, 44*, 125–134.

Jessor, R., Chase, J. A., & Donovan, J. E. (1980). Psychosocial correlates of marijuana use and problem drinking in a national sample of adolescents. *American Journal of Public Health, 70*, 604–613.

Kandel, D. B., Kessler, R. C., & Margulies, R. Z. (1978). Antecedents of adolescent initiation into stages of drug use: A developmental analysis. In D. Kandel (Ed.), *Longitudinal research on drug use: Empirical findings and methodological issues* (pp. 73–99). New York: Wiley.

Lipsey, M. W., & Derzon, J. H. (1998). Predictors of violent or serious delinquency in adolescence and early adulthood: A synthesis of longitudinal research. In R. Loeber & D. Farrington (Eds.), *Serious and violent juvenile offenders: Risk factors and successful interventions* (pp. 86–105). Thousand Oaks, CA: Sage.

Mahoney, J. L. (2000). School extracurricular activity participation as a moderator in the development of antisocial patterns. *Child Development, 71*, 502–516.

Mahoney, J. L., & Stattin, H. (2000). Leisure activities and adolescent antisocial behavior: The role of structure and social context. *Journal of Adolescence, 23*, 113–127.

National Research Council and Institute of Medicine. (2002). *Community programs to promote youth development*. Committee on Community-Level Programs for Youth. Jacquelynne Eccles & Jennifer A. Gootman (Eds.), Board on Children, Youth, and Families, Division of Behavioral and Social Sciences and Education. Washington, DC: National Academy Press.

Polakowski, M. (1994). Linking self- and social control with deviance: Illuminating the structure underlying a general theory of crime and its relation to deviant activity. *Journal of Quantitative Criminology, 10*, 41–78.

Posner, J. K., & Vandell, D. L. (1994). Low-income children's after-school care: Are there beneficial effects of after-school programs. *Child Development, 65*, 440–456.

Rotheram, M. J. (1982). Social skills training with underachievers, disruptive, and exceptional children. *Psychology in the Schools, 19*, 532–539.

Silvia, E. S., & Thorne, J. (1997). *School-based drug prevention programs: A longitudinal study in selected school districts*. Research Triangle Park, NC: Research Triangle Institute.

Tierney, J., Grossman, J., & Resch, N. (1995). Making a difference: An impact study of Big Brothers/Big Sisters. Philadelphia: Public/Private Ventures.

Tobler, N. S., & Stratton, H. H. (1997). Effectiveness of school-based drug prevention programs: A meta-analysis of research. *Journal of Primary Prevention, 18*, 71–128.

U.S. Departments of Education and Justice. (2000). *Working for children and families: Safe and smart afterschool programs*. Washington, DC: U.S. Department of Education.

Wills, T. A., & Shiffman, S. (1985). Coping and substance use: A conceptual framework. In S. Shiffman, & T. A. Wills (Eds.), *Coping and substance use* (pp. 1–24). Orlando, Fl: Academic.

22

Building Effective
Practices and Policies
for Out-of-School Time

Jane Quinn
The Children's Aid Society, New York

The journey to productive adulthood has become an increasingly complex assignment for young people—as has the work involved in directing, guiding, and supporting youth along that road. Labor economists and child development specialists both observe that successful adult life today requires an unprecedented set of technical and interpersonal skills. For example, in their groundbreaking book, *Teaching the New Basic Skills: Principles for Educating Children to Thrive in a Changing Economy,* labor economists Richard Murnane and Frank Levy (1996) outlined the qualifications deemed essential by today's business leaders:

- Literacy and numeracy at a minimum ninth grade level;
- Problem-solving abilities;
- Critical thinking skills;
- Knowledge of and comfort with technology; and
- Ability to work in groups with people of varied backgrounds.

Similarly, child psychiatrist James Comer has written extensively about the developmental expectations of today's society and economy, noting that young people growing up in 21st-century United States need to acquire "a higher level and greater number of skills" (Carnegie Council on Adolescent Development, 1992, p. 18) in order to succeed in adulthood. Comer's analysis provides a warning label, however. He cautions that, at the very time that

479

societal needs and expectations are rising, developmental supports and opportunities provided to youth by their families, schools, and communities are generally decreasing. Murnane and Levy (1996) offered similar caveats, noting that only about one half of our country's 17-year-olds possess the level of "new basic skills" needed to advance to the next step, be it further education or entry into the labor force.

The nonschool hours represent a critical building block in promoting young people's learning and development. The sheer amount of time is staggering—representing about 40% of waking hours (Timmer, Eccles, & O'Brien, 1985)—and so is the untapped potential. The nonschool hours (not only after-school time but also before-school, holidays, weekends, and summers) can provide opportunities to advance young people's growth in all of the development domains—cognitive, social, emotional, physical, and moral—by engaging youth in meaningful experiences that they themselves chose. Young people want and need such opportunities. When asked, most young people say they want "voice and choice" and also "fun and friends" in their free-time activities (S. W. Morris & Company, 1992). The voluntary nature of activities during the nonschool hours is of course one of their hallmarks and strengths, setting them quite apart from what happens during the regular school day.

The relationship of the school day to the rest of the day is not just one of contrast but of complementarity. The research of Reginald Clark (1988), beginning in the 1980s, established quite clearly that young people's out-of-school experience either contributed to or detracted from their school success. For example, Clark found that economically disadvantaged youth who spent between 20 to 35 hours per week engaged in constructive learning activities performed far better in school than their more passive peers. Organized youth programs represented one key component of constructive learning activities, as did reading for pleasure, talking with knowledgeable adults, and playing strategy games such as chess and checkers. Clark described constructive learning activities as those that encouraged young people to practice and apply their academic skills, especially reading, writing, and speaking.

ASSESSING THE CURRENT LANDSCAPE—
COMMENTARY ON CROSS-CUTTING THEMES

Although the authors in Part III of this volume approach the after-school and nonschool hours from different perspectives (theoretical, relational, programmatic, and systemic), they outline common themes and challenges that are worthy of concerted attention and additional comment: quantity of programs, quality of programs, focus and intended outcomes, staffing, other infrastructure, financing and sustainability, knowledge development.

Common Themes and Challenges

Quantity. Several authors in this volume (Pittman et al., chap. 17; Weisman et al., chap. 21; Vandell et al., chap. 20) noted the expansion in the number of after-school programs over the past 10 to 15 years, aided in no small measure by increases in public funding (most notably, the Federal 21st-Century Community Learning Centers). To date, this expansion has largely occurred in school-based programs, as dictated by the federal legislation that guided the effort from 1997 through 2001. Legislative changes authorized by Congress in late 2001 through the No Child Left Behind Act now permit 21st-century dollars to be spent on community-based programs, as long as they are at least as accessible as school-based programs (U.S. Government Printing Office, 2001). In the absence of another national study of before- and after-school programs (similar to the one conducted by Seppanen, deVries, & Seligson, 1993, for the U.S. Department of Education), it is difficult to know the extent to which after-school programs have proliferated during the past decade, apart from the 21st-Century-funded efforts. A future research agenda for the field would certainly include such national mapping.

Quality. Every author in this section analyzed issues around program quality—probably the number one opportunity and challenge in today's after-school landscape. Although the dimensions and measures of program quality are quite well established—through the efforts of such groups as the National School-Age Care Alliance (NSACA) and the National Institute on Out-of-School Time (NIOST)—relatively few programs meet quality standards and even fewer have become accredited through the Advancing and Recognizing Quality (ARQ) assessment system developed collaboratively by NSACA and NIOST. State licensing processes established in many states often have the effect of overregulating around issues of facilities and adult-to-child ratios while under-attending to the dimensions of quality outlined by Vandell and Shumow (1999)—staff–child interaction and developmental nature of activities.

Focus and Intended Outcomes. Although the authors in this section clearly favor a holistic approach to development—one that supports young people's growth in all of the developmental domains—the fact of the matter is that a major portion of the recent growth in after-school (and summer) programs is the result of school-based remedial efforts that have a very narrow focus, usually on raising test scores. Although these programs may offer attractive names, such as "Lighthouse" or "Power Hour," they are often based on notions that are antithetical to quality in after-school programs. For example, these programs may be mandatory, repetitive, rigid, and dull—not offering the voice, choice, fun, and friends that young people desire; and not offering the challenging content, engaging processes, and nurturing relationships advocated by NSACA and NIOST as part of a well-balanced after-school program. In this volume and elsewhere, Vandell and colleagues (1999) have documented a set of plausible outcomes from high-quality after-school programs that include improvements in work habits, social relations, emotional adjustment, and academic achievement. McLaughlin (2000) documented a similar set of outcomes as a result of adolescents' regular participation in community-based youth development programs, including higher education and career aspirations and greater sense of responsibility to the community. It is painful to watch substantial public dollars flow into narrow remedial programs in the face of such strong evidence about positive outcomes that can be achieved through implementation of high-quality programs across the elementary to high school age spectrum.

The chapter by Weisman and colleagues (chap. 21, this volume) is instructive because the authors outline a set of broad and seemingly realistic outcomes that they examined in the context of the goals and objectives established in the initiative described, such outcomes as (a) decreases in the number of unsupervised after-school hours, (b) increases in attachments of young people to prosocial adults, (c) increases in young people's involvement and investment in constructive learning activities, (d) increases in academic performance, (e) increases in beliefs against substance use and illegal behaviors, and (f) improved social skills. In this case, the initiative's designers and its partners (grantees and evaluators) had a very clear idea of intended outcomes and these outcomes seemed sensible, given the nature of the interventions that the initiative sought to support and foster.

Staffing. There is general agreement, in these pages and elsewhere (Carnegie Council on Adolescent Development, 1992), that the single most important contributor to program effectiveness is the quality of adult leadership (paid or volunteer). Whether the authors are considering adult mentors or paid full-time staff, they make a convincing case for investments in careful recruitment, orientation, training, and ongoing support for the adults who work with young people in after-school and other nonschool hour programs. Pittman et al. (chap. 17, this volume) rightly point to the progress made in selected cities to invest in after-school workforce development. Efforts at the individual city level, such as the 14-site BEST initiative (Building Exemplary Staff Training), have been complemented at the national level by major staff development initiatives sponsored by youth organizations such as Boys and Girls Clubs of America, Camp Fire USA, Girls Incorporated, and the YMCA of the United States. Over the past 10 to 15 years, staff development has increasingly come to be viewed as a necessary investment and as a legitimate cost of doing business in the youth development and after-school fields.

Infrastructure Development. The monumental challenges involved in achieving program quality described by authors in Part III will require additional investments in the work outlined by Pittman et al. (chap. 17) at the city level and by other authors at the organizational level. The chapters by Vandell et al. (chap. 20) and by Weisman et al. (chap. 21) describe programs that differ in quality, often by virtue of whether or not they are connected to other programs and to the research and practice knowledge base. Rhodes and Spencer (chap. 19) describe the kind of centralized program supports that undergird successful "matches" in mentoring programs, and Weisman et al. (chap. 21) cite specific social skills curricula that help to ensure program quality. Overall, a picture emerges of isolated programs struggling, often unsuccessfully, to find the right path, and of connected programs that are robust, thriving, and on the road to continuous improvement. Getting more programs on this road to success will surely require greater investments in the kinds of infrastructures described in this section—staff development, program development, curriculum development and evaluation, and knowledge development and dissemination.

Financing and Sustainability. Pittman and colleagues (chap. 17) offer an astute analysis of the challenges facing after-school providers as they seek to finance and sustain their work. Although collectively the after-school and youth development fields have made substantial progress over the past 10 years in generating new public and private dollars to underwrite program expansion, the Pittman chapter documents the major dilemmas—of the categorical nature of much of the available funding, which presents formidable barriers to practitioners trying to foster a holistic developmental approach; of the need for increased investments of public dollars at a time when most public sources are experiencing significant budget deficits; and of the complexity faced by municipal leaders (and other planners) as they work to leverage available federal funding.

Knowledge Development. Throughout this section, authors cite the research–practice connection as a critical nexus—whether it is the Vandell team visiting programs to examine quality, the Blyth team (see Walker et al., chap. 18) examining actual practice to extract useable theories, the Weisman team (chap. 21) studying program effects in a state-funded program, or the Pittman group (chap. 17) spending time in four cities to understand both the progress and work ahead at the municipal level. As several authors recount, the past decade has witnessed a strengthening of the bond between researchers and practitioners as research intermediaries like the Chapin Hall Center for Children and Pub-lic/Private Ventures have turned their considerable skills toward youth development and after-school program evaluation.

THE ROAD AHEAD—ADDRESSING OPPORTUNITIES
AND CHALLENGES THROUGH POLICY AND PRACTICE

The past decade provides important clues to the central opportunities and challenges on the road ahead—(a) the continued importance of program quality; (b) managing growth through appropriately balanced attention to quantity and quality; (c) continued public debate about the role and expec-tations of after-school programs; (d) increased attention to other aspects of the nonschool hours, especially summer; (e) financing and sustainability; and (f) knowledge development.

Building effective policies and practices in the after-school arena will re-quire concerted collective action. As a first step, youth advocates must rec-ognize the interrelated nature of policy and practice, and work to ensure that best practice informs public and social policy. Second, we must build the army of youth advocates and help practitioners understand that, be-cause high quality programs operate in a public policy context, every direct service program bears some responsibility for contributing to a multilevel (federal, state, and local) policy agenda. Third, as we look ahead, it is impor-tant to have a vision of our destination. In my view, our destination should be this: a fully aligned set of public policies supporting the implementation of high-quality after-school programs that are universally available and that promote children's learning and development. Here are specific recommen-dations—first policy and then practice—that can help to guide collective action directed toward this destination over the next several years.

Federal Policy

As we survey the current terrain of federal policy, the two most important vehicles for addressing quantity and quality of after-school programs are the 21st Century Community Learning Centers (21st CCLCs) program and the Younger Americans Act. Despite several similarities in philosophy and ap-proach, these initiatives currently stand at very different places in the legis-lative process and therefore require different kinds of attention.

The work ahead with the 21st CCLCs program at the national level is to ensure that the level of funding authorized by Congress is actually appropri-ated each year, and to ensure that the intent of Congress is actually honored when the funds are allocated by the state Departments of Education. To be specific, the No Child Left Behind legislation that was passed by Congress in December 2001 authorized expenditures of $1,250,000 billion for fiscal year

2002, with increases of $250 million every year through fiscal year 2007 (for a total of $2.5 billion by 2007). However, in the current fiscal climate, there is no guarantee that Congress will actually appropriate expenditures at these authorized levels. The After-School Alliance, the National School-Age Care Alliance, and other youth advocacy groups have made full appropriation of 21st CCLCs dollars a key legislative priority. But simply securing the fully authorized amount of the 21st CCLCs monies is not enough. Youth advocates must work to make sure that funds are spent as intended—that is, with a focus on academic enrichment and a broad array of youth-development activities. The central challenge here will be achieving the kind of programmatic balance outlined in the legislation, given the standards-and-sanctions orientation of other parts of No Child Left Behind and given the Bush Administration's early response to the first year evaluation of the 21st CCLCs program conducted by Mathematica Research Associates (U.S. Department of Education, 2002). This evaluation, as preliminary as it is (based on data collected during the 2000–2001 academic year), was cited by administration officials as justification for proposing a $400 million cut to the program. Many practitioners, myself included, understood that Mathematica's early findings provided useful formative data about three central issues: program quality, participation, and partnership. The programs, all school-based, studied by the Mathematica team consisted of academic help (homework assistance, tutoring, state test preparation) coupled with sports, recreation, arts, and interpersonal support such as mentoring. Schools and school districts ran the majority of the programs and many of the program leaders were day-school teachers, in part because during the initial years (consistent with the federal legislation supporting the work during this period), partnerships with community resources such as youth-serving organizations were encouraged but not required. And the majority of students participated at a very modest rate (on average, about 32 days per year for middle-school students and 58 days per year for elementary school students). Based on these factors, it is quite easy to see how the funded programs could be improved: (a) by offering more challenging and engaging content; (b) by encouraging more regular participation; and (c) by requiring schools to partner with community agencies with the capacity to offer an array of activities and services that are different from, yet linked to, what happens during the regular school day. Because the proposed cuts were not made to the 21st CCLC appropriation in 2003, many funded programs will have an opportunity to use the Mathematica findings to work on needed program improvements.

Not as far along on the legislative track but potentially as powerful (if not more) is the Younger Americans Act (YAA), cited earlier in this volume by Pedersen and Seidman (chap. 5). Modeled on the Older Americans Act, which provides a nationwide network of supportive services for senior populations, YAA provides incentives for communities to plan, implement, and be accountable for strategies that prepare young people for productive adulthood. Specifically, the proposed legislation sets forth a national youth policy to assure that youth have access to the full array of core developmental resources, including: (a) ongoing relationships with caring adults; (b) safe places with structured activities in which to grow and learn; (c) services that promote healthy lifestyles, including those designed to improve physical and mental health; (d) opportunities to acquire marketable skills; and (e) opportunities for community service and civic participation. Leading the charge nationally for enactment of this legislation is the National Collaboration for Youth, an interagency coalition of national youth-serving organizations. To date, over 80 national organizations have signed on to support YAA (National Collaboration for Youth, 2001a). According to the Congressional Research Service, the estimated cost of enacting YAA as introduced in the 107th Congress (H.R. 17 and S. 1005) would be $750 million in fiscal year 2003 (National Collaboration for Youth, 2001b). Several aspects of this legislation make it noteworthy:

- By establishing a national youth policy, it fills a critical public policy gap in our country;
- It is designed to mobilize local communities around youth development, using Federal resources as an incentive to leverage broader local support;
- It delivers 95% of appropriations directly to state and local programs;
- It focuses on all youth but provides more intensive support for young people in communities where the need is greatest;
- It engages young people as active participants in decision making, including program design, implementation, and evaluation;
- It encourages use of proven programmatic methods and materials; and
- It creates a federal advisory committee to help coordinate national youth policy.

The central challenge with the YAA is enactment. Although to date, YAA has received wide bipartisan support, it has gotten stalled in Congress in the aftermath of competing priorities following September 11.

State Policy

At the state level, youth advocates have important work to do in offering both input and oversight to their state education officials around the expenditure of 21st-Century grant dollars. Specific assignments can include providing public comment to draft requests for proposals, applying to be peer reviewers, and serving on task forces and advisory groups. In addition, because approximately 5% of each state's allocation is earmarked for training, technical assistance, and program evaluation, experienced providers can play an important role in teaching others how to implement high-quality programs and in helping to design evaluation approaches that address realistic and multifaceted outcomes.

Given the variation of state policies around after-school and youth development programs, it is difficult to generalize about what is or should be happening at the state level. A few states have leaped ahead of others in the levels of funding provided for after-school programs (California is the current leader in this regard) and in the rigor with which policymakers have approached the development of state frameworks (New York's adoption of a youth development framework across state agencies is one notable example). Several states have made creative use of major federal funding streams—such as Temporary Assistance to Needy Families and Child Care Development Block Grant monies—for after-school programs.

A seemingly underutilized source is the Master Settlement Agreement (MSA), popularly called the tobacco settlement, which is slated to provide some $205 billion to state treasuries over the 25-year period from 2000 through 2025. According to a recent report from the National Conference of State Legislatures, only 5% of the tobacco settlement dollars allocated thus far has been spent on smoking prevention and only 3% went to programs for children and youth (Dixon, 2002). Although many groups—including labor unions, health professionals, and tobacco farmers—are competing for this money, youth advocates have a highly plausible case to make in persuading their state legislators to allocate a higher percentage for youth smoking prevention, and after-school and other youth development programs. By applying the best available current knowledge, states could make wise use of tobacco settlement monies by supporting broad-scale implementation of proven approaches to smoking prevention (such as life skills training programs that build adolescents' knowledge and resistance skills). A sensible additional strategy would be for states to invest in broader youth development approaches that provide healthy alternatives for young people during nonschool hours and that have demonstrated their protective effects against several kinds of high-risk behavior, including use of cigarettes and other substances.

Over the past 10 years, state-level advocacy groups have made important strides in educating policymakers and in helping to enact youth-friendly legislation. In New York State, the Coalition for After-School Funding organizes an annual lobbying day in Albany that attracts nearly 1,000 youth advocates, parents, and young people who hold a public rally and press conference, and then meet with their state legislators to encourage expanded funding for after-school programs. In California, very effective state-level organizing has been greatly assisted by a consortium of private foundations that has supported public awareness campaigns and polls showing wide public support for expansion of after-school programs. One critical feature of most successful state-level advocacy campaigns is the role played by young people in advocating for increased public investments in after-school and youth development initiatives.

The critical link between policy and practice is experienced most acutely at the state level, where the majority of licensing and regulatory decisions about after-school programs are made. One of the most important steps that state agencies could take is to provide incentives for programs to become accredited through the ARQ (Advancing and Recognizing Quality) process, which represents the state-of-the-art in after-school program practice. Because this process is time and labor intensive, many practitioners and program administrators are hesitant to commit agency resources to this effort. But policymakers want some assurance that they are making wise investments of public dollars, and the objective nature and rigor of the ARQ process can provide such assurance. State child-care licensing agencies have a potentially powerful quality assurance vehicle in ARQ by providing monetary incentives for programs to become accredited and status differentials (such as competitive advantage in responding to requests for proposals) for programs that are successful.

Probably the best single source of ideas about state policy around after-school programs is the recent study from The Finance Project (Langford, 2001) entitled "State Legislative Investments in School-Age Children and Youth." This publication documents the growing interest of state legislatures across the country in out-of-school time programs, noting that in recent years, 46 of the 50 states enacted legislation explicitly referring to supports and services for school-age children and youth; and that collectively, state legislatures created 215 statutes that provide for out-of-school time and community school initiatives. Despite this optimistic picture, the report (Langford, 2001) provided the following cautionary note: "... it is not clear whether state legislative support for out-of-school time and community school initiatives is simply a funding fad that will fade over time or whether it is a system-building investment that will provide for sustainable services for school-age children and youth" (p. 8). Several factors—including political transitions at the state level, reauthorization, and annual appropriation processes, linking new programs with existing supports and services, and the changing federal context—are all cited as factors that will help to influence whether this recent spate of state legislative activity is a fad or an investment. This publication provides an important guide for youth advocates about how to learn from past successes at the state level and how to smooth the potential bumps in the road ahead.

Local Policy

Many of the lessons learned from successful federal and state advocacy efforts are mirrored at the local level. Citywide coalitions have tackled the after-school policy agenda in many locations; capacity-building intermediary organizations have been created in a dozen or more cities; and local tax levies have been passed in several cities, providing permanent funding from general public revenue sources. One of the most successful after-school innovations at the municipal level is the Beacons, launched with general tax dollars in New York City over 10 years ago and now being replicated in several cities, including Denver, Minneapolis, Oakland, Philadelphia, and San Francisco. The Beacons represent another stellar example of the intersection of policy and practice because, in order to implement these school-based youth and family development programs in a large number of sites, each city had to make important policy changes, including interagency agreements and budgeting provisions. Other municipalities have crafted citywide after-school initiatives, with names like After School Matters (Chicago), the 2:00-to-6:00 After-School Initiative (Boston), the 6-to-6 Initiative (San Diego), and LA's BEST (Better Educated Students for Tomorrow). What these efforts share is municipal (often mayoral) leadership that results in interagency cooperation and substantial commitment of public financial resources. These and other efforts have been documented in several places, including publications of The Finance Project (1999) and the National League of Cities Institute for Youth, Education, and Families (n.d.), and they represent a solid base of policy and practice on which to build future work.

Practice

As we look ahead to invent our future in the out-of-school field, we want alignment between policy and practice and also between research and practice. We actually know a great deal about what constitutes effective practice, much of which is outlined in this volume. At the program level, practitioners would do well to attend to these and other recent research findings that have documented such key elements as (a) quality of adult–child and peer interaction; (b) nature of activities, particularly whether or not they are well balanced, engaging and offering opportunities to develop new skills; and (c) the importance of participation patterns, particularly the consistent finding that "dosage makes a difference." Although this latter finding is not new (see, e.g., Girls Incorporated, 1991), it has been highlighted in an important recent study of after-school programs conducted in multiple sites around the country by Public/Private Ventures and the Manpower Demonstration Research Corporation for the Wallace-Reader's Digest Fund (Grossman et al., 2002). One of the key findings of this study was that, on average, youth participated in after-school programs slightly less than 2 days per week. This actual participation pattern stands in stark contrast to the picture many policymakers, parents, and practitioners hold in their minds of young people, active and engaged, during the bulk of their nonschool hours. The authors offer a couple of additional thoughts about participation:

> While this participation rate could suggest that students might not be attending often enough for programs to achieve their goals of strengthening youth's academic and social skills, it is important to understand that many of the participants attended these programs over an extended period of time. More than a third (35%) of the enrollees participated in all four semesters that were covered by this study and, overall, 84% participated in two or more semesters. These participation patterns suggest the possibility of a cumulative effect of less intensive participation over time. (p. iii)

Later in the report, the authors offer this insight:

> When considering the extent of participation ... and its potential benefits, it is also important to keep in mind that many of the youth were engaged in other activities in addition to ESS [Extended-Service Schools].... However, even while they said they spent much of their after-school time in supervised settings, a non-trivial proportion of their time was unsupervised—more than half of the youth typically spent some part of their after-school hours each week without adult supervision. (p. 14)

Many after-school programs do not in fact know which children participate in which programs over what period of time, making it hard for them to assess their potential or actual impact. Recent advances in technology, through the development of specialized management information systems, allow practitioners to track the participation of individual youth, providing useful data for program planning and evaluation.[1]

However, tracking participation does not make a lot of sense if the overall quality of after-school programs is poor. One of the most promising avenues for improving program quality is the development of enrichment curricula designed specifically for use in the nonschool hours. Several of the best known and most highly regarded curricula—such as FOUNDATIONS (2002) and KidzLit—focus on building children's literacy skills by taking an enrichment

---

[1]For example, the Wallace-funded Extended-Service Schools sites used a management information system known as Youth Services, originally developed by CitySpan for the San Francisco Beacons.

approach to reading, writing, and speaking. The key ingredients of an enrichment approach are exposure to new ideas, hands-on experience, and engaging activities (Quinn, 2002). *FOUNDATIONS* (2002) and *KidzLit* activate these ingredients by making different kinds of carefully chosen books available to children for reading and discussion, and organizing a wide variety of "connected" activities that encourage children to relate the books to their own lives and experiences, play with new vocabulary words, and apply the ideas about which they are reading. For example, if students have read a book about celebrations in Latino cultures, they might discuss celebrations within their own families, build a piñata in the arts portion of the program, and then plan a culminating activity such as a party that incorporates the kinds of food, music, and games about which they have read. Both *FOUNDATIONS* (2002) and *KidzLit* base their approaches on the best available research from multiple fields, including literacy development and child development. In addition, *FOUNDATIONS* (2002) has been the subject of a rigorous evaluation conducted by the Rand Corporation and has been shown to produce a variety of positive results, including substantial and statistically significant gains in both math and reading scores between the fall pretest and spring posttest.

Literacy is not the only topic covered by such centralized after-school enrichment curricula. There are excellent math enrichment programs and resources, such as *Figure This* and *KidzMath*. For science enrichment, there are *Girls Inc.'s Operation SMART* (Science, Math, and Relevant Technology), and *World in Motion*. And there are several well regarded and evaluated life skills curricula, such as *Overcoming Obstacles* (see Appendix for a listing of after-school enrichment curricula and contact information).

Adopting these kinds of high-quality enrichment curricula offers multiple benefits for after-school programs. The materials are flexible and adaptable, allowing group leaders to use the curricula as a guide and jumping off point rather than as a script to be rigidly adhered to. Because many have been field-tested in multiple and diverse after-school sites, they have broad applicability in engaging young people in constructive and developmentally appropriate learning activities. Also, because these curricula are designed to be used in informal settings, they work well within an intentionally "balanced" after-school program that combines academic enrichment with other kinds of enrichment (recreational, cultural, and social) and academic support (such as homework help). One additional key benefit is that use of these curricula is cost effective. Local programs can deploy their precious financial resources to purchase materials and to train, supervise, and compensate staff—rather than on the much more expensive aspects of developing program curricula from scratch.

Because few of these curricula have yet been the subject of rigorous evaluation, this work represents fertile ground for philanthropic investment and for researcher and practitioner collaboration. The strongest of these curricula—those that are research-based, have been field-tested in multiple settings and have shown themselves to be engaging and interesting to young people—would be the best candidates for such investments. One caveat, however, is that these programs should not be asked to substitute or compensate for weak core instructional programs during the regular school day. This is a clear and present danger in this era of standards-based reform, high-stakes testing, and evidence-based approaches to curriculum selection. A more realistic and appropriate approach would be to assess after-school curricula and programs on the basis of how much value they added to young people's overall learning and healthy development.

Finally, we cycle back to staff quality—the *sine qua non* of after-school programs. If we are to mine the deepest veins of the after-school terrain, we cannot afford to pay our workforce less than parking lot attendants. And we cannot afford to leave our direct service workers adrift on Tuesdays at 3 p.m. as they face 20 young charges. Viable alternatives exist—to compensate our staffs fairly for the important work they do and to support their daily efforts through organized training, supervision, and provision of carefully selected programmatic resources and materials.

CONCLUSION

If all our nation's children are to achieve productive adulthood, they will need to have ongoing access to developmental supports and opportunities throughout childhood and adolescence, during the nonschool hours as well as the regular school day and during the summer months as well as the regular school year. Our knowledge is imperfect but it is growing—as is public support for the kinds of work described in this volume. The high levels of public support documented by the After-School Alliance and other advocates have contributed substantially to more enlightened public policies that recognize the importance of the nonschool hours in promoting children's learning and development. The major progress we have made over the past 10 years should encourage all of us—policymakers, practitioners, researchers, funders, parents, and young people—to work together to advance the inspiring vision of "after school for all."

APPENDIX: AFTER-SCHOOL ENRICHMENT CURRICULA USED BY THE CHILDREN'S AID SOCIETY COMMUNITY SCHOOLS

1. The Activities Club
Tel: 1-800-873-5487; **Website:** www.activitiesclub.com
Contact: The Activities Club
   • Thematic after-school clubs, homework help manuals, and other support materials.

2. The Comic Book Project
Tel: 718-263-6377
Contact: Dr. Michael Bitz, Director
- Literacy enrichment program for sixth through eighth graders in which youth create their own comic books. This program is still in pilot stage and is not currently available for purchase.

3. Figure This!
Tel: 1-202-667-0901; **Website:** www.figurethis.org
Contact: Marjorie Schacter, Senior Account Manager
- Fun and challenging math problems, based on the NCTM standards, designed to help middle school students strengthen higher order math skills.

4. Foundations
Tel: 1- 888-977-KIDS; **Website:** www.foundations-inc.org
Contact: Malik Stewart, Curriculum Specialist
- Literature-based yearlong curricular themes for K–6, developed especially for after-school programs. CAS uses this as one of our two core literacy programs in after-school (the other is KidzLit).

5. Junior Achievement
Tel: 1-212-907-0027; **Website:** www.ja.org
Contact: Alex Vasquez, Manager for School Management Group
- Activity modules for K–12 on business and economic skills.

6. KidzLit: An After-School Reading Program
Tel: 1- 800-666-7270; **Website:** www.devstu.org
Contact: Fran Chamberlain, Director, After-School Literature
- Children's literature and teachers' guides developed for use in after-school programs with children in Grades K–8. CAS uses this as one of our two core literacy programs in after-school (the other is Foundations).

7. KidzMath: An After-School Math Program
Tel: 1- 800-666-7270; **Website:** www.devstu.org
Contact: Megan Weber
- Fun, interactive math games for children ages 5 through 8. Programs for older kids are in development.

8. Operation Smart: Science, Math, and Relevant Technology
Tel: 1- 800-374-4475; **Website:** www.girlsinc.org
Contact: Sally Baker of Girls Inc., New York City
- After-school science program for girls ages 9 through 11. Girls Inc. also offers other excellent programs for girls' empowerment and development.

9. Overcoming Obstacles
Tel: (212) 406-7488; **Website:** www.overcomingobstacles.org
Contact: Tara J. Funk, Professional Development Director
- A life skills curriculum for middle and high school youth that helps young people make reasoned decisions, set and meet goals, communicate effectively, learn conflict resolution, and develop sound study skills. The activities incorporate literacy skills.

10. Project Adventure
Tel: 1-978-524-4500; **Website:** www.pa.org
Contact: Project Adventure, Massachusetts
- An "Adventure Education" program (both recreational and academic-based models available) that helps children build self-esteem and strengthen their social, teamwork, and leadership skills.

11. Putumayo "World Playground: A Musical Adventure for Kids"
Tel: 1-800-995-9588; **Website:** www.putumayo.com
Contact: Putumayo, New York
- Multicultural education curriculum incorporating world music.

12. 24 Game
Tel: 1- 800-242-4542; **Website:** www.24game.com
Contact: Mary Geschel
- A fun math game that reinforces basic skills, mental mathematics, problem solving, pattern sensing, concentration, and critical thinking. Available in Levels K–12.

13. World In Motion
Tel: 1-724-772-8514
Contact: Kathleen O'Connor Byrnes, K–12 Program Manager for SAE International
- Hands-on engineering design program for Grades 4 through 6, in which children are challenged to build three toys: a balloon-powered car, a fan-powered sailboat, and a rubber-band-powered rolling toy. All challenges allow children to explore science, math, and technology. The program is free and all materials for up to 34 children are included.

REFERENCES

Carnegie Council on Adolescent Development. (1992). *A matter of time: Risk and opportunity in the nonschool hours.* New York: Carnegie Corporation of New York.

Clark, R. M. (1988). *Critical factors in why disadvantaged children succeed or fail in school.* New York: Academy for Educational Development.

Dixon, L. (2002). *Analysis of states' allocation of tobacco settlement revenue*. Retrieved March 18, 2003, from the National Conference of State Legislatures Web site: http://www.ncsl.org/programs/health/hpts/tsrreport.htm

The Finance Project. (1999, September). *Creating dedicated local revenue for out-of-school time initiatives*. Washington, DC: Author.

FOUNDATIONS, Inc. (2002, December 2). *Improvements in math and reading scores in students who did and did not participate in the FOUNDATIONS After School enrichment program during the 2001–2002 School Year*. Retrieved March 18, 2003, from http://www.foundationsinc.org/ExtendedDayFolder/conclusions.asp

Girls Incorporated. (1991). *Truth, trust and technology: New research on preventing adolescent pregnancy*. New York: Author.

Grossman, J. B., Price, M. L., Fellerath, V., Jucovy, L. Z., Kotloff, L. J., Raley, R., & Walker, K. E. (2002). *Multiple choices after school: Findings from the extended-service schools initiative*. Philadelphia: Public/Private Ventures and Manpower Demonstration Research Corporation.

Langford, B. H. (2001). *State legislative investments in school-age children and youth*. Washington, DC: The Finance Project.

McLaughlin, M. W. (2000). *Community counts: How community organizations matter for youth development*. Washington, DC: Public Education Network.

Morris, S. W., & Company. (1992, January). *What young adolescents need and want from out-of-school programs: A focus group report*. Unpublished paper.

Murnane, R. J., & Levy, F. (1996). *Teaching the new basic skills: Principles for educating children to thrive in a changing economy*. New York: The Free Press.

National Collaboration for Youth. (2001b. *The Younger Americans Act: State allocations*. Retrieved March 18, 2003, from http://www.nydic.org/nydic/YAAnew/C4allocaions.html

National Collaboration for Youth. (2001a). *The Younger Americans Act: Organizations supporting the Younger Americans Act*. Retrieved April 30, 2003, from http://www.nydic.org/nydic/YAAnew/B4organizations.html

National League of Cities Institute for Youth, Education, and Families. (n.d.). *Expanding afterschool opportunities: Action kit for municipal leaders* (Issue No. 4). Washington, DC: Author.

Quinn, J. (2002). Youth work's vitamin E. *Youth Today, 11*(5), 54.

Seppanen, P., deVries, D., & Seligson, M. (1993). *National study of before- and after-school programs* (Office of Policy and Planning, U.S. Department of Education). Retrieved March 18, 2003, from http://www.ed.gov/offices/OUS/PES/esed/ b4%26aftr.html

Timmer, S. G., Eccles, J., & O'Brien, J. (1985). How children use time. In F. T. Juster & F. B. Stafford (Eds.), *Time, goods and well-being*. Ann Arbor: University of Michigan, Institute for Social Research.

U.S. Department of Education, Office of the Under Secretary. (2002). *When schools stay open late: The national evaluation of the 21st-Century Community Learning Centers Program (first year findings)*.

U.S. Government Printing Office. (December 13, 2001). *No Child Left Behind Act: Conference report to accompany H.R. 1*.

Vandell, D. L., & Shumow, L. (1999). After-school child care programs. *The future of children: When school is out, 9*(2), 64–80.

About the Editors

Joseph L. Mahoney is Assistant Professor in the Department of Psychology at Yale University. His research focuses on social adjustment during the school years with particular interest in children's and adolescents' use of out-of-school time. At Yale, he directs the Social Policy and Intervention Laboratory and the Yale Study of Children's After-school Time. He is a faculty member of the Yale Bush Center for Social Policy and Child Development, and a member of the National Board of Directors for the Horizons National summer enrichment program, and is affiliated with the Yale Child Study Center. He is also a member of the National Academy of Science's Committee on Family and Work Policies and recently received the Public Policy Award from the Smith Richardson Foundation. He earned his PhD in Developmental Psychology from the Center for Developmental Science at the University of North Carolina at Chapel Hill in 1997 and completed postdoctoral training from the Psychological Institute at Stockholm University in 1999.

Reed W. Larson is the Pampered Chef Ltd. Endowed Chair in Family Resiliency and a Professor in the Departments of Human and Community Development, Psychology, and Educational Psychology at the University of Illinois at Urbana-Champaign. His research focuses on the daily experience of adolescents and their parents. He is author of *Divergent Realities: The Emotional Lives of Mothers, Fathers, and Adolescents* (with Maryse Richards) and *Being Adolescent: Conflict and Growth in the Teenage Years* (with Mihaly Csikszentmihalyi). He has also conducted research on adolescents' media use, time alone, experience with friends, and school experience. He was recently the chair of the Study Group on Adolescence in the 21st Century, sponsored by the Society for Research on Adolescence. His current area of interest is adolescents' experience in extracurricular activities, community-based programs, and other structured, voluntary activities in the after-school hours.

Jacquelynne S. Eccles is on the faculty at the University of Michigan. She has served on the Society for Research on Adolescence (SRA) Council and is now President of SRA. She was also President of Division 35 of APA, a member of the DBASSE Committee of the National Academy of Science (NAS), and chair of the NAS Committee on After School Programs for Youth. Her awards include the Spencer Foundation Fellowship for Outstanding Young Scholars in Educational Research, the APS Cattell Fellows Award for Outstanding Applied Work in Psychology, and SPSSI's Kurt Lewin Award for Outstanding Research. She has conducted research on topics ranging from gender-role socialization and classroom influences on motivation to social development in the family, school, peer group, and wider cultural contexts.

About the Authors

Amy L. Anderson is an Assistant Professor of Criminal Justice at the University of Nebraska at Omaha. Her research interests include the social context of crime, juvenile delinquency and other deviant behavior, and criminological theory.

Megan L. Babkes is an Assistant Professor in the School of Sport and Exercise Science at the University of Northern Colorado. She earned a BA in Psychology from the University of Washington, an MS in Exercise Science from the University of Oregon, a PhD in Kinesiology from the University of Northern Colorado, and completed a postdoctoral research fellowship at UCLA in Social Psychology with the International Center for Talent Development before returning to Colorado. Her areas of research focus on the role of significant others in the psychosocial components (perceptions of competence, motivation, and emotional responses) of youth achievement. Specifically, she is interested in the nature and impact of parental, sibling, and peer influences in sport and other talent domains, such as music, art, and dance. She also studies the impact of Special Olympics and other physical domain activities on individuals with mental retardation and their families. Dr. Babkes is committed to integrating the fields of psychology, kinesiology, and special education through research and service and enjoys using her knowledge in both volunteer and professional endeavors. She currently serves on the Social Psychology Committee for the Association for the Advancement of Applied Sport Psychology, teaches skiing and sailing with National Sport Center for the Disabled, and consults with numerous youth sport organizations in the Western United States.

Bonnie L. Barber is a Professor of Family Studies and Human Development at the University of Arizona. She completed her PhD in Developmental Psychology at the University of Michigan in 1990. Her research interests include adolescent and young adult social relationships across life transitions, long-term benefits of activity participation, and positive adolescent development in divorced families. She has also studied the effectiveness of empir-

499

ically based curricula for divorced mothers with adolescents in the United States and Australia, and collaborated on a U.S. outcome evaluation of programs for youth and families at risk. The Spencer Foundation, the William T. Grant Foundation, and the National Science Foundation have funded her current longitudinal research on adolescence and the transition to young adulthood.

Lynne M. Borden is an Associate Professor and Extension Specialist with an emphasis in youth development. She is in the Division of Family Studies and Human Development, School of Family and Consumer Sciences at the University of Arizona. Her research focuses on youth development, specifically on community youth development, community programs that promote the positive development of young people, and public policy. She also works with communities to strengthen their community-based programs through evaluation and training. She is one of co-editors (Villarruel, Perkins, & Keith) of the *Community Youth Development: Programs, Policies and Practices,* which examines community youth development from multiple perspectives. She received a PhD in Human Resources and Family Studies from the University of Illinois at Urbana-Champaign in 1997.

Sean L. Bryner is a Probation and Parole Officer in Martinsburg, West Virginia, and an Adjunct Professor in Mathematics at Shepherd College. He is currently working on his Master's of Arts in Criminology and Criminal Justice at the University of Maryland. His research interests include community corrections and crime prevention programs.

David M. Casey is currently a community and policy research coordinator at the University of Calgary, in the Department of Community Health Sciences within the Faculty of Medicine. He is involved in research that focuses on the design and evaluation of interventions to promote the health of high school students. He earned his PhD in Human Development and Family Sciences from the University of Texas at Austin in 2001. He has conducted research examining participation in out-of-school activities among children and adolescents from low-income families, particularly participation in activities during the summer months. His research interests also include time use, delinquent behavior, and prevention of delinquent behavior among school-age children and adolescents.

Joan L. Duda is a Professor of Sports Psychology in the School of Sport and Exercise Sciences at The University of Birmingham, UK, and an Adjunct Professor in the Department of Psychological Sciences at Purdue University. She completed her BA (1977) in Psychology and Women's Studies at Rutgers University, her MS degree (1978) at Purdue University, and her PhD (1981) at the University of Illinois at Urbana-Champaign. Dr. Duda is a Past-President of the Association for the Advancement of Applied Sport Psychology and has also been a member of the executive boards of the North American Society for the Psychology of Sport and Physical Activity, the Sport Psychology Academy, and the International Society for Sport Psychology. She was editor of the *Journal of Applied Sport Psychology* and is on the Editorial Board of the *Journal of Sport and Exercise Psychology*, the *International Journal of Sport Psychology*, and the *Psychology of Sport and Exercise Journal*. Dr. Duda has published extensively on the topic of sport motivation and the psychological dimensions of sport and exercise behavior and is the editor of Advances in Sport and Exercise Psychology Measurement (1998). She was named Visiting International Scholar by the Australian Sport Psychology Society in 1997. Dr. Duda has been a mental skills/performance excellence consultant for over 15 years, working with athletes and performers at different competitive levels, is certified as a consultant by the Association for the Advancement of Applied Sport Psychology, and is listed on the U.S.A. Olympic Registry (1996–2004).

Christopher Dunbar, Jr. is an Assistant Professor in Educational Administration at Michigan State University. He received his PhD from the University of Illinois at Urbana-Champaign. His research has focused on alternative education for African American children. His book, *Alternative Schooling for African American Youth: Does Anyone Know We're Here?* (Peter Lang Publishers, 2001), is about an alternative school designated for students who have been unable to successfully matriculate through traditional public school. He has authored scholarly journal articles and studies and has also presented his research at several professional conferences. His research interests include examining the intersection between school choice policy and educational opportunities for disruptive students. His most recent work has focused on urban school principals and the impact of zero tolerance policy on their administrative responsibilities. He currently teaches courses on research inquiries, organizational theory, and the intersection of schools, families, and communities.

Stephanie A. Gerstenblith is an Associate at Caliber Associates, Inc., in Fairfax, Virginia. She received a PhD in Criminology and Criminal Justice from the University of Maryland College Park in May 2000. She is currently working on a variety of projects, including an evaluation of a school-based Internet safety program. Dr. Gerstenblith worked for 5 years on the evaluation of Maryland's After School Community Grant Program (MASCGP). Her research interests include delinquency prevention and program planning and evaluation.

Denise C. Gottfredson is a Professor at the University of Maryland Department of Criminology and Criminal Justice. She received a PhD in Social Relations from The Johns Hopkins University. Gottfredson's research interests include delinquency and delinquency prevention, and particularly the effects of school environments on youth behavior. She is the author of *Schools and Delinquency* (Cambridge University Press, 2001) and several influential summaries of effective school-based prevention strategies. She currently directs evaluations of Baltimore City's Drug Treatment Court and Maryland After School Opportunity Grant Fund Program, both of which address important policy questions for the state of Maryland. She is Co-Principal Investigator on an evaluation of the Strengthening Washington, DC Families Program and directs a grant to work with the prevention community in the state of Maryland to increase the use of research-based prevention practices.

David M. Hansen is a postdoctoral research associate in the Department of Human and Community Development at the University of Illinois at Urbana-Champaign. The focus of his research is on the learning experiences of adolescents in out-of-school extracurricular and community-based activities, and other structured, voluntary activities. He has published book chapters and articles examining adolescent development in the context of after-school activities and the context of part-time employment during high school. He holds a PhD in Human and Community Development from the University of Illinois at Urbana-Champaign.

James E. Hunt is a doctoral student in Family Studies and Human Development at the University of Arizona. He received his Master's Degree from the University of Arizona in 2002, and is currently a research assistant and academic advisor there. His research interests include adolescent steroid use, sports participation, issues of male body image, drug use, risk behaviors, and media influences on development.

Aletha C. Huston is the Pricilla Pond Flawn Regents Professor of Child Development at the University of Texas at Austin. She earned her PhD in Psychology from the University of Minnesota. She is a Principal Investigator in the assessment of child and family impacts of the New Hope Project, a study of the effects on children and families of parents' participation in a work-based program to reduce poverty. Dr. Huston is a member of the MacArthur Network on Successful Pathways Through Middle Childhood, and she is an Investigator in the NICHD Study of Early Child Care, a longitudinal study following a national sample of children from birth through middle childhood. She edited *Children in Poverty: Child Development and Public Policy* and has written numerous articles on poverty and children. She is the first author of *Big World, Small Screen: The Role of Television in American Society,* which won the Award for Distinguished Contribution to Psychology and the Media from The Division of Media Psychology of the American Psychological Association in 1992. She has won numerous research awards, including the Urie Bronfenbrenner Award for Lifetime Contributions to Developmental Psychology in the Service of Science and Society, the Nicholas Hobbs award for Research and Child Advocacy from the American Psychological Association, and the Award for Distinguished Contributions to Public Policy for Children from the Society for Research in Child Development.

Merita Irby is Co-founder of the Forum for Youth Investment, a U.S. initiative of the International Youth Foundation (IYF) dedicated to supporting U.S. organizations that invest in young people. As Deputy Director of the Forum, she is responsible for overall implementation and integration of the Forum's strategies, of increasing connections, building capacity, and tackling the challenges across the allied youth fields. Prior to joining IYF, Merita served as Special Assistant to the Director of the President's Crime Prevention Council, chaired by former Vice President Al Gore. At the Council, she facilitated a working group of representatives from seven federal departments and three agencies in developing an integrated, common agenda for youth intervention, prevention, and development programs to streamline information for local communities. Previously, as Program Officer for Research and Evaluation at the Center for Youth Development, she directed a multisite study on school collaboration with youth organizations and developed technical assistance tools and strategies for collaboration and organizational development. Her interest in youth development began as a Senior Research Associate at Stanford University where she worked on a 5-year study of community-based urban youth organizations and co-authored *Urban Sanctuaries: Community Organizations in the Lives and Futures of Inner-City Youth.* She has published extensively and produced video films on youth development education programs. She received her Master's in Public Policy from the John F. Kennedy School of Government, Harvard University. She began her career as a classroom teacher in Central America and in inner-city schools in the United States.

Janis Jacobs is Vice Provost for Undergraduate Education and International Programs at The Pennsylvania State University. She received her doctorate from the University of Michigan and she currently holds academic appointments as Professor of Human Development and Family Studies and Professor of Psychology. Dr. Jacobs' research and writing focus on the development of social cognitive processes during childhood and adolescence. She has published numerous articles and chapters related to the formation of judgment biases in real-world decisions and to gender differences in achievement motivation, self-perceptions of achievement, and parents' influence on achievement.

Melissa A. Kellstrom is a Juvenile Counselor in the Investigations Unit of the Maryland Department of Juvenile Justice. She is currently working on her Master's of Arts in Criminology and Criminal Justice at the University of Maryland and her thesis examines after-school programs and their effects on high- and low-risk students. Her research interests are juvenile delinquency and delinquency prevention.

Margaret Kerr is Professor of Psychology at Örebro University in Sweden, and Co-Director of the Center for Developmental Research, together with Professor Håkan Stattin. She recently served a 4-year term as Newsletter Editor for the European Association for Research on Adolescence, and is now a member of the Executive Committee. Her research focuses on internal and external adjustment in adolescents and its role in the life course. Currently, she and Professor Stattin are conducting a 7-year longitudinal study of all youth between 10 and 18 years in an entire Swedish community. Her published work has looked at behavioral inhibition and social withdrawal and their roles as risk or protective factors for problems including delinquency and depression, and, more recently, parental monitoring and other family management strategies. Professor Kerr earned her PhD in the Psychology Department at Cornell University, and then completed a postdoctoral research fellowship with Richard Tremblay at the University of Montreal, Canada. Her current research interests include adolescents' choices of developmental contexts and parent–child relationships and their role in preventing delinquency.

Ben Kirshner is a doctoral student at the Stanford University School of Education (Child and Adolescent Development). He currently works as a research assistant with the John W. Gardner Center for Youth and Their Communities. His dissertation research examines how young people's views of self and society develop as they engage in civic activism. Ben has written and presented on youth's experiences in after school community centers, youth–adult research partnerships, and youth civic engagement. Ben is also the co-editor of "Youth Participation: Improving Institutions and Communities," a special issue of the journal *New Directions for Youth Development* (with Jennifer O'Donoghue & Milbrey McLaughlin, Jossey Bass, 2002).

Douglas A. Kleiber is Professor and Director of the School of Health and Human Performance at the University of Georgia. He received a PhD in Educational Psychology from the University of Texas at Austin in 1972 and an

AB in Psychology from Cornell University in 1969. He has taught previously in the Department of Leisure Studies at the University of Illinois and in the Department of Psychology at St. Cloud State University in St. Cloud, Minnesota. He was head of the Department of Recreation and Leisure Studies at the University of Georgia from 1989–1991. He has published over 70 articles in refereed journals, as well as 15 chapters and 3 books, dealing mostly with the psychology of recreation, sport, and leisure, especially as related to developmental transitions. He recently completed a book entitled *Leisure Experience and Human Development* for Basic Books/Westview Press. He is a Founding member of the American Psychological Society and a past President of the Academy of Leisure Sciences.

Richard M. Lerner is the Bergstrom Chair in Applied Developmental Science and the Director of the Applied Developmental Science Institute in the Eliot-Pearson Department of Child Development at Tufts University. A developmental psychologist, Lerner received a PhD in 1971 from the City University of New York. He has been a fellow at the Center for Advanced Study in the Behavioral Sciences and is a fellow of the American Association for the Advancement of Science, the American Psychological Association, and the American Psychological Society. Prior to joining Tufts University, he was on the faculty and held administrative posts at Michigan State University, Pennsylvania State University, and Boston College, where he was the Anita L. Brennan Professor of Education and the Director of the Center for Child, Family, and Community Partnerships. During the 1994–95 academic year, Lerner held the Tyner Eminent Scholar Chair in the Human Sciences at Florida State University. Lerner is the author or editor of 55 books and more than 360 scholarly articles and chapters. He edited Volume 1, on "Theoretical Models of Human Development," for the fifth edition of the *Handbook of Child Psychology*. He is the founding editor of the *Journal of Research on Adolescence and of Applied Developmental Science*. He is known for his theory of, and research about, relations between life-span human development and contextual or ecological change. He has done foundational studies of adolescents' relations with their peer, family, school, and community contexts, and is a leader in the study of public policies and community-based programs aimed at the promotion of positive youth development.

Heather Lord is a doctoral student at Yale University. She received her BS in Human Development from Cornell University in 2002. She has spent the past year as a fellow at the Yale Bush Center for Social Policy and Child Development, and Project Coordinator for the Yale Study of Children's After-School Time. Her research interests include out-of-school arrangements and the prevention of antisocial behaviors as well as implications of that research for public policy.

Shaoli Lu is a student in Quantitative Methods in the Social Sciences Program at Columbia University. Her research interests include delinquency prevention, experimental design, and applied statistics.

David Magnusson is Professor Emeritus in the Department of Psychology at Stockholm University. He is an internationally recognized researcher who has made important contributions with regard to both theoretical issues in relation to the interactionistic research paradigm and the study of the adjustment process. He holds several honorary degrees from universities across Europe, and he has been the chairman of the longitudinal network for longitudinal research in the European Science Foundation.

Mary S. Marczak is a Youth Development Evaluator and Researcher at the Center for 4-H Youth Development, University of Minnesota. Her current position entails conducting applied research on quality youth development efforts and examining the impact of a large youth-serving organization. Dr. Marczak has worked extensively with community-based projects and organizations in an effort to better understand the perceived impact of their effects on communities, organizations, policy, programs, and individuals. Prior to coming to Minnesota, Dr. Marczak was at the University of Arizona, Department of Family Studies and Human Development, where she conducted research on quality parent–child and young adult relationships. Her current research focuses on effective youth development program practices, effective community-wide approaches to youth development, and linkages between individual, family, and community outcomes.

Hugh McIntosh is a doctoral student in Human Development at The Catholic University of America. His research interests include developmental assessment, identity formation, and other aspects of the transition from adolescence to adulthood.

Milbrey McLaughlin is the David Jacks Professor of Education and Public Policy at Stanford University. She received her BA from Connecticut College in Philosophy and her EdM and EdD from Harvard University in Education and Social Policy. Professor McLaughlin is Co-Director of the Center for Research on the Context of Teaching, an education research center supported by both federal and foundation funding. Its program of research analyzes how teaching and learning are shaped by their organizational, institutional, and social cultural contexts. Dr. McLaughlin is Director of the John W. Gardner Center for Youth and Their Communities, a partnership between Stanford University and Bay Area communities to build new practices, knowledge, and capacity for youth development and learning. Prior to joining the Stanford faculty, McLaughlin was a Senior Social Scientist at the

Rand Corporation, where she worked on problems of policy implementation and planned change in education, most particularly the Change Agent study. Dr. McLaughlin is the author or co-author of books, articles, and chapters on education policy issues, contexts for teaching and learning, productive environments for youth, and community-based organizations. Her selected recent books include *Community Counts: How Youth Organizations Matter for Youth Development* (Public Education Fund Network, 2000), *Urban Sanctuaries: Neighborhood Organizations in the Lives and Futures of Inner City Youth* (with Merita A. Irby & Juliet Langman, Jossey Bass, 1994), and, *Identity and Inner City Youth: Beyond Ethnicity and Gender* (with Shirley Brice Heath, Teachers College Press, 1993).

Edward Metz received his doctorate from The Catholic University of America in 2003. His current research focuses on how and whether school-based required community service affects high school students in the area of civic engagement.

Martha Montero-Sieburth is a visiting Senior Faculty Member at Webster University, Leiden, The Netherlands, and is an Associate Professor in the Department of Leadership in Education at the University of Massachusetts–Boston where she teaches in the Leadership in Urban Schools Doctoral Program and the Educational Administration Master's Program. She served as Acting Chair and Associate Chair of the Department during 2001–2002, while the College underwent the National Council Association of Teacher Education (NCATE) and is now on sabbatical. Her expertise is in the areas of anthropology and sociology of education, curriculum and instructional development, and bilingual, multicultural, and international education. Formerly, she was the Director of Educational Research at the Mauricio Gaston Institute at the University of Massachusetts–Boston, Program Manager for Multicultural Educational Experiences at the Harvard Medical School, Associate Professor at Simmons College, Visiting Scholar at the Stone Center for Research on Women at Wellesley College, Adjunct Faculty at Lesley College, and Instructor at Boston University. She taught at the Harvard Graduate School of Education as Assistant and later Associate Professor in the Division of Teaching, Curriculum, and Learning Environments from 1984–1991. She has conducted international consultancy in education in Guatemala, Honduras, Costa Rica, Mexico, and Colombia.

Nikos Ntoumanis is a Lecturer in Sport and Exercise Psychology at the University of Birmingham, UK. His research interests focus on achievement motivation in physical activity contexts. He has a particular interest in the psychological experiences of children in sport and physical education. He earned his MSc in Sports Science at Loughborough University, UK, in 1995, and his PhD in Medical Sciences from the University of Exeter, UK, in 1999. He is the author of the book *A Step-by-Step Guide to SPSS for Sport and Exercise Studies*. He has received the third prize in the Young Investigators competition at the Second Annual Congress of the European College of Sport Science (1997) and the first prize at the 7th Congress of the Greek Society of Sport Psychology (2002).

Jennifer O'Donoghue is a doctoral student at the Stanford University School of Education in Administration and Policy Analysis. She received her BA from Wesleyan University in Psychology and her MA from the Hubert H. Humphrey Institute at the University of Minnesota in Public Policy, with concentrations in Community and Public Work and Democratic Education. Her research interests include community-based education and public engagement of traditionally marginalized groups (immigrants and refugees, low-income communities, urban youth), youth participation and development, and citizenship and democracy. She is currently studying the characteristics of community-based youth organizations that mediate urban youth's engagement in social or community change efforts. She has written and presented on democratic education, youth and adult civic engagement, youth's experiences in after-school community centers, and youth–adult research partnerships. She is the co-editor of "Youth Participation: Improving Institutions and Communities," a special issue of the journal *New Directions for Youth Development* (with Benjamin Kirshner & Milbrey McLaughlin, Jossey Bass, 2002) and *We Are the Freedom People: Sharing our Stories, Creating a Vibrant America* (with D'Ann Urbaniak Lesch, Center for Democracy and Citizenship, 1999).

Susan O'Neill is a Senior Lecturer in Psychology at Keele University, UK, where she is Associate Director of the Unit for the Study of Musical Skill and Development and Director of the MSc in Music Psychology. She was awarded a Visiting Research Fellowship at the University of Michigan from 2001–2003 to work with members of the Gender and Achievement Research Program. Her research interests include motivation, identity, and gender issues associated with young people's engagement in music. As a consultant she has developed professional training programs for music practitioners and teachers, and contributed to the policy planning for youth music programs. Dr. O'Neill is currently Director of the Young People and Music Participation Project funded by the Economic and Social Research Council. She has published widely in the fields of music psychology and music education. Her other contributions to edited books include *The Social Psychology of Music* (1997), *Music and Emotion: Theory and Research* (2001), *The Science and Psychology of Music Performance* (2002), and *Musical Identities* (2002), all published by Oxford University Press.

D. Wayne Osgood is Professor of Crime, Law and Justice, and Sociology at Pennsylvania State University, University Park. His research interests include a variety of topics concerning crime, delinquency, and other deviant behaviors, adolescence and the transition to adulthood, time use, and statistical methods.

Corliss Wilson Outley is Assistant Professor in the School of Kinesiology and Leisure Studies at the University of Minnesota, where she also serves as Faculty Member and Advisor to the Youth Development Leadership Program jointly sponsored by the Center for 4-H Youth Development and the College of Education and Human Development. Since joining the school in 1999, Outley has taught undergraduate and graduate courses in research and evaluation, positive youth development and urban recreation programming, and leisure and human development. Dr. Outley received her PhD from Texas A&M University's Department of Recreation, Park, and Tourism Sciences. She has been involved for many years in research dealing with the relationship between race/ethnicity and leisure behavior, especially where it intersects with youth, social class, and leisure planning and management. During this period, she has been affiliated with the National Recreation and Park Associations (NRPA) Youth Development and Recreation Consortium, and has served as a consultant to the Minneapolis Youth Coordinating Board and the NRPA's National Urban Youth Initiative.

Sara Pedersen received her PhD in the community psychology program at New York University in 2003. Her primary research interests involve investigating patterns of positive adolescent development. Specifically, she is interested in understanding the key aspects of nonacademic settings and interpersonal transactions that may facilitate the development of positive self-evaluations and academic achievement among disadvantaged youth. Her dissertation identified trajectories of structured out-of-school activity participation among disadvantaged urban youth and examined the relations among such trajectories and positive development in the areas of self-esteem, academic achievement, and delinquency.

Andreas Persson is a doctoral student in Psychology at Örebro University. He earned his Bachelor's Degree in Psychology at Örebro University in 2001. His research interests include youths' choices of leisure contexts and the influence of peers on adolescent development.

Karen Pittman is the Senior Vice President at the International Youth Foundation (IYF). She established the Forum for Youth Investment, a U.S. initiative of IYF. The Forum supports organizations that invest in young people by promoting a "big picture" approach to planning, research, advocacy,

and policy development among the broad range of national organizations
that help communities invest in children, youth, and families. A sociologist
and recognized leader in the youth development field in the United States,
Ms. Pittman started her career at the Urban Institute, conducting numerous
studies on social services for children and families. Later, she worked 6 years
at the Children's Defense Fund (CDF), promoting its adolescent policy
agenda. In 1990, she left CDF to become a Vice President at the Academy
for Educational Development where she founded and directed the Center
for Youth Development and Policy Research. In January 1995, Ms. Pittman
accepted a position within the Clinton Administration as Director of the
President's Crime Prevention Council. A widely published author, she has
written three books and dozens of articles on youth issues and is a regular
columnist and public speaker. During her career, she sat on numerous boards
and panels, including the E. M. Kauffman Foundation, the Carnegie Council on Adolescent Development, Search Institute, and the Family Resource
Coalition. Recently, she served as a consultant to the Chief State School Officers, Learning First Alliance, White House Conference on Teenagers, Department of Education, Aspen Institute, and the Carnegie Corporation's
High Schools for a New Society Initiative. Currently, she sits on the boards
of the Educational Testing Service, American Youth Work Center,
High/Scope Foundation, and National Center for Children and Poverty,
and is a member of the W. K. Kellogg Foundation's Youth Initiative Partnership Advisory Council, California Tomorrow's Equity and Access in
Afterschool Project Advisory Group, and the National Academy of Science's Forum on Adolescence. She continues to serve as Senior Vice President of the International Youth Foundation.

Jill K. Posner is an Educational Psychologist whose research interest focuses
on child care, and the intersection between health and psychology in developing countries. She is currently based at the University of Wisconsin, Madison, consulting for the Center for Health Policy and Evaluation.

Gwynn Powell is Assistant Professor in the Department of Recreation and
Leisure Studies at the University of Georgia. She received a doctorate in
Park, Recreation, and Tourism Management from Clemson University in
2001 and specializes in training of staff for informal learning settings such as
summer camps.

Jane Quinn joined the Children's Aid Society as Assistant Executive Director for Community Schools in January 2000. In this capacity, she leads
and oversees local and national work to forge effective long-term partnerships between public schools and other community resources, using the 10
CAS community schools in New York City as both a model and a base for

national adaptation. Ms. Quinn came to CAS from the DeWitt Wallace–Reader's Digest Fund, where she served as Program Director from January 1993 to November 1999. This national foundation's sole focus is the education and career development of young people, especially those growing up in low-income communities. Prior to that, she directed a national study of youth organizations for the Carnegie Corporation of New York, which resulted in the publication of a book entitled *A Matter of Time: Risk and Opportunity in the Nonschool Hours*. Ms. Quinn served from 1981 to 1990 as director of program services for Girls Clubs of America, a national organization based in New York. In prior years, she held positions in Washington, DC, at the DC Health Department and the Center for Population Options. In addition, she was a caseworker for the Juvenile Protective Association of Chicago, and Family Counseling Center, Catholic Charities of Buffalo, NY. Ms. Quinn received a master's degree from the University of Chicago School of Social Service Administration and a bachelor's degree in economics from the College of New Rochelle. She did postgraduate work in nonprofit management at the Columbia School of Business (Institute for Not-for-Profit Management).

Marika N. Ripke is currently a postdoctoral research associate for the MacArthur Foundation's Network on "Successful Pathways Through Middle Childhood" in the Department of Human Ecology at the University of Texas at Austin. She earned her PhD in Human Development and Family Sciences from the University of Texas at Austin. She is currently assisting with the development and organization of a national conference and edited book on the theme "Building Pathways to Success: Research, Policy, and Practice on Development in Middle Childhood." She is also involved in assessing the effects of participation in the New Hope Project, a work-based antipoverty demonstration program on parents and their children.

Jean Rhodes is Professor of Psychology at the University of Massachusetts in Boston. She has conducted extensive research on both natural and assigned mentoring relationships in adolescence. Dr. Rhodes is a Fellow in the American Psychological Association and the Society for Research and Community Action, a member of the John D. and Catherine T. MacArthur Foundation Research Network on Transitions to Adulthood, and a research consultant to the National Mentoring Partnership. She has published three books and more than 30 articles and chapters on the topic of youth mentoring.

Larry A. Scanlan is a Principal Scientist at the International Center for Talent Development in the UCLA Department of Psychology, where he uses qualitative and quantitative methods to study the life-span consequences of talent development, commitment sources in talent development, and the use of technology to enhance the development of talent. His first career was with Raytheon, formerly Hughes Aircraft Company, where he held positions as Head of Human Factors Research, System Engineering Manager, and Senior Program Manager. Research areas included target acquisition performance and modeling, visual search behavior, and operator performance in complex systems. He has a PhD in Engineering Psychology from the University of Illinois and a BS in Electrical Engineering from California State University at Northridge. Dr. Scanlan received the first George Briggs Dissertation Award from Division 21 of the American Psychological Association and the Best Student Paper Award at the 17th Annual Meeting of the Human Factors and Ergonomics Society. He has served on a number of school district committees and has been a Boy Scout adult leader.

Tara K. Scanlan is a Professor in the Department of Psychology and Founding Director of the International Center for Talent Development at UCLA. Dr. Scanlan studies motivation and emotion in youth sport, adolescent, and elite athletes, as well as the consequences of developing one's talent. She is particularly interested in the motivational issue of what creates commitment to an endeavor—be it sport or some other enterprise such as art, music, and education. Commitment is the desire and resolve to persist in a sport or some other activity, and at more elite levels, it involves the dedicated pursuit of excellence. Her work on the consequences of talent development focuses on the life-long influences of extracurricular activity participation during the formative adolescent years. Her research is characterized by a mix-methods approach. Dr. Scanlan publishes research and applied articles, and is a frequent keynote speaker to diverse international and national audiences. She is a Past President of one of the largest sport psychology organizations in the world—The Association for the Advancement of Applied Sport Psychology (AAASP)—and is a Past President of the North American Society for the Psychology of Sport and Physical Activity. She was ranked as one of the 10 leading sport psychologists in North America, was cited for having the greatest number of classic references in the leading research journal in sport psychology, is a Fellow in AAASP, has been a member of the Editorial Board of the Journal of Sport and Exercise Psychology since its inception in 1979, and serves as a reviewer for several journals. Dr. Scanlan was selected to be a William Evans Visiting Fellow, one of the highest honors bestowed on foreign scholars by the University of Otago, New Zealand. She also was selected to be the 1999 Australian International Scholar in Sport Psychology and recently served as the Chair of the Social Psychology Area at UCLA.

Edward Seidman is Professor of Psychology at New York University. Previously, he has served as Vice President and Dean of Research, Development, and Policy at Bank Street College and as a Professor in the departments of Psychology at both the University of Illinois at Urbana-Champaign and the University of Manitoba. He is the recipient of numerous awards, including as a Senior Fulbright–Hays Research Scholar (University of Athens), Distinguished Contributions for Theory and Research in Community Psychology, and several national awards for his exemplary research in delinquency prevention. He has served on a variety of professional and scientific panels in a number of different capacities, including being President of the Society for Community Research and Action. He is the editor or co-editor of a number of volumes and monographs including the *Handbook of Community Psychology, Handbook of Social Intervention, Redefining Social Problems,* and *Culturally-Anchored Methodology*. He has done extensive research in the mental health, juvenile justice, and education arenas with particular emphasis on innovations, prevention, and policy. His current research focuses on understanding the nature of the positive developmental trajectories of economically at-risk urban adolescents and how these trajectories are altered by the social contexts of family, peer, school, and neighborhood, and their interaction.

Jennifer N. Shaffer is Assistant Professor of Administration of Justice at Arizona State University West. Her research interests include the causes and consequences of victimization, the social context of crime, interpersonal violence, and the relationships between crime and victimization.

Lee Shumow is an Associate Professor in the Department of Educational Psychology and Foundations at Northern Illinois University. Her research interests focus on family and community influences on child and adolescent development. Dr. Shumow is active in the American Educational Research Association Special Interest Group on family, school, and community partnerships.

David A. Soulé is a faculty research assistant and PhD candidate in the University of Maryland Department of Criminology and Criminal Justice. David received an MA in Criminology and Criminal Justice from the University of Maryland–College Park. He is currently the co-principal investigator and project manager for the evaluation of the Maryland After School Opportunity Fund Program (MASOFP), a program which aims to assist the state in the development of effective after school programs for youth. David previously worked for 2 years on the evaluation of Maryland's After School Community Grant Program (MASCGP). His research interests include juvenile delinquency, delinquency prevention, and program evaluation.

Renée Spencer is Assistant Professor of Social Work at Boston University. She has published several articles and book chapters on adolescent development, relational theories, and qualitative research methods.

Håkan Stattin is Professor of Psychology at Uppsala and Örebro Universities in Sweden. Currently, he is President of the European Association for Research on Adolescence. He directs the Solna Project, a birth-to-maturity longitudinal study. He is also Co-director of the Center for Developmental Research at Örebro University, together with Professor Margaret Kerr. They are conducting a number of long-term and short-term longitudinal projects including a 7-year longitudinal study of all youth between 10 and 18 years in an entire Swedish community. In addition, he has recently completed a successful whole-community prevention program to reduce youth alcohol use. Professor Stattin earned his PD. in Developmental Psychology at Stockholm University. He is probably best known for his past research in two areas: delinquency development and pubertal maturation in adolescent girls. His works include an authored book (with David Magnusson, 1990), *Pubertal Maturation in Female Development*. In addition to these topics, his current research focuses on adolescents' choices of developmental contexts and parent–child relationships and their role in preventing delinquency. His recent work on parental monitoring is particularly noteworthy.

Margaret R. Stone is a research faculty member in the Department of Family Studies and Human Development at the University of Arizona. She received her PhD in Human Development from the University of Wisconsin–Madison in 1994 and has been associated with the Michigan Study of Life Transitions since 1998. Her research involves an examination of the intersection between adolescent social development, social cognitive development, and intergroup relations. She is particularly interested in the peer "crowd" as an emergent social category through which adolescents forge interpretations of their peer world and of their own social identities.

Deborah Lowe Vandell is a Professor in the Department of Educational Psychology at the University of Wisconsin–Madison, where she is affiliated with the Wisconsin Center for Education Research, the Institute for Research on Poverty, and the Waisman Center on Mental Retardation and Human Development. Professor Vandell serves on the Steering Committee for the NICHD Study of Early Child Care and Youth Development. She is a member of the National Academy of Science Committee on Family and Work Policies. She also has served as on the Maternal and Child Health Research Committee at the NICHD and as an associate editor for the journal *Child Development*. Much of her research has focused on early child care and on school-age child care. Children's relationships with their parents, siblings, peers, and teachers have provided another unifying theme to her work. She received a BA in psychology from Rice University, an EdM from Harvard University, and a PhD in Psychology from Boston University.

Margaret K. Vernon is a graduate student in Developmental Psychology at The Pennsylvania State University. Her general research interests include academic achievement and self/identity development during adolescence. More recently she has become interested in exploring the ways in which extracurricular activities serve as contexts for adolescent development.

Francisco A. Villarruel is a University Outreach Fellow at Michigan State University; a member of the Leadership Team and Research Associate of the Institute for Children, Youth, and Families (ICYF); and an Associate Professor of Family and Child Ecology at Michigan State University. He is the co-editor of *Making Invisible Latino Youth Visible: A Critical Approach to Latino Diversity* (with M. Montero-Sieburth, Falmer Press, 2000) and *Community Youth Development: Programs, Practices and Policies* (with D. F. Perkins, L. M. Borden, and J. G. Keith, 2003). A recent report by Villarruel and co-author N. Walker, ICYF's Associate Director, received international attention for its analysis of disproportionate treatment of Latino and Latina youth by the U.S. justice system entitled: ¿Dónde Está La Justicia?: A Call to Action on Behalf of Latino and Latina Youth in the U.S. Justice System—the first national study on Latino youth in the U.S. Justice system.

Joyce Walker is a Professor and youth development educator at the Center for 4-H Youth Development at the University of Minnesota. Her teaching, research, and policy interests focus on community-based education and youth programs that involve young people in the nonschool hours. She coordinates the Youth Development Leadership MEd Program, a professional studies degree program in the College of Education and Human Development designed for practicing youth workers. She is director of a community-based initiative to support training and professional development for youth workers thru the Minnesota Youth Work Institute. Professor Walker has served on the national board of Camp Fire USA. Her work has been recognized with the Distinguished Service Award from the U.S. Department of Agriculture, the Distinguished Faculty Award from the University of Minnesota Extension Service, and the Anselm Strauss Award for Qualitative Family Research. Professor Walker has degrees from Miami University, Northwestern University, and the University of Minnesota.

Kathrin C. Walker is Coordinator of Research Programs in the Department of Human and Community Development at the University of Illinois at Urbana-Champaign. She serves as Project Director for a qualitative study of youth development programs. She is also a doctoral student in Educational Psychology, specializing in program evaluation. Her thesis research examines the nature of youth worker practice.

Shannon C. Womer is a part-time instructor and graduate student at the University of Maryland. She received an MA in criminology from the University of Maryland and is currently completing PhD requirements. Her research interests include juvenile delinquency, delinquency prevention, school-based delinquency prevention efforts, and criminological theory.

James Youniss is the Wylma R. and James R. Curtin Professor of Psychology at the Catholic University of America. For the past decade, his research has been focused on youth who do community service and on its relationship to political-moral development. He and Miranda Yates have published two books on the topic: *Community Service and Social Responsibility in Youth* (University of Chicago Press, 1997) and *Roots of Civic Identity: International Perspectives on Community Service and Activism in Youth* (Cambridge University Press, 1999). He and his colleagues have recently collected longitudinal data from students in three high schools, tracking their service and extracurricular activities in order to determine how they contribute to students' political-moral identity.

Author Index

A

Aaron, P., 7, 20
Abeles, H. F., 257, 263, 269, 270
Aber, J. L., 94, 95, 106, 108
Adams, G., 8, 19, 67, 69, 82, 112, 125, 437, 455
Adler, P., 36, 40
Adler, P. A., 36, 40
Adler, T. F., 186, 208, 236, 237, 238, 240, 249,
251, 252, 254, 290, 305
Ageton, S. S., 54, 62
Agnew, R., 50, 53, 58, 60, 61, 211, 233
Akande, A., 317, 326
Albanese, A. L., 15, 19
Albrecht, R. R., 281, 282, 286, 288, 306
Alfeld-Liro, C., 92, 108, 260, 263, 271, 272
Allen, J. P., 7, 18
Allen, L., 95, 106, 108
Allen, V., 219, 233
Allison, K. W., 91, 107, 139, 154
Ames, C., 314, 315, 325, 326
Andersen, R. E., 31, 38, 40
Andersen, S., 332, 334, 340, 350
Anderson, A. L., 60, 61, 63
Anderson, D. R., 71, 81
Anderson, P. M., x, xii, 119, 128
Anderson Moore, K., 72, 81
Andre, T., 34, 35, 41, 165, 181, 195, 209
Andree, K. V., 321, 326
Andreoli, K. G., 38, 40
Andrews, D. W., 51, 62
Anshel, M. H., 24, 40
Aparecida de Carvalho, V., 458, 476
Arbreton, A., 432, 433

Arbreton, A. J. A., 177, 181, 237, 254, 265,
273, 432, 433
Argyle, M., 262, 271
Aries, P., 23, 28, 40
Armstrong, N., 296, 306, 317, 320, 327
Arthur, M. W., 460, 465, 476, 477
Averill, P. M., 292, 293, 294, 298, 305
Azmita, M., 123, 125

B

Babkes, M. L., 7, 19, 278, 292, 293, 294, 298,
305
Bachman, J. G., 29, 43, 46, 50, 51, 52, 53, 57,
58, 59, 63, 64, 71, 81, 91, 109, 212,
233, 459, 476
Bahr, H. M., 27, 41
Baker, E., 459, 461, 476
Baker, G., 412, 417
Baksh-Soodeen, R., 138, 154
Balague, G., 315, 329
Baldwin, C. K., 13, 19
Bales, S., 131, 155, 406, 418
Balsano, A. B., x, xii, 119, 128
Bandura, A., 238, 252
Banez, G. A., 320, 326
Barber, B. K., 338, 350
Barber, B. L., 5, 6, 7, 16, 18, 19, 70, 71, 82, 85, 89,
92, 93, 95, 106, 107, 173, 180, 186,
187, 188, 189, 190, 196, 197, 203,
205, 206, 207, 208, 209, 235, 236,
239, 252, 256, 259, 268, 270, 332, 350
Barnes, G. M., 93, 108
Barnes, K., 31, 40
Barnett, N., 313, 326

Barry, H., III, 53, 64
Bartko, W. T., 365, *371*
Bartlett, S. J., 31, 38, *40*
Barton, B. A., 92, *107*
Bates, J. E., 47, 58, *63, 64,* 68, 69, 71, *83,* 438, 456
Bates, J. F., 8, 9, 17, *22*
Batt, M. C., 114, 124, *127*
Beals, K. P., 278, 290, 308
Becker, B., 85, *107*
Behrman, R. E., 67, 71, *84,* 438, *455*
Beier, S. R., 420, *433*
Belden Russonello & Stewart, 437, *455*
Belle, D., 47, *62,* 405, *417,* 421, *433*
Belsky, J., 439, *455*
Bempechat, J., 121, 123, *125*
Benson, P. L., x, *xii,* 91, *107,* 119, *128,* 399, 407, *417,* 421, *422, 433, 434*
Bentler, P. M., 61, *63*
Berger, B. G., 237, *254*
Berglund, M. L., 8, 16, *19,* 406, *417,* 459, *476*
Bergman, L. R., 6, *21,* 365, *371*
Bergund, M. L., 112, *125*
Berkley, J. Y., 135, *154*
Berndt, T. J., 52, 61, *64*
Bernstein, L., 437, *456*
Biancarosa, G., 387, *397*
Bianchi, S., 31, *43*
Biddle, S. J. H., 296, *306,* 317, 318, 320, 321, *323, 326, 327, 328, 329, 330*
Bingenheimer, J. B., 420, *435*
Bissell, J. S., 10, *18*
Bjelobrk, D., 119, *128*
Blacking, J., 261, *269*
Blank, M., 384, *396*
Blechman, E. A., 428, *433*
Bloom, D., 70, 79, *82*
Bluck, S., 161, *181*
Blum, R. W., 10, *18,* 408, *417*
Blumenfeld, P. C., 237, 238, 239, *253, 254,* 263, *265, 270, 273*
Blumer, H., 426, *433*
Blyth, D. A., x, *xii,* 119, *128*
Bo, I., 211, *233*
Bobek, D. L., x, *xii,* 119, *128*
Bogdan, R., 170, *183*
Bogenschneider, K., 412, *417*
Bontempo, A. N., 420, *433*
Borden, L. M., 111, 112, 118, 122, *127, 128*
Borgenschneider, K., 123, *125*
Bos, J. M., 68, 70, 73, 76, 77, 79, *82, 83*
Botcher, J., 53, *62*

Botvin, E. M., 460, 461, *476*
Botvin, G. J., 459, 461, *476*
Boulton, M. J., 264, *272*
Boyle, J. D., 264, *271*
Boynton-Jarrett, R., 67, *82*
Bradley, C. B., 37, *41*
Brandstädter, J., 160, *180*
Bray, S. R., 281, 282, 289, *305*
Bredemeier, B. J. L., 313, 323, *329*
Bressler, J., 431, *435*
Briar, S., 50, *62*
Brimhall, D., 72, *82,* 112, *125*
Brindis, C., 121, *125*
Brock, T. W., 70, 73, 76, 77, *82*
Brody, G. H., 239, *254*
Brooks-Gunn, J., ix, *xii,* 4, 5, 12, *22,* 134, *155,* 401, 406, 408, *418,* 422, *434*
Brown, A., 89, *107*
Brown, B. B., 6, 7, *19,* 20, 21, 160, *182,* 189, 190, *197,* 203, 205, 208, 209, *210,* 269, *269*
Brown, B. V., 72, *81*
Brown, J. D., 256, *269*
Brown, U., 114, *125*
Brustad, R. J., 7, *19,* 278, 290, 291, 292, 293, 294, 296, 298, *305*
Bry, B. H., 461, *476*
Buchanan, C. M., 268, *270,* 357, *371*
Buckley, S., 25, 33, 40, *42*
Bumbarger, B., 112, *126*
Bump, L. A., 280, *307*
Burk-Braxton, C., 92, *107*
Burraston, B., 17, *19,* 190, *208*
Burtless, G., 73, *82*
Burton, D., 280, *307*
Burton, J. M., 257, *270*
Burton, L. M., 91, *107,* 139, *154*
Busch-Rossnagel, N., 164, *182*
Butcher, J., 37, *40*
Byrnes, J., x, *xii*

C

Cahill, S., 29, *41*
Cairns, B. D., 7, 12, 15, *21,* 231, *233*
Cairns, R. B., 7, 15, *21,* 85, 89, *108,* 186, 190, 196, 204, 208, 209, 231, *233, 235,* 253
Caldwell, L. L., 13, *19,* 32, *42*
Calvert, M., 131, *156*

Camino, L. A., 134, 135, *154,* 160, 175, 177, 178, *180,* 405, *417*
Campbell, K., 256, *269*
Campbell, P. S., 255, *270*
Canada, G., 119, *125*
Cantor, D., 460, 464, 475, *476*
Capizzano, J., 8, *19,* 67, 69, 82, 112, *125,* 437, *455*
Caplow, T., 27, *41*
Carlini-Cotrim, B., 459, *476*
Carlson, S., 411, *417*
Carpenter, P. J., 278, 290, 291, 292, 293, 294, 296, 299, *305,* 308
Carr, S., 316, *326*
Casey, D. M., 77, *83*
Caspary, G. L., 66, *82*
Catalano, R. F., 8, 15, *19,* 111, 112, *125, 126,* 205, *209,* 406, *417,* 459, 460, 465, *476, 477*
Cauce, A. M., 87, *107*
Cavallo, D., 24, *41*
Cave, G., 422, *433*
Chadwick, B. A., 27, *41*
Chalip, L., 292, 293, 296, *305*
Chamberlain, J., 32, *41*
Chase, J. A., 459, *477*
Chase Smith, J., 131, 132, *155*
Chassin, L., 205, *208*
Chatzisarantis, N. L. D., 321, *330*
Chavez, V., 114, *126*
Checkoway, B., 406, 409, *417*
Cheskin, L. J., 31, 38, *40*
Chi, L., 323, *329*
Christmas-Best, V., 131, *155,* 406, *418*
Cicchetti, D., 85, *107*
Claes, M., 260, *271*
Clark, R. M., 480, *494*
Clark, S., 115, *125*
Clark-Kauffman, E., 68, 75, *82*
Clasen, D., 6, *19*
Clawson, M. A., 263, *270*
Clore, G., 161, *182*
Coatsworth, J. D., 6, *21*
Cochran, M. M., 211, *233*
Cohen, D. A., 46, *62*
Cohen, J., 213, *233*
Cohen, L. E., 50, 56, *62*
Cohen, P., 213, *233*
Cohen, P. A., 461, *476*
Cohn, P. J., 280, 281, 282, 283, 286, 287, 289, *305*
Coie, J. D., 231, *233,* 461, *476*

Cole, C., 47, *62*
Cole, K. A., 136, *155*
Cole, K. C., 91, 95, 102, *108*
Cole, M., 139, *154*
Coleman, J., 333, *350*
Coleman, J. C., 432, *434*
Coll, C. G., 47, *63*
Colletti, J., 256, *272*
Colley, A., 263, *270*
Collins, A., 66, *83*
Collins, W. A., 6, *19*
Comas-Diaz, L., 114, *125*
Comber, C., 263, *270*
Compas, B. E., 320, *326*
Conger, R. D., 13, 14, 17, *20*
Connell, J. P., 368, *371*
Cook, T., 13, 14, *20*
Cooney, G. H., 32, *43*
Cooper, C. R., 123, *125*
Cooper, H., 34, *41,* 423, 425, *433*
Cooper, M., 258, *273*
Coopersmith, S., 283, *305*
Corasaniti, M. A., 438, *456*
Corbin, C. B., 313, *330*
Corbin, J., 170, *183*
Cosden, M., 15, *19*
Costa, F. M., 91, *107*
Costa-Giomi, E., 259, *270*
Costello, J., 135, *154*
Coyle, K., 121, *125*
Crawford, P. B., 92, *107*
Crespo, C. J., 31, 38, *40*
Crnic, K., 120, *126*
Crosby, D. A., 66, 68, 69, 73, 77, 79, *82, 83*
Cross, C. T., 10, *18*
Cross, G., 23, *41*
Crosse, S. B., 460, 464, 475, *476*
Crouter, A. C., 8, *21,* 236, 239, 244, *253*
Crowe, P. A., 48, *63*
Csikszentmihalyi, M., 4, *19,* 30, *41,* 177, *180,* 292, 293, 294, 296, 297, 298, 299, *305*
Cucuzzo, N., 313, *328*
Curran, P. J., 205, *208*
Curtis, J. E., 37, *41*
Cury, F., 318, 321, *326, 327, 329*
Czeh, E. R., 460, 464, 475, *476*

D

Damon, W., xi, *xii*
Daniels, S. R., 92, *107*
Darling, N., 421, 427, *433*

Daughtery, S., 33, *43*
David, T. B., 114, *125*
Davidson, W. S., 422, *433*
Davis, L., 392, *396*
Deasy, R. J., 258, *270*
DeCarbo, N. J., 264, *271*
DeCarlo, K. J., 290, *307*
Dechausay, N., 387, *397*
Deci, E. L., 290, *305*
DeGrazia, S., 23, *41*
DeKnop, P., 325, *329*
Delgado-Gaitan, M., 121, *125*
Deliège, I., 257, *270*
Dell'Angelo, T., 119, *128*
Delpit, L., 115, *125*
Delzell, J. K., 264, *270*
Dempsey, J. M., 321, *327*
Denner, J., 121, 123, *125*
Dennis, W., 259, *273*
DeNora, T., 261, *270*
Dent, C., 48, *64*
Derzon, J. H., 460, *477*
Deutsch, N. L., 90, 93, 94, 102, 105, *107*
Devereux, E., 28, 36, 40, *41*
deVries, D. K., 437, *456*, 481, *495*
Dewey, J., 406, *417*
Dieffenbach, K., 278, *306*
Dishion, T. J., 17, *19*, 51, *62*, 190, *208*, 212, 231, 232, *233*
Diversi, M., 131, *155*, 350, *351*, 406, *418*
Dixon, L., 487, *495*
Dodge, K. A., 8, 9, 17, *22*, 47, 58, *63*, *64*, 68, 69, 71, *83*, 438, *456*
Dolcini, M. M., 189, 205, *208*
Domitrovich, C., 112, *126*
Donovan, J. E., 459, *477*
Dorfman, L., 114, 119, *126*
Dowling, E. M., x, *xii*, 119, *128*
Downey, G., 424, *433*
DuBois, D. L., 92, *107*, 113, *126*, 422, 423, 425, *433*
DuBois, W. E. B., 114, *126*
Duda, J. L., 296, 301, *306*, 314, 315, 316, 317, 319, 320, 321, 322, 323, 324, *327*, 328, *329*
Dunbar, C., 112, 113, 114, 115, 120, *126*
Duncan, G. J., 68, 70, 73, 75, 76, 77, 79, *82*, *83*
Dunér, A., 214, *233*
Dunn, J. C., 322, *327*
Dunn, J. G. H., 322, *327*
Durand, M., 318, *329*

Durlak, J. A., 16, *19*
Dusenbury, L., 460, 461, *476*
Dweck, C. S., 314, 318, 325, *327*
Dworkin, J. B., 5, 12, 16, *20*, 86, 87, *107*, 164, *180, 181*

E

Eccles, J. S., ix, x, *xii*, 4, 5, 6, 7, 8, 10, 11, 12, 13, 14, 15, 16, 17, *18, 19, 20*, 38, *41*, 49, 64, 67, 70, 71, *82*, 85, 89, 92, 93, 95, *106, 107, 108*, 118, 121, *126*, 134, 135, *154*, 173, *180*, 185, 186, 187, 188, 189, 190, 196, 203, 205, 206, *207, 208, 209*, 235, 236, 237, 238, 239, 240, 248, 249, 250, 251, 252, *252, 253, 254*, 256, 259, 260, 263, 265, 266, *268, 270, 271, 272, 273*, 290, 304, *305, 306*, 332, 350, *350*, 357, 358, 360, 365, 370, *371*, 399, 408, 411, *417*, 421, *433*, 438, 442, 444, 454, 455, *455*, 470, 476, 480, *495*
Eckert, P., 190, 205, *209*
Eckland, B. K., 7, *20*
Eder, D., 190, *209*
Edlind, E., 34, 35, *41*
Eicher, S., 6, *19*
Eklund, R. C., 280, 281, 282, 283, 286, 288, 289, *306*
Elder, G. H., Jr., 7, 13, 14, 17, *20*, 334, 350, *350*
El-Khouri, B. M., 365, *371*
Elkind, D., 27, *41*, 162, *180*
Elliot, D., 7, *20*
Elliott, D., 54, *62*
Elliott, S., 465, *476*
Engle, R. A., 136, *155*
Engstrom, D. M., 66, *82*
Entman, R. M., 114, *126*
Epstein, J., 325, *327*
Epstein, J. S., 260, *270, 271*
Erickson, M. L., 51, *62*
Erikson, E. H., 171, *180*, 188, *209*, 331, 332, 335, 350, *350*
Ewing, M. E., 37, *41*, 311, 312, *327*
Eyferth, K., 29, *43*, 164, *182*

F

Famose, J. P., 318, 321, *326, 329*
Farley, T. A., 46, *62*
Farmer, T., 7, 12, 15, *21*
Farrell, M. P., 93, *108*

Farrell, P., 174, *181*
Fashola, O. S., 438, *455*
Fawcett, S. B., 135, *154*
Feather, N. T., 237, *253*
Feldman, S. I., 424, *433*
Fellerath, V., 490, *495*
Felson, M., 50, 56, 58, 59, 62
Feltz, D. L., 281, 282, 286, 288, 299, *306*
Ferber, T., 350, *351*, 380, 397, 422, *434*
Ferrer-Caja, E., 290, *309*
Feshbach, S., 30, *43*
Fetterman, D. M., 132, 134, 135, *154*
Fielding, M., 132, 135, *154*
Figlio, R. M., 96, *109*
Finch, L. M., 280, 281, 282, 283, 286, 288, 289, *306*
Fine, G. A., 190, 205, *209*
Finn, J. L., 406, 409, *417*
Fischer, L., 256, *269*
Fisher, C. B., 12, *21*, 136, 139, *155*
Fisher, J. L., 135, *154*
Fisher, K., 161, *182*
Fitzgerald, M., 256, *271*
Flaherty, B. P., 212, *233*
Flanagan, C., 357, *371*
Flannery, D. J., 50, 57, 62
Flay, B., 48, *63*, 64
Fletcher, A. C., 7, 14, *20*, 334, 350, *350*
Flynn, C. A., 90, 93, 94, 102, 105, *107*
Foley, D. E., 115, *126*
Folkestad, G., 260, 262, *271*
Ford, D. H., 186, *209*
Fortney, P. M., 264, *271*
Foster, E. M., 71, *82*, 365, *371*
Foster, W., ix, *xii*, 134, *155*, 406, 408, *418*, 422, *434*
Fountain, D. L., 432, *433*
Fox, C., 260, *272*
Fox, K. M., 296, *306*, 317, 318, 320, *326*, *327*, *329*
Fox, M., 422, *435*
Francisco, V. T., 135, *154*
Fredricks, J. A., 92, 93, *107*, *108*, 240, *253*, 260, 263, *271*, *272*
Freedman, M., 423, *433*
Freedman-Doan, C., 237, *254*, 265, *273*
Freeman, T., 132, 142, *155*
French, S. E., 94, *108*
Friedlander, D., 73, *82*
Friedman, R J., 87, *107*
Friedman, S. L., 174, *180*
Frith, S., 260, *271*

Frumkin, P., 160, *181*
Fry, M. D., 301, *306*
Fuligni, A. J., 47, 50, *62*, 205, *209*
Fullan, M., 132, *155*
Fuller, B., 66, *82*
Furstenberg, F. F., 6, 13, 14, *20*, *21*, 160, *182*, 421, *433*
Futterman, R., 186, 208, *209*, 236, 237, 240, 251, *252*, 290, *305*

G

Gabriel, K. P., 7, *18*
Galambos, N. L., 57, 62
Gambone, M. A., 177, *181*, 368, *371*
Gansky, S. A., 37, *41*
Garbarino, J., 113, *126*
Garcia-Coll, C., 15, 17, *21*, 120, *126*, 438, *455*
Garton, A. F., 237, *253*
Gauthier, C. A., 66, *82*
Gauvain, M., 160, 161, 162, 163, 174, *181*
Gennetian, L. A., 66, 68, 69, 75, *82*
George, F. E., 461, *476*
Gibbons, J. L., 32, *43*
Gibson, C., 77, 79, *83*
Gill, D., 281, 282, 283, 285, 288, *307*
Gill, D. L., 296, 299, *306*
Gilligan, C., 346, *350*
Gillock, K. L., 121, *126*
Glancy, M., 173, *181*
Glendinning, A., 432, *434*
Glenn, S. D., 301, *306*
Glynn, N. W., 92, *107*
Godbey, G. C., 206, *209*
Goff, S. B., 186, 208, *209*, 236, 237, 240, 251, *252*, 290, *305*
Gold, M., 50, 51, 61, *62*
Goldman, S., 136, *155*
Gollwitzer, P. M., 161, *181*
Gonzales, N. A., 87, *107*
Gonzalez, N. E., 121, *126*
Goodman, C., 24, *41*
Goodyear, L., 131, 132, *155*
Gootman, J. A., ix, x, *xii*, 4, 5, 7, 10, 11, 12, 15, 16, *20*, 38, *41*, 67, *82*, 118, *126*, 134, 135, *154*, 185, *209*, 259, 270, 304, *306*, 350, *350*, 360, 370, *371*, 399, 408, 411, *417*, 421, *433*, 438, 442, 444, 454, 455, *455*
Gore, A., x, *xii*
Gore, T., x, *xii*

Gottfredson, D. C., 459, 460, 462, 464, 475, 476
Gottfredson, G. D., 458, 460, 464, 465, 475, 476
Gottfredson, M. R., 57, 58, 62
Goudas, M., 296, 306, 320, 321, 323, 327, 330
Gould, D., 278, 280, 281, 282, 283, 286, 287,
     288, 289, 299, 306, 313, 327
Graham, S. E., 121, 125
Granger, R. C., 70, 73, 76, 77, 79, 82, 83
Grant, L., 36, 42
Graziano, A., 259, 271
Greathouse, S., 34, 41
Green, L., 255, 264, 271
Greenberg, J. B., 121, 127
Greenberg, M. H., 66, 82
Greenberg, M. T., 112, 126
Greenberger, E., 32, 41
Greenfield, P., 31, 43
Greenleaf, C. A., 278, 306, 324, 328
Greeno, J. G., 136, 155
Gregory, A., xi, xii
Gresham, F., 465, 476
Griffin, M. R., 281, 282, 287, 306
Gross, E., 31, 43
Gross, J. B., 296, 299, 306
Grossman, J. B., 7, 20, 113, 128, 419, 422, 423,
     424, 426, 430, 431, 432, 433, 434,
     437, 455, 459, 477, 490, 495
Grotevant, H. D., 350, 351
Guilamo-Ramos, V., 114, 127
Guillory, M. M., 38, 40
Guivernau, M., 324, 328
Gunn, A. D. G., 32, 44
Gurney, R., 337, 346, 351
Gustafson, S. B., 219, 233, 234
Gutin, B., 313, 328
Gutman, L. M., 121, 126

H

Habermas, T., 161, 181
Haddock, G., 320, 328
Haensky, P., 34, 35, 41
Haertel, E. H., 31, 44
Haertel, G. D., 31, 44
Hagan, J., 61, 62
Hahn, A., 7, 20
Haith, M. M., 161, 181
Hall, G., x, xii
Hall, H. K., 314, 319, 320, 327, 328
Halpern, R., 24, 25, 26, 29, 33, 34, 36, 38, 39,
     40, 41, 412, 417

Ham, M., 37, 42
Hames, K., 421, 427, 433
Hamilton, S. F., 421, 427, 433
Hamm, J. V., 455, 456
Hanks, M. P., 7, 20
Hansen, D., 5, 12, 16, 20, 164, 180, 181
Hantman, I., 460, 464, 475, 476
Hardesty, J. L., 92, 107
Hardy, S. H., 24, 41
Hargreaves, D. J., 255, 256, 260, 263, 270, 271,
     272, 273
Harland, J., 264, 271
Harms, T., 13, 20
Harold, R. D., 237, 238, 239, 253, 254, 263,
     265, 270, 273
Harpalani, V., 119, 128
Harrell, J. S., 37, 41
Harris, E., 131, 132, 155
Harris, J. C., 290, 292, 293, 294, 296, 297, 306
Harris, K. J., 135, 154
Harrison, A. C., 264, 271
Hart, R., 132, 134, 135, 136, 155
Harter, S., 96, 107, 238, 253, 290, 306
Hartley, K., 264, 271
Hasbrook, C. A., 301, 306
Haskins, R., 66, 82
Hatcher, J. L., 72, 81
Hatzigeorgiadis, A., 322, 328
Haubenstricker, J., 296, 299, 307
Hawkins, J. D., 8, 16, 19, 111, 112, 125, 126,
     205, 209, 406, 417, 459, 460, 465,
     476, 477
Hayes, M., 256, 271
Haynie, D. L., 53, 54, 62
Heath, S. B., 163, 178, 180, 181, 410, 417
Hendra, R., 79, 82
Hendry, L. B., 432, 434
Hepper, P. G., 255, 271
Hermandez Jozefowicz, D., 268, 270
Herrera, C., 423, 425, 431, 434
Herrling, S., 7, 18
Hersch, P., 113, 119, 126
Hetland, L., 258, 271, 273
Heymann, S. J., 67, 82
Hilbert, S. M., 422, 435
Hill, D., 255, 273
Hill, P., 262, 271
Hill, R., 27, 41
Hirsch, B. J., 90, 93, 94, 102, 105, 107, 108
Hirschi, T., 53, 57, 59, 62, 115, 126, 212, 233,
     458, 477

Holland, A., 34, 35, *41*, 165, *181*, 195, *209*
Holloway, B. E., 423, 425, *433*
Hom, H. L., 316, 317, *327, 328*
Horn, M. C., 188, 197, *208*
Horn, T. S., 281, 282, 283, 286, 287, 301, *306,*
            307, 321, *327, 328*
Horowitz, R., 257, *270*
Horsch, K., 131, 132, *155*
Howe, M. J. A., 263, *271*
Howell, J. C., 460, *477*
Hoyle, R. H., 292, 293, 294, 298, *307*
Hruda, L. Z., 92, *108,* 260, 263, *271, 272*
Huard, R. D., 163, *181*
Huddleston, S., 296, 299, *306*
Hughes, J., 191, *209*
Huizinga, D., 54, *62*
Hultsman, W. Z., 14, *20*
Hundleyby, J. D., 53, *62*
Hunt, J. E., 196, *209*
Huston, A. C., 66, 68, 69, 70, 71, 73, 76, 77, 79,
            81, 82, 83
Hutson, R. Q., 66, *82*
Hyman, C., 231, *233*

I

Inman, J. W., 313, *329*
Irby, M. A., 123, *127,* 132, 140, *155,* 368, *371,*
            380, *397,* 407, 408, *418,* 422, *434*
Irvine, J., 115, *126*
Islam, S., 313, *328*
Ivaldi, A., 260, *272*

J

Jaccard, J., 114, *127*
Jackson, E. L., 14, *20*
Jackson, J. F., 123, *125*
Jackson, S. A., 280, 281, 282, 283, 286, 288, 289,
            306
Jacobs, E. V., 13, *20*
Jacobs, J. E., 8, *20,* 55, 56, 61, *62,* 92, *107,* 238,
            239, 240, 248, 249, 250, 251, 252,
            253
Jacobs, S. L., 197, *208*
Jacobson, K. C., 188, 197, *208*
Jansen, E., 257, *273*
Jarrett, R. L., 14, *20*
Jeffs, T., 409, *417*
Jenkins, R., 120, *126*
Jensen, G. F., 51, *62*

Jessor, R., 91, *107,* 459, *477*
Jimenez, N. V., 121, *125*
Johns, D. P., 37, *40*
Johnson, A., 431, 432, *433*
Johnson, C. D., 26, *42*
Johnson, M., 71, *83*
Johnson, R., 139, *155*
Johnson, W. R., 281, 282, 283, 287, *307*
Johnston, L. D., 29, *43,* 46, 50, 51, 52, 53, 57,
            58, 59, *63,* 212, *233*
Jones, J., 316, *326*
Jones, M., 119, *127*
Jones, M. B., 7, 13, *20*
Joseph, A. P., 256, *271*
Jozefowicz, D., 187, *208*
Jucovy, L. Z., 490, *495*
Judd, C. M., 337, *351*
Junger, M., 53, *63*

K

Kaczala, C. M., 186, *208, 209,* 236, 237, 240,
            249, 251, 252, 254, 290, *305*
Kagan, S. L., 66, *82*
Kahne, J., 89, *107*
Kandel, D. B., 459, *477*
Kantner, J. F., 57, *64*
Keating, D. P., 161, *181*
Keefe, N., 47, *63,* 438, *455*
Keefer, N., 15, 17, *21*
Keeler, B., 278, 290, *308*
Keith, J. G., 112, *128*
Kelly, J. R., 29, *42*
Kemper, T., 428, *434*
Kemple, J. J., 79, *82*
Kendzierski, D., 290, *307*
Kerr, A. W., 320, *328*
Kerr, M., 213, *234*
Kerrebrock, N., 68, *83*
Kessler, R. C., 459, *477*
Key, R. J., 29, *42*
Kimiecik, J. C., 321, *327, 328*
Kimm, S. Y. S., 92, *107*
Kincheloe, J. L., 262, *271*
Kinder, K., 264, *271*
Kinderman, T., 205, *209*
Kinney, D. A., 15, *20,* 189, 190, *208, 209*
Kirby, D., 121, *125*
Kirshnit, C. E., 37, *42*
Kleiber, D. A., 29, 32, *42,* 49, 50, *63,* 186, *209,*
            256, *271, 272,* 292, 293, 296, *305,*
            421, *434*

Kleitman, S., 196, 209
Knox, V. W., 68, 75, 82
Knudsen, J., 136, 155
Kohn, A., 38, 42
Kolb, A., 411, 418
Kolb, D. A., 411, 418
Konopka, G., 405, 418
Kort, T., 257, 273
Kotloff, L. J., 490, 495
Kourtessis, T., 321, 330
Krane, V., 278, 306, 324, 328
Kraus, R., 23, 42
Kraut, R., 31, 43
Krehbiel, G., 461, 476
Kreisel, P. S. J., 290, 291, 292, 293, 294, 296, 297, 298, 299, 309
Krisberg, B., 460, 477
Kriska, A. M., 92, 107
Kroll, W., 281, 282, 283, 286, 287, 288, 307
Kronsberg, S. S., 92, 107
Kubey, R., 256, 272
Kulik, C. C., 461, 476
Kulik, J. A., 461, 476
Kvaraceus, W. C., 60, 63
Ky, K. N., 258, 273

L

LaBelle, T., 409, 418
Lacourse, E., 260, 271
Laird, R. D., 8, 9, 17, 22, 47, 64, 68, 69, 71, 83, 438, 456
Lamberty, G., 120, 126
Lamborn, S. D., 7, 20, 22
Landers-Potts, M., 36, 42
Langford, B. H., 390, 396, 488, 495
Langman, J., 123, 127, 132, 141, 155, 178, 181, 368, 371, 407, 408, 418
Lanza, S., 8, 20, 92, 107, 238, 239, 250, 253
Larner, M. B., 438, 455
Larson, R. W., 3, 4, 5, 6, 7, 8, 12, 16, 20, 21, 27, 30, 41, 42, 47, 49, 50, 63, 86, 87, 92, 107, 118, 126, 160, 161, 163, 164, 180, 181, 182, 185, 209, 237, 239, 253, 256, 259, 272, 292, 293, 296, 305, 336, 346, 351, 358, 363, 371, 408, 418, 422, 428, 434, 438, 455
Laub, J. H., 68, 84
Lauman, B., 136, 155
Laurencelle, L., 313, 329
Layzer, J. I., 66, 83

Lazarus, R. S., 279, 307
Leavitt, T., 7, 20
Lecanuet, J.-P., 255, 272
Lee, J., 24, 42
Lee, M., 322, 328
Leff, S. S., 292, 293, 294, 298, 307
Leffert, N., x, xii, 119, 128
Leming, J., 260, 272
Lenox, K. F., 231, 233
Leone, C. M., 49, 63
Leppla, D. A., 264, 270
Lerman, R. I., 71, 73, 76, 83
Lerner, R. M., ix, x, xii, 12, 21, 119, 128, 136, 139, 155, 160, 164, 180, 182, 186, 209, 422, 434
Leventhal, A., 189, 205, 208
Levesque, R. J., 6, 21
Levine, L., 259, 273
Levin-Epstein, J., 66, 82
Levy, F., 479, 480, 495
Lewis, R. K., 135, 154
Lewit, E. M., 68, 83
Lewthwaite, R., 281, 282, 283, 285, 286, 288, 289, 290, 291, 292, 293, 297, 298, 303, 308
Linde, C., 136, 155
Linder, S., 27, 42
Lindner, K. J., 37, 40, 312, 328
Lindsay, J. L., 34, 41
Linebarger, D. L., 71, 81
Linney, J. A., 135, 155
Linssen, J., 257, 273
Linver, M. R., 68, 83
Lipsey, M. W., 460, 477
Lirgg, C. D., 281, 282, 286, 288, 306
Little, P. M. D., 131, 132, 155
Liu, K., 92, 107
Lobel, M., 278, 291, 292, 293, 294, 296, 299, 305, 308
Lochbaum, M. R., 317, 321, 328
Lochman, J. E., 231, 233
Loder, T. L., 90, 93, 94, 102, 105, 107
Loeber, R., 51, 63
Lonczak, H. S., 8, 16, 19, 112, 125, 406, 417, 459, 476
London, A. S., 68, 75, 82
Longhurst, K., 299, 307
Loomis, I. S., 111, 129
Lopez, C. M., 135, 154
Lopez, E., 123, 125
Loprest, P., 73, 83

Lord, S., 268, 270
LoSciuto, L., 422, 435
Love, J. M., 437, 456
Lovko, A. M., 47, 63
Lu, S., 459, 462, 476
Lupkowski, A., 34, 35, 41
Luthar, S. S., 85, 107
Lutz, W., 118, 126

M

Ma, P., 384, 397
Macallair, D., 119, 127
MacDonald, R. A. R., 260, 272
Macias, S., 15, 19
MacIver, D., 357, 371
MacKinnon, C. E., 239, 254
Madzey-Akale, J., 408, 418
Maggs, J. L., 57, 62
Magnuson, K., 77, 79, 83
Magnusson, C., 219, 234
Magnusson, D., 13, 17, 21, 49, 59, 63, 212, 213,
        214, 215, 219, 224, 230, 232, 233,
        234, 365, 371, 438, 455
Mahoney, J. L., 6, 7, 8, 10, 12, 13, 15, 17, 21,
        49, 59, 63, 85, 89, 91, 95, 106, 107,
        108, 190, 196, 209, 212, 213, 215,
        230, 232, 233, 235, 236, 253, 365,
        371, 408, 418, 438, 455, 458, 471,
        477
Malcarne, V. L., 320, 326
Males, M., 119, 127
Malina, R. M., 37, 42
Manos, T., 313, 328
Mapp, K., 10, 18
Margulies, R. Z., 459, 477
Markstrom, C., 92, 108
Markstrom-Adams, C., 120, 128
Marsh, H. W., 7, 21, 111, 127, 173, 182, 196, 209
Marshall, N. L., 15, 17, 21, 47, 63, 438, 455
Martens, R., 279, 280, 281, 282, 283, 285, 287,
        288, 307, 309, 313, 328
Martin, B., 260, 272
Martin, D. H., 46, 62
Martin, K. A., 281, 282, 289, 305
Marx, F., 15, 17, 21, 47, 63, 438, 455
Mascolo, M., 161, 182
Mason, C. A., 87, 107
Masten, A. S., 6, 21
Mauldin, T., 27, 42
Mayer, S. E., 135, 155

McAdo, H. P., 120, 126
McCarthy, C., 115, 127
McCartney, K., 15, 17, 21, 47, 63, 432, 434,
        438, 455
McClanahan, W. S., 423, 425, 431, 434
McClelland, G. H., 337, 351
McCord, J., 17, 19, 212, 232, 233
McDaniel, A. K., 131, 156
McDermott, R., 136, 155
McHale, S. M., 8, 21, 236, 239, 244, 253
McLanahan, S., 365, 371
McLaughlin, M. W., 8, 12, 15, 22, 111, 123,
        127, 131, 132, 140, 153, 155, 160,
        182, 357, 363, 368, 371, 405, 406,
        407, 408, 412, 418, 482, 495
McLellan, J. A., 8, 22, 190, 210, 235, 254, 333,
        334, 336, 340, 345, 351
McLoyd, V. C., 70, 73, 76, 77, 79, 82, 83, 120,
        127
McMahon, R. J., 17, 19
McMurray, R. G., 37, 41
McNeal, R. B., 7, 14, 22, 105, 108
McPartland, J. M., 422, 434
McPherson, G. E., 257, 259, 272
Medrich, E. A., 25, 33, 40, 42
Meece, D. W., 17, 22, 58, 63
Meece, J. L., 186, 208, 209, 236, 237, 238, 240,
        251, 252, 290, 305
Meeks, C. B., 27, 42
Mekos, D., 7, 14, 20, 334, 350, 350
Melaville, A., 384, 396
Melnick, M. J., 93, 108
Mergen, B., 28, 42
Meschke, L. L., 29, 42
Metz, E., 334, 336, 351
Meucci, S., 132, 137, 155
Michalopoulos, C., 70, 74, 75, 76, 79, 82, 83
Midgley, C., 186, 208, 236, 237, 240, 251, 252,
        290, 305, 357, 371
Miell, D., 260, 272
Miller, A., 317, 328
Miller, J. Y., 205, 209
Miller, K. E., 93, 108
Mistry, R., 77, 79, 83
Mitra, D., 134, 155
Moll, L. C., 121, 127
Mollard, W., 412, 417
Montero-Sieburth, M., 114, 120, 124, 127
Moore, S., 337, 346, 351
Morris, P. A., 68, 73, 74, 75, 76, 79, 82, 83
Morris, S. W., & Company, 480, 495

Morrison, G., 15, *19*
Morrow, K. V., 408, 409, *418*
Mortimer, J. T., 32, *43*, 71, *83*
Mory, M. S., 189, *208*
Mott, J. A., 48, *63*
Mounts, N. S., 7, *20*
Murnane, R. J., 479, 480, *495*
Murphy, R., 377, 384, *396*
Murray, L., ix, *xii*, 134, *155*, 406, 408, *418*, 422, *434*
Muuss, R. E., 52, 61, *63*

N

Nagaoka, J., 89, *107*
Najaka, S. S., 460, *476*
Neimeyer, R., 161, *182*
Nettles, S. M., 422, *434*
Neville, H. A., 113, *126*, 422, *433*
Newcomb, M. D., 61, *63*
Newcomb, R., 259, *273*
Newman, F. M., 7, *22*
Newman, K. S., 71, *83*
Newman, R. P., 377, 384, *396*
Newton, M., 316, 324, *328*
Nicholls, J. G., 290, 301, *307*, 314, 315, 317, 319, 320, 322, 323, 324, 325, *327*, *328*
Nieting, P. L., 33, *42*
Nixon, H., 276, *307*
Noack, P., 29, *43*
Noam, G. G., 387, *397*, 406, *418*
Nolen, S. B., 319, *328*
Nord, C. W., 111, *129*
North, A. C., 255, 256, 260, *271*, *272*, *273*
Notaro, P. C., 420, *435*
Ntoumanis, N., 320, 322, 323, *328*
Nurmi, J., 161, *182*
Nye, B., 34, *41*

O

Oakes, J. M., 112, *127*
Obeidallah, D., 91, *107*, 139, *154*
O'Brien, J., 89, *107*, 480, *495*
O'Brien, K., 49, *64*
Offord, D. R., 7, 13, *20*
Ogbu, J., 115, *127*
Olsen, J. J., 111, *126*
Olson, L. K., 322, *327*
O'Malley, P. M., 29, *43*, 46, 50, 51, 52, 53, 57, 58, 59, *63*, 212, *233*

O'Neill, S. A., 256, 257, 259, 260, 261, 263, 264, 265, 266, 267, 268, *271*, *272*, *273*
Ooms, T. J., 66, *82*
Opie, I., 23, *43*
Opie, P., 23, *43*
O'Regan, M., 256, *271*
Orlandi, M. A., 91, 95, 102, *108*
Osgood, D. W., 8, *20*, 29, *43*, 46, 50, 51, 52, 53, 54, 55, 56, 57, 58, 59, 60, 61, 62, *63*, 92, *107*, 212, *233*, 238, 239, 250, *253*
Otto, L. B., 7, *22*
Outley, C. W., 122, *127*

P

Pagano, M. E., 90, 93, 94, 102, 105, *107*, *108*
Paik, H., 30, 31, *43*
Paine-Andrews, A., 135, *154*
Palmer, D. J., 424, *435*
Papousek, M., 255, *272*
Parker, S., 190, *209*
Parncutt, R., 257, *272*
Parra, G. R., 113, *126*
Parson, E., 186, *209*
Parsons, J. E., 249, 251, *254*
Passer, M. W., 281, 282, 283, 285, 286, 288, 292, 293, 297, *307*, *308*
Patashnick, M., 319, *328*
Patrick, H., 92, *108*, 260, 263, *271*, *272*
Patterson, G. R., 17, *22*, 51, *62*, 68, *83*, 212, 231, *233*
Pedersen, S., 85, 93, 95, 106, *108*
Pensgaard, A. M., 281, 282, 283, 287, *307*
Penuel, W. R., 132, 142, *155*
Perez, S., 161, 163, *181*
Perkins, D. F., 111, 112, 118, 122, *127*, *128*
Peters, E., 32, *43*
Petersen, A. E., 119, *128*
Petersen, D. M., 50, 53, 60, *61*
Peterson, D. M., 211, *233*
Peterson, J. L., 445, *455*
Peterson, M., 259, *271*
Petlichkoff, L. M., 278, 299, *307*, *309*
Pettit, G. S., 8, 9, 17, *22*, 47, 58, *63*, *64*, 68, 69, 71, *83*, 438, *456*
Philliber, S., 7, *18*
Phillips, D. A., x, *xii*, 174, *182*
Piaget, J., 161, 162, *182*
Pianta, R. C., 426, *434*
Pierce, K. M., 455, *456*

Pierce, W. J., 281, 282, 283, 286, 289, 307
Piliavin, I., 50, 62
Pittman, K., 350, 351, 370, 371, 376, 377, 380,
        381, 383, 384, 390, 393, 397, 422, 434
Poe-Yamagata, E., 119, 127
Polakowski, M., 458, 477
Pollard, J., 465, 476
Poole, M. E., 32, 43
Porkka, K. V., 313, 328
Porter, S. Y., 263, 264, 269
Posner, J. K., 8, 22, 49, 53, 64, 65, 67, 68, 71, 83,
        90, 108, 112, 127, 236, 239, 254, 438,
        456, 459, 477
Poulin, F., 190, 208, 212, 232, 233
Poulin, R., 17, 19
Power, T. G., 292, 293, 294, 298, 305
Pratt, C., 237, 253
Pratt, M., 31, 38, 40
Pratto, D. J., 260, 270, 271
Presser, H., 66, 67, 83
Price, M. L., 490, 495
Primus, W., 66, 82
Proshansky, H., 113, 127
Pugh-Lilly, A. O., 113, 126
Putnam, R. D., 421, 429, 434

Q

Quinn, J., 5, 22, 68, 69, 83, 87, 88, 90, 92, 93, 94,
        105, 108, 112, 127, 370, 371, 406,
        418, 491, 495
Quinn, T., 89, 90, 107
Quint, J., 422, 433

R

Radocy, R. E., 262, 272
Radziszewska, B., 48, 64, 162, 182
Raitakar, O. T., 313, 328
Rajic, A. M., 313, 329
Raley, R., 437, 455, 490, 495
Ramos, B., 114, 127
Rapoport, R. N., 132, 134, 135, 136, 155
Rasanen, L., 313, 328
Raskoff, S., 350, 351
Rauscher, F. H., 258, 259, 273
Ravizza, K., 278, 280, 281, 282, 283, 286, 287,
        288, 289, 291, 292, 293, 296, 297,
        298, 308
Raymore, L. A., 206, 209
Reaney, L., 72, 82, 112, 125

Redner, R., 422, 433
Reichel, H., 214, 234
Reid, J. B., 17, 22, 231, 233
Reis, O., 335, 346, 347, 349, 351
Reisner, E., 10, 18
Reno, J., 39, 43
Resch, N., 113, 128, 426, 434, 459, 477
Resnick, M. D., 405, 418
Reuman, D., 357, 371
Reyes, O., 121, 126
Reynolds, A. J., 368, 371
Rhodes, J. E., 113, 118, 128, 408, 418, 420, 422,
        424, 425, 426, 430, 434
Richards, M. H., 37, 42, 49, 50, 63, 86, 87, 107,
        346, 351
Richardson, J., 48, 63, 64
Richter, K. P., 135, 154
Riess, S. A., 24, 40, 43
Riley, D., 53, 64
Riley, R. W., 39, 43
Rinehart, P. M., 408, 417
Ripke, M. N., 77, 83
Rivera, A., 95, 106, 108
Rivkin, F., 280, 307
Rivkin, M. S., 28, 36, 43
Roach, A., 410, 417
Roberts, G. C., 281, 282, 283, 287, 307, 312,
        314, 315, 317, 318, 319, 320, 321,
        323, 324, 328, 329
Roberts, W., 432, 434
Robinson, J. P., 31, 43
Roder, A. E., 425, 434
Rodman, H., 47, 62
Roehlkepartain, E. C., 421, 434
Roeser, R., 268, 270
Roffman, J. G., 90, 93, 94, 102, 105, 107, 108,
        113, 118, 128
Rogoff, B., 162, 182, 427, 434
Roizen, J. A., 25, 33, 40, 42
Romich, J., 77, 79, 83
Rosenfeld, W. D., 420, 433
Rosenthal, D., 337, 346, 351
Rosenthal, R., 432, 434
Rossi, R., 33, 43
Roth, J. L., ix, xii, 4, 5, 12, 22, 134, 155, 401,
        406, 408, 418, 422, 434
Rotheram, M. J., 461, 477
Rubin, V., 25, 33, 40, 42
Rucks, V. C., 14, 20
Rudinger, G., 29, 43, 164, 182
Ruh, J., 15, 17, 21, 47, 63, 438, 455

Russell, D. G., 278, 290, 300, *308*
Rutter, M., 122, *128*
Ryan, A. M., 92, *108*, 260, 263, *271, 272*
Ryan, J. A. M., 8, 16, *19*, 112, *125*, 406, *417*,
    459, *476*
Ryan, R. M., 290, *305*

S

Sabo, D. F., 93, *108*
Sabry, Z. I., 92, *107*
Sage, N., 205, *209*
Saito, R., 399, *417*
Sameroff, A., 13, 14, *20*
Sampson, R. J., 68, *84*
Sanderson, W., 118, *126*
Sanik, M. M., 29, *42*
Sapp, M., 296, 299, *307*
Sarrazin, P., 318, 321, *326, 327, 329*
Savin-Williams, R. C., 52, 61, *64*
Scales, P. C., *x, xii*, 119, *128*, 421, *434*
Scanlan, L. A., 278, 290, 300, *308*
Scanlan, T. K., 278, 279, 280, 281, 282, 283,
    285, 286, 287, 288, 289, 290, 291,
    292, 293, 294, 296, 297, 298, 299,
    300, 303, *305, 307, 308*, 313, *329*
Scarpa, J., 72, *84*
Schellenberg, G., 255, *273*
Scherbov, S., 118, *126*
Schiefele, U., 239, *253*
Schinke, S. P., 91, 95, 102, *108*
Schiraldi, V., 114, 119, *126*
Schlegel, A., 53, *64*
Schmidt, G. W., 278, 290, *308*
Schmitt, K. L., 71, *81*
Scholnick, E. K., 174, *180*
Schorr, L. B., 111, *128*
Schulenberg, J., 71, *81*
Schultz, J. A., 135, *154*
Schumacher, R., 66, *82*
Schuster, M. A., 46, *62*
Schwab, M., 132, 137, *155*
Schweder, A. E., 8, 12, *21*
Scrivener, S., 79, *82*
Seefeldt, V., 37, *41*, 311, 312, *327*
Sefton, J. M., 290, 291, 292, 293, 294, 296, 297,
    309
Seidman, E., 85, 93, 94, 95, 104, 106, *108*
Seifriz, J. J., 323, *329*
Seligson, E., 421, 422, *434*
Seligson, M., 481, *495*

Selman, R., 162, *182*
Seppanen, P. S., 437, 456, *481, 495*
Shah, P., 384, *396*
Shannahan, M. J., 212, *233*
Shaw, G. L., 258, 259, *271, 273*
Shaw, S., 32, *42*
Shephard, R. J., 312, 313, *329*
Sherman, R. F., 139, *155*
Shields, D. L. L., 313, *329*
Shields, M. K., 67, 71, *84*
Shiffman, S., 459, *477*
Shonkoff, J. P., x, *xii*, 174, *182*
Shumow, L., 47, 48, 64, 407, *418, 481, 482, 495*
Shurrin, C. S., 321, *328*
Sickmund, M., 45, 46, 52, *64*
Silbereisen, R. K., 29, *42, 43*, 131, *155, 164,
    182*, 406, *418*
Silverberg, S. B., 68, *83*
Silvia, E. S., 460, *477*
Simon, J. A., 280, 282, 283, 287, *307, 309*
Simons, J. P., 278, 280, 290, 291, 292, 293, 294,
    296, 299, *305, 308*, 313, *329*
Sims, B., 86, 87, *107*
Sipe, C. L., 384, 397, 423, 424, 425, 431, *434*
Skinner, E. A., 174, *182*
Skipper, J. K., 260, *271*
Skroban, S., 460, *476*
Slicker, E. K., 424, *435*
Sloboda, J. A., 257, 261, 263, *270, 271, 273*
Smith, A. L., 7, *19*, 278, 292, 293, 294, 299,
    305, 309
Smith, C., 38, *43*, 313, *328*
Smith, D. E., 280, *307*
Smith, K., 69, *84*
Smith, M., 409, *417*
Smith, R., 111, 123, *129*
Smith, R. E., 278, *309*, 312, 313, 325, *326, 329*
Smith, S. M., 377, 384, *396*
Smith, T. J., 368, *371*
Smoll, F. L., 312, 313, 325, *326, 329*
Smollar, J., 189, 197, 204, 205, *210*, 336, *351*
Smyth, L., 180, *181*
Snow, J., 324, *328*
Snyder, H. N., 45, 46, 52, *64*
Soep, E., 178, *183*
Sonkowsky, M., 422, *435*
Soulé, D. A., 459, 462, *476*
Spears, B., 24, *43*
Spencer, M. B., 119, 120, *128*
Spencer, R., 419, *435*
Spencer, T. R., 119, *128*

Spielberger, C. D., 279, 280, *309*
Spielberger, J., 135, *154*
Spink, K. S., 299, *307*
Spitalny, K. C., 420, *433*
Spracklen, K. M., 51, *62*
Spray, C. M., 321, *330*
Spreeman, J., 281, 282, 283, 286, 287, *306*
Stachura, M. E., 313, *328*
Stattin, H., 8, 12, 17, *21*, 49, 59, *63*, 91, 95, 106,
        108, 212, 213, 214, 215, 219, 224,
        230, 232, *233, 234*, 438, *455*, 471,
        477
Stein, G. L., 278, 280, 281, 282, 283, 286, 287,
        288, 289, 291, 292, 293, 296, 297,
        298, *308*
Steinberg, L. D., 7, *20*, 32, *41*, 57, *64*
Stephens, D. E., 292, 293, 294, 296, *309*, 323,
        329
Stevenson, H. W., 47, 50, *62*
Stice, E., 205, *208*
Stiles, D. A., 32, *43*
Stone, J. R., 32, *43*
Stone, M. R., 6, 7, 16, *18, 19*, 85, 89, 92, 95, *106*,
        186, 189, 203, 205, *207, 209, 210*
Stoneman, Z., 239, *254*
Stouthamer-Loeber, M., 51, *63*
Stratton, H. H., 460, *477*
Stratton, R. K., 281, 282, 283, 286, 289, *307*
Strauss, A., 170, *183*
Streitmatter, J., 119, *128*
Styles, M. B., 408, 409, *418*
Su, Y., 7, 8, *22*, 190, 205, *210*, 235, *254*, 333,
        334, *351*
Suárez-Orozco, C., 113, 118, *128*
Subrahmanyam, K., 31, *43*
Sundeen, R. A., 350, *351*
Sutton-Smith, B., 28, 40, *43*
Swanson, D. P., 119, *128*
Swanson, R. A., 24, *43*
Swenson, L. P., 92, *107*

T

Taimela, S., 313, *328*
Tangney, J. P., 30, *43*
Tarpley, T., 32, *43*
Tarrant, M., 256, *273*
Taylor, A. S., 422, 431, *435*
Taylor, C. S., 119, *128*
Taylor, S. J., 170, *183*
Taylor, S. N., 46, *62*

Telema, R., 313, *328*
Templeton, J., 5, 6, 7, 17, *19, 20*, 185, 209, 259,
        270, 358, *371*, 470, *476*
Templin, T. J., 322, *327*
Terry, R., 231, *233*
Tevendale, H. D., 92, *107*
Theeboom, M., 292, 293, 294, 299, *309*, 325,
        329
Thiede, K., 89, *107*
Thomases, J., 376, 381, 383, 384, 390, 393, *397*
Thorne, J., 460, *477*
Tierney, J. P., 7, *20*, 419, 422, 423, *434, 435,*
        459, *477*
Timmer, S. G., 49, *64*, 480, *495*
Tobler, N. S., 460, *477*
Toles, M., 135, *154*
Tolman, J., 370, *371*, 376, 380, 381, 383, 384,
        390, 393, *397*
Topitzes, D., 131, *156*
Tortu, S., 460, 461, *476*
Tout, K., 8, *19*, 67, 69, 72, 82, 84, 112, *125,*
        437, *455*
Tracy, P. E., 96, *109*
Trammel, M., 376, 381, 383, 384, 390, 393, *397*
Traub, J., 392, *397*
Treasure, D. C., 314, 315, 317, 319, 320, 323,
        324, 325, *329*
Trehub, S., 255, *273*
Tremblay, J., 313, *329*
Tremblay, M. S., 313, *329*
Trevarthen, C., 255, *273*
Trotta, L., 38, *44*
Trudeau, F., 313, *329*
Tucker, C. J., 8, *21*, 236, 239, 244, *253*
Turetsky, V., 66, *82*
Tyler, R. W., 408, 409, *418*
Tzetzis, G., 321, *330*

U

Ullman, D. G., 47, *63*

V

Valentine, J. C., 423, 425, *433*
Vandell, D. L., 8, 10, *18, 22*, 47, 48, 49, 53, *64*,
        65, 67, 68, 71, *83*, 90, *108*, 112, *127*,
        407, *418*, 438, *455, 456*, 459, *477*,
        481, 482, *495*
Vandell, L., 236, 239, *254*

Van Den Bos, J., 91, *107*
Vanderryn, J., 91, *107*
Vandivere, S., 72, *81*
Van Horn, C. E., 38, *44*
Van Manen, M., 405, *418*
van Well, F., 257, *273*
Vargas, W. G., 68, 75, *82*
Vásquez-García, H., 120, *126*
Vaughn, K., 259, *273*
Vazsonyi, A. T., 50, 57, *62*
Vealey, R. S., 280, *307*
Ventura, A., 77, 79, *83*
Vergun, P., 33, *43*
Verma, N., 79, *82*
Verma, S., 3, 6, *21*, 27, *42*, 160, *182*, 239, *253*,
    363, *371*
Viikari, S. A., 313, *328*
Villarruel, F. A., 112, 118, 119, 120, *127*, *128*
Villeneuve, M., 260, *271*
Vlachopoulos, S., 317, *326*
von Eye, A., 119, *128*
Voss, H., 7, *20*
Vygotsky, L. S., 162, *183*, 427, *435*

W

Walberg, H. J., 31, *44*
Walker, J., 408, *418*
Walker, K. E., 437, *455*, 490, *495*
Walker, N. E., 112, 119, *128*
Wallace, J. M., Jr., 50, 57, 58, 64, 91, *109*
Wallack, L., 114, *126*
Wallerstein, J. S., 424, *435*
Wandersman, A., 135, *155*
Wang, C. K., 321, *330*
Wankel, L. M., 237, *254*, 290, 291, 292, 293,
    294, 296, 297, 298, 299, *309*
Warren, C., 10, *18*
Wasik, B. H., 120, *126*
Way, N., 115, 119, *129*
Wehlage, G. G., 7, *22*
Weigand, D. A., 316, *326*
Weinberg, R., 281, 282, 286, 287, 289, *306*
Weinberg, R. A., 12, *21*, 136, 139, *155*
Weinstein, C. S., 114, *125*
Weinstein, D., 260, *273*
Weisman, S. A., 459, 462, *476*
Weiss, M. R., 278, 290, 292, 293, 294, 298, 299,
    301, *305*, *306*, *307*, *309*, 313, *325*,
    327, *329*
Weissbourd, R., 10, *18*

Wells, A. M., 16, *19*
Wentzell, A. B., 301, *306*
Werner, E., 111, 123, *129*
West, J., 72, 82, 112, *125*
White, D. R., 13, *20*
White, P. T., 37, *41*
White, S. A., 316, *330*
Whitehead, J. R., 313, 315, 321, 322, *326*, *327*,
    328, *330*
Widemeyer, W. N., 281, 282, 289, *305*
Wiergersma, A., 53, *63*
Wigfield, A., x, *xii*, 8, *20*, 92, *107*, 237, 238,
    239, 250, *253*, *254*, 263, 265, 266,
    270, *273*, 357, *371*
Williams, E. L., 135, *154*
Williams, L. L., 50, 57, *62*
Williams, P. A., 31, *44*
Williamson, M. H., 27, *41*
Willits, F., 173, *181*
Willms, J. D., 313, *329*
Wills, T. A., 459, *477*
Wilson, D. B., 460, *476*
Wilson, J. J., 460, *477*
Wilson, J. K., 29, *43*, 46, 50, 51, 52, 53, 57, 58,
    59, *63*, 212, *233*
Wilson, N. C., 300, *308*
Wilson, R., 6, *21*
Wilson, S., 160, *182*
Wilson, W. J., 113, *129*
Winner, E., 258, *273*
Witt, P., 39, 40, *44*
Wolf, D. P., 258, *273*
Wolfgang, M. E., 96, *109*
Womer, S. C., 459, 462, *476*
Wood, G., 161, *182*
Woodruff, K., 114, *126*
Wright, E., 259, *273*
Wright, J. C., 71, *81*
Wynn, J. R., 135, *154*, 387, 388, *397*

Y

Yates, M., 7, 8, *22*, 180, *183*, 190, 205, *210*,
    235, *254*, 332, 333, 334, 336, 340,
    351
Yeung, W. J., 68, *82*
Yin, Z., 316, *328*
Yohalem, N., 370, *371*, 376, 380, 381, 383, 384,
    390, 393, *397*
Yoon, K. S., 237, *254*, 265, *273*
Yoshikawa, H., 95, 106, *108*

Youniss, J., 7, 8, 22, 131, *155*, 180, *183*, 189, 190,
        197, 204, 205, *210*, 235, *254*, 332,
        333, 334, 335, 336, 340, 345, 346,
        347, 349, *351*, 406, *418*

Z

Zani, B., 54, *64*
Zanksy, S. M., 420, *433*

Zaslow, M. J., 72, *84*
Zeldin, S., 131, 136, 139, *156*, 160, *180*
Zelnik, M., 57, *64*
Zetterblom, G., 214, *233*
Zill, N., 111, *129*, 445, *455*
Zimmerman, M. A., 420, *435*
Zippiroli, L., 438, *455*
Zisi, V., 321, *330*
Zwingmann, C., 32, *44*

Subject Index

Note. Page number followed by *n* indicates footnote.

A

Ability
 beliefs about nature of sport, 318
 distinguishing from effort, 301
 relation to success, 317–318
Academic achievement
 maternal employment and, 68
 out-of-school experience and, 480
 participation in activities in general and, 7–8,
  95–96, 99
 participation in after-school programs and, 9,
  39, 450–452
 participation in music activities and,
  257–260
 participation in paid work and, 71–73
 participation in religious youth groups and,
  102–103
 participation in school-based activities and,
  89–90
 participation in sports and, 103–105, 312
 peer context and, 202–203
Academic activities, 241
Academic peer context, 197–198, 200–203
Achievement goal theory, 313–315
 motivational climate and, 315–316
Achievement strategies, in sports, 320–321
Action research agenda, 368
Activities, *see also* After-school activities; Community-based programs; Extracurricu-
  lar activities; Neighborhood youth
  programs; Organized activities;
  Out-of-school programs; Structured

 activities; Unstructured activities;
  Youth development programs
 choice of, *see* Activity choice/selection
 in community-based youth programs,
  409–411
 participation in, *see* Activity participation
 as peer contexts, 197–198, 200–203
 as peer group niches, 204–205
 structure of, *see* Structure
Activities Club, The, 492
Activity choice/selection, 13–17
 demographic and familial influences on, 14
 determinants of, 357
 gender and, 239
 individual characteristics and, 14–16
 in middle childhood, 236–240, 250–252
 parental encouragement and, 235, 239–240
 program resources and, 16–17
 reasons for, 15
 role of self-beliefs in, 186–188
 self-perceptions of competence and,
  238–239
 task values and, 237–238
Activity participation
 academic achievement and, 95– 96, 99
 access issues, 355–356
 among adolescents, 75–76, 86–88
 among middle-age children, 75
 consequences of, 358–360
 continuing participation, 356–357
 development of initiative and, 361
 effect of welfare reform on, 65–66

factors affecting, 13–17
gender differences and, 241–245
identity and, 190–203, 342–343, 347, 354–355
income and, 69–72, 79– 80
in low-income families, 72–73, 80
by low-income, urban adolescents, 86–88
mother's perception of child's competence, task values and, 248–249
peer group norms and, 189–190
positive emotional experience and, 354
psychological well-being and, 78–79
rate of, 490
role of parents in, 355
school attachment and, 361
self-esteem and, 95–96, 98–99
self-perception of competence and, 245–248
social identity and, 194
task values and, 245–248
who participates, 354–357
Adolescent Pathways Project (APP), 93–104
Adolescents, *see also* High school
activity selection and, 15
capabilities of, 161–162
child care and, 68–69
choosing to work, 32–33, 71–72
continuing activity participation by, 356–357
development of youth programs and, 405–406
developmental outcomes and activity participation among, 75–76
developmental tasks of, 6
effect of participation in structured activities on, 79–80
emerging identities, 188–189
extracurricular activities and, 35
features of high-quality after-school programs for, 438
identity formation in, *see* Identity formation
mentoring, 425–429
opportunities for being adventurous, 29
parent supervision during after-school hours and, 60
parental limits on unsupervised socializing with peers and, 56–57
participation in extracurricular activities and, 15n4
participation in music activities, 264–268
peer group norms, 189–190
problem behavior and enjoyment of activities, 60–61

programs for in Chicago, 387–388, 394
programs for in Kansas City, 386
synergies and development among, 203–205
time use of, 383–384
urban, *see* Urban adolescents
Adult care, 47
Adult supervision, 48, *see also* Parent supervision
of organized activities, 4, 33, 360
problem behavior and lack of, 51–52
socioeconomic class and, 421
Adults, *see also* Youth–adult research collaborations
attachment to prosocial, 462, 465
building supportive relationships with, 11–12
community service and connecting youth with, 333–334
creating contextual connections for youth, 412
role in helping children develop initiative, 162–163, 168–169, 174–180
Advancing and Recognizing Quality (ARQ), 481
Advocacy for out-of-school programs, 393
state-level groups, 487–488
Affordability, activity selection and, 14
African Americans, *see also* Community youth development
activity participation among adolescent, 86–87, 97
double consciousness and, 114–115
neighborhood-based activity participation and, 90, 102
rates of physical activity among girls, 92
religious youth group participation by adolescent, 102
role of community in socializing youth, 112–116
unstructured socializing and problem behavior among, 58–59
After-school activities (formal), 5, 8–10, 33–37, *see also* Activities; Child Haven; Hamilton School After-School Program
assumptions underlying, 458–459
as care arrangement, 47
effect of World War II on, 25–26
enrollment levels, 437
expanded opportunities for learning/development in, x, 378–381
features of high-quality, 438

federal policy on, 484–486
funding for, 376–378, 437–438, 483–486
goals of, 440, 453
growth of, 437–438
implementation of, 459–461, *see also* Maryland After School Community Grant Program
importance of program director, 453–454
infrastructure development of, 483
knowledge development and, 483–484
link to community, 442–444
link to families, 441, 443, 453–454
mandate for, 376
narrow range of schools and, 380–381
outcomes of, 39–40, 380–381, 481–482
participant ages in, 380–381, 384
problem of fragmentation in, 377–378
provision of by nonschool agencies, 35–37
quality of, 10, 438–439, 453–455, 481, 490–491
quantity of, 481
reduction in antisocial behavior and, 458–459
in schools, 5, 34–35
staff training for, 441, 443, 453–454
staffing, 482–483, 492
state policy on, 486–488
unstructured socializing and, 59–60
youth–adult research collaborations and, 153
After-school activities (informal), 26–33, *see also* Youth centers
choice to work and, 32–33
impact of electronic media on, 30–32
loss of safety/rise in risk and, 28–30
After-School Alliance, 38, 485, 492
After-school enrichment, curricula, 490–494
After-school hours
adult supervision during, 4, 33, 48, 51–52, 60–61, 68, 360, 421
at-risk behavior and, 45–46
care arrangements, 47–48
policy implications, 58–61
relationship of time use to problem behavior, 50–58
socializing with peers, 49–50, 59
structure of, 48–49
After-School Initiative, 488
After School Matters, 387–388, 394, 488
Agency, 135, 332
Aggression
participation in organized activities and, 7, 9

in sports, 322–323
Alcohol use
participation in organized activities and, 7
participation in team sports and, 92
peer context and, 201–202
All Stars, 470–471
Alternative education, minority students and, 112n2, 115–116
American culture, after-school sports and, 312–313
Annenberg Foundation, 377
Anxiety
competitive trait, 282–283, 285–286
sport participation and, 320, 359
state, 279–280
APP, *see* Adolescent Pathways Project
ARQ, *see* Advancing and Recognizing Quality
ARQ (Advancing and Recognizing Quality) process, 488
Asian Americans, activity participation among adolescents, 87
Asset-based approach, to youth program development, 407
Attainment value, 188, 237
Attendance and activities log, 463–464, 473
Audience, for youth–adult research collaborations, 138–139, 148
Authoritarian parents, role in developing children's initiative, 163
Availability, activity selection and, 14

B

Barrio, youth socialization and, 114
Basic knowledge, 136n4
Beacons, 488, 490n1
Behavior, *see also* Criminal behavior; Problem behavior
at-risk, 45–46
plasticity of, ix–x
program characteristics and changes in, 465–470
program structure and, 458
prosocial, 332
Behavior management system, 471–472, 474
Behavior Problem Index, 445
Belonging, opportunities for, 11
BEST (Better Educated Students for Tomorrow), 488
BEST (Building Exemplary Staff Training), 482

Big Brothers Big Sisters of America, 419–420,
    422–423, 430
Boy Scouts, 5, 36
Boys, *see also* Gender
    effect of participation in structured activities
        on, 77–79
    in enjoyment literature, 292
    identity clarity in, 345–346
    music activity participation and, 263–264,
        266–267
    neighborhood-based activity participation
        and, 90, 101
    rate of normbreaking among, 226–227
    religious youth group participation among,
        103
    social identity and sports participation in,
        193, 195–197
    in stress literature, 281
    unstructured socializing and problem behav-
        ior in, 57
Boys and Girls Clubs of America, 5, 36
    mentoring and, 422
    participation by urban adolescents, 90–91
    social class and participation rates at, 69, 88
    staff training and, 482
Brainstorming phase, planning and, 166–167
Breakfast Club, The, 191

C

California, after-school program policy in,
    487–488
Camp Fire USA, 5, 482
Carnegie Corporation, 377
Carnegie Council on Adolescent Development,
    377
Causal analysis, 369
Causal modeling, 368
CBOs, *see* Community-based organizations
CCLCs, *see* 21st Century Community Learning
    Centers
Challenges
    instrumental, 170
    interpersonal, 170–171
Chapin Hall Center for Children, 377, 387, 394,
    484
Charles Stewart Mott Foundation, 376–377, 382
Chicago
    After School Matters, 387–388
    Chapin Hall Center for Children, 377, 387,
        394, 484

Chicago Community Trust, 394
Child care, developmental changes in options
    for, 67–69
Child Care and Development Fund, 376
Child Care Development Block Grants, 487
Child care subsidies, 66, 70, 80
Child Haven, 438, 440–442
    child functioning at, 450–453
    children at, 445–447
    observation of children's experiences at,
        447–450
Childhood, *see also* Adolescents; Middle child-
        hood
    developmental tasks of, 6
    extracurricular activities during, 8
    historical change in leisure time in, 23–26
    redefinition of, 23
Childhood and Beyond study, 241
Children, capabilities of, 161–162, *see also* Ado-
        lescents; Childhood; Low-income
        children; Middle childhood; Urban
        adolescents
CitySpan, 490n1
Civic-mindedness
    community service and, 334
    participation in organized activities and, 8
Clubs, 6
    academic, 191
    community youth development and, 118
    identity formation and participation in,
        348–349
CNYD, *see* Community Network for Youth De-
        velopment
Coaches
    interaction with in sports and enjoyment,
        298–299
    interaction with in sports and stress,
        287–289
    motivational climate and, 316, 325, 359
Coalition for After-School Funding, 487
Co-curricular activities, 34
Cognitions and worries, stress and, 284, 286
Cognitive outcomes
    mentoring and, 427–428
    of participation in music activities, 258–260
Comic Book Project, The, 493
Committee on Community-Level Programs for
        Youth, 438
Communication, music activity participation
        and, 260–261
Communities That Care Youth Survey, 465

Community
    link of after-school program to, 442–444
    music-making and, 261–262
    role in socializing youth, 112–117
    uneven commitment to out-of-school time
        by, 381–382, 384–385
Community-based organizations (CBOs), af-
        ter-school programs run by, 90–91,
        93, 105
Community-based programs, 6–7, 401, see also
        Youth development programs
    features facilitating development, 38–39
    positive development and, x–xi
Community centers, 69, see also Youth centers
Community-neighborhood collaborations with
        youth development programs, 412
Community Network for Youth Development
        (CNYD), 389
"Community Programs to Promote Youth Devel-
        opment," 377, 385
Community service
    defined, 336
    gender and participation in, 334
    identity formation and, 331–335, 340, 343,
        345, 348
    social-cause, 334
Community youth development, 116–117, see
        also Youth development programs
    building, 121–124
    models for future research, 122–124
    policy foundation for, 121
    programming foundation for, 117–119
    research foundation for, 119–121
Community Youth mapping, 137
Competence
    age-related differences in sources of informa-
        tion regarding, 301
    self-perceptions of, 238–239
Competence motivation theory, 290
Competition
    enjoyment and, 295, 297–298
    extracurricular careers and, 36
    organized activities and, 355
Competitive State Anxiety Inventory (CSAI),
        280
Competitive State Anxiety Inventory-2
        (CSAI-2), 280
Competitive trait anxiety (CTA), 282–283,
        285–286
Computer game playing, 31
Concentration of poverty effects, 113

Congressional Research Service, 486
Consensual validation, 205
Content of activities, program selection and, 16
Contextual connections, in youth development
        programs, 411–413
Continuity, program, 387–388
Conversations, mentoring and, 427
Coping/emotional release, enjoyment and, 295,
        297
Cost-effectiveness analysis, of mentoring, 432
Creative thinking, music activity participation
        and, 257–258
Criminal behavior, see also Behavior; Problem
        behavior
    after-school hours and, 45–46
    leisure and, 29–30
    maternal employment and, 68
    youth center participation and, 17, 212,
        222–224
Crowd identity, 189
CSAI, see under Competitive State Anxiety In-
        ventory
CTA, see Competitive trait anxiety
Cultural capital, 258
Culture
    activity selection and, 14
    leisure, 190
    minority youth, 115
Curricula, after-school enrichment, 490–494

D

DAT, see Differential Aptitude Test
Decision making, retaining adolescents and, 15
Demographics
    activity selection and, 14
    family, 207
Depression, sports participation and, 196
Detroit, repairing recreation infrastructure in,
        391–392
Development
    during adolescence, 203–205
    adult supervision and, 48
    after-school programs and opportunities for,
        378–381
    community programs facilitating, x–xi,
        38–39
    developmental systems view of, ix
    expectations for, 479–480
    features of organized activities that pro-
        mote, 10–13

mentoring and, 425–427
out-of-school time and, 3–4
peer social norms and, 190
play and, 24
youth–adult research collaborations and, 152
Developmental assets, 422
Developmental contextualism, 117
Developmental imperative, 379–380
Developmental intentionality, 399–401
activities and, 409–411
contextual connections and, 411–413
engagement and, 403
ethos of positive youth development,
404–407
generating engagement, 413–414
goodness of fit and, 404
intentionality and, 401–403
relationships and, 408–409
research implications of, 414–417
shaping learning opportunity, 407–412
Developmental outcomes of activity participation, 358
Developmental profiles, 302–303
Developmental status, activity selection and,
14–15
Developmental tasks, organized activities and,
6–10
Differential Aptitude Test (DAT), 207
Discipline management system, 471–472, 474
Divorce, impact on children's recreation, 29
Double consciousness, 114–115
Drop-in centers, 91, see also Youth centers
Drug use
participation in organized activities and, 7
peer context and, 57, 200–201
prevention of, see Maryland After School
Community Grant Program
unstructured socializing and, 58–59

E

Earned Income Tax Credit (EITC), 66
Ecological nutrients, x
Ecological validity
in stress literature, 283
in youth–adult research collaborations,
139–140, 148–150
Efficacy, 361
promoting development and, 11–12
Efficiency, of program procedures, 471

Effort
distinguishing from ability, 301
relation to success, 317
Ego involvement, in achievement goal theory,
314–315
Ego orientation
aggressive tendencies and, 322–323
beliefs about causes of success and, 317–319
motivational climate and, 323–324
positive and negative affect and, 319–320
practice avoidance and, 321
relation to anxiety, 320
Egocentrism, 162, 173
EITC, see Earned Income Tax Credit
Electronic media, impact on after-school leisure
activity, 30–32
Elementary school children, after-school enrichment for, 493
Elite athletes
in enjoyment literature, 293
stress and, 284, 287, 289
Emotion, music activity participation and,
260–261
Emotional climate, in after-school programs,
448
Emotional development, mentoring and,
425–427
Emotional responses, 277–279
examining developmentally, 300–303
motivation and, 278
to organized activities, 355
to participation in sports, 276, see also Enjoyment; Stress
Employment, impact on families, 66–67
Employment programs, experimental studies of,
73–78
Empowerment evaluation, 132
Empowerment, of minority youths, 116–117
Engagement, 403, 408
generating, 413–414
research agenda for, 416
Engineering after-school enrichment program,
494
Enjoyment (in sports), 313
breadth of literature, 291
competitive outcomes and, 295, 297–298
coping/emotional release and, 295, 297
defined, 290
as emotional response, 277–279
examining developmentally, 300–303

intrapersonal sources of, 294–297
mastery and, 295–296, 304
measuring, 290
motivational goal orientation and, 295–296
participation motivation and, 299–300
personal movement experiences and, 295, 297
review of literature, 291–299
situational sources of, 295, 297–298
social recognition and, 295, 298
sources of, 295
travel opportunities and, 295, 298
Enrichment, see After-school enrichment
Entrepreneurship
  Junior Achievement program, 493
  social, 160
Environments, see also Motivational climate
  emotional climate, 448
  identity formation and, 113–114
  intermediary, 387
  performance climate, 315–316
  youth program, 410?411
Ethics, of youth–adult research collaborations, 151–152
Ethnicity
  activity participation rates and, 97–98, 100
  activity selection and, 17
  identity clarity and, 340–341
Ethnography, 123, 139, 364
Ethos of positive youth development, 404–407
European Americans
  activity participation among adolescent, 86–87, 97
  neighborhood youth group participation by adolescent, 101–102
  religious youth group participation by adolescent, 102
  unstructured socializing and problem behavior among, 58–59
Evaluation, of mentoring, 422–425, 432–433
Expectancy-value theory, 186–188, 245, 290
Experience-sampling techniques, 363
Experiential learning, 411
Experimental evaluation studies, 365–366
Expertise/knowledge, in youth–adult research collaborations, 136–137, 145–147
Extracurricular activities, 6–7, see also Activities
  during childhood, 8
  participation in adolescence and, 15n4
  peer contexts for, 199–200
  in school, 34–35

Extracurricular careers, 36

F

Family, see also Mothers; Parents
  impact of employment on, 66–67
  influence on activity selection, 14
  link to after-school programs, 441, 443, 453–454
  music-making and, 261–262
  normbreaking among girls and status of, 215–216
Family Investment Program, 79
Federal policy on after-school programs, 484–486
FFA (Future Farmers of America), 159–160, 361
  development of initiative and, 164–174
  role of adult leaders in, 174–180
Figure This!, 491, 493
Finance Project, 488
Focus groups, 363
Forum for Youth Investment, 376n1, 382, 386n3
FOUNDATIONS, 490–491, 493
4-H, 5
Fragmentation, after-school programs and, 377–378
Friends, time spent with, 28
Fun, stress and lack of, 286
Funding
  for after-school programs, 376–378, 437–438, 483–486
  for out-of-school programs, 390–391

G

Gender
  activity participation rate differences and, 97–98, 100–101, 241–245, 250–251
  activity selection and, 17, 239
  community service participation and, 334, 345–346
  music activity participation and, 263–264, 266–267
  neighborhood-based activity participation and, 90, 94, 101–102
  normbreaking and, 226–227

self-beliefs and sports participation differences and, 187–188
sexual activity and sports participation and, 93
social identity and sports participation and,
193, 195–197
sports participation and, 93, 103–104, 106,
193, 195–197
stereotypes and parent's activity choices for
children, 355
unstructured socializing and problem behavior and, 57
Girl Scouts, 5, 24, 36
Girls, *see also* Gender
advanced sexual activity among, 213,
219–224, 230
after-school enrichment program for, 493
cross-sectional study of effects of youth center participation on, 224–228
effect of participation in structured activities
on, 77, 79
in enjoyment literature, 292–293
identity clarity in, 345–346
music activity participation in, 263–264, 266
neighborhood-based activity participation
and, 90, 94, 101
normbreaking and heavy peer involvement
in, 216–219, 230
normbreaking and youth center partipation
in, 214–216, 230–232
normbreaking rates in, 226–227
normbreaking with girlfriends who are youth
center goers, 227–229
participation in youth centers, 211–216,
230–232
social identity and sports participation in,
193, 195–197
sports involvement and, 93, 193, 195–197
in stress literature, 281–282
unstructured socializing and problem behavior in, 57
Girls Incorporated, 482, 491
Goal orientations
implications in youth sport, 317–323
individual differences in, 315
motivational climate and, 324
Goodness of fit, 408
intentionality and, 404
Greater Resources for After-School Programming
project (GRASP), 376, 382–384
Group activities, 242–243
Guilt, as source of stress, 286

H

Hamilton School After-School Program, 438,
443–444
child functioning at, 450–453
children at, 445–447
observation of children's experiences at,
447–450
Harvard Family Research Project, 377
High-risk areas, after-school programs and targeting, 60
High school, *see also* Adolescents
activity participation during, 100–101, 104
after-school enrichment programs for,
493–494
music participation after transition to,
264–268
sports participation in, 103
High/Scope Educational Research Foundation,
386n3
Hobbies, 242– 243
Homework
amount assigned, 34
time spent on, 27
Human ecological approach to youth development, 117

I

Identity
activity participation and, 190–203
crowd, 189, 203–205
neighborhoods and formation of, 113–114
participation in music activities and, 260
person–environment fit and, 356–357
role of in activity participation choices,
186–188
social, 189, 191–195, 332
Identity affirmation, 186
Identity formation (in adolescence), 12,
188–189, 203–205, 331, 335–349
activity participation and, 354–355
changes in identity clarity over time,
339–340
community service and, 331–335
differences among identity clarity groups,
347–349
factors associated with identity clarity in,
340–347
measuring clarity in, 337–338
personality traits and, 338

relationship with mother and, 335
Identity group, 191–195
Ideology, adolescent search for, 332
Immigrants, change in leisure time and, 24–25
Income, activity participation and, 69–72, 79–80
Independence, increase in importance of, 27
Individual sports, *see also* Sports; Team sports
    enjoyment and, 293
    participation in, 241, 243–245
    stress and, 282
Industry, 171, 332
Informal activities, after-school, *see* After-school
    activities (informal); Youth centers
Information systems, for out-of-school programs,
    393
Infrastructure development, of after-school pro-
    grams, 483
Initiative
    activity participation and, 8, 361
    defined, 160
    development of, 12, 163–164, 173–174
    developmental antecedents for, 161–163
    role of adults in developing children's,
        162–163, 168–169, 174–180
Inquiry-based reform, 132
Institute of Medicine, 10, 377, 438
Institute for Social Research, 36
Instrumental challenges, 170
Instrumentality, 171–172
Intentional balance, 403
Intentionality, 180, 401–403, *see also* Develop-
    mental intentionality
    research agenda for, 416
Intermediary environments, 387
Internal states, self-regulation of, 171–172
Internet surfing, 31–32
Interpersonal challenges, 170–171
Interpersonal conflict, stress and, 289
Interviews, qualitative, 364
Intrapersonal sources
    of emotional response, 278–279
    of enjoyment, 294–297
    of stress, 283–287
Intrinsic value, 237
Irvine Foundations, 377

J

John W. Gardner Center for Youth and Their
    Communities, 142, 377
Junior Achievement, 493

K

Kansas City, teen programs in, 386
KidzLit: An After-School Reading Program,
    490–491, 493
KidzMath: An After-School Math Program,
    491, 493
Knowledge
    after-school programs and development of,
        483–484
    local, 136n4
    in youth–adult research collaborations,
        136–137, 145–147

L

Laboratory experiments, on stress, 281
Large-scale surveys, on community youth de-
    velopment, 123
Latchkey children, 30, 47, 59
Latinos, *see also* Community youth develop-
    ment
    activity participation rates among adoles-
        cent, 87, 97, 106
    neighborhood-based activity participation
        and, 90, 94, 101–102
    religious youth group participation by ado-
        lescent, 102
    role of community in socializing youth,
        112–116, 121
Leadership
    development of, 118, 122
    Mediational Model of, 325
    for out-of-school programs, 392, 394–395,
        405–406
    retaining adolescents and, 15
Learning experience, 409
Learning opportunity, shaping, 407–412
Leisure activities, historical change in, 23–26
Leisure culture, 190
Lessons, 6, 48
Life skills curriculum, 494
Life Skills Training materials, 460
Lions-Quest Skills for Adolescence, 470
Literacy enrichment program, 493
Local policy on after-school programs, 488
Longitudinal fixed effects models, 365
Longitudinal studies, 364–365
Looking glass self, 426

Low-income children, *see also* Children; Urban adolescents
  effect of structured activity on, 71
  need for after-school programs for, 438
  participation in paid work, 73
  participation in structured activities, 72–73, 80

M

MacArthur Task Force on Middle Childhood, 377
Making the Most of Out-of-School Time (MOST), 394
Manpower Demonstration Research Corporation, 489–490
Maryland After School Community Grant Program (MASCGP)
  attendance and activities log, 463–464, 473
  background, 458, 461–463
    objectives of, 462
    observation form questions, 474
    program sample, 464–470
  goals of, 462
  implementation standards for, 472
  implications of, 470–472
  measures of program implementation, 463–464
  program director interview questions, 475
Master Settlement Agreement (MSA), 487
Mastery, 315–316
  enjoyment and, 295–296, 304
Mathematica Policy Research, Inc., 9
Mathematica Research Associates, 485
Mathematics
  enrichment programs, 493–494
  music activity participation and, 259
"Matter of Time, A," 377
Media
  impact on after-school leisure activity, 30–32
  motivational climate and, 316
Mediational Model of Leadership, 325
Mental difficulties, stress and, 284, 287
Mentoring, 17, 360, 419–433
  background on, 419–420
  community youth development and, 118–119
  enhancing social and emotional development through, 425–427
  evaluating, 422–425
  growth in, 422
  improving cognitive skills through, 427–428
  loss of natural mentors, 421–422
  matching partners, 431–432
  natural, 420

  quality of implementation of, 460
  recruiting mentors, 431
  reduction in antisocial behavior and, 459
  relationship length, 423–424, 430–431
  relationships that enhance development, 429–433
  role modeling and shaping and, 428–429
  training for mentors, 425, 430
  understanding, 425
Metacognition, 161–162, 172
Methodological issues, 362–369
  alternative view of best research practices, 366–369
  experimental evaluation studies, 365–366
  longitudinal studies, 364–365
  qualitative studies, 363–364
  quantitative survey studies, 364–365
  quasi-experimental evaluation studies, 365–366
Michigan Study of Life Transitions, 188, 190–203
Middle childhood, *see also* Childhood
  activity choices in, 235–240, 250–252
  activity participation and developmental outcomes in, 75
  activity participation in, 100–101, 104
  after-school enrichment for, 493–494
  after-school programs and development in, 9
  gender differences and trends in activity participation in, 241–245
  mothers' perceptions of child competence, task values, and children's activity participation in, 248–249
  relation among activity participation, perceived competence, and task values, 245–248
  research on activity participation during, 240–241
  sports participation in, 103
Mixed-method research, 363
Mood of American Youth survey, 27
Moral functioning, in sports, 322–323
Moral-political awareness, community service participation and, 332–333
MOST, *see* Making the Most of Out-of-School Time
Mothers, *see also* Parents
  identity formation and relationship with, 335
  perception of child's competence, task values and children's activity participation, 248–249, 251

Motivation
    emotional response and, 278
    participation, 299–300
    self-perceptions of competence and, 238
Motivational climate
    achievement goal theory and, 315–316
    cognitive, behavioral and affective
        concomitants of, 323–324
    goal orientations and, 324
    modifying, 325
    sports and, 323–324, 359, 361
Motivational goal orientation, enjoyment and,
    295–296
Mozart effect, 258–259
MSA, see Master Settlement Agreement
Multi-arts perspective, 257
Music
    community and, 261–262
    listening to, 27
    religious music-making, 262
    self-education and, 255
Music activities
    academic achievement and participation in,
        258–260
    cognitive outcomes and participation in,
        258–260
    communicative functions of participation in,
        260–261
    emotion and participation in, 260–261
    factors sustaining involvement in instrumen-
        tal, 267–268
    family and, 261–262
    friendships/peers and participation in,
        262–264
    importance of, 257–264
    mother's perception of and child's participa-
        tion in, 249
    multi-arts perspective on, 257
    participation in, 100, 241–245
    participation in after transition to high
        school, 264–268
    self-perception of competence in, 245–248,
        250–251
    structured, 255–256
    task values and, 237
    youth identity and, 260

N

National Collaboration for Youth, 486
National Conference of State Legislatures, 487

National Education Association, Commission
    on the Reorganization of Secondary
    Education, 24
National Education Longitudinal Study
    (NELS), 87–88
National Institute on Out-of-School Time
    (NIOST), 481
National League of Cities Institute for Youth,
    Education, and Families, 488
National Longitudinal Study of Adolescent
    Health, 54
National Research Council, 10, 38, 377, 385, 438
National School-Age Care Alliance (NSACA),
    38, 481, 485
National Study of Delinquency Prevention in
    Schools, 464
National Survey of America's Families (NSAF),
    6, 72–73
National Youth Survey, 54
Natural mentors, 420
    loss of, 421–422
Nature, 258
Negative affect, 319–320
Negative feelings, stress and, 284, 286
Neighborhood mapping, 364
Neighborhood youth programs
    as alternatives to school-based, 105
    participation by urban adolescents in,
        90–91, 96–97, 101–102
Neighborhoods, identity formation and,
    113–114
NELS, see National Education Longitudinal
    Study
Neurotic personality, identity clarity and,
    340–341, 348
New Hope Project, 74, 76–79
New York, after-school program policy in, 487
New York Times, The, 392
NIOST, see National Institute on
    Out-of-School Time
No Child Left Behind Act (2001), 376, 481,
    484–485
Nonexperimental mediation analyses, 77–78
Normbreaking, youth center participation by
    girls and, 214–219, 230–232
NSACA, see National School-Age Care Alliance
NSAF, see National Survey of America's Families

O

Obedience, decline in importance of, 27

Obesity, effect of television watching on, 31
Observation form questions, 474
Occupational identity measure, 207
Open Society Institute, 377
Operation Smart: Science, Math, and Relevant
    Technology, 491, 493
Organized activities, *see also* Activities
    balance between adult-structured and
        child-organized, 40
    breadth/diversity of, 5
    community programs, 6–7
    competition and, 355
    defined, 4–5, 353
    developing initiative and, 163–164
    developmental tasks and, 6–10
    drop-outs, 37
    educational achievement and, 7–8
    emotional responses to, 355
    extracurricular activities, 6–7
    factors affecting participation, 13–17
    features of that promote development, 10–13
    important factors in, 360–362
    as peer contexts, 197–203
    problematic, 17
    program impact, 17
Outcomes
    of after-school programs, 39–40, 380–381,
        481–482
    cognitive, 258–260, 427–428
    developmental, 358
Out-of-school programs
    advocacy for, 393
    building capacity in, 388–390
    building city-level infrastructure for, 388–392
    creating continuity in, 387–388
    ensuring quantity of, 387
    identifying resources for, 390–391
    information systems for, 393
    local leadership and, 394–395
    quality of, 385–388
    sustaining public will for, 392–393
Out-of-school time, *see also* Activities; Af-
        ter-school activities; Out-of-school
        programs
    developmental opportunity and, 3–4
    policy recommendations for, 37–39
Overcoming Obstacles, 491, 494
Ownership
    in developing initiative, 175, 178–179
    of youth–adult research collaborations,
        137–138, 147–148

P

Parents, *see also* Mothers
    activity choice and, 235, 239–240, 251–252
    interactions with in sports and enjoyment,
        298
    mentoring and improved relationships with,
        425–427
    motivational climate and, 316
    role in activity participation, 355
    role in developing children's initiative,
        162–163
    role in sustaining musical involvement
        among children, 268
    as sources of stress, 288
Parent supervision, *see also* Adult supervision
    after-school hours and, 60– 61
    problem behavior and, 68
Parks, 23
Participant observation, 363–364
Participation motivation, 299–300
Participatory action research, 132
Peacemakers Program, 470
Pedagogical method, 411
Peer group norms, 189–190
    sharing, 186
Peers
    activities as peer contexts, 197–198,
        200–203
    after-school programs and relationships
        with, 450–452, 454
    crowd identities, 203–205
    delinquency and, 30
    developing initiative and, 162
    enjoyment and interaction with, 299
    identity clarity and, 340, 342, 347–348
    influence on behavior, 70
    motivational climate and, 316
    organized activities as contexts for,
        197–203
    parental limits on unsupervised socializing
        with, 56–57
    power of, 360–361
    problem behavior and socializing with, 51,
        53–54, 212–213, 216–219
    role in participation in music activities,
        262–264
    socialization into normbreaking behavior
        among girls and, 216–219,
        227–229, 232
    socializing with, 49–50, 54–57

Perceived Motivational Climate in Sport Questionnaire-2 (PMCSQ-2), 316
Perceptions of Success Questionnaire (POSQ), 315
Performance achievement
    defined, 294, 296
    enjoyment and, 294, 296
Performance climate, 315–316
Performance expectations, stress and, 284–286, 289
Permissive parents, role in developing children's initiative, 163
Persistence, 135
Personal movement experiences, enjoyment and, 295, 297
Personal Responsibility and Work Opportunity Reconciliation Act (PRWORA; 1996), 66
Personality factors
    identity formation and, 338, 340–341, 345, 348
    stress and, 283–286
Person–environment fit, identity and, 356–357
Person-in-environment approach, to youth development, 117
Physical activity programming, 38
Physical difficulties, stress and, 284, 287
Pizza Parlor Phenomenon, 296
Plan, children's ability to, 161
Play
    development and, 24
    spontaneous, 36
    unstructured outdoor, 28–29
Playgrounds, 23
PMCSQ-2, see Perceived Motivational Climate in Sport Questionnaire-2
Policy
    on after-school programs, xi, 484–489
    for community youth development, xi, 121
    relation to practice, 489–492
    youth–adult research collaboration and, 153
Positive affect, 319–320
POSQ, see Perceptions of Success Questionnaire
Poverty effects, 113
Practice, relation to policy, 489–492
Problem behavior, see also Behavior; Criminal behavior
    activity structure and, 49
    adolescent employment and, 76
    after-school programs and, 458–459
    heavy peer involvement and, 212–213, 216–219
    measure of, 96, 98
    organized activities and reduced, 7
    peer socializing and, 50
    prevention of, see Maryland After School Community Grant Program
    relationship of time use to, 50–58
    structure and, 471
    unstructured socializing and group differences in, 57–58
    youth centers and, 17, 359
Program director
    importance of role of, 453–454
    interview questions, 475
Program effects, 368
Program evaluation, theory-based models of, 368–369
Program–youth fit, 404
Project Adventure, 494
Prosocial activities, 191
Prosocial behaviors, community service and, 332
PRWORA, see Personal Responsibility and Work Opportunity Reconciliation Act
Psychological adjustment measures, 206–207
Psychosocial competencies, participation in organized activities and, 7–8
Psychosocial development, out-of-school activity involvement and, 93–104
Public/Private Ventures, 384, 423, 484, 488
Public schools
    after-school programs and, 33–34
    reform of, 24–25
    youth of color in, 115–116
Putumayo "World Playground: A Musical Adventure for Kids," 494

Q

Qualitative studies, 363–364
    in enjoyment literature, 292
    on stress, 281
Quality
    of after-school programs, 10, 481, 490–491
    of after-school programs for low-income children, 438–439, 453–455, see also Child Haven; Hamilton School After-School Program
    measuring program implementation, 459–461, see also Maryland After

School Community Grant Program
of out-of-school programs, 385–388
program selection and, 16
of youth center programs, 359–360
Quantitative survey studies, 364–365
in enjoyment literature, 292
on stress, 281
Quantity
of after-school programs, 481
of out-of-school programs, 387
Quasi-experimental evaluation studies, 365–366
Quasi-partnerships, in youth–adult research collaborations, 135, 143–144
Questions
observation form, 474
use of guiding, 176, 178–179

R

Race, *see also* African Americans; European Americans; Latinos
activity participation rates and, 97– 98, 100
unstructured socializing and problem behavior and, 57–58
Rand Corporation, 491
Randomized trial experimental studies, 365
Randomized trial policy evaluations, 366
Rational Recreation Movement, 23–24
Reading for enjoyment, 27–28
Reading habits, identity clarity and, 340, 342
Reading programs, 493
Recreation
caveat regarding planning, 471
increase in problem behavior and participation in, 469–470
repairing infrastructure of in Detroit, 391–392
Recreation agencies, 36
Recreational games, 36
Recruitment, of mentors, 431
Redwood City (California), Youth Engaged in Leadership and Learning in, 142–143, 145–147, 149
Relationships, partnerships between youth and adults, 408–409, *see also* Mentoring
Religion, music-making and, 262
Religious institution-based activities, 361
participation by urban adolescents, 91–92, 95–97, 102–103
Research, *see also* Methodological issues

best practices, 366–369
on community youth development, 119–121
developmental intentionality theory and, 414–417
Resilience, models of, 122–123
Resources
activity selection and, 16–17
identifying, 390–391
Retention, staff, 388–389
Retrospective studies, on community youth development, 123
Risk, evolution of after-school programs and sense of, 28–30
Risky peer context, 197–202
Role modeling, mentoring and, 428–429
Routine activity theory, 46
evidence supporting individual, 52–54
relationship of time use to problem behavior, 50–58

S

Safe and Drug-Free Schools and Communities Program, 460
Safety
evolution of after-school programs and sense of, 28–30
promoting development and, 11–12
SAIC, *see* State Anxiety Inventory for Children
Sampling, 150, 365, 368
San Francisco, building capacity in out-of-school programs, 389–390
School attachment
activity participation and, 361
sports participation and, 196–197
School involvement, activity participation and, 191
Schools
after-school programs and narrow range of, 380–381
after-school programs sponsored by, 5
length of school day, 33–34, 37–38
participation by urban adolescents in activities at, 89–90, 96–101, 104–105
Search Institute, 422
Second Step, 470
Selection bias, 368
Selection issues, 365
Self-beliefs, role in activity participation choices, 186–188

Self-care, 47–48, 61, 67–68
Self-concept of sports ability, 207
Self-determination theories, 290
Self-esteem
    activity participation and, 8, 95–96, 98–99
    defined, 283
    mentoring and improvement in sense of, 426
    self-perception of competence and, 238
    sports participation and, 103–105
    stress and, 283, 285
Self-expression, music and, 256, 261
Self-perception of competence, 238–239
    activity participation and, 245–248
    in music, 245–248, 250–251
    in sports, 245–248, 250–251
Self-Sufficiency Project (SSP), 74–76, 79–80
Service activities, 361
Service learning, 124, 406
Sexual activity
    participation in youth centers and advanced,
        213, 219–224
    peer socializing and, 57
    sports participation and, 93
Significant others, as sources of emotional re-
        sponse, 278–279
Situational motivation, 50
Situational sources
    of emotional response, 278–279
    of enjoyment, 295, 297–298
    of stress, 284–285, 287
6-to-6 Initiative, 488
Skill building/development, 135
    activities for, 470–471
    after-school programs and, 39
    promoting, 11–12
    sport participation and, 320–321
Skill level, activity selection and, 14–15
Skillman Foundation, 391–392
SMART Moves prevention program, 91
Social capital, mentoring and increases in, 428
Social-cause service, 334
Social competence promotion programs,
        461–463, 467–468, 470
Social contexts, adolescent behavior and, 68
Social development, mentoring and, 425–427
Social entrepreneurship, 160
Social functioning, after-school programs and,
        450–452
Social identity, 189, 191–195, 332
    activity participation and, 194
    sports participation and, 192–193, 195–197

Social norms, promoting development and posi-
        tive, 11
Social recognition, enjoyment and, 295, 298
Social relatedness, 332
Social skills training, 459
Social Skills Training System Elementary Level
        Student Form, 465
Socialization, activity selection and, 15
Sociocentric perspective, 173
Socioeconomic class
    activity participation and, 69–72, 87–88
    after-school supervision and, 421
    rate of participation in paid work and,
        71–72
    self-care and, 67
    unstructured socializing and problem behav-
        ior and, 58
Sociogenesis, 204–205
Spontaneous play, 36
Sport commitment model, 290
Sport motivation theories, 290
Sports, *see also* Enjoyment; Individual sports;
        Stress; Team sports
    achievement goal theory and, 313–315
    agency-sponsored, 312
    American culture and after-school, 312–313
    anxiety and participation in, 313, 320, 359
    beliefs about nature of sport ability, 318
    beliefs about purposes of participation in,
        318–319
    criticism of organized, 38
    defined, 276, 311
    effects of participation on, 78
    emerging identity and, 188–189
    emotional response to participation in, 276
    enjoyment and participation in, 313
    enjoyment literature and, 293
    identity exploration and participation in, 16
    implications of goal orientations in youth
        and, 317–323
    individual differences in goal orientation
        and, 315
    moral functioning and aggressive tendencies
        in, 322–323
    motivational climate and, 315–316,
        323–324, 359, 361
    music activities and, 262
    participation rates in, 36, 275–276, 311–312
    risky peer context and, 198–202
    school attachment and participation in,
        196–197

self-beliefs and gender differences in partici-
    pation in, 187–188
self-esteem and participation in, 103–105
self-perception of competence in, 245–248,
    250–251
skill development and, 320–321
social identity and participation in, 192–193,
    195–197
socialization of immigrants and, 24
task values and, 237
youth associations of, 36
Sports competence beliefs, 93
Spread of effect, 13n3
SSP, see Self-Sufficiency Project
Staff, after-school program, 482–483, 492
    retention of, 388–389
    training of, 441, 443, 453–454
Stage–Environment Fit, 357
Standards, program, 386–387
State anxiety, 279–280
    measuring, 282–283
State Anxiety Inventory for Children (SAIC),
    280
"State Legislative Investments in School-Age
    Children and Youth," 488
State policy on after-school programs, 486–488
Status, value of, 322
Stress (in sports)
    breadth of literature, 280–283
    cognitions and worries and, 284, 286
    competition outcomes and, 288
    defined, 279
    elite athletes and, 284, 287
    as emotional response, 277–279
    examining developmentally, 300–303
    intrapersonal sources of, 283–287
    measuring, 279–280, 283
    mental difficulties and, 284, 287
    performance expectations and, 284–286, 289
    personality dispositions and, 283–286
    physical difficulties and, 284, 287
    review of literature, 283–289
    situational sources of, 284–285, 287
Structure
    behavior changes and program, 458
    defined, 48–49
    developing initiative and providing, 176–177
    importance of, 360
    need for, 60, 474
    organized activities and, 4
    problem behavior and, 51, 471

promoting development and, 11
Structured activities, see also Activities
    defined, 47, 76
    effects of participation in, 70–71
    participation by low-income children in,
        72–73, 80
    unstructured vs., 47–50
Subject matter content, of activities, 410
Subsidies
    child care
    for structured activities, 81
Substantive theory, 368
Success, beliefs about causes of, 317–318
Supportive relationships, promoting develop-
        ment and, 11–12, see also Mentoring
Surveys
    on community youth development, 123
    quantitative, 364–365

T

Tact, 405
TANF, see Temporary Assistance to Needy Fam-
        ilies
TARGET principles, 325
Task and Ego Orientation in Sport Question-
        naire (TEOSQ), 315
Task involvement, in achievement goal theory,
        314–315
Task orientation
    beliefs about causes of success and, 317–319
    motivational climate and, 323–324
    positive and negative affect and, 319–320
    prosocial attitudes and, 322–323
    relation to anxiety, 320
    skill development strategies and, 321
Task values
    activity choice and, 237–238
    activity participation and, 245–248, 251
    mother's perception of and child's activity
        participation, 248–249
Teaching the New Basic Skills (Murnane &
        Levy), 479
Team, insights into working as, 172–173
Team sports, see also Individual sports; Sports
    developmental tasks and, 6
    enjoyment and, 293
    gender and participation in, 193, 195–197
    growth in participation in, 36
    mother's perception of and child's participa-
        tion in, 248–249

participation in general in, 241, 243–245, 250
school, 312
stress and, 282
Television
participation in school-based activities and time spent watching, 90
time spent watching in general, 30–32, 49
violence on, 38
Temporary Assistance to Needy Families (TANF), 376, 487
TEOSQ, see Task and Ego Orientation in Sport Questionnaire
Theory-based models of program evaluation, 368–369
Time use, relationship to problem behavior, 50–58
Tobacco settlement, after-school programs and, 487
Training
after-school staff, 441, 443, 453–454
of mentors, 425, 430
in youth–adult research collaborations, 151
Transportation, activity participation and, 69, 391
Travel opportunities, enjoyment in sport and, 295, 298
Tutoring, 459, 461
21st Century Community Learning Centers (21st CCLCs), 5, 9–10, 66, 376, 427, 481, 484–485
24 Game, 494

U

Unstructured activities, 4–5, see also Activities
structured vs., 47–50
Urban adolescents (low-income)
building better activities for, 105–106
contexts and correlates of activity participation among, 88–93
neighborhood-based activity participation among, 90–91, 96–97, 101–102
psychosocial development of, 93–104
rates of out-of-school activity participation among, 86–88
religious institution-based participation among, 91–92, 95–97, 102–103
risk factors for psychosocial development of, 85

school-based activity participation among, 89–90, 96–101, 104–105
team sports participation among, 92–93, 95–97, 103–104
Urban youth, community role in socializing, 112–116
U.S. Department of Education, 437–438, 460

V

Values
attainment, 237
intrinsic, 237
self-concept and, 238–239

W

Wallace-Reader's Digest Funds (Wallace Foundation), 377, 394, 490
Welfare reform, 66
effect on activity participation, 65–66
experimental studies of, 73–78
impact of employment on families, 66–67
income levels and, 69–70
policy implications for out-of-school experiences, 80–81
Well-being, activity participation and psychological, 78–79
What About You? survey, 465
Whites, see European Americans
Work
choice to, 32–33
effects of paid, 71–72
participation of low-income adolescents in paid, 73
unstructured socializing and, 60
Working Toward Peace, 470
Works Progress Administration, 25
World In Motion, 491, 494
World War II, evolution of after-school programs and, 25–26

Y

YELL, see Youth Engaged in Leadership and Learning
YEP, see Youth Ethnographers Project
YMCA, 5, 36
mentoring and, 422
social class and participation at, 69, 88
staff training at, 482

Younger Americans Act (2001), 85–86, 484–486

Youth–adult research collaborations, 134–135, 143–144, 361

    youth as research assistants, 133–134, 136–138

    youth as research informants, 133–138

    youth as research partners, 133–134, 136–138

Youth centers

    advanced sexual activity among girls and participation in, 213, 219–224

    criminal behavior and participation in, 212, 222–224, 231–232

    cross-sectional study of effects of participation in, 224–228

    drop-in, 91

    music activities at, 262

    normbreaking among girls and, 214–219, 227–232

    problem behavior and, 212, 359

    problems regarding participation at, 17

Youth development, in research collaboration, 135–136, 144–145

Youth Development Framework for Practice, 389

Youth development programs

    activities, 409–411

    contextual connections in, 411–413

    engagement and, 403

    environment, 410–411

    ethos of positive youth development, 404–407

    generating engagement, 413–414

    goodness of fit and, 404

    intentionality and, 401–403

    pedagogical method, 411

    relationships and, 408–409

    research/practice implications, 414–417

    shaping learning opportunity, 407–412

    subject matter control in, 410

Youth Development Strategies, Inc., 386n3

Youth Engaged in Leadership and Learning (YELL), 142–153

Youth Ethnographers Project (YEP), 140–153

Youth IMPACT, 153–154

Youth mapping, 137

YouthNet, 386

Youth organizations, 5

Youth Services, 490n1

YWCA, 5, 36, 88

Z

Zone of proximal development, 427